D0787309

MY FAVORITE BURGUNDIES

MY FAVORITE BURGUNDIES

Clive Coates, MW

UNIVERSITY OF CALIFORNIA PRESS

Berkeley   Los Angeles   London

University of California Press, one of the most distinguished university presses in the United States, enriches lives around the world by advancing scholarship in the humanities, social sciences, and natural sciences. Its activities are supported by the UC Press Foundation and by philanthropic contributions from individuals and institutions. For more information, visit www.ucpress.edu.

University of California Press
Berkeley and Los Angeles, California

University of California Press, Ltd.
London, England

Library of Congress Cataloging-in-Publication Data

Coates, Clive.
    My favorite burgundies / Clive Coates.
        pages cm.
    ISBN 978-0-520-27662-8 (cloth : alkaline paper)—
ISBN 978-0-520-95660-5 (ebook)
    1. Wine and wine making—France—Burgundy.   2. Vineyards—
France—Burgundy.   I. Coates, Clive. Wines of Burgundy.   II. Title.
TP553.C563   2013
663'.2—dc23   2013025530

Manufactured in the United States of America.

22   21   20   19   18   17   16   15   14   13
10   9   8   7   6   5   4   3   2   1

The paper used in this publication meets the minimum requirements of ANSI/NISO Z39.48-1992 (R 2002) (*Permanence of Paper*).♾

CONTENTS

MAPS

PREFACE

I should begin by explaining what this book is, and what it is not. It is not a textbook about the wines of Burgundy. There are no chapters of the history and the geography of the region. Nor is there a village-by-village, vineyard-by-vineyard commentary, and a comprehensive listing of all the main growers and their wines. This I have done twice before: in *Côte d'Or*, published in 1998, and in *The Wines of Burgundy*, which appeared ten years later. Moreover, since 2008, my friend Jasper Morris has brought out his *Inside Burgundy*. This is a path well tilled.

My Favorite Burgundies should be regarded as a companion piece to *The Wines of Burgundy*. The latter is still valid. There have not been many major changes since *The Wines of Burgundy* appeared in 2008. The villages and the vineyards remain the same. So, very largely, do the domaines. The main changes are that we have five more vintages, and everyone is five years older. A handful of exploitations have evolved—the main ones being Lafon, Liger-Belair, Roulot, and Rousseau. These have been noted in the profiles which follow.

I am in the very lucky position of being able to take part in regular, extensive tastings of the major wines of Burgundy in bottle. What *My Favorite Burgundies* is, is an account of the opportunities which have come my way since *The Wines of Burgundy* went to press and my appreciation of the wines offered. I have split these occasions into three parts: Vineyard Profiles, in roughly south to north order; Domaine Profiles, in, apart from the first piece on the Hospices de Beaune, alphabetical order; and Vintage Assessments, in reverse chronological order.

While the list of wines offered is extensive, it does not pretend to be exclusively comprehensive. Production in fragmented Burgundy is meagre and stocks retained at the domaine tiny, normally just a few bottles kept back for birthdays and anniversaries. If you were the proprietor of an 80-hectare growth in the Médoc, you could well put aside five hundred bottles for future reference. And collectors would not find it impossible to acquire more than six or twelve bottles of any wine they desire. But with Burgundy it is different. If the wine that you seek a note on is not here, I can only apologize. There are limits to how greedy you can get. I have found my friends in Burgundy extremely generous, only equalled by the liberality of my friends with extensive cellars elsewhere. But the grower may simply not have the wine, or may be disinclined to offer it for tasting. Or, when the wines have come from stocks in the United States and elsewhere, the wine may not have been cellared in the first place.

You may also wonder why a certain domaine or vineyard or vintage has been included in this book while others are absent. Here again it is also a question of opportunity. In the case of the vineyards and domaines, I have organised many myself and the rest have been tastings with groups of friends in Guilford, Connecticut, and other venues, mainly in the United States. I have included nearly all the estates to which I awarded the top three-star rating in *The Wines of Burgundy*. I have included many of the top vineyards but not, for instance, any *grand cru* Chambertins. The Guilford group went through the Gevrey card in the mid-2000s, and you will find these notes in *The Wines of Burgundy*. These occasions seemed to be too recent to repeat, so we put these aside in favour of other tastings. As far as the vintages are concerned, what appears in this book is, in the main, the five vintages that we tasted at three years on (2005–2009) and the five at ten years on (1998–2002). This follows on from earlier vintages reported on in *The Wines of Burgundy*.

Marking. You will notice that some wines are marked and some not. The reason for this is that I find it simple enough, where only one vintage is on the table, to place the wines in a rigid hierarchy. Yes. Wine A deserves 17.5; Wine B, alongside it, earns 18.0. When it comes to a mixture of vintages, I personally find this sort of marking more difficult. Vintages vary in quality, and I often find myself noting as more important, for instance, that Wine A, from a celebrated year, is marginally disappointing, while Wine B is an unexpected success compared with what one might expect. The thing, of course, is to read the words.

The University of California Press, being the publishers they are, send out commissioned and submitted books to outsiders for a peer review. I don't know who my two peers are (though I have a suspicion of who one is). But they came up with a number of suggestions about how my manuscript could be improved;

they also pointed out a couple of mistakes. I have taken their comments on board, and the book is better as a result. My thanks to them.

I would like to thank the following, without whom these opportunities I have had to taste fine Burgundy would not have occurred, and without whose friendship, the world would be an unhappier place:

Firstly, in Burgundy: Becky Wasserman and Russell Hone, and all my friends the growers, particularly those whose domaines are profiled in this book, and those others who submitted samples for our tastings.

In Britain and Beaune: Roy Richards, Jasper Morris, Toby Morrhall, Hew Blair, Lindsay Hamilton, Julie Petitjean, Zubair Mohammed, Christopher Moestue, and Neil Beckett.

In Connecticut: Bob Feinn, Gregg Cook, George and Jeri Sape, Jack and Thelma Hewitt, Alvin and Linda Wakayama, Jim and Debbie Cianciolo, Bruce and Pam Simonds, Keith and Judy Edwards, Doug Barzeley, and Roger Forbes.

Elsewhere in the United States: Tony and Judi Dietrich, Arlette and Bob Cataldo, Kevin and Mary-Virginia Hill, Joel and Joan Knox, Jim Kelley, Clay Cockerell, Joe Saglimbeni, Harold Wood, Tom Black, Marshall Katz, Jim and Elaine Israel, Don Scott, Bob Conrad, Jim Finkel, and David Hamburger.

A number of the pieces in this book have appeared in a prior form in *Decanter Magazine*, *The World of Fine Wine*, and the late and lamented *Quarterly Review of Wine*. I thank the editors of these magazines for their permission to use what I had written for them as the basis for the pieces which follow.

And finally, of course, I need to thank all the team at the University of California Press: Rich Nybakken, Leslie Larson, and Francisco Reinking; and Amy Smith Bell, Bea Hartman, Tanya Grove, and David Peattie of BookMatters; finishing up with (and not least) Caterina Polland, who sends out the royalty cheques.

PART ONE

Vineyard Profiles

BURGUNDY

To Dijon

To Paris

Yonne

Auxerre

Chablis

Dijon

Côte de Nuits
(detailed in map below)

Côte de Beaune
(detailed in map below)

Saône-et-Loire

Chalon-sur-Saône

Côte Chalonnaise

Mâconnais

Côte Mâconnais

Mâcon

Lyon

Côte de Nuits

Marsannay

Fixin

Brochon

Gevrey-Chambertin

Morey-Saint-Denis

Chambolle-Musigny

Vougeot

Vosne-Romanée

Flagey-Echézeaux

Nuits-Saint-Georges

Chaux

Prémeaux

Magny-les-Villers

Comblanchien

Pernand-Vergelesses

Corgoloin

Aloxe-Corton

Savigny-lès-Beaune

Ladoix

Chorey-lès-Beaune

Côte de Beaune

Beaune

Pommard

Saint-Romain

Monthelie

Volnay

Auxey-Duresses

Meursault

Saint-Aubin

Puligny-Montrachet

Chassagne-Montrachet

Dezize-lès-Maranges

Santenay

Chagny

Sampigny-lès-Maranges

Remigny

Cheilly-lès-Maranges

To Lyon

N

| 0 | | 4 kilometers |
| 0 | | 2 miles |

MAP 1 Burgundy

Puligny-Montrachet, Les Folatières, 2006

LES, OR EZ FOLATIÈRES, is Puligny's largest first growth, at 17.65 hectares. It lies on the same altitude as Les Caillerets, Chevalier-Montrachet, and Le Montrachet itself, but to the north, between 250 and 300 metres above sea level. It includes the *lieux-dits* of En La Richarde, a recent addition, Peux Bois, and Au Chaniot—all of which are at the southern end.

While many would argue that Caillerets is possibly the best of the Puligny *premiers crus*, Folatières is certainly among the very best. Those further upslope—Le Garenne, La Truffière, Les Champs Gain, and others—are lighter and less fine, and in lesser years can be a bit thin. Clavoillon, below, produces a more four-square wine. Only Clos de la Garenne, next to Folatières, Perrières, Combettes, and Champ Canet, further north towards Meursault, plus Pucelles, which marches with Bienvenues-Bâtard-Montrachet, can match the elegance of Folatières, and only in Clos de la Garenne (owned by the Duc de Magenta and exclusive to Maison Jadot) will you find a wine with the same depth of character.

As you would expect in Burgundy, though essentially limestone, the geology is complex. The lower and eastern part of the Folatières *climat* is made up of a compact, hard, erosion-resistant lower Bathonian rock, found and quarried a couple of kilometres away in Chassagne-Montrachet. The surface soil is rich in stones and rather thin. The uppermost part consists of compact limestones and dolomites equivalent to the Comblanchien rocks of the Côte de Nuits, and also found in the rocky outcrop between Genevrières and Narvaux in Meursault. The soils are once again thin and rich in stones. Between the two lies a thin strip of marl abundant in large mussel-like fossils. Erosion is more commonplace here, so rendering the shalier soils found here more concave. Downslope there is a distinct fault, below which the limestone resembles that of the hill of Corton. You can see the fault in the upper part of Le Montrachet. (My thanks to Francoise Vannier-Petit, local geologist, for this information.)

But, while this geology is instructive, what effect does this have on the wine? Eric Rémy,

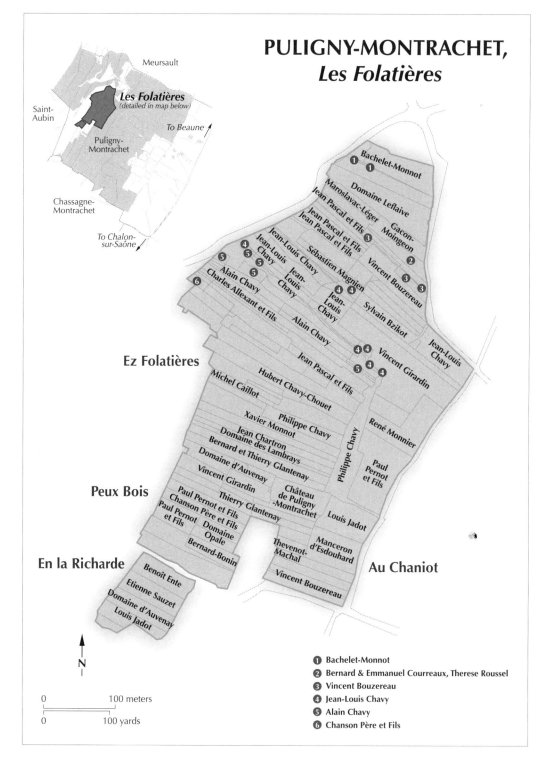

PULIGNY-MONTRACHET,
Les Folatières

Meursault

Les Folatières
(detailed in map below)

Saint-Aubin

To Beaune →

Puligny-Montrachet

Chassagne-Montrachet

To Chalon-sur-Saône →

Bachelet-Monnot ❶
❶

Domaine Leflaive

Maroslavac-Léger

Jean Pascal et Fils

Jean Pascal et Fils ❸

Gacon-Moingeon

Jean Pascal et Fils
Jean Pascal et Fils

Jean-Louis Chavy

Sébastien Magnien

Vincent Bouzereau

❷

Jean-Louis ❹ Chavy

Jean-Louis Chavy ❺
Chavy ❺
Alain Chavy ❺
❺
Charles Allexant et Fils ❻

Jean-Louis Chavy
❹ ❹
Jean-Louis Chavy

Sylvain Bzikot

❸
❸

Jean-Louis Chavy

Alain Chavy

Ez Folatières

Michel Caillot

Hubert Chavy-Chouet

Jean Pascal et Fils
❹ ❹
❺ ❹ ❹

Vincent Girardin

Jean-Louis Chavy

Philippe Chavy

Xavier Monnot

Jean Chartron
Domaine des Lambrays

Bernard et Thierry Glantenay

Domaine d'Auvenay

Vincent Girardin

René Monnier

Philippe Chavy

Paul Pernot et Fils

Peux Bois

Paul Pernot et Fils
Chanson Père et Fils
Paul Pernot et Fils

Thierry Glantenay

Domaine Opale

Château de Puligny-Montrachet

Louis Jadot

Bernard-Bonin

En la Richarde

Benoît Ente

Etienne Sauzet

Domaine d'Auvenay

Louis Jadot

Thevenot-Machal

Manceron d'Esdouhard

Au Chaniot

Vincent Bouzereau

N ↑

| 0 | 100 meters |
| 0 | 100 yards |

❶ Bachelet-Monnot
❷ Bernard & Emmanuel Courreaux, Therese Roussel
❸ Vincent Bouzereau
❹ Jean-Louis Chavy
❺ Alain Chavy
❻ Chanson Père et Fils

MAP 2 Puligny-Montrachet, *Les Folatières*

regisseur of the Domaine Leflaive, says that in the southern part of the *climat* there is a little more clay: hence powerful but elegant wines with good fruit; while the more stony northern section makes more mineral wines. Franck Grux of Olivier Leflaive Frères points out that upslope the surface soil is very thin. It can get very hot and dry; and the fruit can rapidly degenerate into super-ripeness, producing wine which is heavy and superficial on the follow-through: too *primeur* for comfort. I incline to the view that the best sector is that on the same latitudinal line as the Caillerets, rather than further upslope. Here are the most complete Folatières.

Those who have vines here, in rough south to north order, include Philippe Chavy, the Château de Puligny, Domaine des Lambrays, Jean Chartron, Réne Monnier, Paul Pernot (in part), Vincent Girardin, and Sylvain Bzikot. Folatières is a full wine, meaty, mineral, and with plenty of weight of fruit and good grip. It ages well. The best, in the best vintages, require seven or eight years to mature. I asked the growers in the early months of 2010 whether they would be interested in participating in a comparative tasting, and I chose 2006, one of the best of the recent vintages, though perhaps one which is more vintage- than *terroir*-representative. They responded enthusiastically, though some did not have a single bottle to spare for the tasting.

The tasting was held at Hotel/Restaurant Le Montrachet in Puligny itself. My thanks to André Berthier, chef sommelier, and his colleagues for setting up the tasting.

TASTING NOTES

Bachelet-Monnot   From 2014   17.0
43 ares. Bottled after 18 months. 30 percent new oak.

Slightly heavy nose, with a touch of sulphur and at the same time some evolution. Better on the palate. Much cleaner. Fullish body. Very good grip. Plenty of depth. Properly dry. Quite a meaty wine. Long and satisfying. Very good indeed.

Bernard-Bonin   From 2014   18.5
16 ares. 18 months. 30 percent new oak.

Clean, crisp, racy, high-class nose. Subtle and flowery. Medium-full body. Ripe, complex, lovely fruit. Very well-balanced. Lots of depth and distinction. Very fine. Just about ready.

Vincent Bouzereau   Now to 2018   15.0
20 ares. 11 months. 20 percent new oak.

Delicate nose. There doesn't seem to be a lot of depth here. On the palate medium to medium-full body. Clean and enjoyable. But not really the concentration and dimension of a top *premier cru*. Balanced but a bit slight. Good at best.

Sylvain Bzikot   From 2014   17.0
40 ares. 15 to 18 months. 40 percent new oak.

Ripe nose, a touch exotic. Fullish, open, balanced, and just about *à point*. Good grip. Plump. Quite rich. An attractive wine which is long on the palate and just about ready. Very good indeed.

Michel Caillot   Now to 2017   15.5
17 ares. 12 months in cask, followed by 12 months *en cuve*. 100 percent 1-year-old casks.

Quite evolved and a little tropical on the nose. Full and rich, but does it lack a little grip? Better on the palate. Fullish, abundant, decent acidity. Not too exotic, but it could have done with a little more finesse. Balanced and quite concentrated nevertheless. Good plus.

Jean Chartron   Now to 2017   17.0
45 ares. 12 months in cask and then 3 in vat. 30 percent new oak.

Attractive, cool, and minerally on the nose, but a little lightweight. Medium to medium-full body. Good attack, ripe and racy with a touch of new oak. Lacks a little energy on the follow-through but by no means short. Very good indeed.

Chàteau de Puligny   From 2014   17.5

52 ares. 12 months plus 3 months *en cuve*. 15 percent 600 litre new oak casks.

Firm, quite closed nose. But good depth and grip underneath. Lots of class too. Full body, backward, meaty, and profound. Very good grip. It is just a little four-square at present, but it needs time. Fine.

Alain Chavy   From 2014   17.5

1.35 ares. 15 to 16 months. 25 percent new oak.

A slight touch of sulphur on the nose. Better on the palate. Youthful. Medium-full body. Lots of energy and plenty of depth. Lovely balanced, classy fruit, and very good grip. Fine.

Hubert Chavy   Now to 2018   18.0

60 ares. 12 months. 25 percent new oak.

From magnum. Lovely rich, ripe nose. A touch more exotic than most. Lovely fruit. Medium-full body. Subtle, balanced, vigorous, and very complex at the end. Very long and classy indeed. Fine plus.

Jean-Louis Chavy   Now to 2018   18.5

1.03 ha. 14 months. 30 percent new oak.

Lovely subtle nose. Delicate, complex, classy fruit. Not a blockbuster. Indeed quite understated. Very harmonious, long, and complex. Very fine.

Philippe Chavy   From 2014   19.0

30 ares. 11 months. 30 percent new oak.

The nose is quite hidden. Fullish and a bit four-square on the palate. But a lot of depth and vigour. Still very young. Fullish, classy, very good grip. Got better and better in the glass. Very fine plus.

Maison Joseph Drouhin   Now to 2017   15.5

Usual purchase not disclosed. 11 months. 30 percent new oak.

Just a touch of sulphur on the nose. Ripe and rich and quite exotic on the palate. Fullish body.

Not the greatest of class but good energy. Good plus.

Benoit Ente   Now to 2018   17.0

27 ares. 12 months. 20 percent new oak.

Classy if not very concentrated on the nose. Fullish, clean, racy, and energetic on the palate. Finishes better than it starts. No lack of depth or finesse. Very good indeed.

Vincent Girardin   Now to 2020   19.0

1.40 ha. 18 months. 20 percent new oak.

Very lovely nose. Lots of class. Subtle and complex. Balanced and definitive. Medium-full body. Ripe, multidimensional, especially at the end. Very lovely. Very fine plus.

Thierry Glantenay   Now to 2020   19.5

50 ares. 14 to 16 months. 20 percent new oak.

Classy nose. Still closed. Fullish body. Balanced, and full of fruit. This is really very fine indeed. Multidimensional.

Louis Jadot   Now to 2019   18.5

24 ares. 20 months. 20 percent new oak.

Delicate nose. A little more marked by the oak than most. Medium-full body. Ripe, clean, and well-balanced. Gently oaky on the palate but long and classy. Very fine.

Domaine des Lambrays   From 2014   19.5

29 ares. 12 to 14 months. 50 percent new oak.

Full, concentrated, very well-balanced nose. This is profound and youthful. Full-bodied. Ripe, rich, and vigorous. Lots of wine here. Lots of depth and lots of class. Very lovely finish. Needs time. Very fine indeed.

Maison Louis Latour   Now to 2017   15.0

Usually buy the equivalent of 10 *pièces*. 12 months. 50 percent new oak.

Not a great deal on the nose. Medium-full body. Somewhat four-square. Not a lot of either class nor dimension, but decent grip and length. Good.

Domaine Leflaive
From 2014 18.5

1.07 ha. 12 months in cask, then 6 to 8 months in tank. 20 percent new oak.

From magnum. Good balanced fruit on the nose. Fullish body. Ripe. Good grip. Good depth. Lots of energy and a long way from being ready for drinking. Lots of dimension and concentration. Very fine.

Maison Olivier Leflaive
Frères
Now to 2018 18.5

Usually buy the equivalent of 8 to 10 *pièces*. 15 to 18 months. 25 percent new oak.

From magnum. Subtle nose. There is more here than seems at first. Classy and very harmonious. Lovely fruit. Fullish body. Ripe and complex and multidimensional. Very lovely, long, lingering finish. Very fine.

René Monnier
From 2014 19.5

82 ares. 14 months. 30 percent new oak.

From magnum. Complex, subtle nose. Still not fully evolved. But classy and promising. Beautifully balanced. Fullish body. Poised, energetic, and very high class. Very fine indeed.

Jean Pascal et Fils
Now to 2018 18.0

63 ares. 11 months. 25 percent new oak.

Attractive peachy fruit on the nose. Good grip. Ample and very Puligny. Medium-full body. Succulent, pure, balanced, and classy. Lovely finish. Fine plus.

Pernot
Drink soon 13.5

3.08 ha. 11 months. 40 percent new oak.

Not a lot of depth or class on the nose. A bit of sulphur too. I feel this is one of those 2006s that was picked a little late. It is a little concocted. Others liked it more than I did. Three voted it as one of their favourites.

Maison Remoissenet
Père et Fils
From 2014 18.0

Usually buy the equivalent of 5 *pièces*. 16 months. 40 percent new oak.

Ripe, racy, and classy on the nose. Profound and stylish. Lots of dimension. Full-bodied. Youthful. Very good depth. A big wine with lots of energy. Needs time. Fine plus.

Etienne Sauzet
Now to 2017 17.0

27 ares. Plus the equivalent of 9 *pièces* bought as *négociant*. 18 months. 25 percent new oak.

Lovely fruit on the nose. Ripe, clean, and harmonious. Nicely racy. Medium-full body. Balanced. Good grip. It just seems to tail off a bit at the end. Very good indeed but not fine.

I took a consensus of the group's preferences. The four most favoured wines were those of Vincent Girardin, Domaine Leflaive, Olivier Leflaive, and Remoissenet—the last two being merchant wines (but where such merchants were heavily involved in the local viticulture and were bought in as fruit). The Lambrays sample, plus one or two others, were late arrivals and sampled seperately. Note that Chanson and Faiveley, who can today offer you Folatières, did not possess their parcels in 2006.

En primeur, Puligny-Montrachet, Les Folatières, 2006, was offered at 240 to 275 pounds sterling per six bottles, ex cellars, to customers in Britain, $450 or so per sixpack in the United States. As well as the above, the following also produce Folatières: the Domaine d'Auvenay in Saint-Romain, Jean-Michel Gaunoux and Château Genot-Boulanger, both in Meursault, and the Domaine Maroslavac-Léger in Puligny. The wine may also be carried by other merchants.

Chassagne-Montrachet, Les Caillerets, 2007

APART FROM MORGEOT, a name which can be given to any *premier cru* vineyard downslope from the little road which connects Chassagne and Santenay, and to all the land immediately upslope from Fairendes, close to the village, to Clos Pitois on the Santenay border—a surface area of 52 hectares—and apart from the mainly red wine vineyard of Clos-Saint-Jean, Les Caillerets is Chassagne's largest *premier cru*. It is also widely recognised as the best.

The *climat*—which includes the subdivisions of En Cailleret, Chassagne, Vigne Derrière, and Les Combards—covers 10.68 hectares and lies at an altitude of between 250 and 280 metres above sea level immediately to the south of the village itself. For some of the growers, such as Guy Amiot and his son Thierry, it is literally their back garden.

As you might expect from the name Caillerets, the soil is predominantly stony and shallow. Up at the top of the slope, there are outcrops of bare rock. He we find mainly a white marl. This gives the wine weight. Lower down, there is more surface soil and it is calcareous, pro-ducing a wine of steely elegance. A blend of the two, everyone says, makes the best wine.

At best, and there is plenty of best, as the sixteen or so owners include most of the "first division" in the village, this is a Chassagne white—the transformation from Pinot to Chardonnay having taken place in the 1940s and 1950s, according to the late Albert Morey, who claimed to have been one of the pioneers in this respect—of real elegance, without the four-square character of a Morgeot, but with more weight and staying power than, say, an Embazées or a Romanée. Only (Grandes) Ruchottes can rival it. It requires a year or two more than most of the other first growths to come round, but then, as one might expect, it will hold up longer. The most successful vintages are not at their apogee until they are eight years old and still more than satisfactory at age twelve or even fifteen.

The 2007 vintage, which was the subject of the tasing below, was an early harvest following a precocious spring, but then a generally mediocre summer. But the weather wasn't

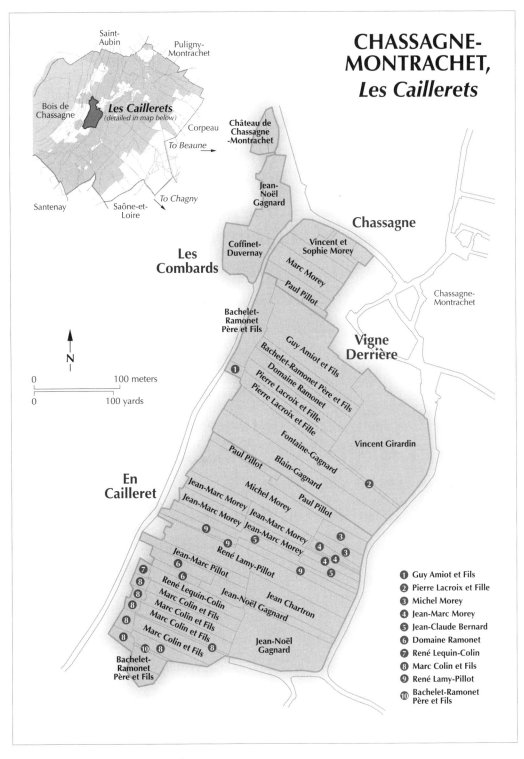

CHASSAGNE-MONTRACHET, *Les Caillerets*

Saint-Aubin

Puligny-Montrachet

Bois de Chassagne

Les Caillerets
(detailed in map below)

Corpeau

To Beaune →

Santenay

Saône-et-Loire

To Chagny

Château de Chassagne-Montrachet

Jean-Noël Gagnard

Chassagne

Coffinet-Duvernay

Vincent et Sophie Morey

Les Combards

Marc Morey

Paul Pillot

Chassagne-Montrachet

Bachelet-Ramonet Père et Fils

Guy Amiot et Fils

Vigne Derrière

❶

Bachelet-Ramonet Père et Fils

Domaine Ramonet

Pierre Lacroix et Fille

Pierre Lacroix et Fille

Vincent Girardin

Fontaine-Gagnard

Paul Pillot

Blain-Gagnard

N

0   100 meters

0   100 yards

En Cailleret

Jean-Marc Morey

Michel Morey

Paul Pillot

❷

Jean-Marc Morey

Jean-Marc Morey

Jean-Marc Morey

❾

❾

René Lamy-Pillot

❺

❸

❹ ❸

❹ ❹

❺

Jean-Marc Pillot

❻

❼

❻

❽

René Lequin-Colin

Marc Colin et Fils

Jean-Noël Gagnard

Jean Chartron

❽

❽

Marc Colin et Fils

Marc Colin et Fils

❽

Marc Colin et Fils

❿ ❽

❽

Jean-Noël Gagnard

Bachelet-Ramonet Père et Fils

❶ Guy Amiot et Fils
❷ Pierre Lacroix et Fille
❸ Michel Morey
❹ Jean-Marc Morey
❺ Jean-Claude Bernard
❻ Domaine Ramonet
❼ René Lequin-Colin
❽ Marc Colin et Fils
❾ René Lamy-Pillot
❿ Bachelet-Ramonet Père et Fils

MAP 3 Chassagne-Montrachet, *Les Caillerets*

all *that* bad. There was some sun and heat, if intermittent, and not too much rain, even if it was largely gray. Unlike in many vintages, the Pinots matured in advance of the Chardonnays. Those in Chassagne who did not start on their whites until the second week of September (September 10 was a Monday) were able to benefit from, finally, a change to dry, stable weather and an evaporating north wind. This concentrated the flavours without reducing the acidity—which, before malo, was very high. The result was white wines of more definition and greater weight and depth than their red counterparts. It is difficult to generalize—which is best?—between the 2005, 2006, and 2007 whites. In each vintage there are some lovely wines, and they are now just about ready.

The following tasting took place at the Restaurant-Hotel Montrachet in Puligny in January 2011. My grateful thanks to the growers for participating and to Thierry and his team for setting things up. I asked the growers to note their three favourites among the thirteen wines on offer. Just about every wine received at least one vote (and far as I could make out, no one voted for their own wine). Marginally ahead of the rest was the wine of Marc Colin and his family. This, as you will see below, was one of my *least* favourites. *De Gustibus!*

All wines, unless otherwise stated, are "*proprietaire*" and produced by the *lutte raisonnée*.

TASTING NOTES

Bachelet-Ramonet, Père et Fils
Now to 2018   15.5

55 ares. 18 to 20 percent new wood. Bottled after 16 months.

Restrained nose at first. Ripe, cool, fresh, and minerally as it evolved. Medium-full body. A little oak. Good acidity. Not the greatest finesse, but good weight and energy. Good plus.

Blain-Gagnard
Now to 2020   18.0

56 ares. 15 percent new wood. Bottled after 11 months.

Fresh colour. Youthful nose. A touch of oak. Flowery, minerally, balanced, and attractive. Medium-full body. Long, positive, and stylish. This has depth and finesse. Fine plus.

Château de Chassagne, Maison Michel Picard
Now to 2018   15.0

11 ares. 50 percent new wood. Bottled after 12 months.

The colour is a little more evolved than most. On the nose this is full, rich, ample, and quite oaky. A fullish quite powerful wine. Good grip nevertheless. Got better as it evolved but nevertheless a little clumsy. Another year in bottle won't do it any harm.

Coffinet-Duvernay
Now to 2017   17.0

25 ares. 50 percent new wood. Bottled after 17 to 18 months.

Flowery-herbal nose. Not a lot of oak. Some evolution. Perhaps a slight lack of energy. On the palate quite forward. Medium body. But very elegant. The fruit is most attractive. Harmonious and very good indeed, if not for the long term.

Marc Colin et Fils
Now to 2017   14.5

73 ares. One-third new wood. Bottled after 15 months.

I find something slightly scented on the nose, which puts me off. Some botrytis? Less so on the attack, but it comes back on the finish. Medium to medium-full body. Decent fruit and grip. Little evidence of oak.

Fontaine-Gagnard
Now to 2020   19.0

56 ares. 30 percent new wood. Bottled after 12 months.

Ripe, reasonably substantial, flowery, balanced nose. Good intensity and flair here. Fullish, ample, and concentrated on the palate. Excellent grip. Lovely purity and harmony. Just the very slightest touch of oak. A yardstick example.

Jean-Nöel Gagnard Now to 2019 17.5

1.06 ha. Culture biologique. 30 percent new wood. Bottled after 18 months.

Ample colour. A little evolution. But on the nose still a little reticent. Medium to medium-full body. Rich, concentrated, attractive, and well-balanced. Good depth. Good class. Long and positive. Fine.

Maison Louis Latour Now to 2018 15.5

Merchant wine. Latour buys the equivalent of 14 barrels (i.e., more or less the equivalent of 1 ha). 50 percent new wood. Bottled after 16 months.

Fresh, ripe nose with a touch of oak. Medium body. Balanced, attractive, and *à point*. Good follow-through, but essentially a delicate wine. It tails off a bit. Good plus.

Lamy-Pillot Now to 2017 15.5

Magnum. 55 ares, *en fermage* from Madame Fernand Chauve since 1997. No new wood in this vintage.

Light, flowery nose. No evidence of oak, but some evolution. Medium to medium-full body. The acidity in evidence. Reasonable length, but a touch clumsy. Better as it evolved but good plus at best.

René Lequin-Colin Now to 2020 18.5

19 ares, *en fermage*. Biodynamic from 2010. 20 percent new wood. Bottled after 15 months.

Good substantial nose, with at first a touch of SO_2 (sulphur dioxide), but this blew off. Fresh, plump, full-bodied, rich, and concentrated. Very good grip and lovely fruit. Real depth. Will still improve. Very fine.

Marc Morey Now to 2016 15.5

20 ares. 25 to 30 percent new wood. Bottled after 15 months.

Soft, fruity nose. Plump and attractive if without any real depth. Fully developed. Medium body. Decently positive and harmonious. Very slightly oaky. Long enough but a bit neutral at the end. Good plus.

Vincent et Sophie Morey Now to 2019 16.5

35 ares. 45 percent new oak. Bottled after 11 months.

Broad-flavoured nose with a touch of oak and some evolution. Fullish, rich, and quite powerful. This will still improve. Indeed, it got better and better in the glass. Very good plus. One of the group favourites.

Paul Pillot Now to 2018 16.5

49 ares. 20 percent new wood. Bottled after 16 to 18 months.

At first the nose was a bit neutral and four-square, but it opened up and brightened up on aeration. Medium to medium-full body. Good grip. Only very slightly oaky. Good energy. Will improve. Very good plus. Another group favourite.

Three important domaines did not make their wines available for tasting: Guy Amiot et Fils (62 ares), Ramonet (35 ares in two parcels), and Jean Chartron of Puligny (30 ares). In addition, Vincent Girardin owns just under 1 hectare, which he bought from the Domaine Duperrier Adam in 2008.

Meursault, Les Genevrières, 2008

GENEVRIÈRES is the second largest of the Meursault *premiers crus*, and, with Charmes and Perrières, one of the "big three." It lies on two levels on either side of the Route des *Grands Crus*; the upper part, the *dessus*, being on the same latitude as the Perrières, and on the slope; while lower down, next to the upper part of Les Charmes, and on flatter land, is the Genevrières *dessous*.

Between Perrières and Genevrières *dessus* is a minor road which reaches up towards the unofficial *deuxièmes crus* of Narvaux, Tillets, and so on, which lie above the first growths, and this is a good place to stop and survey the lay of the land. I often take groups of clients here. To the south, the soil in Perrières is covered in limestone debris the colour of weak milky coffee. To the north, this part of the Genevrières shows a similar rocky aspect, but both the earth and the stones have a more red-brown colour. This is a result of the preponderance of iron in the soil. Lower down on the one side is Charmes: less limestone debris, proper stones the size of golf balls, and muddier in colour.

The soil in Meursault Genevrières *dessous* is similar to the Charmes, but with the iron-based brown shift in colour.

All this makes, or so it should, a difference in flavour. Perrières is minerally, Charmes is flowery, and Genevrières has a spicier, more opulent character, often with a touch of cirtus peel or candied fruit. The upper part is minerally, the lower more fleshy. Most growers, particularly if they are fortunate enough to have their vineyards in the *dessus*, will insist to you that this upper vineyard produces better wine than the *dessous*. They are right. It has more definition. Here the soil is Bathonian, a Callovian limestone, in parts mixed with an Argovian white marl. Upslope the surface layer is thin and the rock is hard; lower down it is deeper, redder in colour, and crumbly—what the French call *lave*.

The white wine from Genevrières has long been considered among the best in Meursault, even if, until the 1930s, whites did not fetch the equivalent prices of reds. Back in 1816, André Jullien rated it third after Perrières and Goutte

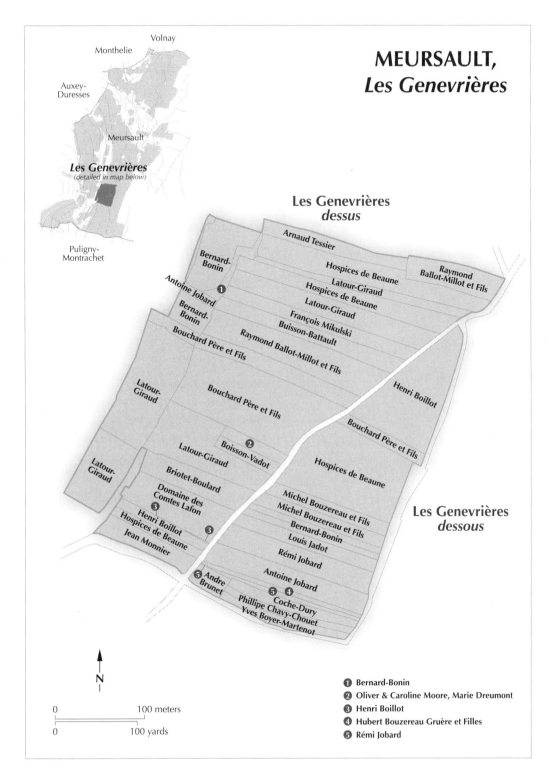

Volnay

Monthelie

Auxey-
Duresses

Meursault

Les Genevrières
(detailed in map below)

Puligny-
Montrachet

MEURSAULT,
Les Genevrières

Les Genevrières
dessus

Arnaud Tessier

Bernard-
Bonin

Hospices de Beaune

Latour-Giraud

Hospices de Beaune

Latour-Giraud

Raymond
Ballot-Millot et Fils

Antoine Jobard

1

Bernard-
Bonin

Bouchard Père et Fils

François Mikulski

Buisson-Battault

Raymond Ballot-Millot et Fils

Latour-
Giraud

Bouchard Père et Fils

Henri Boillot

Bouchard Père et Fils

Latour-Giraud

Boisson-Vadot

2

Hospices de Beaune

Latour-
Giraud

Briotet-Boulard

Domaine des
Comtes Lafon

3

Michel Bouzereau et Fils

Michel Bouzereau et Fils

Bernard-Bonin

Les Genevrières
dessous

Henri Boillot

3

Hospices de Beaune

Jean Monnier

Louis Jadot

Rémi Jobard

Antoine Jobard

5 Andre
Brunet

5 **4**
Coche-Dury
Phillipe Chavy-Chouet
Yves Boyer-Martenot

N

0   100 meters

0   100 yards

1 Bernard-Bonin
2 Oliver & Caroline Moore, Marie Dreumont
3 Henri Boillot
4 Hubert Bouzereau Gruère et Filles
5 Rémi Jobard

MAP 4 Meursault, *Les Genevrières*

d'Or (and Combettes in Puligny, which he mistakenly places in Meursault).

Dr. Lavalle, almost fifty years later, appoints Perrières as a *tête de cuvée,* while Genevrières *dessus,* Charmes *dessus,* and Bouchères and Goutte d'Or were *premières cuvées.*

The combined Genevières vineyard measures 16.48 hectares, of which about 9 are in the *dessus.* This is roughly half of Les Charmes, but then Genevrières doesn't run all the way down to the Meursault-Puligny road (which Charmes does); Limouzin lies beneath it. The largest owner is Bouchard Père et Fils, with 2.65 hectares, followed by Latour-Giraud with 2.39 hectares. Only one other possesses more than 80 ares. In total, there are some thirty exploitants, if you include three or four merchants who regularly list the wine. In addition, there is the Hospices de Beaune, the third largest owner with 1.92 hectares. They produce two *cuvées*: the largest one (1.48 ha) being half *dessus* and half *dessous,* called after its benefactor Félix Baudot; and the smaller Cuvée Humbolt (56 ares) coming entirely from the lower part. As you travel up from the Meursault-Puligny road to the upper road—what I call the first growth—you pass the cross denoting a Hospice vineyard.

In January 2011 I invited the locals to participate in a blind tasting of the 2008 vintage. We sampled fifteen wines, one or two late-comers being sampled separately. I asked the growers to name their top three. The results were rather inconclusive. Every wine got a vote. I was the only one to vote for my clear favourite, the Jadot example.

Could you tell the difference between the wines from the *dessus* and the *dessous*? And were those from the *dessus* better? Looking at my notes (it was of course a blind tasting and the wines were all mixed up), I think the answer to both questions is a marginal yes. Certainly the wines from the upper part showed a more minerally aspect and seemed to have more future. Other growers which have a high reputation include Ballot-Minot, Henri Boillot, Coche-Dury, Rémi Jobard, and Jean Monnier.

TASTING NOTES

Domaine Bernard-Bonin   Now to 2016   17.0
77 ares. Half in the *dessus,* half in the *dessous.* 50-year-old vines. 25 percent new oak. Batonnage. Bottled after 18 to 19 months.

Good fruit on the nose. Fresh and stylish. Ripe and balanced. Not the greatest concentration, but ample and reasonably profound. The finish is positive and elegant. Very good indeed. Just about ready.

Domaine Guy Bocard   Now to 2018   17.0
18 ares. In the *dessous.* 45-year-old vines. 5 percent new oak. A "little" batonnage. Bottled after 20 months.

Good fresh nose with a touch of sherbert lemons. Attractive. Just about mature. Medium to medium-full body. Balanced, fruity, and elegant. Very good indeed.

Domaine Bouchard Père et Fils   From 2015   17.5
2.65 ha. In the *dessus.* 27-year-old vines on average. 13 percent new oak. No batonnage, but they roll the barrels about. Bottled after 13 to 14 months.

A bit tight on the nose still. Not much oak. Some ripeness though. Rather better on the palate and as it opened out. Medium-full body. Yes, there is a touch of oak. Good grip. Still youthful. Finishes well. Classy indeed. This will keep. Fine.

Domaine Michel Bouzereau et Fils   From 2014   16.5
52 ares. In the *dessous.* 25-year-old vines. 25 percent new oak. Batonnage. Bottled after 16 months.

Good colour. Still quite closed. But good depth here. Medium-full weight. Good grip. This will still improve. Just a touch of oak. Very good plus.

Domaine Hubert Bouzereau et Filles   From 2016   18.5
10 ares. In the *dessous.* 60-year-old vines. 25 percent new oak. Batonnage. Bottled after 15 months.

Clean flowery nose. Nicely pure and elegant. Medium to medium-full weight. Good concentration. Plenty of vigour and depth. Long. Complex. Very fine. Still needs time.

Domaine Boyer-Martenot Now to 2016 16.5

19 ares. In the *dessous*. 45-year-old vines. 33 percent new oak. Batonnage. Bottled after 11 months.

Stylish nose. Good depth. Ripe flowery fruit. Just about ready. Medium to medium-full body. Fresh and balanced. Not the greatest complexity and dimension but very good plus.

Domaine Buisson-Battault Now to 2016 15.5

63 ares. In the *dessus*. 45-year-old vines on average. 20 percent new oak. 3 batonnages. Bottled after 18 months.

Round somewhat spicy-*agrumes* (candied peel) nose. Quite developed. Medium weight. Fully ready. Decent balance but no great weight or concentration. Quite stylish. Good plus.

Domaine Darviot-Perrin From 2014 17.5

41 ares. In the *dessus*. 50-year-old vines on average. 33 percent new oak. One batonnage every two weeks until the malo-lactic fermentation is finished. Bottled after 18 months.

Quite a delicate but stylish nose. Ripe, flowery, and sherbert lemony. Medium to medium-full body. Balanced, clean, and elegant. Only just about ready. Finishes well. This is fine.

Domaine Louis Jadot From 2015 19.0

29 ares. In the *dessus*. 20-year-old vines. 25 percent new oak. No malo-lactic. No batonnage. Bottled after 18 months.

Fresh, youthful, stylish nose. Clean and positive. Lovely purity. Medium-full body. Excellent, very complex, very harmonious fruit. Long and multidimensional. Very elegant. Will last well. A lovely wine. Very fine indeed.

Domaine Antoine Jobard From 2015 18.0

50 ares. In the *dessous*. 36-year-old vines. 20 percent new oak. No batonnage. Bottled after 23 months.

Classy, balanced nose. Good depth and weight. This is a fine example. Pure and concentrated. Lovely fruit. Very good grip. Elegant and vigorous and plenty of potential. Fine plus.

Domaines des Comtes Lafon Now to 2018 17.5

55 ares. In the *dessus*. 25 percent vines of 18 years, 75 percent 65-year-old vines. 40 percent new wood. 3 or 4 batonnages. Bottled after 18 months.

Firm, full, and profound on the nose. Rich and ripe. Medium-full body. A nice touch of new oak. Well balanced. Not quite the grip and power on the palate that the nose had suggested, but fine enough. Just about ready.

Domaine Latour-Giraud From 2015 17.5

2.39 ha. In the *dessus*. 35-year-old vines. 25 percent new oak. Batonnage. Bottled after 18 months.

Restrained nose. Still youthful. Good class though. Concentrated, composed, fresh fruit. Good energy. Just a touch of oak. This still needs time and has a fine future.

Domaine Michelot Drink soon 12.0

40 ares. In the *dessus*. 45-year-old vines. 15 to 20 percent new oak. Batonnage. Bottled after 15 to 20 months.

This is rather a common wine. No evidence of any new oak. The fruit is raw and coarse. Quite high acidity. Rather a dead sulphury background. A bad bottle? Jean-Francois Mestre, today's proprietor, didn't seem unduly concerned.

Domaine Francois Mikulski Now to 2018 16.0

58 ares. In the *dessus*. 42-year-old vines. 16 percent new oak. 3 batonnages early on. Bottled after 18 months.

Broad ample nose, showing a little new oak. Balanced and full of fruit, if just a little four-square. Softer on the palate. A touch of candied peel and spice. Good acidity. Very good finish. Just about ready.

Domaine Alain Patriache Now to 2016 17.0

12 ares. In the *dessus*. 60-year-old vines. 40 percent new oak. 3 batonnages. Bottled after 6 months.

Nutty, oaky nose. Yet not much depth and concentration underneath. Medium body. Ready. Clean, balanced, and stylish. Very good indeed.

Volnay, Les Santenots, 2005

SANTENOTS IS AN ANOMALY. It lies within the commune of Meursault, but with some minute exceptions, Pinot Noir rather than Chardonnay is grown here. Of course it is on the north side of Meursault, adjacent to Volnay Les Cailleretes—the authorities have for years allowed the wine to be called Volnay. And no one would disagree for a minute that the red grape produces by far the more interesting wine.

The vineyard has probably always been planted in Pinot Noir. We have evidence from Thomas Jefferson that red wines made twice the price of whites in this part of the world (so the inhabitants of Volnay were able to enjoy white bread, while those of Meursault could only afford black bread). It is quite clear that this is red wine soil, as opposed to what you find in Perrières and Genevrières at the other end of the village. Jasper Morris cites a reference to Santenots dating from 1218, when the Abbaye de Tart ceded vineyards to the Abbaye de Citeaux. Sadly, it seems that whether the vineyard produced white wine or red is not stated. Subsequently the *climat* was rated a *tête de cuvée* by Lavalle in 1855, alongside Champans and Caillerets, but superior to Clos de Chênes and Taillepieds—a rating I have always felt was a grave error of judgment.

Santenots, at 27.4 hectares (for red wine in 2005 production: 1,118 hectolitres; 29.1 in total surface for both colours in the books), is by far the largest vineyard in Volnay. The heart is the 8.8 hectares Santenots du Milieu, shared by amongst others, Lafon and Jacques Prieur, the latter under the title Clos des Santenots. Upslope is the Santenots Blancs (2.9 hectares). Here a few misguided souls (in my view) persist with Chardonnay—the Marquis d'Angerville, Bitouzet-Prieur, Monthélie-Douhairet, there may be others. These are labelled Meursault, Santenots. To the south lies the Plures (10.4 hectares). This is good land, producing, according to Dominique Lafon, wine with less structure but perhaps more finesse than the Santenots du Milieu. Downslope, and denigrated by critics, is the 7.6 hectare Santenots de Dessous. It is not worthy of *premier cru* status, says Morris, pointing out that any white wine from here would be merely village Meursault.

The soil structure is complex. At the top of the slope, as in the Clos de Chênes on the other side of the road, there is Bathonian scree and debris over the mother rock, which is hard. There is not much surface soil. The soil is red in colour, and there are quite a number

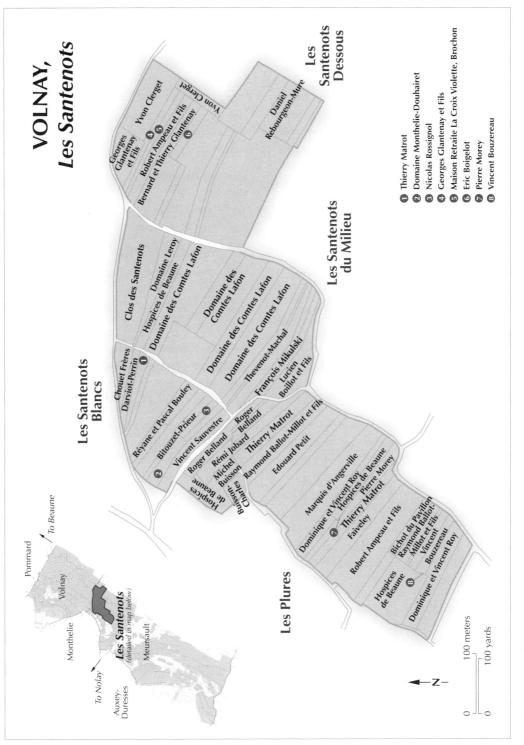

VOLNAY, *Les Santenots*

To Beaune

Pommard

Volnay

Monthelie

Les Santenots
(detailed in map below)

To Nolay

Auxey-
Duresses

Meursault

Les Santenots Blancs

Georges Glantenay et Fils

Yvon Clerget

Robert Ampeau et Fils ❹ ❺

Bernard et Thierry Glantenay

Yvon Clerget ❻

Les Santenots Dessous

Daniel Rebourgeon-Mure

Clos des Santenots

Domaine Leroy

Hospices de Beaune

Domaine des Comtes Lafon

Chouet Frères Darviot-Perrin ❶

Réyane et Pascal Bouley

Bitouzet-Prieur ❸

Vincent Sauvestre

❷

Roger Belland

Rémi Jobard

Michel Buisson

Charles Buisson-de Beaune

Hospices de Beaune

Domaine des Comtes Lafon

Domaine des Comtes Lafon

Domaine des Comtes Lafon

Thevenot-Machal

François Mikulski

Lucien Boillot et Fils

Les Santenots du Milieu

Roger Belland

Thierry Matrot

Raymond Ballot-Millot et Fils

Edouard Petit

Marquis d'Angerville

Dominique et Vincent Roy

Hospices de Beaune

Pierre Morey

Thierry Matrot ❼

Faiveley

Robert Ampeau et Fils

Bichot du Pavillon

Raymond Ballot-Millot et Fils

Vincent Bouzereau

Hospices de Beaune ❽

Dominique et Vincent Roy

Les Plures

❶ Thierry Matrot
❷ Domaine Monthelie-Douhairet
❸ Nicolas Rossignol
❹ Georges Glantenay et Fils
❺ Maison Retraite La Croix Violette, Brochon
❻ Eric Boigelot
❼ Pierre Morey
❽ Vincent Bouzereau

N

0   100 meters
0   100 yards

MAP 5 Volnay, *Les Santenots*

of stones. There is a lot more clay than in the Caillerets or Champans (and indeed elsewhere in Volnay), for over the Bathonian rock there is Oxfordian or Argovian crumbly limestone—what the French call *lave*.

All these *climats* are about 240 to 280 metres above sea level. In the Santenots this produces a very individual Volnay. Not the pure, elegant wine you find in the Caillerets at the top (the 60 *ouvrées,* for instance), nor at the bottom of the Clos des Chênes or in the Taillepieds, where the wines are mineral and both more linear and lusher, nor indeed in the Champans, where from the best domaines such as d'Angerville we have depth and size while remaining essentially round as well as rich. Santenots are—and I don't want to denigrate them by any means—somewhat less aristocratic. Yet they can be very lovely, among the greatest of the Côte de Beaune.

According to the list I was given by the local *syndicat des producteurs*, there are just over thirty owners and lease-holders in the Santenots, including the Hospices de Beaune, who produce the *cuvées* Jehan de Massol and Gauvain. The domaines of Comtes Lafon, Jacques Prieur, and Ampeau are the most signicant—all looking after more than a hectare.

The following examples of 2005 were sampled, courtesy of the Montrachet Restaurant in Puligny, who set the whole thing up blind (my thanks to them) in January 2012. The group as a whole voted the wine of Pierre and Anne Morey in first place. Other growers which should be noted include Nicolas Rossignol-Jeanniard, Leroy, Ballot-Millot, Vincent Sauvestre, Remi Jobard, and Sylvie Esmonin in Gevrey-Chambertin.

TASTING NOTES

Maison Albert Bichot,
Domaine du Pavillon   Now to 2019   15.0
30 ares. In the Pleures. 30-year-old vines. Cold-soaking at 14°C for 4 days. Destemmed. 35 percent new oak.

Medium to medium-full colour. Soft, fruity nose. But there doesn't seem to be much back-

bone here. Medium body. Quite fresh. A pleasant example with reasonable style but only village depth. Just about ready. Good at best.

Domaine Eric Boigelot   Now to 2020   15.0
30 ares. In the *dessous*. 50-year-old vines. Cold-soaking for 12 days. Destemmed. 15 percent new oak.

Medium to medium-full colour. Soft, forward, fruity but not very sophisticated nose. Medium body. Ripe and balanced. But not a great deal of grip and dimension. Fruity and agreeable but lacks depth. Good at best.

Domaine Réyane et
Pascal Bouley   Now to 2020   16.0
9 ares. In the Santenots Blancs; 35-year-old vines. Cold-soaking for two days. Destemmed. 1-year-old barrels.

Medium to medium-full colour. Quite a forward but stylish, balanced nose. Medium body. Not much tannin. Plump, fresh, fruity, and attractive. But forward. Shouldn't a Santenots have more to it than this? Very good though.

Domaine Vincent Bouzereau   From 2014   16.0
20 ares. In the Pleures. 60-year-old vines. Cold-soaking for 5 days. Destemmed. One-third new oak.

Medium-full colour. Fresh, balanced nose. A little unforthcoming at first. Medium to medium-full body. Good fruit. Decent grip. A slight lack of fat and succulence, so a touch astringent. But the wine has class and depth.

Domaine Bernard et
Thierry Glantenay   From 2016   16.5
68 ares. In the *dessous*. 30-year-old vines. No deliberate cold-soaking. 20 percent stems retained. 20 percent new oak.

Fullish colour. A touch stewed on the nose at first but better on evolution and on the palate. Quite full body. Ripe and rich. The tannins are quite sophisticated. Needs time to soften but there is good grip. Potentially very good plus.

Domaine Georges Glantenay
et Fils   From 2014   14.5
51 ares. In the *dessous*. 45-year-old vines. No deliberate cold-soaking. One-third of the stems retained. 40 percent new oak.

Medium-full colour. Somewhat sweaty on the nose at first. A bit of sulphur here. Medium-full body. A touch sweet and a touch astringent. Reasonably fresh but it lacks a bit of style. Quite good plus.

Domaine des Comtes Lafon   Now to 2020   17.0
3.78 ha. In the *milieu*. 40-year-old vines. Cold-soaking at 12°C for 4 or 5 days. Destemmed. 30 percent new oak.

Medium-full colour. Ripe, round, attractively balanced but forward nose. Medium to medium-full body. Plenty of fruit and good backbone. Very well put together. An elegant, engaging wine. If with a little less vigour than I would have expected, especially when I discovered whose it was. Just about ready. Very good indeed.

Domaine Thierry Matrot   From 2015   16.5
87 ares. 3 parcels, 2 in the Pleures, 1 in the Santenots Blancs. 32-year-old vines. Cold-soaking at 15°C for 3 to 6 days. Destemmed. 10 to 20 percent new oak.

Medium to medium-full colour. Some development. Fruity-spicy nose. Not a lot of refinement at first, but it developed in the glass. Classier and fresher on the palate. Medium to medium-full body. Balanced. Long. Stylish. Very good plus.

Domaine Mikulski   Now to 2019   14.0
90 ares. In the *milieu*. 50-year-old vines. Cold-soaking for 4 days. Destemmed. 30 percent new oak.

Medium-full colour. A rather sweet, bland nose. Lacks grip. Not much backbone either. Some SO₂. Only light to medium weight. The fruit is not bad, and the wine is fresher on the palate than the nose would suggest. Just about ready. Only quite good.

Domaine Pierre Morey   From 2015   17.0
35 ares. In the Pleures. 35-year-old vines. Cold-soaking for 8 days at 16°C. Destemmed. 50 percent new oak.

Fullish colour. Firm, substantial, rich, robust nose. The tannins show at present giving the wine a certain earthiness. Medium-full body. Ripe and fresh, even rich and meaty. Very good indeed. A Santenots for the future.

Christophe Pauchard,
Domaine de la Confrerie   From 2017   18.5
38 ares. In the Santenots Blancs. 50-year-old vines. Cold-soaking for 4 days at 12°C. Destemmed. 20 percent new oak.

Fullish colour. Good depth and style here on the nose. Fresh, rich, and classy. Fullish body. Some new oak. Rich and ripe on the palate. Quite concentrated. Very well-balanced. Lots of depth, and, above all, style. Lovely finish. A very fine wine from a grower I have to confess I had never heard of.

Domaine Jacques Prieur,
Les Santenots   Now to 2018   15.5
56 ares. In the Plures. 30-year-old vines. No deliberate cold-soaking. Destemmed. 45 percent new oak.

Medium-full colour. Soft, fruity, fragrant, mature nose. Good balance and class. Medium to medium-full body. Fresh and ripe if without a great deal of personality and depth. Good plus. Just about ready.

Domaine Jacques Prieur,
Clos des Santenots   From 2016   18.0
1.19 ha. In the *milieu*. 40-year-old vines. No deliberate cold-soaking. Destemmed. 100 percent new oak.

Full colour. Still youthful. Closed in on the nose. Rich, ripe, and tannin. Even a bit dense at present. Almost Pommard-ish. Full-bodied. Backward. Concentrated. Very good grip. Lots of wine here. Plus very good, ample, almost fat fruit. Fine plus. Needs time.

Domaine Rebougeon-Mure   From 2017   18.5
26 ares. In the *dessous*. 57-year-old vines. Cold-soaking for 6 days at 14°C. Destemmed. 30 percent new oak.

Medium-full colour. Little development. Fresh, abundant, ripe nose. Some new oak. Plenty of class and definition. Rich and with nice ripe tannins. Fullish body. Very good grip. Lots of sophisticated fruit. Harmonious, subtle, and complex. Very fine. Needs time.

Nuits-Saint-Georges, Les Saint-Georges

THE 2005 AND 2006 VINTAGES

DOWN AT THE BOTTOM of the middle section of Nuits-Saint-Georges, underneath Les Vaucrains and Les Chaines-Carteaux, and between Les Cailles and Les Didiers, lies the 7.52 hectare vineyard of Les Saint-Georges, widely considered, not only by the town itself, which has adopted the name as its suffix, to be Nuits' best *climat*.

It could also be Nuits' oldest. The Abbé Courtepée, writing before the French Revolution, stated that it was already planted with vines in the year AD 1000. In 1023 the land was given by Humbert, archdeacon of Autun, to the Chapitre of Saint-Denis, whose base was up in the hills in nearby Vergy. Dr. Morelot (1831) states that Les Saint-Georges was clearly the best vineyard in the commune. The historian Lavalle, twenty-four years later, placed the wine at the same level as Corton and Clos des Lambrays. Others since have called it unjust that the land was not ruled as a *grand cru* by the authorities in 1936.

Yes, perhaps, I would answer. But justifiably—clamour to be promoted?

Much of the vineyard territory in Les Saint-Georges is clearly not Richebourg. So if you promote this vineyard, how many more will follow suit? And this part of Nuits the vines are planted east-west—this is how the *climat* is divided. There are fifteen plots and thirteen owners. Most of the plots are small: only Thibault Liger-Belair, with over 2 hectares; Henri Gouges, with just over 1; and the Hospices de Nuits, with just under 1 hectare, are substantial. The rest make a token few *pièces* only.

The vineyard lies at an altitude of beween 245 and 260 metres above sea level, exposed to the east on a gentle slope of around 7 percent. The soil is a reddish-brown, relatively deep mixture of very stony, limestone debris, together with a little clay that has been washed down from the plateau above over the aeons. The mother rock underneath is Bathonian, the earliest era found in the Côte d'Or. In contrast, Les Vaucrains, above, contains more white oolite and a fraction of sand. Les Cailles, on the same level to the north, also has this sand element but more overflow from the land above.

This produces what Professor Saintsbury,

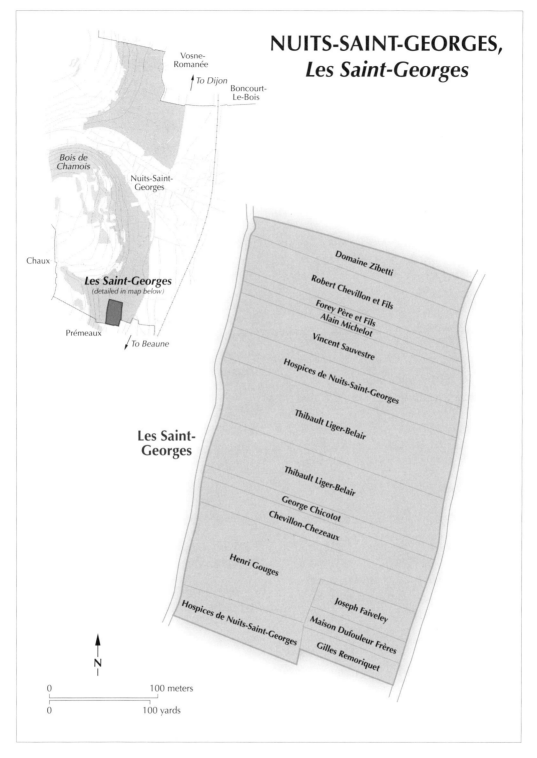

NUITS-SAINT-GEORGES,
Les Saint-Georges

Vosne-
Romanée

To Dijon

Boncourt-
Le-Bois

*Bois de
Chamois*

Nuits-Saint-
Georges

Chaux

Les Saint-Georges
(detailed in map below)

Prémeaux

To Beaune

**Les Saint-
Georges**

Domaine Zibetti

Robert Chevillon et Fils

Forey Père et Fils
Alain Michelot

Vincent Sauvestre

Hospices de Nuits-Saint-Georges

Thibault Liger-Belair

Thibault Liger-Belair

George Chicotot

Chevillon-Chezeaux

Henri Gouges

Joseph Faiveley

Maison Dufouleur Frères

Hospices de Nuits-Saint-Georges

Gilles Remoriquet

N

| 0 | 100 meters |
| 0 | 100 yards |

MAP 6 Nuits-Saint-Georges, *Les Saint-Georges*

writing about Hermitage, called "a manly wine." In the Gouges cellar the Vaucrains is more brutal, but the Les Saint-Georges is the most backward. The wine is well-coloured, solid, and tannic when young, and requires a decade at minimum before it even begins to round off. Frequently in the protracted adolescence it is frankly not very enjoyable. You just have to wait. But if you give it time, your patience will be rewarded. You will find a wine of richness, depth, and concentration which will last and last, getting steadily more and more mellow and fascinating. A Gouges 1959 Les Saint-Georges, generouly provided for the meal which followed, was mellow and splendidly complex, classy and vigorous: an absolutely delicious bottle.

And, compared with an equivalent Vosne-Romanée, it won't have cost you an arm and a leg.

In February 2011 I invited the growers to join me for a tasting of the 2005 and 2006 vintages. One declined, another I could not reach. My thanks to the team at Faiveley for allowing us to use their premises and providing a *casse-croute* afterwards.

TASTING NOTES

Maison Béjot, Domaine Vincent Sauvestre
En fermage from the Audidier-Maitrot family of Corgoloin.

2006   From 2016   16.0
Good, full, youthful colour. Somewhat flat, overblown nose. Lacks a bit of fruit and grip. Better on the palate. Medium-full body. A touch of oak. Rather more alive and succulent than the nose would suggest. Positive finish. Very good.

2005   From 2018   15.0
Fullish colour. Firm, slightly harsh nose. Rich underneath but a little ungainly. Medium-full body. Quite sweet. The tannins a mixture of richness and rusticity. So a bit unbalanced and unstylish. Reasonable but not really convincing fruit. Good at best.

Domaine Chevillon-Chezeaux
45 ares *en fermage* from the Frisby family of Hitchin, UK. 100 percent destemmed. 6 days cold-soaking. 25 percent new wood. Bottled after 16 months.

2006   From 2017   15.5
Fullish colour. Just a little hard and perhaps astringent on the nose. This is a bit old-fashioned. Slightly dry. Fullish body. Some tannin. Decent fruit but not the fat and potential richness of the best. Good plus.

2005   From 2018   16.0
Fullish, youthful colour. Medium weight nose. Slightly tough fruit here. Medium-full body. Decent ripeness, balance, and style. Quite high acidity. Not exactly rich, nor as classy as some. Very good.

Domaine Robert Chevillon et Fils
63 ares of 75-year-old vines *en fermage* from the Misserey and Deharveng families of Compiegne and Neuilly-sur-Seine. Very largely destemmed. A brief period of cold-soaking. 30 percent new wood. Bottled after 15 to 18 months.

2006   From 2018   16.0
Full colour. A bit closed-in on the nose. Medium-full body. Just a touch astringent. Decent fruit but not a great deal of richness. Good grip. Youthful. Will it ever have the charm and excitement? Very good at best.

2005
Not offered.

Domaine Georges Chicotot
22 ares. 100 percent whole-cluster vinification. 6 days cold-soaking. 25 percent new wood. Bottled after 16 months.

2006   From 2018   17.5
Fullish colour. Round, accessible, stylish, balanced nose. Fullish body. Ripe tannins and very good grip. An elegant, vigorous wine with plenty of depth and a lovely finish. Fine.

2005   From 2022   18.0
Full colour. Firm, closed nose. But plenty of depth and vigour. Fullish body. Some tannin.

Very good grip. This is a rich meaty example. Lots of energy. Needs time. Fine plus.

Domaine Dufouleur Frères

16 ares. 100 percent destemmed. No deliberate cold-soaking. Around 30 percent new wood. Bottled after 18 months or so.

2006   From 2020   17.5
Full, vigorous colour. Firm, full, oaky nose. Full body. Some tannin. Very good grip. This has depth and concentration and quite a lot of new oak. Rich and ripe on the follow-through. A good sturdy example in the best sense of the word. Fine.

2005   From 2018   18.0
Fullish colour. Quite a mellow, succulent, gently oaky nose. Rich and classy. Medium-full body. Well-mannered. Harmonious. More accessible than most. Not a monster and all the better for it. A stylish wine. Fine plus.

Domaine Faiveley

23 ares of average age 60-year-old vines. 100 percent destemmed. 5 days natural cold-soaking. 50 percent new wood. Bottled after 15 months.

2006   From 2018   17.5
Medium-full colour. Ripe, balanced, vigorous nose. But not a blockbuster. Quite substantial on the palate though. Some tannin. Good grip. A little sturdy. But a long, vigorous finish. Fine.

2005   From 2018   17.0
Fullish nose. Youthful. At first it seemed to lack a bit of succulence, but it got richer as it evolved. Medium-full body. A little tannin. Just a hint of astringency, yet good grip and a balanced, ripe follow-through. Very good indeed.

Domaine Régis Forey

19 ares planted in 1983 *en fermage* from the Naudin and Laporte families. 100 percent destemmed. 4 days natural cold-soaking. 100 percent new wood. Bottled after 16 months.

2006   From 2020   16.5
Full colour. Rich, full, quite tannic nose. Firm but not brutal. Full body. Good tannins. Good

grip. Ripe and rich. Just a little *sauvage* at the end. But very good plus. Needs time.

2005   From 2019   17.0
Very full colour. Firm, rich but quite tannic nose. A big wine here. Some tannin on the palate. But underneath good style and grip. The structure of the wine tends to overwhelm the fruit but very good indeed nonetheless.

Domaine Henri Gouges

1.03 ha, planted 1961. 100 percent destemmed. 2 to 3 days natural cold-soaking. 20 to 25 percent new oak. Bottled after 16 to 18 months.

2006   From 2020   18.5
Full, immature colour. Quite a firm nose. Plenty of substance. But the tannins are ripe and rich. Full-bodied. Quite some tannin. This is a backward wine, but there is harmony and depth here. Lovely long finish. Very fine.

2005   From 2020   18.5
Very full, backward colour. Broad-flavoured, fullish nose. Ripe and rich, with a suggestion of new oak. Fullish body. Some tannin. Backward. Very fresh. Lovely balanced fruit on the follow-through. Long, very stylish, and very fine.

Hospices de Nuits-Saint-Georges

2 parcels totalling 95 ares, producing Cuvée Georges Faiveley and Cuvée des Sires de Vergy, the former from the best parcels and oldest vines. 100 percent destemmed. 6 to 8 days cold-soaking. 100 percent new wood. Bottled after 17 months.

2006, Cuvée Georges Faiveley   From 2018   18.5
Full, youthful colour. Fresh, balanced, well-mannered nose. I like the poise here. Medium-full body. Very good tannins. Lovely very rich fruit. Energetic and very classy. Not a suggestion of over-oaking here. Lovely long finish. Very fine.

2005, Cuvée Georges Faiveley   From 2020   19.0
Full colour. Firm and closed-in but very classy on the nose. Fullish body. Balanced. Very con-

centrated. Excellent grip. Fresh and harmonious, rich and complex on the follow-through. A classic. Excellent.

Domaine Thibault Liger-Belair

2.10 ha. 33 percent of the stems retained. 7 days cold-soaking. 40 percent new wood. Bottled after 15 to 18 months.

2006   From 2018   18.5
Good colour. Still youthful. Fresh, round nose, no hard edges. Plump and fruity. Fullish body. Rich. Lots of succulent fruit. Very good grip. Stylish. Good depth. Not a bit *sauvage*. Long. Very fine.

2005   From 2022   18.0
Very full, youthful colour. Firm, backward nose. But marvelous concentrated fruit and very sophisticated tannins. Very good grip. Full, nicely *sauvage*—in the best sense—so a very typical middle Nuits-Saint-Georges. A sturdy wine. Rich at the end. Fine plus.

Domaine Alain Michelot

19 ares planted 1978. 100 percent destemmed. 4 to 5 days cold-soaking. 30 percent new wood. Bottled after 16 months.

Declined to submit samples.

Domaine Gilles Remoriquet

19 ares. 45-year-old vines. 100 percent destemmed. A brief cold-soaking. 30 percent new wood. Bottled after 15 to 20 months.

2006   From 2018   18.0
Medium-full colour. Ripe, succulent, gently oaky nose. Lots of quality fruit here. Medium-full body. Some tannin. Very good grip. Quite rich. This is long, complex, and harmonious. Stylish too. Fine plus.

2005   From 2022   18.5
Very full, youthful colour. Rich and ripe on the nose. Classy too. But closed-in. Full, concentrated, rich, and oaky on the palate. This is a very stylish example. Concentrated, complex, and potentially velvety. Lovely finish. Very fine.

Domaine Edouard Zibetti

Unable to run to earth.

I asked the assembled growers to nominate three favourites in each vintage. The group preferences in the 2006 vintage were for Thibault Liger-Belair in first place, with Robert Chevillon, Dufouleur Frères, and the Hospices de Nuits as equal second. In 2005 the vote went to the Hospices, with Thibault Liger-Belair in second place and Georges Chicotot third.

Vosne-Romanée, Les *Premiers Crus*

NOWHERE IS WINE more noble than in Vosne-Romanée. Between the Nuits-Saint-Georges *premier cru* of Boudots to the south and the walls of the Clos de Vougeot at the northern end lie the 240 hectares of Vosne-Romanée vineyard: the most valuable piece of vinous real estate in the world.

Fifty-eight hectares of this is *premier cru*, and there are twelve of these; six of them lie just above the *grands crus*; the other six on the same altitude or a little further down the slope. The *climats* are listed, as was the tasting whose notes are below, roughly in south-north order.

MALCONSORTS The 5.86 hectares of Malconsorts or Aux Malconsorts (never *Les*) lie beween Nuits-Saint-Georges, Aux Boudots, and the *grand cru* of La Tâche. The vineyard is roughly rectangular, with the north-south distance shorter (just under 200 metres) than the east-west extent. Given its location, you might expect a Nuits-Saint-Georges robust earthiness, but it is fairer to say that it is Boudots which has a Vosne character than the other way around. Malconsorts, however, is certainly full, if indeed sturdy, and at its very best not far behind La Tâche in richness. The Domaine Thomas used to be the principal landholder, but their domaine was sold, and here in Malconsorts divided between the Dujac and de Montille estates in 2005. These both produce excellent wine. So do Lamarche, Bichot (Clos Frantin), and Alain Hudelot-Noëllat. The best wines, however, today come from Sylvain Cathiard.

AU DESSUS DES MALCONSORTS Just over 1 hectare of vineyard—the Au Dessus—lies above Malconsorts itself. The wine is lighter and has less class and definition than its illustrious neighbour. I rarely come across it. Dominique Mugneret and Gilles Remoriquet in Nuits-Saint-Georges are two of the proprietors.

CHAUMES Downslope from Malconsorts lies Chaumes, at the same altitude as the village itself. It is a little larger, at 6.46 hectares, and roughly square, with—as everyone will tell you if they have vines in the vicinity—the best wines coming from the northwest corner where Chaumes touches La Tâche. And, yes, there are some lovely Chaumes from up here. But in general,

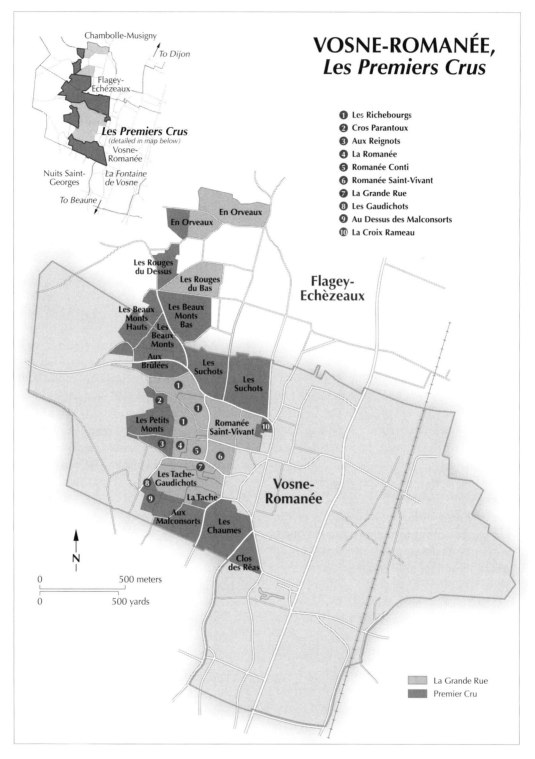

VOSNE-ROMANÉE,
Les Premiers Crus

1 Les Richebourgs
2 Cros Parantoux
3 Aux Reignots
4 La Romanée
5 Romanée Conti
6 Romanée Saint-Vivant
7 La Grande Rue
8 Les Gaudichots
9 Au Dessus des Malconsorts
10 La Croix Rameau

Chambolle-Musigny

To Dijon

Flagey-
Echézeaux

Les Premiers Crus
(detailed in map below)
Vosne-
Romanée

Nuits Saint-
Georges

La Fontaine
de Vosne

To Beaune

En Orveaux

En Orveaux

Les Rouges
du Dessus

Les Rouges
du Bas

Flagey-
Echèzeaux

Les Beaux
Monts
Hauts

Les Beaux
Monts
Bas

Les
Beaux
Monts

Aux
Brûlées

Les
Suchots

Les
Suchots

Les Petits
Monts

Romanée
Saint-Vivant

Vosne-
Romanée

Les Tache-
Gaudichots

La Tâche

Aux
Malconsorts

Les
Chaumes

Clos
des Réas

N

0   500 meters
0   500 yards

La Grande Rue
Premier Cru

MAP 7 Vosne-Romanée, Les *Premiers Crus*

Chaumes has less intensity and volume. In terms of its distinction, Chaumes is a second-division *premier cru*, and this is reflected in the prices the wine attracts. The best addresses include Arnoux, Confuron-Gendre, Lamarche, Liger-Belair, Grivot, Gros Frère et Soeur, Méo-Camuzet, Daniel Rion, and Jean Tardy.

CLOS DES RÉAS Further downslope, but at a higher altitude than its north and south village wine neighbours, a wall surrounds the Michel Gros 2.12 hectare monopoly of Clos des Réas. This is the only first growth *en monopole*. In theory, you would expect, like Chaumes, a lesser wine here, in first-growth terms. But this would be to forget the economies of scale the monopoly allows and to overlook the genius behind Michel Gros's winemaking. Clos des Réas is not a heavyweight, but it is a wine that has all the pure fragrance and supreme elegance of Pinot Noir at its most supreme. In several vintages it was voted the best wine at the tasting.

GAUDICHOTS Most of the best of the Gaudichots vineyard was absorbed into La Tâche in the 1920s and 1930s, leaving just over a hectare, divided into three or four separate pieces at the sides and above the *grand cru*. Some is owned by the Domaine de la Romanée-Conti and normally (perhaps some now goes into the Cuvée Duvault-Blochet?) sold off in bulk. Régis Forey is the main source of domaine-bottled wine. The merchant Nicolas Potel had one cask of a superb 1999. This is a full, sturdy, masculine Vosne-Romanée.

REIGNOTS Above La Romanée lies the 1.62 hectare vineyard of Aux Reignots. The slope is steep, the soil stony and only inches deep, and the *climat* divided up into various different parcels like a staircase. The wine is very elegant but in cooler years can lack a little succulence. Louis-Michel Liger-Belair of the Château de Vosne-Romanée has the lion's share of this first growth, and it lies just above his *grand cru*.

Among the other names, I can recommend Sylvain Cathiard and Robert Arnoux.

PETITS-MONTS Next door, above Richebourg, you will find Aux (or Les) Petits-Monts, very similar to look at but, at 3.67 hectares, quite a bit larger. Like most of Burgundy, there are far too many owners, and those with the most substantial parcels produce the best wine. Véronique Drouhin's wine should be on anyone's list. She has two parcels of very old vines, totalling just under half a hectare and cultivated biodynamically. Liger-Belair, Régis Forey, and Robert Sirugue, an estate whose reputation had not been much to be proud of until recently, should be noted. Mongeard-Mugneret is the name of another major owner here, but I do not recommend his wines. The Domaine de la Romanée-Conti is a further proprietor but sells its wine off in bulk. The wines here have much in common with those of Reignots: purity, finesse, and a silky texture rather than bulk. The parallel is with La Romanée rather than Richebourg.

CROS PARANTOUX Next door to the north, also above Richebourg, is the 1.01 hectare Cros (not "clos") Parantoux. Following phylloxera and the subsequent economic difficulties, the land had been allowed to return to nature. It was owned by the Camuzet family, but they were absentee landlords. Towards the end of the Second World War, Henri Jayer, one of the Camuzet's sharecroppers, was entrusted with developing the vineyard once more, and his successor, Emmanuel Rouget, is now the majority landowner, with the Méo-Camuzets, as they have become, the proprietors of the rest. The vines are old, and though this is also an upslope wine, it seems to have much more of a Richebourg character than the two I have described immediately above. Here we do have velvet rather than silk, and plenty of richness and volume. The wine is much coveted by collectors (not all of whom deserve a wine as good as this, sadly) and so very expensive.

CROIX-RAMEAU A bite out of the bottom northeast corner of Romanée-Saint-Vivant, opposite the village cemetry, gives us the 0.60 hectare La Croix-Rameau, the smallest *premier cru* in the commune. The most important grower here is Lamarche, and like the rest of Lamarche's wines, quality has revived here to the heights of what it used to be in the 1950s and 1960s—that is very high indeed. This is a wine with a true *grand cru* flair, and Lamarche, together with its neighbours, such as the Cacheux-Blée family, is lobbying to have the land redesignated Romanée-Saint-Vivant; so far with no success, but wheels such as these turn slowly.

BRULÉES With Les (or Aux) Brulées, 4.53 hectares, we come to what are generally regarded as the three best first growths—I'd today add Malconsorts to make four. This one is schizophrenic, given that it is divided into two sections by the road going up to Concoeur, and so having a northeast-facing slope opposite one that is inclined to the south. From either side, however, we have a wine of voluptuous richness and backbone, quality and depth, and the ability to last. On the southern side, facing northeast, note the wines of Méo-Camuzet, Michel Gros, and Gerard Mugneret; facing them lie those of Confuron-Gendre, Engel (now the Domaine Eugenie), Grivot, J. P. et M. Guyon, Bruno Clavelier, Leroy, and Liger-Belair.

SUCHOTS Les Suchots occupies a flattened-egg sort of mound between Richebourg and Romanée-Saint-Vivant, and Echézeaux, and is the largest of the Vosne-Romanée *premiers crus*. There are just over 13 hectares. This is the most noble of all the first growths. In the best hands we really do get *grand cru* quality. The wine is full-bodied, less lush than Brulées, less finely spirited (in a racehorse sense) than Beaumonts, but of great breeding nonetheless. Look out for the examples of Arnoux (very old vines at the western end of the *climat*), Gérard Cacheux, Cathiard, Confuron-Cotéditot, Grivot, Hudelot-

Noëllat, Jadot, Lamarche, Liger-Belair, Gérard Mugneret, and the Domaine de l'Arlot.

BEAUMONTS Variously written as two words (Beaux Monts) and with or without the prefix Aux or Les (French nomenclature is consistently inexact), this vineyard lies above Brulées and Echézeaux and measures 11.39 hectares. You could term this an upslope *climat* except that the altitude only rises to just over 300 metres rather than 325 as in Reignots and Petits-Monts. The vineyard also inclines well to the south and the partly marly soil is deeper. These factors are confirmed in the character of the wine which is rich and full, with considerable flair and perfume and a good acidity. The best sources include Gérard Cacheux, Bruno Clavelier, J. J. Confuron, Confuron-Gendre, Dujac, Grivot, Hudelot-Noëllat, Jadot, Leroy, and Daniel Rion.

Two more, small *premiers crus* remain, both upslope from Echézeaux and of minor importance: the 2.62 hectare Les Rouges and the 1.79 hectare En Orveaux. These are proper upslope wines: cooler, medium-full rather than full-bodied, elegant and intense rather than rich and succulent, for the altitude stretches up to 325 metres in the former, while the latter faces distinctly northeast. I know of only one producer of Les Rouges (Grivot), and this is the least good (but what a high overall standard!) of his six first growths (it's also the cheapest). The star in the Orveaux is the brilliant Sylvain Cathiard. The Guyon brothers also have a small holding.

Much as we would all appreciate the opportunity to drink *grand cru* Vosne-Romanée, anyone will gain enormous pleasure as well as enlightenment by comparing two of the first-division first growths for the same cost, or indeed three of the second division. Etienne Grivot sums up the best as follows: Suchots is the most aristocratic, Beaumonts is the most classic, and Brulées softer and more voluptuous. I would add that Malconsorts is the most majestical.

TASTING NOTES

The Connecticut Wine Group sampled the following wines at the end of March 2009. The perspicacious will note that the *crus* have been listed in a rough south-to-north order.

Malconsorts, Domaine Cathiard, 2002
From 2014

Full colour. Splendidly rich nose. Aspects of caramel and mocha. Fullish body. Concentrated, vigorous, balanced, and very classy. Intense and very lovely. Very fine.

Malconsorts, Domaine Hudelot-Noëllat, 2002
From 2013

Medium-full colour. Attractive, plump nose. Again a little mocha. Medium-full body. Good grip. Balanced. Nicely concentrated. Good finesse. Very good indeed but not fine.

Chaumes, Domaine Liger-Belair, 2002
From 2013

Medium-full colour. Laid-back, composed, classy nose. Lovely harmony. Medium to medium-full body. Balanced. Intense. Concentrated. By no means a blockbuster but very long and vigorous. Gently oaky. Very fine.

La Croix Rameau, Domaine Lamarche, 2002
From 2014

Medium-full colour. Ripe nose. Nicely succulent. Even rich. Fullish. Some tannin. Classy. Balanced. Lovely fruit. Good concentration and energy on the follow-through. Fine plus.

La Grande Rue, Domaine Lamarche, 2002
From 2015

Yes. By this time a *grand cru*. But not when it comes to the earlier vintages. And we had never assessed this *climat* before. Full colour. Full, firm, rich, and concentrated on the nose. Lots of depth. High-quality. Full body. Structured and vigorous. Very good tannins. Very good grip. A lot of intense, high-quality wine here. Very lovely rich fruit. Very long. Excellent.

Clos des Réas, Domaine Michel Gros, 2002
Now to 2020

Medium-full colour. Just a bit of reduction on the nose at first, but basically laid-back, ripe, and generous. Medium body. Rich. Gently tannic and very good grip. The reduction hides the finesse, and one wonders if it is not just a little loose-knit for the vintage. Yet long on the palate.

Aux Reignots, Domaine Liger-Belair, 2002
From 2013

Full colour. A little reduction on the nose at fist, but this blew away. A bigger, richer wine than his Chaumes. Fresh. Medium-full body. Good grip. Most attractive fruit. Gently oaky. Long and fine quality, but his Chaumes has more finesse.

Petits Monts, Domaine Veronique Drouhin, 2002
Now to 2020

Medium-full colour. Fragrant, stylish, ripe nose. Medium-full body. Lovely rich abundant fruit on the palate. Very fresh. Very harmonious. Classy and intense. Delicious. Fine plus.

Cros Parentoux, Domaine Méo-Camuzet, 2002
From 2015

Very good colour. The nose is quite marked by the new wood, but the wine is rich, fat, and caramelly. Full body. Very good acidity. Very, very concentrated. Very ripe, rich fruit on the palate. Lots of energy. Long. Fine plus to very fine.

Aux Brulées, Domaine Engel, 2002
From 2014

This seems to have shut down a bit. Medium-full colour. Not much nose. Better on the palate. Medium-full body. Fresh, laid-back, concentrated fruit. Gently oaky. Intense. Long. Fine.

Aux Brulées, Domaine Michel Gros, 2002
From 2014

Fullish colour. Very lovely nose. Rich and concentrated, without being a blockbuster. Gently oaky. Fullish body. Ripe tannins. Very good grip. A bigger, richer, more concentrated wine than his Clos des Réas. This is very lovely. Very fine.

Beaux Monts, Maison Jadot, 2002   From 2015

Fullish colour. Ample, rich, abundant nose. Fullish body. A most attractive, rich, concentrated wine on the palate. Harmonious, classy, and intense. Some tannin. Gently oaky. Long. Very lovely. Very fine.

Suchots, Domaine de l'Arlot, 2002   Now to 2020

Medium-full colour, some development. Whole-cluster nose. Medium to medium-full body. Similar on the palate. Lacks fat. Some of the tannins are a bit astringent. Not for me.

Suchots, Maison Jadot, 2002   Now to 2020

Fullish colour. Ample, rich, abundant nose. Not a lot different from their Beaumonts. On the palate a little less concentrated and much less intense. Balanced and fruity but a little loose-knit. Only very good.

Cuvée Duvault-Blochet, Domaine de la Romanée-Conti, 2002   From 2015

Full colour. Firm, full aristocratic nose. Very lovely profound fruit. Certainly *premier cru* worthy if not as rich or as concentrated on the follow-through as the best of the above. Ample. Very good grip. But fine rather than very fine.

The group vote was overwhelmingly for the Cathiard Malconsorts as the best wine of these 2002s. The most favoured of the also-rans were the Méo-Camuzet Cros Parentoux, the Gros Brulées, and the Liger-Belair Chaumes.

Chaumes, Domaine Méo-Camuzet, 1999   Now to 2020

Very good colour. Not nearly as much pronouced oak as in the 2002 Cros Parentoux. Full body. Some tannin and oak on the palate. Pronounced acidity. Quite rich. But not a lot of charm. Ripe but slightly austere. Very good indeed.

Chaumes, Domaine Robert Arnoux, 1999   Now to 2020

Full colour. Still immature. Ripe nose. Good depth, class, and interest. Medium-full body.

Gently oaky. Fresh. Balanced. Not great but ripe; complex and subtle at the end. Fine.

Clos des Réas, Domaine Michel Gros, 1999   From 2010

Full colour. Still immature. Soft, intense, laid-back nose. Fresh. Just about ready. Lovely cool classy fruit. Very gently oaky. Long and complex. Fine plus.

La Grande Rue, Domaine Lamarche, 1999   From 2013

Full colour. Still immature. Rich, concentrated nose. Fullish body. Some new oak. Quite a big wine, which still needs time. Some tannin to resolve. Rich but slightly austere. But the finish is fresh and classy. Fine.

Petits Monts, Domaine Veronique Drouhin, 1999   Now to 2020

Medium to medium-full colour. Ripe, fragrant, complex, and classy on the nose. Medium-full body. Very good balance and grip. Still a little tannin to resolve but getting there. Long, intense, and very stylish. Lovely. Fine plus.

Cros Parentoux, Domaine Méo-Camuzet, 1999   From 2013

Full colour. Rich, fat, oaky nose. Much like the 2002 and quite different from the Chaumes 1999. Still a little tight but full-bodied, rich, and concentrated. Lots of fruit. A wine with an agenda, but a good agenda. Fine—or even better, according to your taste. Long on the finish.

Cros Parentoux, Domaine Henri Jayer, 1999   Now to 2020

Full colour. The sample was slightly corked (and we had no back-up bottle), but one could see a rich wine, less oaky and concentrated than the Méo but with very lovely fruit and very fine grip. Fine plus at least.

Aux Brulées, Domaine Méo-Camuzet, 1999   From 2013

Very full colour. Rich, fat, oaky, concentrated, and tannic on both the nose and the palate. Good grip. A little adolescent but good structure. Plenty of depth and class. Lovely finish. Fine.

Beaux Monts, Maison Louis Jadot, 1999   From 2013

Full colour. Still youthful. Slightly tight and adolescent on the nose and the attack. Fullish. Good fruit and grip and concentration. But a bit lumpy today. Fine at least.

Beaux Monts, Domaine Daniel Rion Père et Fils, 1999   Now to 2020

Full colour. Still youthful. The nose is a bit tight with some reduction. Medium body. Fresh and balanced but a little unsophisticated. Cleaner at the end than at the beginning. Good long finish. Very good plus.

Beaux Monts, Domaine Grivot, 1999   From 2013

Very full colour. Immature. Brilliant nose. Super elegant and complex. Very fine laid-back textured fruit. Intense and classy. Full body. Backward. Still some tannin. Profound and intense. Excellent. The best of the 1999s by a long way.

Beaux Monts, Domaine Dujac, 1999   Now to 2020

Fullish colour. Some sign of maturity. Round, ripe, rich, sweet but fresh nose. Very Dujac. Lovely style. Medium to medium-full body. Balanced. Lovely fruit. Long, complex, and classy. Fine plus.

Cuvée Duvault-Blochet, Domaine de la Romanée-Conti, 1999   From 2013

Fullish colour. Rich and concentrated and slightly oaky on the nose. Rather more dimension than the 2002 today. Fullish body. Very lovely fruit here. Very good tannins and very good grip. Classy and profound. Long on the palate. Fine plus.

This time it was the Clos des Réas which got the overwhelming group vote. Honorable mentions to the Duvault-Blochet, the Méo Cros Parentoux, and the Méo Brulées.

Malconsorts, Domaine Cathiard, 1998   Now to 2018

Fullish colour. Barely mature. Attractive, plump nose. Medium to medium-full body. Ripe, full of fruit. Balanced, long, and seductive. Very good indeed if without the dimension of the 1996. Now ready.

Cros Parentoux, Domaine Emmanuel Rouget, 1998   Now to 2020

Full colour. Attractive, plump, fruity nose. Not too oaky. Fullish body. Very good tannins. Ample, round, yet still firm and youthful. Very good intensity and vigour, though a little four-square as it evolved. Very fine at first; only fine on aeration.

Reignots, Domaine Régis Forey/ Bouchard Père et Fils, 1998   Now to 2020

Full colour. Classy nose. Very well-balanced fruit here. On the palate a little four-square, with hints of astringency about the tannins. Yet very good fresh fruit at the same time. A curate's egg of a wine.

Suchots, Domaine Robert Arnoux, 1998   Now to 2020

Fullish colour. Some tannin on the nose. Slightly hard, with an absence of richness. Better on the palate. Ample fresh fruit, if without the greatest of class and depth. But long and succulent. Very good.

Beaux Monts, Domaine Leroy, 1997   Now to 2014

Fullish colour. No undue maturity. Clean, fresh, and very classy, for a 1997, on the nose. But quite evolved. Medium-full body. Fresh and *à point*. The attack is very good, but then it tails off a bit. Very 1997! A lot better than most though. Fine for the vintage.

Beaux Monts, Domaine Daniel Rion Père et Fils, 1997   Now to 2014

Full, youthful colour. Good fresh nose. Really quite classy. Medium to medium-full body. Fresh and ripe and plump and positive. This is really very good indeed for the vintage. Lovely finish.

Malconsorts, Domaine
Cathiard, 1996   Now to 2020
Full, immature colour. Ripe, succulent, and very lovely on the nose. Much better than the 1998. Fullish. Very good grip. Lovely fruit. The tannins are now soft, but the wine still needs a bit of time to round off. Very fine finish. Fine plus.

Malconsorts, Domaine
Hudelot-Noëllat, 1996   Now to 2018
Fullish, still youthful colour. Decent nose. But an absence of real concentration, depth, class, and intensity. Medium to medium-full body. Decent balance, structure, and style but lacks the flair of the very best. Very good. Just about ready.

Malconsorts, Domaine
Lamarche, 1996   Now to 2020
Medium-full colour. Plenty of class and depth on the nose. Rich and succulent on the palate. Fullish body. Still some tannin. Very clean and very good depth. Lovely fruit and an impressive finish. Fine plus. Will still improve.

Petits Monts, Domaine
Veronique Drouhin, 1996   Now to 2020 plus
Fullish, youthful colour. Aromatic, fragrant nose. Not a blockbuster but attractive, balanced fruit. Medium to medium-full body. Just a touch of tannin. Very intense fruit. Rich and ripe. Just about ready. Fine plus.

La Grand Rue, Domaine
Lamarche, 1996   From 2014
Full, immature colour. Closed-in nose, but full, rich, concentrated, and profound. A big, tannic, backward wine with lots of depth and energy. Just needs time but could be really fine.

Gaudichots, Domaine
Régis Forey, 1996   Now to 2020
Full colour. Still youthful. Just a little dry and clumsy on the nose. And similar on the palate. The tannins are a bit astringent and this makes for an inflexible wine. Very good indeed at best. Give it a couple of years to see if it softens.

Reignots, Domaine Régis Forey/
Bouchard Père et Fils, 1996   From 2010
Full immature colour. A lack of flair, balance, and class on the nose. Four-square. Higher toned than the Gaudichots above. Slightly less tannic. So a better wine. But not brilliant. Very good indeed. Just about ready.

Aux Brulées, Domaine Engel,
1996   Now to 2025
Medium-full colour. Still youthful. An evolved nose compared with most of these 1996s. Exotic. Ample. Succulent. Medium-full body. Excellent grip. Long and lovely. Just about ready. Fine plus.

Cros Parentoux, Domaine
Méo-Camuzet, 1996   Now to 2020
Fullish colour. Still youthful. Slightly firmer and richer than the Rouget below. More concentrated too. But more "modern." Not too much so though. Fullish body. Rich. Oaky. Very good attack but slightly less impressive on the follow-through. There is a touch of astringency from the tannins. Will a couple of years improve it?

Cros Parentoux, Domaine
Rouget, 1996   Now to 2020
Full immature colour. Ripe, plump, succulent nose. No undue structure or new oak. I prefer this to the Méo: it has more flexibility. Rich, intense, and concentrated. Fullish body. Long and lovely. Very fine. Better still in two years time.

Beaux Monts, Maison Dominique Laurent,
1996   See note
Full, immature colour. Rather stewed and also rather corked. Not very good, I think.

Beaux Monts, Domaine Leroy,
1996   Now to 2014
Full, immature colour. Ripe, concentrated, aromatic nose. Touches of new oak. This is surprisingly flat on the palate, letting the acidity dominate. Medium body. Ripe tannins. But somewhat vegetal at the end. Just about ready.

Suchots, Domaine Confuron-Cotiditot, 1996   Now to 2020 plus
Medium-full colour. A little development. Sweet, whole-cluster nose. Quite classy though. Medium-full body. Balanced. Good intensity. Long on the palate. Yet not the class and depth of the best. Very good indeed to fine. Just about ready.

Suchots, Domaine Hudelot-Noëllat, 1996   Now to 2020 plus
Medium-full colour. A little development. Like the Malconsorts, this is neat, mature, fresh, and balanced. Medium to medium-full body. Fine but it lacks the depth and flair of a great wine. Classier than the Malconsorts though. Long, attractive finish. Just about ready.

Suchots, Maison Louis Jadot, 1996   From 2014
Very full, immature colour. Firm, cigar-boxy nose. A bit of a monolith but rich and full as well as firm and full of fruit. Very good grip. Intense. Long. Potentially fine plus, and it got better and better in the glass.

Malconsorts, Domaine Cathiard, 1995   Now to 2025
Fullish colour. Only a hint of maturity. Lovely fragrant, intense, rich nose. Very composed. Very classy. Fullish body. Now just about ready. Very long. Very fine.

Chaumes, Domaine Tardy, 1995   Now to 2020
Fullish colour. Barely mature. Attractive, plump nose. Medium to medium-full body. Ripe and full of fruit. Balanced, long, and seductive. Very good indeed.

Aux Brulées, Domaine Engel, 1995   Now to 2020 plus
Medium to medium-full colour. Fully mature. Soft, rich, ripe, and concentrated on the nose. Medium body. Round. Full of fruit. Ample. Classy. Fully ready. Fine plus.

Beaux Monts, Domaine Grivot, 1995   Now to 2020
Full immature colour. Quite a firm nose still. Full, classy, and very concentrated. Full body.

Some tannin. Excellent concentration on the palate. Splendidly profound. Lovely intense fruit. This is very fine, indeed brilliant. It will still improve.

Suchots, Maison Louis Jadot, 1995   Now to 2020
Full colour, barely mature. Rich, concentrated, slighly earthy, backward nose. Full body. Lots of depth and concentration here. Intense. Still firm. Still some tannin. Real energy and dimension. Very fine though a bit adolescent at present.

Clos des Réas, Domaine Michel Gros, 1993   Now to 2020 plus
Medium-full mature colour. Lovely aromatic nose. Ripe, concentrated, and sweet. Lots of class and harmony. Excellent balance. Very lovely ripe, concentrated, succulent fruit on the palate. Real depth and class. Fine plus to very fine. Just about ready.

Chaumes, Domaine Tardy, 1993   Now to 2020 plus
Fullish colour, now mature. Firm on the nose but rich, concentrated, and profound. Unexpectedly fine. Fullish body. Rich, concentrated, and quite sweet on the palate. Slightly earthy. Lots of depth and a lovely finish. Only just ready. Fine.

Beaux Monts, Domaine Leroy, 1993   Now to 2013
Full colour. Barely mature. Ripe nose but no real personality or depth. Indeed a touch vegetal on the palate. Medium body. Fresh but slightly raw and one-dimensional compared with these other 1993s. Very good at best.

Beaux Monts, Domaine Daniel Rion Père et Fils, 1993   Now to 2018
Full, very fresh colour. Rich, ripe, ample, but slightly reduced nose. Not hard. Medium body. Very fresh and fruity on the palate (the reduction soon blew away). Most attractive fruit. Rather more class than the other vintages of this wine. Long on the palate. Very good indeed.

Cros Parentoux, Domaine
Henri Jayer, 1993 Now to 2020 plus

Fullish colur. Still very youthful. Slightly earthy but more flexible than the Méo. Less concentrated but better mannered. Less earthy as it evolved. Rich. Concentrated. Fat. Ample. Very fine.

Cros Parentoux, Domaine
Méo-Camuzet, 1993 Now to 2015

Very full colour. Barely mature. Concentrated but not over-extracted nose. Very oaky, though. Better on the palate. Vigorous. Balanced. Rich but still a little tough. Will it ever round off? Very good indeed but no better—nor would it be very food friendly.

Suchots, Domaine
Mongeard-Mugneret,
1993 Drink soon if at all

Medium-full colour. Rather astringent on the nose and lumpy and coarse on the palate. Full and rich but four-squre and with quite a lot of acidity lurking in the background. Poor.

Clos des Réas, Domaine
Michel Gros, 1991 Now to 2016

Medium to medium-full colour. Fully mature. Soft aromatic nose. Round, mellow, and balanced on the palate. Not as rich or as concentrated as the 1993 but *à point* and very lovely.

Malconsorts, Domaine
Hudelot-Noëllat, 1990 Now to 2018

Full, mature colour. Ripe, plump, slightly tarty nose. Lacks real purity and finesse. Some oak. Medium body. Ripe and seductive. Balanced and fresh. Attractive if not that classy. Fully ready. Very good indeed.

Malconsorts, Domaine
Charles Thomas/Maison
Moillard-Grivot, 1990 Now to 2015

Full mature colour. The nose is rather too four-square, indeed slightly over-macerated. Full but lumpy attack. Good grip though. Better at the end. Good at best.

Chaumes, Domaine Tardy,
1990 Now to 2020 plus

Fullish mature colour. Quite a substantial nose. Full and rich but slightly earthy. Fullish, quite some tannin but the tannins fully resolved. Ripe and rich. Not the delicacy, intensity of sheer class of the Clos des Réas but lots of wine here. Good concentration. Good definition. Fine.

Clos des Réas, Domaine
Michel Gros, 1990 Now to 2020 plus

Fullish mature colour. Very lovely nose. Fragrant, mellow, rich, and concentrated. Beautifully put together. Splendid fruit. Very fine quality.

Beaux Monts,
Maison Drouhin, 1990 Now to 2020 plus

Full, mature colour. High-toned, fragrant, classy nose. Medium to medium-full body. Very ripe, indeed rich. Very intense. Very lovely. There is real finesse here. Lovely finish. Fine plus.

Suchots, Domaine
Hudelot-Noëllat, 1990 Now to 2020

Full colour. Fuller than the Malconsorts. No undue maturity. Once again rich but more profound and above all more class. Medium-full body. Balanced. Rich. Complete. Fine.

Malconsorts, Domaine Cathiard,
1989 See note

The colour was fine, but the wine finished.

Petits Monts, Domaine
Veronique Drouhin, 1989 Now to 2016

Full vigorous colour. A little tight on the nose, surprisingly. Good fragrant fruit underneath. But slightly four-square, even rigid. The Beaux Monts 1990 above is much better.

Beaux Monts,
Domaine Leroy, 1989 Now to 2015

Full, barely mature colour. Fragrant, ripe, and rich on the nose but lacks definition and finesse. Full and balanced on the palate but slightly rigid and no more than very good.

Clos des Réas, Domaine Michel Gros, 1988   Now to 2016

Fullish mature colour. Slightly more austere than the 1990. But ripe, fresh, and classy. Medium-full body. Very good structure. Ripe tannins. Complex and intense. Rich and succulent. Elegant and very long on the palate. Very fine.

Petits Monts, Domaine Veronique Drouhin, 1988   Now to 2015

Medium-full mature colour. Rather more together than the 1989. Balanced and plump, with no austerity or hardness. Medium-full body. Ripe. Round. Balanced. Fresh and complex. A lovely laid-back wine. Very fine.

Beaux Monts, Maison Camille Giroud, 1988   Now to 2014

Medium to medium-full colour. Soft, spicy nose. Very mellow. Some stems in the vinification here? Medium body. Fully evolved. Not a bit too lean. Good grip, intensity, and class. Very good indeed.

Suchots, Domaine Confuron-Coteditot, 1988   Now to 2014

Medium-full, mature colour. Rich, fat, ample, spicy nose. Sweet. Medium body. Vigorous and attractive, if not very classy. Very good indeed.

La Grande Rue, 1986   Past its best

Decently full fresh colour. The nose too is fresh and vigorous if without any great nuance or class. But on the palate it is lumpy and coarse. Past its best, and it was never much good in the first place.

Clos des Réas, Domaine Michel Gros, 1985   Drink soon

Good colour. Good class, weight, and depth on the nose. Now mellow. The acidity shows a bit, and I prefer the 1988, let alone the 1990. This is very good, but it is now drying up a bit and losing its succulence.

Petits Monts, Domaine Roland Vigot, 1985   Past its best

Medium-full, quite vigorous colour. The fruit has got a bit thin, and astringency shows.

Suchots, Maison Drouhin, 1985   Drink quite soon

Medium to medium-full colour, fully mature. Fresh, succulent, ripe nose. Lovely fruit on the palate. Balanced, fresh, rich, ample, and classy. Holding up better than a lot of 1985s. Fine.

Suchots, Maison Drouhin, 1983   Now to 2013

Decent, mature colour. Slightly earthy nose. Ripe, ample, rich, spicy, and slightly cooked. Fullish. Rather more vigour than the 1985. Better grip. Very clean. Most attractive. Fine plus.

Clos des Réas, Domaine Michel Gros, 1978   Now to 2013

Medium colour. Fully mature. Ripe, rich, spicy, mellow, aromatic nose. Medium-full body. Soft, stylish, balanced, and silky-smooth on the palate. Lovely long finish. Still bags of life. Delicious.

Beaux Monts, Maison Drouhin, 1978   Now to 2015

Medium-full, fully mature colour. A hint of mint or eucalyptus on the nose. Medium to medium-full body. Clean, ripe, classy fruit. This is a fine example, and it will still keep well.

Beaux Monts, Maison Sichel, 1971   Was very good, but now a bit past it

Good colour. The nose is a bit dried out now. But the fruit is still decently classy.

Suchots, Maison Bourée, 1971   See note

Full colour. Old and dried out, and never very special, I think.

Clos des Réas, Domaine Gros, 1969   No hurry to drink

This is very fine. Fullish body. Lovely intense, ripe, naturally sweet fruit. Splendid balance. Still very fresh. Delicious.

Reignots, Domaine du Château de Vosne-Romanée, 1969   Will last well

Again very lovely. Fresh, balanced, and elegant. Intense, poised, and harmonious. Multi-dimensional.

Malconsorts, Maison Coron, 1959   See note

Now a little coarse at the end, but not too dried out. Was at least more than respectable in its prime. Good positive finish.

Clos des Réas, Maison Bouchard
Père et Fils, 1955   See note

The colour is still fresh, as is the nose. Lovely fruit. Mellow. Gently getting towards the end, but still ripe and elegant and long on the palate. Fine old Burgundy.

Clos des Réas, Domaine   No hurry to
Gros, 1949   drink up

The colour is still fresh. This is a splendid wine. Amazing freshness and intensity. Ripe, sweet, vigorous, and very elegant. Very lovely indeed.

Malconsorts, Domaine
Charles Thomas/Maison
Moilllard-Grivot, 1947   Drink up

Medium-full colour. No undue age. Just a little faded on the nose, but mellow and profound on the palate. Rich and ripe. Fine plus.

Beaux Monts, Domaine
Charles Noëllat, 1945   See note

Full colour. Still vigorous. The nose is a little tired. On the palate the wine is big, full, fleshy, and without any undue astringency. But the wine oxidised fast in the glass. Was fine once upon a time.

Romanée-Saint-Vivant

THE ROMANÉE-SAINT-VIVANT owners are as follows: Domaine de la Romanée-Conti (5.29 hectares); Leroy (0.99 ha); Domaine de Corton-Grancey (Louis Latour) (0.76 ha); Jean-Jacques Confuron (0.50 ha); Christophe and France Poisot, wine made by by Franck Follin-Arbelet (0.49 ha); Hudelot-Noëllat (0.48 ha); Robert Arnoux (now Arnoux-Lachaux) (0.35 ha); Domaine de L'Arlot (0.25 ha); Wilfred Jaeger, leased to the Domaine Dujac (0.17 ha); and Sylvain Cathiard (0.17 ha). In total, the surface area is 9.44 hectares.

There have been two major changes in recent years. What is now exploited by the Domaine Dujac belonged until 2005 to the Domaine Charles Thomas. The Poisot vines used to be farmed by Denis Mugneret until his retirement in 2001. In those days much of the fruit was then sold to Maison Joseph Drouhin and sometimes to Maison Louis Jadot.

Romanée-Saint-Vivant is the closest *grand cru* to the village of Vosne-Romanée, the vines running down behind the church at the northern end of the village to the courtyard of the old abbey of Saint-Vivant, now (having been the property of the Marey-Monge family) belonging to the Domaine de la Romanée-Conti and housing their new offices. The incline here is gentle, the altitude between 265 and 250 metres and the exposure to the east. The soil is heavier than it is further up the slope in Richebourg and Romanée-Conti, and there is more of it: a brown clay-limestone mixture mixed with pebbles on a Bajocian marl base.

For 650 years the land was the property of the local abbey, a Clunaic dependency. In the sixteenth century the bottom end of the parcel known as the Clos-des-Quatre-Journaux was detached. This is the section now owned by Jaeger, Arnoux, Poisot, Arlot, and Cathiard. During the Revolution the rest was acquired by Nicolas-Joseph Marey of Nuits-Saint-Georges, known as Marey the younger, for 91,000 francs. The Marey-Monge family (as they were to become) sold off part of their inheritance in 1898 to Louis Latour and Charles Noëllat. The latter segment is now shared by Leroy, Alain Hudelot, and the Domaine J. J. Confuron. They retained the rest until 1966, when a lease was granted to the Domaine de la Romanée-Conti.

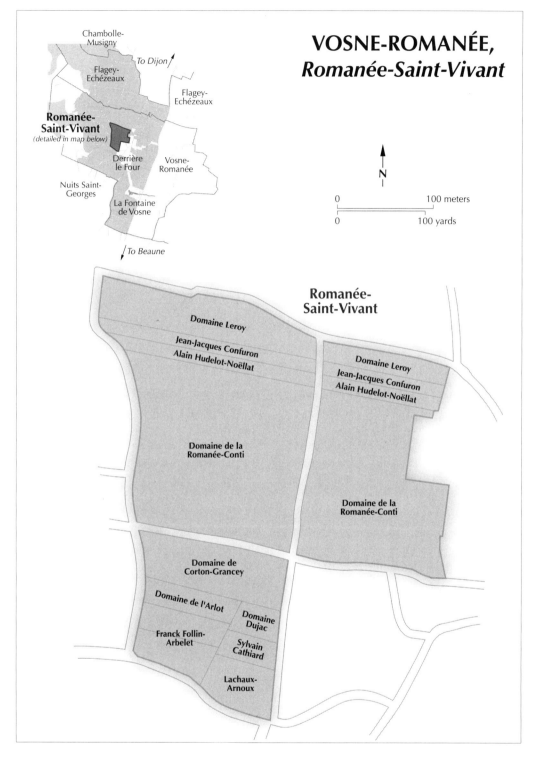

MAP 8 Vosne-Romanée, *Romanée-Saint-Vivant*

The Neyrand family, heirs of Mlle Geneviève Marey-Monge, last of her line, sold this to the Domaine de la Romanée-Conti after her death in September 1988, for, it is understood, about 60 million francs.

Romanée-Saint-Vivant is the lightest, the most delicate, and the most feminine of the Vosne *grands crus*. For me there is a distinct resemblence to Musigny. At its best, it is an exquisitely perfumed wine, silk where Richebourg is velvet but no less intense, no less beautiful. While in the Domaine de la Romanée-Conti lineup the Richebourg is usually the superior, elsewhere, *chez* Leroy or Hudelot-Noëllat, this is not always the case. It is a question of personal taste.

TASTING NOTES

The following Romanée-Saint-Vivants were tasted by the Guilford, Connecticut, group in March 2011.

Domaine Robert Arnoux, 1999   Now to 2025
Full colour. Still very youthful. Very fine, fresh, ripe, rich nose. Lovely balance. Great style. Medium-full body. Very vigorous. Very pure. Very composed. Ripe and very elegant. Lovely long finish. This is great wine. Just about ready.

**Maison Champy Père et Fils,
1999**   Now to 2020 plus
Medium-full colour. The nose was a bit unforthcoming at first. Fragrant, refined but quite delicate. Medium-full body. Fresh and very stylish. Very fine.

Maison Joseph Drouhin, 1999   Now to 2025
Fullish colour. Still very youthful. Ample, soft, round, and succulent on the nose. Very good grip. Lots of class. Medium-full body. Velvety and voluptuous. Lovely balance. Very fine indeed. Just about ready.

**Domaine Alain Hudelot-Nöellat,
1999**   Now to 2025
Good fullish colour. Ripe, concentrated, fresh, succulent nose. Lots of class. Lots of depth. Very lovely. Medium-full body. Ripe, exotic, potentially voluptuous, and old viney. Lovely balance. Very classy. Very complex. Long very vigorous finish. Just about ready. Very fine indeed.

Maison Louis Jadot, 1999   From 2016
Fullish colour. Still youthful. Full, rich, concentrated, high-quality nose. Very vigorous; even powerful. Full-bodied, rich, tannic, backward. High-quality. Profound and multidimensional. Lovely cool, classy follow-through. Still needs time. Excellent.

Domaine Leroy, 1996   Now to 2030
Medium-full colour. Some evolution. Fragrant fruit. Composed and classy and harmonious. Full body. Concentrated. Very lovely fruit and lots of energy. Very persistent. Very fine indeed.

**Domaine de la Romanée-Conti,
1996**   Now to 2030
Fullish, mature colour. Ripe, accessible nose. Some evolution now. Fully ready. Full body. Rich, concentrated, and more youthful on the palate than it seemed to be on the nose. Cool, balanced, ripe fragrant, and very intense. Very elegant. Very fine indeed.

Domaine Robert Arnoux, 1995   Now to 2020
Very full mature colour. Ripe, slightly spicy, fragrant nose. But without the size of the 1999. Fully developed on the palate. Medium-full body. Good balance. Attractive succulent fruit. Long on the palate. Fine. *À point.*

Domaine Robert Arnoux, 1993   Now to 2020
Fullish colour. Still youthful. Ripe, concentrated, classy, and composed on the nose. Now soft and delicious. Medium-full body. Very ripe. Soft and silky but with plenty of depth and energy. Very, very lovely fruit on the follow-through. Very fine indeed.

Maison Joseph Drouhin, 1993   Now to 2025
Full, youthful colour. Very lovely fragrant nose. Fresh. Balanced. Very good acidity. Ripe, profound, and complex. This is a very lovely, very elegant example. Very fine indeed.

Domaine J. J. Confuron, 1990   Now to 2020 plus
Fullish colour. Barely mature. Rich, fat, gently oaky, and exotic on the nose. Ample and seductive but just a touch of rigidity on the palate. Not quite the grip at the end, but there is lovely fruit here and it improved in the glass. Very fine.

Domaine de la Romanée-Conti, 1988   Drink soon
Fullish colour. No undue maturity. Fragrant, complex, and delicate on the nose, showing very lovely fruit. But on the palate it doesn't live up to the nose. There is an element of astringency here. And the wine is a bit rigid. Are there better bottles? This is no more than "very good indeed."

Domaine Alain Hudelot-Nöellat, 1985   Now to 2018
Medium-full mature colour. Ripe, succulent, fresh, balanced nose. Very attractive. Medium-full body. Soft and mellow but vigorous and with very good grip. Not a blockbuster but harmonious, long, complex, and classy. Fine plus.

Domaine de la Romanée-Conti, 1985   Now to 2020 plus
Fullish mature colour. Firm, round, rich, spicy nose. A touch of roast chestnuts. Fullish body. Rich and ample. Complex and pure and classy. Lots of energy. Very fine plus.

Domaine de la Romanée-Conti, 1983   Now to 2020 plus
Full, firm colour. Some maturity but not as much as the 1985. Rich, full, concentrated nose. A lot of depth and dimension here. On the palate not the greatest class and not as pure as I would have liked. On the one hand, an intensity and a depth not in the 1985. On the other, slightly rigid and astringent. It needs food. The finish is a little dry and austere. Lots of life still. Better as it evolved. Fine plus.

Domaine Marey-Monge, bottled by the Domaine de la Romanée-Conti, 1969   Now to 2018
Four to five centimetres of ullage. Full mature colour. Lovely ripe, fragrant nose. Still fresh. Still most attractive. Vigorous, silky-smooth, and very classy. Fullish body. Ripe and succulent and profound. Long, gentle follow-through. Lovely.

Domaine Marey-Monge, bottled by Maison Thorin, 1962   Drink soon
Good fullish colour. Interesting spice on the nose. Sweet, ripe, and roast-chestnutty. Medium-full body. On the palate, though not astringent, shows some odd flavours. The wine oxidised fast in the glass. Somewhat rigid at the end. Could have been fine in its prime.

Maison Joseph Drouhin, 1959   Drink soon
Low shoulder fill and rather a light, well-matured colour. Nevertheless, this is still fresh and elegant and shows plenty of interest. Ripe, intense, sweet, and classy. A surprising amount of thrust, belying the colour and the fill. Very fine.

Domaine Louis Latour, 1952   Past its best
Four to five centimetres of ullage. Fullish, mature colour. Stightly sweet on the nose. Very volatile. Big, rich, and very ripe. Quite a chunky wine. But too volatile to be acceptable.

Maison Henri de Bahezre, 1929   Past its best
Surprisingly good colour for a wine of this age. Slightly dried out on the nose though, just a little decay, and the fruit is drying out. Originally fullish.

Richebourg

THE OWNERS of Richebourg are as follows: Domaine de la Romanée-Conti (3.51 hectares); Leroy (0.78 ha); Gros Frère et Soeur (0.69 ha); A. F. Gros (0.60 ha); Anne Gros (0.60 ha); Thibault Ligier-Belair (0.52 ha)—this was leased out on a sharecropping basis to Denis Mugneret until the 2001 vintage; Méo-Camuzet (0.35 ha); Grivot (0.32 ha); Mongeard-Mugneret (0.31 ha); Alain Hudelot-Noëllat (0.28 ha); and the Clos Frantin (Albert Bichot) (0.07 ha). In total, the surface area is 8.03 hectares.

There have been a number of changes in recent years. The Leroy vines were acquired from Charles Noëllat in 1988. This was also the vintage when Jean-Nicolas Méo reclaimed his patrimony: formerly the land had been sharecropped by Henri Jayer. The A. F. Gros parcel has been passed down from her father, Jean Gros; and the Anne Gros vines from *her* father, François. Up until 1971, the domaine-bottled part of what was then the 2 hectare Gros parcel, all in one piece, was sold as Domaine Louis Gros.

Of all the nonmonopoly *grands crus* of Burgundy, Richebourg rates with Chambertin

and Chambertin, Clos de Bèze, just after Le Musigny, as the region's finest. Some of the richest, most sumptuous Pinot Noir–based wines in the world are made here, and not only from the Domaine de la Romanée-Conti, which owns around 45 percent of the land.

Richebourg lies immediately to the north of La Romanée and Romanée-Conti and upslope from Romanée-Saint-Vivant. It is made up of two *lieux-dits*: Les Richebourgs and Les Véroilles-Sous-Richebourg (see map 9). While the aspect of Romanée-Conti faces due east, that of Richebourg inclines just a little towards the north at its upper end. Lying between 280 and 260 metres of altitude, the gradient is similar to that of Romanée-Conti, as is the soil structure, a pebbly clay-sand mixture with a low sand content, mixed with limestone debris, lying on the rosy Premeaux rock of the lower Bathonian period.

Originally owned by the monastery of Citeaux, the majority of Richebourg was sold off as a *bien national* in 1790. By 1855 the owners included MM Frantin (who owned the bulk of Les Véroilles), Marey (already a proprietor

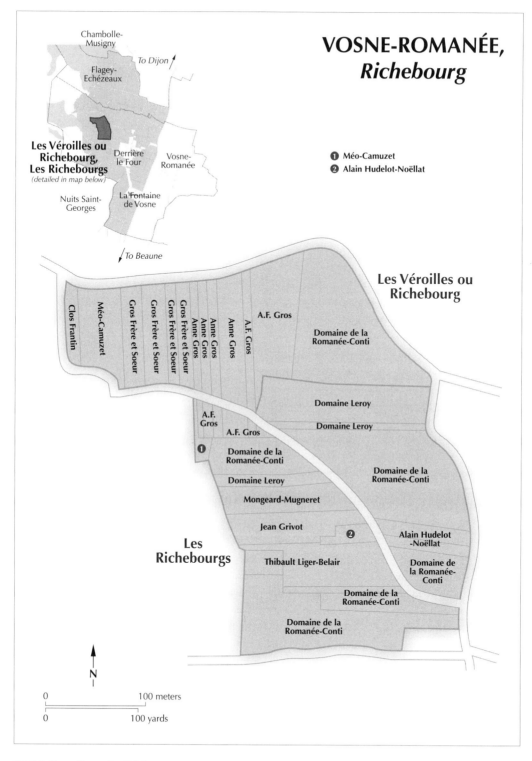

MAP 9 Vosne-Romanée, *Richebourg*

before the Revolution), Duvault-Blochet (ances-tors of the Villaines of the Domaine de la Romanée-Conti), Liger-Belair, Lausseure, and Marillier. As with La Tâche and Gaudichots, the proprietors of Les Véroilles (by this time the name had been changed by them to Les Véroilles ou Richebourg) were able to prove to the Court of Appeal in Dijon in the 1920s that their wine had been sold as Richebourg and at the same price for long enough to warrant this section being officially included within the *grand cru*.

Today all Richebourg is domaine-bottled by the owners. But this has only relatively recently been the case. After the division of the Gros estate in 1963, merchants could continue to buy fruit or wine, especially from Francois Gros, father of Anne, the latter not taking over until 1988. I have rarely seen a Richebourg with Francois's name on the label. Up to this same vintage some of the non-Jayer part of the Méo-Camuzet domaine was sold off to outsiders, as was part of the Liger-Belair estate.

My view on Richebourg today can be sum-marised as follows: top marks to the Domaine de la Romanée-Conti for consistency and sheer breed and *terroir* expression. Superstar of the 1970s, 1980s, and early 1990s: Jean Gros (the wine was made by his son Michel). Today's superstar: Anne Gros.

Richebourg is fuller, fatter, richer, more intense and generous, but more masculine and long-lasting than Romanée-Saint-Vivant. At its best it can offer an explosion of flavours: coffee and chocolate when young, violets when mature; all within a velvet textured conucopia of small black and red fruits. I count some Richebourgs amongst the greatest Burgundies I have ever tasted. "Sumptuous" said Camille Rodier more than seventy years ago. How I agree!

TASTING NOTES

The following Richebourgs were sampled by the Guilford, Connecticut, group in March 2011.

Domaine Gros Frère et Soeur, 1999
Now to 2020

Very full colour. Still youthful. Quite a high-toned nose. Lots of ripe fruit and very good grip. Evolved fast in the glass, and not exactly favourably. There was even a hint of oxidation. Fullish body. Very ripe—almost over-ripe. Yet good grip. Fine but without the depth, dimen-sion, and class of a great example.

Domaine Leroy, 1999
From 2015

Medium-full mature but vigorous colour. Ripe, rich meaty nose, slightly clunky at first, lacking high tones. Full-bodied, earthy, and opulent on the palate. Improved on aeration. Lovely finish. It lacks the sheer finesse for great, but it's very fine and will still improve.

Domaine Méo-Camuzet, 1999
From 2015

Very full colour. Still immature. The nose is full and oaky, and at first it seemed to lack grace. Richer and lusher as it evolved and became less tight. Full body. The tannins just about resolved. Concentrated and meaty. Very rich and very good grip. Needs another five years. Improved in the glass. At present, better with food. Very fine if not great.

Domaine Denis Mugneret et Fils, 1999
Now to 2025

Fullish colour but some development. Slightly pinched on the nose at first. Full and rich underneath but not the definition and finesse of most. Medium-full body. Better on the pal-ate than on the nose. This does show top *grand cru* quality. Long, rich, velvety fruit. Very good grip. Seductive and very fine.

Domaine de la Romanée-Conti, 1999,
From 2016

Fine full, barely mature nose. Rich, opulent, spicy, almost exotic nose. Full body. Still some tannin to resolve. Very ripe and rich and con-centrated. A lot of depth. A powerful example. Real drive and persistence. Very fine indeed. Still needs five years.

Domaine Anne Gros, 1996   Now to 2030

Very fine full colour. Still immature looking. Lovely, laid back, really concentrated, and high-quality nose. Full body. Vigorous. Splendid fruit. A profound wine with very good grip, lots of energy and real finesse. Only just ready. A great wine, I wrote at first. After twenty minutes the leanness of 1996 began to show itself. So only "very fine indeed."

Domaine Liger-Belair, 1966   Now to 2020

Very full, barely mature colour. Very ripe, almost sweet, chocolaty nose. Essentially soft, silky, and very seductive. Fullish body. Rich. Still a bit of tannin to resolve and a little rigid. A wine for food. But lovely fruit and very good balance. Just about ready. Fine quality.

Domaine Denis Mugneret et Fils, 1996   Now to 2016

Good full, mature colour. On the nose the acidity is quite dominant. On the palate it is fullish bodied, with a certain dry astringency. Lacks succulence and richness. No charm. And it won't improve. Good at best.

Domaine A. F. Gros, 1995   Now to 2020

Medium-full, mature colour. Somewhat four-square on the nose. The tannins do not seem to be really sophisticated. But rather better on the palate. Medium-full body. Despite being a little lumpy, there is ample, fresh, attractive ripe fruit. No enormous depth though. Fine.

Domaine Anne Gros, 1995   From 2015

Fullish colour. Still very youthful. Splendidly pure, concentrated, closed-in nose. A lot of depth and class here. Fullish body. Still some tannins to resolve. Marvelous fruit and great vigour. A great wine. Better still in 2016.

Domaine Jean Gros, 1993   Now to 2030

Splendidly youthful colour. Cool, pure, old-viney and very high-class nose. Full body. Brilliant fruit. Splendid tannins and grip. This is velvety and very concentrated. Marvelous energy and loads of dimension. Indisputably a great wine.

Domaine de la Romanée-Conti, 1993   Now to 2025

Fullish mature colour. Attractive fresh, very stylish, composed nose. Fullish body. Very ripe. Very seductive and fully ready. Long and complex and vigorous and subtle. This is very fine plus.

Domaine Jean Grivot, 1990   Now to 2020

Full, barely mature colour. Firm, slightly earthy-spicy nose. Full and youthful. Still a little tannin to resolve. Very good grip, surprisingly so for a 1990, but this makes it a touch austere, if not rigid. Ripe and long and classy but not exactly complete. Very good indeed.

Domaine Jean Gros, 1990   Now to 2025 plus

Full, vigorous colour. Rich, concentrated, plummy-blackberry nose. Profound and very impresive. Full body. A very lovely wine with plenty of depth and grip and still great vigour. Marvelous ripe, lingering finish. Very fine indeed.

Domaine Jean Grivot, 1988   Drink soon

Very full, immature colour. Odd nose. Pungent sweet-sour, rich, but vegetal-soupy and even a suggestion of soy sauce. Fullish, but I'm not really sure there is much pleasure to be had here. I'd had the wine a month previously *chez* Grivot and noted it as "a gyspy of a wine." This is a worse bottle.

Domaine Jean Gros, 1988   Now to 2025 plus

Full, barely mature colour. Very lovely nose. Multidimensional, very very classy, and very very harmonious. This is indisputably a great wine, even finer than the 1990. Full body. Very good grip. Not as big a wine as the 1990 but splendidly composed and very long on the palate.

Domaine de la Romanée-Conti, 1988   Now to 2017

Fullish, fully mature colour. Quite an animal nose. Plus a touch of the stems. Fullish body. Just a little rigid and even astringent. Very good grip. Ripe and ample if not exactly rich and velvety. Slight austerity at the end. Better with food. Fine but not great.

Maison Roland
Remoissenet, 1985   Now to 2020

Full colour. No undue age. At first a little reduced. But when this blew off, one could see a very impressive wine underneath. Ripe, classy, fresh, silky-smooth, fragrant nose. Full-bodied, rich, and vigorous. Sweet and very lovely. Quite substantial. Very good grip. Very fine indeed. From magnum shortly after, courtesy of John Marsh, the wine was even better: indeed great.

Domaine de la
Romanée-Conti, 1985   Now to 2020 plus

Good fullish colour. Now mature. Rich, fat and creamy on the nose. Lots of depth and energy here and a touch of spice. Fullish body. Even more concentrated and vigorous than the Romanée-Saint-Vivant. Splendid finish. Very fine indeed.

Domaine Jean Gros, 1978   Now to 2018

Good colour. Slightly pinched, bitter-earthy nose. Somewhat reduced. Medium-full body. When the reduction blew off, one could see a quite sweet, fresh, and intense wine with good fruit. Much better than the nose would indicate. Nice and pure and vigorous. Fine plus.

Domaine Charles Nöellat, 1978   Now to 2015

Fullish, mature colour. Aromatic nose. Quite spicy. Good complex fruit. No lack of interest if a little dry on the follow-through. Plumped up in the glass. Soft, fragrant, classy, and balanced. Medium bodied. Fine plus, but it aged in the glass.

Maison Roland Remoissenet, 1978   Now to 2020

Magnum, courtesy of John Marsh. Full, vigorous colour. Marvelous nose. Rich, aromatic, and gently oaky. Very ripe, succulent, and multidimensional. Full body. Was quite a tannic wine, but these tannins now fully absorbed. Splendidly rich and energetic. Not a trace of age. Excellent.

Domaine Jean Gros, bottled
in the UK by Avery's, 1969   Drink soon

Fullish colour. No undue age. This bottle was a bit corked. But one could see a big, robust wine with ample fruit and plenty of depth.

Domaine de la
Romanée-Conti, 1969   Drink soon

Medium to medium-full mature colour. Lovely, soft, sweet, fragrant nose. Fully evolved yet still fresh. Now lightening up on the palate. But elegant and balanced, subtle, long, and lovely. Very fine plus.

Domaine de la
Romanée-Conti, 1952   Now to 2020

Four to five centimetres of ullage. Full mature colour. Rich, full, ripe, vigorous, and very lovely on the nose. Quite a substantial wine. Succulent, profound, and very classy indeed. This is a great wine, and there is no hurry to finish it up.

Domaine Charles Vienot, 1949   Will still keep

Huge colour, mature but very deep. Full, rigid, slightly volatile, and astringent on the nose. Better on the palate and with food. Full-bodied, fat, ripe, rich, and voluptuous. No great style but smooth and enjoyable.

Domaine Charles Vienot, 1947   Drink soon

In contrast to the 1949, the colour here is barely medium. Soft, fragrant, almost sweet nose. Juicy and stylish. Medium weight. Fragrant but rather delicate now. Yet not dried out and still classy.

Echézeaux and Grands-Echézeaux

ECHÉZEAUX LINES UP after Corton and Clos de Vougeot as the third largest red wine *grand cru* in Burgundy. There are nearly 38 hectares (ha): production can be as much as 1,200 hectolitres (158,000 bottles).

The principal proprietors are as follows (I have asterisked the best): *Domaine de la Romanée-Conti (4.67 ha); Mongeard-Mugneret (3.80 ha) (some leased off); *Gros Frère et Soeur (2.11 ha); *Emmanuel Rouget (1.43 ha) (exploiting the land of Georges, Henri, and Lucien Jayer); *Lamarche (1.32 ha); *Mugneret-Gibourg (1.24 ha); *Domaine de Perdrix (1.15 ha); *Domaine du Clos Frantin (1.00 ha); *Jean-Marc Millot (0.87 ha); *Joseph Faiveley (0.87 ha); *Anne Gros (0.85ha); *Arnoux-Lachaux (0.82 ha); *Jean-Yves Bizot (0.72 ha); *Dujac (0.69 ha); *Comte Liger-Belair (0.62 ha); *Grivot (0.57 ha); *Eugenie, formerly Engel (0.55 ha); Jayer-Gilles (0.54 ha); *Joseph Drouhin (0.53 ha); *Jadot (0.52 ha); *Duband (0.50 ha); Jacky Confuron-Cotetidot (0.48); *Bouchard Père et Fils (0.39 ha); *Régis Forey (0.38 ha); and Jacques Prieur (from 1996) (0.34 ha). In total, there are eighty-four proprietors.

The *climat* lies upslope and to the south of Grands-Echézeaux and the Clos de Vougeot. However, unlike the Clos, it does not run down all the way to the Nationale. The lower slopes are merely village wine, sold as Vosne-Romanée *tout court*. The Vosne-Romanée *premiers crus* of Beaumonts, Brûlées, and Suchots separate Echézeaux from Richebourg and Romanée-Saint-Vivant.

Within Echézeaux there are a number of *lieux-dits*, not seen on labels but important locally to locate a grower's vines. Above Grands-Echézeaux are Les Poulaillères, where the majority of the Domaine de la Romanée-Conti's vines are situated, and Echézeaux-du-Dessus. On the Chambolle-Musigny border lies En Orveaux. At the top of the slope are Les Champs Traversins and Les Rouges-du-Bas. Below the *premier cru* of Les Beaumonts (*Bas*), of which a morsel is classified as Echézeaux, are Les Loächausses and Les Criots-en-Vignes-Blanches. Lower down still, next to Les Suchots, are Clos-Saint-Denis and Les Treux. While lowest of all, outside the wall of Clos de Vougeot, lies Les Quartiers-de-Nuits, part of which is

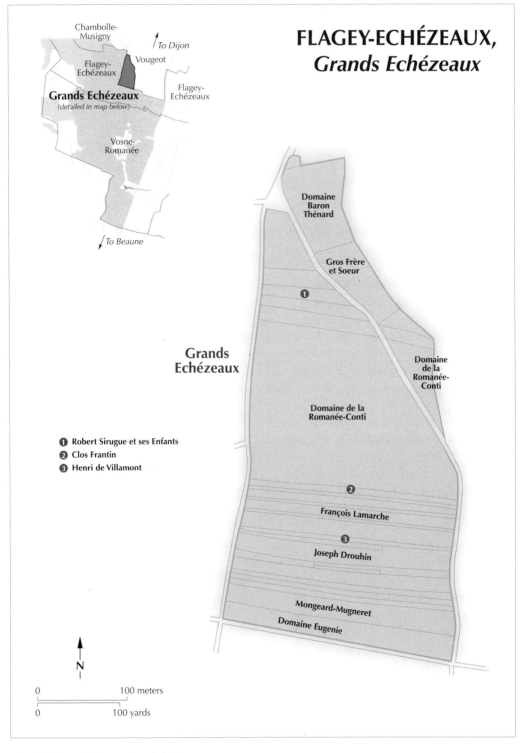

Chambolle-
Musigny

Flagey-
Echézeaux

Vougeot

To Dijon

Flagey-
Echézeaux

Grands Echézeaux
(detailed in map below)

Vosne-
Romanée

To Beaune

FLAGEY-ECHÉZEAUX,
Grands Echézeaux

Domaine
Baron
Thénard

Gros Frère
et Soeur

❶

**Grands
Echézeaux**

Domaine
de la
Romanée-
Conti

Domaine de la
Romanée-Conti

❶ Robert Sirugue et ses Enfants
❷ Clos Frantin
❸ Henri de Villamont

❷

François Lamarche

❸

Joseph Drouhin

Mongeard-Mugneret

Domaine Eugenie

N

| 0 | 100 meters |
| 0 | 100 yards |

MAP 10 Flagey-Echézeaux, *Grands Echézeaux*

classified as Echézeaux, the rest simply as village Vosne-Romanée.

Naturally, in such a large vineyard the *terroir* varies considerably. At its highest point the *grand cru* reaches 300 metres, at its lowest 250. Upslope the incline is steep (up to 13°) and the surface soil thin with the underlying rock often visible. The stone here is Bajocian, friable in parts, hard in others as in Les Rouges du Bas, sometimes pure, sometimes with an important clay content. Lower down the incline is flatter, the soil richer and deeper and the drainage less efficient. By and large, high up on the slope, and where there is sand as well as marl, as in Les Champs Traversins, you will find a more high-toned, somewhat less dense, refined wine. Lower down, as in Les Treux, despite it being next to Grands-Echézeaux, the soil is heavier and more humid, the wine more four-square.

Is there then, as in Clos de Vougeot, a difference in quality between the different sections? The answer is certainly yes, but to a lesser degree, for the very bottom of the slope is not *grand cru*. However, there is a difference in my view between the *lieux-dits* to the north and those on the Les Suchots side. In general, the former produce the best wine. The two best sub-*climats* are Les Poulaillères and the Echézaeux du Dessus. As always in Burgundy, the degree of competence of the wine-maker is paramount. Moreover, many of the landholders possess a number of different parcels within the conglomerate *climat*. Furthermore, none of the important producers goes as far as to name the *lieu-dit* on their labels.

Grands-Echézeaux is rather small: just over 9 hectares. Production is similarly about a quarter of that of Echézeaux (290 hectolitres: 34,000 bottles). Here the principal proprietors are (I have asterisked the best): *Domaine de la Romanée-Conti (3.53 ha); Mongeard-Mugneret (1.84 ha) (some of which is leased off); Domaine Thenard/Bordeaux-Montrieux (1.15 ha) (which often used to be sold in the past through Maison Remoissenet Père et Fils); *Eugenie, formerly Engel (0.50 ha); *Joseph Drouhin (0.47 ha); Henri de Villamont (0.43

ha); *Gros Père et Soeur (0.37 ha); *Lamarche (0.30 ha); *Domaine du Clos Frantin (0.25 ha); and *Jean-Matc Millot (0.20 ha). In total, there are twenty-one proprietors.

Grands-Echézeaux forms a roughly triangular piece which fits into and squares off the southwest corner of Clos de Vougeot. On the other two sides it is bounded by the much more extensive Echézeaux. Originally it belonged to the Abbey of Citeaux but, unlike the Clos de Vougeot itself, it seems to have led a secular existence since at least the seventeenth century, one of the prerevolutionary proprietors being the influential Marey family. Relatively flat, at 260 metres, the brown soil is quite deep, a chalky limestone mixed with clay and pebbles on a Bajocian limestone base. Here we have a similarity to Le Musigny.

Generally regarded, and priced accordingly, as superior to Echézeaux, Grands-Echézeaux is a richer, more structured wine with greater intensity and definition, and a black fruit, gamey flavour: rustic in the best sense. It can be firm, even hard in its youth, less obviously generous than either Echézeaux or the more refined *grands crus* of Vosne-Romanée. It needs time. But the best are clearly as good as the best Clos de Vougeots. And a lot more interesting than the least good. *Chez* Engel, before Philippe's untimely death, one always tasted his Clos de Vougeot after the Echézeaux and before the Grands-Echézeaux; this being his inverse order of preference, despite his Clos de Vougeot coming from a very well-favoured part of that vineyard. I normally agreed with that hierarchy.

The reputation of Echézeaux, however, is that of a second division *grand cru*, without the concentration and finesse of its grander neighbour. Many local growers, judging by their prices, consider it no superior to their top Vosne-Romanée *premiers crus*: Aux Brûlées, Les Suchots, Cros-Parentoux, and so on. As I have written in the past, in many cases the customer would be better off with a top *premier cru*, though he or she might not find it any cheaper.

This is certainly true of most merchant wine. But when you look up the list of the main owners and notice the names of Rouget/Jayer, Mugneret-Gibourg, Faiveley, Lamarche, Anne Gros, Liger-Belair, Grivot, Dujac, and Eugenie-Engel, not to mention Domaine de la Romanée-Conti itself, you begin to think that from these sources you should surely get first-division wine. And that is what you usually get.

TASTING NOTES

The following wines were gathered by Tom Black for an event set up by L'Eté du Vin, a charity raising money for Cancer Research in Nashville, Tennessee, in April 2009.

Grands-Echézeaux, Domaine de la Romanée-Conti, 2005   From 2015
Fullish, youthful colour. Slightly sweaty on the nose. It doesn't sing. Medium-full body. Not unduly tannic. Good grip. But not as rich or as succulent as 2005s should be. A badly stored bottle?

Grands-Echézeaux, Domaine de la Romanée-Conti, 2004   Now to 2020
Good colour. Now a little maturity. Fresh, really quite ripe nose. Balanced and succulent. Good class and intensity. Medium-full body. Really fine for the vintage. Will still improve.

Echézeaux, Domaine Dujac, 2003   Now to 2012
Very good colour. Still immature. Ripe, exotic, fat, rich nose. Fullish body. Soft tannins. Very good grip for the vintage. A lush wine. Unexpected freshness. Long. Just about ready. Fine. Best enjoyed soon.

Grands-Echézeaux, Domaine de la Romanée-Conti, 2003   Now to 2020
Very full, rich colour. Fat, ample, ripe but not over-ripe nose. Full body. Succulent. Unexpectedly classy for a 2003. Very good grip. Very fine for the vintage.

Echézeaux, Domaine Dujac, 2002   Now to 2016
Medium to medium-full colour. I would have expected somewhat more. Classy fruit on the nose, if an absence of real concentration or indeed vigour. But balanced. They could have done better here. A missed opportunity. Just about ready.

Grands-Echézeaux, Domaine de la Romanée-Conti, 2002   Now to 2020
Medium to medium-full colour. Not as full as I would have expected. Lovely nose but less grip and intensity than other top 2002s. Medium to medium-full body. Balanced. Classy. But only very good for the vintage. Quite forward too.

Echézeaux, Domaine Dujac, 2001   Now to 2014
Good colour. Now mature. Bigger and more vigorous than the 2000. Firm nose, a little sturdy. Fuller and richer than the 2000 but not as stylish. A little over-extracted it seemed at first, with the 2000 showing more charm. But this got better and better in the glass. Fine quality. Just about ready.

Grands-Echézeaux, Domaine de la Romanée-Conti, 2001   Drink soon
Lighter and more developed colour than the 2000, which is curious. Light nose. Somewhat too soft on the palate. A lack of grip, concentration, and volume. Not short though. But the 2000 is much better.

Echézeaux, Domaine Dujac, 2000   Drink soonish
Medium-full, mature colour. Ripe, spicy nose. No great depth but clean and classy. Lacks a little vigour, but that is the vintage. Soft and a little weak, compared to the Engel, on the palate. But fresh and pleasant. Essentially a bit loose-knit and one-dimensional, though.

Echézeaux, Domaine Engel, 2000   Now to 2015
Medium to medium-full colour. Now mature. Aromatic, classy nose. A touch of mocha. Not a bit weak. Medium body. The tannins now absorbed. Good energy for a 2000. Good class too. Fine.

Grands-Echézeaux, Domaine de la Romanée-Conti, 2000   Now to 2015
Good colour. Now some maturity. Ripe, quite rich nose. Nicely fat and composed. No lack of concentration and depth. Fresh too. Medium body. Balanced. Plenty of wine for a 2000.

Long. Complex. Stylish. Fine plus for the vintage. Just about ready.

Echézeaux, Domaine Dujac, 1999

Now to 2016

Fullish colour. Still very youthful. Ample, rich, spicy nose. Plenty of depth and concentration and lots of fruit. Slight ground-coffee elements. Medium-full body. Fully *à point*, indeed soft. Round and most enjoyable. But the 1998 is fresher and more vigorous and better.

Echézeaux, Domaine de la Romanée-Conti, 1999

Now to 2020 plus

Full colour, barely mature. Nose still a little unformed. Fullish, energetic. Very lovely pure fresh fruit. Very classy. Long, complex, and very lovely indeed. Very fine for an Echézeaux. Just about ready.

Grands-Echézeaux, Maison Potel, 1999

Now to 2015

Very good colour. Full and still youthful. Plump, accessible nose. No undue tannins, yet not a bit slight. Medium-full body. A slight lack of backbone but sweet and succulent and fully ready. Long. Very good indeed.

Grands-Echézeaux, Domaine de la Romanée-Conti, 1999

Now to 2030

Very fine, full, immature colour. Very lovely, rich, concentrated, very cassis nose. Even richer than the 1998. Fuller. More aromatic. More spicy. The tannins now soft. Classy. Vigorous. Complex. Very lovely follow-through. Very fine for the vintage. Just about ready.

Echézeaux, Domaine Dujac, 1998

Now to 2018 plus

Medium-full colour. Just a little fresher-looking than the 1996. Richer and more vigorous on the nose, with a touch of mocha. Fresh. Profound. Fullish body. Very ripe. Lovely fruit. No austerity. Better than the 1996. Very long and harmonious. Fine plus.

Echézeaux, Domaine de la Romanée-Conti, 1998

Now to 2020 plus

Full, barely mature colour. Firm, still a bit closed-in on the nose. But very classy and profound underneath. Fullish body. Ripe tannins, now absorbed. Lots of vigour and energy. Very long and lovely. Very fine. Only just about ready.

Grands-Echézeaux, Domaine de la Romanée-Conti, 1998

Now to 2028

Fine full, fresh colour. Fuller, fatter, and richer than the 1996. More concentrated. Full, rich, ample. The tannins now absorbed. Very lovely fruit. Long. Complete. Complex and profound. Very fine, and superior to both 1995 and 1996.

Echézeaux, Domaine de la Romanée-Conti, 1997

Now to 2014

Medium colour. Mature. Soft but fresh nose. Medium body. No great depth or complexity and a lack of real grip and vigour. Good length and class nevertheless. Fine for a 1997.

Grands-Echézeaux, Domaine René Engel, 1997

Now to 2013

Good full, vigorous, but just-about-mature colour. Fresh nose for the vintage. Nice and plump and fruity. Not as enjoyable on the palate. Fullish body. Plenty of fruit. But a bit astringent. Yet very good indeed for the vintage. Better with food.

Echézeaux, Domaine Dujac, 1996

Now to 2016

Medium-full colour. Still youthful. Ripe, very Dujac nose. Balanced, fragrant, and just a little sweet. Medium-full body. Soft. Just a little loose-knit but plenty of fruit, depth, and energy. Fine. *À point*.

Echézeaux, Domaine de la Romanée-Conti, 1996

Now to 2020

Full colour. Just about ready. Cooler, firmer, and classier than the Dujac. This is very fine. Medium-full body. Complete. Ripe. Harmonious. No undue acidity. Very long and lots of finesse. Rather more charm than the Grands-Echézeaux.

Grands-Echézeaux, Domaine de la Romanée-Conti, 1996

Now to 2018

Full, very vigorous colour. Slightly austere on the nose. Good acidity. Medium-full body. No undue tannins. Elegant. Slightly cool. It lacks a bit of fat and generosity. But it's certainly classy.

Echézeaux, Domaine
René Engel, 1995 Now to 2020 plus

Full colour. Barely mature. Round, rich, plump nose. Good class and depth. Not a bit hard. Medium-full body. Very ripe. Lots of energy. Lots of depth. Very fine.

Grands-Echézeaux, Domaine
René Engel, 1995 Drink soon

Medium-full colour. Now some maturity. Soft, ripe, rich, stylish nose. Medium to medium-full body. Unexpectedly loose-knit and lacking grip. Somewhat short and one-dimensional. Yet the fruit is enjoyable. Very good. (After the above, I wonder if this was a bad bottle.)

Grands-Echézeaux, Domaine
de la Romanée-Conti, 1995 Now to 2015

Full, barely mature colour. Softer and more stemmy and spicy than the 1993. Ripe. Vigorous. Medium to medium-full body. Curiously not the greatest grip and energy. Ripe, fresh, elegant fruit nevertheless. But a lack of punch.

Grands-Echézeaux, Domaine
René Engel, 1993 Now to 2030

Full colour. Still very youthful indeed. Splendid nose. Rich, concentrated, full, intense, profound, and classy. Full body. Concentrated, complete, and very lovely. Real depth and dimension here. Very, very fine. My wine of the tasting.

Grands-Echézeaux, Domaine
de la Romanée-Conti, 1993 Now to 2020 plus

Fullish, mature colour. Concentrated, rich, youthful nose. Plenty of depth. High-quality. Fullish body. Very good grip. Slightly chunky. But very good fruit and lots of energy. Lovely finish. Will still develop. Fine. But the 1990 is better.

Grands-Echézeaux, Domaine
de la Romanée-Conti, 1991 Now to 2015

Medium to medium-full colour. No undue age. Soft, complete, *à point* nose. Composed and stylish. Very harmonious. Medium body. Soft and round. Long and delicious. The 1990 is better, of course, but this is very delicious.

Grands-Echézeaux, Domaine
de la Romanée-Conti, 1990 2011 to 2020 plus

Full, youthful colour. Rich, full, aromatic, vigorous nose. Lots of depth and class here. Full body. Not a bit too roasted. Excellent grip. Very lovely fruit. Quite chunky but no lack of elegance. For food. Fine.

Grands-Echézeaux, Domaine
de la Romanée-Conti, 1989 Now to 2013

Full, youthful colour. Lovely, rich, full, sweet, concentrated nose. Lots of depth. High-quality. Fullish body. Good fruit. The 1985 is sweeter and more vigorous, but this is fine.

Echézeaux, Domaine
René Engel, 1988 Now to 2018

Full, youthful-looking colour. Rich, nicely abundant nose. Not a bit austere. Fullish body. Just a little tannin. Ripe, balanced, and classy. Will still improve. Fine.

Echézeaux, Domaine de
la Romanée-Conti, 1988 Now to 2018

Full, youthful-looking colour. Round, ripe, clean, pure, and classy nose. Medium-full body. Not a bit too lean or austere. Indeed, the follow-through is quite sweet. Very harmonious. Long. Lovely. Fine plus.

Grands-Echézeaux, Domaine
René Engel, 1988 Drink soon

Full colour. Still youthful. Somewhat reduced and artisanal on the nose. But better on the palate. Full body. Fully mature. Slightly chunky but good fruit if no real class. Better with food. Good plus.

Grands-Echézeaux, Domaine
de la Romanée-Conti, 1988 Drink soon

Very full, vigorous, mature colour. Lovely nose. Full, energetic, rich, concentrated, and meaty. But on the palate rather more austere than the 1985 and the 1989 and a bit astringent. Best with food.

Grands-Echézeaux, Domaine
Gros Frère et Soeur, 1985 Now to 2015

Medium to medium-full colour. Fully mature. Not a lot on the nose. Ripe and fresh but a bit ungainly. Good follow-through but an absence of velvet. Good plus.

Grands-Echézeaux, Domaine de la Romanée-Conti, 1985   Now to 2015

Fullish, vigorous, mature colour. Good ripe, succulent nose: fresh, ample, and stylish. A delicious, medium-full bodied fragrant mature wine. Elegant, long, and complex. No hurry to drink. Fine quality.

Grands-Echézeaux, Domaine de la Romanée-Conti, 1983   Drink soon

Mature but not aged colour. The nose lacks freshness. It is funky but unstylish. Medium body. Loose at the end and a bit flat. Unexciting.

Grands-Echézeaux, Domaine de la Romanée-Conti, 1979   Drink up

Light to medium colour. Fresher than the 1978. Light, faded nose. Loose-knit. Now getting hollow. Never that special.

Grands-Echézeaux, Domaine de la Romanée-Conti, 1978   See note

An old colour for a 1978. Old nose too. Now vegetal. Too old. I think this is due to bad storage. I've had better than this. There are hints here of something interesting.

Grands-Echézeaux, Domaine de la Romanée-Conti, 1976   Drink soon

Still quite a vigorous colour. Typically, slightly chunky 1976 nose. On the palate some sweetness but the structure is a little rigid. No undue astringency though. Yet it lacks suppleness. Better with food.

Grands-Echézeaux, Maison Leroy, 1966   Drink soon

Medium-full colour. No undue age. Soft, fragrant nose. Gentle and stylish. Medium weight. Losing its fruit on the palate. Attractive nonetheless. Good follow-through still.

Grands-Echézeaux, Maison Leroy, 1964   Drink soon

Very good, vigorous colour. Full nose but older than the 1959. Still fragrant but beginning to loosen up. Medium weight.

Grands-Echézeaux, Domaine Engel, 1962   Drink soon

Medium-full colour. No undue age. Ripe nose. Good fruit. Nicely spicy on the palate. Balanced but not very concentrated, nor as stylish as the wine became in the 1990s. Good though.

Grands-Echézeaux, Maison Leroy, 1959   No hurry to drink

Good vigorous colour. Still rich and even sweet on the nose. Fullish. Aromatic. Ample and full of energy. Long and complex and classy. Good intensity. Fine quality.

Grands-Echézeaux, Maison Bouchard Père et Fils, 1955   See note

Very well-matured colour. Now light. Quite an old nose. And similar on the palate. A bit past its best. Yet it was very good in its prime.

Grands-Echézeaux, Domaine de la Romanée-Conti, 1955   Very good but drink soon

Well-matured colour. Fragrant, old nose. Quite rich and ripe. No lack of elegance. On the palate still fruity but the acidity is beginning to dominate. Medium weight.

Clos de Vougeot, 2005

BURGUNDY IS LIGHT ON IMAGES, while in Bordeaux, most of the *château* facades are known to wine-lovers all over the world, for the images are depicted on the labels on the bottles. Burgundy has only two immediately recognizable to outsiders: the interior courtyard of the Hospices in Beaune and the Château of the Clos de Vougeot.

Like much of Burgundy, the origins of the Clos de Vougeot are ecclesiastical. In 1098, Robert, Abbot of the Clunaic Benedictine abbey of Molesmes, near Langres, north of Dijon, decided to form a new order. He felt strongly that the original virtues of poverty, chastity, and obedience, laid down by the founding saint, had become too relaxed. The top ecclesiastics slept in comfortable beds, wore sumptuous clothes, and ate and drank like gluttons. Nor, it seems, were they very enthusiastic about celibacy. Robert only managed to persuade some twenty of his order to join him, but they duly left Molesmes and settled in marshy land some 15 kilometres east of Nuits-Saint-Georges. From the Latin name of the reeds (*cistus*) which surrounded their new monastery came the name of this new order: the Cistercians. Not having suitable land in the vicinity for the vine, the monks followed a little river, the Vouge, upstream until they reached the Côte. There amongst the mixed farming prevalent at the time, they saw vines. They bought a parcel of land, enclosed it within a wall, and set about constructing a winery and living quarters for those who would be responsible on the spot for tending the vines and making the wine. This edifice, much modified since, is today's Château du Clos de Vougeot.

The vineyard remained in church ownership, if not in ecclesiastical management, for parcels had been rented off to local laymen, until the French Revolution. Like most of the land owned by the church, the Clos was sequestered by the state, and on January 17, 1791, it was auctioned off to a Jean Foquard, a Parisian banker. He failed to settle the bill, and the authorities were forced to ask the old cellar master to continue to run the estate while they sought an owner with more reliable finances.

Eventually the Clos passed to Jules Ouvrard, local *député* in the post-Restoration parliament

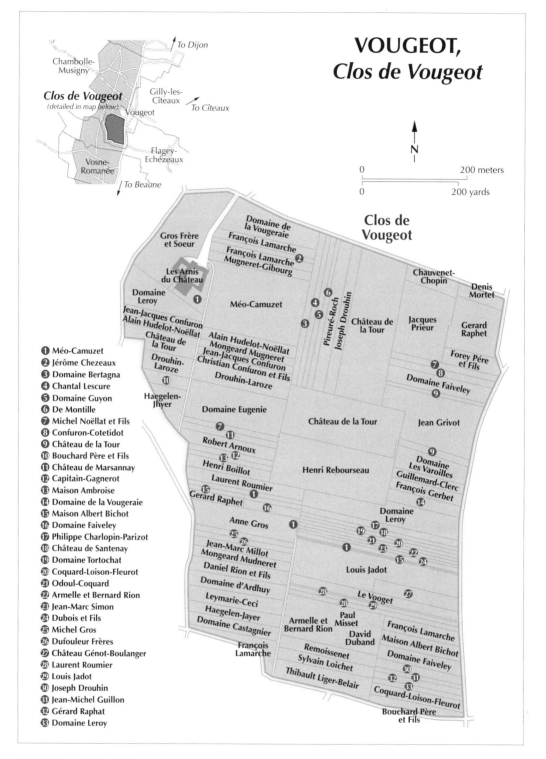

VOUGEOT,
Clos de Vougeot

To Dijon

Chambolle-Musigny

Clos de Vougeot
(detailed in map below)

Gilly-les-Cîteaux

To Cîteaux

Vougeot

Flagey-Echézeaux

Vosne-Romanée

To Beaune

N

| 0 | 200 meters |
| 0 | 200 yards |

Clos de Vougeot

Gros Frère et Soeur

Domaine de la Vougeraie

François Lamarche

François Lamarche ❷
Mugneret-Gibourg

Les Arnis du Château

Chauvenet-Chopin

Denis Mortet

Domaine Leroy ❶

Méo-Camuzet

❻
❹
❺

Pireuré-Roch

Joseph Drouhin

Château de la Tour

Jacques Prieur

Gerard Raphet

Jean-Jacques Confuron
Alain Hudelot-Noëllat

❸

Château de la Tour

Alain Hudelot-Noëllat
Mongeard Mugneret
Jean-Jacques Confuron
Christian Confuron et Fils

Forey Pére et Fils

❼ ❽

Drouhin-Laroze

Domaine Faiveley ❾

Drouhin-Laroze

❿

Haegelen-Jhyer

Domaine Eugenie

❼

Château de la Tour

Jean Grivot

Robert Arnoux

❶❸ ❶❷

Henri Boillot

Laurent Roumier

❾

Henri Rebourseau

Domaine Les Varoilles
Guillemard-Clerc
François Gerbet

❶❺

Gerard Raphet

Domaine Leroy

❶❹

Anne Gros ❶

❶❻

❶❼ ❶❽

❷❺ ❷❻

Jean-Marc Millot
Mongeard Mudneret

Daniel Rion et Fils

❶❾ ❷❶

❷❸

❷❹

❷❷

❶

Louis Jadot

❶❺

Domaine d'Ardhuy

Leymarie-Ceci

Haegelen-Jayer

Domaine Castagnier

François Lamarche

Armelle et Bernard Rion

Paul Misset

David Duband

❷❽

❷❽

Le Vooget ❷❼

❷❾

François Lamarche

Maison Albert Bichot

Remoissenet
Sylvain Loichet

Domaine Faiveley

❸⓪

Thibault Liger-Belair

❸❷ ❸❶
❸❸

Coquard-Loison-Fleurot

Bouchard Père et Fils

❶ Méo-Camuzet
❷ Jérôme Chezeaux
❸ Domaine Bertagna
❹ Chantal Lescure
❺ Domaine Guyon
❻ De Montille
❼ Michel Noëllat et Fils
❽ Confuron-Cotetidot
❾ Château de la Tour
❿ Bouchard Père et Fils
⓫ Château de Marsannay
⓬ Capitain-Gagnerot
⓭ Maison Ambroise
⓮ Domaine de la Vougeraie
⓯ Maison Albert Bichot
⓰ Domaine Faiveley
⓱ Philippe Charlopin-Parizot
⓲ Château de Santenay
⓳ Domaine Tortochat
⓴ Coquard-Loison-Fleurot
㉑ Odoul-Coquard
㉒ Armelle et Bernard Rion
㉓ Jean-Marc Simon
㉔ Dubois et Fils
㉕ Michel Gros
㉖ Dufouleur Frères
㉗ Château Génot-Boulanger
㉘ Laurent Roumier
㉙ Louis Jadot
㉚ Joseph Drouhin
㉛ Jean-Michel Guillon
㉜ Gérard Raphat
㉝ Domaine Leroy

MAP 11 Vougeot, *Clos de Vougeot*

Who Owns What in Clos de Vougeot?
(Surface area in hectares)

Château de la Tour	5.48	Jean-Jacques Confuron	0.52
Méo-Camuzet	3.03	Guy Castagnier	0.50
Rebourseau	2.21	Leymaie-Ceci	0.50
Louis Jadot	2.15	Michel Noëllat	0.47
Paul Misset	2.06	Arnoux-Lachaux	0.45
Leroy	1.91	Bouchard Père et Fils	0.45
Grivot	1.86	Génot-Boulanger	0.43
Gros Frère et Soeur	1.50	Sylvain Loichet	0.42
Gerard Raphet	1.47	Remoissenet	0.42
Domaine de la Vougeraie	1.41	Philippe Charlopin	0.41
Domaine d'Eugenie	1.37	Chauvenet-Chopin	0.35
Lamarche	1.35	Henri Boillot	0.34
Faiveley	1.29	Jean-Marc Millot	0.34
Jacques Prieur	1.28	Bertagna	0.33
Drouhin Laroze	1.03	Yvon Clerget	0.32
Anne Gros	0.93	Francois Gerbet	0.31
Joseph Drouhin	0.91	Régis Forey	0.30
Bernard et Armelle Rion	0.91	Chantal Lescure	0.30
R. Dubois et Fils	0.83	De Montille	0.29
Dominique Laurent	0.80	Hervé Roumier	0.27
Thibault Liger-Belair	0.73	Christian Confuron	0.25
Hudelot-Noëllat	0.69	Confuron-Cotétidot	0.25
Bichot (Clos Frantin)	0.63	Château de Marsannay	0.21
Mongeard-Mugneret	0.63	Tortochot	0.21
Prieuré-Roch	0.62	Jérome Chézeaux	0.20
Laurent Roumier	0.60	Michel Gros	0.20
Domaine de Varoilles	0.60	Jean-Michel Guillon	0.19
Domaine d'Ardhuy	0.56	Bertrand Ambroise	0.17
Daniel Rion	0.55	Capitain-Gagnerot	0.17

and also owner of the Domaine de la Romanée-Conti. This wine was made at the Clos. Ouvrard died in 1860, and the Clos was divided into six parts to enable it to be sold. Six soon became fifteen, and inexorably the Clos became more and more morcellated. Today there are over 80 proprietors and some 120 different parcels. The Château belongs to the local wine promotional organisation, the Chevaliers du Tastevin.

The Clos de Vougeot is notorious for being a *grand cru* whose land stretches all the way down to the main Nuits-Dijon highway. Surely, we argue, the land at the bottom cannot produce *grand cru* wine? On either side we have mere village Vougeot or Vosne-Romanée. Of course, this is an anomaly. But today it is set in stone and there is little we can do about it. And as Jean Grivot, who has vines which stretch up from the main road about two-fifths of the way up, will point out: "When the weather is hot, you need fruit from the more humid, water-retaining lower slopes. When the weather is against you, you need the better drained upslope wines." Back in the Middle Ages, as today at Maximin Grunhaus in the Moselle, we are told that there were three *cuvées* of Clos de Vougeot: that from the upper part, reserved for the Abbot and favoured guests, that from the middle, for the monks, and that from the lower slopes, sold off in bulk. Well, this is the story.

There is in fact no historical basis for it, as far as I can tell.

While the whole of the Clos de Vougeot is separated into *lieux-dits,* there are only two that you will regularly see on wine labels: Le Grand Maupertuis (both Anne Gros and Michel Gros) and Le Musigni (Gros frère et Soeur). The former lies behind the *château,* as you approach it, adjacent to Grands-Echézeaux; the latter is the parcel between the drive-in and the wall with Le Musigny itself.

The altitude of the Clos de Vougeot varies from just over 240 metres down by the main road to over 260 just behind the *château,* but it undulates north to south as well as declining west to east. At the top, as you might expect, the suface soil is thin—barely 35 centimetres—and the underlying rock is Bajocian. Further down, the surface soil layer becomes deeper and there is more clay present, while at the bottom it is yet deeper, with alluvial admixtures. Below the wall, the main road lies on a higher elevation, which both prevents rainwater from efficiently draining away and also provides the threat of a frost pocket. You can find the same problem both up in Gevrey-Chambertin and below the village of Vosne-Romanée.

The largest owner of land within the Clos today is the Château de la Tour, with almost 5.5 hectares out of just over 50. Theirs is the only wine matured and bottled within the Clos, in a nasty nineteenth-century building of no architectural merit whatsoever situated halfway up the slope on the northern side. The wine used to be good, fell off a bit, but is now improving. This is the only proprietor to offer a *vieilles vignes* as well as a normal *cuvée.* Others with more than 1 hectare whose wines can be recommended include Méo-Camuzet, Louis Jadot, Leroy, Grivot, Gros Frère et Soeur, the Domaine de la Vougeraie, the Domaine Eugenie (Engel as was), Lamarche, Faiveley, and Drouhin-Laroze.

Those with less than 1 hectare that I would look out for include: Hudelot-Noëllat, Lachaux-Arnoux, Bertagna, Bouchard Père et Fils, Confuron-Coteditot, J. J. Confuron, Drouhin, Clos Frantin (Albert Bichot), Anne Gros, Michel Gros, Denis Mortet, Mugneret-Gibourg, and Thibaut Liger-Belair.

I consider, and prices seem to agree with me, that Clos de Vougeot is what I term a "second division" *grand cru*—that is, on a par with Corton, Echézeaux, and Charmes-Chambertin, rather than Richebourg or Chambertin. Clos de Vougeot is rarely a really great wine. I can only remember two such bottles: a 1937 Camuzet (predecessor of today's Méo-Camuzet) and Jean Gros's (father of Michel) 1985, the last vintage from vines planted in 1902. I still have a couple of bottles of this. If you look at the notes which follow, and those in the vintage assessments section, you will see that while I might often give 18.5 to a Clos de Vougeot, I rarely manage to award anything higher. No, Clos de Vougeot is a second-division *grand cru.* But it is ample and generous, succulent and slightly spicy, and should be thoroughly enjoyable. And of course, as there is plently of it, relatively speaking, it is a popular wine. In a great vintage such as 2005, there are a very large number of lovely wines.

TASTING NOTES

The following samples of Clos de Vougeot, 2005, were tasted in Burgundy in February 2010 by myself and the proprietors themselves. It was a root day, though clear and sunny (see "Biodynamism" in part four of this book). This meant that the fuller-bodied wines tended to be a bit closed and clumsy. It made the tasting harder work than usual.

Arnoux (now Arnoux-Lachaux)   From 2015 18.5
Good colour. Ripe, plump nose. High-quality. Fresh and concentrated but not hard or aggressive. Medium-full body. Good ripe tannins. Plenty of energy. Rich, balanced, and stylish. Very fine.

Bouchard Père et Fils   From 2013 16.5
Medium to medium-full colour. Quite an evolved nose. Not as substantial as some. But ripe and balanced and attractive. Medium to medium-full body. Good acidity. Fruity but without quite enough depth, concentration,

and, in paticular, intensity. Elegant and harmonious though. Very good plus.

Philippe Charlopin From 2014 16.0
Good colour. Fullish, quite tannic nose. Just a little stewed. Plus a touch of reduction as it developed. Medium-full body. Some tannin but not too aggressively so on the palate. Good grip. But a touch four-square and a slight lack of richness. Very good.

J. J. Confuron From 2013 17.0
Medium colour. Fresh, medium weight, fruity nose. Quite oaky. Very stylish without being a blockbuster. Ripe, fresh, succulent, and seductive. Balanced and positive at the end. Very good indeed.

Joseph Drouhin From 2014 17.5
We had two bottles and they were both corked. But I managed to assess the second before the corkiness dominated the wine too much. Medium colour. Graceful, fruity nose. Not a blockbuster but intense and fragrant. Medium to medium-full body. Very ripe and harmonious. Lovely complex fruit. Seductive. Long and full of interest.

R. Dubois et Fils From 2017 18.5
Very good colour. Lovely rich, full, concentrated, high-class nose. Multidimensional fruit. Lots of vigour and promise. Full body. Good tannins. A wine of depth and backbone which needs time. Splendid finish. Excellent.

Joseph Faiveley From 2016 18.5
Good colour. Very elegant, composed, fullish nose. Lots of depth and dimension here. Lovely fruit. Full body. Very good grip. Classy tannins. Profound and concentrated. Lots of energy and a lovely long finish. Very fine.

Francois Gerbet From 2016 16.0
Good colour. Ripe nose. Some tannin here. And a touch of gingerbread. Slightly earthy. Fullish body. Quite tannic. Needs time. Good grip. This is a chunky example. There is no lack of depth and dimension, but a slight absence of richness. Very good at best.

Jean Grivot From 2017 18.5
Every time I went back to this wine I marked it higher. Knowing that Grivot's wines never exactly sing in their youth, I was not surprised to find out what this was when I saw the results. Very good colour. Good structure on the nose. Fresh, rich, but rather closed-in. Very good energy and concentration. Full body. Tannic. A big, backward wine. But there is very lovely fruit here and a very lovely finish. Got better and better in the glass. Very fine.

Anne Gros From 2015 18.5
Medium-full colour. Soft, ripe, fruity, intense, and classy on the nose. Medium-full body. Quite accessible. A touch of oak. Succulent, rich, but essentially quite forward. But very lovely complexity and lots of dimension. Very fine.

Michel Gros From 2015 18.0
Medium-full colour. The nose is a bit unforthcoming, but on the palate this is beautifully balanced and very elegant. Medium-full body. Good tannins. Good grip. There is plenty of energy and distiction here, but today it is a little austere. Fine plus.

Gros Frère et Soeur From 2017 19.0
From magnum. Good colour. Full, firm nose. Plenty of depth, concentration, and class. But quite backward. Still a touch raw. Full body. Very good tannins. Rich, concentrated, and energetic. Delicious multidimensional fruit. Excellent finish. This is very special.

Lamarche From 2016 19.0
Medium-full colour. Ripe, concentrated nose. Very good tannins. Lots of depth and dimension. Very good style and very lovely fruit. Full body. Very well-integrated tannins. Lovely harmony and splendid energy. Delicious finish. Very fine indeed.

Thibault Liger-Belair From 2016 18.5
From magnum. Very good colour. The nose was a little reduced at first, but this soon resolved itself. Fullish body. Quite sturdy. Rich, balanced, and concentrated. No lack of class.

Very good tannins. Lots of rich fruit. Fat and succulent. Stylish and energetic. Lovely finish. This is very fine.

Dr. Georges Mugneret   From 2015   19.0

Medium-full colour. Fresh, pure, ripe, fragrant nose. Good substance without being a blockbuster. Balanced and stylish. Medium-full body. Very good tannins. Lots of class. Lots of energy. Very harmonious and very complete. Especially lovely on the finish. Very fine indeed.

Jacques Prieur   From 2013   15.0

Good colour. A little more evolved on the nose than most. This is round as well as ripe. Medium to medium-full body. A certain astringency in the background. This doesn't have the grip of the majority. Decent fruit and class but not enough harmony, personality, and energy. Good at best.

Rebourseau   From 2016   17.5

Medium-full colour. No lack of substance on the nose but the character is a little hidden at first. At first I thought it lacked a little richness. But there was plenty on the palate. Medium-full body. The tannin dominates still, but this is no long-term problem. Good grip and no lack of energy and fruit. Finishes long and classy. Fine.

Armelle et Bernard Rion   From 2015   18.0

Medium to medium-full colour. Ripe, unaggressive, stylish, balanced fruit on the nose. Quite forward, it seemed at first. More vigour to it as it developed. Medium to medium-full

body. Good grip and good energy. Plenty of dimension on the follow-through. Fresh and elegant. Long on the palate. Fine plus.

Daniel Rion et Fils   From 2013   16.0

Good colour. Some development here on the nose. There is a lack of real vigour. Soft, fruity, ripe, easy to appreciate. Medium body. Soft tannins. Balanced and attractive. But not really serious. Very good at best.

Château de la Tour   From 2016   16.5

Medium-full colour. Backward nose. Quite sturdy. But good, firm, balanced fruit. Plenty of energy and depth. Medium-full body. Quite tannic. This makes it tough-going at first. But there is good grip here and the finish is promising. Just needs time. Very good plus.

Vougeraie   From 2014   18.0

Medium-full colour. Fresh, stylish fruit on the nose. Good harmony and depth. Good, engaging personality, without being a blockbuster. Medium-full body. Lovely rich, ripe fruit. Very harmonious and classy. Lovely finish. A wine that is very comfortable in its own skin. Fine plus.

Overall the growers' favourites were Arnoux, Anne Gros, Lamarche, Liger-Belair, and Dr. Georges Mugneret. I was impressed by how many voted for (had they guessed?) their own wines, and I have discounted this in the summary just above.

Chambolle-Musigny, Les Amoureuses, 2005

TOGETHER WITH Gevrey-Chambertin's Clos-Saint-Jacques, Chambolle-Musigny, Les Amoureuses is the prime *premier cru* candidate for promotion to *grand cru*. This is already widely acknowledged. You only have to look at the prices. Frédérick Mugnier demanded 250 euros for his 2009, the same price as for his Bonnes-Mares, while his *premier cru* Fuées, a top-drawer site, was a mere 120 euros.

The vineyard measures 5.12 hectares and is divided between fourteen different proprietors. Apart from an anomalous bump above the vineyard road, which lies at the northen end and on the same level as the bottom of Le Musigny, the land is downslope of this road, on a gentle slope of about 8°, between 285 and 255 metres above sea level, descending to an abrupt cliff, both a fault and a quarry, below which are the vineyards of Vougeot.

Where does the name come from? Well, a place where young lovers would go to canoodle, obviously. But Jasper Morris suggests something more prosaic. The soil thickens up in the rain and then sticks to your boots, clinging like young lovers. But you could say that for just about every vineyard in Burgundy!

The soil here is similar but shallower than the lower sections of Musigny above. There is more rock and more limestone on the section closest to the overhang, and there is some sand. But overall, it is very gravelly, mixed with limestone debris—the limestone being less active than elsewhere in the commune, directly over the mother rock, Comblanchien in origin.

This makes a wine which, at its best, is both sublime and ethereal: the epitome of delicacy and finesse. Yet there is nothing feeble about an Amoureuses. Only medium-full bodied it may be, and not quite as glorious as Musigny itself, though in the same mode; but there is an energy and an intensity and the most entrancing fragrance, plus at the end a long, complex, lingering finish. A top Amoureuses from a great vintage is a rivetingly beautiful wine.

TASTING NOTES

The following samples of Chambolle-Musigny, Les Amoureuses, 2005 were assembled by Gregg Cook and tasted at Guilford, Connecticut, in March 2011.

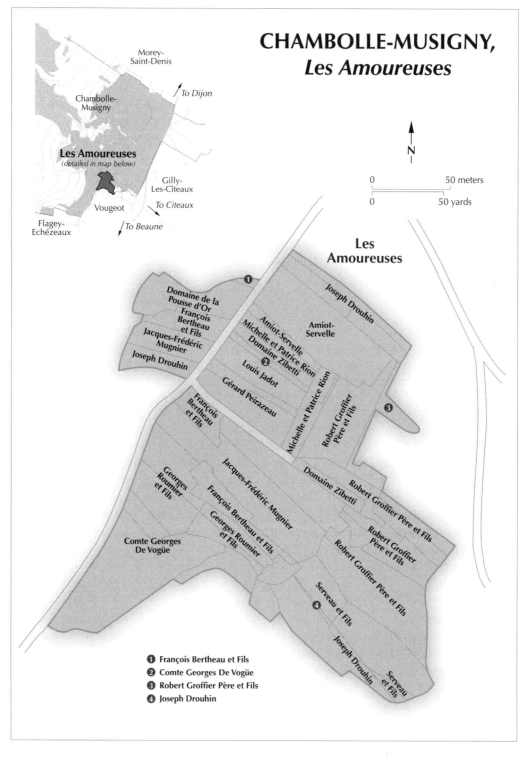

CHAMBOLLE-MUSIGNY,
Les Amoureuses

Morey-Saint-Denis

Chambolle-Musigny

To Dijon

Les Amoureuses
(detailed in map below)

Gilly-Les-Cîteaux

To Cîteaux

Vougeot

To Beaune

Flagey-Echézeaux

N

| 0 | 50 meters |
| 0 | 50 yards |

Les Amoureuses

Joseph Drouhin

Domaine de la Pousse d'Or

François Bertheau et Fils

Jacques-Frédéric Mugnier

Joseph Drouhin

Amiot-Servelle

Michelle et Patrice Rion

Domaine Zibetti

Amiot-Servelle

Louis Jadot

Gérard Peirazeau

François Bertheau et Fils

Michelle et Patrice Rion

Robert Groffier Père et Fils

Georges Roumier et Fils

Jacques-Frédéric Mugnier

Domaine Zibetti

Robert Groffier Père et Fils

François Bertheau et Fils

Georges Roumier et Fils

Robert Groffier Père et Fils

Comte Georges De Vogüe

Robert Groffier Père et Fils

Serveau et Fils

Joseph Drouhin

Serveau et Fils

❶ François Bertheau et Fils
❷ Comte Georges De Vogüe
❸ Robert Groffier Père et Fils
❹ Joseph Drouhin

MAP 12 Chambolle-Musigny, *Les Amoureuses*

Domaine Christian Amiot-Servelle
From 2019 17.5

45 ares, planted in 1944 and 1999, and ripped up after the 2009 vintage. Replanted 2011. Biological from the 2008 vintage. Some stems, depending on the vintage. A week's cold-soaking. 50 percent new oak. Bottled after 15 to 18 months.

Good colour. Lots of wine on the nose. Indeed quite powerful, and with a touch of oak. Fullish body. Rich and succulent. Very good grip. Needs time. But fine quality.

Domaine Francois Bertheau
From 2018 17.5

32 ares, *en fermage*. 100 percent destemmed. A week's cold-soaking. 20 to 30 percent new wood. Bottled after 16 months.

Medium-full colour. Rich, ample, fresh nose. Medium-full body. Good tannins. A supple attractive wine. Balanced and potentially seductive. Fine.

Domaine Joseph Drouhin
From 2019 19.0

59 ares, planted 1971. 40 percent of the stems retained. A week's cold-soaking. 50 percent new wood. Bottled after 16 months.

Medium-full colour. Exquisite nose. The epitome of fragrant Chambolle. Medium-full body. Marvelous balance and great intensity. Very lovely fruit. Very fine plus.

Domaine Robert Groffier
From 2020 18.0

1.0 ha, planted 1968. One-third of the stems retained. 5 days cold-soaking. Two-thirds new wood. Bottled after 16 months, the last 4 in tank.

Good colour. Quite a full, meaty nose. Good depth. Opulent fruit. Quite backward. Fullish body. Rich and gently oaky. Fine plus.

Domaine Louis Jadot
From 2019 18.5

12 ares. Some of the stems rertained, depending on the vintage. No cold-soaking. 75 percent new wood. Bottled after 20 to 22 months.

Good colour. Very lovely, closed-in, concentrated nose. Fullish. Very harmonious. Very profound and very elegant. Splendid fruit. Very fine.

Domaine Jacques-Frédéric Mugnier
From 2019 19.5

53 ares, planted 1954, 1956, and 1966. 100 percent destemmed. 2 to 3 days natural cold-soaking. 10 to 15 percent new wood. Bottled after 18 months.

Fullish colour. Delicious nose. Very, very elegant and harmonious. Very intense fruit here. Great class. Fullish body. Splendidly balanced. Long and sumptuous. Very fine indeed.

Domaine de la Pousse d'Or

20 ares, acquired from Daniel Moine-Hudelot in 2008. The first vintage was 2009.

Domaine Michèle et Patrice Rion

16 ares, *en fermage* from Hervé Roumier (from 2006); the viticulture is in the hands of the Rions. 100 percent destemmed. 4 days cold-soaking. 50 to 70 percent new wood. Bottled after 15 to 18 months.

Hervé Roumier's 2005
From 2019 18.5

Medium-full colour. This is a very lovely wine, which was a surprise as I had not beforehand rated this Roumier highly. Fragrant, intense, classy. Very lovely fruit. Balanced and composed. Very fine.

Domaine Georges Roumier
From 2020 19.5

40 ares, planted 1947. 15 percent of the stems retained. A few days' natural cold-soaking. 33 to 40 percent new wood. Bottled after 16 to 18 months.

Full colour. Rich, full, concentrated nose. Lots of very high-quality wine here. But at present very much in its infancy. Fullish body. Very good grip. Fine tannins. Lots of very profound fruit. Potentially very fine indeed.

Domaine Serveau et Fils
From 2018 17.0

35 ares. No information.

Medium-full colour. Good fruit on the nose. No lack of Chambolle fragrance though not as classy as some. Medium-full body. Balanced. Good grip. Positive finish. Very good indeed.

Domaine Comte
Georges de Vogüé   From 2019   19.5

56 ares, planted 1964 and 1980. 100 percent destemmed. No deliberate cold-soaking. One-third new wood. Bottled after 16 months.

Good colour. Impressive concentration on the nose. Very rich. Full and profound. Full body. Very good grip. Still very youthful. There is a lot of depth and high quality here. Very fine indeed.

The following samples of merchant wines were also sampled:

Maison Alex Gambal   From 2017   17.0

Medium-full colour. Attractive, plump, fresh nose. Very Chambolle. Medium-full weight. Balanced. Stylish. Ripe and supple. Very good indeed.

Maison Pascal Lachaux   From 2018   17.5

Fullish colour. Good meaty nose without losing its Chambolle origins. Fullish. Quite rich and concentrated. Good grip. Good style. Fine

Maison Lucien Le Moine   From 2018   17.0

Fullish colour. At first a little burly and the new oak predominates, but the wine got more civilised as it developed. Rich and fullish. Good acidity. Ripe tannins. Positive finish. Indeed quite elegant. Very good indeed.

Maison Frédéric Magnien   From 2018   17.0

Fullish colour. Quite a full muscular wine for an Amoureuses at first, but like the Le Moine, it softened up in the glass. Indeed, became quite positive and fragrant. Good grip. Long finish. Very good indeed.

Maison Nicky Potel,
Maison Roches de Bellene   From 2018   17.5

Medium-full colour. Ripe, balanced, attractive, fragrant nose. Good Chambolle style here. Medium-full body. Persistent and rich. Elegant and harmonious. Fine.

The following are also proprietors in Chambolle-Musigny, Les Amoureuses.

Domaine Bertagna

8 ares (enough for one large barrel and one small one). Currently uplanted. Bertagna owns the Clos de la Perrière in Vougeot below.

Domaine Chazans (Zibetti family)

12 ares. No information.

Domaine Gérard Peraizeau

25 ares. Robert Groffier is his uncle. Peraizeau makes the wine, which is then largely sold off in bulk. Gerard Peraizeau sells some of his harvest to Benjamin Leroux.

Bonnes-Mares

THE PRINCIPAL PRODUCERS of Bonnes-Mares are as follows: De Vogüé, 2.70 hectares (ha); Drouhin Laroze, 1.49 ha; Georges Roumier, 1.39 ha; Bart, 1.03 ha; Robert Groffier, 0.97 ha; Fougeray de Beauclair, 0.92 ha (this will revert back to Bruno Clair in 2016); Vougeraie, 0.70 ha; Bruno Clair, 0.63 ha; Dujac, 0.59 ha; Naigeon, 0.50 ha; Peraizeau, 0.39 ha; J. F. Mugnier, 0.34 ha; Newman, 0.33 ha; Georges Lignier, 0.29 ha; Hervé Roumier, 0.29 ha; Louis Jadot, 0.27 ha; Auvenay, 0.26 ha; Bouchard Père et Fils, 0.24 ha; Joseph Drouhin, 0.23 ha; Arlaud, 0.20 ha; Hudelot-Baillet, 0.13 ha; and Charlopin-Parizot, 0.12 ha. In total, the surface area is 15.06 hectares.

At the northern end of Chambolle-Musigny, partly overlapping into Morey-Saint-Denis, lies Bonnes-Mares, as far away as it could be, and yet remain within the same commune, from Le Musigny, which lies at the southern end. The most logical derivation of the name is that it is a corruption of Bonnes Mères, "good women"—a reference to the nuns of Notre Dame de Tart, a religious establishment which flourished in the Middle Ages and which gave their name to the Clos which lies next door in the commune of Morey-Saint-Denis. Jasper Morris suggests two alternatives: *marer* is a word for "cultivate." According to Jacques Lardière of Maison Jadot, Jasper also adds: Mares is an old French word for "fairies." Personally I find this more than a little fanciful.

It is a largish vineyard by Burgundian standards and possesses, as you can see, a large number of owners. The 1.52 hectares which lies in Morey are owned by the Clair family, and most of this is leased until 2016 to the Fougeray de Beauclair domaine, after which the parcel will revert to Bruno Clair, making him the second largest domaine in the *climat*. Before the Clair-Daü estate was split in 1985 what is now owned by the Domaine Bart was also part of Clair-Daü. They were then the most important proprietors.

The vineyard lies at 270 to 300 metres above sea level and consists of two quite different types of soil. Above a diagonal line which runs from the top at the Morey end to the bottom

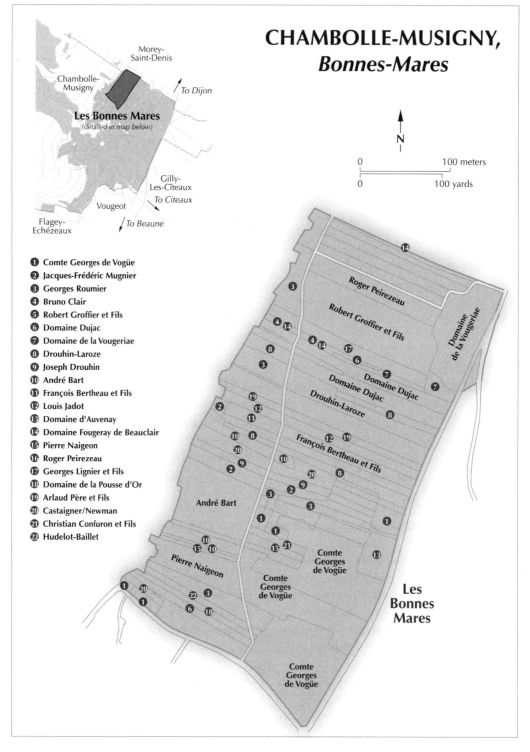

CHAMBOLLE-MUSIGNY, *Bonnes-Mares*

Morey-Saint-Denis

Chambolle-Musigny

To Dijon

Les Bonnes Mares
(detailed in map below)

Gilly-Les-Cîteaux

To Cîteaux

Vougeot

To Beaune

Flagey-Echézeaux

0   100 meters

0   100 yards

N

❶ Comte Georges de Vogüe
❷ Jacques-Frédéric Mugnier
❸ Georges Roumier
❹ Bruno Clair
❺ Robert Groffier et Fils
❻ Domaine Dujac
❼ Domaine de la Vougeraie
❽ Drouhin-Laroze
❾ Joseph Drouhin
❿ André Bart
⓫ François Bertheau et Fils
⓬ Louis Jadot
⓭ Domaine d'Avenay
⓮ Domaine Fougeray de Beauclair
⓯ Pierre Naigeon
⓰ Roger Peirezeau
⓱ Georges Lignier et Fils
⓲ Domaine de la Pousse d'Or
⓳ Arlaud Père et Fils
⓴ Castaigner/Newman
㉑ Christian Confuron et Fils
㉒ Hudelot-Baillet

Roger Peirezeau

Robert Groffier et Fils

Domaine de la Vougeraie

Domaine Dujac

Drouhin-Laroze

François Bertheau et Fils

André Bart

Pierre Naigeon

Comte Georges de Vogüe

Comte Georges de Vogüe

Les Bonnes Mares

Comte Georges de Vogüe

MAP 13 Chambolle-Musigny, *Bonnes-Mares*

at the southern end lies a white marl, rich in fossilised oysters: *terres blanches*. This makes up most of the *climat*. Below it the soil is red-brown colour, heavier and with more clay: *terres rouges*. The upper slopes, as elsewhere, contain very little earth and are largely broken up limestone rock. At the bottom the depth can be as much as 70 centimetres deep.

This leads to a difference in the wines. At the northern end—mainly *terres rouges*—the wines tend to be bigger, more vigorous, muscular, more masculine: denser and more closed-in, even a little four-square. The *terres blanches* produces a more civilised wine. "More spiritual," says Christophe Roumier. Like others, he will make them separately and then blend the two together. The resulting wine is greater than the sum of the parts. In the best hands, like his, we have a wine which not only has the power and the dimension but also the elegance and depth of great Burgundy. Silk and grace: no. That is Musigny. But volume, velvet, and vigour. Bonnes-Mares can be very fine indeed.

TASTING NOTES

The following tasting of Bonnes-Mares took place in Guilford, Connecticut, at the end of March 2012.

Domaine Drouhin, 2002   Now to 2022 plus
Medium-full colour. Barely mature. Fragrant nose. Good grip. This does not have the weight of Jadot. But balanced and elegant. Medium to medium-full body. Just about ready. Ripe and generous, mellow and mineral. At first it seemed to lack a bit of energy, but it was better on evolution. Fine plus.

Domaine Groffier, 2002   2015 to 2030
Medium-full colour. Barely mature. A rather bitter-herbal aspect dominated this wine and detracted from the quality. A lack of generosity about the fruit. Better on the palate. Fullish body. Round, rich, and ripe. Good vigour. The tannins are not very sophisticated though, so the wine does not have the class for great. But long and energetic. Very good indeed.

Domaine Jadot, 2002   2016 to 2030 plus
Medium-full colour. Barely mature. Ripe, concentrated, quite mellow nose. Good rich fruit. Fullish body. Still some tannin. Lovely depth and style. Splendid energy. This is very fine.

Domaine Georges Roumier, 2002   2016 to 2030 plus
Medium-full colour. Barely mature. Brilliant nose. Clean and pure. Concentrated and very, very complete and classy. Quite structured. Some tannin. Excellent fruit. This is still youthful but very profound, complex, and distinguished. Still needs time. Excellent.

Domaine Comte Georges de Vogüé, 2002   2016 to 2030
Fullish colour. Still youthful. Rich, full nose with a touch of oak and chocolate. A little four-square after the Roumier. But lots of energy and a fine, long finish. Better and better in the glass. Very fine.

Domaine Drouhin, 2001   Now to 2020
Medium colour. Now mature. Soft, fragrant, ripe, seductive nose. Lovely fruit in a gentle ambience. Medium body. Good depth. Good intensity. High class. Soft but plenty of wine here and a fine future. Very fine for a 2001.

Domaine Dujac, 2001   Now to 2018
Fullish but mature colour. Ripe, exotic nose. Just a hint of the stems, but more just "different" from the rest. Medium to medium-full weight. A little astringency hovers in the back. Ripe and balanced but a little disjointed. More and more classic Dujac as it developed. Very good indeed but not fine.

Domaine Groffier, 2001   Now to 2020 plus
Ripe, vigorous, full colour. Rich, full plump nose. Good depth. Ample, juicy fruit. Fresh and now velvety. A full, meaty 2001, but not lacking grace. And rather more class than the 2002. Plenty of lie ahead of it. Fine plus.

Domaine Georges Roumier, 2001   Now to 2020 plus
Very full colour. Really suspiciously dense. A big, perhaps too big, 2001. Lots of fruit, but

also quite a lot of unabsorbed tannin. Plenty of energy, but I fear it will never soften up satisfactorily. Fine but not great.

Domaine Comte Georges de Vogüé, 2001
Now to 2020 plus

Full, barely mature colour. Impressive nose. Full and ample but not rigid and four-square. Just rich and succulent. Ripe and seductive and still quite youthful. Lovely fruit. Impressive quality.

Domaine de la Vougeraie, 2001
Now to 2020 plus

Ripe, fullish vigorous colour. Not a lot on the nose at first, but balanced, ripe, and very elegant. Medium-full body. Subtle, generous, excellent grip and class. This is very lovely. *À point* but will last very well. Lots of energy at the end. Very fine.

Domaine Jacques-Frédéric Mugnier, 2000
Now to 2016

Medium to medium-full, mature colour. The nose is of a fully evolved wine. Soft, ripe, fragrant, and classy. Medium-full body. Ripe, gentle, and balanced. Lots of finesse. But a very fine example of a minor vintage at best.

Domaine Georges Roumier, 2000
Now to 2017 plus

Good fullish, vigorous colour. Lovely fruit on the nose. This has depth, vigour, and class. Medium-full weight. Ample, fresh, harmonious, and very stylish. An excellent example of the vintage which will still keep.

Domaine Comte Georges de Vogüé, 2000
Now to 2015

Full colour. Still quite dense. Evolved oaky, spicy, slightly cooked fruit nose. The wine lacks a bit of sophistication. Ripe but too suave. Fresh but a bit artificial.

Domaine Bouchard Père et Fils, 1999
2015 to 2030 plus

Medium-full colour. Just about mature. Fresh, classy, medium-full weight on the nose. Fragrant and harmonious. Medium-full body. Just a touch of tannin still to resolve. Fresh, ripe, elegant, and complex. This is a very lovely wine. Very fine.

Domaine Drouhin, 1999
Now to 2025 plus

Medium-full colour. Just about mature. Quite evolved on the nose. Ripe. Perhaps it lacks a bit of the usual Drouhin sophistication. But an attractive, easy-to-enjoy, medium- to medium-full-bodied wine with a lovely finish. Still very fresh. Fine plus.

Domaine Dujac, 1999
Now to 2025 plus

Medium to medium-full colour. Just about mature. Delicious, soft, fresh, sweet, ripe Dujac nose. More Dujac than Bonnes-Mares. Medium to medium-full body. Very ripe, clean, and stylish. Long, complex, fresh, full of charm. Fine plus.

Domaine Fougeray de Beauclair, 1999
Now to 2020

Medium-full colour. Rich, meaty nose. Good ripe fruit and plenty of weight. But not the greatest of finesse. Medium to medium-full body. Ripe and balanced. Ready. Very good indeed.

Domaine Groffier, 1999
2015 to 2025 plus

Medium-full colour. Still youthful. Ample, rich, flowery-fresh nose. Cool and quite concentrated. Good dimension. Full body. Just a bit of tannin to resolve. Very good grip and plenty of fruit and energy. Less classy as it evolved, but fine nevertheless.

Domaine Jadot, 1999
2018 to 2040

Full, barely mature colour. Splendidly rich, full nose. Very profound. Very concentrated. Still closed-in. This has very lovely, multidimensional fruit. Lots of depth and real finesse. Excellent.

Domaine Georges Roumier, 1999
2016 to 2040

Full, backward colour. Fine full, rich, concentrated nose. Lots and lots of depth. Still very youthful. Still some tannin to resolve. Splendid energy and really aristocratic fruit. Marvelous finish. Brilliant.

Domaine d'Auveney, 1996   Now to 2030 plus

Fullish colour. Very lovely fresh nose. The fruit is very pure. Ripe. Vigorous. Medium-full body. Creamy rich and very composed. Very fine indeed.

Domaine Bouchard
Père et Fils, 1996   Now to 2025

Medium-full colour. Soft, ripe, round, rich, and harmonious on the nose. No undue acidity. Medium body. Ripe, fresh, ready for drinking. Not a blockbuster but intense, long, and classy. Fine plus.

Domaine Drouhin, 1996   Now to 2025

Fullish colour. Just a touch of brown. The nose is ripe and rich. Fullish body. Gently oaky. Profound and classy. Just about *à point*. Good grip. Ample and generous. Fine plus.

Domaine Jadot, 1996   2015 to 2030

Full colour. Rich, ripe, backward, and concentrated. Meaty, but in the best sense. Lots of vigour and depth. Splendid ripe concentrated fruit. Lots of wine, lots of class, and excellently balanced. Will still improve. Very fine indeed.

Domaine Georges Roumier, 1996   Now to 2030

Fine, full, vigorous colour. Lovely pure, minerally, fresh fruit. Medium-full body. Very good grip. Lots of energy. Great class. This is ready but has a splendid future. Very fine indeed.

Domaine Bertheau, 1995   2015 to 2030

Medium-full colour. Attractive plump nose. Lovely fruit. Very well balanced. Medium-full body. A lovely harmonious wine. Long, complex, and vigorous. Very fine.

Domaine Drouhin, 1995   Now to 2025 plus

Medium-full colour. Fully mature. Ripe, soft, accessible nose. Lovely fruit. No great structure. Medium-full body. Balanced. Fragrant. Ripe and intense. Very good class. Long on the palate. Fine plus.

Domaine Groffier, 1995   Now to 2020

Medium-full colour. Still youthful. Odd aspects on the nose, making it not entirely clean. Ample and meaty. Fullish. A bit astringent and lumpy. Very good grip, but not much elegance.

Domaine Jadot, 1995   2015 to 2030

Full colour. Closed nose. Still a bit adolescent. Rich, ripe, and meaty. Just needs time. Full body. Still some tannin. Rich, pure, harmonious, and profound. Very fine.

Domaine Georges Roumier, 1995   2015 to 2040

Very full immature colour. Splendid concentrated closed nose. Crammed with fruit. Yet not a bit too tannic. Marvelous dimension. Excellent grip. Brilliant.

Domaine Dujac Drink, 1994   Soon

Light to medium colour. A lot of reduction on the nose. Really unpleasantly shitty. Light to medium body. Cleaned up a bit on aeration but not enough for me.

Domaine Drouhin, 1993   Now to 2020

Fullish, mature colour. Ripe, fresh, and vigorous on the nose. Very good complex fruit. Medium-full body. Ripe and rich and mellow and seductive. Complex and gentle, but long on the palate. Fine plus.

Domaine Dujac, 1993   Now to 2018

Medium-full mature colour. Good fresh, balanced, ripe, Dujac nose. Stylish and complex. Medium to medium-full body. Plenty of vigour and intensity if no enormous weight. Yet a long finish. Fine.

Domaine Jacques-Frédéric
Mugnier, 1993   Now to 2020 plus

Very good colour. Full and still youthful. Full, rich, ample nose. Splendidly ripe. Fullish on the palate. Very good grip and good energy. Very classy. Long. Very fine.

Domaine Georges
Roumier, 1993   Now to 2025 plus

Very good colour. Full and just about mature. Lovely fresh, high-quality fruit on the nose. Profound and classy. Full body. Intense and complex. Lovely long finish. This is very fine indeed.

Domaine Comte Georges de Vogüé, 1993　　Now to 2030

Very full, youthful colour. Fine, lush, round but quite substantial, ripe nose. Lovely fruit and very classy. Nothing too rigid here. Fullish body. Rich. Youthful. Very fine.

Domaine Jadot, 1991　　Now to 2020 plus

Very full colour. Barely mature. Rich, meaty nose. A touch of sweetness detracts from the class. This is not as pure as the Roumier. Fullish. Quite structured. There is a lot of wine here. And on the palate it is classy, profound, and intense. Very good energy at the end. Very fine.

Domaine Georges Roumier, 1991　　Now to 2020 plus

Full colour. Barely mature. Rich, ripe, cool, civilised nose. Lots of depth and class. This is splendidly concentrated, balanced, and distinguished. Full body. Good tannins. Very good grip. Vigorous and profound. Very fine plus.

Domaine Fougeray de Beauclair, 1990　　Now to 2018

Full, immature colour. Fullish, voluptuous, rich nose. Some class but not as much as there should be. On the palate the wine is rich and ripe but rather lumpy and lacking grip. Rather flabby and sweet at the end. Very good at best.

Domaine Jadot, 1990　　Now to 2030

Full, barely mature colour. Splendid depth and concentration on the nose. Very full body but not a bit rigid. Still very youthful. Fresh, complex, profound, and very lovely, especially at the end. Very fine indeed.

Domaine Georges Roumier, 1990　　Now to 2030

Full colour. Just about mature. Fragrant nose. Full body. Ripe, balanced, and classy. Marvelous depth and finesse. Even more intensity than the Jadot, but a litle more accessible. Excellent.

Domaine Drouhin, 1988　　Now to 2020

Medium-full, mature colour. Elegant, composed ripe fruit on the nose. Medium to medium-full body. Balanced, fragrant, and classy. Not a bit lean. Medium-full body. Lovely long finish. Very fine plus.

Domaine Dujac, 1988　　Now to 2018

Medium, mature colour. Typically Dujac on the nose. Soft, ripe, and fresh, and with nothing lean here. Almost sweet, in contrast. Classy and harmonious but lacks a bit of dimension. Only very good plus.

Domaine Georges Lignier, 1985　　Now to 2020

Medium-full colour. Fully mature. Spice and oak on the nose. Quite classy. Medium to medium-full body. Ripe and sweet on the palate with good grip. Finishes well. Fine.

Domaine Moine-Hudelot, 1985　　Drink soon

Rather a weak, mature colour. A little insubstantial on both the nose and the palate. But reasonably fresh and stylish. Not enough backbone though. Not too coarse. Indeed a pleasant wine.

Domaine Comte Georges de Vogüé, 1985　　Now to 2020

Medium-full colour. Good vigour but fully mature. Ripe, round, succulent nose. Lovely fruit and no undue size. Balanced, plump, quite concentrated, and most attractive. Long and classy. Fine plus.

Domaine Clair-Daü, 1983　　Drink soon

Medium colour. Fully mature. Crisp nose. Good freshness. Quite pure. On the palate, medium body. Clean fruit but a little thin and feeble. Yet there is decent depth and intensity, and it is quite long at the end. Very good indeed.

Domaine Georges Roumier, 1983　　Drink soon

Medium-full, mature colour. Somewhat rigid on the nose. But plenty of fruit here, if a bit lumpy. Medium-full body. Not the greatest class and composure. Better intensity and grip than the Vogüé, but very good at best.

Domaine Comte Georges de Vogüé, 1983　　Now to 2017

Medium-full colour. Fully mature. Slightly toffee-sweet nose. Fullish. It is a little rigid, and it lacks a little class. The fruit is a bit artificial and there is astringency at the end. Good plus at best.

Domaine Clair-Daü, 1972   Now to 2020
Good fullish, mature colour. Ample, ripe, rich nose. This has depth and class and lovely fruit. Good size, without being a blockbuster. Balanced, complex, and stylish. A lovely 1972. Very fine.

Domaine Dujac, 1972   Now to 2020 plus
Medium to medium-full mature colour. Very fresh on the nose. Plump, ripe, stylish, and balanced. Ample and fresh and less evidence of the stems than in most of the rest of the Dujacs. Medium-full body. Very good energy. Very lovely. Fine plus.

Domaine Groffier, 1972   Drink soon
Good colour. Rather lumpy and monolithic on the nose. Obviously heavily chaptalised. Medium-full body. Somewhat solid and unbalanced. Good at best.

Domaine Comte Georges de Vogüé, 1972   Now to 2020
Medium-full, mature colour. Just a little foursquare on the nose. Ample and ripe and stylish on the palate. Medium-full body. Good depth and complexity. Stylish too. Long. Fine.

Domaine Comte Georges de Vogüé, 1969   Now to 2020
Slightly corked but not so much so that one could not judge the wine. Medium- to medium-full colour. Rich, ripe, and ample. Intense and with good grip. Fullish body. Still plenty of life. Fine plus.

Domaine Drouhin-Laroze, 1966   Now to 2020
Medium colour. Fully evolved. Soft, fragrant nose. Medium-full body. Rich, mellow, classy, and vigorous. Plenty of depth and grip. Still plenty of life. Fine plus.

Domaine Georges Roumier, bottled in Beaune by Georges Linton, 1964   Now to 2020 plus
Fullish, vigorous colour. Mature, rich, very concentrated nose. Very lovely fruit. Lots of intensity and vigour. Long. Lots of life ahead of it. Very fine.

Domaine Clair-Daü, 1959   Now to 2020 plus
Very full colour. Splendidly rich, vigorous, sweet, concentrated nose. Full-bodied. Intense and classy. Still very youthful. Excellent.

Maison Bouchard Aîné, 1957   Now to 2018
Medium colour. Fully evolved. Fragrant and classy but now a little suggestion of age on the nose. Medium-full body. Ripe and quite vigorous. Fine.

Domaine Bertheau, bottled in England by Avery's, 1955   Now to 2018
Medium-full, mature colour. Open, accessible, plump, and evolved, yet still has good energy. Sweet and full of charm, if not quite as classy as it could have been. Fine nevertheless.

Domaine Bouchard Père et Fils, Tasteviné, 1952   Drink up
Quite ullaged. Medium colour. Fully evolved. Not much on the nose. The wine is getting towards its end but is still balanced, complex, and classy. Fine. Was even better in its prime.

Maison Bouchard Aîné, 1949   Drink up
Lovely full vigorous colour. Evolved, funky nose. A touch of both oxidation and volatile acidity. Medium body. A little astringent at the end now, but sweet and ripe. Was a fine bottle but now on the downslope.

Maison Jules Belin, 1919   Drink soon
Pure and rarified. Sweet and fragrant. It has lightened up, naturally, but is ample and fresh and lush and delicious. This was the better of two bottles, apparently.

Gevrey-Chambertin, Clos-Saint-Jacques, 2005, 2002, and 1999

TOGETHER WITH Chambolle-Musigny, Les Amoureuses, Gevrey-Chambertin's Clos-Saint-Jacques is the prime candidate for promotion from *premier cru* to *grand cru*. Anyone who has any—and there are five who share the 6.72 hectares—considers the wine superior to anything else in the village save Chambertin and Clos de Bèze and prices it accordingly. *Chez Rousseau* you will be given it to taste after the Charmes, Mazis, and Ruchottes (remember that one always tastes in ascending order of quality), and the wine will be given a little more new wood, as its constitution can take it. All in all, the wine of this *climat* can be quite marvelous, with a voluptuous touch where the Chambertins and Clos de Bèzes are more dignified and more mineral. Happily, all the landholders today produce excellent wine.

Clos-Saint-Jacques lies north and separated from the Gevrey *grands crus*. The slope on which the latter are situated disappears into the hills, the *Combe de Lavaux,* and then reemerges again. Flanked on the one side by Lavaux and Estournelles Saint-Jacques and on the other by

Cazetiers, the Clos itself possesses precisely the correct exposure to the south and east and is well protected from the prevailing westerly winds. It is a little steeper than Chambertin and Clos de Bèze at the upper part of the slope and the altitude is higher—285 to 345 metres above sea level as opposed to 270 to 300. Moreover, as a result of the breeze which issues out of the *Lavaux,* it is marginally cooler. So one needs to harvest four or five days later to get the fruit at the optimum state of maturity.

Clos-Saint-Jacques is even, in the sense of there being no north-south wrinkles, and is divided among the five proprietors in slices from the top to the bottom of the slope. The limestone rock dates from the Bajocian and Bathonian periods. At the top the soil is a light-brown marl mixed with clay, fossils, and sandstone pebbles washed down from the hills behind. In midslope the land becomes a little flatter. Here the limestone is mixed with a little gravel as well as clay and there is more rock. Towards the bottom the incline steepens again before getting flatter. There is progressively

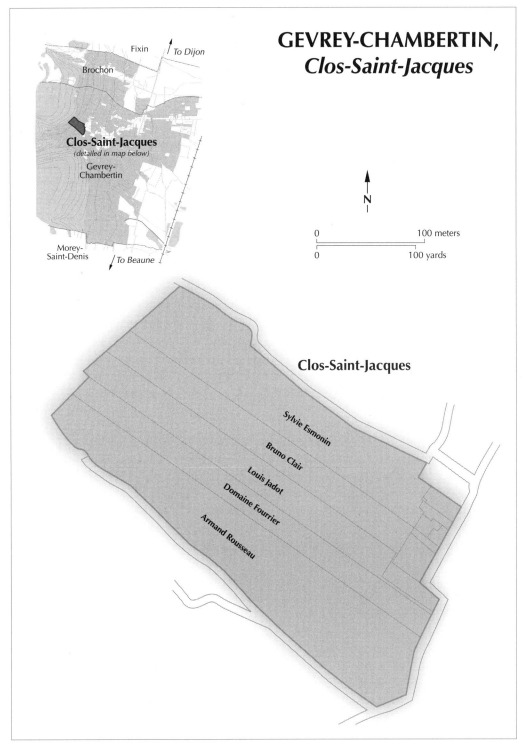

GEVREY-CHAMBERTIN,
Clos-Saint-Jacques

Fixin
To Dijon

Brochon

Clos-Saint-Jacques
(detailed in map below)
Gevrey-
Chambertin

Morey-
Saint-Denis
To Beaune

N

| 0 | 100 meters |
| 0 | 100 yards |

Clos-Saint-Jacques

Sylvie Esmonin

Bruno Clair

Louis Jadot

Domaine Fourrier

Armand Rousseau

MAP 14 Gevrey-Chambertin, *Clos-Saint-Jacques*

more clay and the soil is both stonier and darker in colour. The amount of surface soil is everywhere meagre, even right at the bottom a mere 60 centimetres in depth.

Saint Jacques is of course he who as James or Iago is buried at Compostella in northern Spain, the object of pilgrimage throughout the Middle Ages. In the surrounding wall round the vineyard there is a medieval statue and a small building, a hut some have described as a chapel.

The vineyard was owned, according to the historian and wine writer Jacky Rigaux, by the La Trémoille family in the sixteenth and seventeenth centuries. Perhaps they leased it from the church, for prior to the Revolution it was run by the Jesuits from the College des Godrans. These priests were succeeded by the Seigneur de Jancigny, M. Morizot, a member of the local parliament.

In the nineteenth century the Clos-Saint-Jacques was divided, only to be reassembled by Charles Serre de Meursault. This seems to have been later in the century rather than sooner, for various books on the wines of the region, from Dr. Lavalle in 1855 to Camille Rodier shortly after World War I, all give a number of owners. One of the Serre successors, Louise Boussenot, became the Contesse de Moucheron. It was he who was in charge at the time of the formal classification of Burgundy in 1936.

Moucheron, it seems, was a most unpleasant character. He was, to put it bluntly, a rude, arrogant snob.

He labelled his wine Clos-Saint-Jacques–Chambertin (Sylvie Esmonin has a bottle), which obviously did not go down well in the village. He alienated the tribunal which had been set up to nominate to the newly hatched Institut National des Appellations d'Origine (INAO) what should be *grand cru* and what sould be *premier cru* and so on, refusing to make a formal application, smoking evil-smelling cigars in front of the committee, and walking out in the middle of the deliberations. With him having departed, it is not surprising that anybody could be found to speak up for Clos-Saint-Jacques in his absence. *Premier cru* it became, the locals decreeing that only vineyards touching Chambertin or Clos de Bèze could be considered as *grands crus*. At the time, and indeed even until the early 1950s, the bottom part of the *climat* was planted with lucerne or alfalfa grass.

Following the Count's death in 1952, Clos-Saint-Jacques was put up for sale. Perhaps no buyer could be found who would be prepared to take up the entirety. Be that as it may, in 1954 it was divided into four parts. The domaines Rousseau and Clair-Daü each took about 2 hectares, Pernot-Fourrier and Henri Esmonin, the latter having worked on the estate for Moucheron, each bought around 1 hectare. Of these four—this shows how times have changed—only Esmonin had to go and borrow the money for his purchase. Apparently he was so ashamed about this that forever afterwards he would walk up to his domaine headquarters, situated then as now at the foot of the slope on the Cazetiers side, at 1:15 p.m., when everyone else was at lunch, to ensure that he wouldn't encounter any of his neighbours!

Subsequently, in 1985, when the Clair-Daü domaine was divided, half of their Saint-Jacques, and for a period of twenty years which finished in 2006, a lease on part of the rest, was acquired by Maison Louis Jadot. Today we have five owners: from left to right, as you look up the slope, Rousseau, Fourrier, Jadot, Bruno Clair, and Sylvie Esmonin.

So what is the difference between them? Rousseau's has the greatest reputation, because this is generally the most highly regarded estate. The wine here is rich and succulent, full-bodied but without hard edges, and gloriously profound: it never seems too inaccessible. Jadot's example is even more concentrated and certainly quite tannic. This is a wine can hide under a longer adolescent phase than most. Bruno Clair's bottles are elegant and pure and cool, with a little less fat than Rousseau. The Fourrier wine is very subtle with great finesse but without the volume of Rousseau, let alone

Jadot, while Sylvie Esmonin's Clos-Saint-Jacques, made with 70 percent whole clusters and housed in 100 percent new oak, has splendid depth and intensity. There is an exotic wine here.

TASTING NOTES

March 2011, at a tasting organised by Wine Workshop at the Bar Boulud in New York City, we sampled the following wines:

Domaine Bruno Clair

1.00 ha. Planted 1957 and 1962. Usually destemmed, but some of the stems retained in 2005. No "artificial" cold-soaking. 5 or 6 *pigeages*. Up to 33 to 34°C. Up to 50 percent new oak. Racked in November and prior to bottling 15 to 16 months after the harvest. Not fined but a light *kieselguhr* (diatomaceous earth) filtration.

2005   From 2020

Good colour. Cool, fragrant, classy nose. Medium-full body. Some tannin still to resolve. Just a little more mineral, with slightly less richness and fat than the others, but persistent and full of finesse. Very, very long on the palate. Very fine.

2002   From 2015

Fullish colour. Quite an evolved nose. At first a bit confused, but it settled down after aeration. Full-bodied. Rich and ripe. Very good tannins. Plenty of substance, vigour, and intensity. Potentially very fine indeed.

1999   From 2014

Full colour. Fullish, ample, cool nose. Fresh and vigorous. On the palate there is a slight rustic touch about the tannins compared with the rest and the wine is not as complete. But rich and powerful, youthful and long on the palate. Fine plus.

Domaine Sylvie Esmonin

1.00 ha. Planted 1961 to 1970. 70 percent whole clusters since 2002. No "artificial" cold-soaking. Regular *pigeage* during the fermentation. 100 percent new oak. Bottled after 16 to 18 months.

2005   From 2020

Very good colour. Rich, full, concentrated, spicy nose. Not a bit stemmy, but the use of the stems quite apparent. This is really quite different from the rest. Fullish body, slightly animal. Lots of depth and vigour. Ripe and exotic. Rich at the end. Very fine.

2002   From 2015

Very good, full colour. Rich, very ripe, abundant, seductive nose. Juicy and succulent and almost sweet. Full body. Ample. Exotic. Fat. Spicy. Vigorous and meaty. Very good grip. Lots of wine here. Lovely. Very fine.

1999   From 2014

Fullish colour. The nose is fresh, very energetic, and very lovely. Still very youthful. Fullish body. Cool and classy. Good intensity. Intense and very long on the palate. Very fine.

Domaine Fourrier

0.89 ha. Planted 1910 and *repiqué* since. 100 percent destemmed. 2 to 4 *pigeages* per day in the early stages. No pumping over. Cooled to 15°C after maceration. 20 percent new wood. Not racked until prior to bottling 15 to 16 months after the harvest.

2005   From 2020

Medium-full colour. Closed in, concentrated nose. Fullish body. Backward. Rich, meaty, and multidimensional. Very impressive rich fruit. Marvelous follow-through. A great wine.

2002   From 2015

Medium-full colour. Very lovely fragrant, ripe fruit on the nose. Complex and very, very classy. Medium-full body. Very intense. Splendidly pure and persistent. Very fine plus.

1999   Now to 2025 plus

Fullish colour. Not as pure and classy on the nose than most. There is a very faint touch of decay about the fruit. Medium-full body. Balanced. Classier on the palate than on the nose. Fresher too. Now just about ready. Fine.

Domaine Louis Jadot

1.0 ha. Planted 1957 and 1962. 100 percent destemmed. No formal cold maceration. *Pigeage* but no pumping over (which "would accelerate the fermentation process"). No control over the upper temperature limits of the fermentation. Long *cuvaisons*. 50 to 100 percent new oak. One racking before bottling 18 months after the harvest.

2005   From 2020

Good fullish colour. Rich, ripe, concentrated, high-quality nose. Still quite closed in. Fullish body. Some tannin. Youthful and vigorous. Ample. Balanced. Profound and very complex at the end. Very fine plus.

2002   From 2015

Medium-full colour. Cool, fragrant, understated nose. Very lovely ripe fruit. Lots of finesse. But still a bit austere. Medium-full body. Very impressive follow-through. Persistent and multidimensional. Very fine plus.

1999   From 2015

Full colour. Still very youthful. Fresh, full, vigorous, fragrant nose. Very good grip of acidity underneath. Very lovely fruit. Ripe and profound and nicely plump. Very impresssive finish. Very fine indeed.

Domaine Armand Rousseau

2 ha. Planted 1935 to 1993. 100 percent destemmed but not crushed. 4 to 5 days natural cold-soaking. Maximum temperatures 32 to 34°C. Pumping over at the beginning ("It helps oxygenate"). *Pigeage* there-

after. 60 (in the lesser vintages) up to 100 percent (in 2005) new oak. One racking prior to bottling 18 months after the harvest.

2005   From 2020

Medium-full colour. Very lovely, cool, elegant fragrant nose. Medium-full body. Not a blockbuster. Ripe, balanced, classy fruit. Laid back, composed, and very stylish. Lovely long complex finish. Very fine plus.

2002   From 2015

Medium-full colour. Ample, full, quite fat, and concentrated on the nose. Lovely fruit. On the palate, fullish body. Some tannin. Very lovely fruit. Lots of energy and great finesse. Very fine indeed. Clearly the best of the flight.

1999   From 2015

Fullish colour. Splendid ample, rich, fat succulent fruit on the nose. Fullish body. Some tannin. Very good grip. Lots of energy and depth here. Intense, very classy, very ripe, and very intense. Still needs five years. Very fine plus.

————————

The tasting was blind. Esmonon and Fourrier were voted the best of the 2005s; Rousseau (overwhelmingly) was chosen among the 2002s; and Clair, Fourrier, and Rousseau again took the medals in the 1999 flight.

PART TWO

Domaine Profiles

Hospices de Beaune

ROLAND MASSE—genial, tubby, balding, of medium height, and in his mid-fifties—has ruled over the wine side of the Hospices de Beaune since the 2000 vintage. Prior to this, he spent eighteen years at the Domaine Bertagna in Vougeot.

The Hospices de Beaune wine setup is, as he will willingly concede, an anomaly. The vines are tended by one group of people; the wine is made by the Hospice's own team; but then, following the famous auction on the third Sunday of November, directly after the harvest, the barrels are collected by a third party and matured until bottling by yet another team. On the face of it, it is nonsense. But this is the current status quo, dating back to before there was widespread domaine bottling, and it would be a cruel dent in the *amour propre* of the grand Beaune *négociants* if this were to be rationalized.

The domaine is one of the largest and most important in Burgundy. Over the centuries, since around 1450, the Hospices—originally a religeous foundation set up to provide succour for the poor and the sick of the area—has received donations of land in the Côte d'Or and more recently in the Mâconnais. Today it measures around 62 hectares, of which 58 is in production. The Hospices's very latest acquisitions—three-quarters of a hectare of Saint-Romain *blanc*, and 60 ares of Santenay rouge—were auctioned for the first time in 2009 and 2010 respectively. Most of the holdings are in the Côte de Beaune, and most is village or *premier cru*. But there is a large *cuvée* of Mazis-Chambertin, traditionally the most sought after and expensive of the Hospices wines, and there is additionally some Clos de la Roche and a token amount (four *pièces* in 2009) of Bâtard-Montrachet. The proceeds of the annual sale—the wine has been sold by auction since 1859—are a major source of income for Beaune's large modern general hospital.

So, does it work, and how does it work, this anomalous domaine? First, what control does Masse and his team have over the local *vignerons* who look after the vines? How are they paid?

"We keep the vineyard workers on a very tight rein," says Masse. "It's the main job of my number two, Stéphane Lacoste, for most of the year. The *vignerons* are paid *à la tache*, that is for the job, and they are all paid the same, regardless of the prestige of the *climat*. The basic amount they earn only varies according to the size of the plot. Our agreement with each of them is loose; so that if they want to give up, or we are not content with the quality of their work, we can discreetly move on to someone else. But naturally it is usually someone with vines in the neighbourhood, if not next door to ours."

He continues: "Additionally, we pay the vineyard workers a bonus. This is based on the quality of the work that they do and the prices the wines fetch at auction. But not, I hasten to assure you, on the quantity produced. We decide everything: the treatments, the size of the crop, and the date of the harvest. All except three small parcels are ploughed. We no longer use herbicides or pesticides. The yields were substantially reduced during the time of my predecessor, André Porcheret."

"I repeat," says Masse: "We are in control."

Fine, but now we come to a second point: a potential problem. Many of the Hospices de Beaune *cuvées* are made up from vines of different origins within the same commune. Volnay, Cuvée Blondeau, for example, comprises Champans, Taillepieds, Ronceret, and Mitans; the Beaune, Cuvée Nicolas Rollin comes from Cent Vignes, Teurons, Grèves, En Genêt, and Bressandes. Indeed multiple origins are the rule and not the exception. "How do you get over the difficulty," I ask Roland Masse, "that on the appointed date of harvest, some parcels may be ready but others not yet at their optimum?"

"This is something that I have been mulling over for several years," says Masse, "and over the last few vintages we have been arriving at a solution. The first thing to say is that I am against micro-vinifications, and anyway we don't have the very small vats that this would require. I am speaking of red wine here. Obviously you can vinify white wine barrel by barrel. But what we do do, is to nuance the red wine *cuvées* a bit, rationalize them so that, for the sake of argument, if we had two small bits

of Volnay, Ronceret, we'd amalgamate them into the same *cuvée*. Or where we have a lot of wine destined for several *cuvées*, such as in Corton, Clos du Roi, again we'd vinify them all together.

"As far as the vinification is concerned, I am one hundred percent free," says Roland Masse. "We now have double the amount of sorting tables than a few years ago. Some wines are vinified with a percentage of the stems. And not only the Mazis and the Clos de la Roche, but some of the Beaunes and Volnays. It all depends on the quality of the fruit and the concentration of the vintage. The percentage of the stems is usually in the order of 25 to 30 percent. I like to start the fermentation process at temperatures of around 14°C and let the must naturally cold soak for four or five days.

"Unfortunately the winery is all on one level," he says. "We can't do much by gravity. But we have much more gentle pumps these days, and can assure that the berries arrive in the vat whole. From then on, techniques vary according to the vintage. We adapt. In 2008 we treaded down and pumped over. In 2009 only *pigéage* (treading down)."

Now for the most vexed question; the criticism that almost everyone throws at the wines of the Hospices: that they are over-oaked. Even wines that have been collected on the first of January and immediately racked into old oak turn out unbalanced.

"Yes. I accept the criticism," says Roland Masse. "As we are a domaine which does not do its own *élevage,* we do not have much in the way of old barrels. But as we do hold back about 10 percent of our production there is some, and that means that, for example, our Pouilly-Fuissé is vinified in one-year-old wood, and one or two lighter *cuvées* likewise. I wish I *did* have total control of everything. But it would be dangerous to go out on the market for secondhand barrels. You cannot be certain they've been looked after properly."

What do domaines do with them between the bottling of one vintage in the spring and the decanting of the fermentation vat into cask the following October? "I guarantee not only the wine, but the barrel as well," he points out.

There is a further problem. Traditional domaines assemble the wine from the new casks with the old every time they do a racking. What goes into bottle has been homogenized. The Hospices can't do this. Even if they were to secure good one-year-old barrels, how are you going to organise a sale where you will have some wines in new oak and some in old? Most people will want to purchase most of the *cuvées* in one-year-old barrels. This would be impossible unless both the Hospices were able to run as a traditional domaine and the auction was postponed by a year, by which time what was offered would be from a judicious mix of old and new casks. Which, thinking of it, might not be a bad idea. It's the only way round this problem. At the moment it is tragic that what otherwise is now very good wine should be rendered unpalatably over-oaked by the conservatism of today's system. And at least twelve months on, rather than six weeks after the harvest, potential buyers would be able to assess something assessible.

Which brings us to the auction itself. Until 2005 this was a very tedious, drawn-out affair *à la chandelle*, involving little candles being lit as you came to the bidding crunch point. That year the governing body decided to modernize, and Christie's won the contract. They have made it much more open to outside, even private, buyers. Today, the winner of any bid has the option to rest with that single barrel or to buy any further number of barrels within the parcel.

The wine still has to be reared and eventually bottled by someone in Burgundy with a merchants' license. But today this covers a wide number of domaines as well as the traditional *négoce*. The admirably handsome, hugely informative catalogue of Christie's clearly explains how to set about this; and they will put the buyer in contact with a merchant if he or she does not have one to hand already. In 2009, say Christie's, about a third—that is 210 *pièces*—were sold as single-barrel lots.

How much does it cost? We start with the hammer price. To this must be added 7 percent buyer's premium. Then comes 500 euros for the barrel. The fee for the merchant who rears and bottles the wine can either be fixed (advantageous for expensive wines), say, estimated Christie's in 2009, 1,600 euros, or be a percentage of the hammer price, say 30 percent. An average might be 1,500 euros. Divide by 288 and you have your ex-cellars price per bottle, before shipping, duty, and local taxes.

The Volnay, Santenots, Cuvée Gauvin, sold for an average of 3,718 euros in 2008 and 4,350 euros in 2009; the Meursault, Genevrières, Cuvée Baudot for 8,251 euros and 8,500 euros. Using the figures above, I calculate that this works out at, in 2008, at 19.42 to 21.11 euros per bottle for the Volnay, depending whether the merchant's fee was fixed or a percentage (the 2009 prices are 22.43 or 23.45 euros), and 40.99 or 35.76 euros (here paying a fixed *élevage* fee is cheaper) in 2008 for the Meursault (in 2009 42.17 or 38.87 euros).

This compares surprisingly favourably with the prices in the shops. In January 2010, merchants launched their 2008s. Berry Bros., and Rudd, one of the best, especially as Burgundy is concerned, offered various *premier cru* Volnays at between the equivalent of 40 to 50 euros, and Meursault, Genevrières at 40 euros or more, ex-cellars. (I have translated their pound sterling prices back to euros at 1.00 pound to 1.10 euros—the going rate of exchange back in January).

The downsides are as follows: you are shelling out several thousand euros (12,145 euros for the Meursault on the most expensive of the calculations), and you are doing this a year in advance of your merchant's opening offer. Moreover, you have undertaken a purchase of twenty-four cases of wine. Do you really want as much as this? Are you going to get bored with it? Second, the wines are pretty well impossible to assess this early in their developement. Even the experts on the spot, and the UK trade buyers (master of wine or not), let alone you yourself, if you travel down to participate, are really only guessing by instinct and the past track record. So you'll get a good wine (but an oaky one), but perhaps not, as life turns out, the very choicest plum of the vintage.

But the advantages are persuasive: it's your wine—you can even have a personalized Hospices label—which you've chosen yourself at the outset. You have stolen a march on your wine merchant (not that you don't regret denying them the business). And you have supported a very deserving charity. So you are bound to go to heaven. But not until you have consumed every single bottle you have not given away, of course.

Domaine Marquis d'Angerville

VOLNAY

VOLNAY, AS EVERY COMMENTARY on the wines of Burgundy will tell you, produces the most fragrant, elegant, intense, and delicate wines of the whole of the Côte. It is harder, I would suggest, for a winemaker to get their Volnay completely right than, say, the Pommard in the vat next door. The precision has to be even more exact. Yet, paradoxically, there are more top growers in this commune than there are in its red wine neighbours to the north. Among the very, very best is the Domaine Marquis d'Angerville.

It was in 1805, the year of the Battle of Trafalgar, that the Baron du Mesnil, on taking up an appointment as *sous-préfet* of Autun, bought an estate in what was then called "Vollenay." At the time the two administrative centres in the area—and the two bishoprics prior to the Revolution—were Autun and Langres, not Beaune and Dijon. The diocese of Autun together with the nobility of the ancien régime had owned large amounts of land in the Côte de Beaune, which was then sold off to the bourgeoisie in the 1790s and 1800s. Much of this would

already have been leased out to local *vignerons* and *petits bourgeois* farmers, who would have also owned a few vines and the odd cow on their own account. But some of the land would have been under their direct control.

The Baron had a country house, raised up on three floors over the cellars, constructed at the northern end of the village in a little park. The jewel in the crown of the estate, the 2.15 hectare monopoly of the Clos des Ducs *climat*, lies at the end of the garden beyond the swimming pool. The terrace, facing east across the vineyards, commands a splendid view as far as the mountains of the Jura and beyond. It is a fitting site for one of the top estates in the region.

The Angervilles can trace their ancestry back further than most. One Guillaume d'Angerville d'Auvrecher was a companion of William the Conqueror, invader of Britain in 1066. The family comes from near Falaise in Normandy, and it was Jacques d'Angerville's grandfather who married a Mademoiselle du Mesnil towards the end of the nineteenth century. By this time he was a marquis. How far does this title go back, I ask Guillaume, today's marquis? He is not sure. Apparently there were few with this title before the time of Louis XV.

It was their son, Sem, who inherited the estate in 1906 following the death of his uncle, a Baron du Mesnil. Mensil had decreed that Sem could not take over until he had reached the "age of wisdom"—that is, thirty-five years. In fact, Sem cheated and settled in when he was thirty-three. He had no formal knowledge of winemaking. But he had studied fine arts and had been an engraver. He introduced the elegant label the estate still uses today. And it was he who replanted the Clos des Ducs and the rest of the estate after the ravages of phylloxera. Together with Henri Gouges, it was Sem who started the fashion for estate-bottled Burgundy. During the 1920s they were one of the few who spoke out vociferously against the corrupt practices of the local merchants in Beaune. In those pre-appellation days (sadly it was to continue long after the Loi Chapus introduced the *appellation d'origine contrôlée* [AC] system in 1936), it was the custom of many merchants to ship up cheap wine from the south of France, even from Algeria, to blend it in with the local produce. D'Angerville's courage in denouncing this fraud led to no prosecutions, however—merely to his wine being blackballed by the trade.

So, together with Henri Gouges, Armand Rousseau, and a couple of others, he was forced to bottle his own wine and seek out his clients direct. One was the Thienpont wine business in Belgium (and of Vieux Château Certan and other interests in Bordeaux)—1899 Volnay, Champans at 2.85 francs a bottle—another was a triumvirate of Americans: Frank Schoonmaker; Pierce, a merchant in Boston; and the Senator Hollis. Schoonmaker's first visit was in 1935. D'Angerville shipped a lot of 1929 (Volnay, Fremiets at 14 francs), 1933, and 1934 to the United States before World War II. There was even an order, placed but not shipped, in 1939, which was reserved quietly in Volnay until hostilities ended in 1945.

The market, of course, was different then, not so much by comparison with today, but in relation to what it had been in the period before the First World War. During the nineteenth century and beyond, Germany, Austro-Hungary, and Russia were important markets for Burgundy; even, given its size, the United States. Afterwards, with Prohibition on the one side and economic ruin on the other, the Burgundians had to look elsewhere, to Belgium and Switzerland. Great Britain has never been as eager a Burgundian customer as it should be, or as it is for the wines of Bordeaux.

Jacques d'Angerville, son of Sem, was born in 1927 and attended his first vintage in 1945. He was eighteen. He became fully responsible for the wine in 1949 and proprietor of the estate on his father's death in 1952. For most of my generation, Jacques d'Angerville exemplified Volnay. He was the doyen of the village as well as the source of its finest wine. This Angerville was tall, dignified, and white-haired. He seemed a touch reserved when you first encountered him. But you soon began to realise the warmth and passion for his wines that lay underneath, not to mention his awareness of his estate's position in the history of domaine-bottled Burgundy. While, like his father, he had not been to Wine School, he was certainly as knowledgeable about the winemaking process as anyone in the Côte. And of the Burgundian wine economy. For fifteen years he was president of the growers' side of the Comité Interprofessionel de la Bourgogne.

Jacques d'Angerville died in 2003. His successor is his son Guillaume, born in September 1956 (the only good thing to come out of that miserable vintage, so Jacques would allege), and in an earlier career a merchant banker in London and Paris. He and his wife, Pauline, have four children. Alongside Guillaume is his brother-in-law, Reynaud de Villette. They are both assisied by the *maitre de chai* Francois Duvivier, who arrived in 2005.

Today, the Angerville domaine comprises just under 15.0 hectares, almost all of it, except for a 0.4 hectare piece of *premier cru* Pommard, Les Combes Dessus, and some Meursault, in Volnay; almost all of it, except for some village

Volnay and some generic Bourgogne, of *premier cru* status; and all, except for this Meursault, which is in the Santenots, planted to Pinot Noir, apart from 34 ares of Bourgogne Blanc and 40 ares of Aligoté.

Pride of place is the Clos des Ducs, a *monopole*, as I have said, and lying between the Angerville mansion and the Pitures Dessus. The soil here is *terres blanches*, very light in colour and very stony; the incline steep and very well drained, the rock underneath hard, though the depth of soil is relatively deep for a steep hillside vineyard. The result is a consistent volume of wine which is firmer than a Champans or a Caillerets—which are really, as Jacques d'Angerville used to describe it, "the heart of Volnay"—and which takes longer to develop. It has a Pommard touch. But I don't mean this in the slightest to be interpreted in a pejorative context.

The largest Angerville holding is in the Champans, two sizeable chunks totalling a mite under 4 hectares. There is a little more clay in the soil here, which is also redder than elsewhere, but it is also stony and well drained. The Volnay that the Champans produces is also a firm wine, even a touch solid at the outset. It is not quite as distinctive as the Clos des Ducs, but it is rich, structured, and long-lasting for all that.

On the Pommard side of the commune, the Angerville estate owns 1.5 hectare of Fremiets. Here, and across the border in the Pommard *climat* of Jarollières, there is an Oxfordian, marly element in the limestone, and a thin surface of debris over the decomposing rock the locals call *lave*. The result is normally a lighter wine, without either the intensity or the distinction of the Clos des Ducs or the depth of the Champans, but nevertheless in the Angerville cellar one of quite sufficient backbone, if without quite the level of sophistication of tannins.

The Angerville domaine has two further important holdings; in the Taillepieds *climat*, adjacent to Clos des Chênes, and in the Caillerets, below it: 1.07 hectares of the former, 0.45 hectare of the latter. Here Volnay produces its most glorious wines. The soil structure is not *that* different from the Champans, but the wines are less dense-seeming. They are marginally less structured but more intense and concentrated. When these Angerville wines are young, they are vigorous, rich, and intense; when they are mature, they provide a splendid contrast to the Clos des Ducs, wines of great classic elegance, while the Clos des Ducs seems to have evolved into something lush, exotic, and individually perfumed, with an underlying spice. The vines in the Caillerets, planted in 1998 and 2003, are still young.

This is not the end of the Angerville Volnay lineup. The domaine owns vines in L'Ormeau (now called Les Mitans) and Pitures, but these are less regularly offered to the writer on his yearly visits, usually blended together to make a *premier cru*, *tout court*, and sold mostly in the United States. In 2007, Guillaume d'Angerville was able to acquire 53 ares of Clos des Angles, next to the vines he possessed already. This now gives him 1.07 hectares in total and a new wine which he has offered since 2009. I confess to never having even tasted the Angerville Pommard.

The Meursault, Santenots is curious: a white wine made on red wine soil. It comes from 1.05 hectares of Les Plures, part of "greater" Santenots. They make fifteen to twenty barrels a year. Until recently, as with other white wines made in this neighbourhood, I was not at all a fan. It found it rather four-square, somewhat more like a white Monthélie than a Meursault from the Puligny side. "A wine of interest rather than one of great elegance," I once wrote. On the basis of recent vintages, I feel I may be beginning to change my mind. Guillaume d'Angerville has suceeded in producing a crisper, more refined wine than hitherto.

"No. I've never been tempted to replant the Meursault with Pinot Noir," says Guillaume. "I think we have made a lot of progress here. I also feel that the wine interests me more than it did my father. It's a mistake to compare it with a Charmes. It's a quite different wine."

Jacques d'Angerville was famous for having developed his own particular strain of Pinot *fin*, which suitably bore his name. I was told fifteen years ago that there are no clones in the Angerville vineyards. Today, apparently, there are a few, but Guillaume is now replating vine by vine (*répiquage*) with his own *sélection massalle*.

Yields are low. The domaine aims to produce 35–40 hectolitres per hectare (hl/ha). Production was 38 hl/ha in 2009 and 2005, 30 hl/ha in 2008. It is here that it all begins, you will be told: old vines, low *rendements*, little interference, and an absence of manipulation thereafter. Interestingly, the Clos des Ducs vineyard never suffers from hail damage as it is protected by the village and the forest at the top of the hill.

The grapes are completely destalked, cold-soaked at 11°C for three or four days, vinified at a normal temperature (31°C maximum at the end), macerated with the skins for a total of fifteen days, with *remontage* (pumping-over) rather than regular *pigeage* (treading down of the cap), and then matured using about 20 to 25 percent new oak for the top wines, and that only for the initial period of the wine's sojourn in cask. The Angervilles are against what they describe as the abuse of new oak. Thereafter, if necessary, the wine is fined and finally, also if necessary, given a very light filtration before bottling, fifteen to eighteen months after the harvest.

What has Guillaume d'Angerville changed since he took over? "Lots of little things. I am not interested in changing. Just improving. There is a gentler handling of the fruit, so it is merely crushed before it goes into the vat. We've replaced two of the old horizontal *autopigeant cuves* with temperature-controlled, vertical stainless steel ones. And we have pretty well eliminated the use of pumps."

He continues: "When I arrived, there were one or two members of the team who were not quite as competent as they should have been. These [team members] are with us no longer; more because of reaching retirement age than for any other reason. With the new team, plus the introduction of a biological approach— we've been fully biodynamic since 2009—we have much improved the precision of our winemaking. My objective is to follow the lines laid down by my father and to produce wines which are as much as possible the expression of their *terroir*." "Would I like to expand?" he asks himself. "Yes, but really just in Volnay, though I might be tempted if something came up in Meursault or Pommard, even in Monthelie."

The result is a style of wine which, while intense and complex, is subtle and understated rather than flamboyantly expressive. These are wines which when young require concentration on the part of the taster fully to appreciate their own concentration. Length on the palate, individuality of *terroir*, and above all distinction is what Guillame d'Angerville is after. He is also seeking to produce wines for the long term. He considers the prevailing view that a Volnay should be or will be mature after five years, rather than ten, a misnomer. The Angerville wines are stayers, as these tasting notes will amply demonstrate. They are also consistent. And they are first class. The following range of wines was sampled in July 2011.

TASTING NOTES
Volnay, Clos des Ducso

2009   From 2020
Fullish colour. Lovely ample, succulent, indeed lush nose. Ripe tannins. Very good grip. Already quite round. Fullish body. Vigorous but not a bit harsh. Very lovely fruit. Balanced, complex, and very long and fresh at the end. Very fine.

2008   From 2020
Medium-full colour. Somewhat firmer and more classic than the 2009 on the nose. Good backbone. Very classy. Very profound. Fullish body. Some tannin. Very fresh and with lots of energy. Splendid fruit. Very long and multi-dimensional. More depth than the 2009 perhaps. Very fine.

2007   From 2013
Medium to medium-full colour. Some development. Soft nose. Round but no great vigour or balance. Ripe and charming but a bit loose-

knit. Medium body. Soft tannins. Decent grip and nicely positive at the end. Finishes better than it starts. Very good indeed.

2006 From 2016
Very good colour. But the least developed of this first four. Closed-in and very concentrated. Profound and still youthful. Medium-full body. But just a bit clumsy, even aggressive, on the attack. Some tannin still to resolve. The follow-through is rather more civilised. Very good indeed.

2005 From 2020
Very good, youthful colour. Closed-in but superconcentrated and very high-class. The fruit reminds me more of a Côte de Nuits than a Côte de Beaune. Fullish body. Mineral. Some tannin to resolve. A bit adolescent at present on the palate. Lots of wine here. It just needs time. Very lovely.

2004 From 2014
Medium-full colour. Decent roundness on the nose but nevertheless a touch lean and green. Yet fresh and attractive and succulent at the end. Very good indeed.

2003 From 2014
Full colour. Still youthful. Lush. Ripe but not over-ripe. Yet with a touch of cooked fruit and chocolate. Still a little tannin to resolve. But because of very good acidity, there is no sign of astringency. An exotic wine. More Clos des Ducs than 2003.

2002 Now to 2020 plus
Medium-full colour. Still youthful. The nose is balanced, subtle, and very Volnay-ish. But by no means the volume and intensity of the 2005. Long and classy. Just about ready. For me it misses a bit of vigour and concentration, but others liked it better than I.

2001 Now to 2020
Medium to medium-full colour. Some development. Plump, straightforward, ripe, round nose. Good class, balance, and depth. Medium-full body. Good substance for the vintage. Very Volnay fruit. No lack of energy. Fine plus for the vintage.

2000 Now to 2016
A little more colour than the 2001, which surprises me. Yet softer and less depth and concentration on the nose. Medium body. Fresh and ripe, if no real depth or dimension. Balanced though. Very good indeed for a 2000.

1999 From 2015
Full colour. Still youthful. Very lovely nose. Heaps of succulent, ripe, well-balanced fruit, like the 2009. Well supported by the acidity too. Medium-full body. Just a little tannin. Not as cool or precise as the 2009 but very lovely. Fine finish.

1998 Now to 2020 plus
Medium-full colour. Still youthful. Not the exotic ripeness and concentration of fruit on the nose as the 1999. Medium-full body. Good minerality and very good grip. A slight pause in the follow-through, but it finishes classy and long. Fresh, floral, harmonious, and very elegant.

1995 Now to 2020 plus
Fullish, vigorous colour. Fullish, concentrated, still backward nose. Some tannin still, and lots of high-quality fruit. Full body. Quite structured. Firm. The phenolics are similar to those of the 1999. Very good grip. It's a little dense at the moment. A wine for food.

1994 Now to 2020
Very good colour. Full and mature but no sign of age. Fresh on the nose. Just a little lean but high-quality fruit. Fullish body. No astringency. An excellent wine for the vintage. Positive, classy, and precise.

1991 Now to 2020
Fullish colour. Only just about mature. Aromatic nose. Medium to medium-full body. Interesting spices of maturity. No weakness. No astringency. Fine for the vintage. No hurry to drink.

1990 Now to 2030
Very full colour. Still a bit dense. A full-bodied and perhaps somewhat four-square monster of a wine. Rich and concentrated. Lots of grip.

Some tannin too. Perhaps not exactly elegant. Drink with food. Lots of life ahead of it.

1985 Now to 2020

Medium to medium-full colour. Fully mature. A mature, spicy nose, with a touch of the astringent. Some age for a 1985, it has to be said, but perhaps not quite a representative sample. Better on the palate. Clean, ripe, good acidity. Classy and balanced. Medium to medium-full body. Long. Lovely finish. Fine plus.

1983 Now to 2025

Fullish colour. No undue age. Fuller, richer, rounder, fatter, and rather more vigorous than the 1985. Full body. On the palate a touch of astringency. But concentrated and classy and energetic in its somewhat *sauvage* sort of way. Fine plus.

1978 Drink quite soon

Magnum. Produced by Doug Barzelay from his U.S. cellar. Fullish, mature colour. Ripe nose.

Interesting gingerbread, *sous bois* touches. Lots of depth and interest. No astringency except at the very end. Medium-full body. Fresh, elegant, ripe, and balanced. A very lovely floral wine. Very Volnay.

1976 Drink quite soon

Very full, youthful colour. Fresh, vigorous nose if a touch four-square. Better as it developed. Lovely fruit indeed. Not quite the richness and ripeness it once had, nor the complexity, but long and fine, and it just went on getting better and better.

1964 Drink soon

Another bottle from Doug Barzelay's cellar. I feel it would have been better for having been decanted, which often gives a lease of life to wines which have had a long time in bottle. Well-matured colour. Very, very lovely fruit on the nose. Medium to medium-full body. Ripe, rich, fragrant, and now slightly faded. Great class nevertheless.

Domaine Denis Bachelet

GEVREY-CHAMBERTIN

"I DIDN'T START OFF at a very good time," says Denis Bachelet, a slight, somewhat shy, and diffident man in his late forties. "My first vintage was 1983, when there was a good deal of rot. Then there was 1984: a year of rain, low temperatures, and and absence of sun. And then 1985. A very cold winter. As a result of the frost, I made only half my normal crop."

I first visited Denis in the autumn of 1986 to sample these 1985s. He had produced twenty barrels of wine. (He made fifty in 1986.) He had vinified all the village Gevrey and *premier cru* wine together. I admired both this and the Charmes-Chambertin. "Delicious," I wrote. "This is a property to watch." Subsequently, ten years on, I saw the 1983s. The village Gevrey-Chambertin Vieilles Vignes was unexpectedly supple and fruity and free of all taint. The Charmes—or at least the first bottle of it—did seem affected, but another bottle, later that year in London, if not the epitome of elegance, was concentrated and succulent. I seem to have no ten-year-on notes of the 1984s, but the 1985 Charmes was very fine indeed in June 2005.

Denis Bachelet was born in Namur, in Bel-gium, in 1963. His father, of long-established Gevrey-Chambertin stock, had paid a visit to Belgium as a member of the local brass band, La Fanfare de Gevrey-Chambertin, met a young lady, and decided to stay. He became a technician in a chemical factory. Denis is an only child. Brought up in Belgium, he had no ambitions to become a *vigneron*—though he went down to Burgundy occasionally. As he puts it himself, he hardly knew one end of a vine from the other. But out of the blue when he was sixteen, his father asked him if he might be interested in taking over the family estate. "Instinctively, I said yes."

To describe the exploitation as a family estate is putting it a bit grandly. There was a total of 1.8 hectares, though this did include 43 ares in two separate parcels in Charmes-Chambertin, planted just after the First World War by a great-aunt Mouchet. It was all sold off in bulk to the local merchants. Denis arrived in 1979 and enrolled himself for three years in the local wine school. He did a summer term out with neighbour Jean Trapet to get practi-cal experience of viticulture and an autumn with Joseph Roty on the vinification side. What did he make of the incorrigible Joseph, I ask? Denis is as diplomatic as ever. "I learned a lot. And I liked the wine he made." It was Roty who introduced Denis to Becky Wasserman, with whom he has worked in the United States ever since. Right from the start, it was obvious that Denis Bachelet had the vinous equivalent of a gardener's green fingers. At my ten-year-on and three-year-on tastings, his Charmes is invariably one of the best wines on the table. The man has talent.

Slowly but surely, Denis started to put more and more of his wines in bottle—there are cash-flow considerations here—and piece by piece to enlarge the vineyard holdings. The last additions were in 2011, when he added ten *ouvrées*, much of it in Les Evocelles, which is a very well-sited village vineyard in Brochon adjacent to and on the same level as Champeaux and Goulots (both *premier cru*). This now gives him 4.28 hectares: Charmes-Chambertin; *premier cru* Corbeaux; the Evocelles I have just mentioned, which will be declared separately; village Gevrey (mainly in En Derée) from which Denis makes a Vieilles Vignes *cuvée* (the young vine element is sold off in bulk); Côte de Nuits Villages; Bourgogne Rouge; and a little Aligoté, which I rarely taste. All the red wines are splendid examples of what they are, and I often buy the lot.

Bit by bit, too, Bachelet has updated his cellar, which lies opposite the premises of Rossignol-Trapet just off the main Nuits–Dijon road. There is a long wall, and two-thirds of the way down there is a door. This is just the entrance to the cellar. He lives elsewhere with his second wife, Marie Jo, in Saint-Philibert, on the other side of the auto-route. The cellar is organised and tidy. There is a vibrating sorting table, installed in 2003. The vineyards are ploughed several times a year to eliminate the surface roots and force the rest to dig deep and bring up the soil's nutrients. The fruit is destemmed, crushed lightly, given a four- to seven-day cold-soaking before fermentation in cement *cuves*, at a maximum of 32°C; treaded down rather than pumped-over, and matured in 20 or more percent new oak for the better wines. Up until 2009, when his son Nicolas—also an only child—joined him after his studies and internships abroad, the domaine has effectively been a one-man band.

What is the secret? (This is someone whose sole disappointing vintage was 1991, when he was going through a messy divorce—and he more than compensated by a brilliant 1992 and a spectacular 1993). "It was a lot of hard slog at the beginning," Bachelet replies. "But then the wines began to receive compliments, which makes one even more determined to do even better. And as money became a little less tight and I was able to improve the *matériel* in the cellar, the wines got finer and the reception even more enthusiastic. It's an intoxicating *métier*! You start off making the best wine you can. People applaud it. So then you are encouraged to make even better wine. Your passion is continually stimulated. That's what it becomes: a passion!"

He continues: "What am I trying to do? I'm looking for an expression of the *terroir* and a purity of fruit. Don't forget that in the Charmes, for instance, there is hardly 30 centimetres of surface soil before you strike the mother rock. Both my parcels of vines are on the top of a little slope, so drain very well. The fruit can suffer in very dry, hot vintages such as 2003. But because of the old vines, the berries are often *millerandé* which concentrates the character of the resulting wine. You have to adapt what you do to the vineyard. Each soil, each summer, is different. I'm looking for concentration, but not to excess, and also *gourmandise*." (My dictionary translates this as "greed," but that isn't it at all. Perhaps the dreaded word "hedonistic" is what we want here.) "Yes. If I can, I want to produce the magic that is Pinot Noir. In brief: a wine of pleasure."

What does Denis Bachelet do in his spare time? What other passions does he have? "Clive," he responds, "I don't get much spare time." (I almost feel he's accusing me of imagining he lies about doing nothing for most of the day.) "Skiing and sailing I love, and I adore rugby. But mainly, if I have a few hours off, I simply go for a walk in the woods."

I hope look he looks forward to another thirty years of making some of the best wines in Burgundy.

TASTING NOTES

I sampled the following vintages of Denis Bachelet's Charmes-Chambertin in December 2011.

2006 From 2016
Good youthful colour. Attractive round but crisp nose. Good concentration and class for the vintage. Medium-full body. Ripe and fresh. Some tannin still to resolve. Very good grip. Balanced and elegant and positive. Very fine for the vintage.

2005 From 2022
Very good colour. Closed-in nose. Lots of depth and quality but very young. Less tough on the palate than you might expect from the nose. Very rich and concentrated. But not tannic or aggressive. Powerful and intense. Lots of class. Very profound. Very lovely but needs time. Excellent.

2004 Just about ready
Good colour. Some maturity on the nose now. But slightly dry. Sweeter and classier and more seductive on the palate. Medium body. The tannins are now soft. Nice and fresh. Good fruit and class. Long. A lot of refinement for the vintage.

2003 Just about ready
Bachelet had to eliminate lots of over-ripe, burned fruit. Very good colour. A bit dense and tannic on the nose. Full body but quite rich and concentrated on the palate. Cooked fruit and chocolate flavours. Somewhat ungainly but not too dry on the palate. The fruit is quite fresh too. A fine result for the vintage.

2002 From 2017
Very good colour. Lovely nose. Concentrated and very, very classy. Very lovely, ripe complex fruit. Splendid harmony. Still reserved, though no hard edges. Balanced, vigorous, multidimensional, and excellent.

2001 Now to 2017
Here we had a disagreement. Denis prefers this to his 2004. I don't. Good colour. Fully evolved on the nose. Not the greatest finesse, I find. Better on the palate. Medium body but only medium depth. But fresh and agreeable. Decent balance and class. But the least interest so far.

2000 Now to 2017 plus
Good colour for the vintage. This is lighter but not as loose-knit as the 2001. It is sweeter and has more definition. Good positive, enjoyable, juicy fruit. Finishes well. Fine for the vintage.

1999 From 2017
Good colour. Fat and voluptuous on the nose. Full and concentrated. The tannins now just about absorbed, but the wine is still a bit tight. Splendid fruit and energy. Very rich and with lots of dimension. Excellent grip. Lots of finesse. This is very, very fine.

1998 Now to 2020
Medium-full colour. Still youthful. Quite a soft, open, ripe, balanced nose. Very good fruit. Nice and fresh. No hard edges. On the palate this is fully ready. Medium to medium-full body. Attractive fruit if without the depth or energy of the 1999. A lovely wine to drink now. But I've had more concentrated and powerful 1998s.

1997 Now to 2017
Medium to medium-full, mature colour. Really quite a soft nose. Plump and fruity but a little loose-knit. Better on the palate. Good fruit. Quite fresh. Positive at the end. Attractive because it is not too *tendre*.

1996 Now to 2020
Good fullish, fresh colour. The nose is ripe and still youthful. On the palate this shows medium-full body. Good energy and good backbone. The acidity is not too dominant, but it is there. Stylish if slightly four-square. Fine but not compelling. Best with food. Will still last well.

1995 Now to 2020 plus

Good fullish colour. Mature, concentrated nose. A bit tight at first. This is full-bodied, even sturdy. But rich and meaty. Good grip. Just about mature. Concentrated and energetic. Improved in the glass. Still a bit of reserve. But complete and fine. I prefer this to the above.

1994 Now to 2020

Medium to medium-full, mature colour. Soft, evolved nose. No lack of fruit or interest. Even better on the palate. Vigorous. Medium-full body. Good fat and ripe fruit. No astringency and very good grip. Excellent for the vintage. Lots of life ahead of it.

1993 Now to 2020 plus

Good vigorous colour. Plenty of depth and energy on the nose. Good concentration too. There is lots of lovely, fresh, subtle, high-class, ripe fruit here. Lots of depth and very fine harmony. Complex, long, profound, and excellent.

1992 Now to 2017

Soft, medium, mature colour. But fresh and plump on the nose. Medium body. Ripe, balanced, stylish, and positive. This is a most attractive wine. No hint of undue age and with a lovely long succulent finish.

1991 Drink soon

Medium colour. Fully mature. Rather more evolved than the 1992. Light to medium body. Fruity but a bit diffuse. One-dimensional.

1990 Now to 2017

Medium to medium-full colour. More evolved than I had expected. On the nose this is fully mature but without a great deal of energy. Medium body and good fruit. But not the depth and concentration of the best 1990s.

1989 Now to 2020 plus

Good colour. Soft, ripe, spicy nose. Medium-full body. Plenty of interest and attraction here. Good grip. Lovely fruit. Round and with plenty of dimension, balance, and class. Rather better than the 1990. Will still keep well.

1988 Now to 2020 plus

Good vigorous colour. Fresh nose. Not a bit green or austere at all. This is delicious. Fullish body. Ample, rich, ripe, and balanced. Slightly spicy. The most volume, vigour, and depth of the 1990, 1989, and 1988 series and the best wine. Excellent.

1987 Now to 2017

Lightish colour. Fresh but not very voluminous nose. Decent fruit though. Light to medium body. No undue age. Ripe and pleasant if a little one-dimensional. Good balance. Positive at the end. Really fine for the vintage. Can still be kept.

1986 Drink soon

Light to medium colour. Soft nose. On the palate a bit more evolved than the 1987. Lightish body and a bit loose-knit. But still fresh, fruity, and enjoyable. No lack of class.

Domaine Bonneau du Martray

PERNAND-VERGELESSES

IN TOTAL, THERE ARE some 160.19 hectares of *grand cru* land on the slopes of Corton hill. Split up between the three villages, this represents 22.43 hectares in Ladoix, 120.51 in Aloxe-Corton, and 17.26 in Pernand-Vergelesses. Out of the 160.19 hectares, 71.88 *can* produce Corton-Charlemagne: this includes all the Pernand land, 48.57 hectares in Aloxe-Corton, and 6.05 hectares in Ladoix. I say *can*. The growers have the option in the Corton-Charlemagne appellation to plant either Pinot Noir or Chardonnay. And to complicate matters further, they also have the right—though few exercise it—to plant Chardonnay elsewhere on the hill, and to produce Corton *blanc* from it. There is, as Hugh Johnson puts it, a slight Alice in Wonderland air about the legislation on the Corton hill.

If you look at a map, you will see that the area marked Corton-Charlemagne is that facing southwest towards the village of Pernand-Vergelesses and across the valley towards Savigny. The red wine area seems to be that overhanging Ladoix and Aloxe-Corton. In reality, some red wine is produced in the lower slopes of the Charlemagne vineyard, while white wine—Corton-Charlemagne—is made all the way round the hill, albeit at the top of the slope.

As a further complexity, the hill is divided into a number of *climats*, and there will appear, prefixed by Corton on the labels: Corton, Clos du Roi, Corton, Les Bressandes, and so on. Le Corton is a *lieu-dit* in its own right. But Corton *tout court* will be either a mixture of several different *lieux-dits* or a red wine from the En Charlemagne side of the hill. And I must also mention the brand of Maison Latour here, a major proprietor in the area: Château Corton-Grancey.

Charlemagne, Charles the First and Great, as was befitting for a man who was Holy Roman Emperor and effectively the ruler of the Western civilised world, was a giant of a man. He towered over his subjects, dominating them as much physically as by the force of his personality. One of his many domaines and the one producing one of his favourite wines was at Corton, itself named, one interpretation suggests, after an obscure first-century Roman emperor named Othon: Curtis (domaines) d'Othon become contracted to Corton. As with certain vineyards in Germany, the story is related that, noticing the snows were always the first to melt on this particular slope, Charlemagne ordered vines to be planted there, and, lo, these produced excellent wine.

At the time the wine was red, but, as Charlemagne grew older, and his beard whiter, his wife Luitgarde, ever watchful over the dignity of her spouse, objected to the majesty of her emperor being degraded by red wine stains on his beard and suggested that he switched to consuming white wine. White grapes were commanded to be planted on a section of the hill, Corton-Charlemagne was born, and it continues still.

According to the Burgundian historian Camille Rodier, that part of the *vignoble* donated by Charlemagne to the *Collégiale* of Saulieu in AD 775 corresponds exactly to the current domaine of the Bonneau du Martray family, owners of one of the largest domaines and one of the best sections of the hill. Other later owners included Modoin, Bishop of Autun, who donated his Corton vines to the cathedral there in AD 858, the Abbots of Cîteaux, the Knights Templar, the Dukes of Burgundy, Charlotte Dumay, who left her land to the Hospices de Beaune in 1534, and the Kings of France, whose tenure four hundred years ago is still commemorated in the *climat* Corton, Clos du Roi.

The earliest extant document referring to Corton-Charlemagne dates back from 1375 and refers to a lease of the "Clos le Charlemagne" by the Chapitre de Saint-Andoche-de-Saulieu to a local farmer. A century later the abbot tried to wriggle out of this contract. In 1620 the lessee was a M. Esmonin. Again, ten years later, the clergy attempted to have the agreement revoked. In 1791, following the Revolution, the land was sold as a *bien national* and valued at 10,800 livres.

Legend apart, white wine production from the Chardonnay grape on the hill of Corton is a recent development. Julien, in his *Topographie de Tous les Vignobles Connus*, of 1824, makes no mention of white Corton. Le Corton is one of his *vins rouges de première classe*, and the reds from Pougets, Charlemagne, and Les Bressantes [*sic*] among those of the *troisième classe*. There is no note of white Aloxe or Pernand at all.

By midcentury, however, the Chardonnay had arrived. Dr. Lavalle in his *Histoire et Statistique de la Vigne et des Grands Vins de la Côte d'Or*, published in 1855, speaks of Pinot Noir on the midslope and lower lying ground and what he terms Pinot Blanc on the upper parts. In the 16 hectare section of Corton-Charlemagne lying in the commune of Aloxe, MM Gouveau, de Grancey, Chantrier, Jules Paulet, and the Hospices de Beaune are listed as the main proprietors, while in the 19 hectares of land across the border in Pernand only MM Bonneau-Véry (now the Bonneau du Martray family) is worthy of note. "On ne récolte presque que des vins blancs dans ce climat," he states.

By the end of the century, the owners included Louis Latour, who had acquired the Grancey domaine, and Jules Senard, two families who are still important proprietors in the area. Twenty years later, Camilie Rodier brought out the first edition of his classic *Le Vin de Bourgogne*. In the 1948 edition he speaks of the Chardonnay grape being planted more and more widely, in what was by that time formally the appellation of Corton-Charlemagne, "over the previous thirty years." (This is a repeat of what he says in the first edition, which came out in the 1920s.) This grape, he writes, gives white wines of a fine golden colour and full flavour; this flavour combining cinnamon and gunflint.

As with the Charlemagne side of the hill, the Aloxe-facing slopes also largely belonged in ecclesiastical hands in the Middle Ages. The monks of the Abbey of Sainte-Marguerite, up in the neighbouring valley of the river Rhoin near Bouilland, were one of the first to exploit the vinous possibilities of the *climat*, having received a donation of land in 1164. The Cistercians were soon to follow, as were the Templars, just as they were on the other side of the hill.

From the beginning of the seventeenth century on, as the power of the church waned, the land on Corton hill was progressively annexed by the local bourgeoisie, either by buying it outright or by a simple matter of a cash lease rather than a more uncomfortable *métayage* arrangement. During the reign of Louis XV, a number of important acquisitions were made. Two Dijon gentlemen, M. de Vergnette-Lamotte and M. Le Bault, bought a sizeable amount of land from the Abbey at Cîteaux; Mr. Larbalestier, another local, became proprietor of the vineyards of the Abbey of Sainte-Marguerite; and the brothers Thiroux of Beaune took over the famous *climat* of Clos du Roi. Another arrival was M. du Tillet, squire of the village of Serrigny (as well as Aloxe and Pernand). Le Bault was further to increase his domaine. His wife, Jacqueline, as vivacious and intelligent as she was beautiful (there is a fine portrait dating from 1755 by Greuze) was in her own right heiress of 500 *ouvrées* (nearly 21 hectares) in Aloxe. It was the Le Bault family who constructed Corton-Grancey.

It was through Madame La Belle, as he addressed Jacqueline Le Bault, that Voltaire acquired a taste for Corton (and it is to him that we owe our gratitude for having commissioned the Greuze portrait). Voltaire was an admirer, but Madame was not to be tempted. The one-sided passion was to continue for many years, during which many dozens of bottles of Le Bault Corton were despatched to Geneva or Ferney or wherever it was that Voltaire was nursing his frustration at the time. Incidentally, the orders were for both red and white wine, in equal quantities. Sadly, however, Voltaire, great man of many parts, was not a real wine lover. He was knowledgeable about wine, as you would expect a man of his catholicity of interests to be, but the nuances of connoisseurship passed him by. To him, wine was merely a beverage.

The domaine which is now called Bonneau du Martray was probably created out of the ashes of the old ecclesiastical landholdings when these were taken over by the state and sold as *biens nationaux* at the time of the Revolution. It was not the local *vignerons* who benefited; they could not raise the capital. It was

the wealthy bourgeoisie. One such was the Bonneau-Véry family. Dr. Lavalle, whose book on the history and the wines of the Côte d'Or, published in 1855, is an important source work for those like myself who delve into the origins of the top wine estates, lists the Bonneau-Vérys as owning 19.7 hectares of Corton-Charlemagne at the time, which produced an average of 20 hectolitres per hectare. The family owned the totality of the part of the *climat* which lay within the commune of Pernand (or Pernant, as Dr. Lavalle spells it), and together with other land, enjoyed an estate of 24 hectares.

The vines, however, were not yet Chardonnay. They were Pinot Blanc, even Gamay. And they were not very fashionable either. At the time of the Revolution, the red wine parts of Corton sold for 250 to 300 francs an *ouvrée*, the white for barely 150. Some time after 1855, the domaine was split, and one of the heirs sold his share. Later, following the phylloxera crisis, some of the land at the top of the slope was planted with pines rather than vines. During the miserable 1930s, yet another hectare was amputated. Today, therefore, the size of the domaine is 11 hectares, 9.5 of which produce white wine, and 1.5 of which is planted in Pinot Noir.

In 1969 the late Comtesse Jean Le Bault de La Morinière inherited the domaine from her uncle René Bonneau du Martray. Her husband, despite his Parisian residence, was descended from Burgundian stock—one would naturaly expect a connection with the Le Bault family, owners, as I have stated earlier, before the Revolution, but this does not appear to be so (even the family coats of arms are different—and is related on his mother's side to Madame de Sévigné). It was Madame de Sévigné (1626–1696) in one of her many affectionate and revealing letters to her daughter, the Comtesse de Grignan, who uttered the immortal prediction *à propos* the fashion for coffee, the plays of Racine and the wines of Bordeaux. "It won't last!"

In the time of Uncle René, the totality of the Bonneau du Martray harvest was sold to the local *négoce*, and Jean le Bault could well have continued the part of absentee, disinterested landlord. But no. He had different ideas. He set himself to study viticulture and oenology, and, helped by the rising profitability of top-class winemaking in the 1970s, decided to switch over to bottling and marketing his wines on a direct basis. One of the first things he did was to install proper temperature control of the fermenting process. Today the entirety leaves the domaine in bottle, and 80 to 85 percent is exported.

At the end of 1993 there was a dual change of generations at the domaine. Jean-Charles Le Bault de la Morinière, born in 1949, took over from his father, and in the cellars Henri Bruchon, formerly in charge, took his *retraite* and was succeeded by his sons Bernard and Jean-Pierre.

"If one wants to make the finest possible wine," says Jean-Charles, "it is important to be on the spot, to follow the wine's progress on a day-to-day basis. When I took over, I decided I had to live in Pernand-Vergelesses, not just go down on the weekend. I also realized that I needed to know more about the winemaking process, so I enrolled at Dijon and took an oenology degree. I wanted to know why we did things. Sometimes when I questioned the Bruchons, I got no satisfactory answer; merely that that was the way we had always done it."

He continues: "We gave up fertilizing and the use of herbicides. We now plough the vineyard, as in the old days. The soil is less compacted and more alive. I decided to reduce the yield—by 15 to 20 percent. My father was furious when we only made 32 hl/ha in 1995! The average yield over the last decade has been 39 hl/ha for white, 5 or 6 less for the red wine. We fine and filter much less, not at all if we can get away with it. When necessary, we pick over the same parcel more than once during the harvest. From 1995 we have been stirring up the lees of the Corton-Charlemagne. We have stopped heating the cellar to induce early malos.

"The changes in the way the red wine is made have been more drastic," he explains. "The grapes are now entirely destemmed.

There is a sorting table. We cold-soak for a few days. Our approach to the *élevage* in cask is altogether more flexible. But I don't like to control the temperature of the fermentation. The wine must be allowed to make itself. Yet I do have a heating unit with which I can prolong high temperatures at the end to extract more noble tannins.

"But the most important changes have been made in the vineyard. It is here," says Jean-Charles, "that the wine is created. Back in the 1970s and 1980s, we replanted with clones. But when I arrived, I said to myself, if it's all clones, what will be the difference? So we changed to *sélection massale* and we now propagate from our own vines. I'm very impressed with the results. In fact, apart from one large piece which was uprooted in 2001 and replanted in 2007, there have been merely the occasional replacements (*répiquage*) in the estate."

In 2003, Jean-Charles appointed Fabien Esthor as *chef de culture*. Esthor is now the most important person in the team, apart from Jean-Charles himself. Gradually, over the years the domaine has become increasingly *biologique*. In 1997 they started experimenting, dispensing with insecticides, using sexual confusion instead. There is now an increasing reliance on ploughing using horses. Or if not horses, which now cover between a quarter and a third of the property, replacing the usual tractors, which weigh four tons, with the new generation using Caterpillar wheels which only weigh 1.4 tons, in order to compact the soil less. With a similar goal in mind, *rognage* (leaf clipping) is largely manual. The domaine expects to be confirmed as biological in 2012 and is already conducting trials on a private basis with biodynamism. The yield of the biodynamic parts of the estate are picked and vinified separately. You can tell, I am told, the difference. As part of this ongoing progress in the vineyard, Jean-Charles had the domaine geologically investigated in 2006. The analysis showed nine different types of soil, naunces within the basic limestone generality. The team has adapted the work accordingly.

The white wine vineyard faces west at the

top of the slope and descends in a series of zig-zags. Up here the soil is a white marl. At the bottom the orientation is southwest. There is no longer any clay in the soil. The wine from here will be richer and fleshier than that from the upper slopes. Just above the church in one of Pernand's steep, winding alleys, an old *manoir* has been converted into one of the most up-to-date wineries in Burgundy. The latest changes have been the addition of a modern set of offices, underneath which is an elegant tasting room, converted out of an older part of the building at the side. There are two pneumatic Bucher presses—installed in 2002. The fruit is pressed, left overnight to lose its gross lees, and then decanted into cask for the fermentation. One-third of the wood is renewed each year. There may be as many as sixteen *cuvées*, which, assuming they are all up to standard, are gradually incorporated together before bottling takes place in March, eighteen months after the vintage. The wine does not spend all its time in cask. Before the second winter, it is returned to the tanks so that it should not become too *boisé* (woody) or dried out.

As far as the white wine is concerned, this is clean, meticulous, intelligent winemaking, and the result is a classy product which is refreshingly leaner than some Corton-Charlemagnes (because the vines face south and southwest rather than east, overlapping the sub-*climats* of En Charlemagne in Pernand-Vergelesses and Le Charlemagne in Aloxé-Corton, and do not enjoy quite as much direct sunlight during the day as do those vines which face more to the east), and has depth, elegance, and harmony. Bonneau du Martray produces the true steely sort of Corton-Charlemagne which is built to last: white Burgundy at its best.

Down at the bottom of the hill is a hectare and a half of Pinot Noir in two almost adjacent parcels which make two small *cuvées*, eventually blended together. In the old days, up to 1978 or so, it was fullish but a bit rustic. It then became more sophisticated but a bit lightweight. Since 1993, it has steadily improved and has now both elegance and depth. Since 2000,

it has been even better. It is now quite the equal of the wines produced in Bressandes and neighbouring *lieux-dit*, which is where most of us would expect to find the best Cortons. Considering the size of the *climat*, *grand cru* Corton is surprisingly hard to find at a really high level of quality. But at least we now have Domaine Bonneau du Martray's to consider.

Jean-Charles and his wife Anne live round the corner, the apartment lying above part of the cellar, and have three children, all relatively newly married. There is also a strictly private bolt-hole in the Morvan. One of nature's true gentleman, one can sense behind the calm, polite exterior, a man of passion and determination. The greatest possible wine is his goal.

What exactly is—or should be—Corton-Charlemagne? I posed the question to Jean-Charles Le Bault de la Morinière. "Corton-Charlemagne, because of its exposition, is a wine of light rather than heat," he says. The wine is not about power and volume ("sugar-power," as Jean-Charles puts it) but minerality, finesse, balance, and acidity. There should be a steely touch. It should be lighter and leaner than Bâtard.

I find the Bonneau du Martray example deliciously cool, pure, and understated, and above all splendidly elegant. It lasts superbly, as the following notes will show admirably, becoming even more enticing and complex as it ages. Of course it is a wine for food. And it is recommended that you decant it. For twenty years now this example has been one of Burgundy's finest white wines.

TASTING NOTES

I sampled the following wines in Pernand-Vergelesses in March 2011.

Corton-Charlemagne

2009   From 2019

Will be bottled in a month. Lovely ripe nose. Acacia flowers. Honeyed but steely. Fullish body. Ample and rich. Very good grip. Splendid fruit. Very gently oaky. Balanced and very elegant. Lovely long finish. Very different but as good as the 2008. But more opulent. Jean-Charles prefers his 2009. But I like the 2008. They are both very fine.

2008   From 2019

Full but closed-in nose. Full body. A wine of splendid depth and concentration. Very gently oaky again. Excellent harmony and great class. Very vigorous. Really steely. A classic. Very, very long on the palate.

2007   Now to 2017

Soft, ripe nose. Good fruit. Quite lush. Medium body. Ripe on the palate. Pure and very fresh. A lovely example if without the depth or sheer class of 2008 or 2009; for drinking quite soon. Very good indeed.

2006   Now to 2020 plus

A little development on the nose. Fuller and more mineral on the attack than the 2007. But accessible and just about ready. A ripe, stylish, attractive wine. Very good grip. Fine.

2005   See note

Rather adolescent on the nose. It seems a bit heavy and clumsy. Fullish body. Evolved on the attack. Ripe but rather four-square. Doesn't sing.

2004   Now to 2020 plus

This is the best wine since the first two. The colour shows some development. Nicely cool and composed on the nose. Good minerally fruit. Medium-full body. Balanced. No lack of depth and complexity. Ripe, classy, and very attractive. Just about *à point* but will keep very well. Lovely. Very fine.

2003   Drink soon

The deepest colour of the range. Spicy nose. Somewhat four-square and heavy with a suggestion of sweetness at the end. Rather better than most 2003s, but not my style.

2002   From 2016

Nicely austere, closed-in nose. Plenty of vigour. Full body. Steely. Youthful. Lots of concentration, indeed power in the best sense. Very

impressive follow-through. Great class and depth. Better still in five years. Very fine indeed.

2001   Now to 2017

Ripe nose. Fully ready. Lovely fruit. Balanced. Classy. Minerally. Nice touch of oak at the end. Medium-full body. Juicy and succulent. Not the greatest grip or concentration but delicious now.

2000   Now to 2020

A more developed colour than the 2001. But a better wine. Fresh nose with a slightly herbal touch. Cooler and crisper than the 2001. Medium-full body. Mineral and classy. *À point* but still vigorous. Lovely finish. Fine plus.

1999   Now to 2020 plus

The colour is really quite developed; almost golden. Yet the wine shows no signs of undue age. Full but closed-in and concentrated on the nose. Much fresher on the palate than the nose would suggest. A mature wine now. Lots of depth, dimension, and complexity. This has grip and backbone. Profound, powerful, and very delicious. Cries out for food.

1998   Now to 2016

Youthful colour. Soft, gently fruity nose with a touch of oxidation. Stylish but without a great deal of dimension and vigour. Crisp. Medium to medium-full body. Good acidity. It has the steeliness of Corton Charlemagne but not the richness. Yet elegant and good depth, if a little small-scale.

1997   Now to 2016

Well-matured colour. A touch of oxidation on the nose. Better on the palate though. This is fuller and more developed than the 1998, but less stylish. Yet I prefer it because it is richer, and there is a good layer of new oak underneath which I don't find in the above. Ultimately there is more vigour here. Good grip. Not exactly refined but balanced enough. A most enjoyable bottle.

1996   Now to 2017

Mature colour. Quite a herbal, well-matured nose. Less to it than I had expected, and again a touch of oxidation on the nose. Like the 1997, this is better on the palate. It is a lot fresher than one might expect. Crisp and peachy with quite high acidity. Only medium to medium-full body. But good fruit and quite complex and elegant. Finishes long. Like the two above, this is good but not great.

1995   Now to 2020 plus

Just about mature colour. Full, steely, pure, and classy on the nose. Vigorous and still very fresh. Full-bodied. Ripe. Profound. Complex. *À point*. Lots of energy. Lovely fruit. Harmonious and delicious. This is most impressive. Very fine indeed.

1990   Now to 2016

Splendidly fresh still. Lovely fruit. Not quite the energy or power of the 1995, but a very deli-cious wine. Balanced, long, complex, and classic. Marvelous vigour for a wine which is now twenty years old. Very fine.

Corton

2002   From 2016

Good colour. Ripe nose. Very fresh and pure. Very good grip. Fullish body, beginning to evolve. Very good tannins. Lots of vigour, lovely fruit, and very classy. Still reserved but very impressive.

1999   From 2015

Full colour. Still youthful. Firm but ample nose. Still some tannin to resolve and these tannins not as sophisticated as in the 2002. Fresh, ripe, succulent, and vigorous. This is fine.

Domaine Sylvain Cathiard

VOSNE-ROMANÉE

I FIRST VISITED Sylvain Cathiard to taste his 1992 vintage. I had already been to sample the 1990 vintage next door two years earlier in his father's cellar—the wines were labled André Cathiard-Molinier—but I had not been very impressed. Much had already been passed down the line. And I didn't take to the man. "*Un homme dur*" (a hard man), as his son puts it.

But in the autumn of 1993, I had much liked what I saw *chez* Sylvain. The cellar was spotless—always a good sign—and the wines were pure and intense, and though Sylvain Cathiard was, and is, bedevilled by a persistent stutter, especially when confronted by someone he did not know—I warmed to the man. "This is a potential star," I said to myself. I have been back ever since. And a true star he has turned out to be.

The domaine begins with Alfred Cathiard. (They are distant relations of the Cathiards at Château Smith Haut-Lafitte in the Graves, both having their origins in the Savoy.) Alfred was born there in 1901, moved to Burgundy, and worked for the Domaine de la Romanée-Conti

and then later for Lamarche between the wars. He began to build up a domaine for himself, which was expanded by his son André, born in 1928. André acquired some Nuits-Saint-Georges, Les Murgers, and then three-quarters of a hectare of Vosne-Romanée, Les Malconsorts, from a Félix Nöellat, in 1970. He also had a lease on some Clos de Vougeot, but this no longer exists. André and his father were already farmers in some neighbouring Malconsorts for the Domaine Thomas-Moillard in Nuits-Saint-Georges (Thomas took all the fruit, as they did of the Nuits-Saint-Georges, Les Thorey) and, from 1941 on, equally for the Thomas-Moillard domaine, the Cathiards performed the same role in Romanée-Saint-Vivant. In 1984 André Galtié, a Thomas nephew, sold 34 ares, his inheritance of the Romanée-Saint-Vivant, each to the Domaine Arnoux, also sharecroppers, and to André Cathiard. Cathiard then sold half (17 ares) back to the Thomas family, leaving him with 17 ares. André and Sylvain's first vintage here was the 1987. The Thomas parcel now belongs to the Domaine Dujac. André Cathiard retired in 1995 and died in 2008.

Sylvain, born in 1953, began to work along-side his father in the 1970s. His first independent vintage was in 1986. Gradually he began to take over more and more, and at the same time he expanded the exploitation: 29 ares of Vosne-Romanée, En Orveau, above Echézeaux, 16 ares of Suchots, 24 ares of Aux Reignots, and some village Chambolle-Musigny, Clos de l'Orme, which lies just under Les Charmes.

With the sale of the Thomas-Moillard domaine to Dujac and de Montille in 2006, he was able to acquire 43 ares of Nuits-Saint-Georges, Aux Thorey in exchange or compensation for the farming arrangement he had had with the Thomases. In all, with his village Vosne and Nuits-Saint-Georges, and his generic Bourgogne Rouge (which is jolly good), Sylvain Cathiard looks after 4.25 hectares.

Right from the beginning, ably supported by his wife, Odette, Sylvain Cathiard's objective, as he puts it, is for "fruit, purity, and elegance." He reduced the yield. He relaxed the extraction. There was more new wood. He stopped fining and filtering. Gradually, when the finances permitted, he improved the *matériel*, the destemmer, the pumps and et cetera, and he bought out his three sisters. He expanded the cellar, which is now, in its small way, one of the most elegant in the region. The wines improved by leaps and bounds.

Sebastian, Odette and Sylvain's only child, was born in 1984 and joined his father in 2005. This young man is a determined character, and of late there has been some tension between father and son.

This rose to a head in the winter of 2010 and 2011, but I am relieved to say has now been resolved. Sebastian, who now owns 40 percent of the exploitation, has from the 2011 vintage taken over complete responsibility for the vineyards and the cellar. There is, as Sylvain puts it, a "contract" between them. Sylvain will continue to deal with the clients and the administration. "And I am there if he needs me. I have been working since I took over in order to have something I could pass on to him. He's now the one in charge. But we had a difficult winter." There is now a hired hand, and this man and Sebastian get on well together.

Odette is from the wilds of the Corrèze, and it is there, in a house that she inherited from her mother, that the two of them go to relax. I feel the peace and quiet of what really is *la France profonde* is something which enriches both and fuels them up for the year to come. I trust the vintages to come from Sebastian will live up to the reputation Sylvain Cathiard has achieved over the past twenty years.

TASTING NOTES

I sampled the following vintages of Sylvain Cathiard's Vosne-Romanée, Les Malconsorts, in March 2011.

2009   From 2020

Bottled three days previously. Medium-full colour. Lovely fruit on the nose. Pure and intense. Fullish body. Delicious fruit. Very noble tannins and very fine acidity. Vigorous, classy, multidimensional, and very fine. But the 2005 is better still.

2008   From 2018

Medium colour. Very enticing, fragrant, high-toned nose. Almost a hint of mint. Medium to medium-full body. Lots of energy. A very profound wine. Slightly lean at first still—this will mellow as the wine ages—but generous at the end. I love this. It just goes to show quite how good some 2008s can be.

2007   From 2014

From magnum. Medium colour. Just a bit of evolution. Ripe, fresh, elegant, ample nose. More volume than one might expect. A bit *tendre* nevertheless, but that is the vintage. Medium to medium-full body. Good grip. Balanced and unexpectedly elegant. Lovely long finish. Excellent for the vintage.

I was allowed to take the rest of the magnum

back home with me. It was delicious, and even better the second day.

2006   From 2017

Medium-full colour. The wines here seem to put on colour in bottle. Rich, spicy nose. Lacks a little, high tones. But fullish body, succulent, and balanced. Just a little tannin to resolve. Plenty of fruit. Plenty of energy. Long and stylish. Lots of dimension. Very fine for the vintage.

2005   From 2019

This is quite superb. Fine colour. Quite closed-in on the nose. Yet classy and profound as well as a bit unforthcoming. Fullish body. Very, very rich and full of abundant fruit. Excellent tannins and very fine grip. This is multidimensional and very fine indeed. Marvelous energy and depth. Very, very long and complex. Brilliant!

2004   Now to 2016

From magnum. Good fullish colour. Some signs of maturity. Quite rich and not a bit too lean and herbal on the nose. Medium-full body. Just a little ungenerous on the attack, but firm and quite rich and succulent on the follow-through: indeed ample. Good grip. Unexpectedly elegant. Very fine for the vintage.

2003   Now to 2016

From magnum. Very full colour. Only a suggestion of maturity. Rich and fat and spicy. But not a bit cooked or pruney. Fullish body. Still a little tannin. I find it a little clumsy as I do even the best 2003s. But there is good grip and energy here.

2002   From 2015

From magnum. Fullish colour. Now some maturity. Still a bit hidden on the nose. But high-class fruit and a very profound wine here. This doesn't have quite the richness and depth of the 2005, but it has splendid energy, and really excellent grip. The tannins are now resolved, but the wine still needs three or four years to soften. Very, very long and complex. Very, very fine.

2001   Now to 2020

From magnum. Excellent colour; as dark as the 2003. Just about mature. Lovely silky-smooth, soft ripe fruit on the nose. Fullish body. Virile, ripe, and rich. Still very youthful. Lots of energy. Lots of depth. This is a really excellent 2001. It has bags of life and is very long and classy and complex at the end.

2000   Now to 2017

From magnum. Good, fullish, mature colour. Soft nose. Fresh. No great depth but accessible and full of charm and interest. Lovely fruit. Medium body. Only just about ready. Positive and delicious. Very fine for the vintage.

1999   From 2014

From magnum. Fullish colour. Barely mature. Still a bit closed on the nose, but splendid richness and concentration. Lots of energy and very fresh. Medium-full body. Very good fruit. Still youthful. It needs a few years to round off. Compared with the 2005, this doesn't quite have the intensity and concentration. Sylvain says he's a bit disappointed. Yet I feel that even if it doesn't quite sing today, it is still pretty damn good.

Domaine Bruno Clair

MARSANNAY

THE SENIOR ESTATE in Marsannay is that of Bruno Clair. Bruno's domaine is the successor and inheritor of the bulk of what was the Domaine Clair-Daü, split up in the mid-1980s. But even before this split, Bruno had set up on his own, mainly by taking on vines in Marsannay itself, replanting land in that commune which had been neglected, and pioneering similar plots in Morey-Saint-Denis and elsewhere. To this, we must add some one-hundred-year-old vines in Savigny-Lès-Beaune, Les Dominodes, passed on by his father. In all, in 1985, a total of 6 hectares, built up between 1979 and 1985.

The history of the Clair-Daü domaine begins in the First World War. Joseph Clair (born 1889) from Santenay met Marguerite Daü (born 1895) from Marsannay. He had been wounded and came back to Burgundy to convalesce. They were married in 1919 and were to produce three children: Bernard, born in 1921; Noëlle, who eventually married a M. Vernet, in 1923; and Monique, who was to wed a M. Bart. Marguerite and her sister Hélène had inherited 8 hectares of vines in Marsannay. But these had

been allowed to degenerate as a result of the phylloxera epidemic. Joseph Clair took them over, replanted the vineyards, and the Clair-Daü domaine was born.

It was Joseph Clair who "invented" Marsannay Rosé. Much of what lay in the local vineyards at the time was Gamay. The wine which resulted left much to be desired and could only be labelled (once the laws of Appellation Contrôlée came into force) as Bourgogne Grande Ordinaire. The purely Pinot wine was sold as Bourgogne Rouge de Marsannay. It would be 1987 before the appellation Marsannay would be decreed. Clair replanted his vineyards with Pinot Noir and was soon able to persuade his clients—and neighours—what a delicious rosé could be obtained therefrom. Bourgogne Rosé de Marsannay was to become the saviour of the commune in the depressed years of the 1930s.

Gradually the domaine was extended. Land was not as expensive then as it is today. An *ouvrée* (there are roughly 24 *ouvrées* to the hectare) from which you would normally expect to produce three-quarters of one *pièce* of wine, cost the same price as the value of that cask.

The first acquisitions were in Gevrey, in 1924 and 1925 in the *premiers crus climats* of Combe-aux-Moines and Estournelles-Saint-Jacques, upslope from the church and the old *château*. In the 1930s the holding in Marsannay was itself extended, some village Gevrey was acquired, and the domaine reached further south to embrace the *climats* of Chambolle-Musigny, Amoureuses, and Bonnes-Mares. More of the latter was acquired in the early 1950s, as was some Clos de Vougeot.

Two more Gevrey-Chambertin *premiers crus* followed later in the 1950s: Cazetiers in 1951 and Clos-Saint-Jacques from the Comte de Moucheron in 1954. In 1960, Joseph Clair successfully competed against Aymar de Nicolay of the Domaine Chandon de Briailles to purchase some venerable vines—already about sixty years old—in Savigny-Lès-Beaune, Les Dominodes. The year afterwards a rich widow in Gevrey sold Joseph and Bernard almost a hectare of Clos de Bèze, and finally in 1970 Bernard took over a two-thirds-of-a-hectare parcel of Clos du Fonteny, and the following year a hectare of Vosne-Romanée (three hundred metres from Romanée-Conti, they proudly claim—but simply village AC).

Bernard Clair started working alongside his father in 1939 and married Geneviève Bardet in 1946 (the couple were divorced in 1972), producing five children. In 1954 the ownership of the domaine was entrusted to a family-owned Société Civile. It was after the death of Joseph Clair in 1971 that the troubles began. The children, it seemed, had never got on that well among themselves, but the lid on family dissension had been firmly held in place by Joseph, from all accounts somewhat of a patriarch.

Things were not too bad at first, but towards the end of the decade the Clair-Daü affair went from bad to worse. Bernard, naturally, wanted to reinvest his profits in the vineyard and in the cellars, to buy new wood and the equipment necessary to control the vinification and maintain the reputation of the domaine. The sisters, one of whose husband's business was failing

to thrive, wanted their money out. Meanwhile, though Bernard, responsible for the vinification, was producing a fine *matière première*, the *élevage* in the cellars was increasingly being mishandled by cellar-master M. Ploy. He was nearly always drunk, remembers Bruno Clair. But he was a dab hand at *boules*.

Matters reached a head in 1981. In frustration, Bernard Clair walked out. In retaliation, the sisters boarded up the front door of his house, for it gave onto the courtyard of the domaine. Clair had to come and go by the rear entrance. Noëlle Vernet took over, assisted—if that is the word—by the now totally incapable M. Ploy. But this was merely a stopgap. The Clair-Daü domaine was up for sale. It was a sad time. The vines were neglected. All the competent people had left. The quality of the wine declined.

Following the death of Joseph Daü, ownership of the Clair-Daü domaine had been nominally divided into four parts. Bernard possessed almost two-thirds of the vines of the Société Clair-Daü. Then there was Roger Trinquier, son-in-law of Hélène, *née* Daü. And there were the two other Clair-Daü children. In 1985, Noëlle Vernet's share, which included the Estounelles-Saint-Jacques and the Amoureuses, plus half of the Clos-Saint-Jacques, among other choice parcels, was sold to Louis Jadot. In addition, Jadot took over a twenty-year *fermage* of Roger Trinquier's part, which included a further section of the Clos-Saint-Jacques and some of the Bonnes-Mares.

Monique Bart departed to run her quarter from a large modern cellar elsewhere in the village, the wines are now being made by her son Martin and his nephew Pierre. This left Bernard Clair, who, not wishing to put all his eggs in his sons' basket, so to speak, kept his 1.6 hectares of Bonnes-Mares and some Marsannay vines for himself. This was rented to the Domaine Fougeray-de-Beauclair, but, following his death in 2006, part of the Bonnes-Mares has been taken back by Bruno. (The rest will follow in 2016.) Since the 1986 vintage, the remainder of the domaine devolved to Bruno

Clair, son of Bernard and Geneviève Bardet: he therefore runs more than half of the original Clair-Daü domaine.

Bruno, born in 1957, is the youngest of the family. There is an elder brother, Michel, a civil servant, and three sisters. He started working at the Clair-Daü domaine in 1978 but, as I have said, left during the family troubles to build up his own domaine. For long his right-hand man has been Philippe Brun, a young man who had worked for Drouhin. They make a fine team.

Since 1986, Bruno has gradually increased his landholdings. The Marsannay vineyards now cover almost 10 hectares. In 2003 he bought a third of a hectare of Corton-Charlemagne. He leases land in Aloxe-Corton and Pernand-Vergelesses. And the land upslope from Clos de Tart and Bonnes-Mares, which he had cleaned up and planted in the early 1980s is fully in production—a delicious white wine called En La Rue De Vergy. Bruno has applied for this to be upgraded to *premier cru*. Subsequently he acquired some Gevrey-Chambertin, *premier cru*, La Petite Chapelle. As from 1999 the Clos-Saint-Jacques, which for a couple of decades had been labelled Geneviève Bardet as a result of the divorce settlement between her and Bernard Clair, appears under Bruno's name. In 2006 the twenty-year lease with Jadot (Roger Trinquier's share) came to its end, and Bruno now vinifies, for instance, all his Clos-Saint-Jacques rather than handing over part of the crop. Now he tends 24 hectares and produces twenty-four different wines.

Bruno Clair, like all good winemakers, is nothing if not flexible. Vinification techniques are adjusted to the vintage, to the fruit which arrives in the first place. The phenolic maturity is of much greater importance than the sugar content. "Look at the 1991," he says. "The alcohol content is minimal. Yet the wine is balanced and most attractive." "Winemakers must follow, not lead and force the wine into a staitjacket," is the Clair philosophy.

To ensure that this fruit is as fine as possible, the vines are pruned short and fertilisation is kept to a minimum. "I hope not to have to do a green harvest. If it is necessary, it means that I have not controlled things properly earlier." One must understand the vines and the *terroir*. This is what everyone will tell you, but if you travel round his vineyards with Bruno, you really do feel that he knows every plant individually and is aware of every subtle nuance and variation in the soils they are planted in. The ripeness of the tannins is more important than the alcohol level of the wine. "With sophisticated tannins," says Bruno, "you can expect wines with finesse. That is what I'm looking for."

On arrival at the winery in Marsannay, a large barn with an underground cellar beneath it, the bunches are usually destemmed, a *saignée*—maximum 5 percent; any more will dry the wine up—is performed in some vintages (in 2000, for example), and after a few days natural cold maceration (somewhat less natural in a warm vintage like 1999), the fermentation allowed to progress up to a maximum of 34°C. There is a regular human *pigeage* in the early stages, and a *cuvaison* of up to three weeks, again depending on the vintage.

Thereafter the lesser wines are kept partly in bulk, in oak *foudres*, partly in barrel; the better wines entirely in small oak of which a third to 50 percent is new and bottled from about fifteen to twenty-one months after the vintage, depending on the wine. The white wines are usually both fined and filtered; the reds not, unless necessary.

So what does he do in his spare time? He and his wife, Isabelle, have a cottage in Brittany. He goes sea fishing in small boats and enjoys tidying up his land. As he says, he has plenty of experience with land *en friche*.

Bruno's wines are structured, elegant, and age well. The colours are not dense black, but the wines have no lack of intensity. I find them nicely austere when they are young, with good grip and plenty of sophisticated tannins. This is a five-star domaine which is a worthy successor to the reputation of Clair-Daü at its best. And it remains the source for the best Rosé de

Marsannay, the most elegant and delicious rosé money can buy.

TASTING NOTES

Most of the following wines were served at a wine weekend at the Hotel Wilden Mann in Lucerne, Switzerland, in December 2010. Bruno and Isabelle were kind enough to open the 1997, 1995, and 1993 when I went up to Marsannay to discuss the text above a couple of months later.

Chambertin, Clos de Bèze

2007   From 2014
Medium-full colour. Ripe, succulent nose. Fresh, charming with no lack of depth and style. Medium-full body. Good grip. Lots of vigour and definition for a 2007. Long, complex, and multidimensional. Will still improve. An excellent example of a 2007.

2006   From 2014
Medium-full colour, denser than the 2007. Quite a developed nose. But without the intensity of the above. Medium body. More succulence than the nose would suggest. No hard tannins. Nicely fresh and charming. Getting smooth and silky. Good depth and vigour. Ripe and seductive. Will still improve. Lovely.

2005   From 2020
Full, rich, immature colour. Ample, vigorous, quite powerful nose. Lots of depth and character here. A full wine; quite tannic but the tannins are very ripe. Excellent grip and vigour. Very profound. Very, very long. Real class. Great harmony and depth. Excellent.

2003   Now to 2018
Medium to medium-full colour. Some development. A touch pruney on the nose. Medium body. Not a great deal of backbone or complexity. Quite fresh. But somewhat one-dimensional.

2002   From 2016
Fullish colour. Fragrant, ripe, complex, classy nose. Medium-full body. Still adolescent. Rich,

full-bodied, and generous, but with very good grip. Just a little hard at the end. Still needs five years. Potentially splendid.

2001   Now to 2020
Good colour. Ripe, open, accessible, fresh, elegant nose. Medium to medium-full body. Soft. Lovely luscious, succulent fruit. Very fine indeed for the vintage and *à point* now.

2000   Now to 2016
Good colour for the vintage. Indeed a little more than the 2001. But more evolved on the nose. Slightly spicy. Quite mature. Even a little cooked. Medium body. Quite fresh but rather more one-dimensional than the 2001. Yet there is a classy, energetic follow-through. Better at the end than on the attack, and not short. Very fine for the vintage.

1999   Now to 2025
Full colour. Still immature. Lovely nose. Rich and smoky, with the flavours of a mature wine beginning to develop. Slight mocha touches. Even a touch gamey. Full-bodied, vigorous, and complex. Ample, rich, and very well balanced. This bottle is a little more evolved than I had expected, but it is still lovely, if not great.

1998   Now to 2020 plus
Magnum. Good colour. Delicious nose. Cool, pure, and with very good acidity and very complex fruit. Medium-full body. Fresh and now *à point*. Subtle and very stylish. Fine plus.

1997   Now to 2015
Medium colour. Now mature. Soft, mellow, sightly spicy nose. Not the greatest of zip and class, but fresher than most. Medium body. Attractive fruit. But a soft, somewhat unenergetic finish. Very good indeed but not one of the best 1997s.

1996   Now to 2025 plus
Magnum. Full colour. Still very fresh. Much less advanced than the 1998. Fullish body. Still youthful. Only just about mature. Lots of depth and vigour. Rich. Indeed no leanness at all. Fuller than the 1998. Just a little more austere, but fine plus. Will last well.

1995 From 2014

Magnum. Full, rich, youthful colour. The nose is still quite firm. But balanced, rich, and full of depth and interest. Full body. The tannins are beginning to mellow but needs to soften further. Plenty of vigour. High-class fruit. Lovely long finish. Excellent.

1993 Now to 2021

Fullish colour. Now mature. Mellow nose. Intriguingly aromatic. Much more evolved than the 1995. Medium-full body. Good grip. Not a very structured example. No great dimension or concentration. Fragrant and stylish but lacks a bit of vigour on the follow-through. Fine but not great.

1991 Now to 2019

Medium-full, fully mature colour. Slightly austere but complex nose. Medium weight. Ripe, aromatic. Soft mellow tannins. This is most attractive and yet another example of how well this at the start much maligned vintage has turned out.

Domaine Dujac

MOREY-SAINT-DENIS

UNLIKE MOST Burgundian estates, whether they have been bottling for a number of decades or only embarked on this path recently, the Domaine Dujac is a recent creation. It dates from 1968. Jacques Seysses, the founder, is in his early seventies and has now taken a back seat in favour of his sons Jeremy and Alec and Jeremy's wife, Diana, a trained wine chemist (oenologue). They have been working as a trio now for a few vintages. Have things changed? Should we expect more radical differences in the wines to come compared with the Dujacs of old? I went up to Morey-Saint-Denis to find out.

Jacques Seysses's father, a rich man in charge of a firm who made biscuits, was a well-known connoisseur of food and wine, at home in three-star restaurants, with a fine cellar of his own. Jacques remembers as a teenager visits to three-star restaurants in Paris and elsewhere. "I can't tell you exactly what was the first great bottle of wine I had," he says. "But it was most likely a Rousseau or a Gouges from one of the great vintages we had immediately after the war. What I do recall was a visit to La Tour d'Argent. My father selected a bottle of La

Tâche 1938 (not a great vintage). It was almost rosé in colour. Our guests were rather shocked. But the aroma and intensity of this wine was remarkable. This must have been in 1958 or so, when I was seventeen. I remember my father ordered that the rest of the stock be reserved for himself."

Jacques tried banking and working in the biscuit business. But his heart was in wine. (Though, to tell the truth, having had ambitions to be an actor when he was fifteen, he would also have liked to become an architect—but this is in retrospect). He spent two years in Burgundy learning the ropes. Land at the time was cheap. Seysses *père* had been an initial investor in the Domaine Pousse d'Or, when it was set up in 1964. They found a run-down property in Morey-Saint-Denis. The first vintage was not the 1968. The wines were too poor to bottle themselves. It was 1969 that the Domaine Dujac arrived on the market. Vines elsewhere were acquired, and within a few years the domaine measured 11.5 hectares spread over eleven different appellations, a typically Burgundian morcellation. With the help of father's entrées into the nation's top restaurants, the Dujac wines soon began to be noticed. Jacques has never had much problem selling his crop.

Jacques remembers the first time the American merchant Colonel Frederick Wildman came to call. "He was a gaunt, rather frightening old man. He didn't say much. And I thought the wines weren't showing very well that day. He tasted around the cellar in complete silence, and, not hearing any grunts of approval, I was beginning to think: well, that's it. He doesn't like the wine. And then suddenly he said: 'I'll take the lot!' I was stunned. But I didn't want to put all my eggs in the one basket, so I said: 'I'll sell you half.'" It was the beginning of a fruitful partnership. Wildmans would represent Dujac in the United States for the next twenty years.

"So, who helped you make the wine in the early stages?" I ask. "Gérard Potel, of the Pousse d'Or; certainly Aubert de Villaine of the Domaine de la Romanée-Conti, but perhaps most importantly, Charles Rousseau of Domaine Armand Rousseau. I soon began to realise the importance of the attention to detail in the vineyard: training high, to maximize efficient photosynthesis, hoeing and ploughing as much as possible, reducing the potential yield from the beginning, and so on. A lot of replanting was necessary." Originally Jacques Seysses was a great believer in clones. He's less convinced now, and he can make his own selection *"massalle"* from the best of his own old vines. At vintage time he soon decided to employ a large number of people to collect the fruit. "They can take more time, and the *triage* (sorting through to eliminate the substandard) is more efficient." In the winery, following the Domaine de la Romanée-Conti, Seysses vinified with all the stems, and matured his wine in new oak, but bottled quite early.

Jacques and his attractive American wife, Rosalind—she came over to work the vintage and never went back—have three children: Jeremy (born 1975) and Alec (born 1977), both involved in the business, and their younger brother, Paul, who runs an embryonic chain of restaurants in Burgundy called My Wok. Both Jeremy and Alec went to university in England—Jeremy to University Collge, Oxford, Alec to the London School of Economics. While working at Mondavi, Jeremy met his future wife, Diana, a Davis graduate, whose family owns the Snowden winery up in the hills above Rutherford in the Napa Valley. She is now the winemaker at the Domaine Dujac, and they have two boys: Aubert (born 2007) and Blaise (born 2009). Whose wines are their yardsticks? I asked Jeremy and Alec. Frédéric Mugnier and Christophe Roumier, they both echoed, and Jean-Marc Roulot for his whites. I was rather dismayed when Jeremy declared that his first remarkable bottle memory was a Château Guiraud 1975. By no means a great wine, in my view! But apparently Jacques had bought quite a lot of it, and it was always wheeled out on birthdays. Jeremy was on more comfortable ground with his recollection of the bottles for his twenty-first: Bâtard-Montrachet 1976 from Ramonet and 1966 La Tâche. Diana's most impressive early wine is a 1993 Aroujo Cabernet, which I confess I have never sampled.

So. Who is in charge now, and has anything radical been changed? "It is a triumviate," says Jeremy, "plus Jacques as the Wise Old Man in the background. Diana makes the wine. But otherwise all three of us are involved in the cellar. Alec is in charge of the picking team and the logistics of the vintage—the vineyard manager is Lilian Robin—while I am more responsible for the commercial side, the allocations and so on. But I decide on the date of the harvest."

Nothing has fundamentally altered as far as the winemaking is concerned, but there have been some subtle changes. "I feel," says Jeremy, "that hitherto our wines were more 'Dujac' than Chambolle, Gevrey, or Morey. We are trying to make the family signature less instantly obvious." Partly, I suggest, this is because under Jacques it was always 100 whole clusters and 100 percent new wood. Since 1999, the domaine destems on occasion. The cellar is now permanently air-conditioned, so is a little cooler, and as a result the malo-lactics are later. This, plus the fact that in the new, enlarged cellar, half the fermentations take place in concrete vats, which retain heat—though it is the later malos which have the greatest influence—results in more colour in the wines than hitherto. The youngest wines, and the village examples are destemmed a little more, and of course see less new oak. "The origins of the wines necessitate us to change our techiques," says Jeremy. "For instance, I find that totally whole cluster fruit doesn't work as well in Gevrey than in the villages further south. However, if we had a parcel where there was lots of *millerandage*, we would not destem at all.

"We tend to add nearly all the press wine; keep the wines on their fine lees a year; then rack—as much to liberate excess carbon dioxide as for any other reason; and bottle in February and March. Getting back to the amount of new oak, we normally now use 40 percent for the village wines, 60 to 80 for the *premiers crus,* up to 100 for the *grands crus.* The tendency is that we use less new oak in the riper vintages, where there is less malo-lactic, more in those less fortunate." But then Jeremy points out that you have to order your casks early, well in advance of the vintage, at a time when you might have no idea whether your vintage is going to be generous or not. And you can't leave a cask unused.

In 2005, Jacques and Jeremy were approached by Etienne de Montille. Through his banking connections—he used to be a merchant banker before returning to Burgundy to take over the family estate on a full-time basis (he also runs the Château de Puligny-Montrachet)—Etienne had heard that the Domaine Charles Thomas was for sale. It was an undertaking he couldn't afford on his own. Were the Seysses interested in sharing the estate? They were. So the Thomas vineyard holdings were acquired and shared, with Dujac basically taking over the northern end, chiefly Romanée-Saint-Vivant, Chambertin, Vosne-Romanée, Les Beaumonts, and a large slice of Vosne-Romanée, Les Malconsorts. Some of these are owned and leased back by outsiders, such as Wilfred Jaeger in

the Romanée-Saint-Vivant. A few lesser parcels were disposed of to help finance the deal, and the first vintage was 2005. The Dujac domaine now covers 15.25 hectares. Hence the extention to the cellar.

The Dujac style has always been one of great elegance and purity, wines of poise and balance, and this has been enhanced of late, as much because the average age of the vines has increased as to any nuancing of the winemaking processes. Though not biodynamic, the viticulture is, and always has been, firmly ecological. Judging by the 2005s and most of the vintages since—though I am rather suspicious about the 2006s (the Clos de la Roche as well as the Clos-Saint-Denis)—the wines are even better than they used to be. What I like about them is that they are always ripe, fresh, and fragrant without ever hinting at excess acidity. This is one of the great Burgundy domaines.

I have been fortunate in the past to have participated in at least three important vertical tastings of Dujac Clos de la Roche, so this time I opted for Clos-Saint-Denis. Before we sat down to taste, I asked Jeremy how he would describe the difference between these two adjacent *climats.*

"Aromatically they are both unmistakably Morey-Saint-Denis," Jeremy began. "That is there are suggestions of nutmeg and cinnamon to go with the cherry-raspberry-strawberry. But texturally they are quite different. Clos de la Roche [where the Dujacs have 1.95 hectares in six parcels with an overall average age of forty-five to fifty years] has more structure, more tannin, and is generally more masculine. There is a minerally graphite aspect I don't find in Clos-Saint-Denis.

"In the Clos-Saint-Denis [1.45 hectares in two parcels; also an average age of forty-five to fifty years], the silky tannins are first and foremost. There is intensity without weight. Texturally there are similarities with Chambolle but in character our Clos-Saint-Denis is quite different. There are aromatic fireworks to be found and a 'peacock's tail' as the wine opens out in the mouth that I find most appealing."

TASTING NOTES

I sampled the following wines in May 2011.

Clos-Saint-Denis

2009   From 2022

Full colour. Impressive nose. Ripe, succulent, profound, classy, and gently oaky. Fullish body. Very classy tannins. Very good grip. Ample and rich and complex. Lots of finesse. Very fine.

2008   From 2020

Medium to medium-full colour. I expected a bit more. A touch of austerity on the nose. More substance than the colour would suggest. More generous on the palate. Medium-full body. Very good tannins and grip. A lovely, subtle combination of fruit and acidity. Lots of originality. Long and very stylish. Very fine for the vintage.

2007   From 2015

Medium colour. Generous nose. Showing no weakness. Ripe, fruity, and positive. Medium body. Fresh and stylish. Balanced and attractive if no real depth. Good finish. Will be ready quite soon. Fine for the vintage.

2006   From 2016

Fullish colour. More than the 2008. Not a lot on the nose at first. But more character on the palate. There is fresh fruit here but at the same time an astringent touch. Decent acidity nevertheless. Medium-full body. But it is an unrelaxed, somewhat four-square wine, lacking style and grace.

2005   From 2017

Full, immature colour. Lovely nose. Quite marked by the new wood. But rich, concentrated, and potentially voluptuous. Full body. Still firm. But now beginning to soften up. Splendid rich fruit. Lots of energy. Complex, harmonious, and very high-class. Excellent.

2002   From 2014

Medium to medium-full colour. Fully mature. Some evolution on the nose. Fresh, ripe, and quite rich; with very good grip. Essentially gentle on the attack now. More vigour and depth on the aftertaste. Lots of class. Yet a bit more forward than many at this level. Lovely.

1999   Now to 2025 plus

Fullish colour. Just beginning to show signs of maturity. Open, accessible, plump nose. Medium-full body. Just about ready. Very fresh. Complex and ample. Composed and harmonious. Perhaps not the greatest power and vigour and concentration, but long on the palate and a most delicious bottle.

1998   Now to 2020

Fullish colour: identical to the 1999. Cooler and less ample on the nose. Medium-full body. On the palate the wine is plump and attractive, but there is less to it than the above. Most enjoyable nevertheless. And *à point* now.

1996   Now to 2020 plus

Medium to medium-full, mature colour. Fresh, complex nose, with a bit more of the stems apparent than most. This is because the fruit is less ample here. On the palate quite full. Certainly vigorous. Interesting sweet-sour flavours. Good grip. Riper than the nose would suggest. Good long finish. Fine.

1995   Now to 2025 plus

Fullish mature colour. Rich, fresh, quite sturdy nose. Plenty of depth and vigour. Fullish and youthful on the palate. Very good energy and grip. Ripe tannins. Fresh, plump, complex, and full of character. Plenty of backbone. Much more complete than the 1996. Good creamy-rich finish. Very fine.

1993   Now to 2025

Medium-full, mature colour. Less weight than the 1995 on the nose. But ripe and round, classy and complex. Medium-full body. Good fruit. Very good acidity. Not as profound as the 1995, but very long and subtle. Lovely.

1991   Now to 2018

Full vigorous colour. Lovely nose. Roses and slight herbal fragrances. Good weight and depth behind it. Medium body. Now beginning to lose its energy at the end. But fresh and balanced and stylish and still with life. Fine, especially for the vintage.

1990   Now to 2020

Medium-full colour. Fully mature. Soft, rich, very Dujac nose. Medium-full body. Alive and complex and *à point*. Less volume than many 1990s at this level, but plenty of depth, vigour, and finesse. Now more than fully ready. Lovely finish.

1985   Now to 2020

Medium-full colour. Fully mature. Aromatic nose. Fresh and concentrated. But gamey nonetheless. A fullish wine which is a little less fresh and has a little less acidity than the 1990.

But it is sweeter and more seductive. Splendidly classy and harmonious. Very lovely.

1980   Drink soon

Medium-full colour. Fully mature. Smoky, oaky nose with a hint of bonfires on the nose. This is now beginning to show a bit of age on the palate. Medium body. Still sweet but geting a little ungainly with suggestions of astringency. Was a fine wine in its prime.

1978   Will still keep

Medium-full colour. Fully mature. Lovely nose. Aromatic, ripe, mature, complex, and vigorous. Lots of depth and interest. This is really fine. Medium-full body. Very fine grip. Excellent fruit. A real treat.

Domaine Fourrier

GEVREY-CHAMBERTIN

SOME FIFTEEN YEARS AGO, when I was composing my book *Côte d'Or*, I commented on the Fourrier domaine. Jean-Marie Fourrier had recently taken over from his father, Jean-Claude. Changes for the better were in progress. I said, in effect, that this was a domaine to watch. A decade further on, in *The Wines of Burgundy*, I gave the domaine two stars: "There are brilliant wines here." Recent visits, culminating with a vertical tasting of his *premier cru* Champeaux, and a comparative tasting of the five Clos-Saint-Jacques, has clearly shown that this accolade is truly merited. The Fourrier estate is one of the very best in Burgundy.

The history begins in the 1930s and 1940s with Fernand Pernot, a *celebataire* whose sister had married a Fourrier. Vineyard plots came from both sides, including a 26 ares parcel of Griotte-Chambertin, and, in 1955, 89 ares of Clos-Saint-Jacques, following the death of the Comte de Moucheron. The wines were sold as Pernot-Fourrier, and I have some fond memories of the wines of the period. Pernot, it would seem, almost forced his nephew, Jean-Claude Fourrier, to take over responsibil-

ity for the estate as he grew older, and it was the latter who ran the domaine from 1969, with Pernot passing away in 1981. Additions to the property arrived from Fourrier's wife's side. She is the daughter of Georges Bryczek of Morey-Saint-Denis.

Under Jean-Claude, it has to be said, the wines were not brilliant. I first arrived to taste in the autumn of 1986. Fourrier's cellar was "damp and dirty and contained little evidence of new wood." He'd bought a couple of new casks recently, but these were the first since 1977. He believed in "long fermentations, to extract plenty of *matière*," and bottled after twenty-two months or more. Some good wines, I commented. A year later I was distinctly underwhelmed by his 1986s, and I put the domaine aside to give me the time to go and see others.

I returned in 1994, having perhaps heard through the grapevine that Jean-Marie was taking over. I saw signs which encouraged me to continue to visit. I have been tasting there ever since. Jean-Claude, it would seem, was not a happy *vigneron*. His own father had died young, affixiated in a *cuve* at vintage time. He had been forced into the role by his uncle, and then been the subject of bad notes from Robert Parker, which resulted in his being abandoned by his U.S. importer. He was only too happy to hand over the responsibility to his son Jean-Marie as soon as he could.

Jean-Marie was born in 1971. On either side of his military service, having qualified as a pilot on his seventeenth birthday—his parents forbade him to drive a car—he completed an internship with Henri Jayer and then with Domaine Drouhin in Oregon. He obviously—as do so many of his contemporaries—reveres the name of Jayer. "What did you learn from the great man?" I asked. Only to be told that one of his first tasks was to go out and apply herbicides to the vineyards, and another was to scrub down the vats with bleach—but then to wash off the bleach with tartaric acid. Moreover, he told me, Jayer criticised him for cleaning the press in the middle of the harvest. There was no need to do this until all the pressings had been completed. And this was in the early 1990s!

Jean-Marie had started to work with his father in 1989 and took over completely in 1994. One of the first things he did was to bottle at eighteen months or so, rather than after two years as his father had done. Another was to reduce the yields. A third was to isolate the Gevrey *premiers crus* and bottle them separately. There are four of them, as well as the Clos-Saint-Jacques. More fine-tuning followed. The vineyards are ploughed. There is a vibrating sorting table. A new vinification cellar with stainless steel vats, which correspond to the volumes of the parcels and is air-conditioned so that there is a constant temperature of 15°C both inside and outside the vats, followed in 2007. "This preserves the aromas in the wine." And much else besides.

Let him speak for himself: "I find that my way of doing things—not forcing the extraction, not raising the temperature at the end of the fermentation, retaining the carbon dioxide, not over-oaking—results in nobler tannins and fresher and more sophisticated fruit." There is total destemming—he tried using some of the stems in 1995 but was dissatisfied with the results. "It may work for Vosne-Romanée but it doesn't work with Gevrey-Chambertin: the tannins can be a bit too hard." The temperatures are allowed to rise to 33°C after a short, natural period of cold-soaking. "One should leave the wine to start its fermentation naturally. If one forces the cold-soaking, one has to add too much sulphur dioxide." There are two *pigeages* but no pumping-over. "Why pump the wine if one doesn't have to? One should respect the solid matter as much as the liquid." And overall a minimal use of sulphur and 20 percent new oak. Since the 2005 vintage, he has waxed the necks of the bottles and ceased the use of corks treated with peroxide, to reduce the risk of premature oxidation.

In the vineyard Fourrier can profit from the largely venerable age of his vines (the Clos-Saint-Jacques dates from 1910), and he uses his the best of own plants for his *massale* selection, convinced that these are far superior than clones. The date of the harvest is dependent on the phenolic ripeness rather than the sugar levels.

The result is precision. And since 2004, even greater quality than before, as the notes below amply demonstrate. There are very lovely wines at the Fourrier domaine today. Jean-Marie Fourrier, now rising forty, is a quietly composed individual, clearly a thinker as well as a doer. There is no bombast. Just a gentle confidence. He is married to a charming and very attractive English lady, Vicki, and they have two children, Louis and Lucie.

The Fourrier domaine occupies 9 hectares, and this is made up as follows:

Griotte-Chambertin (26 ares).

Gevrey-Chambertin, Clos-Saint-Jacques (89 ares).

Other Gevrey *premiers crus*: Champeaux, Cherbaudes, Combe Aux Moines, and Goulots.

Morey-Saint-Denis, *premier cru* Clos Sorbès.

Chambolle-Musigny, *premier cru* Les Greunchers.

Vougeot, *premier cru* Les Petits Vougeots.

Village Gevrey-Chambertin: Including the *lieu-dit* Aux Echézeaux; village Morey-Saint-Denis; and village Chambolle-Musigny.

TASTING NOTES

I sampled the following vintages of Jean-Marie Fourrier's Gevrey-Chambertin, Les Champeaux in January 2011.

2009   From 2020 plus
Bottled eight days previously. Despite this, the wine shows very well indeed. Good colour. Full, ample nose. Rich, quite structured. Fat and classy. Full-bodied. Some tannin. And the tannins are very rich and ripe. Very good grip. Lots of depth and energy. Lovely long finish. This is fine.

2008   From 2018
Good colour. Really quite rich and succulent on the nose. An excellent result. Full and fresh and classy. Not quite as rich and opulent as the 2009. The acidity is more apparent. But medium-full bodied, with good tannins, and a lovely, long finish. This will get more and more generous as it develops.

2007   From 2014
Medium-full colour. Soft cedary-oaky nose. Medium weight. Balanced. But quite forward, without a great deal of tannin. But fresh enough, juicy, and nice and ripe. Finishes positively. Will come forward quite soon. Lots of charm here.

2006   From 2016
A little more colour than the 2007. Good nose. Plenty of class and depth. Not too adolescent, but an absence of real richness. Balanced though, and no lack of finesse. Fullish body. Good tannins. Richer on the palate than the nose would suggest. Ripe, harmonious, and even complex at the end. Very good finish. Fine for the vintage.

2005   From 2017
Full colour. Lovely fragrant nose. Not a blockbuster but very stylish, very harmonious, and very intense. On the palate more backbone and more tannin than the nose suggested. Very lovely succulent fruit. Ripe tannins. Lots of energy and class. Very fine.

2004   Now to 2020
Good colour. A slight touch of reduction at first, but this blew off. Medium body. Attractive ripe fruit if not the finesse of recent vintages. Now just about ready. More substance than the 2007. Good positive, ample, ripe follow-through. Generous for a 2004 and a fine result.

2003   Now to 2018
Good but not monstrous colour. Ripe, spicy, somewhat caramelised nose, but reasonable freshness and style. Medium-full body. The tannins are now soft. The wine is very ripe, with somewhat burned and cooked flavours. No real class but reasonably fresh. Very good plus for the vintage. But I much prefer the 2004.

2002   Now to 2020 plus
Fullish colour. Fragrant nose. Softer and not quite as rich or as intense as the 2005. Not quite as classy either. Medium-full body. This is now getting soft. Only a little unresolved tannin. Balanced. Good energy and depth. Fine but not as sophisticated or as profound as the wines of today.

2000   Now to 2015
Light, mature colour. Very soft nose. Not a great deal of wine here. Reasonably fresh but rather one-dimensional. Easy to drink and charming nonetheless.

1999   Now to 2020
Medium-full mature colour. Attractive nose. Ripe and succulent. Just about ready. Medium to medium-full body. Fresh. Not the greatest depth or vigour, but balanced and most enjoyable. Very good indeed for the vintage.

1998   Now to 2016
Medium colour. Open, charming nose. No great concentration but fruity and attractive. Medium weight. No real backbone. Fully ready. Decent attack but then it tails off just a bit. Very good for the vintage.

Domaine Jean-Nöel Gagnard

CHASSAGNE-MONTRACHET

THE COMMUNE of Chassagne-Montrachet contains some 380 hectares of vineyard (I'm excluding the generic wine) of which 160 hectares or so are *premier cru* and 10 *grand cru*. This is much larger than Puligny, though not as extensive as Meursault. Moreover, in Chassagne, as opposed to Puligny, there is a greater proportion of important self-sufficient wine estates and most of these produce very good wine. One of those with the highest reputation is that of Jean-Noël Gagnard. The wines have been very good for a long time. With a recent extension to the winery and the arrival of daughter Caroline Lestimé in the mid-1990s, further progress has been made. Today the quality is indubitably fine. This is one of the best estates in the commune.

Everybody, it seems, is related to everybody else in Chassagne. If you are not called Morey, or Pillot, or Colin or Gagnard, you are almost certainly related to someone who is. Caroline's cousins, Laurence and Claudine, are married to Richard Fontaine and Jean-Marc Blain. Her paternal great grandfather was a Coffinet. All these are, or were, wine domaines. The original Gagnards, however, were not in the wine-making business. Neither are Caroline's late mother's family, though from nearby in Arnay le Duc.

Jean-Noël Gagnard was born in 1926, his brother, the late Jacques, father of Laurence and Claudine, in 1928. The brothers inherited an estate from the Coffinet side of the family and divided it between themselves in 1960. Caroline, Jean-Noël's daughter, was born in 1966, went to a business school in Paris, then to the Lycée Viticole de Beaune, started work alongside her father in 1989, and began taking charge a few years later. "My first red wine vintage was the 1991. I took over responsibility for the white wines as well the same year." At about this time she married Hubert Lestimé, a Parisian engineer who had graduated from the École Polytechnique, and they now have two boys, Nicolas (born 1996) and Philippe (born 1998).

The Jean-Noël Gagnard estate today measures some 11 hectares, the majority producing white wine. Pride of place is a 36 ares parcel of Bâtard-Montrachet, half of a segment which runs down from the road which separates Bâtard from Montrachet itself, just on the Chassagne side, acquired by an ancestor, Ferdinand Coffinet-Paquelin, in 1892. According to Jasper Morris, there was a Charles Paquelin who kept a *vigneron*'s diary during the French Revolution. This parcel was divided between Jean-Noël and Jacques in 1960. There is just over a hectare (1.06) of Caillerets, perhaps Chassagne's best white wine *premier cru*. The remaining first-growth vines are in Morgeots (32 ares), La Boudriotte (48 ares), La Maltroie (29 ares), Clos de Maltroye (converted from Pinot Noir to Chardonnay in 1990) (34 ares), and Champs-Gain (23 ares), south of the village, plus Chenevottes (49 ares), Blanchots-Dessus (13 ares), and the most recent addition, Chaumées (59 ares), on the northern side. Single vineyard white village wines come from Les Masures (61 ares), Les Chaumes (29 ares), Pot Bois (from 2009) (13 ares), and a parcel of very well-situated vines next to the Château de Chassagne-Montrachet (first harvest 2012) (44 ares). The red wine *premiers crus* consist of Clos-Saint-Jean (recently replanted, so currently young vines) (33 ares), Morgeot (78 ares), and Clos des Tavannes (30 ares) in Santenay. In addition, there are 78 ares of red village Chassagne, bottled as "Lestimé" ("esteemed," a play on her surname).

Recent acquisitions include several parcels of Bourgogne Hautes Côtes de Beaune in La Rochepot which produce a white wine; Sous Eguison, bottled with a screw cap; and a sparkling Cremant de Bourgogne, Blanc de Noir, vintaged since 2008.

Since she has taken over responsibility for the estate, Caroline has gradually expanded her domaine, vinified and bottled all of the first growths separately, improved the *matériel* in the cellar, and engaged Claude Bourgignon as viticultural consultant. For the past ten years the wines have been ploughed, and the vineyard has been *biologique* since 2008. The domaine, controlled by Exocert, is in its second year of certification.

For some reason, though it is now increasingly commonplace in Puligny and Meursault, those in Chassagne mainly bottle after a year rather than later. Not here. The lesser wines are bottled after twelve to fifteen months, the more important after even more months in cask.

After pressing and *débourbage* (allowing the gross lees to settle out), the white wine is fermented in cask, some 25 percent of which is new. The *cave* is not warmed to facilitate the malo, and the wine kept in barrel until blended together before bottling.

A new *cuverie*, installed in 1997, has facilitated the vinification of the reds. Formerly the cellar was cramped. There was not the room above the tanks to enable the *chapeau* of skins and so on to be trodden down. Now there is both *pigeage* and *remontage* (pumping-over). There is a longish *cuvaison*, the grapes having been destemmed, at temperatures of up to 33°C, and the wines are then held in cask (25 percent new again) before bottling, for about twelve to fifteen months. This is classic winemaking, no artificial yeasts, no enzymes; the wine is allowed to make itself.

This is not to suggest there is anything lackadaisical about Caroline Lestimé's attitude. Under the pretty, blonde exterior, there is a woman of intelligence and determination. You feel she might be a hard taskmaster. There are two full-time workers on the estate: a *tâcheronne* (one who works by the job rather than by the hour) plus a part-time girl. Hubert Lestimé works most of the week in Paris but is back in Chassagne at weekends and over vintage time.

"Your cousins," I once said to Caroline, "married *vignerons*. Was this the way you envisaged things when you were younger?" "No," she replied. "This job just seemed the natural thing to do. I was the only child. And it interested me."

The wines have steadily improved throughout the last couple of decades, from what was already a very high level, as the tasting notes below show. They are purer. There is more concentration. There is more definition. I have been enjoying them for as long as I can remember. They are now better than ever.

Caroline Lestimé is a regular attendee at

the ten-year-on tasting, usually supplying her Caillerets or her Bâtard. While I have certainly had one or two prematurely oxidised bottles from here, it is literally only one or two.

TASTING NOTES

I sampled the following vintages of Bâtard-Montrachet in Beaune in December 2011.

2009   From 2019
Bottled February 2011. Quite a delicate nose. But ripe, balanced, stylish, and very gently oaky. Fullish on the palate. Good vigour and intensity. Very good grip. Lovely fruit. Poised, long, and harmonious. Very fine.

2008   From 2015
Lovely fruit on the nose. Unexpectedly ripe for a 2008 in a Granny Smith apple sort of way. But quite broad and evolved on the palate. Good grip and depth but not the greatest of finesse.

2007   From 2017
Round nose. Ripe, ample, and with a touch of spice. Well-balanced. Medium-full weight. Soft, harmonious, and very stylish on the follow-through. Lots of fruit and class. Rather better than the 2008.

2006   From 2016
The nose has a hint of good rich gravy—but in a good sense. Fullish, ripe, and spicy. On the palate there is more weight here than in the 2007. More vigour but not as fresh or as elegant. Very good indeed nevertheless. Clean and poised and still youthful.

2004   Now to 2019
From a magnum. Fresh, quite delicate but stylish on the nose. Good fruit. No great weight or power but certainly complex and with good grip. Medium to medium-full weight. Good finish. Fine.

2002   Now to 2017
From a magnum. Quite an evolved colour. But the nose is still quite youthful. Fullish body. This is rather more advanced than many 2002s at this level. Decent fruit and grip. But not the vigour and quality of fruit I had hoped for. A bit of a disappointment. I prefer the 2004.

2000   Now to 2018
Some evolution on the colour. Rich, ample, honeyed, but not really oxidised on the nose. This is a most attractive mature wine. Fullish, very ripe, but good acidity. Touches of gingerbread. Lots of charm. Nice and fresh at the end. Very good indeed.

1999   Now to 2020 plus
From a magnum. Good fresh colour. Plenty of wine here and lots of depth and high quality. Still youthful. Ripe, fresh, complex, relaxed nose. Lovely harmonious fruit. This is fullish, profound, and very, very long and classy. Brilliant.

1998   Now to 2020
Very fresh colour. The nose likewise still very fresh. Ripe, profound, harmonious, and very classy. Fullish body, rich, and very vigorous. This is even better than the 1999. Real class. Very lovely fruit. Bravo!

1996   Now to 2017
Quite an evolved colour. Some evolution on the nose but not unduly so. Ripe, balanced, and attractive on both nose and palate. Fullish. Good grip. Plenty of ripe, succulent fruit. Complex finish. Fine.

1986   Past its best
The colour is almost orange. Old rather than oxidised. Still a little pleasure to be had. But fading. Was a lightish, classy, fruity wine in its prime.

Domaine Grivot

VOSNE-ROMANÉE

I DON'T LIKE half bottles: stupid size. Not nearly enough for one—let alone two. But for some reason, lurking about in the Château Coates cellar, I owned a half of the Domaine Grivot's Clos de Vougeot 1964. Eventually I opened it at the end of a boozy dinner. My friend said she'd take half a glass up to bed with her. I finished the washing up and relaxed with the rest. It was delicious.

Etienne Grivot disagrees. He was born in 1959, and it never occurred to him that his role in life was not to follow his father, Jean, into the family domaine. But as he grew up, drinking the occasional bottle from years like 1929 and 1937, and wines from the great vintages immediately after the Second World War, he began to realise that the wines the Grivot domaine was producing in the 1960s and 1970s were a shadow of their former selves.

Why? Because they were over-fertilising the vineyards, and as a teacher demonstrated to Etienne when he was doing his studies in the late 1970s (first a BT [*brevet technique*] in general agriculture, and then a BTS [superior] in viticulture and oenology), the soil in Burgundy was becoming increasingly incapable of producing *vins de terroir*, wines which had the magic character and flavour concentration of where they come from.

The origins of the Grivot family lie in the upper reaches of the river Doubs, 100 kilometres to the east in the Jura, but Grivots have been established in Burgundy since the French Revolution. At first they lived in Nuits-Saint-Georges, farming vines at Arcenats in the Hautes-Côtes and at Corgoloin, but raising other crops as well. A branch then moved to Vosne-Romanée and slowly but surely the activities of this side of the family concentrated on wine production. Gaston Grivot, son of Joseph and father of Jean, sold his vines in these lesser areas in 1919 in order to buy an important piece of Clos de Vougeot from an M. Polack. He was one of the first to pursue a proper oenological

---

This section is based on a piece I wrote for *Decanter Magazine* in 2006. That itself was based on articles I had written in *The Vine* in 2002 and 1993.

degree at the University of Burgundy in Dijon in the 1920s. And he had the foresight to marry Madelaine, daughter of Émile Grivot of Nuits-Saint-Georges, in 1927—no close relation, but surely a distant cousin—who brought vines in Pruliers and Roncières with her as a dowry.

Jean Grivot, the present head of the family, was born in 1928. He too studied at Dijon, married a Jayer, Yvonne, inheriting vines in Chambolle, Vosne-Romanée, Les Rouges, and Échézeaux from her and her sister Jacqueline, and, in 1984, acquired a parcel of land in Richebourg, formerly owned by the Vienot estate, dividing it with Jean Mongeard. The vines here were not in the most pefect of conditions. And it takes time to get them in order. But the majority of the vines date from the late 1930s. Since 2006, the vineyard, like other Grivot land in Vosne-Romanée has been ploughed by a horse, Pirate. See the tasting notes below. Little by little, therefore, a sizeable (by Burgundian standards) domaine has been created. There are currently 40 parcels of vines spread over 14.8 hectares. And twenty-two different wines. From 1959 all has been sold in bottle.

As early as 1978, Etienne persuaded his father to abandon chemical fertilisation. He didn't join the domaine until after he'd finished his military service in 1981. But right from the beginning, he persuaded Jean Grivot to let him take charge of at least one wine. Gradually over the decade he took over.

"I see the evolution of Domaine Grivot in four phases," he says. "Between 1982 and 1986 I forged my opinions. I talked and tasted with my friends and contemporaries, among them Dominique Lafon and Christophe Roumier. We were all in the process of taking over well-reputed estates, but we all felt we could and should improve things." It was at this period that he met Marielle Bize, the tall, elegant, slender, younger sister of Patrick, of Domaine Simon Bize in Savigny-Lès-Beaune. "Patrick," says Etienne, "asked if he could come to taste with a client. Later, I went back to sample his wines. I saw Marielle. 'This is the woman I want

to marry,' I said to myself." They were married in 1987 and have two children: Mathilde (born 1989), a horse rider, and Hubert (born in 1991), destined to take over, eventually, from his father.

Phase two begins with his introduction to Guy Accad. "Accad was incompetent as a communicator, rude and ungainly as an individual, but a genius when it came to soil analysis and what was vital to do to regenerate the life therein: how to persuade the vines to get the maximum out of their environment. He also had very definite views over vinification. And it is here that the controversy lies." It is difficult to appreciate today how original Guy Accad was at the time. Alongside Claude Bourguignon and his groundbreaking book *Le Sol, La Terre et Les Champs*, Accad was the first to demonstrate the importance of the vines' environment and the role it had to play.

But Accad was also a strong advocate of long, indeed prolonged, cold-soaking before vinification. This occurred naturally in the old days, when harvests took place in October, for the grapes were gathered at 10°C and it took a week for the fermentations to get under way. But it did not produce the succulent, juicy, easy-to-appreciate wines critics and buyers liked to find when they sampled them in cask, especially if you followed the Accad edict to block the onset of the fermentation for a week or more.

"My father was all in favour," says Etienne. "The wines I began to produce reminded him of those of his youth. I too was utterly convinced that my 1987s, not an easy vintage, were distinctly superior to most of my friends. But they tasted odd, different, and almost everyone found them un-Burgundian." He still rankles at what he sees as the unjust desertion he experienced following his first few Accad vintages, and the fact that he was left, as the most prominent Accadian, to justify all the Accad wines, good or bad. "In fact, I began to feel I was the only one making *bad* wine in the 1987–1992 period. We also lost three-quarters of our clients." He continues: "Gradually I began to modify, to take the best of Accad (we are still friends, and I would trust no one else to do my soil analysis) and jettison the rest. I wanted the liberty to make Grivot wines, not Accad wines. This began in 1993."

The fourth phase followed on logically. In 1998, Etienne began to make somewhat more generous wines. "It was I who had changed. I was approaching forty, more mature, more relaxed. The wines became more serene and supple, without compromising their freshness and potential to age, because I was more at ease." He began vinifying at a slighly higher temperature, 31° rather than 28°C. The wines became less monolithic. "Let the wine make itself, particularly in the better years." And (which we didn't touch on) because a decade of Accad techniques in the vineyard was now resulting in better fruit from more "grown-up" vines. Gradually he ceased the use of insecticides and herbicides. Gradually the domaine became totally biological. Since then, the Grivot wines have been truly excellent.

It was with the 1998 vintage, coincidentally, that the Institute of Masters of Wine in London commenced an annual Burgundy tasting sponsored by the Domaines Familiaux et Tradition, a group of top estates. Grivot sends along his Vosne-Romanée, Les Beaumonts, and sometimes something else. It is consistently among the top-three wines on the table.

What of the future? "One is never satisfied. This is an obsession: to improve. And I don't think I will ever give up. I certainly don't have to for many, many years. I'm hardly fifty. And Hubert is still a young man. Like me, he is assuming that one day he will take over. But nobody's forcing anything on him." He continues: "But we all need changes. Changes of scene and occupation. I need freshness. I'm a very curious person. I don't understand those of my colleagues who never take a holiday. That's absurd. We go to Canada [the Grivots have a house on Lake Masson, about an hour away from Montreal] every summer for three or four weeks. One gets back regenerated." He also flies helicopters.

"Do I have a philosophy of wine? Let's make a parallel. *Terroir* is like what a composer of music has created. The winemaker is like the conductor. You have fine *terroirs*, like great pieces of music. But you need a fine interpreter. In fact, being a winemaker has a lot in common with being a conductor. Though I wouldn't describe myself as especially passionate about music, I would like to have been a conductor. The power of being in charge intrigues me.

"As far as winemaking is concerned, I'm looking for harmony and balance: freshness is primordial. I don't want wines which are too spontaneous. I like a wine which is slow to develop. What I have learned over the years is that some vintages need fermenting at a different temperature to others." He says, "At Domaine Grivot we destem 100 percent; we've had a sorting table since 2000; there is cold-soaking, but not in such an exaggerated way as before; we use anything from 20 to 80 percent new oak; in our cold cellars the malos are often late to complete; and we bottle after eighteen months without fining—except on the rare occasions when it is necessary—and, since 1988, without filtration. Are we late or early pickers? Neither. I pick when I think it is the right time. But I hate *sur-matirité*. What my neighbours do doesn't concern me. My 1997s are very fine because I picked very early, to preserve the freshness."

Etienne Grivot is tall and fit, an attractive-looking man, gently greying, intelligent and thoughtful. (In the 1980s I wrote a piece on Vosne-Romanée growers for an American wine magazine, *Wine News*. Etienne was featured on the cover. He received several proposals of marriage!) This Grivot is not, you would think, easily aroused (which is not for a minute to suggest he lacks passion. He's just got it under control). He only once got really belligerent during our conversation. Back in the early 1990s, as I knew, the Institut National des Appellations d'Origine (INAO) had asked him to experiment with a concentrating machine. What did he think of them? He is fundamentally against. "They destroy the harmony of the wines: all the wines taste the same; they are banal!"

I think there is now a fifth phase apparent at the Grivot domaine. The wines since 2005 or so are even more relaxed—less introverted, as Etienne would put it. And even more distinctive and profound.

The Grivot domaine currently includes the following:

Grands Crus Richebourg (32 ares); Clos de Vougeot (1.86 hectares); Echézeaux (85 ares).

Vosne-Romanée *Premier Cru*: In Les Beaumonts, Les Brulées, Les Chaumes, Les Reignots, Les Rouges, and Les Suchots.

Nuits-Saint-Georges *Premier Cru*: In Les Boudots, Les Pruliers, and Les Roncières.

Village Vosne-Romanée: Including Les Bossières.

Village Nuits-Saint-Georges: Including Les Charmots and Les Lavières.

Village Chambolle-Musigny La Combe d'Orveaux.

As I begin to take my leave, I ask him one more question. "Do you have a frustrated ambition, Etienne?" He thinks for a minute. "I would have liked to have been someone really famous."

But in the wine world you are, Etienne. You really are.

TASTING NOTES

The following tasting of the Domaine Grivot's Richebourg took place in Vosne-Romanée in February 2011, the day of Jean Grivot's eighty-third birthday.

2008   From 2020

Good colour. Slightly austere on the nose at present. But plenty of richness underneath. It will get more generous as it develops. No oak apparent. Full body. Ripe and succulent on the palate. Excellent grip. A noble wine. Lots of depth and real class. Excellent.

2007   From 2015

Good colour for the vintage. Ample, round, juicy nose with just a touch of new oak. Medium body. Soft, balanced, ripe, and most attractive. Long and already delicious. Plenty of intensity and lots of finesse for a 2007.

2006   From 2017

Very good colour for the vintage. Lovely rich, generous, very slightly oaky nose. Already most seductive. Fullish body. Some tannin. Very good grip. This has a definition missing in most 2006s, good as they may be. Lots of dimension. Very fine indeed for the vintage.

2005   From 2020

Excellent colour, still very youthful. Not too closed-in on the nose. Marvelously concentrated, intense, and vigorous. A really profound wine. Essence of Pinot. Full-bodied, subtle, multilayered, and splendidly classy. This is a great wine. Effortless harmony and a very lovely lingering finish.

2004   From 2014

Very good colour with just a hint of evolution. The nose is beginning to soften and show some of the spices of maturity. The tannins lack just a bit of class. Medium to medium-full body. Good acidity. Ripe but not that rich. Balanced but not velvety. Good energy though. This will soften well. Very fine for the vintage.

2003   From 2014

This has 14° plus of alcohol, while the rest of these Richebourgs are between 13.1° and 13.4°. Full, firm nose. Still very youthful. Splendidly fresh for a 2003. Only a bit of the cooked fruit of the vintage, and nothing pruney or Rhônish. Very impressive richness. Full body. Ripe tannins and very good acidity. Somewhat foursquare but elegant for a 2003, and long and positive at the end.

2002   From 2014

Medium-full colour. Now mature. Softer, more evolved, and less profound than I had expected on the nose. A little loose-knit for a 2002. Better on the palate. Lovely, elegant, harmonious, delicious fruit. Not the volume and backbone of the 2005, but very complex and with an excellent long finish.

2001   Now to 2020

Medium-full colour. Now mature. If anything a little more substance and vigour than the 2002. Soft, fragrant, fresh nose. Medium to medium-full body. Balanced, stylish, good intensity. Very long and complex. It shows the class of the *climat*. Lovely finish. Just about ready.

2000   Now to 2018

Good youthful colour for the vintage. But rather more evolved, less fresh, and less classy on the nose than the 2001. More vigorous on the palate than the nose would indicate. Medium body. Good grip. No great dimension but plenty of wine here. Long and satisfactory. Very fine indeed for the vintage.

1999   From 2017

Medium-full colour. Just about mature. Rich, ripe, ample, fragrant nose. Now getting soft, but no lack of vigour. Still a little adolescent on the palate. Quite a solid, four-squre and tannic attack. This needs time. At present it is not as relaxed as the wines of the next century. Yet the follow-through and finish are splendidly rich and concentrated. It just needs time.

1998   From 2014

Quite a full colour after the 1999: vigorous too. Full plump nose. No lack of depth and dimension here. Full body, especially for the vintage. Some tannin and these tannins are slightly more rigid than in the wines of today. Very good grip but a slight absence of real richness. I fear it will always lack a little generosity.

1997   Now to 2017

Very good full, youthful colour for the vintage. Ripe, soft, almost sweet nose. Etienne picked early, and it shows. Medium body. Very fresh. Very stylish. Not the greatest depth and dimension, or even class. But very fine for a 1997. Now *à point*.

1996   From 2014

Very full colour. Just a touch of brown at the rim. Splendid nose, full and rich, fat and generous. Fresh but absolutely no excess acidity. Full body. Some tannin. Still just a little rigid. Very good grip. Lots of wine here. It still needs to soften. But essentially very classy, very long, and lots of dimension. Perhaps in the long run it will be better than the 1995.

1995   Now to 2025 plus

Fullish, fresh colour. Very lovely, slightly gamey nose. Fresh, complex, profound, intense, and classy. Fullish body. A lot less rigid than the 1996. Lots of energy and depth. Harmonious and long on the palate. Rather more seductive than the 1996. Just about ready.

1994   Now to 2018

Medium-full colour. Still youthful. The nose is still fresh and classy if without great richness and dimension. But it's got a lot more to it than most. Indeed, a super example of the vintage. Fresh and stylish. Balanced and positive. Even complex. A really excellent 1994.

1993   Now to 2025 plus

Medium-full, mature colour. Supple, aromatic nose, beginning to show some of the flavours of maturity. Very relaxed and harmonious. Nothing rigid here. Medium-full body. Good grip. Complex fruit. Intense, classy and multidimensional. This is absolutely *à point*. Very fine indeed. Will keep very well.

1991   Now to 2020

Medium to medium-full colour. Fully mature. Not a wine of enormous weight and tannic structure, but fragrant and complex, supple and subtle. Fully evolved. Yet riper on the palate than on the nose. Very good follow-through. A delightful wine. Very lovely.

1990   Now to 2025

Full colour. Just about mature looking. Full, rich nose. A slight touch of burned sugar. But also a little rigid. On the palate full-bodied, rich, sweet but again a little clumsy. Plenty of depth, complexity, and richness on the follow-through. Sweeter and more structured than the 1993, but the 1993 has more class and harmony. This is a wine for food, like the 1996.

1989   Now to 2019
Medium to medium-full colour. Quite a lot of maturity. The nose is soft and mellow, gently plump. But not a great deal of freshness, fragrance, and intensity. Ripe and rich though and by no means short. On the palate fresher and more positive than on the nose. Delicious to drink if without the sheer class of the more recent vintages.

1988   Now to 2015
Medium-full colour. Still quite youthful. The nose is soft, with a taint of old vegetable soup. This was made under the Accad regime, and I remember the wine, still not having achieved its malo, being somewhat reduced and sulphury a year on. Does not lack interest but a gypsy of a wine.

1987   Drink soon
Fullish, mature colour. Seems to have more to it than the 1985. Classy nose. Ripe and fully matured. But still fresh. Medium body. Good depth if no great weight. Classy and intense. Long and fragrant. Most enjoyable.

1985   Now to 2015 plus
Grivot's second vintage of their Richebourg. Also the year that Etienne and Marielle got married. Medium-full colour. Fully mature. Ripe, aromatic, somewhat gamey nose. There is a hint of the exotic here. Still very fresh and now silky-smooth. Medium-full body. Rich, ripe, and intense. Very persistent. Lovely. Will still keep very well.

Domaine Anne Gros

VOSNE-ROMANÉE

AS WILL BE EXPLAINED more fully in the next chapter, there are four Gros estates in Vosne-Romanée. Confusingly, one is called Domaine Anne Gros and another is Domaine A. F. Gros (A. F. standing for Anne-Francoise). Moreover, in the early years of Anne's responsibility in the early 1990s, her wine appeared as Anne et Francois Gros, Francois being the name of her father. It pays to pay attention. In earlier articles on the Groses, I have sometimes included a family tree.

This Anne—our Anne for the purposes of this chapter—was born in 1966, the only child of Francois and Dany Gros. Francois had inherited his share of the estate when it was split in 1971. He sold some of his wine in bulk to the local *négociants* and bottled the rest. The percentage varied from year to year. As he got older and began to have health problems (he died in 2004), the percentage of domaine-bottled wine declined. Anne studied at Beaune and Dijon, and spent a month at Rosemount Estates in Australia—it was as a result of their both being ancient *stagières* at Rosemount that she met her other half, Jean-Paul Tollot-Beaut (they have three children)—and took over in 1988. She immediately started bottling everything, at first under the joint name as I have mentioned above. A new label, with her first name alone, appeared in 2001.

From the outset it became apparent that a new talent had arrived in a village not lacking in very fine winemakers. I feel fortunate that I was a customer before prices began to rocket and while it was still possible to buy a dozen of, say, the Richebourg. Today, such is the demand, you will be rationed, and the wines will cost you twice as much. (I say this with regret, but not as a complaint: the wines deserve to attract high prices.) For almost twenty-five years the Domaine Anne Gros has been one of the few incontestable three-star domaines in the Côte d'Or.

But not only is the lady competent, she is also very charming. Quite the opposite of the prima donna, she has a sense of humour which is both wicked and self-deprecating. And the most enchanting smile. The estate covers 6.5 hectares, of which all but the Hautes-Côtes are very old vines. Firstly there are 60 ares of

Richebourg. There are 93 ares of Clos de Vougeot, in the Grand Maupertui, and 76 ares of Echézeaux, in the Loächausses, the latter farmed by cousin Bernard (Gros Frère et Soeur) until 2007. But sadly there are no *premiers crus*. We have village Vosne-Romanée in Les Barraux, above Les Brulées (39 ares); village Chambolle-Musigny in La Combe d'Orveaux (1.10 hectares); and, the first vintage being 2001, 1.63 hectares of Bourgogne Hautes Côtes de Nuits, from Concoeur, an area above Vosne the Gros family seem to have taken over in its entirety, in both colours.

The fruit is destemmed, vinified at temperatures up to 32°C, but without cold-soaking, Anne preferring not to interfere, stored in from 25 percent new wood for the generics up to as much as 90 percent for the *grands crus*, racked rarely, and bottled in December after fourteen to fifteen months. The cellar, which Anne wondered was too large when it was first constructed in 1999, is now being enlarged.

That said, there is no "recipe." Anne Gros's instinct is to let the wine make itself; to "go with the flow." As she points out, this can cause more problems. It would be easier to be more rigid. But she won't. The reason for bottling in December—and it doesn't have to be December—is that this is usually the time when the wine is properly integrated: the fruit is "in place."

These are not blockbuster wines. Nor is the percentage of new wood in those at the top of the hierarchy at all obvious, let alone dominating. The wines are excellently harmonious, with a vigour and above all an impressive persistence of the most classy fruit. They are medium-full in colour and medium-full in weight, but they are brilliantly intense and exceptionally long lasting. See the note below on the Clos de Vougeot, 1989.

Meanwhile, up in the hills of the eastern Minervois, not far from Saint-Jean de Minervois, she and Jean-Paul have an estate at Cazelles, presently measuring 14 hectares, with another hectare recently planted. It is a splendid example of juicy Minervois: sturdy, freshly balanced, and full of fruit. Well worth seeking out.

Does she have any spare time to indulge in outside passions? Not much. Cazelles has one full-time employee on the spot, and she and Jean-Paul try to get down once every couple of weeks. In Vosne, too, you get the impression of a more or less one-man (lady) band. "I find I spend lots of time with clients, for we do a lot of private business," says Anne. "But increasingly I get inundated by all the paperwork. I'd love to have more spare time!" she says ruefully.

And in Vosne-Romanée, next to the winery, there is a *gite* (a small self-catering apartment for hire by the night—minimum two in this case—or the week). Vosne is a quiet village. Where better to spend the night than surrounded by great vineyards. I'm sure you'd sleep like a log! Write to Anne Gros at La Colombière, 21700 Vosne-Romanée, France. Or consult www.anne-gros.com.

TASTING NOTES

I sampled the following wines in Vosne-Romanée in February 2012.

Clos de Vougeot, 2010   From 2020
Bottled December 2011. Medium-full colour. Very lovely, gently oaky fruit on the nose. Medium-full body. Concentrated, fullish, and vigorous, with excellent grip. Classy tannins and very fine stylish fruit. Lots of depth and distinction. Minerally at the end. Very fine.

Richebourg, 2010   From 2022
Bottled December 2011. Rather more concentrated and less together than the Clos de Vougeot at present. A lot of depth here. Fullish. A little tight. Some tannin. Yet very ripe and with very good grip. A great deal of energy. More body and more dimension. Splendid finish. Excellent.

Clos de Vougeot, 2009   From 2022
Good colour. Rich, luscious, potentially velvety nose. Fresh, ripe, and generous. Medium-full body. Good ripe, classy tannins. Lots of vigour and lots of depth. Harmonious and very long on the palate. Excellent.

Richebourg, 2009　　　　　From 2024

Good colour. The nose is rather more closed-in than the wine above. But this has more volume and quite a lot more tannin. Fullish body. Very lovely succulent fruit. Splendid energy. Needs time. A great wine.

Clos de Vougeot, 2008　　　　　**From 2015**

Medium to medium-full colour. Fragrant nose. By no means a heavyweight. Medium to medium-full body. Most attractive balanced fruit. Just a little tannin to soften. Harmonious and delicious. But quite forward.

Richebourg, 2008　　　　　From 2018

Medium-full colour. Rich nose, quite meaty for a 2008. Fullish body for the vintage. Some tannin. Very fresh. Ripe, complex, elegant, and profound. There is quite a bit more to this than the Clos de Vougeot. Very long and very lovely.

Clos de Vougeot, 2007　　　　　Now to 2020

Medium colour. Soft nose. Some of the flavours of maturity. But fresh. Medium body. Ripe and succulent. Stylish, long, positive, and most attractive. Now just about ready.

Richebourg, 2007　　　　　From 2015

Medium colour. Rather more backbone and vigour here. But it doesn't show as well. There is a certain astringency which dominates. The softer Clos de Vougeot seems better balanced. Yet there is plenty of energy here. We'll see.

Clos de Vougeot, 2006　　　　　From 2015

Medium to medium-full colour. The nose is a bit earthy, but the wine has good volume and richness. Good concentration and depth with a touch of mocha. Rather more attractive on the palate than on the nose. Good grip. Good energy. Long. Fine.

Richebourg, 2006　　　　　From 2017

Medium to medium-full colour. Rich, full, vibrant nose. Rather firmer and more positive than the Clos de Vougeot. Fullish body. Very concentrated. Very classy indeed. Splendid fruit. Real vigour. Delicious.

Clos de Vougeot, 2005　　　　　From 2015

Medium-full colour. Still youthful. Very lovely nose. Concentrated, precise, very complex, very classy. Medium-full body. Fresh and succulent. Composed and subtle. Long and profound. Very concentrated. Excellent.

Richebourg, 2005　　　　　From 2017

Fullish colour. Much more closed-in than the above. Splendidly concentrated, aristocratic fruit. Fullish body. Still some tannin to resolve. A really profound, multidimensional wine. Splendid energy and marvelous class. Magnificent!

Richebourg, 2004　　　　　Drink soon

Medium colour. Good fruit on the nose. But not much depth or class and a bit earthy and astringent as it developed. Medium body. Better on the aftertaste, but not the usual Richebourg distinction.

Clos de Vougeot, 2003　　　　　Now to 2018

Fullish colour, but not exaggeratedly so. Rich, cooked nose. Ripe and fat and succulent. Fullish body. Very good acidity for a 2003. Long and seductive. Still youthful. Ready but will last well.

Richebourg, 2003　　　　　Now to 2020

Fullish colour. Full, rich luscious nose. Very ripe. Most attractive. Even more seductive and opulent than the wine above. Full body. Very good grip. Very lovely. Not a bit like an average 2003 because no lack of class. And long and complex. Delicious.

Clos de Vougeot, 2002　　　　　Now to 2025

Medium-full colour. Some touches of maturity now. Smooth, ripe, subtle, harmonious nose. Medium-full body. Ripe and fresh. Just about ready. Very well-balanced. Stylish fruit. Very good vigour. Lots of depth and class. Very fine.

Richebourg, 2002　　　　　From 2017

Fullish colour. Rich, concentrated, still backward nose. Great energy and depth here. Very fine tannins and very fine grip. This still needs five years. But it is really excellent. Marvelous follow-through.

Clos de Vougeot, 2001　　　Now to 2018

Medium colour. Soft, ripe, charming nose. Medium body. Good fruit. Good grip and structure for the vintage. No weakness. Vigorous at the end. Most enjoyable.

Richebourg, 2001　　　Now to 2021

Medium to medium-full colour. Richer, fatter, and with more energy than the Clos de Vougeot. Fuller and fresher. More structure and a better grip. Plenty of wine here. Long and vigorous. A really fine 2001.

Richebourg, 2000　　　Now to 2016

Medium colour. Mature nose but no great depth, size, or energy behind it. A pleasant, quite fresh, fruity wine. But one-dimensional. Not a patch on the 2001.

Clos de Vougeot, 1999　　　Now to 2025

Fine, full, vigorous colour. Only barely mature. Rich, ample, concentrated nose. Fullish body. Ripe and round and succulent. Vigorous but *à point*. Balanced and complex and long on the palate. Perhaps not the greatest finesse but quite delicious.

Richebourg, 1999　　　Now to 2030

Similar colour. The basic difference is sheer class. This is a little fuller and more concentrated. Perhaps a bit richer and more vigorous. But the breed here is remarkable. Quite brilliant.

Clos de Vougeot, 1998　　　Now to 2018

Medium colour. Soft, fully mature nose. Medium body. No great weight or vigour here but fresh and pleasantly fruity. I've had more complex and more concentrated 1998s.

Richebourg, 1998　　　Now to 2020

Medium-full, vigorous colour. This has more to it than the Clos de Vougeot. Ripe, energetic, complex, and stylish. Finishes positively. But fine rather than great.

Richebourg, 1995　　　Now to 2025 plus

Full colour. Just about mature. Rich, vigorous nose. Quite a backbone here. But rich and opulent. Not a trace of astringency. Just lots of energy and sumptuous fruit. Very lovely. Very fine. Lots of life ahead of it.

Clos de Vougeot, 1989　　　Now to 2020 plus

Magnum. Fullish, mature colour. Vigorous nose, especially for a 1989. Lovely and rich coupled with a certain balancing austerity (a word I thought I would never write about a 1989). Fullish. Ripe. Very good grip. Lots of depth and class. Lots of dimension. A very lovely wine indeed.

Domaine Michel Gros

VOSNE-ROMANÉE

VOSNE-ROMANÉE is a commune rich in *grand cru climats* and a village replete with growers of the highest quality. One of the longest-established of this first division, owners inter alia of the monopoly of an excellent *premier cru*, Clos des Réas, and no less than 2 hectares, one-quarter, in the best part of Richebourg, one of the grandest *grands crus* of them all, is the Gros family. There are now four separate Gros exploitations: Domaine Michel Gros, Domaine Gros Frère et Soeur, Domaine Anne Gros, and Domaine A. F. Gros.

The dynasty begins with Alphonse Gros, born in 1804 at Chaux, a hamlet in the hills behind Nuits-Saint-Georges. He married a Latour and arrived in the village of Vosne in the 1830s, where he bought a substantial house, later divided, which had formerly belonged to the Abbey of Citaux prior to the Revolution. In 1860 he acquired the 2-plus hectare walled vineyard of the Clos des Réas, a triangular *climat* at the southern end of the village, downslope from Malconsorts and Chaumes, and like them, a *premier cru*.

Following his retirement a few years later, responsibility passed to Louis-Gustave, one of his two sons, who had married a Mlle Guenaud, and it is under the name Gros-Guenaud that the wine was first sold. Louis-Gustave must have been one of the first small growers to sell his wine direct. In a price list of November 1, 1868, he points out that as there are no middlemen between him and his clientele, he is able to offer his wines 20 to 30 percent cheaper than the *maisons de commerce*: the Clos des Réas at 5 francs a bottle for the 1858, 3.50 for the 1861 and 1862, and 2.50 for the 1864, in minimum quantities of twenty-five bottles per order, delivered to the railway station at Vougeot or at Nuits. He adds that the 1868 vintage is a good one, which the consumer would do well to stock up on.

The domaine continued to expand. In 1882, Louis-Gustave acquired 2 hectares of land in Richebourg, up in the Veroilles section of the *climat*, between Cros Parantoux and Brulées. In 1920, Louis-Gustave's grandson Louis Gros—the domaine was now trading under the name of his father (Jules) Gros-Renaudot—bought two substantial parcels of Clos de Vougeot from the heirs of Léonce Bocquet, one directly under the vineyard of Musigny in the northwest corner of the *grand cru* adjacent to the *château*, called Clos de Vougeot, Le Musigni [*sic*], the other a little further south but also at the top of the slope, called Grand Maupertuis. Bit by bit he assembled a 3 hectare parcel of Echézeaux in the *lieu-dit* Les Loächausses. Some Grands-Echézeaux followed and, in 1967, a further few rows of Clos de Vougeot, next to the Grand Maupertuis was bought by Jean Gros, son of Louis, from Madame Machard de Grammont, *née* Dufouleur.

Louis Gros died in 1951, and for a while the domaine continued to be run in common by his four children: Gustave, Jean, François, and Colette. François did the paperwork and managed the finances, Jean looked after the vines, and Gustave ran the cellar. Sadly none of the three men seems to have enjoyed the best of health. Nevertheless, with the exception of Gustave, who died in 1984 (Francois died twenty years later), this generation still survives, though it has been the next who have been making the wine for some time.

In 1963, when François got married, the Gros-Renaudot domaine was split up. Jean received the Clos des Réas and part of the Clos de Vougeot Maupertuis, the rest of the Maupertuis went to François, and Gustave and Colette, neither of whom had married, pooled their interests together under the name Gros Frère et Soeur, and took over the Grands-Echézeaux and the larger Musigni section of the Clos de Vougeot. The Richebourg was divided.

In the early 1990s, Jean Gros officially retired (though the wine had for some time been made by his eldest son, Michel), and his estate was divided amongst his children. Michel retained the Clos des Réas and the Clos de Vougeot, while his sister Anne-Françoise took on the Richebourg. This is made by her husband, François Parent of Pommard, and is sold under the lable A. F. Gros. Meanwhile, the second son of Jean and Jeanine Gros, Bernard, had been responsible for the Gros Frère et Soeur exploitation since the early 1980s. In 1988, François's daughter Anne took over from her father. This means that today there are four Gros estates, labelled respectively Michel Gros,

Gros Frère et Soeur, A. F. Gros, and Anne Gros. All have vines in the Hautes Côtes, at Concoeur, just above Vonse-Romanée—Domaine Jean Gros being a pioneer here—as well as in the Côte d'Or.

In 1997, the Écard family (GFA des Arbaupins) asked Michel Gros to look after their vines in Nuits-Saint-Georges and Vosne-Romanée, including *premier cru* land in Vignerondes and Murgers in the former commune and Brûlées in the latter. More recently, he has acquired some village Nuits-Saint-Georges Les Chaliots. Together with his inheritance and land he has bought in Vosne-Romanée, Chambolle-Musigny and Morey-Saint-Denis in the 1990s, this brings Michel Gros's estate up to 18 hectares.

Pride of place, together with the Clos des Réas monopoly (2.12 hectares), is the Clos de Vougeot. This is Jean Gros's 1967 purchase: 20 ares. In 1967 the vines dated from 1902, the first generation planted after the phylloxera epidemic. Sadly the parcel was deeply affected by the frosts of January 1985. The wine from this vintage, what little there was of it, is quite brilliant, but the vines had to be ripped up the following year. Michel replanted with the 115 clone on 161-49 rootstock in 1987. By 2002 the vines were beginning to reach a respectable age, and the wine is now of serious *grand cru* quality.

Michel Gros made his first vintage in 1975. Though his mother, Jeanine, originally from the Jura, runs the business side of Domaine Jean Gros—she has also been mayor of Vosne since 1971, one of her first duties being to marry Aubert de Villaine, co-owner of the Domaine de la Romanée-Conti, to his American wife, Pamela—father Jean seems to live a life of leisure. He prefers hunting to winemaking, as does his brother François. In twenty or more years of regular visits to Domaine Jean Gros, I have never succeeded in meeting him. (Originally I surmised Madame Jeanine was a widow. I mentioned this in *The Vine*, and though I corrected the mistake as soon as it was pointed out to me, I was rather dismayed to see the error repeatedly copied by other writers who should have known better.)

Michel prefers to maintain the harvest within limits by pruning short and rubbing off excess buds early in the season, rather than by green-harvesting in late July, a process whose efficacy he regards with a certain healthy scepticism. The fruit is entirely destemmed, after which the vinification takes place in a variety of vats, mainly cement, following a gentle crushing of about half of the fruit. There is no prior *maceration à froid*, but *pigeage* twice a day, and temperatures up to a maximum of 34°C. Where necessary, Michel is a member of an increasingly large group of winemakers who will perform a sort of reverse osmosis on the must in order to concentrate it. This he prefers to doing a *saignée* (bleeding). After a *cuvaison* of ten to twelve days, the fermented wine is lodged in oak casks of which up to 100 percent is new for the Clos de Vougeot, 50 percent for the Clos des Réas and the other first growths, and 30 percent for the village wines. It is racked but once only and bottled twenty-two to twenty-three months after the vintage.

All this is what you might expect when you get to know Michel, a kind but somewhat shy man at first, but one whose character is evidently both perfectionist and cautiously conservative. (When I asked him what changes he had made since he took over from his father, he was able to offer little except the installation of cooling systems.) Where there is a break with the norm, is that he is a firm believer in selected yeasts. There is a more efficient transference of sugar to alcohol, in his view, and the resulting wine has more finesse.

I find Michel's wines very pure in their expression of Pinot. There is an essence of fruit, an intensity of flavour, and a breed in these wines which is wholly admirable. I have been buying them myself for ages.

TASTING NOTES

Vosne-Romanée, Clos des Réas

The following wines were served at a dinner at Restaurant Bouley, New York, in March 2010.

The bottles had come direct from Michel Gros's cellar.

2007   From 2013

Medium colour. Gentle, fragrant, subtly oaky nose. Medium body. Fresh. Good acidity. No great concentration, but good fruit and balance. Very elegant. Now quite soft but still a touch raw, so it will still benefit from a couple of years.

2006   From 2014

Medium-full colour. A little tannin and a bit of new oak on the nose. No great grip, however. Medium to medium-full body. Better grip on the palate than the nose would suggest. Quite rich. Good fat for 2006. Plenty of depth. Positive finish. Fine for the vintage.

2005   From 2017

Very good colour. Firm, closed-in nose. Needs time. Full body. Some tannin. Currently adolescent. Still unformed but a lot of depth and potential. Very fine. An altogether more masculine wine than the two above.

2004   From 2014

Good colour. Somewhat lean on the nose. Rather less obvious oak than in the wines above. Good tannin and good grip, but it needs several years to round off and become more generous. Medium-full body. Well balanced and not too green. Fine for the vintage albeit that it lacks a bit of sex appeal at the moment.

2003   Now to 2020

Good but not excessively deep colour. Roasted nose. Rich and concentrated and oaky. Not too cooked and reasonably fresh. Medium-full body. The tannins are now integrated. Opulent, fat, and rich on the palate, with surprisingly good balance. Lovely, even for those who generally dislike this vintage: me, for example.

2002   From 2014

Medium-full colour. Not a blockbuster, but this wine never is. Lovely nose. Real breed. Hardly a touch of oak and beautifully balanced. Subtle and complex. Medium-full body. Beginning to soften. But still needs three years. Marvelous fruit and harmony. Lots and lots of dimension. Very, very long at the end. Very lovely.

2001   Now to 2018
Medium to medium-full colour. Lots of interest on the nose. Ripe and quite complex. Good balance and now just about *à point*. Just a smidgen of new oak. Good depth and balance. No weakness. Long. Fine plus for the vintage.

2000   Now to 2015
Medium colour. Ripe, open, and charming, if a little one-dimensional. Medium body. No great depth but fresh, balanced, and sufficiently complex. No lack of class. Good acidity if an absence of fat and concentration. Fully ready: indeed delicious now. Very good indeed.

1999   From 2013
Good full, youthful colour. Full, fat, rich, firm nose. Some tannin still to be absorbed. Fullish body. Ripe and rich. Very good grip. Still needs a year or two to soften up. Lots of energy. A lovely wine which is at least fine plus for the vintage. But the 2002 is more elegant and more intense. This is less precise.

1998   Now to 2020
Medium to medium-full colour. Just about mature. The nose is now soft. Ripe and elegant. Medium-full body. Maybe it could have done with a bit more weight and energy, but it is balanced and subtle and long on the palate. Intense and classy. Fine plus for the vintage.

1997   Drink soon
Magnum. The only real disappointment in this series. Surprisingly full colour. Somewhat earthy, even bitter on the nose and on the palate. Reasonable acidity—indeed fresher than most—but no great depth or elegance. Not a very relaxed wine, and the finish is rather flat and lumpy.

1996   Now to 2016
Very good colour. Still youthful. Ripe, fresh, complex, and elegant on the nose, though not very rich. Medium-full body. On the palate there is an absence of generosity. It is stylish and vigorous but a little austere. I don't think

now that it will ever round off satisfactorily. Better with food.

1995   Now to 2020 plus
Fullish, mature colour. Lovely ripe, rich, succulent nose. Lots of depth. Medium-full body. Good integrated tannins. Lovely concentrated fruit. Very good grip. This is very complete and harmonious. Lots of energy. Very long and very fine.

1994   Now to 2014
Medium to medium-full colour. Fully mature. Soft nose. No lack of fruit, nor undue acidity. Just a bit one-dimensional. Fresh on the palate. Medium body. Balanced and fruity. Still vigorous and really quite sophisticated for a 1994. Very fine for the vintage. No hurry to drink.

1993   Now to 2020
Very good colour. Ripe, rich, and without the slightly lean aspect which you find in some of the 1993s. There is a nice meatiness here. A bigger wine than the 1995. Still a suggestion of unabsorbed tannin. This is like a blend of 1995 and 1996, but bigger and more concentrated than either, if just a bit rugged. Good depth and grip. The 1995 is finer, but this is fine plus.

1992   Drink soon
Medium colour. No undue age. Soft, ripe nose. Not much volume or depth on the palate, but fresh, ripe, and certainly stylish. Better with food.

1991   Now to 2020
Good fullish, vigorous colour for its age. An ample, round, energetic, fullish-bodied wine with a touch of oak. Good grip and lots of depth. Plenty of wine here. Delicious. Still lots of life ahead of it.

1990
Surprisingly, no more colour here than in the 1991. Round, ripe, fullish, and rich. But I have seen rather more energetic bottles recently. This example shows a little age. It is lightening up and the acidity is beginning to show on the finish. The 1991 is better today.

1989   Now to 2016

Fresh but only medium to medium-full colour.
Red fruit—cherries, for instance—on the nose.
Cool and elegant as it evolved. Good depth.
Fuller than most 1989s and nicely fresh. Hold-
ing up well. Fine.

1988   Now to 2020 plus

Good fullish colour. Lovely cool, composed
nose. Intense and classy. Not a bit austere, as
you will find in some 1998s. Fullish body, balanced, vigorous, and very long on the palate.
Real breed here. Very fine.

Domaine des Comtes Lafon

MEURSAULT

THERE ARE FEW ESTATES in the Côte d'Or—if we exclude the merchant domaines: Bouchard Pere et Fils, Drouhin, Jadot—which are equally successful in Chardonnay as in Pinot Noir. Offhand, I can only think of eight or nine. But one such is the Domaine des Comte Lafon in Meursault. In 2013 the man in charge, Dominique Lafon, turned fifty-five and celebrated his thirtieth vintage. Having been to the local wine schools, and done a vintage in California, he joined his father René in 1981, as junior partner, worked alongside him in 1982, and was in charge from 1983. "Yes," he reminds me, "That was the year we had real noble Botrytis in some of our vineyards. So I produced some Meur-Sauternes. You, Clive, thought it was disgusting. But some people, like Jasper Morris, were kinder!"

René Lafon was an engineer. He had had a fight with his relations back before the war. They had wanted to put up the domaine for sale. René was adamant that he should retain it, so he bought out the rest of the family. The vineyards were leased out on a *metayage* (share-cropping) basis, Lafon *père* returning at vintage

time to receive his share of the fruit. After vinification the wine was stored in the cold, deep, humid Lafon cellar beneath the winery. It matured slowly. The wines could take their time to evolve, and did not dry out, even after two years in cask. This is one of the first clues to the Lafon success: Time.

"I had a good grounding from my father," Dominique recalls. "At the École Viti in Beaune I was a bit confused at first. I didn't know enough to challenge what I was being told—such that machine harvesting was better than manual collection of the fruit—or other practices we did not follow at the domaine. But I instinctively knew some of them to be wrong. Nevertheless, I don't want to criticise them too much. I learned a lot of useful things."

René Lafon's philosophy, as he put to me once, I find exemplary: "To have the courage to do nothing." This, if you like, is the second clue to the success of the domaine.

Some of the sharecroppers were more competent than others. Dominique has nothing but respect for Pierre Morey, who looked after most of the Chardonnay parcels. "I had absolute confidence in what Pierre would render unto us." says Dominique. "You only had to look at the vines to know that they were being properly looked after. But some of the others! Early on, at vintage time, this man turned up with a couple of skips of Volnay fruit. I looked at the grapes. I was horrified. A good part was unripe. A lot more was rotten. 'Do you really expect me to accept this?' I asked him. 'Look,' he says, 'the weather hasn't been very good, as you know. But the unripe fruit will give you acidity, the over-ripe will give alcohol, and the good grapes will give you the fruit. The sugar bags will do the rest!'"

Sharecropping leases normally run on a nine-year basis. One of the first things Dominique did was to give his leaseholders their notice. Slowly but surely, during the course of the 1980s decade, the vines reverted to him. He was now responsible for all the crop. Not half.

In the meanwhile, he got a job with the celebrated American wine broker Becky Wasserman. "I worked with Becky from 1982 to 1986. This was one of the best times of my life." he says. "Not only did I get an invaluable insight into what happens to my wine after it leaves my cellar, but I was able to go and taste and compare notes with all the other growers that Becky was dealing with, and also go with her to the USA and help sell her portfolio."

What did he change at the domaine? "We started to go biodynamic in 1995. I did a few experiments at first, and then became fully convinced. So from 1998 we have been completely biodynamic. Secondly, there was a lot to do in my red wine vineyards. You can't change things completely overnight. It's a slow process. But by 1989 I felt we were beginning to get there. One thing I threw out was the old crusher-destemmer. It really chewed up the fruit. With its replacement we get much more sophisticated tannins."

In 1995 he was invited to take on a lease from by Dr. Desormais, who had bought a parcel in Puligny-Montrachet, Les Champ-Gains. Subsequently, Dominique decided—temporar-ily, as it turned out—that further expansion in the Côte de Beaune, if it were to turn up, would be beyond his means. So he decided to prospect elsewhere. In 1999 an estate in Milly-Lamartine in the Mâconnais was acquired: 7 hectares. Four years later a further 7 hectares came up for sale in Uchizy and Chardonnay, further to the north. This made the whole Mâconnais venture much more profitable, for the expansion only required one more full-time *vigneron*. More lately, in 2009, Dominique has leased another 7 hectare parcel in Viré-Clessé and is now in charge of the Château de Viré: a total of 21 hectares.

Lafon's arrival in Southern Burgundy didn't half shake up some of the locals. As I wrote at the time: "It has taken an outsider to demonstrate the real possibilities of Chardonnay in the Mâconnais." Then in the autumn of 2010 a golden opportunity arose. The firm of Labouré-Roi in Nuits-Saint-Georges decided to sell their 7 hectare domaine in Meursault, René Manuel. Foreign investors were found, and Dominique struck a deal with his good friend Jean-Marc Roulot of the Domaine Guy Roulot to share the ensuing lease. Briefly this gives Dominique some *premier cru* Poruzots and Bouchères for the first time, while Roulot takes on the Clos des Bouchères. They are sharing the 2.7 hectare Clos de la Baronne, in the domaine's back garden. And Dominique has taken on, on his own account, a 1.8 parcel of well-placed, old vine Bourgogne Blanc.

Meanwhile, Dominique has separated those wines and vineyards he owns or expoits personally—these include the Champ-Gains referred to earlier, some Meursault, Narvaux, Beaune, Epenottes and Volnay, Lurets (it's under Caillerets), plus other village and generic parcels—from the family domaine. In total, there are 4.5 hectares. These are housed in the old René Manuel cellar, where he also has a merchant's licence. He has bought in Mâconnais fruit to vinify himself.

The Comtes Lafon Meursault domaine now covers 17 hectares, if we discount the Puligny.

There are 32 ares of Montrachet, at the exteme southern end, Meursault, *premier cru* in Les Perrières, Les Genevrières, Les Charmes, and Les Gouttes d'Or (vines now approaching proper maturity, for Dominique replanted the parcel after he reacquired it in the late 1980s), plus village Meursault, including the *lieu-dit* Clos de la Barre, directly behind the *château*. In red there are Volnay, *premier cru* in Santenots-du-Milieu, Champans and Clos de Chênes, plus Monthelie, Les Duresses, *rouge* and a little young vine *blanc*, drunk by the harvesters at vintage time.

The perspicacious amongst you will notice that I have not mentioned the Desirée. This was the old cadastral name of a parcel of first-growth Plures, planted in Chardonnay but adjacent to the Santenots-du-Milieu. The Lafons were the only ones to retain the name after the *appellation d'origine contrôlée* (AC) was introduced in 1936, so it was sold as a village wine. This is red wine soil. I have never liked the wine. Too tarty. So I was interested to hear Dominique say to a few years ago: "You'll be very pleased, Clive. We have uprooted the Desirée and we are going to replant it with a better clone and root-stock." I look forward to sampling it in due course.

What is the difference between Charmes, Perrières, and Genevrières? They are, after all, adjacent. To explain why, you just have to look at the soil. In the Perrières it is shallow and almost entirely decomposed limestone rock, dirt cream in colour. Next door in Genevières it is much redder; there is more iron in the composition. On the other side of the road, there is a little more depth—much more so lower down—and the colour is a brown mud, with bigger stones, some the size of a tennis ball. This gives a minerally, racy character to the Perrières, and a touch of citrus peel to the slightly fuller and certainly richer Genevrières, while the Charmes is softer and more flowery. Any one of them can be the best Meurault in the Lafon cellar. It depends on the vintage.

"Genevrières is the *cuvée* which gives me the most problem," says Lafon. "It is unforgiving. The slightest mistake on my part and you will see it in the wine. With my other wines an error is less unmistakable. Genevrières is jealous of its *terroir* expression." But, he adds: "When I get it right, its my favourite of the three." He continues: "Charmes is perhaps the easiest. The harvest is more regular in both quantity and quality than the other two. While I am instictivly a Perrières man, I often find the Charmes—as the name suggests—utterly charming."

"Can you explain this Count business?" I ask Dominique. Some 125 years ago, France elected its first socialist government, one of whose intentions was to disestablish the Church. Naturally, a noisy lobby arose to try (unsuccessfully as it turned out) to defeat this proposal. The leaders were appointed Counts by the Pope of the time. There is one Count Lafon, René Lafon's older brother Jacques, but as Jacques has no children, Dominique eventually will become the Count. In the meanwhile, René, Dominique, and even his son Guillaume could all call themselves Count (christain name) Lafon, if they wish. In fact, they don't bother.

Ask him about his artistic preferences and Lafon will start talking about Land Art. Explain, I ask. "It's ephemeral art, if you wish," says Dominique. "The two leaders in this field are Andy Goldsworthy and Richard Long. Let's say you go into a wood in the autumn and you make a magnificent patchwork with the most brightly coloured leaves. You leave. Two days later the wind and the rain will have utterly destroyed what you have created. Or, to give you another example: You take a field and you walk up and down, always in the same place, a thousand times. After a while you will have created a path. Go away, and the path reverts to nature. The concept intrigues, fascinates me." "Ah," I say brightly. "A sandcastle." "Absolutely," says Dominique. "It's the impermanence which is compelling. I make wine. That's impermanent too. So are the creations of a master chef."

We also talk about music. Apart from Pop, which doesn't really interest him, Dominique professes to like all music. His answering machine currently plays Miles Davis's "Kind of Blue." "But it is the expertise, the artistry of the musicians which moves me, more than the style. In this, as in everything else, I like to be surprised." And what would he do if he were not to be a winemaker? "I'm an outdoorsman. I could only be some other sort of agriculturalist." And what red wine would he drink, for preference? "Well, if I were forced to drink nothing but (Chambolle-Musigny) Amoureuses for the rest of my life, I don't think I would complain!"

Lafon is refreshingly dispassionate about his own wines. He feels he didn't quite pull it off with his 1999 whites. He prefers his 2000s. He is less enthusiastic about his 2002s than I am about the white wine vintage as a whole—or indeed about his Charmes (see tasting notes below). This scepticism is healthy. It makes a refreshing change from a great many domaines which cannot brook one iota of comment less than laudatory. You can talk turkey with Dominique.

I have found few examples of prematurely oxidised wine here, and this is a domaine whose three top *premiers crus* and Clos de la Barre I regularly cellar.

Today the Lafon wines, for decades amongst the very best in white, are now equally brilliant in red. A comparison of his 1990 Volnay, Santenots-du-Milieu with, say, the 1999 or the 2005 is telling. But don't dismiss all the pre-1990 reds. A Santenots 1978, enjoyed at lunch *chez* the Lafons a few years ago, was dreamy-delicious, everything you would expect this most elegant of communes to come up with. And a magnum of Santenots 1992, consumed at lunch after the tasing below, was *gouleyant*, fresh, round, and full of fruit, without a hint of undue age.

TASTING NOTES
Meursault, Charmes

The following wines were sampled in Meursault in June 2002.

2009　　　　　　　　　　From 2014

Bottled a month ago. Quite a powerful nose, but that is the sulphur added at the time of the bottling. Rich, fat, full-bodied. Good grip. Plenty of depth. Lovely fruit. This a keeper in 2009 terms. Lots of energy. Fine.

2008　　　　　　　　　　From 2016

Fullish nose. Lots of vigour and depth. Very good acidity. Quite fat on the palate. Indeed a bit more development than I had expected. More dimension than the 2009. More energy and concentration at the end. Better than the 2009, and it will last longer.

2007　　　　　　　　　　Now to 2017

Fresh colour. Very lovely flowery nose. Great style. Balanced in a delicate sort of way. Elegant and harmonious. Perhaps it lacks a little vigour but ripe and delicious now.

2006　　　　　　　　　　From 2013

Still has a fresh colour, though there is a little more here than in the wines above. A fat, ample, succulent wine. A lot plumper than the 2007. Full and very rich. The good acidity stops it being heavy. Vigorous follow-through and long on the palate. Needs food.

2005　　　　　　　　　　From 2015

Fresh colour. Quite a firm, indeed hidden nose. A bit tight still. Full, rich, concentrated, and powerful. A small crop, and it shows. Lovely follow-through. Real depth and energy. This is long and classy, and still a little adolescent, but a very fine wine which will keep very well.

2004　　　　　　　　　　Now to 2014

Fresh colour. Fully developed on the nose. Very flowery and really quite dry. Plump, medium bodied, mature, and stylish. This is *à point* and most attractive. Juicy fruit on the palate. Good vigour. Long. Fine.

2003　　　　　　　　　　Drink soon

No undue weight or age on the colour. The nose is full and surprisingly fresh. Spicy. Nutty. Full-bodied. A more than respectable example of this difficult vintage. Good fruit. No lack of grip. But a slight heaviness at the end. Holding up well. Would go well with foie gras.

2002 From 2015

The colour is still very fresh indeed. It is less developed than the 2005. The nose is a bit subdued, but it shows a great deal of concentration, depth, and style. Fullish body. Great harmony and spendid depth and class. Very lovely crisp, minerally, flowery fruit. Multidimensional. Great energy. Will still improve. Clearly the best wine of the decade. Very fine indeed.

2001 Drink soon

Soft, plump, flowery nose. Nicely ripe if without any great depth or concentration. Medium weight. Still fresh if a bit one-dimensional. A wine which despite being the least good of the decade, has no lack of attraction and charm.

2000 Now to 2018

Still a very fresh colour. The nose has quite a bit more weight, depth, and concentration of fruit than the 2001. And more vigour and interest too. Fullish body. Quite a lot of succulence and vigour. Elegance too. Ready but will keep well. Fine plus. Dominique has always preferred this to his 1999. It has never gone through an adolescent phase, he says.

1999 Now to 2016

Still a very fresh colour. Very lovely nose. Full-bodied. Very fresh. Very vigorous. Lovely fruit. It's a firmer, more structured wine than the above. The attack is fine but the follow-through is a little hard, without the attractive plumpness of the 2000. A wine for food. Fine.

1998 Drink soon

Quite an evolved colour. There is just a touch of fade on the nose. This makes it round and ripe with an illusion of sweetness. But lowers the grip. Medium-full body. Ripe and fresh on the palate. Indeed, after a quarter of an hour the whole thing was livelier than it had appeared to be at the outset. Plenty of fruit and enjoyment to be had. Positive finish. Bigger than the 1997 but less stylish. No hurry to drink.

1997 Drink soon

Now some suggestion of age on the colour. Attractive, aromatic nose with the savour of a well-matured wine. Medium-full body. Ripe, round, and fruity. No enormous energy but balanced. Still fresh at the end. Very good indeed.

1996 Now to 2016

Fresh colour. Lovely nose. Very good concentration and good grip. But no undue leanness. Just a suggestion of the herbal and mineral which gives it complexity. Fullish body. Vigorous and individual. Just a bit hard at the end. Needs food. Fine plus.

1995 Now to 2020

Mature colour. Full, firm, rich, masculine nose. Plenty of depth. Quite powerful. This is *à point* now and very lovely. Fullish body. Concentrated. Lots of depth and dimension. Lots of energy. Very good grip. Lovely finish. Very fine. Will still last very well.

1994 Now to 2015

No undue age on the colour. The nose is still fresh too. This was a potentially fine vintage compromised by rain at the last minute. Medium to medium-full body. Good plump, fresh, even vigorous fruit. Ripe and ample. Much better than you would expect (and I prefer it to the 1997) and still holding up very well indeed. Lacks a bit of dimension and concentration but most enjoyable.

1993 Now to 2017

Mature colour. Not a very pronounced nose at first. But it is fresh and full of interest in a slightly herbal sort of way. Medium-full body. Youthful, crisp, and stylish. Lovely complex white flower finish. Individual and fine plus.

1992 Now to 2015

Some age on the colour now. Soft, plump, ripe, gentle but still vigorous on the nose. An attractive wine with no lack of dimension. Medium-full body. Honeysuckle flavours. Good fresh acidity. Very ripe and fruity. Very elegant. Fine.

1991   Drink up

The colour is still very fresh. As is the nose. Plump and with a vigour here as a result of the very small crop. On the palate medium to medium-full body. A mixture of youth and age in the flavours. This is less good on the follow-through but enjoyable nevertheless.

1990   Drink soon

Well-matured colour. Fresh, ample, vigorous, flowery nose. Medium to medium-full body. Ripe, complex, good grip. On the attack this seems to have depth and harmony and to be holding up well, but it's a bit rigid at the end compared with the 1992. Fine nevertheless.

1989   Now to 2016

Well-matured nose. Full, ripe, rich, aromatic, spicy nose. Very lovely, complex, well-matured wine. Lots of depth and class. This is very lovely, even after all this time. Quite a full-bodied, structured, masculine wine. Needs food. Lovely though perhaps the 1992 is more elegant.

1982   Will still keep well

Developed colour but by no means too much so. Delicious nose. Ripe, distinguished, full-bodied, mature, and very subtle. The fruit is fresh and very concentrated. Splendid grip. Great class. Lots of vigour. A really excellent wine with not a trace of age.

1979   Drink soon

Just a little more colour than the 1982. Ripe ample nose. Full-bodied and still fresh, if not as precise as the above. Just a little astringency at the end. A little rigid too. Yet at first very good with food. It tailed off in the glass though. This was bottled by Lafon *père* after two years in cask.

Domaine Lamarche

VOSNE-ROMANÉE

THE 11 HECTARE Domaine Lamarche has had its ups and downs—the latter perhaps inevitable during a period where until relatively recently profit was hard to come by—but is now definitely on the up. Progressively since 1990 or so, quality has moved from "good" to "very fine." In a village replete with overachievers, it is a relief that such an important establishment, and possessor of one of the four *grand cru* monopolies in the commune of Vosne-Romanée, now produces wines as good as they should be.

The Lamarches begin with Jean-Constant, born in Sombernon in the Hautes Côtes in 1835, who married a local lady and installed himself in the village. She brought with her some vines as a dowry, and all the generations since have gradually expanded the estate. These two produced Henri, who I will call for the sake of convenience Henri 1, born in 1871, and two other male children. Henri 1 married into the Chambolle-based Grivelet family, thereby gaining more land, and was also a barrel maker. His son Henri 2, born in 1903, was, alongside the Domaine de la Romanée-Conti (DRC) and that of the Gros family, one of the first to start selling wine in bottle to the restaurant trade. He was also a broker and cellar master for the Marey-Monge estate, owner of what is now the DRC's parcel in Romanée-Saint-Vivant. Under his aegis the Lamarche domaine was further enlarged.

His uncle Edouard, rich and widowed, and with no successors of his own, on the occasion of Henri 2's marriage in 1933 to Jeanne Demur (she brought with her land in Pommard), bought him the vineyard of La Grande Rue as a wedding present. He also left money to his two nieces, daughters of his brother Alfred. At the time it was thought that the girls had had the best of the arrangement. Henri 2 had three children. The eldest, Elizabeth, married Joseph Moissenet of Nuits-Saint-Georges, and it is their successors who look after the Pommard vines. Then Francois, born in 1944, and finally Geneviève, born in 1949. Francois retired in 2007. His daughter Nicole is now in charge of the wines and the cellar, while Geneviève's daughter, Natalie, works alongside her aunt Marie-Blanche on the commercial side. Did Marie-Blanche, like her predeccesors, bring a dowry of vines? "No. I come from the Lorraine. I was born in Metz."

La Grande Rue is a thin strip of land lying between La Tâche and Romanée-Saint-Vivant,

La Romanée-Conti, and La Romanée. The wine it produces has been classed, if not quite as highly as Romanée-Conti and Richebourg, right at the top of the tree, at least in the very next rank—that is, alongside La Tâche and Romanée-Saint-Vivant, by the Abbé Courtépée in the eighteenth century, and his successors Dr. Denis Morelot and Jules Lavalle in the nineteenth. It belonged before the French Revolution to a wealthy Nuits family, the Lamy de Samereys, was sold as a *bien national* to the influential Marey family (who seem to have been involved in just about all the top vineyards in the Côte d'Or at some stage in their history), and then passed by marriage to Louis-Charles Bocquillon, Comte Liger-Belair, and then to Bocquillon's son-in-law Joseph de Champeaux, proprietor of the Château de Vosne-Romanée. It was Champeaux's successors, in the straitened times of the 1930s, who were forced to put La Grande Rue on the market.

One hundred and fifty years ago, La Grande Rue measured 1.33 hectares. It seems to have grown since. Current records put it at 1.65 hectares. Over the years since the Lamarche acquisition parcels have been exchanged with the Domaine de la Romanée-Conti, for there were vines in La Tâche belonging to the Lamarches and vines in La Grande Rue owned by the DRC. Things have now been tidied up.

But why was La Grande Rue not appointed *grand cru* in 1936 alongside the rest? It seems to have been Henri Lamarche's decision not to apply. He feared he would have to pay higher taxes. It was Marie-Blanche, wife of Francois, who was the driving force behind the application for reclassification. She started this in 1984. The decree was finally issued on July 8, 1992.

The domaine is rich in enviable parcels of all that is best in the immediate neighbourhood. In the Clos de Vougeot (two-thirds at the top, one-third lower down), the Lamarches own 1.35 hectares; in Grands-Echézeaux 30 ares; in Echézeaux, from the three *lieux-dit* of Champ Traversin, Cruots, and Clos-Saint-Denis, there are 1.32 hectares. There are four *premiers crus* in Vosne-Romanée: Chaumes, La Croix-Rameau,

Malconsorts, and Suchots; and one in Nuits-Saint-Georges, Les Cras. In addition, there is village Vosne, Bourgogne, Hautes Côtes de Nuits and Bourgogne Rouge and Aligoté.

Slowly but surely, since he took over completely upon the death of his father in 1985, Francois, aided by the capable and energetic Marie-Blanche, began to invest in the quality of the Lamarche wines. The two wish they had been able to spend more money sooner, but there were the inevitable financial constraints. Firstly, the harvest was reduced. Figures quoted by Jean-Francois Bazin (La Romanée-Conti, 1994) show yields of as much as fifty casks of La Grande Rue in some of the more abundant vintages in the 1970s: far, far too much. In 2009 there were twenty-four.

A new *cuverie* was installed in 1990, and at the same time a general cleaning up of the cellar. One of the downsides of tasting *chez* Lamarche twenty-five years ago was the smell of drains in the farthest part of the *cave*, where the top wines were stored. This part of the cellar lay underneath the main drain running outside under the road. Naturally this did no good to the wine. There was an extension of the cellar and the offices in 1991. New, more sophisticated temperature control of the winemaking process was introduced in 1998.

Nicole, *diplomé* in oenology, joined her father Francois in 2003. Naturally at first he was in charge. In 2006 the roles were reversed, and in 2007 Nicole made the wines on her own. One of the first things she did was to change her consultant: she wanted someone more expert who shared her objectives. Attention was required in the vineyard. From 2010 the vines are being cultivated biologically. The barrel suppliers were altered: more Francois Frères and a bit of Remon and Seguin-Moreau; less Rousseau, which she found adapted less well to the wine. There is less new wood than hitherto, but the effect is a more sophisticated oaky background in the wine. Now that the cellar is better equipped, the domaine can better nuance things such as cold-soaking before the fermentation starts, and the length and temperature of the fermentation and maceration. Not to mention the amount of new wood, which today averages 50 percent for the top wines. Each vintage brings with it its own recipe.

"My overriding objective," says Nicole, "is to respect the Pinot Noir. Of all the varieties, it is the most complex. In order for it to express its *terroir*, we must respect the environment and keep the viticulture traditional." Yes, she adds, in answer to my question, it would be nice to revert to horses for the ploughing, as they do in the neighbouring La Tâche. "Perhaps in the future. It's very expensive."

"La Grande Rue, in my view, is a more feminine wine than La Tâche. It is closer to Romanée-Saint-Vivant. The age of the vines is now getting venerable, but there is still much to do; more personality to extract. For instance, not all the *porte-greffes* [root-stocks] are the optimum ones for the *climat*."

Lamarche is now a top domaine, with wines which express themselves through their subtlety rather than their power. Since 1999, and more especially since 2005, the quality has been top-notch. This is now a three-star domaine.

TASTING NOTES

The following vintages of La Grande Rue were tasted in Vosne-Romanée in November 2010.

2010
Start of the harvest: September 24
Still very young, and the malo-lactic fermentation yet to take place. Good colour. Medium-full weight. Good grip and concentration. Ripe and fresh. Seems very good indeed at the very least.

2009   From 2021
September 12
En masse. Racked two or three weeks ago. Will be bottled in the spring. Good colour. Rich, indeed opulent nose. Some oak in a roasted chestnut sort of way. Good fresh acidity. Not a bit aggressive. Succulent, rich, balanced, very seductive. Lovely long complex finish. Very fine for the vintage.

2008   From 2018
September 26
Medium to medium-full colour. Quite oaky on the nose. By no means a blockbuster. Indeed quite gentle. Though fresh, the acidity is not a bit dominant. Medium body. Ripe, good grip. Just a little tannin. Lacks a bit of real vigour and concentration, but it is long and elegant. An attractive bottle with a positive finish. Fine plus.

2007   From 2016
September 7
Medium colour, a little development. Soft, fruity nose. Not weak but lacking a bit of backbone and energy. Ripe and fresh though. More to it on the palate. Decent volume and vigour. Good grip. No lack of dimension or richness. Long on the finish. This is very fine for the vintage.

2006   From 2016
September 23
Medium colour. Some development. Gentle, ripe, oaky nose. Balanced and attractive but a little one-dimensional. Quite forward. Once again, better on the palate. Medium to medium-full body. Good grip. Good vigour. Good dimension. The tannins are ripe, and the wine fresh and positive. Finishes very well. Very fine for the vintage.

2005   From 2020
September 17
Splendid colour. The nose has gone into its shell a little. But full, firm, rich, and concentrated. Lovely touch of oak. Lots of dimension. Very fine grip. Full body. Very good tannins; this has a lot of depth. This is a much bigger wine than the 2009. Real energy. Very high quality and a marvelous finish. A great wine.

2004   From 2014
September 25
Good colour. Quite full. Only a little development. At first this was a little pinched and vegetal on the nose. But it got a bit more civilized as it developed. Better on the palate. Quite full. Less oaky than the wines above. Some weight—more so than the 2006—but less attractive. The tannins are a bit dry, and the wine lacks

charm. I hope it will mellow as it ages. But I doubt it.

2003   Now to 2023
August 30

Fine, full, youthful colour. Ample, voluptuous nose. Rich and fullish but soft and fat. Very good acidity for the vintage. And not a bit cooked or pruney. On the palate this is full-bodied, rich and full of summer pudding fruit, supported by very good grip. Most attractive. Very fine for the vintage. Only just about ready.

2002   From 2016
September 22

Good colour. Classy nose. Less oaky than the recent vintages. Balanced and profound. Fullish body. Cool. Very harmonious. Subtle and very long on the palate. Very lovely fruit. Quite delicious. Can be enjoyed now, but all the better in five years' time. Very fine for the vintage.

2001   Now to 2018
September 22

Good colour. No undue development. Attractive, fresh, fruity nose. Really quite a lot of depth here for a 2001. Medium weight. Good fruity attack. Good acidity. No great vigour or concentration on the follow-through. But a wine of charm. Fine for the vintage.

2000   Now to 2015
September 16

From magnum. If anything, this has a deeper and more youthful colour than the 2001. But more developed on the nose: even a little bit oxidised. Less flesh. Medium weight. A slight touch of astringency yet decent grip. This does not have the class or balance of the wine above. Not short but rather ungainly.

1999   Now to 2020
September 20

Medium-full colour. Just about mature. Ripe, full, quite concentrated, quite gamey. Good grip. But it doesn't have the flair of the post-2002 vintages. On the palate full body but somewhat robust, cooked, and "hot." Decent grip and vigour, and it still needs a couple of years. But only "very good indeed" for the vintage. The maceration was prolonged too long.

1998   Now to 2020
September 22

In contrast, this is delicious. Good, quite vigorous colour. Very good nose. Fresh, sophisticated, balanced, and profound. Medium-full body. Good tannins. Most attractive fruit and good grip. It doesn't have the volume of the 1999, but it's a much better wine with a lovely finish. Very fine for the vintage.

1997   Now to 2016
September 20

Medium colour. Mature. No undue age. Soft, ripe nose. But it lacks vigour. Medium weight. Fresher than most 1997s but a little one-dimensional. Ripe and pleasant through and positive at the end. Very good for the vintage.

1991   Now to 2020
October 1

From magnum. Very good colour. Quite full and still vigorous. Fresh nose. Good grip. Mature and complex and plenty of energy. Fullish body. Lots of depth. Very slightly lean perhaps, but a lovely profound wine which will still keep well. Fine plus for the vintage.

1969   Now to 2017
October 6

From half bottles. These varied. Luckily I had one of the better examples. Fullish, fully mature colour. Lovely fragrant, mature, subtle Pinot on the nose. Still fresh. Elegant, complex and fine, with very lovely fruit. Aged quite fast in the glass but an impressive wine.

1955   Drink soon
October 6

The colour is fully mature if not even a bit aged. Soft, ripe nose. Subtle, gentle, and very classy. Medium-full body. Getting towards its end but still very lovely, and, as it turned out, lasting better in the glass than the 1969. Quite a robust wine originally, but it has matured well. Very fine.

Domaine Clos des Lambrays

MOREY-SAINT-DENIS

SINCE THE INAUGURATION of *appellation contrôlée* (AC) in Burgundy in the 1930s, and the classification of land into *grand cru, premier cru,* and so on, there have been frequent minor adjustments to the original legislation, nibbling at the edges in order to redefine the status, usually upwards, of a particular parcel of neighbouring vines. It is easy to see where Clos de Vougeot begins and ends, less so with Clos de la Roche, which has grown in size quite substantially in sixty years. Many other *grands crus* and *premiers crus* have been expanded and, especially in the Côte Chalonnaise but also in the Côte d'Or, entirely new *premiers crus* have been invented, at the whim, it seems to us outsiders, unaware of the decade of lobbying that had preceded it, of the legislator's pen.

However, only twice have we seen the creation of an entirely new *grand cru*; with La Grande Rue in 1992 and Clos des Lambrays in 1981. Both of these, as it happens, are monopolies, as they were in the 1930s (in the case of Lambrays quasi-monopolies, see below). The Lamarche family, proprietors then and now of La Grande Rue, either just couldn't be bothered

or feared that they would have to pay higher taxes.

But what of the Clos des Lambrays? This is a less well-known *climat*. It has been a *grand cru* now for thirty years, but it is only recently that it had any sort of reputation. Did perhaps the authorities make a mistake? A glance at the map, confirmed by a visit in person, will demonstrate that there is a good prima facie case for the Clos des Lambrays always deserving to have been classed *grand cru*. Remember that this is a classification of the potential of the land to make grand wine, not an assessment of the quality in bottle.

Clos des Lambrays, entirely walled as the designation *clos* would suggest, lies immediately to the north of Clos de Tart, though it continues further up the hill. The land undulates in two directions. It inclines from west to east, and it also turns round the slope so there is a descent from south to north. Across the road which leads up from the village of Morey-Saint-Denis, past the Ponsot headquarters, eventually to arrive at a quarry up in the hills, lies Clos-Saint-Denis. Beyond that is Clos de la Roche.

All are at the same level of altitude, have the same sort of protection from the prevailing westerly wind, share the same aspect to the east, and are comprised of more or less the same soil structure, a limestone-marl mixture. Moreover, as I have said, Clos des Lambrays is a monopoly, or nearly. There are economies of scale here, that is if the wine were ever to be called into question. So why was it not decreed to be a *grand cru* in the first place?

Like most of Burgundy, the origins of the vineyard are ecclesiastical. The *seigneurie* of the village of Morey was ceded to the nearby and recently established monastery at Cîteaux by the local lord, Savaric de Vergy, in 1120. A document dating from 1258 refers to the Frères Lambrays and their wines. Papers from the Cîteaux archives confirm that Clos des Lambrays (the name obviously taken from the family who worked the vineyard) was the property of the abbey in 1305. There are further documents dating from 1349.

The name then disappears from the records. No doubt simply because the relevant papers have been lost. We next hear of Lambrays in the Revolution when, like its neighbours, the vineyard is sequestered and sold off. Unlike Clos de Tart, however, it was very quickly morcellated. There were soon as many as seventy-four different proprietors, we are told (though as there are a mere 8.7 hectares, I find this somewhat exaggerated). What is more indisputable is that the quality fell in reputation. Dr. Morelot (1831) mentions all the other Morey *grands crus* save Lambrays.

Rescue, however, was on hand in the person of Louis Joly, a merchant in Nuits-Saint-Georges. He started buying up some of the fragments in the early 1830s. There is a *terroir* (land register) dating from 1836 where he is listed as possessing 4.84 hectares. By 1855, according to the historian Lavalle—who places the wine alongside Bonnes-Mares and Clos de la Roche as a *première cuvée* (Clos de Tart is graded higher as *tête de cuvée*), indicating that quality has been restored—Joly ownes 7 hectares, and it would seem that this is the entirety

of the *climat*. Joly had restored both the reputation of the wine and the monopoly. He was also to renovate the *château*, parts of which date from the seventeent century (the cellar is medieval), and laid out a splendid secluded, shady garden.

Ten years later, he sold Clos des Lambrays to Albert Sébastien Rodier, director of a fellow Nuits-Saint-Georges merchant company, Maison Henri de Bahèzre. It was this celebrated negociant—Henri de Bahèzre enjoyed a powerful reputation at the time—who properly established Clos des Lambrays as a *grand cru* and took it up to its present size.

After the First World War, sadly, the business, now in the hands of Rodier's grandsons Camille and Albert, went into decline. The brothers did not get on. Albert was left struggling and undercapitalised with the business while Camille found a new career as an author (never has there been a wine writer more apt to plagiarise without acknowledgment) and cofounder with Georges Faiveley of the Confrérie des Chevaliers de Tastevin.

Fortunately Albert had a rich mistress. This was the sculptress Renée Cosson. She had a fortune in her own right and had married a wealthy Parisian banker. M. Cosson had "neither the time nor the inclination to live in Morey," according to Charles Quittanson, who has written a monograph on Clos des Lambrays. Renée Cosson, however, was quite willing to buy out the Cossons and take over as proprietor and *chatelaine* at the nearby *château* in 1938.

More hard times were to follow, sadly, and Madame Cosson, passionate about her vineyard, was obdurate. As, one by one, the old pre-phylloxera vines began to give up the ghost, she refused to replace them. She also failed to compost the vineyard. She would not allow Albert Rodier to chaptalise, insisted on very long *cuvaisons*, and kept the wine, if it had not found a buyer, several years in cask. In 1979 there was still some unbottled 1973 in the cellar. The *rendement* fell to 10 hectolitres per hectare.

The wine, despite this, could be truly magnificent, and I can testify to this personally. Alexis Lichine was a customer. On separate occasions at the Prieuré in Cantenac in the late 1970s and early 1980s, I was lucky enough to be able to share with him the 1945, the 1947, the 1948, and the 1949. I regard them as some of the finest Burgundies I have ever drunk. The label, I recall, was designed by the Alsacien Hansi, a friend of Renée Cosson.

None of Renée Cosson's children—one at least being Albert's—was willing to take over, and in the 1970s she put the property up for sale. In 1974, at the time of the oil crisis, it failed to find a buyer at the equivalent of $20 million U.S.

Renée Cosson died in May 1977, and in 1979, for the equivalent of $10 million U.S., it was rumoured, the heirs sold the vineyard and *château* to a consortium which consisted of the brothers Fabien and Louis Saier, originally from Alsace (they were also already owners of a 28 hectare domaine which included vineyards in Morey-Saint-Denis, Aloxe-Corton, and Mercurey), Roland Pelletier de Chambure, a member of an old Burgundian family, and Robert Margnat. The new owners appointed Thierry Brouin, born in 1948, an *oenologue* who had worked for the Institut National des Appellations d'Origine (INAO), as manager, and put in for promotion to *grand cru*. This was granted on April 27, 1981.

Why had the Cossons and Rodiers, owners at the time, not put Clos des Lambrays forward for *grand cru* in the 1930s? No one is quite sure. The answer seems to be, as with La Grande Rue, sheer inertia, together with a worry that they'd pay more tax.

The new management had much to do. Brouin had to replant much of the northern part of the vineyard—some 2.44 hectares—and fill in the holes elsewhere. Just over half the surface area today consists of vines planted in the early 1980s. The house and park were restored. The cellars were modernised. In all, a great deal of money was spent.

As the new vines came into fruition, the question arose: What to do with their wine?

The solution was simple: a second wine, Morey-Saint-Denis, *premier cru*, called Les Loups. A citizen of Morey is not called a Moreysien but a *loup*, a wolf. The entire 1991 harvest was downgraded. In most vintages some 30 to 40 percent is declassed.

The Saier consortium then ran into difficulties. Margnat had already been bought out. Then Roland Pelletier de Chambure, in his old age, wanted to relinquish his share. The Saiers bought this, but at the height of the market in 1988, at a price which subsequently they found hard to support. Clos des Lambrays was for sale again: ironically, just when it seemed that the wine was once again beginning to show its true potential.

The saviours this time were German: Günther Freund, who died in November 2010 at the age of eighty-eight, and his son Joachim. Their fortune was based on poster-site advertising, where in Germany they were number one. At the end of 1996, and for a sum equivalent to $9 million U.S., they found themselves in charge of the largest *grand cru* parcel under a single proprietor.

The Freunds had no intention of being absentee landlords. The building which formerly housed the offices was extended and changed into a private apartment for the Freund family, and a personal cellar constructed. On the other side of the courtyard, whence the offices have now been moved, a *salle de réception* was installed. The garden, with its mature trees, including a cedar planted in 1637, was thankfully left untouched. The future of Clos des Lambrays was assured.

The vineyard measures 203 *ouvrées*, which is precisely 8 hectares 70 ares 48 centiares. To be even more precise, it is not truthfully the monopoly of the Clos. One *ouvrée* (420 square metres) at the bottom is owned by Jean Taupenot-Merme and his wife, who live below, but I believe they normally mix the produce of this into one of their Morey-Saint-Denis *premiers crus*. I have never seen it offered separately. But my friend Nigel Bruce tells me that he has seen the 2005 on offer in Hong Kong.

The soil is a deep red-brown marl, rich in iron. The clay content gets higher as you move downslope, thus the *cuvées* from the bottom give the body and the power, those from the top the finesse. Nevertheless, as Brouin will point out, while Clos de Tart resembles Bonnes-Mares in its red fruit character, Clos des Lambrays exhibits black fruit—"those small cherries we call *aigres-douces* [sweet-sour], plus *mûres* [bramble] and liquorice"—rare in the Côte de Nuits but similar, I would add, to its northern neighbours, Clos-Saint-Denis and Clos de la Roche. (But see the final paragraph below.)

In order to avoid erosion, as at Clos de Tart to the south but rarely elsewhere in the Côte d'Or, the vines are planted north-south, not east-west, with a density of eleven thousand vines a hectare.

Thierry Brouin understands his Clos by heart, and he is an adept winemaker. It is *triage* (the sorting through of the fruit to eliminate anything rotten, bruised, or unripe) which is the key to great wine, he says. And the *tri* here is severe. After a short natural cold-soaking, the wine is vinified with all its stems, at a maximum of 34°C, with regular *pigeage* until the fermentation has come to its end, and a long maceration. It then goes into 50 percent new wood from François *frères* in Saint-Romain, where it stays for fifteen to eighteen months. There is no fining: occasionally a very light filtration.

In Morey, the Domaine des Lambrays produces a village wine from vines upslope from the *clos*, a *premier cru* and the *grand vin* itself. It also offers two delicious *premier cru* Pulignys from 37 ares of Les Caillerets and 29 ares of Les Folatières. But what of the Clos des Lambrays itself? If the old wines were majestic—see my comments above—have we had anything resembling them under the Saier and Freund regimes? Well, not immediately. They missed a trick in 1990, and the 1993 and 1995, by the rigorous standards we are entitled to judge *grand cru* Burgundy by, are not as fine as they should have been, indeed not "fine" by my standards. But the 1988 was, as was the 1989. And vintages since 1996 and more particularly those of

the 2000s have certainly been equal to the very best the top vineyards of Morey-Saint-Denis can offer.

The vines now average sixty years old, and two-thirds of them are now ploughed with a horse. As next door at the Clos de Tart, the *cuvées*, six to eight of them, correspond to sections of the vineyard. Sometimes one from the top seems the best, sometimes one of those from lower down. But a blend is better than the sum of the parts. And, moreover, this will show the signature of the Clos. In recent years, as the vines have got older and older, I have found the essential character of the wine move just a little towards that of Clos de Tart. Twenty years ago I would have described the wine as red fruity. Today it is definitely more of a black fruit wine. It is a brilliant wine today.

TASTING NOTES

I sampled the following vintages of Clos des Lambrays in Morey-Saint-Denis in February 2011.

2009   From 2020 plus

At present *en masse*, waiting for bottling in March. Very good colour. The nose is a little subdued by the recent adjustment to the sulphur levels. Delicious ripe fruit nevertheless. Fullish without being a blockbuster. Rich, abundant, classy, and persistent. Very finely balanced. Very graceful. Very fine.

2008   From 2018 plus

Slightly less colour than the 2008. Earthy-minty nose. But ample, fullish, fresh, and with very good backbone. Underneath the slight austerity on the palate, this is really quite rich. Very good tannins. Black fruit–flavoured and very fine for the vintage.

2007   From 2016

Surprisingly good colour. Lots of depth on the nose. This has a volume and depth which few 2007s possess. Very classy fruit, with just a touch of the new wood. A marvelous example of the vintage. Lovely harmony and great class.

2006   From 2016

Very good colour. Just a hint of development.
Fullish, quite firm nose. Rich and succulent.
Fresh and classy. Plenty of depth. Just a hint of
new oak on the palate. Fullish body. Very good
tannins. Fresh, generous, profound, and seductive. Very lovely.

2005   From 2018

Very fine colour. Somewhat aloof but very
classy nose. Profound and slightly austere, but
with great finesse and distinction. Medium-
full body. Very well-integrated tannins. On the
palate rich and harmonious and multidimensional: more generous than on the nose. Marvelous finish. Excellent.

2004   From 2014

Good colour. Just a little development. The nose
is a little lean and vegetal. But on the palate
there is good weight and rather more richness
than you might expect from the nose. Good
tannins. The finish is again a little green, but
the wine will improve as it rounds off. Lacks a
little charm nevertheless.

2003   From 2013

Very good colour. Still youthful. Fine nose.
Unexpectedly classy. Fresh, fat, rich, and generous. Not a bit too stewed and pruney. Really
quite stylish. Some tannin still to resolve. But
these are ripe. Oaky, voluptuous, and surprisingly fresh. Excellent for the vintage.

2002   From 2013

Medium-full colour. Still youthful. Fullish,
ample, plump, and well-balanced on the nose.
Lots of complexity and nuance. On the palate
this is approaching maturity. Medium-full
body. Lots of energy and depth. Very poised.
Very lovely. Very long on the palate.

2001   Now to 2020 plus

Surprisingly good colour. Just a little maturity.
Fresh, gentle, plump, fruity nose. Not a blockbuster but no lack of depth or dimension. Lots
of fruit and no lack of class. *À point* now and
quite delicious.

2000   Now to 2015

Medium colour. Now just about mature. Ripe
and fruity and stylish on the nose. But it doesn't
have the freshness, vigour, and volume of the
2001. On the palate ripe and plump. Only
medium body. But a most enjoyable wine. A lot
better than most.

1999   Now to 2030

Excellent full, youthful colour. Fresh, rich, concentrated, and multidimensional nose. This
was Thierry Brouin's biggest yield (45 hl/ha
after a green harvest). Excellent complexity and
dimension. Still youthful. On the palate fullish body, very good tannins, lots of vigour. Not
quite as classy as the 2002 and 2005, but very
seductive. Very long and surprisingly fresh at
the end. Just about ready.

Domaine Leroy

VOSNE-ROMANÉE

ALMOST A CENTURY AND A HALF ago, in 1868, François Leroy set himself up as a wine merchant in his native village of Auxey-Duresses, just round the corner from Meursault. The business was expanded by his son Joseph, who took over at about the turn of the century, and further developed by the next generation in the person of Henri, born in 1894, who entered the family affair in 1919. Henri diversified into *eaux de vie* and cognac, establishing a model distillery at Ségonzac and as well as fine wine, sold lesser bulk wine to Germany, where it was made into *sekt*, and brandy in the same direction particularly to Asbach. During the 1930s Henri became firstly a client of the Domaine de la Romanée-Conti (DRC) and then a good friend of Edmond Gaudin de Villaine, the *gérant* and co-owner with his brother-in-law Jacques Chambon.

These were hard times. The DRC was a bottomless pit necessitating yearly expensive investment on the one hand but yielding no profit on the other. It seemed inevitable that it would have to be sold. And if it were to pass out of the Chambon-De Villaine hands, Henri Leroy and his friend knew only too well, it would be the start of the slippery slope. Before too long the vineyards of Romanée-Conti and La Tâche would be as morcellated as that of Clos de Vougeot.

Some years later, in 1942, with the financial structure of the domaine having been changed to a *société civile*, Jacques Chambon decided to sell out. Henri Leroy bought the Chambon share and became co-owner of the Domaine de la Romanée-Conti. For the meantime, however, he was content to take a back seat, at least officially. It was not until 1950, after Edmond Gaudin de Villaine's death, that he became co-*gerant* alongside Edmond's son, also Christened Henri. The two were to run the DRC jointly until 1974. Henri Leroy passed away on February 21, 1980. As he had commanded, the domaine's Richebourg 1952 was opened after his funeral in his memory.

Henri Leroy and his wife, Simone (*née* Brun), had two daughters: Pauline (born 1929) and Marcelle (universally known as Lalou, born 1932). It was the latter, adored and adoring younger daughter, who was to inherit her father's passion for wine. Lalou, born in Paris, was brought up in Meursault, in the mansion today occupied by her daughter Perrine. "From the word go I was fascinated," she says. "I was a cellar rat, watching and helping the *cavistes* rack the wines, taste them, bottle them. My mother kept calling me to come out of the cellar to play with my friends like a normal schoolgirl, but as soon as I could I crept back." Henri Leroy, his attention diverted by the DRC, had somewhat neglected his *négociant* business. Lalou remembers 1937s still in cask long after the war. In 1955 she persuaded her father to let her take over. She was twenty-three. "He gave me *carte blanche*," she says. "I started as I meant to go on. I bought finished wine, and only that which pleased me. I insisted on having no contracts, no moral obligations. If the wine wasn't *extra*, I didn't buy it."

The turnover of Leroy wines has always been modest, the stock to back it up enormous: totally uneconomic. But it has always been subsidised: firstly by the bulk German business, later by the Leroy sales exclusivity of the DRC wines. Except for the UK and the United States, this all passed through Leroy. Three-quarters of the Leroy turnover came from selling DRC wines.

In 1974 the co-managership at the DRC passed down a generation, to Lalou, representing her sister (they both owned 25 percent) and Aubert, son of Henri de Villaine, representing his brothers, sisters, and cousins (there are ten of them). From the start this was a fiery relationship. Lalou is not an easy character: emotional, insecure, arrogant, temperamental, and combative, she must have been a trial to the pacific, intellectual Aubert. It was a fire awaiting a match. Early in 1992, following a boardroom dispute, Lalou was relieved of her position as co-*gérante*, and the Domaine de la Romanée-Conti took over responsibility for selling and marketing its wines throughout the world.

Meanwhile, at the other end of Vosne-Romanée, lay the headquarters of the Charles Noëllat domaine. The landholdings were impressive: nearly a hectare of Romanée-Saint-Vivant, over a hectare and a half of very well-placed Clos de Vougeot, 78 ares of Richebourg, substantial *premier cru* vineyard in Nuits-Saint-Georges, Les Boudots and Vosne-Romanée, Aux Beaux Monts and Aux Brûlées. Charles Noëllat had died in 1969, and despite some of the land passing to the other members of the family, notably what are today the Alain Hudelot-Noëllat and J. J. Confuron estates, the residue still amounted to 12 hectares. But it was moribund. Quality was unremarkable and inconsistent. Yet the potential was high. "Yes, the wines they produced were terrible," says Lalou. "But the quality of the vines were great. All honour to Charles Noëllat. The vines were old, reproduced by *sélection Massale*. And in the Romanée-Saint-Vivant they are particularly superb, giving very small fine berries. Yardstick Pinot Noir fruit. I have never seen anything so fine in all of Burgundy."

In 1988 the estate came on the market. It is said that AXA were interested. But Leroy made a better offer. Subsequently, in July, Lalou and Pauline sold one-third of their interest in Leroy to their Japanese agents Takashimaya in order to finance the 65 million franc acquisition of Charles Noëllat, including buildings and stock. (After a number of years offering the plums of this stock around the trade, the residue was sold at jumble sale prices in an auction in Dijon in 1992.)

At a stroke, the addition of the Charles Noëllat domaine to that of Leroy, mainly based in Auxey and Meursault but with tiny holdings in Chambertin, Clos de Vougeot (at the bottom), and Musigny, transformed it into one of Burgundy's major players. But things did not stop here. In 1989, for 19 million francs, Lalou acquired the Gevrey-based 2.5 hectare Domaine Philippe Remy. This added 40 ares of Chambertin, 57 ares of Latricières, 67 ares of Clos de la Roche, as well as *premiers crus* in Gevrey-

Chambertin, Les Combottes, and village land in Gevrey and Chambolle. It neatly complemented the Noëllat estate. A year later Lalou increased her holding in Le Musigny by buying a parcel from the Moine-Hudelot family. Some Corton, both red and white, has followed, as has some Volnay, Santenots. Today the domaine measures just under 22.5 hectares.

At the same time, in her own right, Lalou has made further acquisitions. High up on the plateau above Saint Romain is an ancient farm—records go back to a donation from Raynaud, *seigneur* of Saint Romain, to Messieurs de La Ferté in 1180—known as the Domaine D'Auvenay. It used to belong to Henri Leroy's bachelor brother. It is here that Lalou lives with her husband, Marcel Bize, who sadly died in 2004. While she occupied herself with wine, he ran the farm, biodynamically, of course.

Under the name of Auvenay, Lalou has added on to the land in Auxey and Meursault that she inherited from her father: 51 ares of Puligny-Montrachet Les Folatières in 1989, 6.4 ares of Criots in 1990, 16.3 ares of Chevalier-Montrachet (from Jean Chartron) in 1992, 26 ares of Bonnes-Mares in 1993, and, then 26 ares of Mazis-Chambertin (Lalou had always bought the wine) from the Collignon family in 1994. A further purchase occured in 2011: 7 *ouvrées* of Bâtard-Montrachet and some village Puligny, Les Enseignères. The total is now just about 4 hectares. Vinification of this is quite separate from that of Domaine Leroy. In 1994 a brand new *cuverie* was installed up at Auvenay.

In many ways the seemingly hard-nosed Lalou Bize is the last person you would expect to be seduced by any new fad. That biodynamism is not a fad is proven by the fact that the Domaines Leroy and Auvenay have joined the increasing number who have gone not just *biologique* but the full way.

Nicolas Joly's Coulée de Serrant at Savennières was Lalou's Road to Damascus. "I shall never forget," says Nicolas. "There was Lalou, dressed up as if she had just stepped out of some *maison de haute couture* in Paris, on her knees, running the soil of the Coulée de Serrant through her fingers, and exclaiming, 'Ça, c'est la vérité.'" Actually, Lalou maintains she was probably wearing jeans.

"The soil was alive," says Lalou. "Everything was alive, and in place, in harmony with one another: the earth, the plants, the fruit and the wine. I really do believe that cosmic rhythms should determine when we do things. And that we should encourage the vine to build up its own resistance and allow it to express its own *terroir*. So we have proscribed all chemical treatments except very minimal doses of sulphur against oidium and copper sulphate against mildew." In 1993, to avoid further compacting the soil with yet another tractor treatment, Lalou sprayed against mildew by helicopter. Sadly, this proved ineffective, and as a result her crop was reduced almost to nothing.

In many ways the Leroy winemaking methods are deeply traditional. When she took over at what was to become the Domaine Leroy, Lalou inherited some magnificent examples of old, high-quality Pinot Noir vines but vineyards which were in many cases only half full. Yields naturally were cut to shreds, averaging 15 hectolitres per hectare (hl/ha) or so. She took her time about replacing the holes with new vines, these being propagated by *selection massale* from her own plants. Pruning is excessively strict. But now, except in 2008, when she lost a majority of her crop to rot and mildew and in some cases made only 11 hl/ha, yields are 25 hl/ha or so, a little more economic. As much as possible, the land used to be ploughed using horses. But this proved too hard to manage. Half the time the animals and their ploughmen did not turn up. They have been replaced with very light baby tractors which weigh less than a horse. For the past ten years the Leroy vines have not had their excess folaige clipped back in the summer, Lalou believing this stresses the plant. Instead, the shoots of two vines are looped round one another. It makes it easy to identify a Leroy vine.

In the cellar there is no destemming, a severe *triage*, two pumpings-over at the beginning of the fermentation and then two or three *pigeages* a day—there were automatic plungers, but they have now reverted to *pigeage à pied*—and a long *cuvaison* at temperatures up to 33°C. Each vat at Vosne-Romanée is equipped with an internal temperature-controlling stainless steel coil. After the *cuvaison* the press wine is incorporated, the lees are retained, and the wine transferred to cask. One hundred percent new wood is used. There is no filtration, and not always a fining either. Lalou Bize says she wants to preserve the fruit, so bottling tends to be early, often after only twelve to fifteen months or so.

The range of the Domaine Leroy wines is a roll call of all that is great in Burgundy, the monopolies excepted, of course. There are eight red wine *grands crus*: Chambertin, Richebourg, Romanée-Saint-Vivant, Musigny, Clos de Vougeot, Latricières-Chambertin, Clos de la Roche, and Corton, Renardes. And there is some Corton-Charlemagne. Add to this eight *premiers crus*, from Gevrey-Chambertin, Les Combottes to Volnay, Santenots, and some very good single-vineyard village wines, and we have a mouthwateringly impressive list. And quality is generally very high indeed, if perhaps not as invariably "extra!" as Lalou will pronounce, they are when you taste alongside each other out of cask. But the prices! There is absolutely no concession here. Nevertheless, there being more than enough millionaire collectors about, what Madame Bize produces is snapped up the moment it is put on the market.

The following Leroy wines were sampled in Nashville, Tennessee, courtesy of my friend Tom Black, in April 2010.

Corton-Charlemagne

1995   Drink soon   14.0

Very fresh colour. Curiously flat and anonymous yet fresh enough. But by no means the depth and interest of a *grand cru*. Just very dull.

1993   Drink up   12.5

Quite a developed colour and at first an interesting if slightly oxidised nose, together with a touch of oak. Plenty of depth, it seemed, and good grip. But it fell away rapidly in the glass. After twenty minutes it was barely drinkable.

1992   Now to 2014   16.0

Youthful colour. Plump attractive nose. Round and flowery-fruity. Medium to medium-full body. Not a great deal of concentration and depth. But fresh and balanced. Very good.

1989   Now to 2017   18.0

Full, fresh colour. Rich nose. Youthful and fresh. Elegant and with good fruit. But not a great deal of depth at first. Improved as it developed. Still young. Nicely steely. Very classic. Lots of energy still. Held up well in the glass. Fine plus.

Clos de Vougeot

2005   2020 to 2040   19.0

Full, immature colour. Full, rich, concentrated, pure, stylish nose. Fullish body. Very energetic. A lovely, classy wine and one of the best wines of the tasting. This is very poised, harmonious, and classy. Splendid finish. More to it than the 2002. Very lovely.

2003   Drink soon   12.0

Very full colour. Not much sign of maturity. Strangely, exotic nose. Slightly sweet-sour. As well as caramelised. Fat and rich but tarty. No grip underneath. I don't like this at all.

2002   2015 to 2035   18.5

Medium-full colour. Just about mature. Rich, clean, fresh, stylish nose. Not a blockbuster, it seems. Fullish body. Still some tannin. Lots of vigour and grip. Lots of depth and class too. Very well put together. A very fine Clos de Vougeot. Still needs five years.

2001   Now to 2020   17.0

Medium colour. If anything, this is browner at the rim than the 2000. Some depth on the nose. More volume than the 2000. But no great finesse. Spicy though, and this gives it interest. Some richness, some fat, some body. Now fully ready. Good energy at the end. Very good indeed.

2000   Now to 2015   15.5
Medium-full, mature colour. Quite full and fruity, if no great depth and finesse. A bit superficial, in fact. Medium to medium-full body. Ripe, still fresh, generous, and balanced. But like most 2000s, a lack of dimension.

1999   Now to 2030   19.0
Fine, full, immature colour. Rich, abundant, harmonious, three-dimensional nose. Very lovely fruit here. Fullish body. Quite meaty, very ripe, and rich on the palate. Lots of energy. The finish is very impressive. Very, very lovely. Only just about ready. One of the best wines of the tasting.

1998   Now to 2020   17.5
Medium-full colour. Just about mature. Soft, round, ripe, attractive nose. Lots of charm. Medium-full body. Fresh and harmonious. Not the greatest depth and vigour, but lovely balance and lovely fruit. Long and fresh and absolutely *à point*.

1996   Drink soon   16.5
Fullish, immature colour. Not as rich or as full as the 1993 and the acidity is a little dominant. Yet very fresh and elegant, at least at first. Medium-full body. On the attack there is very good fruit and complexity, class, and balance. It is a lovely wine. But it needs drinking soon and with food. Keep it and the acidity will begin to dominate.

1993   Now to 2025   19.0
Splendid full, immature colour. The nose is still closed. Very rich and concentrated. Some tannin still to resolve. On the palate this is essence of wine—it was a microscopic crop. Excellent fruit and grip. Velvety rich. Fine acidity. Very, very long and complex. Only just ready. Brilliant.

1991   Now to 2020 plus   18.0
Fullish, vigorous colour. Lovely nose. Even better on the palate. Fullish body and lots of vigour. Very good grip. Classy and harmonious, unlike the wines older than this. Long. Still fresh and sweet. Better than 1990 and 1989. Fine plus.

1990   Now to 2017   17.0
Very good colour. Still very young. Lovely nose. Rich, full, complete and intense, slightly oaky. On the palate not as exciting. Full-bodied, sturdy, unrelaxed. There is energy here but not distinction. A wine for food.

1989   Drink soon   14.0
Very good colour. The nose reminds me of a sweet counter: rather artificial fruit. Medium body. Lacks real balance and class. Somewhat four-square and dry at the end.

1985   Drink soon   16.5
Fine, full, vigorous colour. Lovely pure, fresh, succulent nose. Fullish body on the palate. Not as splendid as the nose. Somewhat astringent. The finish is elegant, but the wine is beginning to fall apart. Very good plus at best.

1959   Past its best
Fullish, mature colour. Fragrant, sweetly-rich if not very vigorous or very elegant any more. There was a hint of mushrooms as it developed. Was better a decade ago.

The following range of Leroy and Auvenay wines was offered at a tasting and dinner at Restaurant Benoit, New York, organised by Wine Workshop, in March 2012. The wines are all Domaine Leroy unless otherwise stated.

Vosne-Romanée, Aux

Beaux Monts, 1999   2015 to 2030   18.5
Fine colour. Firm nose, still closed. Rich and profound. Full-bodied, rich, and oaky on the palate. Lots of energy and grip. Lots of depth. Very lovely. Very high-class. Will still improve.

Richebourg, 1999   2015 to 2040   20.0
Fullish colour. Just about mature. Still quite closed on the nose. But lots and lots of depth

and concentration. Very intense and very high-class. Full-bodied. Not yet ready. A very impressive, profound, multidimensional wine. Excellent grip. Marvelous fruit. Splendid long finish. Indisputably great.

Vosne-Romanée, Aux
Beaux Monts, 1998   Now to 2020 plus   18.0
Medium-full colour. Quite a difference in weight and maturity to the 1999. Medium to medium-full body. Soft, graceful, fresh, and fragrant. Good energy. Very classy. Opened up in the glass. *À point*. Delicious.

Clos de Vougeot, 1988   Now to 2020 plus   18.0
Medium colour. Some development. More so than the Bonnes-Mares. Ripe, open, accessible. Attractive, fragrant, juicy fruit. Elegant and harmonious. But not the vigour of the Bonnes-Mares or the depth. Yet a lovely long finish. Fine plus.

Bonnes-Mares, 1988
(Auvenay)   2015 to 2030   19.0
Medium-full, just about mature colour. Still quite closed on the nose. Rich, fat, and concentrated. Lots of wine here. Lots of energy. Some tannin too. Very good grip. Lovely fruit. Will still improve. Splendidly fresh all ther way through. Very fine indeed for a 1998.

Chambertin, 1998   2015 to 2030   19.5
Medium-full colour. Still quite youthful. Interesting exotic nose with a touch of coffee. Certainly rich and opulent. Fine balance and high quality. Full-bodied. Splendid grip and concentration. Very, very rich and youthful. Only just about ready. Indeed it will still improve. Excellent.

Mazis-Chambertin, 1997
(Auvenay)   Now to 2020 plus   18.5
Medium-full, mature colour. Spicy nose, soft and round. Lacks just a little grip but fresher than most 1997s. Fullish for the vintage. Vigorous too. Fresh and juicy. Ripe and with excellent grip. Very classy. There can't be many 1997s better than this.

Mazis-Chambertin, 1996
(Maison Leroy)   Now to 2020   18.0
The only bottle not made by Leroy, but brought in as wine. Full, vigorous colour. Still closed on the nose. Rich and full-bodied. Perhaps a little solid. Good acidity. But a little astringency. And an absence of succulence. Rather better with food, but it lacks sex appeal.

Romanée-Saint-Vivant,
1996   Now to 2020   18.5
Fullish colour. Some development. Rich, fat, and ample on the nose. But it doesn't have the intensity and class I expected. Fullish body. *À point* now. Splendid fruit. Very good grip. And indeed no lack of elegance. More to it than appeared on the nose, and a lovely long finish. But very fine rather than great.

Clos de Vougeot, 1995   Now to 2030   19.5
Medium-full colour. Just about mature. Rich, fresh, harmonious nose. Round and concentrated. Very good grip and class. Fullish body. Just about ready. Lots of vigour. Very lovely fruit. A lovely wine, very long on the palate.

Volnay, Santenots, 1992   Now to 2016   15.5
Full colour. Rich, fat, and vigorous on the nose, especially for the vintage. Lovely ripe fruit. Succulent and balanced. Medium body. On the palate somewhat less vigorous and succulent than on the nose. But balanced and attractive. No hurry to drink.

Clos de la Roche, 1991   Now to 2016   18.0
Good full vigorous colour. Attractive, individual nose. A hint of meat *jus*. Ample, ripe, even fat. Good volume and depth. Medium body. Best on the attack, which is fresh and accessible, balanced and classy. But on the follow-through it tails off slightly. Delicious nevertheless.

Nuits Saint-Georges,
Aux Boudots, 1990   Now to 2019   17.0
Fullish, mature but vigorous colour. A touch of cooked fruit on the nose. Rich, fat, and spicy. With mocha touches. Fullish. But quite sturdy. A meaty wine with a touch of astringency on

the follow-through. Very good indeed, but it is a little unsophisticated. A wine for food.

Latricières-Chambertin,

1990 Now to 2025 19.0

Good colour. No real sign of maturity. Ample, ripe, sductive, spicy nose. Quite high toned. Mocha touches. Rather more civilised than many 1990s today. Fresher. More fragrant. More classy. More harmonious. Fullish body. A lovely 1990 which is still an infant. Very fine indeed.

Chambertin, 1989 See note

Full, vigorous colour. At first I was inclined to say this was corked, but the off-smell was more of damp cardboard than sweaty socks, and it largely blew off after a while in the glass. Not perfect, but rich and concentrated, ripe and intense. Fullish body. Lots of vigour. Could have been a great wine, with rather more energy than most 1989s today.

And I had the following for lunch the next day:

Gevrey-Chambertin,
Lavaut-Saint-Jacques, 1985
(Maison Leroy) Now to 2017 18.0

Medium-full, mature colour. Ample, ripe, vigorous nose. Lots of lovely ripe fruit. Fresh and classy and harmonious. Sweet and succulent. Good grip. Medium-full body. Very smooth and subtle at the end. Will still last. Fine plus.

Vicomte de Liger-Belair

VOSNE-ROMANÉE

THE VICOMTE DE LIGER-BELAIR is both ancient and modern: ancient because it was acquired by Louis Liger-Belair, Napoleonic general, in 1815; and modern in that it was relaunched by his successor Vicomte Louis-Michel Liger-Belair in 2000. Since 1827, the diamond in the crown of the estate has been the monopoly of La Romanée, one of the very few *grand cru* monopolies in Burgundy—and the smallest.

The minuscule *climat* of Romanée lies directly above that of La Romanée-Conti and is separated from it by a path. Further upslope is the *premier cru* Aux Reignots, to the north is Richebourg, to the south La Grande Rue. As all the Burgundian *grands crus* are *appellations* in their own right, La Romanée has its own separate *appellation contrôlée*. At 85 ares it is the tiniest in France. (La Romanée-Conti, which covers 1.81 hectares, is the second smallest.) Like La Romanée-Conti, it is a monopoly, under the exclusive ownership of the Comte Liger-Belair family, as it has been since its creation.

Eighty-five ares, of course, doesn't produce much wine, especially if the vines are old and carefully pruned so that the production is severely limited. The Romanée yield has varied in the last decade from 25 hectolitres to 33. Thirty-two hectolitres is equivalent to 37.8 hectolitres/hectare (hl/ha). And 350 cases of wine.

It is now generally accepted that La Romanée was never part of La Romanée-Conti. What was to become La Romanée was a *lieu-dit* called Aux Échanges (or Aux Changes), part of which was included in Les Richebourgs. At the time its illustrious downslope neighbour was the property of the Prince—let's give him his full name, it sounds so marvelously impressive: Son Altesse Sérénissime Monseigneur Louis-François-Joseph de Bourbon, Prince de Conti. In a map produced for the Prince de Conti in 1760, we can see that this was divided into six parcels, varying from one *ouvrée* (4 ares) to one *journal* (30 ares). Other evidence shows that it was similarly divided two and a half centuries prior to 1760.

One of the subsequent proprietors, in 1791,

was a Madame Lamy de Samery. She was the owner of the one *ouvrée*. Her children emigrated to escape the French Revolution and after she died in 1797, this parcel was confiscated and put up for sale. It was sold to a pair of Dijon wine merchants, Messrs Viénot-Rameau and Bruet-Crétinet. Three years later it passed to Nicolas-Guillaume Basire. He was the father-in-law of General Louis Liger-Belair, who acquired the land upon his marriage in 1815. Over the next twelve years the general, who died in 1824, followed by his adopted successor, Louis-Charles, the son of his sister, slowly pieced together the rest of the *lieu-dit*. This was declared on the land registry in the town hall of Vosne in July 1827 as La Romanée.

The vines of La Romanée form a square, lying at an altitude of between 275 and 300 metres, on a distinct slope. The soil structure is not that different from La Romanée-Conti below except that there is less clay: a *limono-argileux* feeble in the sand fraction, mixed with pebbles and decayed limestone boulders, based on a friable Premeaux limestone rock. The depth of surface soil is shallow.

Cultivation is difficult. There is an odd camber in the slope making the use of tractors inappropriate. Much has to be done by hand. Moreover, the vines are fragile. The *climat* has never been properly disinfected.

La Romanée is not an easy wine to taste from cask. Compared with the Reignots, which can be already round and fat after a year in barrel, La Romanée is austere: "not *hautaine* [snobbish or haughty], but severe." Another word would be "aloof." It has neither quite the aristocratic, aromatic intensity of La Romanée-Conti nor the sumptuousness of Richebourg. But as it matures and begins to throw off the element of reserve it has in its youth, there is splendid perfume in evidence. La Romanée is unmistakably of top-quality *grand cru* lineage.

La Romanée continued for the next century as one of the stars of the Liger-Belair holdings. But as they also owned La Tâche, also purchased first by Viénot-Rameau and then by Basire, it was only number two in the hierar-

chy. The Liger-Belairs had formed a merchant company in 1852 together with Félix Marey, the father-in-law of Louis-Charles. The estate also comprised land in Malconsorts, Chaumes, Reignots, Brulées, and Suchots, all in Vosne-Romanée, as well as Vaucrains in Nuits-Saint-Georges, Clos de Vougeot, and Chambertin. In all 60 hectares, not to mention 15 in Fleurie. Sometimes, God forbid, as records show, the fruit was even turned into a sort of mock champagne!

Sadly, the First World War and the resultant depression hit the Liger-Belair family severely. Comte Henri de Liger-Belair, grandson of Louis-Charles, died in 1924. His wife passed away in 1931. At the time there were two minors among their ten children, and the law prevented a division of the estate as a result. Succession could only be resolved by putting the whole domaine up for sale at auction. In 1933 both La Romanée and La Tâche, plus the less prestigious vineyards, were put up for sale. La Tâche was acquired by Edmond Gaudin de Villaine and Jacques Chambon of the Domaine de la Romanée-Conti. Who was to purchase La Romanée?

One of the members of the Liger-Belair family was Just, a priest (he later became a canon) born in 1904. Another was Comte Michel, grandfather of today's Louis-Michel. "I couldn't let all these family treasures evaporate away," the priest was later to say. "But in those days one didn't compete with a friend, and I knew that René Engel was interested in buying La Romanée. Anyway, away I went to the auction. When the sale was announced, the village people urged me to go ahead. 'Just, we are waiting to hear from you,' they said. I stuck my hand up. I didn't care what it cost me. Engel finally backed down. So, together with my brother, I was able to keep hold of some of the patrimony of my ancestors." They also were able to purchase the Reignots and the Chaumes.

For the time being—and it became a lengthy time being—the family was unable to take an active part in the exploitation of their domaine. Comte Michel died in 1941. His son, Comte

Henry, was otherwise engaged as an army officer—like his ancestor, he was to rise up to the rank of general—and the vineyard parcels were leased out to outsiders.

Though the vines were tended on a sharecropping basis by local *vignerons,* Canon Just continued to take an active interest in his landholdings, making sure the other parcels, which had been abandoned, were replanted after the war. He spent his retirement in Vosne-Romanée, dying at the age of eighty-seven just before the 1991 harvest.

One of the sharecroppers—and that of La Romanée—were the Forey family: father Jean followed by his son Régis. The finished wine was passed around various *négociants*: the cousins at Maison Liger-Belair, Delaunay, Thomas-Bassot, even Leroy (Henri Leroy was another who had wanted to buy La Romanée), and then Bichot, before settling with Bouchard Père et Fils, Bernard Bouchard having married the Canon's sister Milla.

During Régis Forey's time—up to the 2001 vintage—the fruit was destemmed, cold macerated for a few days, and then given a fairly long *cuvaison*, with fermentation temperatures rising to 30° to 32°C. Bouchard Père et Fils provided the new barrels and took delivery of all of the wine once the malo-lactic fermentation had finished.

Louis-Michel Liger-Belair was born in 1973. In view of his father Henry's career, it is not surprising that he only spent the odd holiday week in Burgundy. Paris, Germany, and later Strasbourg was where he was brought up. Nevertheless, at the age of eight he announced that his intention was to take over the family vineyards and to make the wine. Very well, said Count Henry, but in that case you will need to be academically equipped. Louis-Michel studied agricultural engineering in Toulouse, the business of wine in Beaune, and after his military service, a diploma in oenology at Dijon. He is married to Constance, daughter also of an army officer. They have three children and live in the partially restored Château de Vosne-Romanée in the centre of the village.

He took over some of his patrimony in 2000 and responsibility for La Romanée in 2002. For the next three years—that is, until the 2005 vintage—the deal with Bouchard Père et Fils taking over part of the crop in cask after the malos had finished was to continue, so for these vintages there are two separate bottlings of what was originally the same wine. I've tried the two 2002s against each other. I find little material difference.

Since then, Louis-Michel has enlarged the cellar under the *château* and built a new winery next to it. Across the driveway opposite, old barns have been tastefully converted into an office, a tasting room, and a library. In 2006, one of the erstwhile sharecroppers, a M. Lamadon, retired and entrusted Louis-Michel with a lease on his own vines. This gives Louis-Michel vines in Suchots, Petits Monts, Brulées, two Nuits *climats* (Lavières and *premier cru* Cras), as well as Echézeaux. It sounds like a rich bounty! Sadly the parcels are all very small, some so tiny that the wine is only bottled in magnums and sold off for charitable purposes. The estate then comprised 8.6 hectares and made fourteen different wines.

Subsequently, in 2012, Louis-Michel expanded further. The Clos de Grandes Vignes is a unique *premier cru*. It lies on the "wrong side"—that is, to the east—of the main road, in the Prémeaux section of Nuits-Saint-Georges. It comprises 2.21 hectares. Formerly part of the Domaine Charles Thomas, it was acquired by the Châteaux de Puligny-Montrachet. It has now been bought by Louis-Michel.

Louis-Michel is a determined and thoughtful winemaker. The vines have been cultivated biodynamically since 2008, and part of the vineyard is ploughed by a horse, Fanny. "I am looking for wines for drinking, not tasting," he insists. "With the former you just sit back and enjoy the sensation. You might even want to open another bottle. With the latter, you don't even finish up the first! It therefore follows that one must avoid over-extraction. Nothing that doesn't come naturally from the fruit is going to be stable, or indeed attractive."

Louis-Michel Liger-Belair has modified what Régis Forey used to do, wishing to produce a wine that is lighter, more aromatic, less tannic but with more elegant fruit. To achieve this, he has prolonged the cold-soaking to a week and shortened the postfermentation maceration. There is more pumping-over than treading-down. The number of rackings has been reduced to one, delayed as long as possible. The domaine employs mostly new wood, and bottles after sixteen to eighteen months without fining or filtration. "Finally," Louis-Michel told me in 2010—he was referring to his 2009s—"I think I'm getting there." I find his wines subtle, understated, harmonious, and very elegant. Lovely examples of the purity of Pinot Noir.

"Do I have a philosophy?" inquires Louis-Michel. "It's a very grand word for something as simple as wine. Wine is not science. It's a sensation, an emotion, a feeling, an instinct . . . "

TASTING NOTES

I sampled the following range of 2005s—the full range at the time—as well as this vertical of Vosne-Romanée, Les Reignots—Louis-Michel's favourite of his *premiers crus*—in July 2011.

2005

Vosne-Romanée,
La Colombière   Now to 2020

This comes from the big field that lies between the village and the main road. Quite a youthful, medium-weight colour. We had two different bottles. The first was round, ripe, spicy, and had a hint of gingerbread on the nose. Medium-full body. Good fresh juicy fruit. A little tannin but quite soft and approachable. The second bottle seemed fresher, with more volume and vigour. Very good depth and style for a village wine.

Vosne-Romanée,
Clos du Château   Now to 2020 plus

As the title indicates, these are the vines in the back garden in the middle of the village. Youth-ful, medium-weight colour. Lovely nose. Cool. A hint of mint. Still young. Medium-full weight. Good energy. Plenty of definition. Attractive firmness and drive on the follow-through. Classy, positive, and long on the palate. Good as the Colombière is, this is appreciably better. A lovely example.

Vosne-Romanée,
Les Chaumes   2015 to 2030

The vines lie in the northwest corner of the *climat*, directly under La Tâche. Good, fullish, youthful colour. There is a similar touch of mint here as in the Clos du Château. Full-bodied, vig-orous, ample. Ripe and rich—indeed richer than it used to be—and concentrated. Excellent grip. The tannins are now getting soft. This has got a lot of class. Minerally and distinguished. Fine.

Vosne-Romanée,
Aux Reignots   2015 to 2027

Fullish colour. Still youthful. This is more closed, less balanced, and less succulent today. Even a bit harsh on the nose at first. On the palate the fruit is very ripe, almost perfumed. Fresh but not exactly vigorous on the attack. It seems to be more advanced than the Chaumes without the same volume and backbone. But it is very long and classy at the end. Perhaps just a bad day. See the bottle below.

La Romanée   2015 to 2035

This was in the days when Bouchard Père et Fils took half of the crop. Louis-Michel was left with 1,781 bottles. Full, youthful colour. Lovely rich, very concentrated, multidimensional nose. Essence of high-quality fruit. Very good tannins. Fullish body. Harmonious. Subtle. Very classy. A very lovely wine of indisputably high *grand cru* status.

Vosne-Romanee, Aux Reignots

2009   From 2020

Medium-full, youthful colour. Rich, fat, suc-culent, very ripe nose. Very lovely classy fruit here. No hard edges. Fullish body. Ripe. Fine tannins. A meaty example. Lots of energy and depth. This is long, complex, and very fine.

2008　　　　　　　　　　　　From 2020

Fullish, youthful colour. Firm, full, rich, and concentrated on the nose. Nicely austere. Fullish body. Some tannin. But these tannins are very sophisticated. A lot of energy and depth. A splendidly distinguished wine. Very fine plus.

2007　　　　　　　　　　　　Now to 2017

Fine youthful colour for a 2007. Soft, ripe, quite advanced nose. A touch loose-knit. Not a great deal of grip. Classy, juicy, and balanced though. Succulent if somewhat one-dimensional fruit. A pleasant wine for drinking now.

2006　　　　　　　　　　　　From 2016

Fullish, vigorous colour. Something a little ungainly about the tannins on the nose. Closed. Not integrated. A touch of reduction. Fullish. Good grip. When it shakes off its adolescence, it will be fine. Ripe, even rich on the follow-through.

2005　　　　　　　　　　　　From 2020

This is quite a different bottle to the above. Full, concentrated, backward colour. This is very classy. Very rich, multidimensional and splendidly vigorous and balanced. Full-bodied. Very concentrated. A lovely example. But it needs time.

2004　　　　　　　　　　　　Drink soon

Good fullish, vigorous colour. Firm touches on the nose, but good rich, chocolaty bits as well. Medium-full bodied. Good fresh attack. Stylish and balanced. Doesn't go on for very long or have a lot of dimension. But an attractive wine. Fine for the vintage.

2003　　　　　　　　　　　　Drink soon

Full, immature colour. Rich and spicy but not cooked. Just a touch dense. Medium-full bodied. Sumptuous fruit. Not a bit too 2003-ish. Just a little lumpy at the end. Still has vigour. Not exactly elegant but an enjoyable bottle.

2002　　　　　　　　　　　　From 2016

Fullish colour. Still very youthful. A touch of reduction on the nose. But underneath there is high quality if rather closed-in at present. Fullish body. Very good grip. Plenty of fruit and class on the palate. Very good depth and energy. Very fine.

Domaine Ponsot

UP ON THE SLOPES above Clos de la Roche lies a 1 hectare vineyard that produces a wine which is truly unique: a *premier cru blanc* exclusively produced from the Aligoté grape. Elsewhere in Burgundy, only generic wines can be made from the Aligoté, and such is the fashion for Chardonnay that this poor, unfashionable grape variety is increasingly confined to lesser vineyards, the flat lands on the "wrong" side of the main road (which would probably be better suited to potatoes and beets) and hidden corners further up where the microclimate and the aspect are not of the first order. Only in Bouzeron in the Côte Chalonnaise is the Aligoté taken seriously and planted in the full sun and on well-drained rocky soils. Here we have a delicious wine, if one at its best drunk soon after bottling. What comes out of the Clos des Monts Luisants, however, is altogether different. A bottle with all the same depth, interest, class, and aging potential of the best of the Chardonnays of Meursault and Puligny-Montrachet; yet an Aligoté.

The Ponsot family hails originally from Saint-Romain. In 1872 one of their line, a lawyer in Dijon, bought a domaine in Morey-Saint-Denis on behalf of his son, William. William died childless in 1926 but not before his god-child and nephew Hippolyte had been roped in to learn the *metier* and prepare himself for the succession. Hippolyte's grandson, Laurent, born in 1954, has been in charge of Domaine Ponsot since 1983.

It was William Ponsot who created today's Clos des Monts Luisants. The vineyard, which begins some 20 metres below the tree line, is their monopoly. Back in the nineteenth century, Aligoté was widespread, planted alongside the Chardonnay in places as exalted as Corton-Charlemagne. But after the phylloxera epidemic and the economic depression which followed it, growers increasingly filled up their white wine vineyards exclusively with Chardonnay. It ripened better and the wine fetched more money. William Ponsot had different ideas. He would persevere with Aligoté, and so in 1911 the 1 hectare of Clos des Monts Luisants was replanted with this variety.

Some time later, in the late 1930s, his successor Hippolyte decided to add some "Pinot Gouges" to the vineyard. This is mutated Pinot Noir, found by Henri Gouges in his vineyards in Nuits-Saint-Georges, and reproduced by him in the *premier cru* Les Perrières. Gouges allowed Ponsot to take cuttings for his own use, and so for a time 15 percent or so of the *encépagement* in the Clos des Monts Luisants came from this rare and original mutation. (As anyone who has tasted the Gouges wine will tell you, it bears absolutely no resemblance to Chardonnay.)

Some time later, the grape mix changed again: in the early 1950s Laurent's father, Jean-Marie, added some 20 percent Chardonnay. So for a time the wine was made out of all three varieties, with the Aligoté making up around 60 perecnt of the total. In 1992 the old Pinot Gouges were ripped up, and following the 2004 harvest, after Laurent had done various tests, he abandoned the Chardonnay. From 2005, therefore, we have a 100 percent Aligoté wine once again, and still from the original 1911 stocks.

How is the wine made? Firstly, production is severely limited. The yield averages less than 30 hectolitres per hectare (hl/ha). The fruit is collected in wicker hods, the fruit later being transferred to plastic trays. The grapes are not destemmed, and pressed in an old vertical press (today most perfectionists consider that vertical presses are better than horizontal ones). After settling out in bulk, the must is transformed into wine in old wooden barrels, without any deliberate cooling, so temperatures can rise to 30°C or so, and rarely undergoes malo-lactic fermenation. It is then hardly interfered with—no fining, for instance—until bottling, which takes place after twenty-two months. Throughout the process the sulphur level is kept to the barest minimum. If any wines could be considered to be made without the use of sulphur, they are those of Laurent Ponsot.

Does it keep? The answer is a strong yes, and even in vintages where nature has been less than kind. In the best years, twenty years is a minimum: the 1989 is still an infant.

And what dose it taste like? Well, it is not honeyed in the sense of a Meursault. Neither is it peachy in the sense of a Puligny. And of couse it is not oaky. The wine is very fresh, though except in the very lean vintages with no undue acidity. It is flowery, and the fruit flavours are understated and very subtle. Now having sampled the more recent pure Aligoté wines and compared them with what was made before, I agree with Laurent that 100 perecent Aligoté makes the best wine. There is a brilliant complexity and delicacy about today's Clos des Monts Luisants. It is delicious and it really is unique. Yet is is not prohibitively expensive. Ponsot does not sell wines direct to private consumers. But the wine can be picked up at the shop in Morey-Saint-Denis for around 45 euros *toutes taxe comprises.*

TASTING NOTES
Clos des Monts Luisants

The following tasting of twenty vintages of Clos des Monts Luisants was organised by Sylvio Nitzsche in his Wein Kultur Bar in Dresden, Germany, in September 2009. My thanks to him for asking me to lead the tasting.

2007
100 percent Aligoté

Light colour. Closed-in, crisp, high-toned, slightly minty nose. Ripe though not austere. Medium to medium-full body. Just a little less volume than the 2006. Very interesting fruit with a touch of butterscotch. Ripe. Good energy. Not the volume of some of the older wines—but then it's Aligoté only now—but subtle and delicate, long and complex and elegant. Perhaps not for the very long term, but who cares? It's delicious.

2006
100 percent Aligoté

Light, crisp colour. Fragrant, ripe, subtle nose. A touch herbal. Very fresh and quite delicious. Medium to medium-full body. Good acidity. This is very ripe Aligoté, with lots of high tones.

Suggestions of pistachio, angelica, and flowers. Long and complex, harmonious and very lovely. Can be drunk now but will still improve. Compared with other recent vintages, such as the wine below, my one criticism is that it doesn't quite have the same grip or steeliness. But fine quality.

2005
100 percent Aligoté

Light colour. Very lovely nose. Subtle and fragrant but with good size and energy. Rather more substance than the 2006 and 2007. Lots of depth and lots of elegance. Lots of potential. This does not have the volume of the 2002, for instance, but it has rather more nuance. This is as elegant and as intricate as a piece of carved ivory. High-class. Very lovely. And with a splendid future. Very fine indeed.

2004
80 percent Aligoté, 20 percent Chardonnay

Light colour. Soft and quite honeyed on the nose at first. Good freshness. Good complexity. Ripe and flowery. Youthful and fresh. No lack of depth and interest. Not the greatest volume or energy though. So not for the long term. But long, positive, and classy. Very good.

2002
80 percent Aligoté, 20 percent Chardonnay

Youthful colour. Rich, full, quite firm nose. Very good grip. Slightly more four-square than the 100 percent Aligoté wines. Broader too. Perhaps it will last better. But it's less complex. That said, this is a very lovely wine. Vigorous and rich, profound and concentrated and very harmonious. Very good grip. Ready but will last very well. Fine plus.

2001
80 percent Aligoté, 20 percent Chardonnay

Some development in the colour. And on the nose too. Fat and slightly blousy, even a tad oxidised. Toffee touches and a bit heavy. On the palate this is well-developed if not edging towards the end. Flat. Not much pleasure here. Really far too oxidised as it developed in the glass. Drink up.

2000
80 percent Aligoté, 20 percent Chardonnay

Fresh, mid-gold colour. Slightly closed-in on the nose. Some volume. Very subtle. Fullish body. Ripe. Perhaps it lacks a little nuance and depth, but there is good acidity. Quite a meaty wine. Starts better than it finishes. Good at best.

1999
80 percent Aligoté, 20 percent Chardonnay

Fullish, light gold colour. Full nose. At first a little blousy but fresher as it developed. Rich and full but slightly adolescent on the palate. Good grip. The attack is a little heavy—at least at first—but the finish is better. A wine between two stools, so to speak. Full and rich, but just a bit of reduction. Good at best.

1998
70 percent Aligoté, 30 percent Chardonnay

Slightly older colour than some. Mixed-up nose. A touch unclean. At first I feared it was corked, but it cleared up as it developed. No great strength, depth, or class though, but fresher than it seemed at first. Medium body. A bit overblown and over-ripe. Drink soon. Only fair.

1997
70 percent Aligoté, 30 percent Chardonnay

Fresh colour. Fresh on the nose too. Charming if not very profound. Quite high-toned, but with a lack of structure and real vigour underneath. Decently crisp if without depth and nuance. A bit of development at the end on the palate. I think this needs drinking soon. Medium to medium-full body. Fully mature. Ripe. Good but not great.

1996
70 percent Aligoté, 30 percent Chardonnay

Quite a developed colour and quite developed on the nose too. A little four-square. Not much nuance at first, yet plenty of volume. Medium to medium-full body. Fresh. It is at the same time rich, especially at the end, while having the leanness of the other whites of this vintage. Best on the finish. Energetic, ripe, and quite classy. Long and positive. Best with food. Will still keep well. Very good indeed.

1995
70 percent Aligoté, 30 percent Chardonnay

Light gold colour. Muscular and closed-in on the nose at first. It remained a bit pinched for quite some time. I'd carafe this. On the palate, medium body. Interesting, quite fragrant, complex fruit. Well-balanced. Improved in the glass. A wine for food. Long on the finish. Very good indeed.

1994
70 percent Aligoté, 30 percent Chardonnay

Quite a developed colour. Undistinguished nose. Smells like a stale fruit cake. Medium body. It is now falling apart. There is some fruit; a touch of residual sugar; but also some astringency. Past its best. I don't think it was ever very special.

1992
60 percent Aligoté, 25 percent Chardonnay, 15 percent Pinot Gouges

Light gold colour. Ripe, nicey steely, mature, complex nose. Honeyed in a herbal sort of way. A bouquet of flowers. Medium-full body. Individual. Good grip but not a great deal of acidity. Yet not a bit short. Just a slight lack of complexity. Remarkably fresh for a seventeen-year-old wine. Fine.

1991
60 percent Aligoté, 25 percent Chardonnay, 15 percent Pinot Gouges

Quite a developed colour but not too aged a wine on the nose. Well-developed though. Quite full-bodied. Broad-flavoured. Perhaps lacking a bit of elegance. The fruit flavours are a bit kinky, somewhat sweet-sour. Yet I like this wine a lot.

It is individual and balanced, positive and long on the finish. Very poised and harmonious. Will still keep well. Very good plus.

1990
60 percent Aligoté, 25 percent Chardonnay, 15 percent Pinot Gouges

Light mid-gold colour. Very fresh for a nineteen-year-old wine. Ripe, fullish, broad-flavoured nose. Opulent and plump. Mature but still crisp. Fullish body. Rich and meaty in the best sense. Lovely succulent fruit. Plenty of grip and energy and plenty of vigour and volume. This I like a great deal. Ready but absolutely no hurry to finish up. Would go very well with food. Fine plus.

1989
60 percent Aligoté, 25 percent Chardonnay, 15 percent Pinot Gouges

Mid-gold colour. Very lovely, open, fresh, succulent nose. Plenty of wine here, yet not a bit aggressive. On the palate this is full in body, yet soft, ample, and gentle. Yet it is very, very fresh; amazingly so for a twenty-year-old wine. Very subtle and very elegant. Very harmonious. Quite the best of these older wines. Excellent.

1988
60 percent Aligoté, 25 percent Chardonnay, 15 percent Pinot Gouges

Very light gold colour. Lean nose, with highish acidity in a green-herbal sort of way. But lots of energy and bite. Medium to medium-full body. Aspects of crab apples. Good length if a bit one-dimensional and a little austere at the end. Rather more *echt* Aligoté in flavour than some. Long and fresh and very vigorous. Very good quality.

1985
60 percent Aligoté, 25 percent Chardonnay, 15 percent Pinot Gouges

Mid-gold colour. Well-matured on the nose. Ripe, rich, slight hints of petrol, like an old Riesling. On the palate you could find Meursault here. Fat and rich and vigorous as it developed. Kept on and on improving. Very long and lovely. Will keep very well. Fine.

1983

60 percent Aligoté, 25 percent Chardonnay, 15 percent Pinot Gouges

The colour is like that of a very light, fresh Sauternes. And there is a touch of noble rot, now a little aged, on the nose. Rich and full-bodied, a little muscular perhaps. On the palate, though, quite dry. And much more together than I had expected from the nose. Fresh. Slightly ungainly yet not without its attraction. There is an interesting complexity of herbs and ripe yellow plums. An individual wine from an individual vintage. No hurry to finish up.

As you will see, the 1989 was my favourite of the older wines, and the 2005 of the most recent. The group's vote went to the 1996, with the 1985 in hot pursuit, and the 1989 third.

The red Ponsot wines are made in an equally idiosyncratic way. For a start, Laurent Ponsot picks late. He often does not start until all his neighbours have finished. In the vineyard no pesticides or insecticides are employed, and the vines are looked after according to the cycle of the moon. But Laurent makes no claim to being biodynamic. There are no sorting tables; such elimination of the substandard having taken place in the vineyard. After the fruit has been collected, it is lightly dusted with sulphur, but after that no further sulphur is used, and the wines are allowed to ferment and further age without any intervention. The fruit is usually destemmed. There is no new oak, and the wines are bottled late.

All this produces a wine which is very pure and very individual. They keep admirably but are not blockbusters. At the same time they are fragile; vulnerable to exposure to bad storage conditions such as temperatures which are too high. Laurent has "invented" his own deterrent: a white blob of ink on the label which will turn grey and warn the consumer if the bottles have been temperature

abused. Moreover, the vintages since 2008 have been bottled using a special artificial cork.

TASTING NOTES

Clos de la Roche, Vieilles Vignes

The following vintages of Clos de la Roche, Vieilles Vignes were sampled at a Wine Weekend at the Hotel Wilden Mann, in Lucerne, Switzerland, in November 2011. The average harvest in the Clos de la Roche, Vieilles Vignes is 26 hectolitres per hectare.

2009   From 2020

(As a result of hail damage, Ponsot produced 35 percent less than in 2008.) Good colour. Some development. Rich, full, succulent, classy nose. Lovely fruit. Full-bodied, rich, and vigorous on the palate. Very well-balanced. Lots of depth and energy. Still needs time but surprisingly accessible already. Ripe finish. Great class. Very long. Very fine.

2008   From 2020

Good colour. Still youthful. Good intensity and grip on the nose. Medium-full body. Quite pronouced acidity. But fresh and ripe. Lots of vigour and lots of dimension. A splendid wine for food. But it needs keeping. The tannins are as ripe as those of 2009, but the expression of them is a little more austere.

2007   From 2014

Medium colour. Quite developed now. Soft nose. Plump but somewhat lightweight. Medium body. Nice and fresh. Attractive, ripe, and succulent on the palate. Good energy and positive at the end. Needs a year or two. Most enjoyable.

2006   From 2014

Medium colour. Developed. Also soft but slightly more grip and intensity. Very seductive. There is an illusion of oak here which is very curious. And this soft, aromatic, odd flavour is continued on the palate. Medium-weight. Charming and balanced. A bit more to it than the 2007 but similar.

2005

Not presented. Currently the wine is hard as nails and not showing very well.

2004 From 2017

Medium to medium-full colour. Just a touch of the vegetal on the nose. Less ripe than the 2006 and 2007 but more substantial. Yet no lack of fruit and charm. Medium to medium-full body. A lot more interest, succulence, and vigour than most 2004s. Good positive follow-through. Still a bit of tannin to resolve. Fine for the vintage.

2003 From 2017

From magnum. Full colour. Still immature. This is still youthful on the nose. Chocolaty and not a bit Rhônish. Full body. Rich, sweet, spicy, very good acidity. The second magnum was even fresher and more delicious than the first.

2002 From 2021

Medium colour. Looks fully mature, and there is a little mature spice on the nose, which is of medium weight. Reticent at first. Medium-full body. Still a bit adolescent. Some tannin. More energy and power than seemed at first. Very good grip and very good class. Long and very promising, but it needs ten years to get to its best. Very fine.

2001 Now to 2021 plus

Medium to medium-full colour. Fresh, classy, medium-weight nose. Good positive fruit. Soft, round, spicy, ripe, fresh, and balanced. Medium body. Plenty of depth here. A great success. Just about ready.

2000 Now to 2020

Medium, mature colour. Soft, sweet, opulent, and approachable. Medium body. Plenty of depth if not quite the energy of the 2001. Remarkably good for the vintage and plenty of life ahead of it.

1999 From 2017

Very good colour. Rich, full, abundant, lush, and energetic on the nose. This is very delicious. Fullish body. A ripe mocha nose which is always encouraging. Fullish body. Still some tannin to evolve. Real harmony, class, and grip. Will still improve.

1998 Now to 2021 plus

Good fresh, medium-full colour. The nose is a little lean at first, but the wine opened up and gained charm in the glass. Medium-full body. A little reserved but concentrated, pure, stylish, and well-balanced. Lovely finish. Plenty of life.

Domaine de la Pousse d'Or

VOLNAY

LOOK UP FROM THE PLAIN which lies below the village of Volnay, surrounded by its vines in the middle of the Côte de Beaune, and one building sticks out. This is the imposing headquarters of the Domaine de la Pousse d'Or.

What is now the 17 hectare Domaine de la Pousse d'Or has its nucleus in two domaines which were grouped together in 1964. It was then 13 hectares and the land comprised several of the choicest parcels, all of them of significant area, of these two long-standing estates, whose histories can be traced back into the eighteenth century or beyond. It was created through the efforts of one of France's leading *gastronomes* and *oenophiles* of the postwar era, Jean-Nicolas Ferté, and had at its helm, from then until his untimely death in 1997, his favourite niece's husband, Gérard Potel, one of Burgundy's most respected winemakers.

Subsequently the Domaine de la Pousse d'Or was acquired by Patrick Landanger, a businessman involved in the manufacture of surgical and orthopedic instruments. He had originally only been interested in becoming a sleeping partner alongside Potel, though no doubt anticipating that he could use some of his fortune to expand the estate. But after Potel's demise, the property was put up for sale in its entirety and Landanger decided to go for broke. Since then, there have been significant additions to the portfolio; into Corton and Puligny-Montrachet, and more recently a major acquisition in Chambolle-Musigny. Pousse d'Or is now a very important estate.

One of the two estates in which lie the origins of today's Pousse d'Or is that of the Duvault-Blochet family. A century ago this was a giant domaine: the Romanée-Conti itself was part of it, as was the Clos de Tart, and so was what was then called En Bousse d'Or, a 2 hectare monopoly in Volnay. This was acquired by Jacques-Marie Duvault-Blochet from the Dumesnil family in 1857. In all, his estate comprised 100 hectares of prime land.

Duvault-Blochet himself died in January 1874. For the next fourteen years, until November 1886, his landholdings were exploited in common by his successors, the families Guyot, Massin, and Chambon. The Clos de la Bousse d'Or and most of the rest of the Côte de Beaune holdings passed into the hands of Armand Massin after the split in 1886, and when he died in 1913, were left to his sons-in-law MM de Chavigné and Lavoreille.

The headquarters of this domaine—it comprised 25 hectares in 1955 and may well have been even larger in the first place—were in Santenay, in the imposing construction in the Place Jet d'Eau now occupied by the *négociants* Prosper Maufoux and briefly owned by Harveys of Bristol.

Meanwhile, back in Volnay, there was another imposing edifice. In the 1893 Danguy and Aubertin (*The Great Wines of Burgundy*), a sort of Burgundian Cocks and Féret (*Bordeaux and Its Wines*), a photograph of it is described as the Château de Volnay et Clos d'Audignac, the property of M. Delaplanche-Garnier. He too owned a large estate, with vines in Caillerets, Taillepieds, and Clos de Chênes in Volnay, and parcels in Pommard, Meursault, Auxey, and Puligny-Montrachet. This is the building which is the home of today's Domaine de la Pousse d'Or.

We now come to Jean-Nicolas Ferté. Ferté was a gentleman farmer and businessman who hailed from the Aisne. He was a bachelor, a lover of huntin', shootin', and fishin', but above all, passionate about food and wine: a *bon viveur*, a gourmet, a master of the art of good living. He was a member of the Académie des Vins de France, the Académie des Gastronomes and the Club des Cent, a gathering of the richest cream of these wine and food lovers. Ferté knew everybody, all the great chefs and *maître d*'s, all the top winemakers and *château* owners. In his youth he had even organised things so that he did his military service in Burgundy and could visit the likes of the Marquis d'Angerville, Rousseau, Gouges and "*père*" Ramonet—his almost exact contemporary—on his days off.

Ferté had a favourite niece, Françoise, and Françoise had a bright young man whom she intended to marry: Gérard Potel. Ferté decided to "adopt" the young pair—Potel referred to him as "my" uncle—and help them set themselves up. He picked the right man.

Gérard Potel's father's family were well-to-do farmers from Château-Thierry, on the edge of the Champagne area. His mother was Catalan in origin, whose family had spent time in Algeria. Gérard himself was one of eight children and had been brought up near Carcassonne, where his parents produced table wine. He took a degree in agricultural engineering in Paris and then went to Beaune to study oenology under Philippe Trinquet. It was here that he met Françoise and came under the wing of Jean-Nicolas Ferté.

Ferté, of course, was not disposed to invest his largesse in table wine. This was greatly beneath the old man's dignity. The three of them therefore went on the hunt for something suitable, something which would make fine wine. Ferté told all his friends to look out for something on his behalf.

It was through "*père*" Ramonet that the nucleus was found in the Chavigné-Lavoreille estate. Ramonet was someone who never wrote letters. But nevertheless he wrote to Ferté to let him know that this domaine was up for sale. Ferté, however, happened to be on holiday in Morocco, and no one opened his correspondence. So in the end Ramonet telephoned. This was an even more extraordinary occurrence. The old boy *hated* the telephone.

Eventually the message got through. Subsequently a consortium, which included Louis Seysses (father of Jacques Seysses of Domaine Dujac), who had just sold his Biscuits Belin to Nabisco, was set up. They bought about half of the Chavigné-Lavoreille estate, other parcels being snapped up by Matrot, De Montille, Ampeau, and others, and on May 8, 1964, the Domaine de la Pousse d'Or—they had to change the B into a P because the authorities wouldn't allow a title based on the name of a *climat*—came into being.

Why was the Chavigné-Lavoreille domaine put on the market? Because the successors to the original Massin sons-in-law didn't get on.

And the business was not making money. Various parcels of land had been sold off over the years, and the winery in Santenay had just been sold to Harvey's, who had at the time extravagant plans in Burgundy to complement their shareholding in Château Latour (this didn't last long, as neither did the appointment of a young Lavoreille as director of their Burgundian operation).

The Potels installed themselves in Santenay, hired part of what was then Harvey's premises, and started looking for somewhere more permanent to live in and run their estate from. Meanwhile, Gérard continued to make the arduous journey to Carcassonne to supervise proceedings down there.

In Volnay, the daughter of M. Delaplanche-Garnier, a Madame Raoult, had died at the age of ninety-two in 1962. Her house, bequeathed to an association of retired priests, lay closed and empty—though the cellars were leased by Bouchard Père et Fils—for there were no retired priests who could make use of it. In October 1964 it was put up for auction. Ferté and the Potels, having almost bought what is now the Savigny HQ of the Domaine Antonin Guyon, bought it. With it, beyond the garden, came another monopoly, the 80 ares of the Clos d'Audignac.

It was, of course, through Ferté and his friend and fellow member of the Club des Cent, Louis Seysses, that Seysses's son Jacques should come down to Burgundy and get bitten by the winemaking bug. Jacques worked two vintages with Gérard Potel in the mid-1960s. After Louis Seysses had acquired the Domaine Dujac for his son in 1967, he wanted to sell his shareholding in the Pousse d'Or. But only at a profit, which at that stage could not be paid. For a long time, even beyond the death of Jean-Nicolas Ferté in 1978, there was an impasse, the dearth of domestic interest in taking over the Seysses shareholding dropping to zero after the election of François Mitterand in 1981. In 1985 a group of Americans expressed interest, but not on terms to which Gérard Potel could agree. But finally, thanks to the good offices of the Burgundian-based American wine broker Becky Wasserman, who was selling the Pousse d'Or wines in the United States, and to Potel's friendship with Bill Pannell, founder of the Moss Wood estate in the Margaret River area, a consortium of Australians was found to buy up the Seysses interest. Thanks to that marvelous new invention, the fax machine, the whole thing was finalised in six hours, and on the last day of August 1985, Pannell and his associates became shareholders in the Domaine de la Pousse d'Or.

At first things ran smoothly. But then Pannell and his associates decided that they wanted to release their capital, and they sold their shares to a second group of Australians. This new arrangement was less successful. Relations between France and Australia deteriorated during the early years of the 1990s, coming to a head in the autumn of 1997. A board meeting was fixed at which it would be decided that the Australians would withdraw from the consortium. The night before the meeting, at the age of sixty, Potel died of a heart attack.

Patrick Landanger hails from the Haute Marne and was born in 1950. He had no background in wine except for aiding his grandfather in his few rows of *ordinaire* near Langres. "What fascinated me," he says, "is how you put grapes in one end, so to speak, and wine would come out of the other." Landanger took over and expanded his father's surgical instrument business, diversified into orthopedics, and took the company public. He was now a rich man, and he started looking, originally in the Midi, for a wine estate in which he could invest. He heard about the imminent changes at the Posse d'Or and expressed his interest, but eventually found himself, as I have said, sole proprietor rather than sleeping partner.

Right from the start, Landanger was in acquisition mode. The first parcels to come up were two slices on the hill of Corton: 50 ares of Bressandes from a member of the Jaboulet-Vercherre family, and no fewer than 3 hectares of Corton, Clos du Roi, from an English lady,

Madame Crosby, a Latour descendent. Landanger, however, thanks to the interference of SAFER, a government organisation which supervises all sales and can even prohibit some of them, only exploits half of this surface. The rest is rented out to Latour, as it had been prior to the sale.

Subsequently, in 2004 Landanger bought 70 ares of Puligny-Montrachet, Les Caillerets, inevitably from the Domaine Jean Chartron. Jean-Michel Chartron later approached Landanger, hoping to persuade him to sell it back, but Landanger had no intention of relinquishing one of the best parcels of white Burgundy there is.

In 2008 Daniel Moine, with no successors interested in taking over on his impending retirement, decided to put his Chambolle-Musigny domaine up for sale. Though performance under his reign had been mediocre, the potential—with Bonnes-Mares, Amoureuses, Charmes, Feusselottes, and Groseilles—was great, and there was some fierce competion from other interested parties, including, I am told, Dujac. But Landanger emerged as the victor. He hived off some lesser elements of Moine's 5 hectares, including some Gruenchers in favour of Ghislaine Barthod, and in the meanwhile sold his Santenay, Gravières to the Château de la Crée in the same commune. The state of the Moine 2008 fruit (Landanger having taken over in September) was such that he decided not to produce a vintage that year. The first vintage then was the 2009, and it showed very well in cask in September 2010. Landanger's last purchase has been 30 ares of Clos de la Roche. Again, the first vintage was 2009.

"It is a major convenience," Gérard Potel used to say, "that all my parcels are sizeable. Unlike others, I don't have the inconvenience of vinifying in minute quantities."

The most northerly parcel of the "original" (i.e., post-1964) domaine lies across the Pommard boundary in the *premier cru* of Jarollières, just below Rugiens. The parcel here now measures 1.5 hectares, the domaine having enlarged its holding in the early 1990s by 40 ares it used to rent *en métayage* from a American called Harris.

Between the village of Volnay and the main road up to Auxey-Duresses will be found a number of small parcels which collectively (and misleadingly, for this too is *premier cru* land) used to be grouped under the name Le Village. Most proprietors prefer to use any other name which is available, especially if they can then claim the monopoly of it. Lafarge has his Clos du Château des Ducs. The Pousse d'Or has two: the 2.14 hectare Clos de la Bousse d'Or and the 80 are Clos d'Audignac. The vines in the former *climat* average forty years old. The latter, enlarged and flattened by Gérard Potel when he arrived, was replanted in 1965.

In the *premier cru* of Caillerets, at opposite ends, the Domaine de la Pousse d'Or has two large parcels—Bouchard Père et Fils is the other major landholder—and one of these is a monopoly too. At the bottom, eastern end, next to the Champans where there is more soil and where the wines are the most precocious, lies 2.27 hectares of plain Caillerets. Upslope, just under the road, is the 2.39 hectare Clos des Soixante Ouvrées (*monopole*). The vines here have an average age of forty-five years old. Here the soil is meagre, just really broken-up rock. The wines are quite different. The 60 Ouvrées is very silky and archetypally Volnay. The Bousse d'Or is more masculine, more stuctured. Which you prefer will vary with the vintage, and with your palate.

The remaining parcel of the Pousse d'Or, as it was when Landanger arrived, lies in Santenay. Immediately adjacent to the Chassagne border, next to the northern end of the Gravières *climat*, is the 2.10 hectare parcel known as the Clos de Tavannes. Again, there is little soil here. Further south, in the Gravières proper, there was a further extensive holding, partly planted in Chardonnay. But, as I have said, this has been sold off.

What has been changed in the cellar and in the vineyard since Patrick Landanger has taken over? "In the cellar? Everything," he replies. While it was perfectly functional before, the buildings have been completely redesigned, and the winemaking and storage now takes place on a number of levels, rendering the usage of pumps totally unnecessary. There is a sorting machine which has been in use now for three vintages and with which Landanger is very pleased. And no recourse to chemicals or weedkillers in the vineyard. Moreover, vineyard and cellar-work are timed to follow the phases of the moon.

"Biodynamism?" I ask. Is he tempted? "Is it a bit too extreme?" he replies. "I look at some of my biodynamic neighbours. Some of them have immaculate vineyards. Others don't. Perhaps when the present *chef de culture* retires in two years' time, I'll start some tests."

In the cellar there is nothing revolutionary. The fruit is picked in small plastic trays, delivered to the sorting table at the top of the slope across from the château and entirely destemmed. After a week's natural cold-soaking, it is fermented with treading-down twice a day and macerated for about three weeks. Temperatures are confined to a maximum of 32°C, and the wines then go into 30 percent new oak for the entire range. Bottling is after fifteen to eighteen months depending on the vintage, with neither fining nor filtration.

Gérard Potel produced marvelous wines, making his premature death a double tragedy. Landanger took a few years to get it right—not by making nasty bottles, but just competent wine which did not sing. At the outset he employed a manager and a number of vintage consultants, a different one each year, in the pursuit of as much know-how as possible. Consultants, however, have to have the experience of the estate and its vines that they are involved in. And they have to be competent. Jasper Morris (*Inside Burgundy*) speaks of a "tongue-lashing" Landanger received from neighbour Henri Boillot (this was over sloppy practices by the manager, who was subsequently relieved of his responsibilities).

From 2005, however, I think the Pousse d'Or wines are back on track. As well as the notes which follow, I can report very favourably on the performance of the 2009s in cask in September 2010.

The following wines were laid on at a tasting at the Domaine de la Pousse d'Or in June 2010.

TASTING NOTES

2008

Volnay, Clos de la Bousse d'Or   From 2017

Bottled at the end of March 2010. Good colour. Nicely substantial. Still recovering from the bottling. Fullish body. Firm, rich, some tannin. Good grip. A little tight compared with the 60 Ouvrées. But with very good depth and plenty of class. Long and complex. Very good indeed.

Volnay, Caillerets,
Clos des 60 Ouvrées   From 2016

Good colour. Softer and more fragrant than the Bousse d'Or. Lovely fruit. Balanced and harmonious. Medium-full body. Very intense. Lots of depth and vigour. This is long, multidimensional, and of fine quality.

Pommard, Jarollières   From 2015

Medium to medium-full colour. Decent fruit on the nose. But not really a great deal of concentration and intensity. Balanced and ripe and quite stylish though. Medium body. Not a lot of tannin. But not short. Very good.

Corton, Bressandes   From 2018

Medium-full colour. Full, ample, quite closed-in nose. Classy concentrated fruit on the palate. Rich. Fullish body. Vigorous and succulent. Lovely fruit. Long, elegant, and impressive. Fine plus.

Corton, Clos du Roi   From 2019

Fullish colour. Rich, concentrated nose. Lots of depth and very lovely fruit. Fuller, firmer, and more tannic than the Bressandes. Richer and more opulent too. Lots of energy. Very good grip. Very fine.

2007

Volnay, Clos de la Bousse d'Or
From 2013

Medium colour. Soft nose. Not a great deal of backbone and power here; indeed, it is a bit lacking in this department. Medium body. Not much tannin. Decent acidity. But rather too forward and one-dimensional.

Volnay, Caillerets, Clos des 60 Ouvrées
From 2014

Medium colour. A little more fragrant on the nose than the Bousse d'Or. But similarly rather slight. Medium body. This is rather better than the above on the palate. Good depth and good intensity, especially at the end. Balanced, fresh, and positive. Very good for the vintage.

Pommard, Jarollières
From 2012

Better colour than the two Volnays. A little weak on the nose though. Plump on the attack, but then it tails off and finishes a bit astringent. Unexciting.

Corton, Bressandes
From 2015

Good positive colour. And there is decent substance and plumpness on the nose. Medium to medium-full body. Some structure and tannin and no lack of succulent fruit. Good grip, good depth, good finish. Very good indeed.

Corton, Clos du Roi
From 2014

Rather lighter and more developed than the Bressandes. Quite a lot weedier and one-dimensional on the palate. A great disappointment.

2006

Volnay, Clos de la Bousse d'Or
From 2014

Medium colour. A little development. Ripe, round nose with touches of mocha. Medium body. Good open, attractive, juicy fruit. Good acidity too. Classy and balanced. Good positive, vigorous finish. Very good plus.

Volnay, Caillerets, Clos des 60 Ouvrées
From 2016

Good colour. Fuller, richer, and more ample on the nose than the Bousse d'Or. Rather more closed-in. Medium to medium-full body. Good grip. Lovely fruit. Fragrant and minerally. Good energy. Needs time. Very good indeed.

Pommard, Jarollières
From 2014

Medium colour. Decent fresh, vigorous nose. Open and accessible. Stylish and complex. Not quite as much grip and concentration as I would have liked, but a decent follow-through and finish. Good plus.

Corton, Bressandes
From 2014

Medium to medium-full colour. Quite closed-in on the nose. This is still adolescent. Medium body. Decent fruit if without a great deal of dimension. Lacks a bit of distinction and character. Forward. Good plus for the vintage at best.

Corton, Clos du Roi
From 2016

Medium to medium-full colour. Rather more accessible than the Bressandes and much richer and more voluptuous. Not exactly classy but juicy and balanced. Medium-full body. Good acidity. Very good plus.

2005

Volnay, Clos de la Bousse d'Or

Both bottles have a slight element of the lactic on the nose, even a touch of reduction. Is this a long-term problem? Good colour. Underneath one could see a round, rich, ample, fullish wine with very good grip.

Volnay, Caillerets, Clos des 60 Ouvrées
From 2015

Fullish colour. Very lovely, elegant fruit on the nose. Finely poised; beautifully harmonious. Really profound and marvelously ripe. The palate is similar. This is complex and aristocratic. Very fine, even for a 2005.

Pommard, Jarollières
From 2013

Medium-full colour. Very impressive nose. Rich and concentrated. Medium-full body. Good acidity. It doesn't possess the depth and finesse of the 60 Ouvrées but it is a balanced, charming, and already accessible wine.

Corton, Bressandes　　　　From 2015

Full colour. A good, full, quite backward, meaty nose. Plenty of substance and depth if no real *grand cru* class. Fullish body. Good grip. Nicely plump and vigorous. Even opulent. This is very good indeed.

Corton, Clos du Roi　　　　From 2017

Full colour. Quite closed-in on the nose at first. Fullish body. Rich, fat, and succulent. The fruit is much more fragrant than the Bressandes and the wine is rather more classy. It has poise and intensity. Lovely long, elegant finish. Fine plus.

2004

Volnay, Clos de la Bousse d'Or　　　　Drink soon

Medium colour. Attractive, ripe, succulent fruit on the nose. Medium body. On the palate, decent ripe fruit and good acidity. But something is missing. The wine is not dry, but it's a little thin and attenuated on the follow-through. Quite good plus for the vintage.

Volnay, Caillerets,
Clos des 60 Ouvrées　　　　Now to 2015

Medium to medium-full colour. Open nose. Less herbaceous and more succulent than the Bousse d'Or; but the wine is a bit slight nonetheless. Medium body. Quite fresh. No lack of style. Good.

Pommard, Jarollières　　　　Drink soon

Medium colour. Soft, quite plump, sweet nose. Medium body. Reasonable fruit and balance but touches of attenuation at the end. Quite good.

Corton, Bressandes　　　　Now to 2020

Medium to medium-full colour. Nicely plump, fresh nose. Medium-full body. Rich, ripe, succulent, good grip on the palate. This has fat as well as balance. Good vigour. Fine for the vintage.

Corton, Clos du Roi　　　　Now to 2015

Medium to medium-full colour. More developed than the Bressandes. Soft nose. Succulent and ripe. This is less fat and so it is rather drier. Rather less attractive. The finish lets it down even further. Good at best.

2003

Volnay, Clos de la Bousse d'Or　　　　Drink soon

Medium, mature colour. A slightly harsh, bitter, not very pleasant nose. Medium-full body. Ripe. Not too cooked, but the acidity is a bit contrived and the wine lacks class.

Volnay, Caillerets,
Clos des 60 Ouvrées　　　　Now to 2014

Medium, mature colour. Softer, riper, and more pleasant on the nose than the Bousse d'Or. Medium body. Better grip. Good fruit. Even a little class. Good for the vintage.

Pommard, Jarollières　　　　Drink soon

Medium, mature colour. Quite a fresh nose. Decent fruit. Medium body. Slightly astringent on the palate. Otherwise quite positive fruit and grip, if rather one-dimensional.

Corton, Bressandes　　　　Now to 2014

Medium-full, mature colour. Rather more serious on the nose than the wines above. Ripe. Full body. Fresh. Fat and opulent. Decent grip. But a bit ungainly.

Corton, Clos du Roi　　　　Now to 2014

Medium-full colour; just about mature. Somewhat more rugged than the Bressandes on the nose. Better on the palate. But somewhat more cooked and pruney and equally lumpy.

2002

Volnay, Clos de la Bousse d'Or　　　　Now to 2018

Medium, mature colour. Ripe, fragrant, balanced, medium to medium-full nose. Plenty of life and attraction here. Medium to medium-full body. Good depth and plenty of grip and ripe fruit. Good vigorous follow-through. Just about ready. Very good.

Volnay, Caillerets,
Clos des 60 Ouvrées　　　　Now to 2015

Medium, mature colour. Soft, fragrant, balanced, classy nose. Softer than the Bousse d'Or but very lovely individual fruit. But on the palate, only medium body. It lacks the dimension, vigour, and intensity of the above. Merely good.

Pommard, Jarollières
Now to 2019

Medium, mature colour. Fresh, stylish, medium-weight nose. Good balance if no great weight or force. Medium to medium-full body. Ripe. Slightly spicy. Good grip. Finishes positively with good class. Very good.

Corton, Bressandes
Now to 2020

Medium-full colour. Fat, ripe, spicy, succulent nose. Medium-full body. A touch hard still, but good fruit and grip. Lacks a bit of charm at the end, but this may arrive as the wine softens further. Only just about ready.

Corton, Clos du Roi
Now to 2020

Medium-full colour. Similar nose to the Bressandes but more refined. Attractive, fragrant, medium-full bodied wine, with clean, fresh fruit, and a long and complex finish. Classy. Very good indeed.

2001

Volnay, Clos de la Bousse d'Or

Over 80 percent hailed. Not produced commercially.

Volnay, *Premier Cru*
Drink soon

Mainly Caillerets. Lightish, mature colour. Soft, attractive nose. Fragrant and balanced. Light but not too weak. Fresh and by no means beneath one's dignity.

Pommard, Jarollières
Drink soon

Medium colour. Fully mature. A rather firmer nose than the Volnay. Medium body. Fresh. Slight touches of astringency at the end but decent fruit and grip, if not as stylish as the wine above.

Corton, Bressandes
Now to 2017

Medium to medium-full colour. Good fresh, cherrylike fruit on the nose. Nicely abundant for a 2001. Medium to medium-full body. Good grip. Good fresh fruit. Ripe, rich, and stylish with a good follow-through. Very good plus.

Corton, Clos du Roi
Now to 2018

Medium to medium full, mature colour. Compared with the Bressandes, less grip on the nose, but a little more fruit. Once again, classier. Medium-full body. Velvety. Good grip. Lovely elegant fruit. Long. Fine plus.

2000

Volnay, Clos de la Pousse d'Or
Now to 2015

Medium, mature colour. Light, fruity, spicy nose. On the palate, again, light in body but not weak. Fresh and fragrant. Really good for the vintage. Positive all the way through.

Volnay, Caillerets,
Clos des 60 Ouvrées
Drink soon

Medium, mature colour. A little more fragrant on the nose than the Bousse d'Or. But a little weaker on the palate. Less vigour. Stylish though. Good.

Pommard, Jarollières
Now to 2015

Medium, mature colour. A little more substance on the nose than the Volnays. This gives it the benefit of a bit of depth. Medium body. Fresh. Decent class and dimension. Meaty finish for a 2000. Good plus.

Corton, Bressandes
Now to 2018

Medium-full, mature colour. Ample, quite plump nose. Good vigour on the palate. Medium-full body. Quite rich fruit. Good style. Plenty of energy. This is long and very good indeed.

Corton, Clos du Roi
Now to 2018

Medium-full, mature colour. Rich, fat, round, spicy, mocha-ish nose. Medium-full body. Velvety tannins. Very good energy. Lots of finesse. Lovely finish. Fine.

1999

Volnay, Clos de la Bousse d'Or
Now to 2019

Medium to medium-full colour. Mature. Rich, fat, balanced, succulent nose. Fullish body. Riper, plump, round, and balanced. Plenty of energy. This is very good.

Volnay, Caillerets,
Clos des 60 Ouvrées
Now to 2019

Medium-full colour. Just about mature. A touch of oak and a suggestion of over-extraction here.

Fullish body. A bit of residual tannin. Will this ever soften adequately? Very good grip. Lots of succulence and richness, but a bit over the top.

Pommard, Jarollières   Now to 2018

Medium to medium-full colour. Just about mature. Short, ripe, plump, and balanced on both the nose and the palate. Medium to medium-full body. Good structure. Not the greatest elegance but good fruit. Finishes well. Good plus.

Corton, Bressandes   Now to 2020

Fullish colour. Ample, plump, rich nose. Slightly spicy but decent style and depth. Good grip. No lack of substance. Good energy at the end. Very good indeed.

Corton, Clos du Roi

Landanger bought this in 1999, but without the right to the harvest.

Domaine Ramonet

CHASSAGNE-MONTRACHET

IT IS THE SPRING of 1978. A small man, seventy-two years of age and very much a peasant, with an old stained pullover, baggy trousers, and the inevitable *casquette* on his head, arrives at a lawyer's office in Beaune. He is about to buy 25 ares and 90 centiares—enough to make about four and half barrels—of Le Montrachet, the finest white wine vineyard in the world. The vendors are the Milan and Mathey-Blanchet families: gentlepeople. Pierre Ramonet is a man of the soil. Apart from the occasional meal at some of his clients—Lameloise, Alan Chapel, Troisgros, Bocuse—he never ventures outside Chassagne-Montrachet. He hates the telephone. He rarely writes a letter. Such paperwork that needs to be done is achieved by Mother Ramonet, *née* Lucie Prudhon, whom you will never see dressed otherwise than in black, as befits old ladies throughout France, in an old-school exercise book which she keeps in a drawer in her kitchen.

There is the question of payment. "Ah, yes," says Ramonet. He fishes in one pocket for a thick wad of notes, in another for a second,

in the back of his trousers for a third, and so on. The stacks of money pile up on the attorney's desk. He has never seen such an amount of *espèces* in his life. "I think you'll find it all there," says Ramonet, uncomfortable in the formal surroundings of the lawyer's office. And he leaves, anxious to return to the familiarity of his cellar and his vines.

"*Père*" Ramonet was more than a character. He was, to use the old cliché—but it is true in this instance—a legend in his own lifetime. More or less from scratch, by dint of sheer hard work and a genius for wine, he built up one of the finest white wine domaines in Burgundy. Today the name of Ramonet is synonymous with top Chardonnay. The allocations for bottles are fought over, for every collector considers it his or her right to own some. They sell at auction for astronomical sums whenever they appear. On the rare occasions, as in January 1995 at the Montrachet restaurant in New York, when someone puts on a special vertical tasting and dinner, the tickets—and they are not cheap—are over-subscribed ten times.

Ramonet in white is the equivalent of Henri Jayer or the Domaine de la Romanée-Conti (DRC) in red.

Pierre Ramonet died in 1994 at the age of eighty-eight. He is much missed. But his echo lives on, and the wines, in the able hands of his grandsons Noël (born 1962) and Jean-Claude (born 1967) since the 1984 vintage (*mais sous ses ordres*, stoutly avers Noël), continue his reputation. They are very fine. More important, they are also very individual. A Ramonet wine is a Ramonet wine before it is a Chassagne, or a Bienvenue, or a Bâtard . . . or a Montrachet.

The original Ramonets came from the Bresse on the other side of the river Saône from Chalon. A branch settled in Beaune in the nineteenth century, where they were millers. The mill failed, and one of them, Claude, moved to Chassagne, where he became a *tâcheron*—a vineyard worker who is paid by the amount of land he tends rather than by the day as a direct employee—for Colonel Vuillard, owner of the Château de Maltroye.

This second Claude had three children; a daughter who married Georges Bachelet (from whence comes today's Bachelet-Ramonet domaine) and two sons, Pierre (born 1906) and Claude (born 1914). This Claude never married and died in 1977. Pierre married Lucie Prudhon, daughter of the Duc de Magenta's *chef de culture* at the Domaine de l'Abbaye de Morgeot. (For a time the wine was sold as Domaine Ramonet-Prudhon.) They had a single child, their son André (born 1934), father of Noël and Jean-Claude. André has never enjoyed good health, and for some time has been more or less of an invalid. He has never had total responsibility for the Ramonet domaine.

Pierre Ramonet left school at the age of eight to help his father in the vineyard. His first vineyard purchase was in Chassagne-Montrachet, Les Ruchottes, early in the 1930s. Exhibiting at the Beaune wine fair in 1938, he found himself being addressed by Raymond Baudoin, one of the founders of the Revue des Vins de France and adviser to many of the nation's top restaurants. Baudoin had obviously encountered something disagreeable at a neighbouring stand. "Have you got anything to take the taste away?" he asked. And was given some Ruchottes 1934. "Excellent!" pronounced Baudoin. "Do you have any for sale? Can I take away a couple of bottles?" Six months later he arrived in Chassagne with Frank Schoonmaker, one of the first Americans to seize the opportunity provided by the abolition of Prohibition. Schoonmaker took two hundred cases of both red and white—though the Ramonets did not get paid until after the war!

Baudoin was of similar assistance in getting the Ramonet wine onto the lists of the top restaurants in France: Taillevent in Paris, Point in Vienne, the Côte d'Or in Avallon—and this encouraged the opening up of a market for *vente directe*. And of course, after the war, and his settlement of the bill for the 1934s, Schoonmaker continued as the major export customer.

Slowly but surely, the Ramonet domaine began to expand. They now possess vines in seven Chassagne *premiers crus* (Ruchottes, Morgeots, Caillerets, Clos de la Boudriotte, Clos-Saint-Jean, Chaumées, and Vergers), and most of these were acquired in the 1940s and 1950s. In 1955 two adjoining parcels, one in Bâtard (45 ares) and one in Bienvenues (56 ares), were obtained from Henri Coquet.

More recently, the domaine has expanded into Saint-Aubin (Les Charmois) and into Puligny-Montrachet (Champ-Canet and village wine in Enseignières and Nosroyes: the best village appellation vineyards, says Noël Ramonet), and some Boudriottes white has been bought, while they have lost 1 hectare of Morgeot to another branch of the family. The total now exploited is 17 hectares.

An even more recent development, dating from 1998, is the exchange with the Domaine Jean Chartron of Bâtard-Montrachet must for Chevalier-Montrachet must. In this small way, therefore, the Ramonet brothers are merchants. In theory, Noël is responsible in the cellar and his brother Jean-Claude in the vineyard. But in fact it seems to be a joint effort. Neither has had technical training, and so if you ask why they do this, or not do that, you will be unlikely to receive a coherent answer. The approach is empirical and instinctive. But it seems to work.

The Chardonnays are pruned to the Guyot system, the Pinots Noirs *cordon* trained. In the vineyard the yields are kept low, the average age of the vines maintained high, with no *repiquage* after a certain time. This means that, as has happened in Le Montrachet, whole parcels eventually have to be ripped up. The produce of the younger vines can then be vinified apart, and downgraded. This is the case today with half of the Montrachet.

The red wines, village Chassagne, Clos-Saint-Jean, Clos de la Boudriotte, and Morgeots, are partially destemmed, usually 50 percent, cold-soaked for a few days, vinified in cement vats—there is a resistance to stainless steel here—macerated for ten days, and matured using one-third new oak for a year, being both fined and lightly filtered. There is a very noisy cooling unit for temperature control in the cellar. Above ground, what looks like an ugly garage-type hangar stands over an extensive underground cellar hewn out of the rock. But the Ramonets express no interest in being able to cool down or warm up the wine in order to facilitate the malo-lactic. "We like to let nature take its course."

Unusually, the Ramonets do not allow the gross lees to settle out before the fermentation of the white wine begins. "There are elements in the gross lees which are good," maintains Noël. Perhaps as a result of this, the wines are *bâtonné*-ed much less than elsewhere: only once a month for four months. Why? Because they fear that these gross lees would taint the wine. Fermentations are begun in tank, continued in wood—overall about one-third new—at 20 to 25°C, and the finished wine kept on the lees as long as possible before the first racking. A second racking takes place after a year or fifteen months. The white wines, like the reds, are both fined and lightly filtered.

The cellar, both upstairs and downstairs, is not the neatest, most orderly cellar you have ever been into. Odd bits of machinery, adapters for pipes, and boxes of this or that lie all over the place. You feel they have never had a tidy-up or thrown anything out. As you squeeze between a beaten-up truck and a redundant pumping machine to get below to sample the wines, you find that the staircase is used as a cupboard for yet more accumulation of bits and pieces. It is like an ironmonger's nightmare.

But all this seems fitting when you meet Noël Ramonet. The man is in his early forties, stocky, usually unshaven, in a dirty old T-shirt and jeans, with piercing blue eyes, a loud voice, and a preemptory way of expressing himself. Finesse, order and method, and reflection are alien. Energy, passion, and forthrightness is his manner. But when you listen, you realise that this is truly a chip off the old block. He reveres his grandfather. But he has his own full understanding of his *métier*. (He has also got one of the most magnificent—and eclectic—private cellars I have ever seen. All bought; none exchanged.)

"Moins fins mais plus profonds," he will agree with you, when you sample the Chassagne, Morgeots white after the Saint-Aubin, Charmois. And the Boudriottes is more mineral, less fat and heavy, because this is on the semi-*coteaux*, while the Morgeots is in the plain. The Chaumées, despite being young vines, and the Vergers show more finesse. They are properly on the slope. And the Caillerets and the Ruchottes are best of all. "Where the soils are really well drained, as here," explains Noël, "you will always have much less problem with botrytis." This is the heartland of Chassagne white.

Why is there such a sharp contrast between the Bienvenues—composed, accessible, discreet—and the Bâtard—closed, powerful, masculine? After all, the vines are adjacent and the same age. Noël shrugs. You feel he knows the answer. But he can't articulate it. And is his Bâtard his most consistently successful wine, better even than the Montrachet, which can be totally brilliant, but over the seventeen years since the Ramonets have produced it, certainly not always? Is this a question you even dare ask?

I find the Ramonet reds refreshingly direct. They are full, ample, and plump, nicely concentrated but nicely succulent at the same time. Chassagne reds will never be great, and can be over-extracted. But the Ramonets get theirs right.

The whites, on the other hand, are exceptional. They are distinctive, full-bodied, and long-lasting. They are rich and masculine, firm and concentrated. They can be magnificent. And they can also be flawed. This is a result of risks being taken. But often the flaws are by no means disagreeable; they lend individuality; they give character; they add an element of dimension. For me, a great wine often *does* have something just a little bit "wrong" about it. And a squeaky-clean "perfect" wine is very rarely as interesting. But on the other hand, I have only come across one Ramonet wine which I have found prematurely oxidised (for further discussion, see part four of this book, "Observations").

TASTING NOTES

The following wines were sampled at a tasting organised by Tom Black of Nashville, Tennessee, in April 2011. A big thank you to him and his friends who supplied the wines.

Bienvenues-Bâtard-Montrachet, 2005　　Now to 2020 plus
Delicate, youthful nose. Honeyed, concentrated, but understated on the nose. Lovely fruit. Medium to medium-full body. Ripe and balanced, but really quite soft on the palate. Long and classy. Just about ready. But it lacks a bit of power. Fine.

Bâtard-Montrachet, 2005　　From 2018
Ripe, full, nutty nose. A lot of depth. Fullish body. Very gently oaky. Still very youthful. Rich. Full of energy. High-class fruit. Excellent.

Le Montrachet, 2005　　From 2022
This is still very closed and youthful. Marvelous energy and power. Very, very concentrated nose. Full body. Very, very rich and almost solid on the palate at present. Real depth and dimension here. Potentially excellent.

Bâtard-Montrachet, 2004　　Now to 2020 plus
Clean, crisp, and with plenty of depth. Excellent grip. Medium-full body. Flowery and stylish. Lovely fruit. Elegant and balanced. Very fine.

Le Montrachet, 2004　　Now to 2025 plus
Flowery but youthful—indeed a bit ungainly at first—on the nose. Medium to medium-full body. On the palate, really classy. Lovely, racy fresh fruit. Now just about ready. No lack of energy here. Very long at the end. Very lovely.

Bienvenues-Bâtard-Montrachet, 2002　　From 2016
Delicate, youthful colour. Firmer, richer, and more concentrated by some way than the 2005. Fullish body. Very good grip. Elegant and harmonious. Rather more power than the 2005. Lots of depth. Very fine.

Bâtard-Montrachet, 2002　　From 2018
Quite a developed colour. Fullish body. Profound and multidimensional. Very fine fruit. Still very young. This is concentrated and has even more depth than the 2005. Very, very long and classy. Brilliant.

Le Montrachet, 2002　　From 2019
Nutty, fat, and very, very concentrated on the nose. Still very, very closed. Similar on the palate. Immense concentration and depth. Excellent fruit. Still a baby. This is very classy and very profound. Potentially a great wine. Even better than the 2005.

Bâtard-Montrachet, 2001　　Now to 2017
Some evolution on the nose now. Ripe, dryish, not an enormous amount of depth. Medium body. Of all the first flight of Bâtards, this has the least dimension. Yet fresh and enjoyable nonetheless. Not a bit short.

Le Montrachet, 2001　　Now to 2030
Lovely ripe, profound nose. Unexpected depth here. A little evolution on the palate. But lots of energy and class. Marvelously balanced fruit. Brilliant for the vintage. Bags of life ahead of it.

Bienvenues-Bâtard-Montrachet, 2000   Now to 2017

Most attractive, ample, ripe nose. Very classy. Plump and flowery. Medium to medium-full body. Lovely and fresh. Not rich but cool, elegant, racy, and with plenty of depth. Classy finish. Very lovely, especially for a 2000. Better than the Bâtard.

Bâtard-Montrachet, 2000   Now to 2017

Round, ripe, ready, mellow, and full of charm. Medium weight. Fresh and flowery. An attractive wine which is closer to the 2001 in depth than the 1999. Just a bit dull.

Bâtard-Montrachet, 1999   Now to 2025

Fresh, ripe, and concentrated on the nose. Lots of depth. This is very fine. Fullish body. Will still improve. Rich, vigorous, full-bodied, and multidimensional on the palate. Quite powerful even. Excellent.

Le Montrachet, 1999   Now to 2030

Very ripe and concentrated and profound on the nose. Splendidly, concentrated, rich, ripe fruit. Great depth. Still very young. At the end—for this bottle evolved quite fast in the glass—the wine is quite soft, showing lovely fruit. Now just aboiut *à point*. Very fine.

Bienvenues-Bâtard-Montrachet, 1988   Drink soon

Somewhat pinched on the nose. Some developement. Slightly four-square. Medium to medium-full body. Decent grip. But a lack of class.

Le Montrachet, 1998   Now to 2020

Crisp, composed, and flowery, but no great weight on the nose. Accessible and delightful if not greatly serious. Still very youthful on the palate though. Graceful, very fresh. A lovely wine. Just about ready.

Bâtard-Montrachet, 1997   Now to 2018

Fresh and honeysuckle-flavoured on the nose. No undue age. Medium weight. Classy. Medium-full body. Fruit-salady. Good energy and no lack of class. Long, elegant, and complex. A lovely bottle. Totally *à point*. Excellent for the vintage.

Le Montrachet, 1997   Now to 2020

Some development on the colour. But the nose is still very fresh. Full, crisp, steely, and youthful. Fullish body. Now *à point*. Better grip than the 1998 but less ample. This is very classy and very lovely.

Bâtard-Montrachet, 1996   See note

Quite an old colour. Far too old on the palate.

Le Montrachet, 1996   Now to 2020 plus

Very fresh colour. Lovely, flowery, honeysuckle nose. Most seductive and quite delightful. Fullish body. Ripe, round. *À point*. Richer than the 2007. More depth. More vigour. Very fine.

Bâtard-Montrachet, 1995   See note

Quite an old colour. Not quite as faded as the 1996 on the nose, but nevertheless past it on the palate.

Le Montrachet, 1995   Now to 2020 plus

Some development on the colour, yet not over-aged on the nose. Full-bodied. Round and ripe. Fresh, concentrated on the palate, yet just a little rigid. But it improved in the glass. Lovely but not brilliant.

Bâtard-Montrachet, 1994   Drink soon

Youthful colour. Attractive, ripe, ample, and charming on the nose. Surprisingly fresh still. Fullish body. Good concentration. No great dimension but balanced and ripe and no lack of depth. Still holding up well. Fine for the vintage.

Le Montrachet, 1994   Drink soon

Quite a developed colour. Full and fresh, if somewhat spicy and showing some age on the palate. Not the greatest of concentration, depth, or dimension. A bit dull. But that is the vintage.

Bâtard-Montrachet, 1993   Now to 2017

Vigorous, youthful colour. Slightly lean but mature, round, and fullish bodied. This is complex and delicious. A lot of interest, individuality, and dimension. Will still last well. One of the best bottles of the second flight of Bâtards.

Le Montrachet, 1993   Now to 2019

Lovely fresh nose. Full body, rich, and now mellow on the palate. Pure and clean. Ample and ripe and rich and fully ready. No undue austerity. Complex and classy and individual. Fine quality. But is the Bâtard better still?

Le Montrachet, 1991   Now to 2017

Impressive, youthful colour. Ample, fresh nose. Fullish body. Ripe. Very vigorous. Very lively still. Lots of fruit. Really surprisingly ample and elegant, classy, vigorous, and ripe. Delicious. No hurry to drink.

Bienvenues-Bâtard-Montrachet, 1990   Past its best

A little evolution on the colour. Too old on the palate. Just drinkable but has lost most of its fruit.

Bâtard-Montrachet, 1990   Drink soon

The colour is quite evolved. Round, ripe, plump, and well-matured but no undue age. Fullish body. Fresh, ample, and even mineral. But fine rather than great.

Le Montrachet, 1990   Drink soon

Just a little golden on the colour. Ample, round, ripe nose. Fullish on the palate. Slightly rigid. Good grip. But not the grace and depth of the 1991. Fine quality fruit nevertheless.

Le Montrachet, 1987   Past its best

Orange colour. Tired and oxidised.

Le Montrachet, 1985   Drink soon

Just a little development here on the colour. But the nose has become a little vegetal. Fullish body. Somewhat rigid on the palate. Concentrated and very good acidity, but a bit foursquare. Was better five years ago. But other bottles may be holding up better than this.

Bâtard-Montrachet, 1983   Will still keep

Very fresh colour. Splendidly individual all the way through. Lots of dimension here. Very ripe; almost a touch of currants. At the same time, the acidity is excellent. Fullish body. Intriguing. Glorious.

Le Montrachet, 1983   Now to 2020

Fresh if mature colour. Ample, very ripe—almost over-ripe—nose. Very complex. Great depth and complexity. Full body. Splendidy fresh, succulent, balanced, energetic, and multidimensional. Individual and really great. These two 1983s are magnificent!

Bâtard-Montrachet, 1971   Drink soon

Well-matured but not aged colour. A little fade on the nose now. Fullish body on the palate. Beginning to lose its fruit, but no undue oxidation. A little past its best. Finishes a bit rigid.

Domaine de la Romanée-Conti

VOSNE-ROMANÉE

VOSNE-ROMANÉE is the first of the six great—in the sense that it possesses *grand cru climats*—communes of the Côte d'Or as one travels north out of Nuits-Saint-Georges. The village of Vosne is small and tranquil, set a few hundred metres away from the main road, and forms a rectangle, at one end of which lies a modest church and at the other a more imposing town hall. Beyond this rectangle, at the northwest corner of the village, along a little road which abruptly stops at the entrance to the vineyard of Romanée-Saint-Vivant, the traveller will find, not without difficulty if this is his first visit, the red-painted metal gate which leads into the small courtyard of the Domaine de la Romanée-Conti. Beneath the offices to the left lie part of the cellars; a couple of hundred metres away, under what looks like an anonymous garage, lie further cellars, where the wines are made and will spend their first year or so in cask. A short walk in the opposite direction will bring you to the old *manoir* of the abbey of Saint-Vivant, which the domaine took over a couple of dozen or so years ago for use as a second barrel cellar and is now their main offices.

The contrast with the grand country estate atmosphere of the leading growths of the Médoc, or the tourist-attracting rather over-restored buildings of some of the *négociants* in Beaune is very apparent. There are no neon lights, no flamboyant *panneaux*. Visitors, though warmly received when they do arrive, come only by appointment. The casual tourist is discouraged.

Above and behind this small complex of houses, offices, and *chais* lie the vineyards, literally the bedrock on which the fortunes of the domaine are based. Nearest is Romanée-Saint-Vivant, the largest vineyard. Further up the slope is the tiny, gently inclined La Romanée-Conti itself. As the hill curves round to the right to face more northeast than southeast lies the steeper Richbourg. To the left, across the narrow files of vines which make up the *climat* of La Grande Rue, runs the slope of La Tâche, again steep at the top. On either side of this memorable roll call of names are two of Vosne's top *Premiers Crus*, Les Malconsorts, on the Nuits boundary, marching with Les Boudots, in my view Nuits' best site, and to the north

Les Suchots, across which are the various stony Echézeaux vineyards.

The Domaine de la Romanée-Conti owns the entirety of two *climats*, La Romanée-Conti and La Tâche. They possess approximately half of Richebourg, over a third of Grands-Echézeaux and one-seventh of Echézeaux. It also used to "farm" but since 1988 has owned the portion—over half of the appellation—of

→ Vosne-Romanée ← Grand Cru *Holding*	
SITE	SURFACE AREA (hectares)
La Romanée-Conti	1.81
La Tâche	6.06
Richbourg	3.51
Grands-Echézeaux	3.53
Echézeaux	4.67
Romanée-Saint-Vivant	5.29

the Domaine Marey-Monge's Romanée-Saint-Vivant. In addition, the domaine owns 0.68 hectare of Le Montrachet, 0.17 hectare of Bâtard, and 3.43 hectares of *premier cru* and communal Vosne. The last two are not sold under the domaine label but in bulk to local merchants, as is the produce of vines on the more famous slopes which are less than ten years old.

Stricly speaking, the domaine does not "own" all of the above. When the possibility of acquiring the Romanée-Saint-Vivant came up, in order to raise the full amount, it sold off some vines in both Echézeaux and Grands-Echézeaux to the Crédit Mutuel bank. Naturally the deal involved what I imagine is a long lease back in the domaine's favour, and so in reality it makes no difference to the wine.

In 2009 the domaine came to an agreement with the successors of the late Prince de Mérode of the Château de Serrigny. They took a lease on three important parcels of Corton: 57 ares of Clos du Roi, 1.19 hectares of Bressandes, and 51 ares of Renardes. For the time being,

the fruit is vinified as one wine, and labelled simply Corton, but the domaine is not insisting that there will only be the one Corton in future vintages. It is more that they are used to decent-sized parcels of wine. It simplifies life.

From time to time, starting with the 1999 vintages, the younger, but not totally infant, vines' produce is blended together to produce a Vosne-Romanée-Conti *Premier Cru* Cuvée Duvault-Blochet, named after the proprietor in the nineteenth century.

The Abbe Courtepée in the late eighteenth century, echoed by Camille Rodier in the twentieth, said of Vosne-Romanée: "Il n'y a pas de vin commun" (there are no common wines in the village). The wines were famous then, and they are highly regarded now. The mixture of the right exposure, on a well-drained slope facing east or southeast, soil which is essentially an oolitic, iron-rich limestone on a base of marl, rock and pebbles, and vines which lie approximately between 250 and 300 metres above sea level, sheltered from the west and north by the trees at the top of the slope, is as good as you can get. The *grand cru climats*, plumb in the middle of the slope, are the best of all, and the Domaine de la Romanée-Conti has the lion's share of these.

The domaine as it stands today was brought together by Jacques-Marie Duvault-Blochet about a century ago, but its individual constituents have of course an older history. The prime section, La Romanée-Conti itself, can count but nine owners in eight and a half centuries. In the twelfth century it belonged to an influential local family called Vergy. In 1232 Alex de Vergy donated a piece of land known as Le Cloux de Vosne (Cloux is a common *lieu-dit* in Burgundy and denotes a particularly well-regarded piece of ground) to the nearby Abbey of Saint-Vivant, a subsidiary of the great endowment at Citeaux. Almost exactly four hundred years later, in 1631, the site was sold to a Monsieur de Croonembourg (to raise money for a crusade to Palestine, it is said; though it sounds a little late to me for the Crusades).

It was the Croonembourg family who decided to change the name to Romanée. Was there some tangible evidence of Roman occupation at the time? Or was this just in memory of the people who had first introduced the science or art of vine cultivation to Burgundy? The Croonembourgs also bought the neighbouring vineyard of La Tâche, and it was under their ownership that the wines first received renown.

In 1760, after the death of Philippe de Croonembourg, his son André decided to sell his domaine. There was great competition to become owner of La Romanée, then regarded as the best vineyard in Burgundy. After a while, only two contestants remained in the ring: the Marquise de Pompadour, the King's mistress, and one of the King's distant kinsmen, Louis-François de Bourbon, the Prince de Conti. Thanks to the efficacy of his agent, François Joly, it was the Prince who was the victor, much to the chagrin of La Pompadour—but no doubt the King himself was the final arbiter and as has unkindly been pointed out, the Pompadour was then somewhat on the wrong side of fifty and perhaps had less influence on the King then she had previously enjoyed. The price, though, was astronomical, eight thousand gold *livres*, particularly as taxes continued to be payable to the Abbot of Saint-Vivant.

The Prince added his name to La Romanée, and Romanée-Conti it has been ever since. The Pompadour forswore Burgundy and turned to the delights of Champagne.

Conti, however, reserved all the produce of his vineyard for his own pleasure. Not even his friends, who according to Beaumarchais, would go down on their knees in front of him and mockingly plead for an indulgence of one single bottle, would move him from his avarice. La Tâche, now under a separate ownership, was able to take La Romanée-Conti's place as the most sought-after Burgundy in France.

During the Revolution, Conti emigrated and the vineyard was sequestered by the state and sold as a *bien national* in 1793. As John Arlott and Christopher Fielden have pointed out (*Burgundy*, published by Davis-Poynter in 1976), "Even the prosaic valuers . . . dug deeply into

their resources of evocative language when they described it on the Bill of Sale." A celebrated piece of vineyard, they said; the most advantageous position in Vosne; the fruit reaches the most perfect maturity; the site bears its breast to the first rays of the sun which stimulates it with the softest heat of the day; and so on. The document even goes on to claim that the Romanée-Conti vineyard "did not suffer from *coulure* or frost like many of the other climats." This contrasts amusingly with the document of sale under similar circumstances and at the same time which is today preserved, framed at Lafite. Lafite's bill of sale says simply that it was "Le *Premier Cru* du Médoc *et produisant le premier vin*"; the property was in good order—and it also did not suffer from frost.

The purchaser was a Parisian, a Nicolas Defer de la Nouerre, about whom little seems to be known. Subsequently, in 1819, it changed hands again. The new owner was Julien Ouvrard, one time Napoleon's banker, later to be imprisoned for fraud, and already proprietor of Clos de Vougeot and also according to Fielden of properties in Bordeaux (though no famous ones as far as I am aware). The price was once more fabulous. At 78,000 francs, it worked out at 45,000 francs per hectare, at a time when Chambertin, La Tâche, and Richebourg could not attain more than a third of that amount.

Finally in 1869, Romanée-Conti changed hands for the last time. The new purchaser was the aforementioned M. Duvault-Blochet, probably the most important vineyard owner Burgundy has seen since the Revolution. It was he who constituted most of the present domaine by acquiring the holdings in Richebourg and both of the Echézeaux climats, and his domaines extended throughout the Côte d'Or, including the Domaine de la Pousse d'Or in Volnay.

By the time of the Second World War, the domaine was in the hands of two families, both successors to Duvault-Blochet, the De Villaines and the Chambons. In 1942—one can hardly conceive today quite how unprofitable fine winemaking was until only just recently—the Chambons wanted to sell out. Happily, a family friend and good customer was Henri Leroy, a local wine merchant. Leroy was just as horrified by the possibility of the domaine being split up as was Herri de Villaine. He acquired half and jointly ran it with Henri de Villaine until their children, Aubert and Lalou Bize-Leroy, were ready to take over. In 1999, following a board-room argument, Mme Bize ceded responsibility in favour of her nephew Henri Roch.

According to my French dictionary, the name of La Tâche signifies "work which was remunerated" as well as merely a task. *A la tâche* was a form of payment by the job completed rather than by the hour or day, and here perhaps refers to the difficulties of working this particular vineyard so that it would produce its best; perhaps as the cliché puts it: "beyond the call of duty."

In the eighteenth century, according to some records, it was also in the hands of the Croonembourg family. At some time before the Revolution, it belonged to the Chapitre de Nuits and while La Romanée-Conti was off the market sold for the high price of 1,200 francs the *queue*—a Burgundian measurement which like the Bordeaux *tonneau* has no cooperage actuality but which is the equivalent of two 228 litre *pièces* or burgundy barrels. In 1791 it was bought by a M. Marey, whose family also owned part of Romanée-Saint-Vivant. It was acquired by the Domaine de la Romanée-Conti in 1933.

Originally La Tâche only covered 1.5 hectares. However, during the 1930s most of the *climat* of Les Gaudichots was absorbed, for the Domaine de la Romanée-Conti and its predecessors in a series of lawsuits was able to prove that a "local, loyal, and constant" precedent of selling the wine from this additional section as La Tâche had been set, and this was confirmed by the *appellation contrôlée* (AC) regulations when they appeared in 1936. La Tâche now covers 6 hectares.

Romanée-Saint-Vivant takes its name from the Abbey of Saint-Vivant, owners also in the Middle Ages of what is now Romanée-Conti. The abbey acquired part by donation, part by purchase in the mid-thirteenth century, and

were large vineyard holders in the Côte de Nuits and in the Hautes Côtes, more extensively planted with vines in pre-phylloxera times than now.

The wine achieved wide recognition and royal approval when it was used to cure Louis XIV of a fistula, a sort of pipe-like ulcer, though how much was due to the wine and how much to the expertise of the royal surgeon Guy-Crescent Fagon is a matter for conjecture. At the time of the Revolution, all ecclesiastical vineyard holdings were sold off, and part was bought by the Marey-Monge family of Nuits for 91,000 francs. The Domaine de la Romanée-Conti took over management of this parcel in 1966 and have reconstituted about half of this holding since then. In September 1988 they bought it.

One of the present day co-administrators of the Domaine de la Romanée-Conti, representing the large number of members of his family, is Aubert de Villaine, a great-great-great grandson of Jacques-Marie Duvault-Blochet. De Villaine (born 1939), who originally had ambitions to be a poet, is a quietly purposeful, studious-looking, bespectacled man in his early seventies. His mother was Russian. He has an American wife, an art historian, and lives in an attractively converted *manoir* in the village of Bouzeron in the Côte Chalonnaise.

De Villaine started working at the domaine in 1978, working alongside his father Henri and Henri Leroy, who had bought half the domaine from other descendents of Duvault-Blochet in July 1942. De Villaine had previously trained with Leroy S. A. in Auxey-Duresses. He acquired his own property in Bouzeron—of which he is mayor—in 1973, and since then has been the driving force behind the creation of Bouzeron as a separate AC for Bourgogne Aligoté. His example is a classic, and his Bourgogne Rouge, from Pinot Noir, and Blanc, from Chardonnay, are equally delicious. In 1995 he embarked on a new project in the Provence with Jacques Seysses of Domaine Dujac and another friend, not in the wine business. Together they acquired the Domaine de Triennes in the Var near Saint-Maximin-de-Saint-Baune. They transformed the 46 hectare vineyard to Syrah, Cabernet-Sauvignon, Chardonnay, and Viognier. The results are very promising.

Following the departure of Lalou Bize-Leroy, it was decided to appoint Charles Roch, eldest son of Lalou's sister Pauline, as co-*gérant*. Tragically, Charles was killed in an automobile accident a month later. His brother Henri (born 1962), proprietor from a base in Nuits-Saint-Georges of his own small Vosne-Romanée estate, has taken his place.

It was said quite some time ago that the Domaine de la Romanée-Conti was run on biodynamic lines. This was not strictly true until relatively recently. The first trials began in the late 1990s, but it was not until 2007 that it was decided to go fully biodynamic. Aubert de Villaine was determined not to rush things until he was fully convinced.

"We want to get the maximum of character and individuality from the soil and from each vine," I was told on a visit once. As evidence of this, in reaction to the widespread replanting in the early years of this century following the phylloxera epidemic, the owners refused, despite declining yields—in only one vintage during the 1920s did the harvest exceed more than 20 hectolitres per hectare (hl/ha), and again in 1933 only 6 hl/ha—to plough up the vineyard and plant grafted vines in the Romanée-Conti *climat*. They only finally finished replanting in 1946, and it was not until 1952 that the next harvest appeared under Domaine de la Romanée-Conti label. Propagation is done using shoots from their own vineyards. Behind the offices, what at first sight seems to be a *potager* turns out on closer inspection to be a field of newly grafted young vine shoots. These are propagated from the domaine's own vines in Romanée-Conti and La Tâche.

The vineyards are rigorously pruned, and even then, if the harvest looks like being too abundant, some of the young bunches are piteously knocked off. Pruning has traditionally been done by women, wives of the cellar-

workers; the wife of the late André Noblet, erstwhile cellar master, who died in 1986, reserving for herself the vineyard of Romanée-Conti itself. Today the top vineyards are ploughed by horses.

There are a total of twenty-five permanent employees: one per hectare. At the time of the vintage, these are naturally supplemented so that there is a team of sixty pickers, enabling the Domaine de la Romanée-Conti to complete its harvest in eight days.

The *rendement* is normally scant—in a region often notorious for over-production. In the twenty years to 1980, 40 hl/ha was reached occasionally: in 1959, 1970, 1972, and 1973, but never surpassed, and the average yield was a mere 30.8 hl/ha. Elsewhere, almost half as much in a generous vintage such as 2009 would today be the norm. Even in 1989 and 1990, prolific vintages, the domaine harvested no more than 32 hl/ha. And of late, the average harvest has been around 25 hl/ha.

The domaine used to pride itself on the late date of its picking. This was always at least a week after everyone else has commenced their harvest, often a fortnight. In 1978 the Domaine de la Romanée-Conti did not start until October 16, after the rest of Burgundy had finished. Before the real harvest commences, a *passage de nettoyage* is undertaken. Experienced staff work through the rows of vines cutting out anything substandard. I was in Burgundy with a wine tour at the time of the 1987 harvest and took them up to worship at Romanée-Conti. The earth was covered in rejected bunches or half-bunches of grapes not considered up to scratch. Today, as far as I can see, the domaine is no longer a "late picker." "We pick when the fruit is ready," I was told recently.

On arrival at the press house the bunches undergo a *triage*. They are poured onto a conveyor belt, and each is systematically and assiduously picked over to eliminate anything rotten or unripe. This technique—a first in Burgundy—was first introduced in 1977. "Only with the finest fruit can you produce the finest wines." Next the bunches, stems and all, are moved into the wooden vats, where the must undergoes a long *cuvaison*—often for as much as a month. The must is first cooled to 15°C, and there will then be a natural cold-soaking for a few days. Fermentation used to take place at a temperature of between 30° and 32°. Nowadays it is allowed to rise to as much as 35°. The juice from the first pressing is added, and the wine matured entirely in new oak from François Frères in Saint-Romain, increasingly today exclusively from the forests of the Troncais and the Bertranges, for sixteen to twenty months before bottling—it used to be longer. The 1990s were bottled in April 1992. One advantage of such a painstaking *triage* is that the wine can be kept on its lees as long as possible. Often there is not a single racking, as in 1979, 1980, and 1981; otherwise one only. If there is a fining, and this also does not always take place, it is done with white of egg; four whites per barrel. Up to 1985—with the exception of the 1982—the bottling was straight from the cask, and cask by cask without any prior *égalisage* or filtering, into a special heavy, old-fashioned bottle. Today five or six casks at a time are assembled before bottling in order to eliminate any minute bottle variation which might occur.

Of the red wines, the two Echézeaux—particularly the Grands-Echézeaux, which is the more expensive of the two—are burly wines; this is not to say they are not ripe and full of fruit, but they can lack breed. The Romanée-Saint-Vivant—a significant step up—is lighter, softer, much more elegant and more feminine—there is a higher proportion of marl and clay in the soil—while the Richebourg is big, but fat and ripe, and lasts a long time. La Tâche is a classic, but a classic in a Mouton Rothschild sort of way—that is, if Romanée-Conti can be said to be Lafite. The improvement over the Richebourg is immediately apparent. There is more concentration and depth (perhaps the vineyard is older—forty-five years overall is claimed as the average), with more density of fruit.

Finally, at the top of the tree by several leagues, and justifiably therefore at twice the price, is Romanée-Conti itself—a wine of great richness, harmony, concentration, and finesse. Silk rather than velvet as in La Tâche. Throughout the whole range, but especially in these last two, the glorious, true, clean flavour of the Pinot Noir comes shining through. At their best—and there has been a lot of best in the past thirty years—these are yardstick examples of all that is glorious about Burgundy.

TASTING NOTES

Most of the following wines were offered at The Great Wine Seminar, held in West Palm Beach, Florida, in April 2008. The 1993s were sampled at a lunch offered by Harold J. Wood of San Antonio in April 2010.

2001

Echézeaux   Now to 2017
Good colour. Fine, rich, plump nose. Good depth and substance. Slightly raw on the palate still. But very good fruit and a nice touch of underlying oak. Not a bit stemmy. Medium to medium-full body. Ripe, round, balanced, vigorous finish. Fine.

Grands-Echézeaux   Now to 2018
A lighter, more fragrant nose than the Echézeaux. Slightly less weight but more complexity. Very good grip. Lovely fruit. Long and subtle. Lovely finish. Fine plus.

Romanée-Saint-Vivant   Now to 2018
Refined nose with a touch of the herbal. Very elegant. Medium weight. Flowery. A lot of intensity. Very good grip. Fine plus.

Richebourg   From 2014
Rich, fat nose, still a little closed. A much bigger wine than the Romanée-Saint-Vivant. Fat, rich, and opulent, with very good grip. Lots of vigour and intensity. High-class fruit. Lovely finish. Very fine.

La Tâche   From 2014
Full, rich, concentrated nose. Lots of depth. Even more concentration, dimension, and volume than the Richebourg. Really rich. Very lovely, classy, pure Pinot. Excellent.

1999

Echézeaux   Now to 2025
Fullish colour. Rich, ample, concentrated nose. Not a bit stemmy. Full body. Gently oaky. Fat, balanced, and classy. Very long. Very lovely. Fine plus.

Grands-Echézeaux   Now to 2025 plus
Fullish nose. Rather more closed-in than the Echézeaux. More concentrated. More profound. Full body. Very, very rich and voluptuous. Lots of fruit. Balanced, long, complex, and potentially velvety. Very long. Very lovely.

Romanée-Saint-Vivant   Now to 2025 plus
Fullish colour. Aromatic. Slightly leaner on the nose and palate than the Grands-Echézeaux. A little more adolescent. Not quite the same sex appeal at present, but longer, more subtle, and with more finesse.

Richebourg   From 2015
Full colour. A little adolescent on the nose. Rich, profound, and closed-in on the palate. Full body. Some tannin. Very concentrated and lots of energy. Still needs quite some time. Excellent follow-through. Very fine indeed.

La Tâche   From 2016
Full colour. Hidden nose. Really very concentrated; even dense. Quite a bit of tannin. Excellent grip. This has very lovely fruit and has lots of dimension and promise. Splendid quality! Potentially a great wine.

1996

Echézeaux   Now to 2020
Good mature colour. Lovely subtle, fragrant nose. Now incorporating some of the spices of maturity. Fat and seductive and complex and most attractive. Long, ripe, and lovely. Fine.

Grands-Echézeaux   Now to 2020 plus
Good mature colour. Richer nose than the Echézeaux. Fatter and more hidden. Fullish. Good grip. Still has a bit of tannin to resolve. Lots of energy. Lovely fruit. Very long. Very classy. Fine plus.

Romanée-Saint-Vivant   Now to 2020 plus
Good mature colour. Very lovely Musigny-ish nose. Very lovely fruit on the palate. Soft, ripe, and silky-smooth. Medium-full body. Complex, subtle. Very fine. Just about ready.

Richebourg   Now to 2025 plus
Good mature colour. Big, fat, voluptuous nose. Lots of energy and charm. On the palate, still a bit closed. Full body. Some tannin. Rich, ripe, and concentrated. Multidimensional. Excellent grip. Lots of personality. Very fine plus.

La Tâche   Now to 2025 plus
Good mature colour. Really profound, rich nose. Excellent concentration of fruit here. Full body. Lots of energy. Still quite a bit of tannin. Marvelous fruit. Real vigour and depth. Excellent quality.

1993

Echézeaux   Now to 2020 plus
Medium-full colour. Just about mature. Ripe, round, intense, and quite spicy (as opposed to stemmy) on the nose. Mature but vigorous. Medium-full body. Soft, ample, and succulent. Still shows a vestige of tannin. Very good grip and concentration. Lovely finish. Fine plus.

Grands-Echézeaux   Now to 2025
Medium-full colour. Just about mature. Quite a lot firmer and fresher than the Echézeaux. Fullish body. Still some unresolved tannin. Lots of energy. Very lovely cool, cassis fruit. Vigorous, very complex and high-class. Lots of wine on the follow-through. Very fine.

Romanée-Saint-Vivant   Now to 2020
Fullish colour. Just about mature. Soft, fragrant, stylish nose. Fresh, ripe, complex, and very elegant. A soft, round wine on the palate. Medium-full body. This does not have the energy, depth, grip, and sheer style of the Grands-Echézeaux. But very lovely fruit nonetheless. Fine plus.

Richebourg   Now to 2025
Fullish colour. Still youthful. Full, rich, quite spicy nose. Still a little unformed but lots of

depth and concentration. A big wine. Full body. Very concentrated and very vigorous. Still some tannin to resolve. Very profound, lovely fruit, and great energy at the end. Very fine plus. Will still improve.

La Tâche   2015 to 2035
Full colour. Barely mature. Splendidly rich nose. Very concentrated. Marvelous fruit. Quite splendid depth. Full body. Youthful. Concentrated and very energetic. Splendid ripe tannins, which still need to soften. Excellent.

Romanée-Conti   Now to 2035
Fullish colour. More mature than the Tâche. Very lovely fragrant nose. Great class and complexity. Really very beautiful. Medium-full body. Absolutely delicious fruit. Marvelously ripe and intense. Immense length, dimension, and class. Perfect!

1990

Echézeaux   Now to 2020
Fully mature colour. Rich, spicy, and aromatic, if not *that* stylish on the nose. More 1990 than Echézeaux. Full-bodied, concentrated, balanced. Good backbone and depth, in a slightly gamey sort of way. Very good indeed.

Grands-Echézeaux   Now to 2020 plus
Fully mature colour. Quite evolved on the nose, but fresher on the palate. Very lovely fruit. Full body, rich, complex, and luscious. Very long and very lovely. Fine plus.

Romanée-Saint-Vivant   Now to 2015
Fully mature colour. Soft, subtle, and naturally sweet on both the nose and the palate. Medium to medium-full body. Complex and harmonious and very lovely. Fully ready. Fine plus.

Richebourg   Now to 2020 plus
Fully mature colour. Fat, rich, voluptuous nose. Full and aromatic. Very fresh and beautifully balanced. Much more Richebourg than 1990. Lots of wine here. Splendid quality.

La Tâche   Now to 2025 plus
Fully mature colour. Full, rich, profound, and multidimensional on the nose. Very, very lovely, complex, vigorous fruit. Really excellent pure Pinot. Again, much more of the *terroir* than the vintage. A great wine.

Domaine Joseph Roty

GEVREY-CHAMBERTIN

JOSEPH ROTY, who died in 2008, was not the easiest person to do business with. Indeed, to do anything with. Both he and the rest of his family: *madame*, sons Philippe and Pierre-Jean, seem to have an almost paranoiac distrust of outsiders, the local bureaucracy, and other people in general. They do not consort with their neighbours, play no part in Gevrey-Chambertin promotional activities, and are closed to almost all journalists, including myself.

My breakup with Joseph Roty goes back to 1990 or so. I'd learned that a visit *chez* Roty required at least an hour and a half. It was difficult to get an appointment confirmed in the first place, but, once in, even more difficult to get out. Roty never stopped talking, he needed to discuss the world's events with you, show you all his vintage photographs, ask your opinion about this or that grower. He used to stand in your psychological space, and he chain-smoked Gauloise cigarettes; even in his own cellar when someone was trying to taste. Exasperated, I said to him, at the end of a long, tiring, bitterly cold day—for I had come to realise that

one had to position one's Roty visit at the end of one's program—"Please, M. Roty, I'm trying to taste your wine. Will you please shut up, and if you will insist on smoking, please go to the other end of the cellar." Naturally, I've not been allowed back.

But Joseph Roty and his sons do produce very good wines, and if I have not been allowed to sample them from the cask, I have had plenty of occasion to enjoy them in bottle. He deserves at least one star (in the Michelin sense), perhaps two. One of the main reasons is the average age of the vines. Seventy percent are the original post-phylloxera graftings, now over one hundred years old. Yields are consequently very low, averaging 26 hectolitres per hectare (hl/ha). After a severe *triage* (sorting through the fruit to eliminate the substandard), there is a week's long cold-soaking before the fermentation is allowed to commence, and thereafter it takes place at a maximum of 25° to 26°C. This is very low indeed. I know of several who vinify at 28°, but no one else in the Cote d'Or who makes his or her wine at this temperature. In addition, the

Rotys stir up the lees of their red wines (*bâton-nage*), a process more usual in white wines. Naturally, racking and other manipulations are kept to a minimum. There is between 60 and 100 percent new oak for the top wines.

The Roty domaine has recently been expanded with yet more Marsannay. In Gevrey they possess 16 ares of Charmes (under three casks), 12 of Mazis and 8 of Griotte, plus *premier cru* Le Fonteny, and village Clos Prieur and Les Champs Chenys. They offer at least five different *lieux-dit* Marsannays.

These are assertive wines: oaky, very intense, very perfumed, very original. At the outset I sometimes find them a bit sweet, especially in a lineup with other wines from the commune's more "traditional" winemakers. But on their own, as in the tasting notes below, they are immensely seductive and with no lack of harmony or class.

TASTING NOTES

Acker-Merrill, the New York auction house, invited me to preside over the following vertical tasting of Joseph Roty's Charmes-Chambertin, Très Vieilles Vignes in March 2007. It was a memorable occasion.

2003   Now to 2022

Full, rich colour, but, in comparison with the 2002 and 2001, no more intense, which is unusual, as the 2003s are usually very much more dense. Rich, full, oaky nose. Really quite a classic wine for this vintage. Cool and balanced. Full, exotic, oaky, and very concentrated on the palate. Splendid fruit. Excellent grip. This is very fine indeed.

2002   Now to 2018

Very good full colour. Not a very forceful nose. Pretty fruit but not very concentrated. Not much oak. Medium body. Not much backbone or tannin. In fact, rather slight for the vintage. What there is, is not very oaky, but fruity and elegant and quite intense. But I expected a bit more. It seemed to put on a bit more weight as in expanded in the glass, however.

2001   Now to 2018

Splendid immature, full colour. Ripe and rich and it seems rather more successful than the 2002 within the context of the vintages. Medium to medium-full on the palate. Somewhat raw, rather than tannic. Not very oaky. Good acidity. Good depth. A fine example of the vintage, finishing positively. Needs three years to round off.

2000   Now to 2015

Good medium-full colour. A little development. Soft, ripe, very gently oaky nose. An attractive wine, if not a very serious one. Less raw, more developed than the 2001. Much more seductive today on the palate. Medium to medium-full body. Ripe, lush, red fruity. Not a bit short nor lacking intensity. Just about ready. Very fine for the vintage.

1999   Now to 2030 plus

Full, youthful colour. Quite a closed-in nose. But full, concentrated, rich, and classy. No undue oak. On the palate backward, full, very rich, and concentrated. Excellent fruit. Splendid balance, depth, and dimension. Great class too. This is very lovely: a great wine. And it will last and last.

1998   Now to 2020

Full, youthful nose. Indeed, less developed than the 1999. Full, very fresh nose. Good tannins, if not as fat or as concentrated as the 1999. But no lack of depth. Medium-full body. Neat and discreet. Balanced but by no means a blockbuster. Indeed, more or less ready. Elegant. Long. Fine.

1997   Drink soon

Medium colour. Mature. Quite a fresh nose. Seductive, ripe, and cedary. Medium body. Better grip than most 1997s. No real depth or concentration but a most attractive bottle for drinking now.

1996   Now to 2020

Fullish, still immature colour. Quite a firm, austere nose. A little lacking charm. Fullish body. Plenty of acidity. A bit hard. Perhaps this will always lack a bit of generosity, but it improved on aeration. And the finish is long. Give it two years. Very good indeed at best.

1995   Now to 2030
Full colour, still immature. Rich, full, juicy, and not a bit too tannic on the nose. Much better than the 1996. Full body, ample, very fine grip. Still a suspicion of tannin but lovely cool fruit, and a very impressive finish. Will still improve. Very fine.

1993   Now to 2030
Full, immature colour. Splendidly concentrated rich wine, less tannic but fatter than the 1995. Not a bit austere. Very full body. Lots of grip and backbone. Surprisingly voluptuous for a 1993. Lots of energy and real intensity. This is very fine indeed. Better than the 1995. Up with the 1999.

1990   Now to 2020
Fine, full colour, barely mature. Rather a tough, lumpy nose. Full and aggressive, but lacking sex appeal and richness. I don't think this is a good bottle (this was a one bottle tasting and we had no back-up bottles). Fullish body. Good

acidity. No lack of depth and volume. But it doesn't sing.

1989   Now to 2020 plus
Good full colour, still vigorous. Ample succulent nose, with very good acidity and plenty of depth. The attack is fresh, cool, and full of fruit. The middle palate is a little astringent, but the finish is clean, fresh, and ripe. It got cedary and gingerbread spicy as it developed. Very fine. Even better with food.

1988   Now to 2030
Full colour, still very youthful. Fine, full, rich nose. Slightly austere and backward, but absolutely no undue hardness. A serious wine, with very classy fruit. Full-body, the tannins now mature. Good backbone and grip. Very great finesse. Complex and delicious. A great wine.

1985   Now to 2015
Full colour, now mature. Ample, soft succulent nose. It doesn't have the grip and intensity of the 1988, but it is plump and juicy, fresh and harmonious. Medium-full body. Gentle, subtle, and harmonious. Very fine.

Domaine Guy Roulot

MEURSAULT

IS IT GETTING HARDER to produce white wines of purity, complexity, and precision? It is not, I would suggest, harder in the sense of not knowing what to do. But perhaps it is more difficult to be able to do it. Sixty years ago it was not unusual to be vintaging in October. Today these harvests, like 2008, are rare. What was uncommon then was to be starting in August or in the first week of September, as in 2011 and 2007. If you compare the 1945–55 decade with the first ten years of this millennium, you will see that the average start date is almost three weeks earlier today.

"The big difference," says Jean-Marc Roulot, "is that the days are longer and the weather warmer at the beginning of September than they are at the end of the month. So the progress towards optimum maturity is more rapid. The window of opportunity for harvesting white wine grapes has always [been] narrower than for the reds. Now it is getting even more acute. Miss a day or two and the results are not nearly as fine. In a vintage such as 2006, when the foliage was in a far from ideal condition, the problem is even more pronounced. We have to be flexible enough to be able to nuance the collection date of every single parcel. Even if this means changing the plan day by day.... That's why I wouldn't want to expand further than Meursault," Roulot adds. "I would worry that I wouldn't be able to contol it."

There have been, at the very least, six generations of Roulots in Meursault, the earliest traceable being Hugues, registered as a *viticulteur* in 1827, the year he married Marguerite Nudan. Their son, Guillaume, born in 1830, was also listed as a winegrower when he married Marie Garnier in 1856. In those far-gone days, the Roulots were distillers as well as wine producers and even millers. The milling activities were discontinued towards the end of the century, but the distilling still continues today. Paul Roulot, born in 1863, together with his son, Paul-Guillaume, born in 1899 and grandfather of Jean-Marc, today's winemaker, expanded both the winemaking and distillery side of the business, buying new premises for this process on the road to Auxey near the *tonnellerie* Damy shortly after the First World War. Pierre-Guillaume Roulot also bought some vines in the *climat* of Meix-Chavaux at this time, and though originally he worked for a local merchant called Giraud, little by little, as he built up his domaine—some derelict land in the Charmes, for instance, in 1942—he became self-supporting. Paul-Guillaume Roulot died in 1976.

It was his son Guy, though, who really created today's 15 hectare Domaine Roulot. He had the fortune to marry a Coche (Geneviève Roulot is a first cousin of Jean-François Coche and of Alain Coche), and from this side came the Meursault, Tillets, the Auxey-Duresses, Les Duresses, some of the Bourgogne Blanc, and the Bourgogne Aligoté. Guy Roulot bought some Luchets and the Tessons at the end of the 1950s, more Luchets in 1975, and shared a parcel of Meursault, Perrières with Pierre Matrot, a great friend, in the following year. Meanwhile, the couple had produced two children: Michèle in 1951 and Jean-Marc in 1955. They moved into their existing house in the Rue Charles Giraud in 1963.

Guy Roulot was one of the first to consider separately vinifying and bottling not just his *premiers crus* but his other Meursaults, all of which come from the slopes in the same line as first growths, and which in pre–*appellation contrôlée* (AC) times were regarded as *deuxièmes crus*. Not only was he curious to see how the differences between the various plots would turn out after they had had time to mature in bottle, but he intuitively felt that the results would be more individual.

Tragically, Guy Roulot died in 1982 at the early age of fifty-three. The natural successor was Jean-Marc, then aged twenty-seven, but he had another career, that of classical actor, and was naturally reluctant to give it up. So at first he decided to appoint an outsider to take on the day-to-day responsibility. Ted Lemon, a Californian at the time learning his *métier* in Burgundy (and today owner of Littorai), took over for a couple of years and made the 1983 and 1984. On his departure a Roulot cousin, Franck Grux, now winemaker at Olivier Leflaive Frères, was appointed. Franck made

the next four vintages. Finally, in December 1988—Franck having been poached by Olivier Leflaive—Jean-Marc Roulot decided to return to take over full responsibility in Meursault.

In September 1994 he married Alix, daughter of Hubert de Montille of Volnay—they have two children—and for the first few years was in charge of producing the de Montille Puligny-Montrachet, Les Caillerets, which Hubert had just bought from the Domaine Charton.

Does Jean-Marc miss the stage? "Not a bit," he answers, "because I have not given it up. I still escape every now and then. But it is more television and film work these days. The change of air, the different environment, I find very invigorating."

Jean-Marc has continued to expand the Roulot domaine. In 1989 he acquired some Monthelie, Champs Fuillot (*premier cru blanc*), and Les Joueres (village red). Meursault, Bouchères followed in 1996, and some Poruzots in 2003, Meursault, Narvaux the year after (*en métayage*), and in 2010 more Meursault Villages, half a hectare of Auxey-Duresses *blanc* and some Bourgogne Blanc.

Finally, later on in 2010, came the sale of the René Manuel domaine by its owners, the Nuits-Saint-Georges–based firm of Labouré-Roi. Jean-Marc joined forces with Dominique Lafon, found some outside shareholders, and divided up the vineyards. The Roulot domaine now has more vines in Poruzots, the monopoly of the Clos des Bouchères, and half of the Clos de la Baronne—a parcel of village Meursault Blanc in the old René Manuel back garden.

So we now have four *premiers crus*: 26 ares in the Perrières, 28 in the Charmes (in the *bas* but they are very old vines), 42 ares in Poruzots, and 1.38 hectares in Bouchères. In addition, there are the six Meursault *"deuxièmes crus"*: 49 ares of Tillets, which lie above Bouchères; 67 ares of Vireuils, further along towards the commune boundary with Auxey-Duresses; 85 ares of Tessons, lower down; 1.03 hectares of Luchets, again under the Vireuils; adjacent, 95 ares of Meix-Chavaux; and, the most recent purchase, 26 ares of Narvaux.

Of these the most interesting, as well as being the biggest parcel, is the Tessons, christened Tessons Clos de Mon Plaisir by Guy Roulot. Of all the *"deuxièmes"* in the cellar, it has the most depth, the most precision, and the most purity. It is a lovely wine, as the tasting notes which follow will amply demonstrate.

In Monthelie there are 19 ares of *premier cru* Les Champs Fuillot and 36 ares of red Joueres. There are Auxey *premier cru* Les Duresses and Grands-Champs (47 ares). And finally Aligoté, Bourgogne Blanc, and Bourgogne Rouge. All this, as I have said, now makes an estate of 15 hectares.

"Since we went *biologique* in the mid-1990s, I have seen the effects more pronounced in the downslope vineyards—Meix-Chavaux and Charmes," says Jean-Marc. There is more personality and more definition. The domaine has applied for official biological status and has already done a few trials in biodynamism. "I am intruiged by the idea," he says, "but I don't want to be forced into a biodynamic box."

The domaine does its new vine replacements (*repiquage*) with its own *massalle* selection and stopped using herbicides in 1992. The harvest is restrained by the removal of excess buds and double shoots, rather than by recourse to green-harvesting, and there is a severe *triage* at the time of the harvest. More recent developments include a progression to lighter tractors and the introduction of 450 litre receptacles for the bunches at vintage time: much more respectful of the fruit. All in all, the estate and its vines are kept in meticulous order. Eric Bodin, who arrived in 2000, is Jean-Marc's right-hand man.

More changes for the better have occurred in the cellar. In 1987 the Roulot domaine acquired a pneumatic press, giving Jean-Marc even more control of the winemaking process. Since 1993, the *cave*, which is not normally excessively cool, has been *climatisée*. This has been one of the factors which has led to a change in the length of time the wine is kept in wood before it is bottled. Twenty years ago the Roulot domaine always bottled after eleven months, just prior to the next harvest. Following tests—I remember

being given samples and the request, "which did I prefer?"—Jean-Marc decided to keep the *premiers crus* longer, up to eighteen months, with the last six or so months in tank. As the cellar temperature can rise to 16°C in the summer, there were fears originally that this change would not work. I remember pointing out that the extra six months were winter not summer months. Now no one would deny that the wines are all the better for the extra time in cask. The first vintage was 1996. Today all the wines are bottled sixteen months or more after the harvest.

There have been two other major changes in the vinification methods. The grapes are pressed for a shorter time than in most cellars in the village, resulting in less juice but of a higher quality. Indeed, before the pressing they are gently crushed. The result is more acidity without changing the level of pH. Subsequently the wine is not held to settle for the habitual twenty-four hours. Not only are the lees richer and more complex as a result, but Jean-Marc will hold aside part of the very last of this lees and allow it to oxidise a bit, before sulphuring and eventually blending it back with the rest. A sort of vaccination against premature oxidation, perhaps.

Jean-Marc is also suspicious about batonnage. He stirs up a maximum of five or six times in total, and never after the malo-lactic has started.

All the white wines except for the Aligoté are entirely fermented in wood, and of this there is from 15 percent (for the village wine) up to 25 percent (for the first growths) new oak, mainly from the Allier.

I ask Jean-Marc about mildew and oidium. Are these getting to be more of a problem? "Back in the 1980s, when we sprayed by rote, these were less of a concern. But since then, like most, we have switched first to the *lutte raisonnée* and now to the *lutte biologique* in order to have more respect for the environment. We can now take advantage of the much more precise information we receive from the local meteorological stations and the Service de la Protection des Végétaux. At the beginning of the last decade, there was a lot of oidium, particularly in 2004. But these things seem to go in cycles. In the last three years—2009, 2010, and now 2011—there has been much less."

Jean-Marc has very firm views about the sort of wines he is seeking to make. "I prefer if necessary to sacrifice a little volume and power on the palate in order to obtain the *ligne droite* and the purity. Persistence rather than *puissance* (power). What I like is that when one noses the wine, one gets an idea of what is to follow on the palate. I consider it essential that there is a correspondence between the one and the other."

There are not many top-quality *caves* where, as here, one gets the chance to compare such a wine range of the second division of the Meursaults *climats*. But first the Bourgogne Blanc. This is surely one of the finest examples in the whole of Burgundy. I use it myself in my introductory presentations when I take groups around. Simply to demonstrate quite how good a generic wine can be. I remember being in the Roulot cellar tasting the 2007s for the first time some twelve months after the harvest. "Jean-Marc," I said. "This may be the best Bourgogne Blanc I have ever tasted out of cask." "Aha," replies he. "I think my 2004 is even better." So we opened up 2004, 2005, and 2006 to match the 2007. It was a close-run race. In the end we had to agree to differ.

In the Vireuils, I find a peachy fruit. It is a racy wine: a good example. The Narvaux, as it should be, is crisp and racy. The Meix-Chavaux has more structure, is plumper and fatter. You can see that it comes from lower down the slope. This is a nutty wine, sometimes with a honeysuckle flavour. It has more depth. Luchets, which lies in between has the advantages of both, and is yet better. Roulot's is a lovely example.

The Tillets is the most original of all the six "*deuxièmes crus*" in this cellar, for the *climat* lies away from the rest. There is a mineral, flowery raciness here, which is very much to my taste.

Best of all, however, is the Tessons. Here, like the Luchets, we are in midslope. And in the Roulots' hands we have wine of really serious *premier cru* quality. Depth, balance, breed: it's all here. It's the slowest to evolve, needing seven years in the best vintages.

In my view neither Bouchères nor Poruzots are ever going to produce wine with the same amount of sheer finesse as Charmes, Perrières, and, indeed, Genevières (which the Roulot domaine does not possess), but they are priced accordingly. In Jean-Marc Roulot's hands we at least have bottles which are more serious than most, if just a tad four-square. Now that he possesses the 1.4 hectare monopoly of the Clos des Bouchères, and with it all the benefits of a nice large parcel *d'un seul tenant* (in one piece), I look forward to the future with great interest.

If the Tessons is closed-in, restrained, aloof, the Charmes is open and exuberant, oaky and peachy, much more accessible. But it is, ultimately, also the better wine, as it should be. But best of all is the Perrières, as is also logical: firmer, steelier, more closed-in, more mineral. But with greater finesse, more definition, more dimension. All in all, a splendid end to a fine sequence of wines: impressive quality and wines which keep well. The quietly passionate Jean-Marc Roulot is a master.

TASTING NOTES

I sampled the following wines in Meursault in June 2011. All except the last two were Tessons, Clos de Mon Plaisir.

2009   From 2015
Bottled April 2011. Cool, crisp, ripe, succulent, and youthful on the nose. Very good grip. Lovely precision. Fullish body. Very good fruit. Lots of energy. The merest suggestion of new oak. Lovely finish. This will keep really well for a 2009. Very fine.

2008   From 2014
Quite full on the nose. At present there is something a bit heavy here. Full body. Firm. Good vigour and very good grip on the follow-through. But the somewhat four-square-ness

of the attack puts me off. An adolescent period perhaps. But the 2009 is more elegant.

2007   From 2013
Soft, gentle, flowery, stylish nose. A delicate wine it seems. More to it on the palate. Medium to medium-full body. Very lovely ripe fruit. Good vigour. Lots of class. A very pure wine with a lovely finish. Fine plus.

2006   From 2013
Riper, fuller, richer, and lusher on the nose. More opulent than the 2007. But not heavier. Medium-full body. Very fresh. Ample ripe fruit. Well balanced and nicely crisp all the way through. Perhaps the 2007 is more elegant. Perhaps this has more staying power. I prefer the 2007. This doesn't quite have the same precision.

2005   From 2015
Aromatic, spicy nose. A touch of gingerbread. Fullish body. Still adolescent. Rich and concentrated. Good vigour. Plenty of depth. Good attack. Then the follow-through is a bit mixed up. But the aftertaste is fine. Lots of wine here. But a wine for food. Fine plus.

2004   2013 to 2023
Now the colour is beginning to get a bit deeper. But no undue age. Ripe, stylish, ample, quite substantial on the nose. Good depth. Good vigour and very pure. Balanced, classy, and absolutely nothing "off-vintage" about this. Fine.

2003   Drink soon
Fresh colour for the vintage. Unexpectedly good for a 2003. But nevertheless on the palate slightly oily with a suggestion of sweetness. Heavy and clumsy.

2002   Now to 2020 plus
Fresh, youthful colour. Lovely, very youthful, fresh nose. Still quite closed. As it opened up, it showed itself to be fully mature. Fullish body. Perhaps less grip than the nose would suggest. And less complexity and class. Very good

fruit nevertheless and better as it developed. Fine. Another bottle was better. All you would expect. Indeed, very fine.

1999   Now to 2025
Fully mature colour with no sign of age. Soft, plump, succulent nose. Fullish body. Ample, round, fresh, lush, and with a very good grip. Lots of stylish multidimensional fruit. If the first bottle of the 2002 was just a little disappointing, this is a super wine. Absolutely crammed with fruit. Lots of future.

1998   Drink soon
Fresh, mature colour. A slight touch of fade and oxidation on the nose. It has now lost its grip. But a pleasant, soft, juicy wine on the palate, and decent acidity. Lacks a little elegance but a decently positive follow-through.

1996   Now to 2016 plus
Fresh colour. Still very alive and full of interest on the nose and palate. Medium-full body. Good acidity. Not lush but ripe and succulent. Good precision and purity here. Very good indeed.

1990   Drink soon
Light golden colour. Quite some evolution on the nose now. Rather fresher and a lot more interesting on the palate. Fullish body, ripe, a certain residual sugar but good grip. Getting a bit coarse and aggressive at the end.

Meursault, Perrières, 1990   Now to 2016
Mid-golden colour. Quite fresh on the nose. No fade at all. A rather more elegant as well as more complete wine than the Tessons. Very ripe fruit and very good grip. Cleaner, more positive, very properly racy and minerally. A lovely mature wine. Fine plus.

Meursault, Perrières, 1989   Drink soon
Mid-golden colour. Ample nose, more herbal than the 1990. Less richness, less volume. A little more age. This needs drinking soon but is very lovely and subtle. Balanced, cool, and classy. Very fine.

Domaine Georges Roumier

CHAMBOLLE-MUSIGNY

FOR CHAMBOLLES with a difference, wines which are substantial, even sturdy, as well as velvety and elegant, the best source is the Roumier domaine: to be precise, because there are two others in the village, the Domaine Georges Roumier. This is one of the longest-established estate-bottling domaines in the Côte d'Or. And one of the very best of all.

The nucleus of this domaine lies in the dowry of Geneviève Quanquin, who married Georges Roumier in 1924. Georges, who was born in 1898, came from Dun-Les-Places, in the Charollais cattle country near Saulieu. When he arrived in Chambolle, he took over the Quanquin family vineyards, enlarged the exploitation by taking on a small part of Musigny *en métayage* and buying additional land in the commune, and set up on his own, independent of his parents-in-law, who also had a *négociant* business. (This ceased to exist after the Second World War.)

The domaine was further enlarged in the 1950s. More Bonnes-Mares, from the Domaine Belorgey, arrived in 1952. Two parcels of Clos de Vougeot were added in the same year. And

in 1953 the 2.5 hectare monopoly of the *premier cru* Clos de la Bussière in Morey-Saint-Denis was acquired from the Bettenfeld family. In the 1930s this parcel had belonged to the Graillet estate, the residue of which was subsequently to form the base of the Domaine Dujac.

Georges and Geneviève had seven children, five of them boys, and I get the feeling he must have been a bit of a martinet, not willing to let go of the reins. In 1955, Alain, the eldest son, left to take up the position of *régisseur* for the neighbouring De Vogüé domaine. Another son, Paul, became a *courtier*. Jean-Marie, the third, had started playing a part in the domaine in 1954 and eventually took over when his father retired in 1961 (Georges died in 1965). In this year, wishing to keep the domaine intact, the brothers formed a limited company for their inheritance, which together with the sisters' holdings, was rented to the domaine. When he retirered from De Vogüé, Alain retrieved his share, these vineyards now being exploited separately by the widow of his son Hervé and his other son Laurent.

Today the winemaker at the Domaine

Georges Roumier is the fifty-year-old Christophe, son of Jean-Marie. Christophe was born in 1958, studied oenology at Dijon University, did a *stage* at the excellent Cairanne cooperative in the Côtes du Rhône in 1980, and joined his father the year after. The wines were fine in Georges and Jean-Marie's time. They have reached even greater heights under the aegis of Christophe.

In more recent times there have been three significant additions to the Roumier portfolio. In 1977, when the Thomas-Bassot domaine was being sold, a substantial slice of Ruchottes-Chambertin came on the market. Two parcels were quickly snapped up by Charles Rousseau and Dr. Georges Mugneret. The third was acquired by a businessman and oenophile from Rouen, one Michel Bonnefond. At Rousseau's suggestion, Bonnefond entered into a *metayage* arrangement with the Roumiers, and Christophe now gets two-thirds of the yield of this 0.54 hectare parcel. You can find it under both labels. It is the same wine.

In the following year, Jean-Marie Roumier finally managed to buy the parcel of Musigny, just under one-tenth of a hectare (it only produces a cask and a half) which the family had been sharecropping since the 1920s. Seven years later, in 1984, a French merchant in Lausanne, Jean-Pierre Mathieu, bought a small section (0.27 hectare) of Mazoyères-Chambertin. This again is rented *en métayage* to Christophe Roumier. The financial arrangements are a little different here, and Roumier only gets half of the crop, which, like most Mazoyères, is labelled as Charmes—a name easier to pronounce and sell.

Somewhat earlier than this, back in 1968, Christophe's mother, *née* Odile Ponnelle, bought a parcel of land, *en friche*, on the Pernand-Vergelesses side of Corton-Charlemagne, halfway down the slope from the Bois de Corton. The land was cleared and replanted, the first vintage being 1974. It is delicious, but there is little of it: three *pièces* from 0.2 hectare.

The heart of the 12 hectare Roumier domaine, as always, lies in Chambolle-Musigny. A number of parcels in the village, totalling almost 4 hectares, produce a splendid village wine. There are originally six *cuvées* of this, eventually blended together, and within this wine will be the yield of some old vines of Pinot Beurot, a sort of Pinot Gris, the residue of the old days when a few white vines were planted in with the red in nearly every Burgundian *climat* to add balance and complexity to the wine.

Christophe Roumier is fortunate to own vines in the three most famous *premiers crus* in the commune: Les Cras and, since 2005, when it was first separated from the village wine, Les Combottes: 1.76 hectares and 0.27 hectare respectively.

On the other side of the village, just under the northern end of Le Musigny, there is 0.4 hectare of Amoureuses, Chambolle's finest *premier cru*. This plot was planted in three stages, in 1954, 1966, and 1971. The vines in the parcel of Musigny itself, lying nearby, date from 1934. Roumier's most important wine, though, is not this Musigny, or not always, but the Bonnes-Mares. (A *pièce* and a half is difficult to vinify. And though Christophe considers Musigny in principle the grandest *grand cru* in the Côte d'Or, he finds the results of his Musigny less regular.) There are four parcels of Bonnes-Mares, all in the Chambolle part of this *grand cru*, totalling 1.45 hectares.

There are two distinct soil types in Bonnes-Mares. At the Morey end the soil is *terres rouges*. But, coming down the slope in a diagonal line from above the Clos de Tart and continuing south towards Chambolle, the soil changes to *terres blanches* (if you look carefully, you will see a large quantity of small fossilised oysters) and this makes up most of the *climat*. Three of Christophe Roumier's parcels are *terres blanches*, one *terres rouges*. He normally vinifies them separately and blends them together afterwards, today rather sooner than he used to (though he keeps back a separate cask of each to watch how it develops. In 1988 he produced a *vieilles vignes cuvée*). What is the difference?

"The *terres rouges* gives the power, the backbone, the concentration," says Christophe. Wine from the *terres blanches* is more spiritual. From here we get the finesse, the intensity, the definition. But a blend is yet greater than the sum of the parts.

Below the northern, Morey, end of the vineyard and the Clos de Tart, the land sinks into a hollow as it comes down the slope (this is the *premier cru* of Ruchots) and then rises up a little. Here we find the enclosed vineyard of Bussière. Christophe's mother, Jean-Marie Roumier, lived in a house in the middle until she died in 2002.

Finally there is the Clos de Vougeot, which sadly Christophe no longer exploits. Originally there were two parcels, vinified together and both sold under the Georges Roumier label. After 1984, the upper part was taken back by Alain and Hervé, and after the 1996 harvest the second parcel passed to Laurent Roumier. It is certainly a good wine. But in Christophe Roumier's view: "It is not really of top *grand cru* quality." I don't think that is sour grapes. I happen to agree with him.

"I make wines from *terroir* which expresses itself through Pinot Noir," says Christophe Roumier, who today runs the domaine with the assistance of his sister Delphine. (There are two other sisters.) There is a lot more to fine wine than merely the variety it is made from, he will point out. Roumier sees his role as an intermediary, as a facilitator. The *vigneron*'s duty is to allow the vines to produce fruit which, when vinified, will be unmistakably typical of its origins. The winemaker's job is to effect this translation from fruit into wine. But it is a question of control rather than creativity. The creation is being done by the vine, by its location, by Mother Nature: not by man.

Along with most of the progressives in the region, Christophe Roumier has turned his back on weedkilling sprays, preferring to plough the vines. This is sometimes difficult where a vineyard has not been cultivated for some time, as important roots may be cut in the process. But an ancillary benefit where it is done is that the roots are encouraged to penetrate deeper.

The average age of the vines in the Roumier domaine is high, but they don't make a fetish of it. Once a parcel has reached, say, fifty years old, individual vines are not replaced as they die off. So eventually, as fifteen years ago in one part of their Bonnes-Mares, the whole parcel can be cleared, the land disinfected against viral contamination, and eventually replanted. At first the young vines are Cordon trained; when their youthful vigour has died down, this is replaced by the traditional Guyot method.

Pruning is severe, and the harvest is further contained by an elimination of excess buds and shoots during the spring. This is much more effective, says Christophe, than a green harvest later in the season. By then it is too late, he maintains, though he does it to thin out late develping bunches or if there are two adjoining, which might give rise to rot. He has no time for those who systematically green-harvest every year. It shows they didn't restrict the crop properly in the first place. This discipline is reflected in the Roumier harvest: 41 hectolitres per hectare (hl/ha) in village wine, 34 in *premier cru*, 30 in *grand cru* in the last big vintage: 2009. This is the key, says Christophe, to the production of great wine.

The next part of the jigsaw is the quality of the fruit. Trials have convinced Christophe that the ratio of leaves to fruit, and their exposure, is critical. So he prefers a large canopy, trained a little higher than some, at least during the early part of the season. It is also important, he believes, to eliminate the second generation of fruit, the *verjus*.

There is a careful *triage*, both in the vineyard and later when the fruit arrives in the *cuverie* up at the top of the village, but a flexible attitude to the quantity of the stems which are kept. The Bourgogne Rouge and the village Chambolle are usually destemmed. For the rest it depends very much on the vintage, Christophe not deciding until the harvest begins. From 20 to

50 percent of the stems are normally retained. The bigger the wine and the more concentrated the harvest, the higher the amount tends to be. The wine is vinified in open-top wooden, concrete, or closed stainless steel vats. The first two materials are preferable, says Christophe, for the heat generated by the fermentation is slower to dissipate.

Fermentations at the Roumier domaine begin slowly, so there is always a brief period of prefermentation maceration. Thereafter, Christophe likes to prolong the extraction, maintaining the temperature just under 30°C, as long as possible. The temperature level is one of the winemaker's most important points of intervention, Christophe believes. It should not go too high, for you begin to lose the subtleties of the aromas above 33°.

As you would expect from the Roumier approach to *terroir*, this is a domaine which does not approve of a lot of new oak. Thirty percent is about maximum. "I want to taste the wine, not the cask," says Christophe, pointing out that new wood is the best mask for wine faults. The wine is kept on its lees until racking the following September. Until 1993 the wines were fined with one egg white only per *pièce*. But no longer, and it is not filtered either. The 2006 village wine was bottled after fifteen to sixteen months, but normally bottling takes place later, between February and May of the following year.

Christophe Roumier is refreshingly open about the quality of his wines. I have referred already to his view on his Clos de Vougeot and to the irregularity of the Musigny as a direct consequence of the size of the *cuve*. "It should be the best, but it isn't always." In principle, he will tell you, Mazis, in the line of Chambertin and Clos de Bèze, should be better than Ruchottes, which lies upslope. It gets more sun later in the evening in September. The reason Ruchottes has the higher reputation, I suggest to him, is that the three most important producers—Rousseau, the Mesdames Mugneret, and himself—are all highly competent wine-

makers, while in Mazis there are a dozen or so, some good, some less so. The real Charmes, Christophe will also insist, is a better *terroir* than that of the Mazoyères.

The Roumier range begins with the Corton-Charlemagne. The vines are now of a respectable age, and since 1985, at the very least, have been producing wine of really top quality, though Christophe is not a fan of his 2002.

The reds, as I have said, are more muscular than most: full, virile, austere, made to last; not necessarily wines which sing in their youth. Time is required, a decade for the best wines in the best vintages. The series begins with a Bourgogne Rouge (2 hectares). This is a sturdy example, but none the worse for that; even in 2007 it had good structure and good acidity. The village Chambolle follows next. It is a bigger wine than those of Ghislaine Barthod or De Vogüé, and it takes longer to open out. But there is no lack of finesse, no lack of Chambolle fragrance. The Morey, Clos de la Bussière, is firmer and chunkier. It used to have a touch of the rustic about it, but I have noticed this less in the past decade. Again, it lasts well.

You will usually be offered, winemakers normally giving you the wines to taste in their order of preference, the Chambolle-Musigny, Combettes, and the Cras before the Amoureuses. The former is plump, ripe, and full of charm, and the latter magnificent in its austerity: really classy. The Chambolle-Musigny, Les Amoureuses, though, is delicious. Here we really do find distinction and class as well as the supreme fragrance of the commune. It is a fitting example of the village's greatest *premier cru*. In Roumier's hands, clearly a wine of *grand cru* quality.

The next two wines in the range are from the *climats* in Gevrey that Christophe farms *en métayage*, the Charmes and the Ruchottes. The latter is clearly finer than the former. Christophe suggests that the wine benefits, like in its own way that of the Mesdames Mugneret, from the fact that it is made and matured in a "foreign"—that is, in his case Chambolle—cellar and can take up some of these Chambolle nuances. Here we have intensity as well as weight and richness, the lush flamboyance of Gevrey-Chambertin, and all the finesse you would expect in top-quality Burgundy.

The Bonnes-Mares, by contrast, is always much more closed-in; somewhat solid at the outset, much less expressive. It seems to go through more of an adolescent phase, and it is only on the finish—but of course, when a wine is young, the finish is what you should concentrate on—that you can see the breed, the complexity, and the depth. Is this Burgundy's best Bonnes-Mares? It needs at least a decade to come round.

When the Musigny is good, and it usually is, it is brilliant. It has less backbone than the Bonnes-Mares, less density. But it can be equally backward, needing just as much time to come round. Sometimes the Bonnes-Mares has more concentration and a better balance. Sometimes, the reverse is the case. It is a pity there is so little of it. I have sampled it ten times in cask for every occasion I have met it in bottle.

What does Christophe Roumier have to say about Chambolle and his wines? "Yes. Chambolle is the most elegant wine of the Côte. There is nothing original about that statement. But for me the wines are also the most mineral. There is a purity, a fruit, an elegance, and a distinction which come in large part from the extra amount of limestone in our soil, and perhaps the marginally higher altitude. I try to make my wines express this."

In sum, this is one of Burgundy's greatest domaines, and Christophe Roumier is one of its most intelligent and knowledgeable winemakers. The combination of the two produces magic.

TASTING NOTES

The following wines were sampled at a tasting organised by Tom Black of Nashville, Tennessee, in April 2010.

Ruchottes-Chambertin, 1999 — 2015 to 2030
Full colour. Just about mature. Still a little closed on the nose. Full body. Concentrated and backward. Very lovely fruit here. Splendid depth, dimension, and vigour. Long and very lovely. Very fine.

Ruchottes-Chambertin, 1998 — Now to 2020
Fullish colour. Just about mature. Good fresh nose. Nicely rich in a soft sort of way. Ripe, attractive, rich. Very good grip. Fullish body. Long and lovely. Just about ready.

Ruchottes-Chambertin, 1997 — Drink soon
Medium to medium-full colour. Fully mature. Fresher and more stylish on the nose than many 1997s. Medium body. Fruity, though the fruit doesn't have much dimension or vigour. But a decent wine, and still reasonably fresh.

Ruchottes-Chambertin, 1996 — Now to 2020
Full, youthful colour. Fullish, stylish, balanced, fresh nose. Fullish body. Now fully mature. No undue acidity. Indeed, it is soft on the palate. Elegant. Long. Fine plus.

Ruchottes-Chambertin, 1995 — Now to 2015
Medium-full colour. Just about mature. Soft, medium-weight nose. Quite evolved. No great backbone, which is curious. And it lacks a bit of vigour and depth. A strange, atypical 1995. Is this a rogue bottle? Good plus at best.

Ruchottes-Chambertin, 1993 — Now to 2025
From my own cellar. Drunk separately in May 2010. Full colour. Still youthful. Quite firm still on the nose, but an impressive weight, concentration, and depth underneath. It is now finally beginning to soften up and become the rich, generous, multidimensional wine it promised to be at the outset. Very fine.

Ruchottes-Chambertin, 1990 — Now to 2020
Full colour. Just about mature. Rich, full, cool, composed nose. Lovely fruit. Lots of depth. Full body. Rich and vigorous on the palate. Quite a tannic wine, but the tannins now resolved. Very good grip. Yet in the end, it is just a little four-square. Fine plus but not the flair for great.

Ruchottes-Chambertin, 1985   Drink soon

Medium colour. Fully mature. Soft, fruity nose. But now beginning to lose its vigour. Medium body. A most attractive bottle with just a suggestion of fade about it. Yet very elegant and very lovely nevertheless.

Charmes-Chambertin, 1999   Now to 2025 plus

Good full, rich-looking colour. Still very young. Medium-full body. Very lovely concentrated fruit. A very serious Charmes. Cool, classy, and very lovely. Splendid finish. Fine plus.

Chambolle-Musigny,

Les Amoureuses, 1969   Now to 2018

Medium-full colour. Fully mature but not a bit tired. The nose shows similar vigour. Ripe, round, and spicy. Fullish body. Aromatic, long, and very classy. Velvety smooth and very fine indeed.

———————

Bonnes-Mares, 2005   2012 to 2030 plus

Full, barely mature colour. The nose is still closed, but the fruit is very lovely. Lots of depth and dimension. Not a blockbuster. Still very youthful. More to it than the 2002, but not quite the very top class I thought at first, but it continued to improve in the glass. Lots of energy. Full body, great finesse, and lots of dimension. Very fine plus.

Bonnes-Mares, 2004   Now to 2016

Medium-full, mature colour. Elegant if slightly reserved nose. A little lean, yet a fine 2004. Medium-full body. Balanced and classy. No lack of fruit. Vigorous and long on the palate. Fine plus.

Bonnes-Mares, 2003   Drink soon

Fullish, mature colour. Untidy nose. Lumpy and inelegant. More astringent than rich. Indeed, not very nice at all. Sweet on the palate. A concocted, ugly wine. No pleasure here.

Bonnes-Mares, 2002   Now to 2020 plus

Medium-full colour. Fully mature. Rich, fat, succulent nose. Medium-full body. Not a block-buster, but rich, vigorous, and intense. Classy and very lovely. Now approaching maturity. Very fine but not quite brilliant.

Bonnes-Mares, 2001   Now to 2018

Good full colour. Better than the 2002, curiously. Just a little sweaty on the nose. But good depth and substance. This cleared up after a minute. Good fruit. Quite full-bodied. Still a touch of tannin. Good acidity. Surprisingly good if a little lean.

Bonnes-Mares, 2000   Now to 2015

Medium colour. Mature. Ripe, round, fruity nose. More to it than most. Medium body. No tannins. A little one-dimensional but fresh and classy. A wine of charm and purity. Delicious to drink now.

Bonnes-Mares, 1999   Now to 2017

Full, vigorous colour. The nose is still closed. Full body. Rich, still closed-in. Tannic. On the palate this is a bit dry. Was it a bit over-macerated, or is this the storage? Yet the finish is not four-square; indeed, rich and long on the palate. But the grip and intensity is missing. I've had better bottles.

Bonnes-Mares, 1997   Now to 2017

Medium to medium-full colour. Fully mature. A little lumpy and four-square on the nose. Quite substantial for a 1997, but it lacks harmony and class. Decent fruit on the palate. Ripe and sweet. Finishes well. In fact, in the end one of the best 1997s I've had for ages.

Bonnes-Mares, 1996   Now to 2020

Fullish colour. Now mature. Lovely fruity, quite high-toned nose. Medium-full body. Juicy-fruity. Absolutely no undue acidity. Ripe and succulent. Balanced. Not as concentrated and multidimensional as the 1995 but fine plus.

Bonnes-Mares, 1995   2012 to 2032

Medium-full colour. Fully mature. Rich, full, aromatic, and vigorous on the nose. Very lovely fruit. Lots of depth. Fullish body. Still a little tannin to resolve. Very good grip. Lots of wine here. Very elegant and very long on the palate. Marvelous finish. Will still improve. Very fine indeed.

Bonnes-Mares, 1993   Now to 2040

Very full vigorous colour. Marvelous nose. Full, rich, concentrated, and multidimensional. Still youthful. Full-bodied. Just a little tannin. Splendidly profound fruit. Very, very classy, and excellent balance. This is a great wine.

Bonnes-Mares, 1992   Now to 2018

Medium-full colour. Fully mature. Soft, ripe, succulent nose. Still vigorous. Most attractive. Medium to medium-full body. Lots of energy. Lovely fruit. Surprisingly fat and rich. I haven't had as delicious a 1992 as this for ages. Brilliant for the vintage.

Bonnes-Mares, 1991   Now to 2020

Full, barely mature colour. Very impressive nose. Fresh, ripe, concentrated, and very classy. Full-bodied. On the palate the wine is rich and ripe, if with a slight lack of succulence behind it. Just a little austere, but very fine and still showing lots of life.

Bonnes-Mares, 1990

Not shown *chez* Black, but at the 1990 twenty-years-on tasting, elsewhere in the United States on the same visit, marked: "Excellent: Now to 2020 plus."

Bonnes-Mares, 1988   Now to 2020 plus

Fullish, mature colour. Rich, aromatic nose. Generous for a 1988. Fullish body. Very good structure. Ripe tannins and excellent grip. Very profound. This is very lovely indeed. Long on the palate. Very fine.

Bonnes-Mares, 1985   Now to 2015

Medium colour. Fully mature. At its peak, if not just a little past it, on the nose. Yet there is still grip and class. More vigorous than the Ruchottes. Medium-full body. Good succulent fruit. Good grip, depth, and class. Rather better on the palate than on the nose. Lovely. Fine plus.

Domaine Armand Rousseau

GEVREY-CHAMBERTIN

WHEN IT COMES to Chambertin and Chambertin Clos de Bèze, Burgundy is a minefield. Large portions of both vineyards are owned by underachievers. Though several of these—notably Damoy, Drouhin-Laroze, Jean & Jean-Louis Trapet, and their cousins Rossignol-Trapet—have showed welcome signs of progress in the past decade or so, the wines of many of the rest of the growers in the village need to be approached with caution. You are better off with the holdings of outsiders such as Drouhin, Bouchard Père et Fils, and Louis Jadot, all based in Beaune, Faiveley in Nuits-Saint-Georges, and Bruno Clair in Marsannay, or Leroy in Vosne-Romanée, than those of Gevrey-based growers such as Camus, Rebourseau, and Tortochot.

There is, of course, one major exception. This is Armand Rousseau. Rousseau is one of the small number of Burgundy estates to which I would unhesitatingly award three stars. Indeed, as far as Chambertin and Clos de Bèze are concerned, you could even argue that there is Rousseau, and then there are the rest.

There are few finer domaines in the Côte d'Or than that of Armand Rousseau. With land in Le Chambertin itself, Chambertin Clos de Bèze, Mazis, Charmes, Clos-Saint-Jacques, Cazetiers, and Lavaux-Saint-Jacques, all in Gevrey, as well as in Clos de la Roche in Morey-Saint-Denis, this 14 hectare estate can boast some of the finest sites in the northern part of the Côte. The vines are old, the *rendement* low, and the winemaking perfectionistic—and the wines themselves are stunning.

Charles Rousseau himself—he was born in 1923 and took over upon his father's death in a car accident in 1959—is one of nature's gentlemen. Small, ebullient, and shrewd, he is generous with his time and his willingness to impart information. He has the refreshing ability to be dispassionate about the quality of both his own and his neighbours' wines. He will admit that there were problems with rot in 1983, and that as a result of a strange bacteria or enzyme in his cellar his 1978s and 1979s are not up to scratch. This openness, this honesty, though now on the increase, especially among the younger generation, is rarer than one might think. A grower's wines are as precious and as personal as his own children. Criticise them and you wound the proprietor himself. I remember a day I received a rather aggrieved letter from an important French *personnage*. I had written that I had found his 1988s disappointing. He thought that it was presumptuous of me to have said so. But someone, I could have replied, must tell the emperor that he has no clothes on.

Armand Rousseau, Charles's father, was a wine broker before the First World War. He lived in Gevrey and was a middleman between his neighbour, the local growers, and the wine merchants in Nuits-Saint-Georges and Beaune. As such, he must have known the area and its wines as well as anybody. He would have been aware in advance that a parcel of vines would be coming on the market. He would have seen land going to waste as the old original pre-phylloxera *vignes françaises* were not replaced. He saw the opportunity to build up a domaine of his own, and he gradually began to buy.

At first, like his neighbours, he sold his wine in bulk, shortly after the vintage, to the local *négoce*. It was the great Raymond Baudoin, editor of the French magazine *Revue des Vins de France* and consultant to a clutch of the finest French restaurants of the time—to Point in Vienne, Pic in Valence, Darroze in Mont-Saint-Marsan, and Taillevent in Paris, among others—who persuaded Rousseau to set aside some of his best *cuvées* for domaine-bottling and direct sale. During the 1930s the local merchants were over-stocked, sales of wine to them were moribund, and prices were very depressed. Baudoin's pioneering work, to *sortir les vignerons dans le monde*, as he put it, was invaluable. Through the restaurants Rousseau was able to build up a private clientele. Through Baudoin he was introduced to Frank Schoonmaker and began to export. And all this gave him the means further to expand his holdings in Gevrey.

Yet progress was slow. When his son Charles took over in 1959, the size of the domaine was only 6.5 hectares. It has since more than doubled. In 1961 Charles acquired land in Clos de Bèze (this has recently been enlarged by the purchase of a half hectare of vines from the Nousbaum family). In 1965 and again in 1975 he bought his Clos de la Roche; in 1968 more Chambertin to add to his father's holding; in 1978 the Clos des Ruchottes when the Thomas-Bassot estate was wound up. The rest of the Ruchottes was shared between Dr. Georges Mugneret of Vosne-Romanée and a businessman from the north of France who entrusted his share to the Georges Roumier domaine of Chambolle-Musigny and in 1983 yet more Chambertin from Jaboulet-Vercherre. More recently, his son Eric, who has been responsible for the wines for the past fifteen years, has acquired yet more Chambertin and Chambertin, Clos de Bèze. The Clos-Saint-Jacques had been acquired in 1954 from the Comte de Moucheron, then owner of the Château de Meursault. You have to be patient, says Charles. Not everything that comes up is entirely suitable; and today prices are high.

In 2012 a Chinese businessman, Louis Ng, acquired the 1.7 hectare Château de Gevrey-Chambertin, and he has entrusted the vines to Eric Rousseau. Eric will incorporate the 10 ares of Charmes-Chambertin and the 30 of Gevrey-Chambertin, Lavaux-Saint-Jacques into his existing *cuvées*, but will create a new, separate Clos de Château, village *appellation contrôlée* (AC).

Not including the above, there are today 2.56 hectares of Chambertin, 1.42 hectares of Clos de Bèze, 1.06 hectares of Clos des Ruchottes, 0.53 hectares of Mazis (or Mazy as the Rousseaus call this), 1.37 hectares of Charmes and Mazoyères, 2.22 of Clos-Saint-Jacques, 1.48 hectares of Clos de la Roche, 60 ares of Cazetières, 47 ares of Lavaux-Saint-Jacques, and 2.21 hectares of Village Gevrey.

Charles is now well over eighty, and though he shows absolutely no signs of retiring—you'll find him most days in his pokey little office, quite happy to be interrupted for a chat—he has long ceded the reins to his son Eric, born in 1957.

There was a period in the past, towards the end of Charles's stewardship, when I was not alone in feeling that less attention was being paid to the "lesser" (that is, all except the top three) wines in the portfolio. The Charmes and the Lavaux-Saint-Jacques in particular being regularly outclassed by their peers. Eric has taken this under his belt, and this can no longer be held as a just criticism.

Careful winemaking, a short and early pruning and debudding if the *sortie* looks like being prolific—the domaine is dismissive about green harvesting—a rigorous selection, and, of course, old vines in the best sites. It all sounds so simple, but so few manage it!

It all starts in the vineyard. The average age of the vines is deliberately kept high: sixty years in Le Chambertin; forty-five in Clos de Bèze. Every year Eric Rousseau rips out about a sixth of a hectare across his domaine—a few vines here, a few vines there—to maintain this important average. The object, of course, is to keep the harvest low and the concentration of the vines high. In the Clos-Saint-Jacques, for instance, the average *rendement* during the 1990s was under 30 hectolitres per hectare (hl/ha). Even in the prolific 1996 vintage, it was only 35.

As a result, the domaine never has to practice a *saignée*. It is more important, they will tell you, to reduce the crop in the vineyard by having old vines in the first place and then by pruning hard. And finally by a severe *triage* of the fruit. "You should have seen my vineyards in 1986," Charles once told me. "The ground was carpeted with rotten berries which had been eliminated at the time of the harvest. It was necessary to examine every single bunch. As a result, I had to employ fifty harvesters for twelve days to pick the 1986s. The 1985 was collected by half the number in half the time."

Vinification takes place in open stainless steel vats. Some time in the past the domaine used about 15 percent of the stems, not so much for the extra tannins the stems will add to the must, but for physical reasons, to give aeration to the mixture of juice, skins, and pulp. To vinify all the stems would be a grave mistake, in Rousseau's view. You would get too much tannin, and tannins of the wrong, hard, and unripe sort, as well as an excess of bitter acidity. So for many years the fruit was totally destemmed. Nevertheless, in 2009, Eric carried out some experiments using all the stems and was not displeased with the results.

Maceration takes place for about a fortnight, the temperature being controlled at a maximum of 31°C, with *pigeage* and *remontage* (treading-down and breaking up of the pulp, and pumping-over) twice a day. The wine is then decanted into a fresh vat or straight into cask to await the malo-lactic fermentation. There is up to 100 percent new oak from the Allier in the best vintages for the Chambertin, the Clos de Bèze, and the Clos-Saint-Jacques (which, like others who have holdings here, Rousseau considers better than his other *grands crus*), and up to 60 percent for the rest of the top wines. The domaine likes to have the malos completed by early spring, so they can then rack the wine (there used to be second racking in September, but Eric dispensed with this a decade or more ago) and move it to a lower, deeper cellar, where it will lie at a temperature of 15°C during the second winter. Bottling normally takes place between eighteen months and two years after the harvest; the lesser wines in March to May, the top wines sometimes as late as September.

What exhilarates me about Rousseau's wines is their concentration and their class. The concentration, naturally, is readily apparent in rich, structured vintages such as 1999, 2002, 2005, and 2009. The class is not only obvious in these vintages, but in lighter years such as 2000 and 2007. Not being dominated by excessive quantities of unripe tannins, as perhaps you might find in a claret in a less ripe vintage, now that they have softened up wines from these years are really surprisingly good. (Only in 1997, and to a lesser extent in 1998, did I feel Rousseau's wines missed out a bit.) These are the proof of the thesis I have put forward in previous discussions of Burgundy and the Pinot Noir. Go for old vines and expert winemaking in the poorer vintages. You will get much more interesting wine than by buying lesser, village examples in a so-called great vintage.

TASTING NOTES

In April 2008 I was invited by Tom Black of Nashville and his friends to participate in a major retrospective of the Rousseau wines of recent vintages. Here are my notes.

2004, Chambertin　　　　Now to 2020

Medum to medium-full colour. Some evolution. Closed nose. Good quality underneath. Fullish body. Ripe. Good backbone and grip. Good depth too, if not exactly succulent. Vigorous at the end. Needs food. Needs time.

2003, Chambertin　　　　Now to 2015

Medium to medium-full, vigorous colour. Splendid rich nose. Fat but not a bit *midi*-ish. Medium-full body. Full, soft, sweet, ripe, and stylish. Really quite classy and quite long on the palate. Very seductive. Ready.

2002, Charmes-Chambertin　　　Now to 2020

Medium-full colour. Now some maturity. Soft nose. A little sulphur. Sweet and succulent and fruity. Medium body. Round and ripe. Not the greatest of class. But fine and long and softening well.

2002, Ruchottes-Chambertin　　　Now to 2022

Medium-full, fresh colour. Ripe, vigorous, classy nose. Lots of depth and energy here. This is the best Ruchottes for some time. Fullish body. Lovely fruit. Balanced and classy. Very fine.

2002, Clos-Saint-Jacques　　　From 2014

Full colour. A little developement. Splendid rich nose. Lots of concentration and depth. Full body. Lovely fruit. Fresh and ripe and complex. Very succulent. Very fine indeed.

2002, Clos de Bèze　　　From 2015

Full immature colour. Still quite closed on the nose. Profound, rich, full-bodied, and generous on the palate. Very ripe tannins. Very lovely fruit. Great concentration. Excellent.

2002, Chambertin　　　From 2016

Full, immature colour. Still a bit closed on the nose, even after the Bèze. Full, rich, and concentrated. Still quite a bit of tannin. Today it is the Bèze which sings. But this is also potentially excellent.

2001, Mazy-Chambertin　　　Now to 2018

Good colour. Medium weight. Fragrant, elegant, and succulent. A small wine but not superficial. Good balance. Positive at the end. Very good indeed. Just about ready.

2001, Clos-Saint-Jacques　　　Now to 2016

Good colour. Vigorous, ripe, and with plenty of energy on the nose. More austere than the Chambertin. Better on the palate. Decent substance (fuller than the 2000). Ripe, rich, the tannins mellow. Cool, long, fine, but a slight lack of charm nevertheless.

2001, Clos de Bèze　　　Now to 2025

Very good colour. Full, rich, and concentrated on the nose. Quite a step up after the two above. Ripe, fullish body. Lots of depth. This is very fine. A lovely example.

2001, Chambertin　　　Now to 2025

Good colour. Some evolution. Refined nose. Only medium weight. But good class and depth. Stylish, ripe fruit. Quietly successful. Long, fresh, elegant, and very fine. But quite a different wine from the above.

2000, Clos-Saint-Jacques　　　Now to 2017

Medium colour. Mature. Classy, soft, succulent nose. Medium body. Fresh. Good finesse. Not a blockbuster but good depth and even energy. Long. Fine plus.

2000, Clos de Bèze　　　Drink soon

Medium colour. Now mature. Not as much energy and grip as the Clos-Saint-Jacques. Seems a bit weak. This is medium-bodied. Decently fresh but rather slight. Somewhat of a disappointment. A bad bottle?

2000, Chambertin　　　Now to 2020

Medium to medium-full colour. Now just about mature. This is a lot better than the Bèze. Excellent fruit. Very fine grip. Good vigour and energy, especially for the vintage. Classy, long, and very fine. Just about ready.

1999, Clos-Saint-Jacques　　　From 2014

Full colour. Just a touch of maturity. Rich, full, opulent nose. Very lovely fruit on the palate. Fullish body. Ripe tannins. Excellent grip and lots of finesse. Balanced. Fresh and very lovely. Indeed, as good as the Bèze.

1999, Clos de Bèze　　　From 2014

Full, vigorous colour. Fuller than the Chambertin. Richer, fuller, and spicier on the nose. Full body, ample, more evolved on the palate. Fat, rich, and opulent. Not as much finesse but very lovely.

1999, Chambertin　　　From 2015

Fullish, vigorous colour. Fat, rich, succulent nose. Very lovely fruit. Full body. Vigorous. Meaty. Very, very rich. Excellent tannins. Fine grip. This is very, very lovely. Multidimensional and very long on the palate. A great wine.

1998, Chambertin　　　Now to 2022

Lovely nose. Fresh. Concentrated. Plump. Rich. Medium-full body. Excellent fresh fruit. Finely balanced and harmonious. Long and very classy indeed.

1997, Clos-Saint-Jacques　　　Drink soon

Medium-full colour. Still quite fresh. This is quite ripe and sweet and better than the Chambertin. But also without a great deal of depth. Soft but slight.

1997, Chambertin　　　Drink soon

Medium-full colour. Still quite fresh. Soft nose. Rather thin. Disappointing, even if it was a lesser wine.

1996, Ruchottes-Chambertin　　　Now to 2020

Medium to medium colour. Some development. Ripe, elegant, and cool on the nose. Medium to medium-full body. Slightly lean but very classy. Very long. Fine plus.

1996, Clos-Saint-Jacques　　　Now to 2020 plus

Medium to medium-full colour. Some development. Rich, full, and opulent on the nose. Lots of depth. Medium-full body. Very lovely, classy, balanced fruit. Complex and energetic. Very fine.

1996, Clos de Bèze　　　From 2014

Fullish colour. Some development. Seems richer, fuller, and certainly more opulent than the Chambertin. Still has some tannin to resolve. Lots of depth and energy. Today—perhaps it is the bottles—this is more impressive than the Chambertin. A very lovely wine indeed.

1996, Chambertin　　　From 2014

Fullish colour. Some development. Still quite closed on the nose. Firm, full body, very good tannins, but these are not quite resolved at present. Lots of depth, dimension, and energy. Very fine.

1995, Ruchottes-Chambertin　　　Now to 2017

Medium-full colour. Only just mature. Medium-full body. Slightly lean on both the nose and the palate. Reminds me more of a 1993. Lacks just a little charm. Very good indeed at best.

1995, Clos-Saint-Jacques　　　Now to 2020

Full colour. Only just mature. Rich, fat, surprisingly classy, and opulent. Excellent tannins. Fullish body. Very fresh, very harmonious, very long, and very lovely.

1995, Chambertin　　　From 2014

Full, vigorous colour. Fat, rich, voluptuous nose. Rich and multidimensional. Full body. Still very youthful. Excellent. Will still improve.

1993, Clos de la Roche　　　Now to 2018

Medium-full colour. Just about mature. Soft. Gently spicy and fruity on the nose and palate. Medium body. Good grip. Lovely long finish. Fine plus.

1993, Mazy-Chambertin　　　Now to 2018

Medium-full, mature colour. Rich meaty nose. Good grip. Still slightly lean. But ripe and generous on the palate. Good class, vigour, and depth. Medium-full body. Long. Very fine.

1993, Clos-Saint-Jacques　　　Now to 2020 plus

Full colour. Just about mature. Lovely nose. Very fine, classy fruit. Lots of depth and concentration. More austere than the 1995, but more profound. Very lovely fruit at the end. Excellent.

1993, Chambertin   Now to 2025 plus

Full, very vigorous colour. Lovely nose. Rich, full concentrated, and classy. Full body. Lots of depth and real dimension. Very, very lovely. A great wine which is better than the 1990 and the 1995.

1990, Clos-Saint-Jacques   See note

Quite a developed colour. Older than I would have expected on the nose (and older than my own stock). Not much vigour on the palate. Good fruit and grip but without the magic I have enjoyed elsewhere in this wine.

1990, Chambertin   Now to 2020 plus

Full, vigorous colour. Rich, full, fat, concentrated nose. Full body. Very lovely fruit. Lots of depth and dimension. Excellent grip. A profound wine which is more Chambertin than 1990. Excellent.

1989, Clos de Bèze   Now to 2019

Full, mature colour. Lovely, ripe, really quite cool fruit on the nose. Very good grip. Fullish body. Concentrated. Slightly spicy. Certainly a little sweet. But lots of vigour and a very fine wine.

1988, Ruchottes-Chambertin   Now to 2018

Good vigorous colour. Quite soft for a 1988 on both nose and palate. Classy fruit. Good substance. As always with this wine just slightly lean, but elegant and fine plus.

1988, Chambertin   Now to 2020

Full vigorous colour. Splendid nose. Full, rich, concentrated, and of very fine quality. Full body.

Rich, fat, and meaty. Excellent grip. Really fine depth. Very long and complex, and with real class. Very fine indeed.

1985, Mazy-Chambertin   Now to 2020

Full colour. Lovely nose with a touch of coffee. Ripe, round, fullish, and complex. Full body. Lovely fruit. A lot of energy still. Really harmonious. Delicious.

1983, Chambertin   Now to 2018

Full colour. No undue development. Quite spicy on the nose. Medium-full body. Rich, fat, and meaty. This is an individual wine with a lot of interest and dimension. Very good grip. Still plenty of vigour.

1978, Ruchottes-Chambertin   Past its best

Well-matured colour. Even a bit old. This is confirmed on the nose and palate. Classy fruit, but now a bit too astringent for comfort.

1976, Clos de la Roche   Now to 2013

Good full, vigorous colour. Soft, ethereal nose. Lots of style here. Medium body. Ripe and fresh. Balanced and subtle. Lovely finish. Fine quality. Holding up well.

1976, Clos de Bèze   Drink soon

Good, full, vigorous colour. Quite spicy, but full, rich, sweet, and energetic on the nose. Similar on the palate. Lovely fruit and surprisingly fresh and classy. Very fine.

1969, Charmes-Chambertin   Drink soon

Medium-full, fully mature colour. Fully mature—indeed fading gently—on the nose. But sweet and refined. Medium-full body. Good acidity, which is beginning to take over. Very good plus.

Clos de Tart

MOREY-SAINT-DENIS

THERE ARE ONLY FIVE *grand cru* monopolies in Burgundy. Four in Vosne: La Romanée, La Romanée-Conti, La Grande Rue, and La Tâche; and one in Morey-Saint-Denis: Clos de Tart. Most people would include the adjoining Clos des Lambrays but technically it is not, for a small segment is owned by the Domaine Taupenot-Merme opposite. Clos de Tart, directly above the village, and comprising 7 hectares 53 ares 28 centiares, has belonged since 1932 to the Mommessin family, only the third proprietor of this vineyard since the Middle Ages. It is largely such continuity, plus the inevitable bits of luck along the way, which has prevented the morcellation that is so widespread elsewhere. But today the danger is past. Like a first-growth Bordeaux *château*, it would be inconceivable that the Clos de Tart could be split up in the future. The five Côte d'Or monopolies, I feel, are secure.

The history of the Clos de Tart begins with a religious order, founded in 1125, for ladies who wished to live under conditions of piety and chastity similar to the Cistercians. They were called Bernadines. The mother house, Notre Dame de Tart, was established in a village of the same name which lies in the plain between Dijon and Saint-Jean de Losne. As with their masculine counterpart at Cîteaux, the order soon found itself endowed with vineyards: in Dijon, Bouze, Beaune, Pommard, and Meursault. And it was in 1141 that the Hospitaliers de Brochon sold an already established wine estate in Morey—the deeds refer to buildings and a *pressoir* as well as to vines, known then as La Forge—to the young *abbaye* of Notre Dame de Tart situated in a village called Tart l'Abbaye not far from Dijon.

Over the next couple of centuries, the holdings in Morey were increased and consolidated by means of acquisitions and exchanges. At one time there were vineyards in Vosne, but these *biens* were ceded to enlarge the domaine in Morey. It was probably not until the fifteenth century, so the archives suggest, that Tart became a Clos. The brick wall, partly rebuilt and extended in 1939 to include some land which had always been considered part of the *climat*, is still in place today.

At first this was a working order. The young

nuns were allowed, indeed encouraged, to take part in the harvest and to perform vineyard duties such as pruning and leaf-trimming which their sisters in the world outside the order have always undertaken. But, as elsewhere, disciplines eventually relaxed. The Notre Dame de Tart would never be a rich order. For some reason—were the prayers of women considered less effective than those of men?—the Bernadines did not attract the same legacies as did the monastic orders. Yet by the end of the sixteenth century, there are reports of the ladies taking a full part in local society, entertaining the nobility, wearing silk, lace, and jewels and sporting elaborate hair pieces: all this a long way from the ordinances of Saint Bernard! Then came a papal decree that female religious orders should seek safety within the walls of the larger towns. The nuns displaced to Dijon. The abbey at Tart village had been abandoned and later destroyed in the seventeenth century.

Early in 1791, alongside the sale of Romanée-Saint-Vivant (which fetched 583 *livres* the *ouvrée*—an *ouvrée* being roughly one-twenty-fourth of a hectare) and Chambertin (777 *livres*), the domaine of Clos de Tart was sold for 415 *livres* the *ouvrée*. At the time there were 6.17 hectares of vines.

By what one assumes was a mutual agreement between the local bourgeoisie interested in acquiring good vineyards, there was no competition at the auction. The entirety of the Clos de Tart passed to Nicolas-Joseph Marey (1760–1818), a wealthy local wine merchant who had just also bought the whole of Romanée-Saint-Vivant. Perhaps this explains the relatively low prices. Both Romanée-Saint-Vivant and Clos de Tart came fully equipped with press-house, cellar, and all the other dependencies of a self-sufficient winery. Chambertin did not.

Dr. Morelot, in 1831, wrote as follows: "Clos de Tart combines the merits of being both abundant and delicious, closely resembling Chambertin." Together with Clos de la Roche, this was Morey's best wine. Clos-Saint-Denis, in his view, was less fine, and he doesn't men-

tion Clos des Lambrays, much divided at the time.

Dr. Lavalle, successor as general Burgundian pundit to Dr. Morelot, is yet more positive. He cites (1851) one *Tête de Cuvée* in the commune: Clos de Tart, measuring 6.88 hectares and belonging to M. Ferdinand Marey (1802–1869), mayor of Chambolle, chief councillor of Gevrey, and son of Nicolas-Joseph.

Ferdinand bequeathed the Clos de Tart, very suitably, to his daughter Louise, otherwise Mother Saint-Louis, canoness of Saint Augustin; and she in her turn sold the Clos in 1919 to her sister Edith and brother-in-law Hervé de Blic. By this time the Marey wine business was moribund, for from the turn of the century onwards, exclusivity for the production and sale of Clos de Tart had been entrusted to, firstly, Maison Champy, of Beaune, and subsequently Maison F. Chauvenet of Nuits-Saint-Georges.

The origins of the Mommessin *négociant* business date back to 1865, when Jean-Marie Mommessin, originally of Oyé in the Charollais, set up a business specialising in *marc* and other alcohols in the Mâconnais. Turning to wine in the 1920s, his son Joanny set about acquiring vineyards in Pouilly-Fuissé and in the Beaujolais. In 1932, in the middle of an economic crisis which had affected the wine trade as much as everything else, his attention was drawn by a broker he often used to use, a M. Cyrot, to the forthcoming sale of the de Blic wine domaine. This consisted of the Château de Pommard, vines in Pommard, Rugiens, Clos-Saint-Denis, Chambertin, and Clos de Tart. On Tuesday, October 25, he found himself at the townhall in Morey. No one else was interested in the Clos de Tart (the Clos-Saint-Denis and Chambertin vines were acquired by the Groffier family and the Château de Pommard by that of Laplanche), and so Mommessin was able to buy the Clos de Tart without having to undergo a Dutch auction. The price was 400,000 francs, equivalent to roughly 1 million francs today.

The vineyard, neglected by Chauvenet, was in disarray. "I remember we only made eleven barrels in 1933," said the ninety-nine-year-old

Henri Mommessin, son of Joanny, when I last made a comprehensive tasting of the wines in 1997. Mommessin engaged Cyrot, already *régisseur* here and at the Château de Pommard at the time of the Blics, as his local manager, and two of the seven or so hectares were replanted in 1935. Cyrot was succeeded by his deputy Alfred Seguin in 1965, Seguin by Henri Perraut on his retirement four years later, and Perraut by Sylvain Pitiot in 1996.

The Mommessin family divided their vineyard and merchant business activities in the 1990s. Though they sold the latter to Boisset, the Clos de Tart remains firmly their own, divided between the successors of the three children of Joanny Mommessin. For a decade or so Clos de Tart was sold through Boisset, but since the 2007 vintage, it has been sold independently, with some 20 percent going direct to French private customers.

Roughly square, the vineyard of Clos de Tart runs up the slope behind the Tart dependencies and the house of Robert Groffier next door, but only some two-thirds of the way up the slope. Immediately to the north, Clos des Lambrays climbs higher. Above Clos de Tart at the same level as the top of Lambrays is the Morey-Saint-Denis village AC of En La Rue de Vergy, several proprietors of which are lobbying to have elevated to *premier cru*, a promotion which seems logical to me.

Curiously, but repeated next door to the north, the *climat* is planted north to south, to avoid erosion, rather than the normal east-west, up- and downslope. There is a gain in sunlight too, Sylvain Pitiot believes. The soil is the usual Bathonian limestone of the northern Côte d'Or, with very little surface debris, and large amounts of broken-up rock mixed with clay. There have been four different analyses of the terrain in recent years, the last by the great Claude Bourguignon himslf. These have established that there are essentially three types of soil, lying roughly on top of one another. At the top is grey marl; in the middle, occupying the greater part of the *climat*, is *calcaire de Premeaux*, containing the same fossilised oysters (*ostra aculminata*) one finds in Romanée-Conti; while below is *calcaire entroques*, containing fossilised worms.

From this Pitiot produces an initially large number of *cuvées*. In 2008 not only where there six vats from the three diffrent soils, and two each of young vines and *vin de presse*, but he also divided the *terroir cuvées* into those from destemmed and whole cluster fruit.

The average age of the Clos de Tart vines is old. The soil is poor. The result? A harvest of a maximum of 30 hectolitres per hectare. In 1987 a second wine was registered: La Forge du Tart. This comes from the vines which are less than twenty-five years old, but otherwise made in exactly the same way.

On one side of the courtyard, opposite the entrance to an impressive two-level cellar, built in 1855, is the old press house. Here is a huge wooden medieval *presse à perroquet* (parrot press), built in situ, and in continuous use between 1570 and 1924. There are apparently parrot presses and squirrel (*ecureuil*) ones. It all depends on where the people stand to pull the ropes which turn the wheels. The elevation and descent of this press is controlled by a large—2 metres in diameter—vertical wheel at the side. Opposite, replacing the old *cuverie* which contained six 60 hectolitre concrete vats is a battery of stainless steel tanks. There is the usual thermo-regulation, *érafloir* and *table de tri*. The press is now *pneumatique*. Behind this is the first-year cellar, where the wine will rest until the malo-lactic is finished. Downstairs is the splendid vaulted second-year cellar.

How has the Clos de Tart winemaking changed in recent years? Until the end of the 1970s, the wine was produced by the *chapeau immergé* technique. A grill some two-thirds of the way up the vat prevented the skins and so on from rising to the top. There could be *remontage* (pumping-over) but no *pigeage* (treading-down). This resulted in very aromatic wine but was less effective in extracting colour and tannin, yet it suited the domaine style, which was always for wine which was more elegant than muscular.

The domaine reverted to traditional methods at the end of the 1970s, gradually introducing more sophisticated methods of temperature control and movement of the wine, maceration at a maximum of 32°C rather than 35° from around 1990 onwards, and the *table de tri* since the 1996 vintage. At the same time as the temperatures of maceration have been reduced, the time on the skins has been increased, and always, except in weak vintages, has there been 100 percent new oak for the grand vin. Similarly, Sylvain Pitiot prefers natural yeasts. "I am very much against artificial yeasts," he told me on my last visit. "They banalise the wine."

While in the past the fruit tended to be largely destemmed, save for about 10 percent added as much for physical purposes—to aerate the vat—as anything else, Pitiot has recently begun to vinify as much as 50 percent, as in 2009, using whole clusters. "It all depends on the vintage."

In the vineyard the work is as organic as possible, but Pitiot wants to retain the freedom to use some of the organically banned treatments if he is forced to, as was essential in 2008. "I call it *culture integrée*, one up from the *lutte raisonée*." We used to pick later in the old days, he adds. "This gave us firmer tannins—sometimes a bit solid. Now we have more control over the yield, the wines are concentrated but purer and more supple." He adds that he likes long, drawn-out malos. One obtains a more subtle wine.

Pitiot, a lean man with a somewhat cadaverous face, was born in 1950 and is not a native Burgundian. He was originally a mapmaker, having stumbled across the old Larmat maps at an early stage. It is he who is responsible for today's splendid maps of the Côte de Beaune and the Côte de Nuits. He subsequently decided to become a winemaker and worked as a trainee at the Domaine Jacques Prieur, which was where he met his wife. Subsequently he was at the Hospices de Beaune, when he was recruited for the Clos de Tart position.

Clos de Tart has for long been one of the best of the *grands crus* and made particularly excellent wines in the late 1940s and early 1950s. Subsequently it lost a little, though not a lot, of its sparkle. Sylvain Pitiot's arrival brought a much-needed breath of fresh air to the domaine. The new winery, which came into use with the 1999 vintage, plus other refinements, underlined a further sophistication in the winemaking process. Today Clos de Tart has few peers, even among the great wines of Vosne and Gevrey.

What is the essential character of Clos de Tart? Didier Mommessin, in reply to this question in 1997, stressed its finesse, its elegance. Sylvain Pitiot points out the very sunny exposition of the vineyard. As a result, the average natural degree during the past decade has been about 14°. "It's signature? Closer to elegance than power. But more on the side of Bonnes-Mares than Clos de la Roche. In the time of my predecessors, the wine lost some of its punch: it was too delicate. Now we have reduced the harvest we have regained some of this intensity." I would add that Clos de Tart has a typically Morey character, bigger than Musigny and Les Amoureuses, not as full-structured as Chambertin. Alongside its neighbours, the wine has the backbone of Bonnes-Mares and the lushness of Clos de la Roche, but not the soft centre of Clos des Lambrays and Clos-Saint-Denis. There is plenty of wine here, and it keeps well. This is a first-class estate producing one of the very best of Burgundy's *grand cru* wines.

TASTING NOTES

I presented a range of wines of the Clos de Tart, the samples having come directly from the domaine, to the members of the Metropolitan Club, in Washington, D.C., in April 2010. Subsequently I went up to Morey to interview Sylvain Pitiot, and he was kind enough to open up some further bottles.

2008   From 2018
Good colour. Lovely ripe nose. Very good succulent fruit. Medium-full body. Very good

tannins. Excellent grip. Very classy fruit. Rich follow-through. Intense and pure. Vigorous. lovely.

2007 From 2014

Medium colour. Soft, ripe, gentle nose. On the palate good backbone, more than the nose would suggest. Medium to medium-full body. Good grip. Still some unresolved tannin. Ripe and intense for a 2007, and classy too. An excellent result.

2006 From 2017

Good colour. Good substance. Ripe, sophisticated tannins and plenty of fruit on the nose. Lots of style and flair. Quite full body. No shortage of tannins on the palate. These need to soften up. Good grip. Nice ripe finish. A little bit more to it than the 2008 but not as elegant.

2005 From 2018

Good, rich, immature colour. Splendid concentration and depth on the nose. Real drive and dimension. Great class. Full body. Very good tannins. Very fine grip. Rich, vigorous, profound, and very lovely at the end. Quite brilliant.

2004 Now to 2018

Medium colour. Still youthful. A little dry tannin on the nose, but fresh and succulent enough underneath. Medium body. Just lacking a little richness and dimension but now softening. Not great by any means but a pleasant bottle with at least some style.

2003 Now to 2016

Very full colour indeed. Still youthful looking. Ample, rich, slighly chocolaty, but not too baked or pruney on the nose. On the palate, surprisingly fresh and sophisticated. This is due to good supporting acidity. Energetic and positive. A great success.

2002 Now to 2030

Medium-full colour. Still youthful. A little adolescent on the nose. Doesn't sing. Better as it developed in the glass. Medium-full body. Good tannins and concentration. Beginning to

soften up now. Lovely, balanced intense fruit. Great class and harmony. Eclipsed by the 2005 but still very lovely.

2001 Now to 2018

Medium to medium-full colour. Just about mature. Very lovely gentle, fragrant nose with a touch of oak. Fresh and lovely. Medium to medium-full body. Ripe, soft, and round yet with good grip and intensity and no lack of vigour. Really seductive. Very fine indeed for the vintage.

2000 Now to 2018

Very good colour for the vintage. No sign of maturity. Round, supple, ripe, and charming on the nose. More seductive than the 2004. Medium body. Ample, easy to enjoy. Very good fruit. Soft but long and positive. Good depth. Fine for the vintage.

1999 Now to 2030

Fullish, youthful colour. The nose was still a little closed at first. Just about mature on the palate. Medium-full body. Concentrated, abundant fruit. Fat, rich, quite meaty. Lots of energy. Still needs two years to reach its apogee. It will then be excellent.

1996 Now to 2020 plus

Medium-full colour. Now some sign of maturity. Ripe, fresh nose. No undue acidity. Lots of finesse. Full, rich, and ample. Fat and seductive. Very, very lovely for what is now often a disappointing vintage.

1995 From 2013

Full colour, just about mature. Full, firm, tannic and solid on the nose. Quite a big wine. Slightly uncompromising but not too dry. Very rich underneath. Very good grip. Lots of depth and dimension, even class. Needs food. Fine plus. Still needs three years.

1993 Now to 2025

Full, mature colour. Lovely fruit. Just a touch of hard tannins on the nose at first. Fullish, rich, aromatic, and splendidly balanced and understated. Complex and very classy. Better on the palate than on the nose. Lovely finish. Less aggressively tannic on the palate than the 1995. Very fine.

1990   Now to 2025

Full, mature colour. Very lovely, fully mature, spicy and aromatic nose with a touch of residual dry tannin. Complex and perfumed on the palate. Harmonious, especially on the finish.

Fresh, balanced, and multidimensional. Lovely. But the wines today are even better.

1988   Now to 2020

Medium to medium-full colour. Fully mature. A very lovely example. No leanness. Lots of vigour. Still very youthful. Medium-full body. Very well-balanced. Warm, generous, and long on the palate. Very lovely. No hurry to drink.

Domaine Comte Georges de Vogüé

CHAMBOLLE-MUSIGNY

DELICATE, FEMININE, and fragrant, the epitome of finesse; lace, silk, and taffeta; violets and dog-roses; raspberries and blackcurrants with a finish of liquorice; amplitude and generosity; intensity without a trace of hardness. All this has been said by those attempting to describe the taste of Musigny. It goes further: an ode by Keats; the oboe solo from the Sixth Symphony of Beethoven; a Fabergé egg. What is it about Musigny which excites the imagination to such realms of fantasy?

Musigny is indeed an individual and distinctive wine. It is totally dissimilar from the other *grand cru* of Chambolle, Bonnes-Mares. But then the two are separated by the village, the valley of the tumbling river Grosne, and several hundred metres of vineyard. But it is also quite different from its contiguous neighbour, the Clos de Vougeot. Musigny lies higher up the slope, at a point where the rise becomes distinctly steep. The soil is stony and thin, there are barely 30 centimetres of surface earth before you strike the crumbling limestone rock underneath. There is red clay in the upper part of the *climat*, rare in itself, as well as white oolite,

which you will find as the basic mother rock all over the *climat*, but in general there is less clay than further down or in Bonnes-Mares, less nitrogenous matter, and hence more breed, and more definition in the wine, but less structure. Friable is the soil of Musigny, and this contributes to the fragrance of the wine.

And the wine, when it is good, *is* perfumed and silky-smooth, not rugged and masculine. The tannins are there, but they are supple; the vigour is present, but the feel is essentially soft. If Musigny has a similarity with any other *grand cru*, it is with Romanée-Saint-Vivant, just as the wines of Chambolle find their echo in those of Volnay in the Côte de Beaune.

Le Musigny consists of two sub-*climats*, Le Musigny itself and at the same altitude next door to the south, Les Petits-Musigny. In addition, a couple of isolated parcels of the Combe d'Orveau seem to have been able to prove to the authorities that they had always produced Musigny wine and have been added on. Altogether this comprises 10 hectares 85 ares 55 centiares.

Four proprietors own 90 percent of the surface area. The Domaine Jacques-Frédérick

Mugnier owns 10.5 percent, Jacques Prieur 7.05 percent, and Joseph Drouhin 6.2 percent. Other landowners include Louis Jadot, Drouhin-Laroze, Christian Confuron, Joseph Faiveley, the Domaine de Vougeraie, formerly Ponnelle, Georges Roumier, and Lalou Bize. But the lion's share, 7 hectares 24 ares 21 centiares, almost 70 percent and including the totality of Les Petits-Musigny, belongs to the Domaine Comte Georges de Vogüé. Not for nothing does this estate proclaim itself the Domaine des Musigny.

Not many estates in the Côte d'Or can trace their origins as far back as the Vogüé domaine of Chambolle-Musigny. Around 1450, when what was to become today's tightly-knit community of houses was but a straggling hamlet, a Jean Moisson endowed money for the construction of the Chambolle village church. When his granddaughter married a Dijon merchant called Michel Millière in 1528, she brought as dowry the nucleus of the future Vogüé domaine. The deed of marriage settlement is the first extant mention of Musigny vines. The Millières residence—it still exists—lay in the Rue de la Chouette in Dijon. For most of the fifty-two years the late Comte Georges de Vogüé ran the family domaine he lived next door. A bizarre coincidence.

In 1575, again through the female line, the vines passed into the hands of the illustrious Bouhier family, prominent members of the local parliament. And two centuries after that, in 1766, Catherine Bouhier de Versalieu, last of her line, espoused Cerice François Melchior de Vogüé, eldest son of a long-established noble family from the Vivarais. Once again, the Musigny vines are mentioned in the marriage deed.

Six generations on, following the death of the late Comte Georges in 1987, the management of the Vogüé estate passed to the hands of the daughters of the late Elisabeth, Baronne Bertrand de Ladoucette, herself the only daughter of Comte Georges; and the domaine belongs to the Baroness's two daughters, Comtesse Gérard de Caussans and Marie de Vogüé.

Georges de Vogüé took over the domaine on the death of his father in 1925. A man of military bearing, cooly precise, aristocratic but by no means self-important, he was complemented by his resident *régisseur*, Alain Roumier, whose father and grandfather had also occupied the same post. Roumier, who retired in July 1986, was the opposite of de Vogüé. Short of stature, excitable and voluble, every meagre inch the peasant, he was as passionate about his wines and his responsibilities as was his *patron*. Merely the expression was different.

Since the late 1980s, there has been a new *équipe*. The vines are tended by Éric Bourgogne, the wine by François Millet, and the sales by Jean-Luc Pépin. Briefly, after the retirement of Roumier, it was Gérard de Caussans, son-in-law of Madame la Baronne, who was in charge of the marketing and financial management. Tragically he was overtaken by a rapid cancer and his tenure was brief.

Located in one of the thin side roads in the heart of the village, you gain access to the large de Vogüé courtyard through a fifteenth-century porch. Opposite you lie the *chais*. Above the porch and round the sides, in a mixture of architectural styles, is the *château* itself: a grand stone staircase to the main rooms on the first floor, monumental fireplaces, hammer-beamed ceilings, escutcheons of the Moissons everywhere as are portraits of past de Vogüés. But otherwise it is sparsely furnished. Deep beneath the *chai* where the wine is made is the cellar, a vast vaulted room, replete with the barrels of the young wine, and cool and tranquil as all cellars should be. In late 2010 an extension to the cellar was undertaken, below the central courtyard, both to expand the barrel cellar and to increase the space for stock in bottle.

The domaine itself occupies 12.4 hectares. As well as the 7.25 hectares of Musigny, there are 2.75 of Bonnes-Mares, located entirely in the southern, Chambolle end of this *climat*, 58 ares of Amoureuses, one-third of a hectare of *premier cru* Chambolle (Baudes and Fuées), and 1.8 hecatres of village wine. The Musigny vines average forty years—it is all sold as Vieilles

Vignes—the young vine wine being incorporated with the *premier cru* wine and sold as *premier cru tout court*; the rest of the estate's vines average thirty years old.

How do they make the wine? François Millet is wary of committing himself, but, as he will hasten to assure you, flexibility is the key. The first thing is a low *rendement*: 30 hectolitres per hectare is the paramount objective. After that the fruit is largely if not totally destemmed. It depends on the vintage, the origin of the grapes, and the ripeness of the stems themselves. Fermentation takes place at relatively high temperatures—above 30°C rather than below, and where possible, the length of the maceration is prolonged. There is a judicious, but not excessive, use of new wood (usually 30 to 45 percent, though 55 percent in 1990), only a light filtration, and the wines are bottled after a year to eighteen months.

As well as the red wines, the Vogüé domaine produces one hundred cases—and the monopoly—of Musigny Blanc. This is a *rara avis*. Few are permitted to sample it out of cask. It is an odd wine, exclusively Chardonnay, but grown on Pinot Noir soil, but in no way resembling even Nuits-Saint-Georges *blanc*, let alone a Corton-Charlemagne or a Montrachet.

Forty-three ares are planted with Chardonnay, the residue of a period when it was commonplace to mix about one-tenth white grape–bearing vines amongst your red. Old records will show you that in pre-phylloxera times, even a Chambertin *blanc* was occasionally produced. The parcel lies at the top of the slope, close to the border between Petits Musigny and Musigny itself. At present the vines are young. In 1986 half the vineyard was replanted. In 1994 they uprooted the remaining old vines. Currently the produce of this section is sold as Bourgogne Blanc, but it will not be long, I hope, before at least part is once again labelled as Musigny Blanc, an exclusivity of the domaine. That element planted in 1986 would certainly be mature enough to produce *grand cru*. But I imagine they are waiting until all the vines are capable of being called Musigny Blanc.

The wine is most individual. A little four-square, quite heavy in alcohol, yet rather austere, it is full and has a flavour of almond-blossom as well as nuts. You would have difficulty placing it. It does not do well in blind tastings. My experience is limited. I am tempted to say that it is more of a curiosity than an experience, but I am looking forward to the opportunity of being persuaded to change my mind.

Over on the other side of the commune, indeed stradling the Chambolle-Morey border, lies the *grand cru* of Bonnes-Mares. The soil structure is quite different from that of Musigny. North of a diagonal line across the vineyard from the top in Morey (1.52 of the 15.06 hectares lies in Morey-Saint-Denis) to the bottom in Chambolle, the soil is heavier and contains clay, a marl known as *teeres rouges*. South of this the soil is lighter in colour; there is less clay; and there are fossilised oysters. This is the *terres blanches*. All over, the stone and pebble content is high. The effect is a sturdier, less delicate wine than Musigny: richer and more masculine. Yet a first-division *grand cru* without a doubt.

TASTING NOTES

I presented the following range of de Vogüé Musigny to clients of Acker, Merrall's Wine Workshop, in New York at the end of March 2009.

2005   From 2020
Very good colour. Rich, firm, closed-in, concentrated nose. This has now begun to shut in. Full body. Gently oaky. Lots of intense, profound fruit. Vigorous. Very good grip. A big wine, but splendidly put together. Very good tannins. Lots and lots of class. Rather adolescent at present, but a very, very long, lovely finish nevertheless. Very fine indeed.

2004   Now to 2016
Good colour. Fragrant, ripe, medium-weight nose. No great depth or dimension. But charming and already accessible. Medium body. Not a lot of tannin. Lacks a bit of vigour and suc-

culence. I find it a bit one-dimensional and disappointing. Yet balanced and enjoyable. But for a top *grand cru*, even in this vintage, it lacks a bit. Better than the 2000 but less good than the 2001.

2003   From 2013
Very concentrated, deep colour. Rich, ripe, but slightly monolithic on the nose. A certain inflexibility, but not too "southern." Exotic and seductive on the palate. Really very rich indeed. Full body. Some tannin. But the tannins not exaggerated. Surprisingly good acidity underneath. Beginning to soften up and open out. Not classic but very fine all the same.

2002   From 2015
Fine, full, immature colour. Quite a high level of volatile acidity in this bottle (and there was no backup). Despite that medium-full body. Rich and balanced. Excellent grip. Very, very lovely fruit. Not as full-bodied as 2003 or 2005 but marvelously poised and elegant. Very, very long. Excellent quality.

2001   Now to 2020
Medium-full colour. Still youthful. Ripe, open, straightforward, accessible, plump nose. Balanced and attractive. Medium to medium-full body. Abundant. Just about ready. Very lovely Musigny fragrance. Harmonious. *À point.* Unexpectedly fine. An example of how good some 2001s can be in the Côte de Nuits.

2000   Now to 2015
Medium colour. Hints of maturity. Not quite the weight on the nose of the 2001, but lovely fruit. Now mature. Fresh and enjoyable and charming. Medium body. Rather looser-knit than the 2001 by quite a way, and a little disappointing as a result. It's a bit one-dimensional at the end.

1999   From 2013
Fine full colour. Still youthful. Rich, fullish, abundant nose. Still not yet ready, but not too backward and certainly not hard. Fullish body on the palate. Still some tannin. Even still a little adolescent. It doesn't quite sing today.

Very good grip. Yet a zing and an intensity is missing. Curious.

1998   Now to 2025
Fullish colour. Still youthful. The nose is a little reticent, yet there is fine fresh, concentrated fruit here. Medium-full body. Very lovely, vibrant, succulent fruit on the palate. Fragrant and very stylish. Long, consistent, and very lovely. Excellent for the vintage and now just about ready.

1997   Now to 2014
Fuller colour than the 1998 but now just about mature. Plump, slightly cooked nose and palate. Decent grip. Ripe and fat, even sweet. Fresh at the end. Very fine for the vintage. Longer and fresher than most. But nevertheless a lack of real class.

1996   Now to 2018
Full colour. Still youthful and bigger than the 1998. Reticent nose, but very classy. But on the palate a little lean, a little astringent. I much prefer the 1998. This is more structured, but less succulent and less harmonious. Give it another year to see what happens.

1995   Now to 2020
Fullish colour. Just about mature. Slightly smoky nose. Fat, rich, and succulent. Not a bit unduly tannic. Fullish body. A little tannin still to resolve. Very good grip and lots of energy. Ripe and vigorous. Not exactly very rich, but very classy and very long on the palate. A lovely wine, especially with food. Just about ready.

1994   Now to 2017
Quite a full, fresh colour for a 1994 in 2009. Mature but not unduly so. Ripe nose. Good weight. Good depth. Good class. Good fruit. This is plump and fruity and surprisingly fresh and enjoyable. Will still keep well.

1993   Now to 2030
Full, rich colour. Still very youthful-looking. Still very young on the nose for a sixteen-year-old wine, and even a little tight. High quality concentrated fruit on the palate. Harmonious and profound in a slightly austere sort of way.

More concentrated and more volume than the 1995. More depth too. Marvelously vigorous follow-through. Excellent. Only just ready. Will last for ages.

1992   Drink soon
Medium to medium-full colour. Still vigorous. Soft, plump, ripe nose. Similar attack. The fruit is beginning to lose its succulence on the palate. But there is still good weight, grip, and vigour. Still enjoyable.

1991   Now to 2021
Surprisingly good colour. Good, weighty, rich, balanced nose. Lots of depth. Really very fine. Probably the finest really mature wine of the series (not counting the 1969). Fullish body. Fresh, harmonious, and full of fruit. Long, complex, and classy.

1990   2015 to 2030 plus
Full, firm nose. Still firm and monolithic on the nose. Seems a little over-extracted. But not too much so. Just a little rigid. Very full body. Excellent grip. It loosened up, to its advantage, in the glass. Lots and lots of very concentrated wine here. More to it in its monolithic way than the 1993. But very fine? Great? Leave it another five years and we'll see.

The 1990 Vogüé Musigny is a controversial wine, especially in the United States. I have misguessed it on more than one occasion, even taking it for one of Guigal's La-Las about a decade ago. Yet bottles on this side of the Pond do not seem to be as rigid. I still prefer the 1993 but am much more comfortable with the bottles of 1990 I have in my own cellar. Could it have been that the U.S. stock, at some point in its journey from Chambolle onwards, was subject to temperature abuse?

Many thanks to Mark O'Connell for this vin de nuit:

1969   Now to 2010
Fullish, fully mature colour. But absolutely no sign of age. Delicious nose: fragrant, complex, poised, and still very much alive. Very lovely, naturally sweet fruit. Long and one-dimensional. Still very fresh. Very fine indeed. Plenty of life ahead of it.

And to Gregg Cook for the following:

1966   Now to 2018
Magnum. Fine colour. Mature but showing lots of energy. Very fresh and delicious on the nose. Ripe, sweet, concentrated, full-bodied and with a splendid grip. Very classy. Remarkably fresh. Very lovely. Plenty of life ahead of it.

The following wines were presented by Jean-Luc Pepin and myself at The Great Wine Seminar in Miami in April 2011.

2008

Bonnes-Mares   From 2018
Good colour. Ripe, quite concentrated nose, but softer and with less pronounced acidity as many in this vintage. Not a blockbuster. Ample, fullish. Lovely fruit and very good grip. Quite structured. Concentrated, cool, and racy. Very fine.

Musigny   From 2018
Good colour. Fragrant nose. Quite delicate. Fresh and very stylish. Elegant, pure, lacy, and with splendid minerality. A greater dimension than the above.

2007

Bonnes-Mares   From 2016
Good fresh colour. Ripe, expansive nose. Good structure and depth for the vintage. Very lovely fruit. A delicious wine for the medium term.

Musigny   From 2017
Good, youthful colour. Rich, fragrant, quite substantial—for a 2007—nose. Very complex. Rather more to it than the Bonnes-Mares. Lovely finish. Very fine.

2006

Bonnes-Mares   From 2016
Good colour. Spicy and aromatic nose, with just a touch of greenness. Fullish, attractive ripe fruit, but it lacks a bit of elegance and precision.

Musigny   From 2017

Good colour. Fullish, ample, ripe nose. Fullish. Rather more elegance as well as substance than the Bonnes-Mares. Round, succulent, and long on the palate. Doesn't really sing nevertheless.

2002

Bonnes-Mares   From 2020

Fullish, vigorous colour. Very lovely fat, succulent fruit on the nose. Very good concentration. Fullish and ample. Great class and depth. Splendid grip. A lot of *millerandage* here. It shows. Very fine.

Musigny   From 2020

Good colour. Very lovely, persistent, fragrant nose. Great breed. Excellently pure and very delicious complex, subtle fruit. Marvelous energy and balance. Very lovely finish. This is a great wine.

2001

Bonnes-Mares   Now to 2020

Ripe, succulent, and complex. Not as fragrant as the 2002. But lots of wine here. Classy. Very lovely for the vintage.

Musigny   Now to 2020 plus

Slightly more closed-in than the Bonnes-Mares, but fragrant again. A lovely expression of fruit. Quite full body. Good grip. Very long on the palate. A super example.

1999

Bonnes-Mares   From 2016

Very good colour. Ripe, opulent, rich, and almost exotic. Full body. Lots of depth and energy here. Still will improve. Splendid.

Musigny   From 2016

This is a great wine. Fine colour. Still youthful. Rich, very concentrated, intense, and very elegant fruit throughout from start to finish. Fullish body. Both intellectually serious and very seductive. A great wine.

1998

Bonnes-Mares   Now to 2020 plus

Good colour. Cool, ripe, fullish, mineral, and concentrated. Not a bit austere. Lots of depth. Delicious.

Musigny   Now to 2020 plus

Even more seductive and less austere than the Bonnes-Mares. Less obvious acidity. Round and rich and ample and succulent. And, like the above, some of the complexity and flavour of an old Burgundy. Very fine indeed.

These two bottles of 1983 below were from the late Norman Kinsey's cellar and enjoyed in Shreveport, Louisiana, a few days before the wines above. These bottles had not been moved since the outset and were in remarkably youthful condition. I believe that at the time there were more than one bottlings at the domaine. Certainly I have notes which show wines rather less impressive than those below.

1983

Bonnes-Mares   Now to 2018

Again a very fine, fresh colour: very youthful for a nearly thirty-year-old wine. Splendid, very elegant and subtle fruit on the nose. Ripe, fragrant, and multidimensional. Great finesse. Marvelous balance. Impressive depth. A very lovely wine indeed.

Musigny   Now to 2020

Fine fullish, surprisingly youthful colour. Very fresh and pure on the nose. Fullish body. As usual, less sturdy than the Bonnes-Mares. But plump and concentrated, vigorous and harmonious. No undue age at all. Very classy. Very profound. Very fine.

PART THREE

Vintage Assessments

When to Drink Your Burgundy

The following applies to a very good (but not great and super-concentrated) vintage, and to 75 centilitre (cl) bottles. For a great year, multiply by 25 percent. For a lesser year, take off 25 percent. For half bottles, reduce by 20 percent. For magnums, increase likewise.

Village red wines, Côte de Beaune	Start four years after the vintage. Drink over the next six years.
Village red wines, Côte de Nuits	Start five years after the vintage. Drink over the next seven years.
Premiers crus, Côte de Beaune	Start six years after the vintage. Drink over the next ten years.
Premiers crus, Côte de Nuits	Start seven years after the vintage. Drink over the next twelve years.
Grands crus	Start ten years after the vintage. Drink over the next fifteen to twenty years.
Village white wines	Start three years after the vintage. Drink over the next five years.
Premiers crus	Start five years after the vintage. Drink over the next eight years.
Grands crus	Start eight years after the vintage. Drink over the next ten years.

A few words of advice: One of the silliest things I have ever seen written about fine wine—in this case the journalist was writing about Musigny—was that "great wine should be great from the get-go." This is absolute nonsense. Many wines, especially those from the biggest, most concentrated vintages, go through a period of adolescence, and during this period they taste far from great, especially to those unaware that the optimum drinking window may not open up for a decade or more. Meanwhile, a more superficial wine may be all singing and dancing and get all the plaudits. Remember the story of the Ugly Duckling.

About the Assessments

AS I HAVE SAID in the preface, these vintage assessments come largely from two series of tastings. The three-year-on tastings take place at the end of August, twenty-two or so months after the harvest, in the Beaune headquarters of Roy Richards, assembled and sorted by Jasper Morris. A group of us, mainly British Burgundy importers, sample some three hundred wines, arranged in appropriate series, over three days. The tasting is blind, but we normally know what we are tasting—that is, Volnay *Premier Cru* or Clos de Vougeot. When it comes to mixed flights, we will be aware, for example, that the first four are Bonnes-Mares, and the next four Musigny.

To this I add notes on the wines I have sampled at the annual tasting of the Domaines Familiaux, which takes place the previous March—that is, when the wines have had from nine to twelve months in bottle. This is not a blind tasting. Moreover, in April, in the interim, because that is the vintage on the market, I frequently find myself presenting a tasting of wines of the same vintage on my annual visit to the United States. These tastings too are not

blind. This frequently gives me the opportunity to see the same wine twice, if not three times—a help if a sample is corked. My notes are an assembly of all these tasting opportunities.

The ten-year-on tastings take place in the farmhouse of Becky Wasserman, outside Beaune, in June every year, some nine-and-three-quarter years after the vintage. The tasting of the 2002s marks our twenty-fifth anniversary. This is a tasting for our friends, the growers. Outsiders are expressly excluded so that these growers can feel free to discuss their and other's wines without fear of prying ears. Each grower provides three bottles or two magnums of each wine, so we have backups in case a bottle is corked. This is also not a blind tasting.

Sometimes, later in the year, I might find myself with bottles in my cellar of the same vintage which were not on the table in Bouilland. I open these in twos or threes (to give myself a bit of context) at dinner parties in the months which follow, and I have added my notes to those consumed in June. Here, because the tasting comprises a mere one hundred wines

Production in the Côte d'Or, 2005–2009, Five-Year Average
(In hectolitres, excluding generics)

	RED WINES	WHITE WINES	TOTAL
Grands crus	12,644	3,953	16,597
Village and *premiers crus*	172,291	65,728	238,019
TOTAL	184,935	69,681	254,616

or so, ranging from Marsannay to Chambertin, I have not attempted to produce a selection of the best of the vintage, as I have done with the three-year-on tastings.

In addition, over the past few years, I have made separate tastings of the Savigny-Lès-Beaune, *Premiers Crus*. The wines are not only admirable and worthy of consideration, but they also represent excellent value for money: indeed, perhaps the best values in the whole of Burgundy.

For the first time, in 2012, the group also made a comprehensive tasting of the white wines, in this case, of the 2009 vintage. Prior to this, I have added white wine notes which had come my way, but what is in this guide does not at all pretend to be comprehensive.

A note on the optimum drinking assessments: The comments which follow on the wines sampled are exactly as I wrote about them at the time. But I have amended the optimum drinking notes so that they represent the state of play in 2013, when this book is published. This may lead to apparent anomalies. The note, taken say in 2010 or earlier, may say: "Needs two years" or "Still has unresolved tannins." But the optimum drinking will say "Now to 2020." This latter comment is the state of maturity of the wine as this book goes to press. I am sure you will understand.

To put the statistics in the pages which follow into context, here is the five-year average production in the Côte d'Or for the years 2005 to 2009.

Chablis

CHABLIS *GRANDS CRUS*

There are currently almost 5,000 hectares of vineyard in production in the Chablis area. Just over a hundred of these are the *grand cru* vineyards, a continuous slope of undulating vines facing southwest and directly overlooking the town itself.

Looking up at the slope from the town, these *grands crus* are, from left to right: Bougros, Preuses, Vaudésir, incorporating La Moutonne of Domaine Long-Depaquit, Grenouilles, Valmur, Les Clos, and Blanchots. It is generally agreed that Les Clos is the best *grand cru,* producing the most powerful and long-lasting wines, the ones with the most intensity and richest flavour. Valmur and Vaudésir are also highly regarded (Valmur, in particular, also needs time to age). Preuses and Grenouilles produce more floral and delicate wines. Bougros and Blanchots are the least fine.

Opinions on these *grands crus* vary and, quite naturally, it is difficult to find a grower who can be totally objective. Michel Remon—erstwhile owner of the *négociant* Regnard, who could afford to be more dispassionate than most as this firm did not at any time own any vineyards at all—held the following views: he described wine from Blanchots as the most rustic, and he condemned Grenouilles for its lack of class; in his opinion, it was only a *grand cru* because it lies alongside the rest. In his view, Les Clos is racy and the most *nerveux*; Vaudésir is the roundest and richest but occasionally a bit heavy; Preuses is similar but with less style; Bougros produces wine somewhat like it on its upper slopes but is more like Grenouilles on the lower land. Monsieur Remon gave first prize to Valmur—a feminine wine, the most elegant and full of depth.

The now-retired but (before he sold his firm to Champagne Henriot) important grower William Fèvre saw three different categories. Leading the list, he put Les Clos, which he described as intense and long on the palate, with a toasted, gamey flavour. Bougros was *tendre* and *douceâtre* (soft and sweetish) with elements of chocolate. The wine was less steely and more obviously fruity than Preuses. Grenouilles and Vaudésir come somewhere between the two in style—less powerful than Les Clos, with more delicate and floral perfumes and a touch of violets.

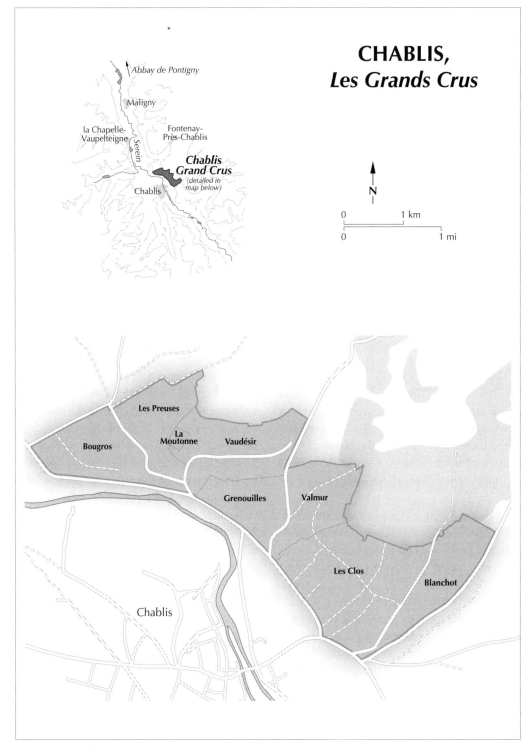

CHABLIS,
Les Grands Crus

Abbay de Pontigny

Maligny

la Chapelle-
Vaupelteigne

Fontenay-
Près-Chablis

Serein

*Chablis
Grand Cru*
(detailed in
map below)

Chablis

N

0   1 km
0   1 mi

Les Preuses

La
Moutonne   Vaudésir

Bougros

Grenouilles   Valmur

Les Clos

Blanchot

Chablis

MAP 15 Chablis, *Grands Crus*

Christian Moreau simply says that Les Clos, Valmur, and Vaudésir are the three finest *climats* and the remainder do not merit *grand cru* prices. Les Clos, he adds, is a combination of the finesse of Vaudésir and the structure of Valmur. Jean-Pierre Simonnet, an important *négociant-éleveur*, finds the quality-price ratio for all the *grands crus* to have ceased to be useful. These wines are difficult to buy, finance, or sell, he will tell you.

I would categorise the *grands crus* as follows:

Blanchots

12.88 ha

SIGNIFICANT OWNERS   Laroche (4.50 ha), Vocoret (1.77 ha), Long-Depaquit (1.65 ha), La Chablisienne (1 ha), Servin (0.91 ha), Vauroux (0.69 ha), Raveneau (0.60 ha), Viviers (0.50 ha), P. Bouchard (0.25 ha), D. Defaix (0.20 ha), Robin (0.20 ha), Billaud-Simon (0.18 ha), Droin (0.16 ha), C. Moreau (0.10 ha), and J. Moreau (0.10 ha).

Blanchot or Blanchots is the most southeasterly *grand cru* and rises up above the road to Fyé, sandwiched between Montée de Tonnerre and Les Clos. The aspect is southeast and the soil drains well. A typical Blanchots is a delicate wine, highly floral, maturing earlier than, say, Les Clos or Valmur. Not having the backbone of these neighbours, Blanchots is more susceptible, I would suggest, to over-production.

Bougros

15.47 ha

SIGNIFICANT OWNERS   Fèvre (6.20 ha), Colombier (1.20 ha), Long-Depaquit (0.52 ha), Robin (0.50 ha), Servin (0.46 ha), Drouhin (0.33 ha), Laroche (0.31 ha), and La Chablisienne (0.25 ha).

There are two distinct wines produced in this, the most northwesterly of the *grands crus*. Most Bougros is fullish-bodied, four-square, bordering on the rustic. It lacks the minerally thrust of a typical *grand cru*. Within the *climat*, however, facing southwest rather than due south, is a very steep section which gives an altogether better wine, combining the power of Bougros with no lack of finesse. William Fèvre, whose estate was bought by Champagne Henriot in 1997, owns a large parcel in this part of Bougros, which they label as Clos des Bouguerots.

Les Clos

27.61 ha

SIGNIFICANT OWNERS   Fèvre (4.15 ha), J. Moreau (3.61 ha), C. Moreau (3.60 ha), Pinson (2.50 ha), V. Dauvissat (1.70 ha), Vocoret (1.62 ha), Long-Depaquit (1.54 ha), Laroche (1.12 ha), Drouhin (1.03 ha), Droin (0.99 ha), P. Bouchard (0.70 ha), Servin (0.63 ha), Raveneau (0.54 ha), Malandes (0.53 ha), La Chablisienne (0.50 ha), L. Michel (0.50 ha), Billaud-Simon (0.44 ha), Duplessis (0.36 ha), Robin (0.20 ha), and Gautherin (0.18 ha).

Les Clos is the largest of the *grands crus* and lies between Blanchots and Valmur, facing south. The soil is rocky and very well drained. Here we have Chablis at its very, very best: firm, austere, racy, mineral, full, and long-lasting, combining depth, intensity, and great elegance. A bottle of Les Clos requires time, but it is worth it. The famous Clos des Hospices, an 0.80 hectare shared monopoly between Christian Moreau and his nephew Louis, lies towards the bottom of the hill.

Les Grenouilles

9.38 ha

SIGNIFICANT OWNERS   La Chablisienne (7.5 ha), Testut (0.55 ha), L. Michel (0.54 ha), Regnard (0.50 ha), Droin (0.48 ha), and R. Gautherin (0.22 ha).

Les Grenouilles forms a triangle at the bottom of the slope, bordered by Valmur to the east and Vaudésir to the north and west. It is the smallest of the *grands crus*. Much of Les Grenouilles is controlled by the cooperative, and most of this is labelled as Château de Grenouilles. This is one of La Chablisienne's flagship wines, vinified, at least sometimes, using new oak, an exotic and nutty wine with size and even muscle. Louis Michel's example is also rich and full-bodied, more ample but less mineral than his Vaudésir. In principle, I prefer both Vaudésir and Valmur and place Grenouilles in the second division. *Chez* Droin, comparing the same wines: the Grenouilles is more powerful but perhaps less elegant.

Les Preuses

10.7 ha

SIGNIFICANT OWNERS La Chablisienne (4 ha), Fèvre (2.55 ha), V. Dauvissat (1 ha), J. Dauvissat (0.74 ha), Servin (0.69 ha), Billaud-Simon (0.40 ha), Simmonet-Fèbvre (0.29 ha), Long-Depaquit (0.25 ha), and Drouhin (0.23 ha).

Les Preuses I rate in fourth place, above Les Grenouilles and Blanchots but lower than Vaudésir and Valmur, and, of course, Les Clos. The *climat* lies on the northwestern edge of the flank of *grands crus*, between Bougros and Vaudésir. This is an undulating vineyard, facing mainly due south, and giving a Chablis which is typically ripe and succulent, balanced, and elegant, but without the steeliness of Valmur and Les Clos.

Valmur

11.04 ha

SIGNIFICANT OWNERS Robin (2.60 ha), Bessin (2.08 ha), Fèvre (1.10 ha), Droin (1.02 ha), C. Moreau (1 ha), J. Moreau (0.99 ha), Raveneau (0.75 ha), Moreau-Naudin (0.60 ha), Collet (0.51 ha), Vocoret (0.25 ha), and La Chablisienne (0.25 ha).

Valmur lies northwestward of Les Clos above Les Grenouilles. Only a small part reaches down to the main road. The aspect is southwest. Valmur is a firm, full-bodied wine; properly steely, it should be backward and austere in its youth, rivalling Les Clos in the time it needs to mature. A top Les Clos is classier and more complete, but Valmur ranks with Vaudésir in a second equal spot in my personal hierarchy.

Vaudésir

16.83 ha

SIGNIFICANT OWNERS Long-Depaquit (2.60 ha), Besson (1.43 ha), Drouhin (1.41 ha), Fèvre (1.20 ha), L. Michel (1.17 ha), Droin (1.03 ha), Malandes (0.90 ha), Gautherin (0.89 ha), Billaud-Simon (0.71 ha), P. Bouchard (0.60 ha), Tremblay (0.60 ha), La Chablisienne (0.50 ha), C. Moreau (0.50 ha), J. Moreau (0.45 ha), Robin (0.25 ha), and Vocoret (0.11 ha). Plus La Moutonne, Long-Depaquit (*monopole*) (2.35 ha).

Lying between Les Grenouilles and Les Preuses, and mainly high up on the slope in the form of a well-protected south-facing amphitheatrical bowl, Vaudésir has long been regarded as one of the best of the *grands crus*. Many consider it as *the* best. The reason, as always, lies in the quality, individuality, and finesse of the fruit. A good Vaudésir shows very subtle floral tones, a little more high-toned than Valmur and Les Clos; slightly more feminine, perhaps, but not a bit lacking the essential Chablis minerality. La Moutonne, a monopoly of Domaine Long-Depaquit, lies in the Vaudésir *climat*.

CHABLIS *GRANDS CRUS*, 2010

It is now clear that in each of the three years—2008, 2009, and 2010—Chablis has produced the best of the white wines of the Burgundy region. What is also clear is that in Chablis, 2010 is superior to 2008, which is itself better than 2009, but that there are some very lovely

→ Size of the Crop ←			
FIVE-YEAR AVERAGE	2008	2009	2010
Production (hl) 5,266	5,209	5,336	4,589
Surface area (ha)	103	103.79	104.48
Yield (hl/ha)	50.6	51.41	44.09

wines in each of the three vintages. Perhaps unlike 2007, 2006, and 2005—none of them as fine as these last three—they will last well.

Summer 2010 was one of contrasts. After a cold winter and a cool, dry spring—much lower temperatures than further south—May was broadly similarly grey and miserable. Not until the beginning of June was there any sun, and that soon disappeared, just when the vines were about to flower. This caused widespread *coulure* and *millerandage*, which would eventually result in a deficit in the harvest of some 16 percent on 2008 and 2009. In July, thankfully, the weather warmed up. It was the sole month of the year where temperatures were above average. Nevertheless, the weather was changeable—hot, dry days alternating with cold, wet ones. August was similar, though sunshine was below average, but better weather prevailed in September and continued right through into late October. The Chablis harvest began during the week of Sepember 20. In some areas, but not on the slopes of the *grands crus*, botrytis threatened to be a problem. *Triage*, both in the vineyard and on arrival in the cellar, was even more crucial than normal.

In retrospect, the vintage was "saved" in the sense that its promising quality was ensured, by the size of the crop. Sixteen percent represents one glass out of the six you will normally get out of a bottle. So the 2010s have, potentially at least, a greater concentration. This gives them a depth and an energy too. And today (global warming?) we no longer get Chablis summers so deficient in warmth that a lack of ripeness becomes a problem (nor do we seem to get frosty springs). Even in 1996, the coolest summer over the past twenty years, some perfectly good—indeed fine—Chablis were produced.

As in 2008, but not 2009, the malos were slow to complete, but not too slow to generate any inconvenience in the cellars. As usual, all but a handful of the 2010 *grands crus* were in bottle by Christmas 2011 or very shortly thereafter, so my annual tasting at the beginning of March found the vast majority in good form. The small size of the vintage has helped to give them a concentration and a depth which leads me to rate them higher than the 2008s, with which otherwise they have much in common.

One thing which stood out—rather more than usual—was the difference in quality between what I consider the least good *grands crus*, such as Blanchots and Bougros, and those from Valmur, Vaudesir, and Les Clos: hardly a fine wine from the first two *climats*, barely a disappointment from the last three.

Another thing, by the way, which became clear from the *fiches techniques* which accompanied all the samples supplied to the Burgundy Wine Board (Bureau Interprofessionnel des Vins de Bourgogne, BIVB) for my tasting was that the only enterprise to freely admit to still picking their *grands crus* (except for their Grenouilles) by machine was the Co-operative, La Chablisienne. After thirty years the machine is dying out in the quality vineyards of Chablis, and a good thing too. Nor is the use of new oak the menace it threatened to be ten years ago. At that time, many domaines offered decidedly oaky wines. In not a single example of the wines I include here did I notice any undue oak. For that, many thanks.

The majority of the wines here will retail in France for 35 to 45 euros a bottle ($55 to $75 in the United States). This is less than the price for a *premier cru* Meursault. Yet sales, the locals complain, are sluggish. Make a note to put Chablis on your shopping list. The best of these last three excellent vintages are splendid value for money.

By the way of a PS, for those travelling in the region: The Hostellerie Les Clos has always been the place to stay. One (Michelin) star food and simple but perfectly adequate and modestly priced bedrooms. I dined there twice on my recent visit. The food was even finer than I have found it to be in the past. Bravo to M. Vrignaud and his team (www.hostellerie-des-clos.fr).

TASTING NOTES

The following wines were sampled in Chablis in March 2012. Those of Vincent Dauvissat and Raveneau were tasted *sur place* as these two distinguished estates don't deign to join the motley at the BIVB. Sadly, the Raveneau cellar was in the process of being racked, so the only *grand cru* in a fit state to be tasted there was the Valmur.

Bougros

Jean-Marc Brocard   16.5
Good style on the nose. Good depth here. Medium-full body. Just a touch four-square but balanced and very good plus.

La Chablisienne   13.0
Somewhat tarty nose. The wine is a bit short on the palate. Ungainly.

Domaine du Colombier   12.0

A lean vegetal touch on the nose. Weak and unstylish on the palate. Even a touch sweet at the end. No.

Bernard Defaix   16.0

Fresh, forward, flowery nose. Quite elegant. Good balance. But very good rather than great. It lacks a little personality.

Joesph Drouhin   16.5

A bit herbal on the nose. Better on the palate. Ripe and balanced. Medium-full body. Stylish finish. Very good plus.

Willam Fèvre   17.5

Nicely flowery on the nose. Composed, balanced, elegant. Long on the palate. Fine.

William Fèvre, Clos Bouguerots   18.0

Clean but slightly neutral nose at first. It's a bit closed-in. Better on the palate. Fruity and racy. Long and complex. Very good style. Fine plus.

Laroche   14.0

Soft, ripe, forward nose. Medium body. A pretty wine. But that's it.

Servin   16.5

Good minerally nose. Fullish body. Ripe. Good style. Still youthful. Very good plus.

Grenouilles

Jean-Paul et Benoit Droin   14.0

Fresh nose, if not exactly stylish. But some fruit. But only quite good, at best.

La Chablisienne   13.0

Rather old, herbal nose. Watery at the end. Superficial.

Testut   17.0

This has good fruit and grip. Ripe, fresh, positive, and attractive. Very good indeed.

La Moutonne

Long-Depaquit   17.0

High-toned, flowery nose. Medium to medium-full weight. Good energy. Ripe and stylish and a long positive finish. Very good indeed.

Preuses

Billaud-Simon   17.0

Soft, quite ripe nose. But at first it seems a little weak. More personality on the palate than seemed on the nose. Long, pure, racy, very good indeed.

Jean-Marc Brocard   18.0

Clean, pure, and racy on the nose. Medium-full body. Very harmonious. Very stylish. Lovely long finish. Fine plus.

La Chablisienne   18.5

Nicely pure and racy on the nose. This is very lovely. Quite rich. Lots of depth and harmony. Lots of energy. Very fine.

Maison Chanson   16.0

Clean, pure, vigorous nose. Just a little bland on the palate. It lacks a bit of raciness. Ripe, fruity, stylish, and forward. Very good.

Vignoble Dampt   16.0

Still a bit closed on the nose. Balanced and agreeable and fruity, if no great distinction. Very good at best.

Maison Faiveley   16.5

Decent fruit on the nose. Ripe, balanced, medium to medium-full body. Positive and energetic. Very good plus.

Nathalie et Gilles Fèvre   16.0

Good flowery fruit on the nose. Still young. Ripe on the palate. But the finish is just a shade sweet. Very good at best.

William Fèvre   17.5

Medium weight. Somewhat herbal on the nose. Nicely racy. Good depth and balance. Long and positive. Fine.

Simonnet-Febvre   18.5

Nicely poised and balanced on the nose. Fullish body. Lots of energy and depth. Very good fruit. Long and vigorous. Very fine.

Raveneau   18.5

Concentrated. Abundant. Full of fruit. Very good grip. Long and mineral at the end. Austere and voluptuous at the same time. Very fine.

Blanchots

Château de Beru   17.0
Quite a full colour. Round, ripe, good concentration. Plenty of depth. Attractive style. Medium-full body. Very good indeed.

Billard-Simon   14.0
Quite ripe fruit on the nose. But less elegant on the palate. A bit tarty.

Pascal Bouchard   17.5
Nice and fresh and steely on the nose. Medium-full body. Balanced. Good purity. Finishes well. Fine.

Jean-Marc Brocard   14.0
A bit vegetal on the nose. Decent fruit on the palate. But should have been more stylish and more concentrated. Quite good at best.

La Chablisienne   17.5
Ripe and stylish and quite substantial on the nose. Medium-full body. Good depth. Good grip. This will last well. Fine at the end.

Laroche   16.0
Green-gold colour. Racy and ripe. Youthful. Good fruit. A touch of lime blossom. Long. Balanced. Very good.

Laroche, Cuvée de l'Obedience   18.0
Ripe and fresh and stylish on the nose. Medium-full body. Good depth. Balanced and succulent and racy. Fine plus.

Long-Depaquit   12.0
Weedy, almost tired Sauvignon on the nose. Rather watery on the palate.

Louis Moreau   15.5
Attractive, quite forward, flowery nose. A touch raw on the palate. This is good plus at best.

Servin   13.0
A little stewed appley on the nose. Medium body. Not much style here.

Simonnet-Febvre   17.0
Round, ripe nose. Medium-full body. Balanced. Nicely racy. Not great, but very good indeed.

Valmur

Jean Collet et Fils   17.0
Good, quite firm nose. Lovely fruit here. Fullish. Rich. Still youthful. Long. Very good indeed.

Jean-Paul et Benoit Droin   18.0
Lovely fruit here. Very well balanced. This has depth and backbone. Backward. Very classy. Fine plus.

William Fèvre   17.5
Stylish fruit here, though not a blockbuster. Rich and concentrated. Good weight and depth. Long and complex. Fine.

Christian Moreau   17.0
Good, classy, fullish, backward nose. On the palate this is balanced and stylish. But it lacks just a little grip. Very good indeed.

J. Moreau et Fils   17.0
An attractive, flowery wine. But just a bit lightweight. Not short though. The fruit is very attractive. Very good indeed.

Louis Moreau   17.5
Full, nicely rich but austere nose. Classy fruit and very good harmony. Ripe. Complex. Long. Vigorous. Fine.

Moreau-Naudet   17.5
Good, stylish depth and concentration on both nose and palate. Rich and succulent. Good energy. Needs time. Fine.

Raveneau   19.0
Firm, backward nose. Rich. But steely. Lovely pure intense fruit. Fullish body. Long. Very fine plus.

Vaudesir

Billaud-Simon   17.0
Decent fruit on the nose, but a slight lack of backbone. Ripe and flowery on the palate. Medium to medium-full body. Long. Very good indeed.

Maison Damien et Romain Bouchard (DRB)   17.0
Good fruit and grip on the nose. Very ripe on the palate. Fullish body. Abundant and ample.

Quite forward. A seductive wine. Very good indeed.

Pascal Bouchard   16.0
Discreet, minerally nose. On the palate the fruit has a touch of sweetness at the end. Full-ish. Ample. But very good; not fine.

Jean-Marc Brocard   See note
This doesn't show well. A *brut* sample. The notes didn't say, so I must assume not. Ripe and fruity. Decent grip. To be reviewed.

La Chablisienne   17.5
Attractive minerally nose. Medium-full body. Good style. Racy and balanced. Ripe and long on the palate. Fine.

Bernard Defaix   17.0
Good classy nose. Still youthful. Medium to medium-full body. Ripe and balanced. Good depth. But very good indeed rather than fine.

Jean-Paul et Benoit Droin   18.5
Good firm nose. Plenty of depth here. Ripe, full-ish body. Full of fruit. Backward. Long. Very fine.

Joseph Drouhin   18.5
Good style on the nose. Medium-full body. Rich and ripe and minerally. Very elegant. Long. Very fine.

William Fèvre   18.5
Ripe, full, stylish nose. Medium-full body. Very good fruit. Quite firm on the palate. Good depth and a lovely finish. Will keep very well. Very fine.

Garnier et Fils   17.5
Soft, high-toned nose. Medium to medium-full body. Very good fruit. Racy and flowery. Complex, stylish, long, and fine.

Maison Olivier Frères   17.5
A bit neutral on the nose at first. Medium-full body. Ample fruit. Very well-balanced. Backward and with good intensity. Fine.

Long-Depaquit   16.5
Good, pure, backward nose. Plenty of elegance here. But less so on the palate. Plump fruit but a bit of a pedestrian finish. Merely very good plus.

Malandes   16.0
Ripe nose. But it lacks a bit of personality and elegance. Better on the palate. Fruity but not very complex. Decent balance. Very good.

Christian Moreau   16.5
Soft nose. Forward, flowery. Medium body. An attractive example but quite forward. Very good plus.

J. Moreau et Fils   15.5
Somewhat hard on the nose. Fruity but lacks a bit of elegance on the palate. Medium to medium-full body. Good plus.

Louis Moreau   18.0
Nicely ripe and steely on the nose. Laid-back. Medium-full body. Mineral. Very good depth. Long. Fine plus.

Les Clos

Pascal Bouchard   17.5
Ample, round, fruity nose. Medium-full body. Balanced. Plump. Good style. Positive finish. Fine.

Jean-Marc Brochard   15.5
Attractive, nicely minerally nose. On the palate, medium body. Not a lot of depth or personality. Good plus.

La Chablisienne   18.0
Good depth and class on the nose. Fullish. Very nicely ripe but dry finish. Very minerally. Balanced. Long. Fine plus.

Maison Chanson   See note
Is this a *brut* sample? The nose is not clean. Medium body. Rather raw. Difficult to judge.

Vincent Dauvissat   19.5
Rich, balanced, full-bodied, profound, and classy. Very lovely fruit. Very complex. Splendid finish. Excellent.

Jean-Paul et Benoit Droin   18.0
Good, discreet, minerally nose. Full body. Very good fruit. Fine balance. Classic and racy. Lovely finish. Fine plus.

Joseph Drouhin 18.5

Good restrained, dry, minerally nose. This is very classy. Medium-full body. Properly austere. Profound. Long. Very fine.

Duplessis 18.5

Very good nose. Steely and discreet. Very good fruit. Plenty of depth. Plenty of energy. Long and complex. Very fine.

Maison Faiveley 14.0

A bit tarty on the nose. Soft and fruity on the palate. Forward. Lacks distinction.

William Fèvre 15.5

Slightly yeasty but fresh and fruity on the nose. Medium to medium-full body. Decent balance but not a lot of class. Good plus.

Garnier et Fils 14.5

Lightweight but pretty nose. Medium body. Decent fruit but no great depth or distinction.

Laroche 18.0

Good nose. Nicely dry and pure. Discreet. Composed. Medium-full body. Lovely fruit. Lots of class. Long and fine plus.

Long-Depaquit 15.0

Soft and fruity but not very classy on the nose. A quite attractive ample wine on the palate. Good balance. Good.

Malandes 17.0

Good classy, minerally nose. Similar on the palate. Quite forward though. It lacks the drive and backbone of the very best. Very good indeed.

Christian Moreau 17.5

A bit closed on the nose. Nicely steely. Medium-full body. Ripe and balanced. Good depth. Fine.

Christian Moreau, Clos des Hospices 16.0

Soft flowery nose. Lacks a bit of style. Ripe and ample on the palate. Good harmony and depth. Very good.

J. Moreau et Fils 16.0

Ample, nicely austere, fruity nose. Medium to medium-full body. Ripe. An attractive wine but it lacks a little depth and class. Very good.

Louis Moreau 18.5

Good nose. Properly minerally. Fullish body. Ripe. Profound. Classic. A lovely wine. Very fine.

Servin 16.5

Round and plump and fruity on the nose. Medium-full body. Decent grip and austerity on the palate. Minerally. Balanced. Long. Very good plus.

Simonnet-Febvre 19.0

Very good nose. Minerally yet full of fruit. Very good intensity on the palate. Full-bodied. Balanced. Lots of energy. Very fine plus.

CHABLIS *GRANDS CRUS*, 2009

Following the 2008 vintage, a year which is looking even better one year on, the 2009s can be considered very nearly—if slightly less consistent—as successful as the 2008s. While elsewhere in the region, especially in the three great communes of Meursault, Puligny, and Chassagne, there are just a few 2009s which show a bit of *sur-maturité*, if not of botrytis, the cooler climatic conditions of the Chablis vineyard, a hundred kilometres to the north, have worked to the wines' advantage. They retain the crisp minerality of true Chablis while at the same time having the richness of the best wines produced further south. In terms of quantity, both 2009 and 2008 are reasonably abundant but not excessively so: indeed, the figures for both vintages are very close to the five-year average.

It was a long, cold winter, but without excessively low temperatures, but it continued cold through March, especially at the end of the month. April and the second half of May, though, were a little warmer than average, leading to an even and successful flowering, unencumbered by spring frost damage, a few days earlier than the average, about ten to fifteen days after the Côte d'Or. July and August were largely warm but interrupted by several quite torrential storms—but thankfully without serious hail problems nor any cryptogamic outbreaks.

So we come to September. Conditions were

already looking promising at the beginning of the month. The development of the fruit had already gained a few days: it was to approach its optimum even speedier. By September 15 the Chablis *vignoble* was ready, and the harvest began at around the same time as the Côte d'Or. The fruit was ripe, healthy, and concentrated, and the picking took place under sunny skies without any serious interruptions for rain.

The 2009 is a sensual Chablis vintage: the essential is ripe, and at the *grand cru* level, concentrated fruit, with plenty of richness. But at the same time the acidities are properly balanced, ensuring the racy steeliness we search for. There is plenty of encouraging purity. Some wines are at present a little four-square, indeed seem heavy, but this may be an illusion. While some had not been bottled at the time of my tasting, most of the rest had not been in bottle long, and might very well appear more relaxed in a few months time. In brief, this is a fine Chablis vintage. Perhaps not as glorious as 2008, but not far short of it. It will give a lot of pleasure. Drink them from 2013 or so—or later—depending on your taste.

TASTING NOTES

The vast majority of the wines below were set up for me to taste blind, *climat* by *climat*, by the local BIVB (Bureau Interprofessionnel des Vins de Bourgogne) in February 2011. My thanks to them. The Dauvissat and Raveneau wines were tasted separately, *sur place*, the next day.

Bourgros

Jean-Marc Brocard   15.0
Not yet bottled. Somewhat lightweight nose. Pretty but a bit superficial on the palate. Forward. Lacks the depth of a *grand cru*. Good at best.

Co-operative La Chablisienne   16.0
Not yet bottled. Ripe, balanced, and pure on the nose. Decent fruit. Medium-full body. Lacks a little definition but very good.

Domaine du Colombier   17.5
Good depth here. Fullish, stylish, minerally, and well-balanced. Good vigour. Long and satisfying. Fine.

Vignoble Dampt   17.5
Clean and pure if not very full and concentrated on the nose. But very good fruit and style and long and positive at the end. Fine.

Bernard Defaix   14.0
Ripe and balanced on the nose, if not very elegant. On the palate it ends with a flavour of boiled sweets. Medium-full body. Quite good at best.

Joseph Drouhin   13.0
Somewhat four-square on the nose. A lack of personality. Decently ripe and balanced. But a little forced. Hard at the end. Only fair.

William Fevre   13.0
Fresh, fragrant, crisp nose. But not enough fruit on the palate. Rather lean.

William Fevre, Côte Bouguerots   16.0
Slightly four-square on the nose, but better on the palate. Fullish. Good grip. Ripe fruit and decent balance. Very good.

Domaine Laroche   16.0
Quite a full, fat example. Ripe and balanced. Just a little four-square, but the finish is positive. Very good.

Long Depaquit   15.5
Medium weight. Fresh and fruity. But it lacks a little personality. Good plus.

Francois Servin   17.0
A racy, lean wine with good energy and style. Positive at the end. Elegant too. Very good indeed.

Grenouilles

Jean-Marc Brocard   14.0
Not yet bottled. Lovely flowery nose. But sadly the palate is less distinguished. Balanced but rather forced and rather coarse. Quite good at best.

Co-operative La Chablisienne,
Château Grenouilles 17.0

Not yet bottled. Steely, nicely lean nose. Ample on the palate. Medium-full body. Ripe, positive, and balanced. Good energy at the end. Very good indeed.

Jean-Paul et Benoit Droin 17.0

Soft, ripe, harmonious nose. Plump, yet properly steely. Almost peachy in its fruit. Balanced, long, and stylish. Tails away just a bit at the end but very good indeed.

William Fevre See note

Lean, coarse, decidedly inelegant nose. Not even really clean. What happened here?

Testut Frères 15.5

A touch of oak here which I find out of place. This gives it an un-Chablisien spicy flavour. Otherwise, reasonable weight and balance.

La Moutonne

Long Depaquit 15.5

Decent crisp fruit on the nose. Medium body. Balanced and fresh but no great dimension. Good long finish though. Good plus.

Preuses

Jean-Marc Brocard 17.0

Not yet in bottle. Fragrant nose. Stylish. Medium to medium-full weight. Nicely flowery. Ripe and positive at the end. Very good indeed.

Co-operative La Chablisienne 16.0

Fullish, rich, ripe, and balanced on the nose. Slightly four-square but long and positive on the palate. Lacks a little grace. Very good though.

Vignoble Dampt 17.0

This has very good fruit and plenty of depth and energy behind it. A bit rigid on the follow-through though. Very good indeed.

Vincent Dauvissat 18.0

Full, fat, backward, and quite powerful nose. Lovely ripe fruit on the palate. Quite a big wine. Needs time. Ample, long. Fine plus.

Maison Faiveley 17.5

Flowery, ripe, elegant, and balanced on both nose and palate. Good positive finish. Lovely fruit. Fine.

Nathalie et Gilles Fevre 17.5

Ripe, balanced, and stylish on the nose. Good energy on the follow-through. Medium-full weight. Very good finish. Fine.

William Fevre 12.0

Somewhat unbalanced and not very clean either. No.

William Fevre (Domaine) 17.5

Steely nose. Very Chablis. Clean and pure. Good depth. Harmonious. Plenty of vigour. Long. Fine.

Francois Servin 12.5

Soft and fruity on the nose, but a bit feeble. Not much personality either. Forward. Disappointing.

Simonnet-Febvre 18.5

Not yet in bottle. Very pure, stylish nose. Lots of depth. Medium-full body. Harmonious. Very good energy. Long and lovely. Very fine.

Blanchots

Pascal Bouchard 16.0

Not yet in bottle. Crisp, lean nose. Good style and grip. This will develop well. Nicely fresh and appley. Very good. Could turn out even better.

Co-operative La Chablisienne 17.0

Not yet in bottle. Attractive, ripe nose. Forward and accessible. But only medium weight and concentration. Balanced and positive. Better on the finish than on the attack. Very good indeed.

Laroche 17.5

Youthful, energetic, nicely profound nose. This has very good fruit and depth. Long and satisfying. Will evolve well. Fine.

Laroche, Reserve de l'Obedience 17.5

Racy, crisp nose. Good depth and character. Good vigour. Youthful. Good fruit. Pure and elegant and long on the palate. Will keep well. Fine.

Long Depaquit   15.0

Ripe. Medium-full weight. Harmonious. Good attack but then it falls away a bit. Good at best.

Maison Lupé-Cholet   14.5

Just a little lean, even thin on the nose. Ripe but a bit superficial on the palate. Decent finish. But a lack of depth. Quite good plus.

Louis Moreau   18.0

Good minerally nose. A backward wine with a lovely style and lots of depth. Good energy. Long on the palate. Fine plus.

Raveneau   18.0

Not yet in bottle. Firm, flowery, clean, and closed-in on the nose. Fullish body. Ample. Very lovely pure fruit. Somewhat austere. Very good grip. Long, complex, and classy. Fine plus.

Francois Servin   17.5

Good, fresh, balanced nose. Attractive, ripe, stylish fruit. Fullish body. Lots of personality and depth. Long on the palate. Fine.

Simonnet-Febvre   14.0

Not yet in bottle. Quite a deep colour. Somewhat overblown nose. Quite a lot of oak. Ripe underneath. Full and fat. But not very stylish. Quite good at best.

Vocoret et Fils   18.5

Nice and pure and steely on the nose. Medium-full body. Ripe and rich and with plenty of depth. Long. Lots of finesse. Very fine.

Valmur

Jean-Marc Brocard   17.5

Not yet in bottle. Ripe, nicely racy, harmonious nose. Medium-full body. Good energy and depth. Lots of style. Fine.

Jean Collet et Fils   18.0

Nice and steely on the nose. Good depth. Ripe, stylish, and balanced. Very lovely fruit. Excellent finish. Fine plus.

Jean-Paul et Benoit Droin   17.0

Lovely, almost ethereal, flowery nose. Very elegant. Medium-full body. Very ripe on the palate. Almost peachy. Long. Very good indeed.

William Fevre   17.5

Very good depth here. A fullish, concentrated, vigorous wine with very good fruit. Perhaps not quite the elegance at the end, but lots of drive. Fine.

Christian Moreau Pere et Fils   16.0

Cool, composed, stylish nose. Very good fruit. Not quite the concentration and grip on the palate. But ripe and easy to drink. Very good.

J. Moreau et Fils   16.0

Slightly closed-in on the nose, but good style and depth. Just a bit solid on the attack. Balanced but an absence of energy and nuance. Very good though.

Louis Moreau   16.5

Slighly austere on the nose. Good grip. Medium to medium-full body. Nice and pure but lacks a bit of fruit. Elegant finish nonetheless. Very good plus.

Raveneau   18.5

Not yet in bottle. Very lovely concentrated nose. Firm. Has a touch of hazelnut. Full body. Rich. Flowery in an orange-blossom sort of way. Individual, delicious. Very fine.

Vaudesir

Pascal Bouchard   12.0

Overblown nose. A bit too rich. Tarty.

Jean-Marc Brocard   16.5

Not yet in bottle. Balanced on the nose but a little rigid, so it lacks nuance. Good energy. Medium-full body. Very good plus.

Co-operative La Chablisienne   16.0

Not yet in bottle. Stylish and pure on the nose. But not as elegant on the palate. Medium-full body. Good grip. But not quite the class. Very good at best.

Bernard Defaix   19.0

Very soft and peachy on the nose. Lovely fruit. Very ripe and elegant. Reasonably forward but with a very lovely follow-through. Very fine plus.

Jean-Paul et Benoit Droin 19.0

Flowery, peachy nose. Harmonious and very elegant. Medium-full body. Persistent. Lots of dimension especially on the finish. Excellent.

Joseph Drouhin 18.5

Soft, ripe, elegant nose. Quite full and firm, but good depth. Very good fruit and grip. Long and positive at the end. Lovely.

William Fevre 18.5

Lovely nose. Flowery and composed. Medium-full body. Ripe and harmonious. Classy fruit. Long and complex and very elegant. Very fine.

Garnier et Fils 17.5

Not yet in bottle. Subdued nose, but nice and minerally. Pure and stylish. Lots of fruit. Quite rich, with a very slight touch of oak. Medium to medium-full body. Long. Fine.

Long Depaquit 16.5

Good depth here on the nose. Plenty of energy. Medium-full body. Balanced. Very good plus.

Domaine de Malandes 16.0

Good steely, profound fruit on the nose. Lacks a bit of sheer class on the palate. But medium-full body and good grip. Very good. May improve as it ages.

Domaine de Maupertuis 18.5

Soft, ripe, pure, and distinguished on the nose. Medium-full body. A subtle wine. Balanced and persistent. Very long. Very fine.

Christian Moreau Père et Fils 19.0

Lovely nose. Very pure, ripe, racy fruit. Balanced, poised, and vigorous. Medium-full body. Lots of depth. Very fine plus.

J. Moreau et Fils 19.5

Very lovely fruit all the way through. Balanced and persistent. Medium-full body. Ripe and long and complex. Delicious. Very fine indeed.

Louis Moreau 17.5

Fresh, pure, elegant fruit on the nose. Medium to medium-full body. Lots of nuance if not a wine for the very long term. Fine finish. Fine.

Les Clos

Pascal Bouchard See note

Not yet in bottle. Somewhat overblown, slightly oxidised nose. Ripe. Medium-bodied. But not at its best. Slightly heavy at the end.

Jean-Marc Brocard 16.5

Not yet in bottle. A slight touch of reduction on the nose. Medium to medium-full body. Good balance. Nice fruit. Very good or better.

Co-operative La Chablisienne 17.5

Not yet in bottle. Fresh stylish nose. Good fruit. Plenty of character. Soft, ripe, and accessible. Medium to medium-full body. Good grip and a positive finish. Elegant, pure, and persistent. Fine.

Vincent Dauvissat 19.5

Very classy, poised nose. Excellent grip. Very lovely, steely character. Ripe underneath. Full body. Very pure. Lovely fruit. Excellent balance. Splendid finish. Very fine indeed.

Jean-Paul et Benoit Droin 17.0

Nicely austere, slightly yeasty nose. Fullish. Good grip. Not the finesse of the very best but good energy and very good indeed.

Joseph Drouhin 17.5

Lovely clean, steely nose. Ample, rich, and full of fruit on the palate. Quite full body. Good energy. But almost too rich. Fine but not great.

Caves Duplessis 15.5

Not yet in bottle. Very poised, racy nose. Soft on the palate. Ripe and fruity. Medium-bodied. An elegant wine, but it tails off. Merely good plus.

Maison Faiveley 16.0

Ripe and ample but not very stylish on the nose. A little bit too rich. Medium to medium-full body. Decent finish but very good at best.

William Fevre 17.5

Good vigorous nose. Ample, ripe, balanced, and accessible on the nose. Stylish fruit on the palate. Medium to medium-full body. Long and vigorous. Fine.

Garnier et Fils 19.0

Not yet in bottle. Lovely nose. Pure and racy. This is classic. Fullish body. Elegant, balanced, clean, and complex. Very lovely long finish. Excellent.

Alain Geoffroy 17.5

Racy, minerally, and very Chablis on the nose. Ripe but steely. Lots of depth. Pure, persistent, and fullish-bodied. Very elegant. Long and lovely. Needs time. Fine.

Lamblin Fils 17.5

Good ripe fruit on the nose. Fullish, ample, balanced, and stylish on the palate. Plenty of wine here. Plenty of depth. Finishes very well. Fine.

Laroche 13.0

Soft nose. Even softer palate. Medium body. Forward. A bit short and one-dimensional. Only fair.

Long Depaquit 13.0

Pretty but rather short and slight. Lacks energy.

Christian Moreau Père et Fils 16.5

Ripe fruit and good grip on the nose. Medium-full body. Persistent, balanced, but not quite the class. Lots of energy though. Very good plus.

Christian Moreau Père et Fils, Clos des Hospices 17.0

Good class, energy, balance, and fruit on the nose. Medium-full body. Good follow-through. An ample wine. Very good indeed.

J. Moreau et Fils See note

Rather reduced. Difficult to judge.

Louis Moreau 16.0

Quite herbal on the nose. Good grip. Medium to medium-full body. Slightly lean, and it lacks a bit of dimension. But clean and balanced and long on the palate. Very good.

Louis Moreau, Clos des Hospices 17.0

Ripe and yeasty and slightly oaky on the nose. Very ripe on the palate. An ample, well-balanced wine. Long. Very good indeed.

Domaine des Malandes 16.0

Good firm nose. Fullish. Very ripe on the palate. This is balanced and vigorous, but it lacks that extra finesse. Very good.

Pinson 14.0

Somewhat overblown on the nose. Ripe but a bit flat. Lacks energy and elan. Quite good at best.

Raveneau 19.5

Not yet in bottle. Really profound, classy nose. Lots of distinction here. Full body. Backward. Lots of vigour. Delicious fruit. Very complex. Splendid finish. Very fine indeed.

Francois Servin 15.0

Delightful, delicate, flowery nose. Very soft on the palate though. Lacks grip and energy. Forward. Good at best.

Simonnet-Febvre 18.5

Not yet in bottle. Firm and fresh on the nose. Good depth. Medium-full body. Lots of very good fruit here. This has grip, depth, and energy. Very fine.

Vocoret et Fils 17.0

Fresh, flowery, stylish nose. Medium weight. Not the greatest of energy and depth. But harmonious and persistent. Very good indeed.

CHABLIS *GRANDS CRUS*, 2008

The 2008 Chablis vintage, as elsewhere in Burgundy, was rescued at the last minute by fine weather which set in from the middle of September. There are two important differences with the Côte d'Or, however. Firstly, the vintage started later—not until the very end of September—so the vines got the full benefit of this change for the better. Secondly, while equally cool and cloudy for much of the summer, especially in August, it was rather less wet. The incidence of rot and incipient mildew was diminished. That said, without the fine weather from September 15, the 2008 vintage would have certainly been mediocre. As it is, we have wines which are very good indeed: classic, minerally Chablis. This is where the 2008 Burgundy whites are at their best.

Following a dry and largely mild winter, the development of the vegetation was somewhat prolonged during a very wet April. There was a frost attack on April 16, but thankfully this seems to have affected only some localized plots up on the plateau among the Petit Chablis vineyards. May was warmer, indeed a little warmer than the average, but it continued to be wet. Hail affected the village of Fleys on September 12. The weather in June was similar: wet but reasonably warm, and a long and drawn-out flowering commenced around September 15. *Coulure* and *millerandage* reduced the potential crop. Things improved towards the middle of July, only for August to be, if no wetter than the average, cool and cloudy, and this continued until September 14, when at last the sun began to shine, and a northeast wind dried up the ripening fruit and stopped any major threat of botrytis. This fine weather continued well into October, enabling growers to wait for full maturity and to take their time over the harvest.

The 2008s took their time to show their true character. As elsewhere in Burgundy, the malolactic fermentations were late, many wines not finished by the time of the 2009 harvest, traditionally bottling-time for many estates. Nevertheless, those I sampled in Beaune and elsewhere in October and November impressed me greatly. So in the early weeks of 2010, I made a date with the local BIVB and on March 2, I sampled seventy-one *grand cru* wines in Chablis. Some domaines had not yet bottled, notably those of Pascal Bouchard, Jean-Marc Brocard, and Louis Michel. But I was not aware of which bottles when I tasted. It would have given too much of the game away! Yet I only noticed one wine whose lack of a star-bright colour indicated a vat sample.

Grand cru Chablis should be full and rich, yet at this stage austere as well as racy, steely, and minerally. What the best of the 2008s possess is very lovely, pure, concentrated fruit, balanced by very good acidity. The 2007s, by contrast, are equally cool and mineral, but they do not have the same weight, depth, and concentration. They will evolve sooner. But the 2008s should keep very well. I happen to like my Chablis young and vibrant, so I will be starting to drink my *grand crus* from 2012 or so. Classicists may prefer to wait until 2015.

TASTING NOTES

As you will see, the standard of wines was impressive. The vast majority of the wines were sampled blind, *climat* by *climat*, at a tasting set up for me by the local BIVB in March 2010. My thanks to them. The wines of Raveneau were sampled separately in situ.

Bougros

Jean-Marc Brocard   15.0

Not yet bottled. Not much on the nose. Pleasant, clean fruit on the palate, but without the depth and elegance of a *grand cru*. Decent follow-through. Good.

Co-operative La Chablisienne   17.5

Ripe, succulent, fullish nose. Lovely fruit. A fullish, ample, well-balanced wine. Good energy. Lots of style. Long and positive. Fine.

Domaine du Colombier   16.5

Decent fruit on the nose. Forward. Delicate. Fresh, racy, and fruity on the palate. Medium to medium-full body. Good follow-through. Persistent and quite vigorous. Very good plus.

Bernard Defaix   18.5

Racy, steely nose. Very good fruit and grip. Ripe and pure. Very good definition. Balanced, vigorous, elegant, and long on the palate. Very fine.

Joseph Drouhin   18.0

Delicate but clean, fragrant nose. Ripe, forward, medium-bodied, but with very elegant and persistent fruit. Fine plus.

William Fevre   14.0

Clean but somewhat neutral on the nose. Slight malic touches. Rather one-dimensional and lacking fruit on the follow-through. Only quite good.

William Fevre, Côte Bouguerots   16.0

Racy, stylish, fruity nose. Forward, balanced, gentle but quite intense on the palate. Good fruit. Long. Very good.

Long Depaquit 15.0

Clean but somewhat neutral nose. Fruity but a little one-dimensional. Lacks persistence. Forward. Merely good.

Francois Servin 14.0

Clean, crisp, very dry nose. But not a lot of depth, it seems. Medium body. Ripe and balanced, but something rather heavy and unstylish here. Quite good at best.

Domaine de Vauroux 13.5

Soft, fruity nose. Not a lot of energy underneath. Slightly oily on the palate. And the fruit is a little bitter as well as not very stylish.

Grenouilles

Co-operative La Chablisienne,

Château Grenouilles 14.5

Somewhat exotically perfumed on the nose. Decent fruit on the attack. Rather hard on the follow-through. Lacks charm as well as style.

Jean-Paul et Benoit Droin 13.5

Clean but forward and nondescript. Rather short.

Louis Michel 13.5

Not yet bottled. Slight touch of reduction on the nose. Light. Pleasant enough. But lacks depth and elegance.

La Moutonne

Long Depaquit 17.0

This was hidden among the wines above. Attractive, flowery nose. Medium body. Racy, steely, balanced, and persistent. Good vigour. Long and promising. Very good indeed.

Preuses

Jean-Marie Brocard 17.0

Not yet bottled. Fullish, plump nose. An ample wine here. Ripe and succulent. Well-balanced. Good style. Vigorous. Very good indeed.

Co-operative La Chablisienne 16.0

Closed-in nose. Just a touch of sulphur. Good depth. A little tight. But good energy. Very good.

Dampt-Dupas 15.0

Plump nose. Clean and fruity. Medium weight. Quite persistent but not the greatest of style. Good.

Faiveley 17.0

Ripe, almost honeyed (in a Chablisien sense) on the nose. A touch of new oak here. Rich, balanced, good fruit. Not my style but well made. Very good indeed.

Nathalie et Gilles Fevre 17.5

Good clean fruit on the nose. Medium body. Ripe, racy, and fruity on the palate. Balanced and persistent. Complex and elegant. Fine.

William Fevre 16.0

Clean nose, but it seems a little dilute. Understated. Medium body. Good grip and persistence. More to it than there seems at first. Very good.

Simonnet-Febvre 15.5

Soft, fruity nose. Good, racy fruit on the palate. But a slight lack of real quality and dimension. Good plus.

Blanchots

Pascal Bouchard 13.5

Not yet bottled. Slightly weak on the nose. Medium body. Lacks grip. Quite pretty fruit. But it tails off.

Co-operative La Chablisienne 17.5

Good nutty nose. Fullish, ripe, succulent, racy, and balanced. Very good follow-through. Lots of depth and energy. Fine.

Faiveley 17.0

Ripe, stylish, flowery nose. Good weight. Quite rich. Certainly vigorous. Fullish body, ample, and persistent. Very good indeed.

Long Depaquit 15.0

A little overblown and herbal on the nose. Better on the palate. Good grip. Quite full body. Has persistence if no great finesse. Good.

Denis Race 16.0

Good rich, firm nose. Plenty of depth and energy. On the palate, less elegance than I hoped to find after the nose. An abundant wine though. Ample and fullish in body. Very good.

Francois Servin   17.5
Attractive but undersated slightly herbal nose. Ripe, integrated. Medium-full bodied. Balanced. Good energy. Lovely, long finish. Fine.

Raveneau   18.0
Very classic. Lovely pure, flowery fruit. Fullish and ample, but very steely. Classy finish. Fine plus.

Château de Viviers   13.0
Not a lot of vigour on the nose. Ripe. Medium body. Lacks style and energy. No better than fair.

Valmur

Jean-Claude Bessin   18.5
Cool, composed, restrained but high-quality nose. Fullish body, concentrated, and profound. Very good grip. Lovely fruit. Lots and lots of energy. Needs time. Very fine.

Jean-Marc Brocard   18.0
Not yet in bottle. Concentrated, quite closed-in but very pure and steely on the nose. Lovely fruit on the attack. Medium-full body. Ripe and succulent. Very good grip. Long. Fine plus.

Jean Collet et Fils   19.5
Fine nose. Steely, pure, intense, and lovely. Medium-full body. Profound. Mineral. Concentrated. Splendidly balanced. Very lovely finish. Excellent.

Jean-Paul et Benoit Droin   18.5
Discreet and classy on the nose. Very lovely fruit and balance. Quite full body. Persistent. Ripe, poised, harmonious, and intense. Long and lovely. Very fine.

William Fevre   17.0
Fullish ample, slightly "puppy fat" fruit on the nose. Medium-full body. Decent grip. Good style and concentration. Best at the end, which is cool, balanced, and persistent. Very good indeed.

Christian Moreau Père et Fils   16.0
Slightly overblown nose. Medium-full body. Ripe and ample. Good grip. Plenty of fruit and

plenty of energy. Lacks a bit of nuance but very good.

Raveneau   18.5
Very pure nose. Full body. Steely but rich. Ample flowery fruit. Ripe and profound. Still very youthful. Long. Very lovely.

Vaudesir

Jean-Marc Brocard   18.5
Not yet in bottle. Not star-bright in colour. Ripe, round, and mineral on the nose. Full and concentrated. Crammed with fruit. Excellent grip. Very profound and very lovely. Very fine.

Pascal Bouchard   16.0
Not yet in bottle. Clean but a little weak on the nose. Good balance and quite racy fruit on the palate. Medium body. But a slight lack of dimension on the follow-through. Very good.

Co-operative La Chablisienne   17.5
Lovely intense fruit on the nose. Steely and complex. Not quite as impressive on the palate, but pure and balanced and certainly fine.

Bernard Defaix   18.5
Very fine, classy nose. Properly mineral. Lots of depth. Lots of energy. Very impressive depth and grip. Long. Complex. Very fine.

Jean-Paul et Benoit Droin   17.0
Clean and stylish on the nose. But it lacks a little intensity. Medium body. Ripe, balanced, and stylish. Nicely racy. Very good indeed.

Joseph Drouhin   15.5
Lightweight nose with a suggestion of oak. Medium body. Ripe. Good grip. Well-made. But the oak masks the minerality of Chablis.

J. Durup et Fils   12.0
This is a bit overblown on the nose and rather cheap on the palate. Too evolved. Disappointing.

Maison Faiveley   17.0
Medium weight. Stylish nose. Harmonious and subtle. Ripe fruit. Good attack. Lacks a little energy at the end but very good indeed.

William Fevre 17.5

A bit inexpressive on the nose. Better on the palate. Medium-full body. Good grip. Pure and intense. Long and racy. Very good depth. Fine.

Garnier et Fils 18.0

Not yet in bottle. More depth of colour than most. Ripe fruit. Some evolution. Ample, quite peachy. Good acidity. Classy and profound. Lots of energy. Fine plus.

Maison Olivier Leflaive Frères 17.5

Youthful, intense, classy nose. Medium to medium-full body. Very good grip. Lovely peachy fruit. Complex, long, and stylish. Fine.

Long Depaquit 16.5

Cool, poised, pure, intense nose. Medium-full body. Ripe and round. Fresh and balanced. But not the energy at the end. Very good plus.

Domaine de Malandes 19.0

Very attractive nose. Ripe, steely, but nutty. Pure and very elegant. Fullish body. Rich. Balanced. Energetic. Lots of depth. Very high-quality. Delicious.

Domaine de Maupertuis 16.5

Balanced and subtle on the nose if no great vigour. Round, ripe, ample, and fruity on the palate. Good acidity. Pure and not short. Very good plus.

Louis Michel 14.0

Not yet in bottle. Not quite the finesse on the nose of some. Fullish, ample, ripe, and balanced nevertheless. But it lacks flair.

Christian Moreau Père et Fils 18.0

Ripe, racy, complex, mineral nose. Medium-full body. Ample fruit. Balanced and abundant. Plenty of energy and intensity on the follow-through. Fine plus.

J. Moreau et Fils 14.0

Clean but rather inexpressive on the nose. Medium weight. Decent fruit and balance. But no real depth or flair.

Les Clos

Pascal Bouchard 14.5

Not yet in bottle. Not a lot on the nose. Ripe if a little evolved on the palate. Medium body. Good fruit. But no real depth or flair.

Jean-Marc Brocard 19.5

Not yet in bottle. Splendid, rich, concentrated nose. Pure, minerally, ripe, and intense. Very lovely fruit. Medium-full body. Very concentrated. Really energetic. Splendid.

Co-operative La Chablisienne 19.5

Perfumed nose. Classy, racy-peachy, ripe nose. Creamy-rich old-vine elements here. Full, intense, round. Lovely balance and very complete. Marvelous finish. Excellent.

Maison Chanson Père et Fils 14.0

Gentle nose. Some evolution. Medium body. Not a great deal of depth or dimension. Lacks concentration. Pretty but not serious.

Jean-Paul et Benoit Droin 18.5

Good class and good depth on the nose. Very good minerality. Medium-full body. Lovely fruit. Very complex and very harmonious. This is intense and very elegant. Very fine.

Joseph Drouhin 16.0

Interesting, slightly herbal nose. Plus a touch of oak. Medium to medium-full body. Good grip and ripeness. Good intensity. But the wood dominates. Well-made but not my style of Chablis.

Cave Duplessis 14.0

Not yet in bottle. Decent balance and intensity on the nose, if not a great deal of class. Fullish body. Broad-flavoured. Decent grip. But it finishes just a little coarse.

J. Durup et Fils 12.5

Rather overblown on the nose. Rather flat in the glass. Medium body. This is going nowhere.

Maison Faiveley 17.5

Graceful, flowery nose. Medium-full body. Balanced, ripe, racy, and quite profound. This is composed and classy. Fine.

William Fevre 18.0

A little reduction on the nose at first. Full, fat, and rich underneath. Full body. Plenty of vigour. Just a hint of oak. Very good grip. Plenty of wine here. Ample, concentrated, and profound. Fine plus.

Garnier et Fils 17.0

Not yet in bottle. Rather neutral on the nose. Medium body. Balanced, and at first just seemed pretty. But the follow-through showed good energy and style and more depth than was apparent at first. Not fine but very good indeed.

Lamblin et Fils 17.5

Stylish nose. Subtle and elegant. Not a blockbuster. Medium-full body. Pure and balanced. Nicely racy and minerally. Very good follow-through. Intense and complex. Fine.

Long Depaquit 11.0

Not a lot on the nose. Light and indeed thin on the palate. This is supposed to be *grand cru*?

Domaine de Malandes 19.5

Lovely high-toned, flowery-herbal nose. Fullish body. Ripe, balanced, succulent, and harmonious. Lots of energy. Multidimensional. Excellent.

Louis Michel 18.5

Ripe, balanced, classy nose. Full body. Rich, ample, succulent, and energetic. Very elegant. Lovely balance. Very fine.

Christian Moreau Père et Fils 17.5

Good, ripe, open, succulent nose. Ample fruit on the palate. Medium to medium-full body. Very ripe but the richness is steely and minerally. Plenty of depth. Fine.

Christian Moreau Père et Fils, Clos des Hospices 16.0

(Potentially better, but the vines are younger here.) Not very expressive on the nose. But composed and classy underneath. Good attack. Pure, ripe, balanced, and elegant. But it tails off a bit on the finish. Very good at best.

Pinson 16.5

Good intensity on the nose if not a great deal of class. Medium-full body. Good balance and plenty of energy. But it lacks the final element of finesse. Very good plus.

Raveneau 20.0

Lovely rich but steely nose. Very profound. Very pure and composed. Lots of energy and lots of depth. Backward. Really concentrated. A great wine.

Francois Servin 15.0

Full, quite concentrated, intense, youthful colour. Broad-flavoured and slightly scented on the nose. Full body. Good grip. Plenty of wine here. But it lacks real flair.

Simonnet-Febvre 13.0

Clean but not very intense on the nose. Medium body. Is there a touch of oak? No great concentration here. Nor grip. The wine is rather feeble and therefore the oak dominates.

The Three-Year-On Tastings

SAVIGNY-LÈS-BEAUNE, *PREMIER CRU*, 2009

Savigny-Lès-Beaune—the *lès*, with an accent, meaning "by" or "near to"—is the most divided *vignoble* in Burgundy. Part of the vineyard lies on the south-facing slope of the Bois de Noël, as it curves round from Pernand-Vergelesses. Opposite, on the northeast-facing incline of Mont Battois—down which the motorway thunders from the Morvan into the plain of Beaune—are the other half of Savigny's *premiers crus*, adjoining those of Beaune. The flatter land between the *premiers crus* is village *appellation contrôlée* (AC), as is an important but normally overlooked chunk of vineyard on south-facing higher ground beyond the village.

The soil on the Bois de Noël consists of gritty, sandy marl covered with ferruginous oolite on the top slopes and red-brown crumbly limestone below. It is not very stony and not very permeable, for the clay content is high. On the Mont Battois slopes the soil is sandier and even less stony, with deep limestone scree on the flatter land below. The result, combined with the orientation, is wines which are quite separate in character. From the Pernand side, the wines have medium weight and are elegant and persistent. The Mont Battois slopes opposite give more structured, earthier, more *sauvage* wines, which get rounder and fatter as the slope turns round and approaches the boundary with Beaune.

PREMIERS CRUS There are twenty-two *premiers crus* in Savigny-Lès-Beaune, in whole or in part. On the Pernand side we have Champ-Chevrey (part of Aux Fourneaux—and the monopoly of Domaine Tollot-Beaut); Les Charnières; La Bataillère (part of Les Vergelesses); Aux Cloux; Aux Fourneaux (part); Les Petits-Godeaux; Aux Gravains; Aux Guettes (part); Les Lavières; Aux Serpentières; Les Talmettes (part of Les Vergelesses); Aux Vergelesses; and Les Basses-Vergelesses. On the Mont Battois slope will be found La Dominode (part of Les Jarrons); Les Hautes-Jarrons; Les Jarrons; Les Bas-Marconnets; Les Hauts-Marconnets; Les Narbantons; Les Peuillets (part); Redrescut (or Redrescul); and Les Rouvrettes (part). These cover 144.02 hectares and produce around 5,350 hectolitres (700,000 bottles) per year of red wine and 275 hectolitres (36,000 bottles) of white.

There is plenty of Savigny, and the village offers some very good sources of wine, as do the merchants in Beaune and other estates elsewhere. Moreover, prices are inexpensive compared with those of either Pommard or Volnay—or, indeed, Beaune itself. All this adds up to very good value—indeed one of the best red wine values in the region: a happy hunting ground for those seeking good Burgundy.

TASTING NOTES

I sampled the following 2009 *premiers crus* at a tasting I set up in May 2012. There were several outstanding wines, especially when one considers the prices demanded. As usual, there were also some disappointments, particularly disheartening in view of this excellent vintage. My thanks to Claude and Francois de Nicolay of Domaine Chandon de Briailles for hosting the tasting.

Savigny-Lès-Beaune, *Premier Cru*, 2009

Le Champ-Chevrey (monopole),
Domaine Tollot-Beaut   From 2017   17.0
Medium colour. Slightly closed on the nose. But good depth and fruit. Rich, ripe. Medium-full body. Nicely generous and abundant. Good depth and energy. Very good indeed.

Les Clous, Maison Champy   From 2016   15.0
Medium colour. Spicy nose. A touch of gingerbread. Medium to medium-full body. Some tannin. Ripe and quite rich. Good grip. A meaty example. Good.

Les Clous, Domaine
Louis Chenu Père et Filles   From 2015   15.0
Medium colour. Plump, fruity nose. Medium body. Not a lot of structure but good style and intensity. Attractive fruit. Balanced, fresh, and long on the palate. Good.

La Dominode,
Maison Chanson   From 2018   17.5
Good colour. Quite closed on the nose. But rich and concentrated underneath. Fullish body,

fat, profound, and concentrated. Plenty of wine here and very good style. Fine for what it is.

La Dominode,
Domaine Bruno Clair   From 2017   17.0
Good colour. Backward nose. Ripe and with good grip. Medium-full body. Good fruit. This is less developed than most. The attack lacks a bit of generosity at present, but this will come. It finishes better than it starts. Very good indeed.

La Dominode,
Domaine Louis Jadot   From 2014   13.5
Medium colour. Light but fresh and fruity, supple nose. Light to medium body. Rather too ephemeral. Only fair.

La Dominode, Domaine
Jean-Marc et Hugues Pavelot   From 2018   17.5
Good colour. Rich, ample, fullish nose. Fullish body. Ripe and generous. A little tannin. Plenty of depth and a lovely rich finish. This is fine.

Les Fourneaux,
Domaine Simon Bize   From 2018   18.5
Very good colour. Rich, quite backward, tannic nose. Ripe and ample. Fullish body. Backward. Lots of depth and class. Delicious. Very fine.

Aux Fourneaux, Domaine
Chandon de Briailles   From 2017   16.0
Very good colour. Ripe nose. Good fruit and character. Very ripe on the palate. Almost sweet. Medium-full body. Some tannin. Generous at the end. Very good.

Les Guettes, Domaine
Arnoux Père et Fils   From 2018   17.0
Full colour. Rich, fat, and vigorous on the nose. Lots of fruit. On the palate, full and rich. A little tannin. Good depth and class. Good follow-through. Plenty of wine here. Very good indeed.

Aux Guettes,
Domaine Simon Bize   From 2017   17.0
Medium-full colour. Good clean, pure fruit on the nose. Medium to medium-full body. Good style. Good energy. Balanced and positive. Very good indeed.

**Clos des Guettes, Domaine
Gagey, Maison Louis Jadot**   From 2017   16.5
Medium to medium-full colour. Ripe nose. A little closed-in. On the palate there is good style especially on the follow-through. Ripe, balanced, and energetic. Very good plus.

**Les Gravains,
Domaine Camus-Brochon**   From 2015   14.0
Medium to medium-full colour. Soft, fruity, forward nose. Similar on the palate. A pretty wine, but without much to it. Quite good.

**Les Gravains, Domaine
Michel et Joanna Ecard**   From 2016   15.0
Medium-full colour. Very fresh. Not a lot on the nose. Medium to medium-full body. Balanced and fruity. But no enormous depth or richness. Merely good.

**Aux Gravains, Domaine
Jean-Michel Giboulot**   From 2015   13.0
Medium colour. The nose is a little overblown. Medium body. Some fruit but rather tarty. And not enough backbone. Lacks class. Only fair.

**Les Hauts Jarrons, Domaine
Louis Chenu Père et Filles**   From 2014   14.0
Light colour. Light forward nose. Quite fresh. Quite pretty. But not a lot here. Quite good at best.

**Les Hauts Jarrons,
Domaine du Prieuré,
Jean-Michel Maurice**   From 2014   13.5
Medium colour. Fresh, fruity, attractive nose. But rather lightweight on the palate. Tails off. Short and unexciting.

**Les Jarrons,
Domaine Pierre Guillemet**   From 2016   16.5
Medium-full colour. Good nose. Ripe, balanced, and stylish. Medium to medium-full body. Balanced and energetic. Rich at the end. Very good plus.

**Domaine Les Lavières,
Camus-Brochon**   From 2017   17.0
Medium-full colour. Still a bit closed-in on the nose. Medium to medium-full body. Good energy and depth. Ripe and balanced and vigorous. No lack of intensity. Very good indeed.

**Les Lavières,
Domaine Chandon de Briailles**   From 2018   18.5
Medium-full colour. Ample, rich, creamy nose. Fullish body. Fat, rich, and with lots of depth. This is admirable. Still a bit of tannin to resolve. Old-vine concentration. Needs time. Very fine.

**Les Lavières, Domaine
Louis Chenu Père et Filles**   From 2016   16.0
Light to medium colour. Crisp, fruity, attractively balanced nose. Medium-full body. Good grip. Ripe and stylish. Not the greatest complexity at the end, but very good.

**Les Lavières,
Domaine Jean-Jacques Girard**   From 2016   13.5
Medium to medium-full colour. Clumsy nose. Rather rigid and astringent. Medium to medium-full weight. Lacks style. Only fair.

**Les Lavières,
Domaine Philippe Girard**   From 2014   12.5
Light to medium colour. A little thin on the nose. And on the palate too. Rather weak and anaemic. Disappointing.

**Les Lavières,
Domaine du Prieuré,
Jean-Michel Maurice**   From 2016   14.0
Medium colour. Some evolution. Slightly weedy on the nose. But a bit better on the palate. Yet more astringent than fruity. Decently positive at the end but quite good at best.

**Les Lavières,
Domaine Seguin-Manuel**   From 2017   16.5
Medium colour. Ripe, fresh, slightly spicy nose. Medium to medium-full body. Quite rich. Good style and depth. Rich finish. Very good plus.

**Les Marconnets,
Domaine Simon Bize**   From 2018   18.0
Good colour. A fullish meaty nose. Plenty of weight and depth on the palate. Still some tannin to resolve. Lots of concentration and energy. Very good fruit and style. Long on the palate. Fine plus.

Les Narbantons,
Domaine Camus-Brochon   From 2017 16.0
Medium-full colour. Quite a closed nose, but no lack of weight and interest here. Fullish body. Rich, balanced, meaty. A little tannin to resolve. But good style and depth. Very good.

Les Narbantons, Domaine
Michel et Joanna Ecard   From 2018 18.5
Good, full colour. Backward nose. But full and rich. Some tannin. A full-bodied, meaty wine with very stylish ripe fruit. This is complex, high-class, and delicious. Lovely finish. Very fine.

Les Narbantons,
Domaine Philippe Girard   From 2017 17.0
Medium colour. Good ripe nose. Medium-full body. Rich and balanced. Ripe and energetic. Attractive, accessible, and stylish. Very good indeed.

Les Narbantons,
Domaine Pierre Guillemot   From 2014 13.0
Light to medium colour. Not much on the nose. Rather thin and nondescript on the palate. Forward. Disappointing.

Les Peuillets,
Domaine Arnoux Père et Fils   From 2016 16.0
Medium to medium-full colour. Ripe, ample nose. Good fruit here. On the palate the attack is fresh and fruity. But there is a lack of grip. Decently positive at the end but very good rather than fine.

Les Peuillets, Domaine
Michel et Joanna Ecard   From 2017 15.0
Medium-full colour. Ample nose. No hard edges. But slightly earthy. Medium to medium-full body. Reasonable balance but not very stylish. Merely good.

Les Peuillets, Domaine
Jean-Michel Giboulot   From 2016 14.5
Medium colour. At first a little reduced on the nose. Medium to medium-full body. A certain astringency, but reasonable fruit and grip. Lacks a bit of flair. Quite good plus.

Les Peuillets, Domaine
Jean-Jacques Girard   From 2017 16.5
Medium to medium-full colour. Quite a rich, ripe nose. Medium body. Pleasant, ripe, succulent, and easy to enjoy. Good positive follow-through. Very good plus.

Les Peuillets,
Domaine Lucian Jacob   From 2014 12.5
Light to medium colour. Light, pretty nose. But rather too weedy and insubstantial on the palate.

Aux Peuillets,
Domaine Lebreuil   From 2016 15.5
Medium colour. Ripe and fresh on the nose. But not a lot of depth or strength. Medium to medium-full body. Fresh and fruity. Quite stylish. Reasonably positive. Good plus.

Les Serpentières,
Domaine Simon Bize   From 2015 14.5
Medium colour. A little reduction on the nose. Medium body. Rather one-dimensional but quite pretty, and balanced as well. Reasonable follow-through. Quite good plus.

Les Serpentières, Domaine
Michel et Joanna Ecard   From 2018 18.5
Good colour. Plenty of depth and structure on the nose. Fullish body. Ample, ripe, rich, and fresh. Really quite sophisticated fruit. Long and vigorous. Very fine.

Les Serpentières, Domaine
Jean-Michel Giboulot   From 2015 14.0
Light to medium colour. Spicy, gingerbread nose. Light to medium body. Quite a pretty wine but a bit lightweight. Reasonable finish. Okay at best.

Les Serpentières,
Domaine Jean-Jacques Girard   From 2014 12.5
Medium colour. Light nose with a hint of reduction. Rather weedy on the palate.

Les Serpentières,
Domaine Pierre Guillemet   From 2016 15.0
Medium colour. Quite a rich nose with a touch of spice. Medium body. Fresh fruit but nothing much to support it. Reasonable style. Good.

Les Serpentières,

Domaine Patrick Javillier   From 2016   15.5

Medium colour. Soft, pretty fruit on the nose. But not much to support it. Medium body. Ripe, balanced, stylish, and positive. Some character. Good plus.

Les Serpentières,

Domaine Lebreuil   From 2018   16.0

Medium colour. Some evolution. Fresh, stylish, balanced nose. Quite backward on the palate. Some tannin. Quite concentrated. Plenty of good wine here. A bit four-square perhaps. Needs time. Very good.

Les Serpentières, Domaine

Jean-Marc et Hugues Pavelot   From 2014   12.5

Fullish colour. Somewhat lean and green on the nose. Thin and weedy on the palate. Disappointing.

Les Talmettes,

Domaine Simon Bize   From 2017   15.5

Medium-full colour. A slight reduction on the nose. Medium-full body. At present a bit sturdy. But there is good fruit and energy here. Will improve. Good plus.

Les Vergelesses,

Domaine Arnoux Père et Fils   From 2018   17.0

Fresh, medium colour. Rich, ample, concentrated, stylish nose. Plenty of depth here. On the palate, fullish body. Balanced. Not quite the intensity of fine, but long, attractive, and very good indeed.

Aux Vergelesses,

Domaine Simon Bize   From 2017   16.5

Medium to medium-full colour. Good rich nose. Fresh and quite concentrated. On the palate medium body. Reasonable fruit: ripe and quite rich. But it lacks a bit of bite. Very good plus but not fine.

Les Vergelesses,

Domaine Lucien Jacob   From 2018   17.5

Light to medium colour. But more to it on the nose than you might expect. Ample, medium-full body, quite fat. Good energy and generosity. Lovely finish. Fine

2009 BURGUNDY

Right from the very beginning, as soon as the fruit, gathered in auspicious conditions—warm and largely free from rain—was in the fermentation vats, it was clear that 2009 had followed the general run of "9" vintages and was very

→ Rating for the Vintage ←	
Red	18.5
White	16.0

good indeed. I had no hesitation, even as early as October 2009, in placing 2009 up with 2005 and 1999 as the very best of the past twenty-five years. The vintage was also quite plentiful, as was 1999. It was a splendid summer. From the middle of May on, the sun shone; it was warm though rarely very hot; it was dry without being parched; and these favourable conditions con-

→ Size of the Crop ← (In hectolitres)			
	RED	WHITE	TOTAL
Grand cru	13,059	4,150	17,209
Village and			
premier cru	188,068	69,453	257,521
TOTAL	201,127	73,603	274,730

tinued through until the end of the harvest and beyond.

Not all was totally perfect, however. There were May hailstorms variously in Morey-Saint-Denis (Laurent Ponsot's Clos de la Roche produced half a normal crop) and the southern end of Gevrey-Chambertin. The southern Mâconnais and the northern Beaujolais were also affected at this time. The flowering in parts of the Côte d'Or was rather drawn out, resulting in the possibility of uneven ripeness at the time of the harvest. (As it turned out, the warm summer, plus judicious green harvesting of the more backward bunches, reduced this potential problem to a minimum.) Halfway through July, there was a very wet weekend which gave rise to fears of an attack of mildew and oidium. And the vintage in Chablis, which otherwise had had an almost perfect summer, was interrupted by two days of rain.

But by and large, the 2009 weather conditions could hardly have been better. August especially, in contrast to recent years, was magnificent. Remember the old saying "Août fait le moût" (August makes [creates] the must). September was warm with a drying north wind, preserving the acidities which in the light of the fine weather and generous harvest might have begun to sink to levels close to dangerously low. In fact, though these levels were not by any means high, apparently the pHs are quite normal. The fruit was so healthy it was hardly necessary to do a *triage*.

Naturally, in view of the benign conditions, it was an early harvest. But not dangerously early, as in 2003. Most importantly, the growers could take their time, as it was not too hot. The harvest started towards the end of the first week of September in the Beaujolais, a few days later in the Mâconnais, and as early as that in some vineyards in the Côte d'Or. By September 14 it was fully under way in the Côte de Beaune, and even traditional late-pickers in the Côte de Nuits such as the Domaine Ponsot were out in their vineyards by September 21. By October 1, all but some vines in the Hautes Côtes remained unharvested. Chablis, meanwhile, started on September 11, stopped because of the rain, started again a week later, and was finished by September 20.

The red wines have naturally high alcoholic degrees without being blockbusters. One grower said that he was going to be careful about prolonging macerations for fear of creating monsters. Others, worried about the size of the crop, have performed a light *saigner* to concentrate the must, or where they feared there might be over-ripeness, have made their team perform overtime and finished their harvest in six days rather than ten.

In contrast to 2008, there was little malic acidity, and the malo-lactic fermentations took place quickly. Colours were very good. The tannins were very ripe, and even at three years on, when you might expect them to be a bit harsh, not aggressive. And there is no lack of grip and definition to go with the inherent richness of the vintage. Moreover, and this is in fact rarer in large, splendidly ripe vintages than you might think (often it is the somewhat less favoured years which excel), there is no lack of *terroir* definition.

My one initial fear was the level of acidity in the top red wines. As I wrote in October 2009: what we may have is a repeat of 1985, where we effectively had two sets of wines. The first matured fast and were fully mature in advance of their tenth birthday. The others had hardly even begun to soften by then, and only began to show agreeably five years after that. Nearly three years on, while there are certainly some which lack a bit of bite, the majority of the 2009s, as I state earlier, do not lack grip.

A great vintage? Not quite. Though there are more than a few single bottles which are indisputably great, overall the 2009s do not have the concentration and depth of the 2005s. The year 1999 is the closest parallel. Yet, as we felt at the three-year-on tasting: 1999-plus. It is a tribute to modern *élevage* that there is a consistency in the 2009 vintage which was not there a decade ago. Moreover—and this is always encouraging—the quality of the generic wines is very high. This is a vintage to stock up with the Bourgognes Rouges of your favourite growers (which you can then have fun offering blind to your guests in three or four years time). I await the three-year-on tasting of the 2010s, a vintage which is showing better and better now the wines are in bottle, and promises to be profound and classic, if a little more austere than the 2009s, with impatience.

The white wines in the Côte d'Or are attractive but not as successful. Yes, there is no lack of ripe, succulent fruit, but here I do have to search more extensively for the sort of reserve I seek; the austerity at this stage that indicates the wine will be better at eight years old than at four. The quality in the Mâconnais as well as Chablis has been to some extent compromised by their local weather conditions. In general, I prefer the 2008s and 2010s in both cases, but there are no long faces. It may be the Côte de Beaune and the Côte Chalonnaise have got the best of it this year, as far as white wines are concerned; but elsewhere growers are nevertheless more than happy. The Beaujolais *crus,* on the other hand, are terrific. These are the best Beaujolais I have enjoyed for many a year.

For the first time, thanks largely to Jasper Morris, the group organised a white wine tasting, which took place *chez lui* in June 2012. This tasting was just of the Côte d'Or wines. The Chassagnes were the most disappointing of the three main villages, but we found some good Pulignys. Of the *grands crus,* the Corton-Charlemagnes left something—indeed much—to be desired, and there were some howlers elsewhere. Overall, the tasting was disappointingly uneven.

The notes on the following red wines come from two main tastings. In March 2012 there was the annual Domaines Familiaux tasting in Paris, and this was succeeded by our own group tasting at the end of August. In June, as I have said, we had already made a comprehensive tasting of the white wines. The latter two tastings were blind; the former open. Inter alia I tasted a number of 2009s on my annual trip to the United States in April. The Domaine de la Romanée-Conti and Domaine Leroy wines were tasted separately in their cellars in Vosne-Romanée.

The Best Red Wines

20.0/20.0

Richebourg, Anne Gros

Richebourg, Hudelot-Noëllat

La Tâche, Domaine de la Romanée-Conti

Romanée-Conti, Domaine de la Romanée-Conti

Chambertin, Rousseau

19.5

Chambolle-Musigny, Les Amoureuses, Vogüé

Romanée-Saint-Vivant, Leroy

Richebourg, Clos Frantin

Richebourg, Domaine de la Romanée-Conti

Le Musigny, Leroy

Le Musigny, Mugnier

Le Musigny, Vougeraie

Clos de la Roche, Ponsot

Chambertin, Clos de Bèze, Rousseau

Chambertin, Leroy

19.0

Vosne-Romanée, Les Brulées, Grivot

Chambolle-Musigny, Les Amoureuses, Mugnier

Grands-Echézeaux, Eugenie

Romanée-Saint-Vivant, Hudelot-Noëllat

Richebourg, Leroy

La Grande Rue, Lamarche

Bonnes-Mares, Bruno Clair

Bonnes-Mares, Drouhin-Larose

Clos de la Roche, Jadot

Chambertin, Clos de Bèze, Bruno Clair

Chambertin, Clos de Bèze, Drouhin-Larose

Chambertin, Camille Giroud

TASTING NOTES

White Wines

Beaune, Clos des Mouches, Domaine Chanson Now to 2018 13.5
Rather a flat nose. Some sulphur. Undistinguished. Medium body. Not much dimension. Forward.

Beaune, Clos des Mouches, Domaine Drouhin Now to 2019 14.5
Round nose. Ample and succulent. Just a little four-square. Medium body. Decent fruit and grip. Not a lot of depth, but quite good plus.

Beaune, Clos des Mouches,
Domaine de la Pavillon
(Albert Bichot) Now to 2017 14.0
Light, brisk nose. But soft and without much bite on the palate. One-dimensional, but some style here.

Meursault, Blagny,
La Jeunelotte, Domaine
Martelet de Cherisy Now to 2019 14.5
Slightly deeper colour than some. Round, ripe nose. Some development. Medium to medium-full body. Decent grip. Some character if no great finesse. Quite good plus.

Meursault, Blagny,
La Piece Sous le Bois,
Domaine Paul Pernot Now to 2016 12.5
Nothing much on the nose. Medium body. Lacks fruit. Dull and forward.

Meursault, Charmes, Domaine
Michel Bouzereau et Fils 2015 to 2024 17.0
A bit closed on the nose. Yet good fruit and depth here. Some development. Very ripe. Yet good grip. The finish is long and vigorous. Medium-full body. Very good indeed.

Meursault, Charmes,
Domaine Buisson-Charles 2014 to 2021 16.5
A soft but quite a concentrated, juicy wine on the nose. Some development but no lack of depth and concentration. Medium to medium-full body. Good pure flowery-peachy fruit. Finishes well. Very good plus.

Meursault, Charmes,
Domaine Coche-Bizouard 2016 to 2025 17.5
Quite a firm nose. Good grip and depth. Plenty of balanced fruit. Fullish body. Very good peachy-flowery character. Very good grip. Quite concentrated. Lots of depth and potential. Splendid finish. Fine.

Meursault, Charmes,
Domaine Faiveley Now to 2019 14.0
Rich, full, backward, concentrated nose with a touch of oak. On the palate though there is a lack of grip and fruit. The attack is a bit hard, though the follow-through is better. Quite good.

Meursault, Charmes,
Domaine Antoine Jobard 2015 to 2022 17.0
Still a bit closed on the nose. Ripe and spicy underneath. Medium to medium-full body. Nice and pure. Balanced and flowery. Very good grip. A classy wine which will last. Very good indeed.

Meursault, Charmes,
Domaine des Comtes Lafon 2015 to 2021 15.5
Soft, ripe, flowery nose. Some development. A touch of H_2S as well as SO_2. Medium-full body. Plenty of fruit. Good grip, if slightly lumpy. Positive finish. Will develop. Good plus.

Meursault, Charmes,
Domaine Francois Mikulski Now to 2020 16.0
Lovely nose. Flowery and a bit peachy. Good grip. Good depth. Medium body. Not a great deal of power. Soft, high-toned, and forward. But stylish. Very good.

Meursault, Charmes, Domaine
de Pavillon (Albert Bichot) 2016 to 2026 17.5
The nose is a bit closed, but flowery and balanced, even classy. Lovely pure fruit on the palate. Fullish body. Balanced and profound. Very good finish. Lots of energy and class. Fine.

Meursault, Les Cras,
Domaine Henri Boillot Now to 2019 14.5
Some development on both colour and nose. Some sulphur. Medium to medium-full body. Decent grip. And a positive finish. Quite good plus.

Meursault, Genevrières,
Domaine Bouchard
Père et Fils Now to 2017 13.5
Decent balance, grip, and class on the nose. But not outstanding. Somewhat hollow and watery on the palate. Lacks freshnes and flair. Disappointing.

Meursault, Genevrières, Domaine
Michel Bouzereau et Fils 2015 to 2020 15.5
Fruity nose but a slight lack of grip. Medium to medium-full body. There is fruit and balance here and a decent follow-through, but it doesn't really convince.

Meursault, Genevrières,
Domaine Antoine Jobard   Now to 2018 14.0
Ample, fullish nose but a lack of real grip. Medium to medium-full body. Quite good fruit but an absence of purity and bite. Quite good at best.

Meursault, Genevrières,
Domaine Rémi Jobard   2016 to 2024 17.5
Nicely flowery, high-toned nose. By no means ephemeral. Medium-full body. Very good fruit. Good grip. Elegant and vigorous. Lovely finish. This is fine.

Meursault, Genevrières,
Domaine des Comtes Lafon   See note
Really quite shitty on the nose. And of course rather astringent on the palate. Medium to medium-full weight. Difficult to judge.

Meursault, Genevrières,
Domaine Francois Mikulski   Now to 2019 14.5
Round, ripe, but just a bit clumsy on the nose. Decent fruit on the attack. But then it tails off a bit. The finish is quite positive though. Quite good plus.

Meursault, Goutte d'Or,
Domaine Buisson-Charles   2016 to 2024 17.0
Ripe, round, peachy nose. Not a lot of depth but attractive if forward. On the palate, not as forward as all that. Long and classy. Very good grip. Very good indeed.

Meursault, Goutte d'Or,
Domaine Coche-Bizouard   2016 to 2026 17.5
Good depth, personality, and class on the nose. Plus the potential for development. Subtle and flowery. Lovely fruit at the end. Fine.

Meursault, Goutte d'Or,
Domaine Arnaud Ente   2016 to 2024 16.0
Good depth and potential here. Still youthful. But only medium-bodied. Not enough weight. Better as it developed though. Good grip. Very good.

Meursault, Goutte d'Or,
Domaine des Comtes Lafon   2016 to 2024 16.0
A touch of sulphur on the nose. But a wine made to last. Good depth here. Attractive fruity style but a slight blunt finish. Very good nevertheless.

Meursault, Perrières, Domaine
Bouchard Père et Fils   2016 to 2024 18.0
Properly steely on the nose. High marks! Fullish body. A bit adolecsent. But balanced and minerally with very good grip. Flowery too. Will develop. Fine plus.

Meursault, Perrières, Domaine
Michel Bouzereau et Fils   2017 to 2027 18.5
Crisp, racy nose. Very typical Perrières. Classy and profound. Fullish body. Concentrated, poised, and backward. Complex and vigorous. This is very classy. Lovely. Very fine.

Meursault, Perrières,
Maison Colin-Morey   2016 to 2024 17.5
Fullish, ripe, quite steely nose. But enough grip? Fullish body. Yes. Plenty of grip on the palate. Ample fruit. Nicely minerally. Fine.

Meursault, Perrières,
Domaine Vincent Dancer   2014 to 2020 16.0
A touch of sweaty animal on the nose. Soft, ripe, and plump. Medium to medium-full body. Good grip. Quite forward. But positive at the end.

Meursault, Perrières,
Domaine Albert Grivault   2015 to 2023 17.0
Open, crisp, flowery-minerally nose. A shade forward but very attractive. Ample. Balanced. Medium-full body. Accessible. Nicely racy. Most enjoyable.

Meursault, Clos des Perrières,
Domaine Albert Grivault   2016 to 2024 17.5
Lovely fruit on the nose. Honeysuckle plus minerality. Fullish body. Somewhat adolescent on the palate. But balanced and profound and very energetic. Fine.

Meursault, Perrières,
Domaine des Comtes Lafon   2016 to 2024 17.5
Rather over-developed, flat and reduced on the nose. But rather better on the palate. Good steely fruit. Medium-full body. A bit adolescent but it has good potential. Long on the palate. Fine.

Meursault, Perrières,
Domaine Roulot   2016 to 2024   17.0
Rich, full, somewhat closed nose. A touch of reduction. Medium-full body. Good grip and vigour. Plenty of steeliness as well. Very good indeed. Perhaps better.

Meursault, Poruzots,
Domaine Buisson-Charles   Now to 2018   14.0
Not a lot on the nose at first. Slightly hard as well as a bit over-ripe. Ungainly.

Meursault, Poruzots,
Domaine Antoine Jobard   2016 to 2024   17.0
A bit hidden at first but fullish, concentrated, and quite profound. Very good grip. Long, classy, will still develop. Very good indeed.

Meursault, Poruzots,
Domaine Rémi Jobard   2015 to 2022   17.0
Good fruit and an attractive wine if slightly more forward than others. Classy, well-balanced, and very good indeed.

Meursault, Poruzots,
Maison Benjamin Leroux   2016 to 2024   17.5
Round, ripe, flowery, and classy. Good grip. Lots of depth. Lovely fruit. This is fine.

Meursault, Poruzots,
Domaine Francois Mikulski   2016 to 2024   17.5
Lots of attractive fruit here. Fresh and balanced. Very good grip. Fullish body. Classy. Still youthful. Fine.

Meursault, Poruzots,
Domaine Roulot   2015 to 2020   16.0
Nothing much on the nose and the palate at first. Medium-full weight. Good grip. Some depth but it lacks a bit of grace and high tones. Yet there is more to this wine than seems at first. Very good.

Meursault, Les Rougeots,
Domaine J. F. Coche-Dury   2014 to 2022   16.5
Ripe and round but with good concentration and grip. Medium-full body. A touch of oak. Quite forward but fresh and stylish. Finishes well.

Meursault, Les Santenots,
Domaine Marquis
d'Angerville   Now to 2019   15.0
Nice, fresh, quite peachy nose. But forward and only medium body. Ripe fruit. Good grip. This has personality and it finishes well.

Puligny-Montrachet, Les Caillerets,
Domaine Michel Bouzereau
Père et Fils   2016 to 2028   19.0
The nose is very lovely. Cool and backward. Ripe and intense and very subtly flowery. Medium-full body. Splendidly put together. Classy and multidimensional. Very fine indeed.

Puligny-Montrachet,
Les Chalumeaux,
Maison Roche de Bellène   2015 to 2025   17.5
Rich, ripe, full, backward nose. There is depth here. A fullish meaty wine. Plenty of grip and plenty of character. Long. Fine.

Puligny-Montrachet,
Clavoillon, Domaine Leflaive   2014 to 2019   15.5
Intense, honeyed nose. Good grip but a touch over-ripe. Fullish body. Just a bit clumsy. Ripe and inviting though. Good plus.

Puligny-Montrachet,
Clos de la Garenne,
Duc de Magenta, Jadot   2015 to 2025   19.0
A bit closed-in on the nose, yet plenty of class and depth underneath. Fine grip and intensity. Very fresh and youthful. Very fine indeed.

Puligny-Montrachet,
Clos de la Garenne,
Domaine Paul Pernot   2015 to 2024   17.5
A bit closed on the nose. Yet class and depth here. Fullish body. Ripe. Very good grip and intensity. Yet just an absence of high tones for great. Just fine.

Puligny-Montrachet,
Les Combettes,
Domaine Jean-Marc Boillot   2014 to 2019   15.5
Laid-back fruity nose. Just a whiff of sulphur underneath. Medium to medium-full body. There isn't the intensity and concentration here

and the sulphur detracts from the class. Good plus.

Puligny-Montrachet,
Les Combettes,
Domaine Carillon   2015 to 2024   17.5
Soft, plump, open nose. Good depth and class underneath. Round, ripe, fresh, and balanced. Medium to medium-full body. Fine, long follow-through.

Puligny-Montrachet,
Les Enseignières,
Domaine J. F. Coche-Dury   2014 to 2020   17.5
On the nose this is quite an evolved wine. But it is firmer on the palate, and there is rather good fruit here. The finish is fine.

Puligny-Montrachet,
Les Folatières,
Domaine Bachelet-Monnot   2015 to 2025   18.0
This is subtle and laid-back on the nose. Very classy. Medium-full body. Soft yet intense. Splendidly classy, complex fruit. Very long. Very concentrated. Lovely.

Puligny-Montrachet,
Les Folatières, Domaine
Pierre-Yves Colin-Morey   2015 to 2025   17.5
Soft, fragrant, subtle nose. Good class. Full body. Plenty of fruit. Still very youthful. Firm on the follow-through but lots of depth underneath. Needs time. Fine.

Puligny-Montrachet,
Les Folatières,
Domaine Joseph Drouhin   2014 to 2021   17.0
Open, accessible nose. Good fruit and depth. Ripe. Easy to appreciate. Medium to medium-full body. Clean. Long. Very good indeed.

Puligny-Montrachet,
Les Folatières,
Domaine Louis Jadot   2015 to 2025   19.0
Rich, quite firm, very concentrated nose. Lots of depth and high-quality here. Fullish body. Some oak. Lots of vigour. A profound, multidimensional wine with an excellent finish. Very fine indeed.

Puligny-Montrachet, Les Folatières,
Domaine Paul Pernot   2015 to 2025   18.5
Ripe, concentrated, gently fragrant, and multidimensional. Medium-full body. Closed-in. Concentrated. Excellent balance. Still very young. Lots of energy here. Very fine.

Puligny-Montrachet, La Garenne,
Domaine Etienne Sauzet   Drink soon   12.0
Some reduction and not entirely clean on the nose. Odd flavours on the palate. The wine is of medium weight and somewhat fruitless. A bad bottle?

Puligny-Montrachet,
Hameau de Blagny,
Domaine Martelet de Cherisy   Drink soon   12.0
A bit of reduction here on the nose. Weedy and four-square on the palate. Slightly astringent at the end. Medium to medium-full body. No.

Puligny-Montrachet,
Clos de la Mouchère,
Domaine Henri Boillot   2014 to 2019   16.0
Quite a lot of built-in sulphur on the nose. Medium-full body. Somewhat empty at the end. Good fruit on the attack and quite ample and long.

Puligny-Montrachet, Les Perrières,
Domaine Carillon   2015 to 2025   18.5
Ripe, fullish, quite firm nose. Good depth and class. Youthful. Fullish body. Nicely concentrated fruit. Very good grip. Disceet and classy. Lovely finish. Very fine.

Puligny-Montrachet, Les Pucelles,
Domaine Leflaive   2014 to 2020   16.0
At first a bit lumpy and reduced on the nose. Medium-full body. Improved in the glass. But very good rather than fine.

Puligny-Montrachet,
Les Referts,
Domaine Bachelet-Monnot   2014 to 2019   15.5
Honeysuckle and syringa on the nose. Soft and fruit-salady. A bit of sulpur underneath. Medium to medium-full body. Slightly loose-knit. It lacks a bit of zip and concentration. Yet stylish.

Puligny-Montrachet, Les Referts,
Domaine Arnaud Ente   2014 to 2021   17.5
Disceet, closed, subtle, and very profound fruit
on the nose. Medium to medium-full body.
Flowery. Very good acidity. Crisp and stylish.
Long. Fine.

Puligny-Montrachet,
Les Referts, Domaine
Jean-Philippe Fichet   2015 to 2025   18.5
Firm, classy nose. Good depth. High-class
fruit. Balanced, ripe, and profound. Fullish
body. Very gently oaky. Long aftertaste. Very
fine.

Puligny-Montrachet, La Truffière,
Domaine Jean-Marc Boillot   2014 to 2020   16.0
A bit flat and four-square on the nose. Better
as it evolved. Ripe and balanced and long and
stylish. Very good.

Puligny-Montrachet,
Sous les Puits, Domaine
Jean-Claude Bachelet   2015 to 2024   17.5
Soft, pleasant, stylish, fruity nose. Medium-
full weight. Good balance. Ripe, elegant fruit.
Plenty of depth and class. Fine.

Puligny-Montrachet, Sous les Puits,
Maison Olivier Merlin   2015 to 2022   17.0
Not quite enough fruit on the nose. But no lack
of it on the palate. Soft and flowery. Touches
of honeysuckle. Good acidity. Long at the end.
Very good indeed.

Chassagne-Montrachet,
Les Baudines, Domaine
Vincent et Sophie Morey   2014 to 2021   17.0
Crisp, minerally, and classy on the nose.
Medium-full body. Good energy. Ripe and pro-
found. Very good indeed.

Chassagne-Montrachet,
Les Blanchots Dessus, Domaine
Jean-Claude Bachelet   Now to 2018   14.5
Firmer and more grip on the nose than some.
Medium to medium-full body. Decent grip, if
not much depth or class. The finish is positive.

Chassagne-Montrachet,
Les Boudriottes,
Domaine Jean-Noel Gagnard   Drink soon   14.0
Ripe, persistent, and stylish on the nose. But
somewhat concocted and caramelised on the
palate. Fresh finish. But overall not very impressive. Quite good at best.

Chassagne-Montrachet,
Les Caillerets, Domaine
Jean-Marc Blain-Gagnard   Now to 2021   17.0
Fresh, flowery nose. Only medium weight, but
balanced. A touch of SO_2 on the palate. But
good grip and substance. Just a touch four-
square at the end. Vigorous nevertheless. Very
good indeed.

Chassagne-Montrachet,
Les Caillerets,
Domaine Yves Colin-Morey   2014 to 2022   17.5
Fresh, delicate but complex nose. Flowery and
classy. Medium weight. Balanced, ripe, and
stylish. Long, vigorous, and with plenty of
finesse. Ripe. Will evolve soon.

Chassagne-Montrachet,
Les Caillerets, Domaine
Richard Fontaine-Gagnard   Now to 2020   14.0
Quite full on the nose. Good depth but rather
four-square. Fullish body. Some grip. But rather
lumpy and astringent. Quite good at best.

Chassagne-Montrachet,
Les Champs-Gain,
Domaine Michel Niellon   2014 to 2022   16.0
Slightly sweaty on the nose. Yet good fruit
underneath. Cleaned up as it evolved. Good
fruit and energy. Medium-full body. Finishes
vigorously. Very good.

Chassagne-Montrachet,
Les Chaumes, Domaine
Jean-Noel Gagnard   Now to 2020   14.0
Some fruit but overall somewhat neutral on the
nose. Medium to medium-full body. Decently
fresh and fruity. Still youthful. Quite good.

Chassagne-Montrachet,
Les Chenevottes,
Maison Chanson Drink soon 12.5
Decent fruit but a lack of flair and grip on the nose. Some sulphur. Rather flat and lifeless on the palate. Poor.

Chassagne-Montrachet,
Les Chenevottes,
Domaine Philippe Colin Now to 2020 14.0
Ample but rather four-square on the nose. Decent but clumsy fruit. Medium to medium-full body. Ripe and pretty but not a lot of depth or class. Quite good.

Chassagne-Montrachet,
Les Chenevottes, Domaine
Jean-Noel Gagnard 2015 to 2023 17.5
Ripe, flowery, attractively balanced nose. Medium to medium-full body. Good grip. Very stylish, ripe fruit. Nicely steely. And it will keep too. Fine.

Chassagne-Montrachet,
Clos-Saint-Jean;
Domaine Baron Thenard Drink up 11.5
Open, evolved, fruit-cake as well as fruit-salad nose. Evolved, watery, and short. Poor finish. No merit here.

Chassagne-Montrachet,
Les Embazées,
Maison Benjamin Leroux Drink soon 13.0
Some oxidation on the nose. Broad-flavoured. Medium body. Lacks fruit. This won't hold up.

Chassagne-Montrachet,
Les Embazées, Domaine
Vincent et Sophie Morey Now to 2020 16.0
Nice austerity on the nose. A bit closed but good depth. Medium to medium-full weight. A touch of oak. A well-made wine for the medium term. Very good positive finish.

Chassagne-Montrachet,
La Grande Montagne,
Domaine Paul Pillot Now to 2017 13.5
Somewhat four-square on the nose. Fullish body. There is substance here but a lack of grace. Not entirely clean. There is a bit of astringency. Decent grip but rather boring.

Chassagne-Montrachet,
Les Grandes Ruchottes,
Domaine Bernard Moreau Now to 2018 14.0
Full and firm on the nose. Good depth. Still youthful. Medium to medium-full body. But on the palate, a bit clumsy and it lacks fruit. One-dimensional at the end. Quite good at best.

Chassagne-Montrachet,
Les Grandes Ruchotte,
Domaine Paul Pillot Now to 2018 14.0
High-toned, flowery nose. Not much substance or grip underneath. Medium body. Decent fruit. But it lacks flair. Quite good.

Chassagne-Montrachet,
Les Macharelles,
Domaine Carillon Drink soon 13.0
Ripe flowery nose. A little four-square. On the palate, medium to medium-full body. Flat and one-dimensional. Unexciting.

Chassagne-Montrachet,
Les Macharelles,
Maison J. Y. Devevey 2014 to 2018 14.0
Good colour. No great class, but there is depth and balance here. Medium-full body. Slightly four-square. Decently positive at the end. Quite good.

Chassagne-Montrachet,
La Maltroie,
Domaine Bernard Moreau Now to 2018 15.0
Rather four-square and closed-in on the nose. Good grip. Similar palate. Good but not great.

Chassagne-Montrachet, Abbaye
de Morgeots, Domaine Jadot See note
Both reduced and prematurely oxidised. Sweet underneath.

Chassagne-Montrachet,
Les Morgeots,
Jean-Noel Gagnard 2014 to 2024 16.0
A little four-square on the nose. But clean enough nevertheless. Better as it evolved. Flowery and

fruity. Fragrant, ripe, and stylish. Medium-full body. Could have had a little more grip, but very good.

**Chassagne-Montrachet,
Les Morgeots,
Laguiche/Drouhin**   2015 to 2024   16.0
Ripe, fullish, vigorous nose. Medium-full body. Good grip and depth. Even class. This will keep well. Very good.

**Chassagne-Montrachet,
Les Morgeots,
Domaine Bernard Moreau**   2014 to 2020   14.0
Ripe but not very forceful nose. A bit more to it on the palate. But a bit rough and ready. Decent fruit and acidity but no real style. Quite good.

**Chassagne-Montrachet,
Les Petits Clos,
Domaine Vincent Dancer**   Now to 2017   14.0
A slight touch of reduction on the nose. Medium-full body. Broad-flavoured. Decent grip but no style. Essentially rather neutral.

**Chassagne-Montrachet,
Les Petits Clos,
Maison Camille Giroud**   2014 to 2020   16.0
Ample, plummy fruit. Medium to medium-full weight. Good acidity and style. Nice and fresh. Not brilliant but very good.

**Chassagne-Montrachet,
Les Petits Clos,
Maison Benjamin Leroux**   Now to 2018   14.5
High-toned, flowery, and quite elegant nose. On the palate, medium to medium-full body. Decent grip but a slight lack of fruit and flair. Finishes better than some.

**Chassagne-Montrachet,
Les Ruchottes,
Domaine Ramonet**   2015 to 2025   18.0
Ripe, succulent. Very well-balanced. Very elegant. Lovely plump fruit. Already most enjoyable. But it will continue to improve. Fine plus at the very least.

**Chassagne-Montrachet,
Les Vergers,
Domaine Philippe Colin**   2014 to 2020   17.0
This has good class, depth, and steeliness. Abundant. Really quite ripe. Quite an exotic finish. But good grip and length. Very good indeed.

**Chassagne-Montrachet,
Les Vergers,
Domaine Fontaine-Gagnard**   See note
Prematurely oxidised. Plump, fruity, and flowery and of decent class originally.

**Chassagne-Montrachet,
Le Vide-Bourse,
Domaine Yves Colin**   Drink soon   13.0
Flowery and fruity. But a lack of definition on the nose. Decent attack. But then it tails off.

**Nuits-Saint-Georges, Clos de
l'Arlot, Domaine de l'Arlot**   Drink soon   13.5
A little reduction on the nose. A lack of flair and fruit here. Medium body. Dull and forward.

**Nuits-Saint-Georges,
Clos de la Maréchale,
Domaine J. F. Mugnier**   Drink soon   13.5
Soft, ripe, forward nose. Merely pretty. Medium body. Reasonable fruit and balance. But it lacks depth.

**Nuits-Saint-Georges,
Les Perrières,
Domaine Henri Gouges**   2014 to 2021   15.0
Attractive fresh, flowery, backward nose. Medium body. Stylish. Good fruit. Decently balanced. Positive at the end. Good.

**Nuits-Saint-Georges, Les
Terres Blanches, Domaine
Michèle et Patrice Rion**   2014 to 2019   14.0
A bit of reduction on the nose. Undistinguished. Medium to medium-full weight. Some grip. Some depth. Quite good.

**Clos Blanc de Vougeot,
Domaine de la Vougeraie**   Drink soon   14.0
Pretty fruit on the nose. But no great distinction. Forward. Medium body. Decent acidity. Quite good.

Morey-Saint-Denis, Les Monts
Luisants, Domaine Dujac   2014 to 2019   14.0
Firm, but rather four-square nose. Good depth. A touch of sulphur. Medium to medium-full body. Quite good.

GRANDS CRUS

Corton-Charlemagne, Domaine
Bonneau du Martray   2016 to 2025   17.0
Still closed but class and depth here on the nose. Fullish body. A little less distinction on the palate. Good acidity. But not as complete as this estate can produce at its best.

Corton-Charlemagne, Domaine
Bouchard Père et Fils   2014 to 2020   15.0
Sweet peppermint on the nose. Medium body. Very ripe. Decent acidity. But too pretty for Corton-Charlemagne. Quite a long finish. But good at best.

Corton-Charlemagne,
Domaine Bruno Clair   2016 to 2024   14.0
Fresh, ripe, plump nose. Lacks a bit of bite and grip. Round and quite rich. But a bit banal.

Corton-Charlemagne,
Domaine Faiveley   2016 to 2023   16.0
Ripe, fresh, backward nose. Nicely austere on the palate, if lacking a bit of personality. Medium-full body. Finishes well. Still young. Very good.

Corton-Charlemagne,
Domaine Follin-Arvelet   2014 to 2019   13.0
Flat nose, lacking bite. Pedestrian. Undistinguished on the palate. Lumpy and quite forward. Medium to medium-full body.

Corton-Charlemagne,
Maison Camille Giroud   2016 to 2025   16.5
Good depth on the nose. Nicely firm too. Quite sweet on the palate. Fullish body. Good depth and style. Good long finish. Very good plus.

Corton-Charlemagne,
Domaine Louis Jadot   Drink soon   13.5
A touch minty-herbal on the nose. Medium body. Lacks grip and concentration. Nothing much here. Forward.

Corton-Charlemagne,
Domaine Patrick Javillier   2017 to 2029   18.0
Nicely steely on the nose. Fullish body. Good depth. Racy and harmonious. Plenty of energy. This is fine plus and will keep well.

Corton-Charlemagne,
Domaine Louis Latour   2014 to 2020   14.0
Backward nose. A bit clumsy. Somewhat artificial fruit flavours. A bit sweet. Lacks bite and concentration. Boring.

Corton-Charlemagne,
Maison Benjamin Leroux   2016 to 2025   16.5
Good firm, backward nose. Very good depth. A big wine. Plenty of fruit. A slight lack of grip, austerity, and class, but better as it evolved. Indeed very good plus.

Corton-Charlemagne,
En Charlemagne,
Maison Sylvain Loichet   2016 to 2025   15.5
Firm, closed nose. Good depth. A wine built to last. A little adolescent on the palate. Good structure but not quite the class. Yet good grip.

Corton-Charlemagne, Le Corton,
Maison Sylvain Loichet   2016 to 2026   17.5
Fullish, ripe, abundant nose. Plenty of fruit here. Medium-full body. Good grip. This is an attractive wine. Finishes well. Fine.

Corton-Charlemagne, Domaine
du Pavillon (Albert Bichot)   2016 to 2025   16.0
Ripe fragrant nose. Quite soft. Medium to medium-full body. Lacks a bit of bite on the attack but a better follow-through. Very good.

Corton-Charlemagne,
Domaine Rollin   2016 to 2027   17.5
Nice and steely. Very pure. Closed-in nose. Very good depth and very lovely fruit. Good austerity. Yet quite accessible for a Corton-Charlemagne. Medium-full body. Good grip. Long and stylish. Fine.

Corton-Charlemagne, Domaine
Christophe Roumier   2015 to 2022   14.0
Fragrant touches on the nose. A bit light for a Corton-Charlemagne. Lacks depth, grip, and personality. Forward.

Corton-Charlemagne,
Domaine Tollot-Beaut 2017 to 2028 18.0
Fresh nose. Good depth. Quite racy. Medium-full body. Nicely steely and austere on the attack. Good depth and concentration underneath. Still young. Classic.

Corton-Charlemagne,
Domaine de Vougeraie 2017 to 2029 18.0
Good nose. Stylish and profound. Full body. Backward. Nicely steely. Very good, slightly austere fruit. Fine, long finish. Lovely.

Corton-Vergennes,
Domaine Chanson 2015 to 2025 15.0
Firm, backward, quite profound nose. Balanced fruit. But only medium body and medium bite. Slightly empty in the middle. Has style though. Good.

Criots-Bâtard-Montrachet,
Domaine Richard
Fontaine-Gagnard 2017 to 2029 18.0
Closed-in nose. Slightly four-square and a touch of sulphur. Better on the palate. Fullish body. Good concentration. Very good grip. There is class and depth here. Fine long finish. Needs time. Fine plus.

Bienvenues-Bâtard-Montrachet,
Domaine Jean-Claude
Bachelet 2016 to 2026 16.5
Fragrant nose. Quite high-toned. Medium-full body. Crisp and fruity on the attack. Fresh and stylish if without the grip of fine, but very good plus.

Bienvenues-Bâtard-Montrachet,
Domaine Faiveley 2017 to 2029 18.0
Fresh nose. Good depth. Still a bit closed. Medium-full body. Good fresh, vigorous attack. Plenty of fruit. The follow-through is concentrated and abundant. Lovely.

Bienvenues-Bâtard-Montrachet,
Domaine Paul Pernot 2016 to 2028 17.5
Ripe, classy nose. Good depth. Medium-full body. Good crisp, fresh fruit. Very good support. Stylish and vigorous. Fine.

Bâtard-Montrachet,
Domaine Bachelet-Monnot 2016 to 2029 18.0
Attractive nose. Positive, balanced, and classy. Still a bit closed-in. The attack is good and crisp. The follow-through complex and classy. Very long. Fine plus.

Bâtard-Montrachet,
Domaine Faiveley 2016 to 2028 17.5
Good nose. Backward but with good depth. Honeysuckle touches on the nose as it developed. Medium to medium-full body. Fresh, balanced, and stylish. Long. Fine.

Bâtard-Montrachet,
Domaine Jean-Noël Gagnard 2014 to 2020 14.0
A bit four-square on the nose. Lacks grip and vitality. Medium-full body. Ripe but somewhat flat. Boring.

Bâtard-Montrachet,
Domaine Pierre Morey Drink soon 13.0
A touch of reduction on the nose. Clumsy. Medium body. Lacks fruit and distinction.

Bâtard-Montrachet,
Domaine Paul Pernot 2014 to 2020 14.0
Awkward nose. Not exactly pure. A bit loose-knit. Some astringency waiting in the wings. Lacks bite.

Bâtard-Montrachet,
Domaine Etienne Sauzet 2015 to 2026 17.5
Firm nose. Good depth. Good class. Youthful. Medium-full body. Round, ripe, honeysuckle fruit. Good acidity. This is an attractive wine.

Chevalier-Montrachet, Domaine
Bouchard Père et Fils 2018 to 2030 plus 18.0
Closed-in on the nose. Lots of energy. Lots of concentrated fruit on the nose. This needs time. Full body. Very lovely clean, balanced fruit. Good oaky base. Long and energetic. Very fine.

Chevalier-Montrachet,
La Cabotte,
Bouchard Père et Fils 2018 to 2030 plus 19.0
Splendid depth but still very tight on the nose. Very, very impressive. Full body. Splendid

vigour. Really profound and multidimensional. Excellent grip. Still very, very young. Exceptional.

Chevalier-Montrachet,
Domaine Philippe Colin   2016 to 2028   18.5

Classic nose. Lovely ripe, gently oaky, very concentrated Chardonnay. Still very young. A somewhat feminine version after the Bouchard examples. Medium-full body. Lovely balanced fruit. Round, ample, very good acidity and length. Lovely.

Chevalier-Montrachet,
Domaine Vincent Dancer   2016 to 2024   14.0

Ripe and expansive but slightly funky on the nose. Fullish body. Good attack at first. Flowery. But it lacks a bit of bite and fell apart in the glass.

Chevalier-Montrachet,
Les Demoiselles, Domaine
Louis Jadot   Drink soon   12.5

Rather overblown on the nose. Some oak. A lack of concentration. Medium body. Weak and fruitless and already cracking up. Can this really be a representative bottle?

Le Montrachet, Domaine
Bouchard Père et Fils   2019 to 2030 plus   19.0

Full rich nose. Very tight and closed-in. Some oak. Very concentrated fruit. Full body. Very, very youthful. But lots of grip and vigour and very classy and profound. Excellent finish. Most impressive.

Le Montrachet,
Domaine Marc Colin   2018 to 2030 plus   19.0

The fruit is full on the nose with a slight herbal touch. On the palate and after development, this was most impressive. Very stylish, ripe, flowery fruit. Very pure and balanced. This is very lovely.

Le Montrachet,
Domaine Marquis de
Laguiche/Drouhin   2019 to 2030 plus   20.0

Ample nose, just a bit more accessible than Bouchard. Fullish body. Balanced, harmonious, very intense, and classy. The finish is really distinguished. Excellent.

Le Montrachet,
Domaine des Comtes Lafon   2016 to 2026   16.0

Quite a lot of new wood masks the flavour and character of the wine on the nose. Plus there is a bit of reduction. I don't find the grip, depth, and class I am expecting in Le Montrachet. The follow-through is a bit weak. No better than very good today.

Le Montrachet,
Domaine Baron Thénard   2016 to 2028   17.5

Rich, ripe, abundant, and multidimensional on the nose. A really flamboyant wine. On the palate, gentle ripe fruit, but the wine lacks the sheer class and depth of Montrachet. Fine at best.

Red Wines

Mercurey, Clos des Myglands,
Domaine Faiveley   From 2015   15.5

Medium-full body. Round and ripe and plump and well-balanced. Stylish. Quite forward.

CÔTE DE BEAUNE

Savigny-Lès-Beaune, La Dominode,
Domaine Bruno Clair   From 2019   16.5

Ripe, stylish, round, and medium-full-bodied. Very good tannins. Lovely character. Very good indeed.

Savigny-Lès-Beaune, Les Fourneaux,
Domaine Simon Bize   From 2018   16.0

Good fruit. Nicely intense without being rustic or aggressive. Rich. Fine for what it is.

Savigny-Lès-Beaune,
Les Guettes, Domaine Gagey,
Maison Louis Jadot   From 2017   16.5

Good colour. Very lovely, gentle, quite rich, old-viney concentration on the nose. Fullish body. Good tannins. Lots of concentration and intensity for a Savigny. Long and delicious.

Savigny-Lès-Beaune, Les Lavières,
Domaine Chandon de Briailles   From 2017   15.5

The stems are evident but this is an attractive stylish wine. Ripe, fresh, but almost a touch sweet. Very good grip at the end.

Savigny-Lès-Beaune, Les Narbantons,
Domaine Leroy   From 2019 16.0
Medium-full body. Some tannin. Typically
Savigny in that the attack is a little brutal. It's
a meaty wine. But there is no lack of fruit here.
Good grip. Positive at the end.

Savigny-Lès-Beaune,
Les Peuillets, Domaine
Rodolphe Demougeot   From 2019 16.5
Good colour. Round, ripe, rich, fat and spicy on
the nose. Good grip. The tannins are sophisticated. Profound and classy for a Savigny. Very
good indeed.

Savigny-Lès-Beaune, Les Talmettes,
Domaine Simon Bize   From 2019 16.0
Firmer and more tannic than the Fourneaux.
More structure and depth. Very good energy
and lovely fruit. Rich. Fine for what it is.

Pernand-Vergelesses,
Ile des Vergelesses,
Domaine Chandon de Briailles   From 2018 17.5
This is a very classy wine. Very good grip.
Medium-full body. Lots of personality. Lovely
fruit. Fine.

Pernand-Vergelesses, Ile des
Vergelesses, Domaine Rapet   From 2016 17.0
Good, fullish, immature colour. Fresh, elegant,
cool nose. Very stylish on the palate. Medium-
full body. Rich and ripe. Intense and harmonious. Very composed. Very good indeed.

Beaune, Boucherottes,
Maison David Butterfield   From 2017 15.0
David Butterfield is Canadian. He is married to
Jacques Lardière's daughter Juliette. This wine
is quite a substantial example. Good colour.
Some tannin. The nose is a bit subdued, but
there is good fruit here and no lack of energy.
Pommard-ish, in fact. Finishes well. Good.

Beaune, Boucherottes,
Domaine A. F. Gros   From 2017 14.0
Medium-full colour. Light, but quite rich, oaky
nose. Medium body. Lacks a bit of succulence
but attractive fruit and good freshness. Quite
good.

Beaune, Boucherottes,
Domaine Jadot   From 2016 16.0
Good colour. Rich, ripe nose. Fullish body. Suc-
culent. Fresh, ample, and stylish. Good grip.
Long. Very good.

Beaune, Bressandes,
Maison David Butterfield   From 2017 15.5
Good colour. Attractive plummy, cherry fruit.
Fullish body. Quite oaky. Good tannins. Fresh,
ample, and vigorous. Stylish too. Good plus.

Beaune, Bressandes,
Domaine des Croix   From 2018 16.0
Medium-full colour. Fresh, but nicely fat and
rich on the nose. Medium-full body. Good grip.
Good tannins. No lack of energy here. This will
develop. Long on the palate. Very good.

Beaune, Clos des Feves,
Domaine Chanson   From 2016 14.0
Medium to medium-full colour. Fresh nose.
No great weight but a little closed. Medium
weight. Good balance and structure. Decent
fruit. Quite good.

Beaune, Clos des Mouches,
Domaine Chanson   From 2017 14.5
Medium to medium-full colour. Good fruit on
the nose. Some oak on the palate. Medium body.
Decent balance and a positive follow-through.

Beaune, Clos des Mouches,
Domaine Drouhin   From 2018 16.0
Ripe fruit. Good class and personality. Rich.
Quite fat. Not too spicy. Medium to medium-
full body. Very good.

Beaune, Clos du Roi,
Domaine Henri Boillot   From 2018 15.5
Medium-full colour. Good weight and depth on
the nose. Succulent too. Medium-full weight.
Less developed than most. There is concentra-
tion and depth here. This has potential.

Beaune, Clos du Roi,
Domaine Tollot-Beaut   From 2016 14.5
Medium to medium-full colour. Fresh and
fruity on the nose, if no great substance.
Medium weight. Decent fruit and freshness

on the palate. Balanced and quite stylish at the end.

Beaune, Clos des Ursules,
Domaine Jadot   From 2018   17.0
Medium colour. Soft, plump, quite mellow nose. More substance on the palate. Very good tannins and very good grip. Rich and profound. Lovely fragrant fruit. Fine plus. I marked this rather lower at the three-year-on tasting, but most tasters gave it a much higher mark. Perhaps I was asleep on the job.

Beaune, Coucherias,
Domaine Francois Labet   From 2017   16.0
This is quite serious. Fullish. Fresh. Ripe. Stylish and balanced. Very good.

Beaune, Cras,
Domaine Camille Giroud   From 2016   13.0
Medium colour. Some development. Rather bland on the nose. Some weight on the palate but not much depth or class. Lacks richness.

Beaune, Epenottes,
Domaine Jean-Marc Boillot   From 2017   14.5
Medium colour. Soft, round, fruity nose. Quite advanced. Good fruit on the palate. Medium weight. Fresh and balanced. No hard edges. Quite stylish. Quite good plus.

Beaune, Epenottes,
Domaine Dominique Lafon   From 2018   14.5
Light to medium colour. A bit reduced on the nose. Medium to medium-full body. Good structure and grip. Fresh. Quite good plus.

Beaune, Grèves, Vigne de
l'Enfant Jesus, Domaine
Bouchard Père et Fils   From 2016   14.0
I didn't like this at the three-year-on tasting but elsewhere I noted it as gentle and fruity, quite stylish, and reasonably balanced.

Beaune, Grèves,
Domaine Bellène   From 2016   12.0
Medium-full colour. A bit closed on the nose. Rather earthy as it developed. On the palate, rather astringent and lumpy. Unattractive.

Beaune, Grèves,
Domaine des Croix   From 2017   15.5
Medium to medium-full colour. Black cherries and chocolate on the nose. Medium-full body. Good tannins. Balanced and vigorous. Good fruit, good depth, and good energy at the end.

Beaune, Grèves,
Domaine de Montille   From 2016   13.5
Soft. Ripe. But a slight absence of real grip. Merely pretty. Medium body. Feeble.

Beaune, Grèves,
Domaine Tollot-Beaut   From 2016   14.0
Sweet and spicy. Medium to medium-full body. Lacks a bit of style. Quite oaky, even rich. But rather raw and edgy.

Beaune, Pertuisots,
Domaine Jean-Yves Devevey   From 2017   14.5
Medium to medium-full colour. Plump nose. Still closed. Medium body. A touch astringent. Decent fruit and grip. Finishes better than it starts.

Beaune, Teurons,
Maison David Butterfield   From 2017   15.5
Good colour. Attractive plump nose with a touch of oak. Good backbone. Medium to medium-full body. Ripe and stylish. Good grip. Good plus.

Beaune, Teurons,
Domaine Rossignol-Trapet   From 2015   13.5
Medium colour. Rich and quite oaky on the nose, if without a great deal of substance. Medium body. Forward. Fresh but lacks depth.

Beaune, Toussaints,
Domaine Remoissenet   From 2017   15.0
Medium to medium-full colour. Fresh, attractive, spicy nose. Medium to medium-full body. Ripe and seductive. Balanced and positive at the end. Good.

Beaune, Tulivans,
Domaine Hervé Murat   From 2016   14.0
Lightish colour. Light and rather weedy on the nose. But decent fruit. Better on the palate. Medium body. Fresh, fruity, and positive.

Volnay, Vendages Sélectionnées,
Domaine Michet Lafarge   From 2017   15.5
Lovely fruit. Ripe and stylish for a village wine. Very civilised. Lovely long finish.

Volnay, Caillerets,
Domaine Louis Boillot   From 2017   15.5
Medium-full colour. Ample nose. Quite high volatile acidity. No lack of substance. Medium-full body. A little dense. Some oak. A bit astringent at the end. Good acidity but a slight lack of richness. Still young though.

Volnay, Caillerets,
Domaine Bouchard Père et Fils   From 2017   17.0
Medium-full colour. Closed-in on the nose. But plenty of depth here. Medium to medium-full body. Plenty of fruit. Not quite the depth and grip of some. But plump and generous. Very good indeed.

Volnay, Caillerets,
Clos des 60 Ouvrées,
Domaine de la Pousse d'Or   From 2018   17.5
Medium-full colour. A touch of reduction at first but this quickly blew away. Medium-full body. Good grip. Good vigour. Ripe and succulent and energetic. Full, classy, positive follow-through. Fine.

Volnay, Carelle Sous la Chapelle,
Domaine Jean-Marc Boillot   From 2017   15.5
Medium-full colour. Good depth on the nose but a little closed-in. Medium-full body. Ripe. Good tannins. Needs to soften. But the follow-through is stylish, balanced, and vigorous.

Volnay, Champans,
Domaine Marquis d'Angerville   From 2020   17.5
Fullish, rich, energetic, and profound. Lots of wine here. Lots of depth. Fine.

Volnay, Champans,
Domaine des Comtes Lafon   From 2017   17.5
Medium-full colour. Vigorous, classy, harmonious nose. Quite profound. Medium-full body. Lots of depth and dimension. Very good grip. Very long on the palate. Fine.

Volnay, Champans,
Domaine de Montille   From 2016   15.0
Medium colour. Some development. A little weak and thin on the nose. Medium to medium-full body. Good acidity but not enough ripeness and generosity. Finishes better than it starts though.

Volnay, Chevret,
Domaine Henri Boillot   From 2017   17.0
Medium-full colour. Soft, oaky, ripe nose. Medium-full body. Ripe tannins. Good grip. Very composed fruit. Balanced. Long. And very good indeed.

Volnay, Clos des Cave des Ducs,
Maison Benjamin Leroux   From 2017   16.5
Medium to medium-full colour. Slightly closed-in on the nose. Good substance and energy on the palate. Medium-full body. Fresh, succulent, and balanced. Very good follow-through. Long and stylish.

Volnay, Clos du Château des Ducs, Domaine Michel Lafarge   From 2016   16.0
Medium to medium-full colour. Good Pinot depth on the nose. Still youthful. Medium-full body. A little four-square but ripe enough. Good grip and balance. Seems to lack a bit of personality at present but this will come.

Volnay, Clos des Chênes,
Domaine Buffet   From 2019   18.5
Medium to medium-full colour. Very elegant, gently oaky, balanced nose. This is very lovely. Fullish body. Excellent grip and very lovely fruit. Complex and classy and lots of dimension. Very fine.

Volnay, Clos des Chênes,
Domaine Michel Lafarge   From 2022   18.5
Medium-full colour. Rich, ripe, and ample on the nose, with a touch of oak. Firm, profound, and classy. Full-bodied. Lots of dimension. Very lovely finish. Very fine.

Volnay, Clos des Chênes,
Domaine des Comtes Lafon   From 2018   17.0
Medium-full colour. Soft, plump nose. There is some richness and vigour here, and no lack of elegance, if no real depth. Medium-full body.

Oaky on the palate. Good grip. This is long and ripe at the end.

Volnay, Clos des Ducs,
Domaine Marquis d'Angerville   From 2022   18.5
Even firmer and richer than their Champans. More vigour. More depth. This is very lovely. Splendid finish.

Volnay, Clos de la Bousse d'Or,
Domaine de la Pousse d'Or   From 2017   17.0
Medium-full colour. Rich, round, ample, ripe nose. Medium-full body. Nice and ripe and succulent. A touch of oak. Some tannin. Balanced, long, and stylish. Very good indeed.

Volnay, Fremiets,
Domaine Marquis d'Angerville   From 2015   15.5
Soft, flowery, ripe, stylish nose. No great weight or grip, but ample and balanced and classy. Quite forward.

Volnay, Fremiets,
Domaine Henri Boillot   From 2016   16.5
Medium-full colour. Soft, round, ripe, gently oaky nose. Medium to medium-full body. Balanced. Attractive round tannins. Elegant and already quite short. Long on the palate. Very good plus.

Volnay Fremiets,
Domaine Francois Parent   From 2016   17.0
Medium colour. Some development. Fresh, balanced, stylish nose. Medium-full body. Some oak. An elegant vigorous wine. Long, succulent, and delicious. Quite accessible already.

Volnay, Les Lurets,
Domaine Dominique Lafon   From 2018   17.5
Medium-full colour. Fresh, clean nose. Still a bit closed. Plenty of succulent fruit here. Good depth and integration. Positive and classy. Needs time.

Volnay, Santenots du Milieu,
Domaine Arnaud Ente   From 2016   13.5
Medium-full colour. Strangely scented nose, a bit sweet. On the palate the wine is a bit thin, unripe, and astringent. Lacks charm. Medium body.

Volnay, Santenots du Milieu,
Domaine des Comtes Lafon   From 2019   18.0
Fullish colour. Very ripe. Even a bit sweet. Rich and fat. Concentrated and profound. Fullish body. Fine plus.

Volnay, Santenots du Milieu,
Domaine Leroy   From 2021   17.5
Good colour. Quite a closed wine. Very good backbone. Concentrated fruit. Fullish body. Harmonious, classy, and very good grip. Fine.

Volnay, Santenots du Milieu,
Domaine Francois Mikulski   From 2017   15.0
Medium-full colour. Some development. Fresh, plump nose. Attractive fruit. Not so good on the palate. Somewhat charmless. Lacks succulence and not very stylish either. Good at best.

Volnay, Taillepieds,
Domaine Buffet   From 2018   17.5
Medium-full colour. Attractive, gentle, balanced, oaky nose. Fullish body. Some tannin. Balanced and classy. Long on the palate. Fine.

Volnay, Tailepieds,
Domaine de Montille   From 2019   17.5
Medium-full colour. Backward nose. But good style. Medium-full body. Plenty of energy. Very good fruit and grip. Long and positive. Fine.

Pommard, Argillières,
Domaine Lejeune   From 2016   14.0
Medium colour. Rather lumpy, four-square nose. Reasonable depth and substance, even energy on the palate. Yet a bit inflexible and lacking class.

Pommard, Clos des Epenaux,
Domaine Comte Armand   From 2019   17.0
Medium colour. Fresh nose. Stylish fruit here. Medium to medium-full body. Plump, attractive, balanced fruit on the palate. Positive and vigorous all the way through.

Pommard, Epenots,
Domaine Francois Parent   From 2016   14.0
Medium-full colour. Fresh, fruity nose, but no great substance. Medium body. Spicy and fruity on the attack. Decent grip, but lacks a bit of depth.

Pommard, Fremiers,
Domaine Louis Boillot   From 2015 13.0
Medium-full colour. High toned nose. Lean and astringent on the palate. Weak. No.

Pommard, Grand Clos des
Epenots, Domaine de Courcel   From 2017 15.5
Medium-full colour. Ripe nose. Some tannin. Good substance. A touch astringent on the palate after a decently vigorous attack. Reasonable finish.

Pommard, Grands Epenots,
Domaine Michel Gaunoux   From 2015 14.0
No great style here on either the nose or the palate. Not exactly oxidised but it lacks vigour and grip. Ample and fullish but flat and lacking class.

Pommard, Grands Epenots,
Domaine Pierre Morey   From 2020 15.5
Quite full body. Rich and ripe. A little tannin. Very good fruit but the structure sticks out a bit. Very good grip though. May well turn out better than the note today.

Pommard, Hospices de Beaune,
Cuvée Dames de la Charité,
Maison Benjamin Leroux   From 2016 14.0
Medium-full colour. Soft, gentle, oaky nose. A bit thin and astringent on the palate, especially on the attack. The follow-through is better.

Pommard, Jarollières,
Domaine Jean-Marc Boillot   From 2016 14.0
Medium colour. Fresh nose, but just a little thin. Pretty but a bit one-dimensional. Medium body. The fruit is not too bad on the palate.

Pommard, Jarollières,
Domaine de la Pousse d'Or   From 2017 14.5
Medium-full colour. Slightly four-square nose. Even a touch vegetal. On the palate, good substance. Some tannin. Good grip. No great class but quite good plus.

Pommard, Pezerolles,
Domaine A. F. Gros   From 2017 15.5
Medium colour. Plump, ripe nose. Some tannin but not dense. Medium weight. Ripe tannins. Fresh. Good acidity. A positive finish if without great class or personality.

Pommard, Pézerolles,
Domaine de Montille   From 2019 16.0
Medium colour. Decent fruit on the nose. Good energy and grip here, if not the finesse of their Taillepieds. Good backbone. Very good.

Pommard, Rugiens,
Domaine Henri Boillot   From 2016 15.5
Medium-full colour. Just a little dense and reduced on the nose. Better on the palate. Not quite enough richness but good grip. Not astringent. And positive at the end.

Pommard, Rugiens,
Domaine Bouchard Père et Fils   From 2016 14.5
Medium to medium-full colour. Some development. Medium weight on the nose. Decent fruit but a lack of depth. Medium body. Quite fresh. Quite stylish.

Pommard, Rugiens,
Domaine Buffet   From 2015 13.0
Medium-full colour. Attractive fruit on the nose. Not too dense or tannic. But somewhat soupy on the palate. A bit concocted. Medium weight.

Pommard, Rugiens,
Domaine de Courcel   From 2017 16.0
Medium-full body. Round, ripe nose. Medium-full body. A little astringent at first but good grip and depth. Slightly sweet. Positive finish. Very good.

Pommard, Rugiens,
Domaine Faiveley   From 2018 17.0
Medium-full colour. Fresh nose. Good substance. Medium-full body. Ripe and vigorous and well-balanced. Very good fruit and grip. Good attack and long and stylish at the end. Very good indeed.

Pommard, Rugiens,
Domaine Michel Gaunoux   From 2019 17.0
Rather better than the Epenots. Much fresher. Fullish and vigorous. Very good grip. Very long. Indeed classy. Very good indeed.

Pommard, Rugiens,

Domaine Lejeune From 2017 16.5

Medium-full colour. Fresh nose. Balanced and quite stylish. Medium-full body. Some tannin. Ripe and generous. Good depth and class. Very good plus.

Pommard, Rugiens,

Domaine de Montille From 2015 14.0

Medium colour. Rather a weak, evolved nose. Fresh and fruity, but only lightish body. But better on the palate than on the nose.

Pommard, Rugiens, Domaine

de Pavillon (Albert Bichot) From 2018 17.5

Medium to medium-full colour. Spicy, bonfire-smoky nose. Medium-full body. Ripe, nicely rich, and opulent. Good grip. Nothing too bulky here. Lots of style and dimension. Long finish. Fine.

Côte de Nuits

Nuits-Saint-Georges,

Maison Louis Jadot From 2020 16.0

Good colour. Ripe, fullish, plump, and stylish on the nose. Plenty of depth, fruit, and interest on the palate. Very good indeed for a village wine.

Nuits-Saint-Georges,

Domaine Méo-Camuzet From 2018 16.0

Quite firm. Rich and plump. Not too much oak. Good fruit and style. Very good.

Nuits-Saint-Georges,

Premier Cru,

Domaine Michel Gros From 2018 16.0

Medium-full colour. Plump, medium-full oaky nose. Good grip. Medium-full body. Good ripe tannins. Nice fresh, stylish fruit. Not a blockbuster but classy and balanced. Finishes well.

Nuits-Saint-Georges,

Aux Boudots, Domaine Grivot From 2022 18.5

Medium-full colour. A lovely firm, rich wine. Stylish vigorous fruit. This is really fine this year. Full and multidimensional at the end. Lots of finesse.

Nuits-Saint-Georges,

Aux Boudots, Domaine Leroy From 2022 18.0

Potentially velvety. Rich, fat. Very good acidity. Full body. Classy. Long and multidimensional. Needs time. Fine plus.

Nuits-Saint-Georges, Les Cailles,

Domaine Bouchard Père et Fils From 2019 16.5

Somewhat dumb on the nose and a little reduced. Medium to medium-full colour. Soft and oaky, almost sweet. Good grip. Medium body. Seductive and long on the palate. Very good plus.

Nuits-Saint-Georges, Les Cailles,

Domaine Robert Chevillon From 2020 18.5

Medium-full colour. Ample, rich, concentrated nose. Fullish body. Very Rich. Lots of depth and dimension. Splendid fruit. This is vigorous and very fine.

Nuits-Saint-Georges, Les

Chaignots, Domaine Bellène From 2021 18.5

Full colour. Backward nose. Lots of depth and concentration. A touch of oak. Fullish body. Very good tannins. Excellent fruit. Very long and harmonious. Very fine.

Nuits-Saint-Georges,

Les Chaignots,

Domaine Henri Gouges From 2021 17.5

Medium-full colour. Abundant fruit but some evolution and not the greatest of grip on the nose. Medium-full body. Good fruit and balance. Elegant too. Lovely finish. So fine even if it does lack a bit of thrust.

Nuits-Saint-Georges,

Les Chaignots, Domaine

Dr. Georges Mugneret-Gibourg From 2021 18.5

Fullish colour. Rich, fullish, firm, vigorous nose. This is very delicious. Fullish body. Very fresh. Very composed. Very good tannins. Elegant and multidimensional. Very fine.

Nuits-Saint-Georges,

Clos des Argillières, Domaine

Michèle et Patrice Rion From 2019 17.5

Medium-full colour. Medium weight on the nose. Fresh fruit but slightly rigid. Better on the palate. Fullish body. Plenty of energy. Ripe tannins. Very good grip. Plenty of fruit and personality. Classy. Very typical well-made Nuits-Saint-Georges. Fine.

Nuits-Saint-Georges, Clos de l'Arlot, Domaine de l'Arlot From 2018 15.0
Fullish colour. Quite a supple nose. But some reduction here. Medium to medium-full body. Slightly astringent at the end. Lacks a bit of class and vigour.

Nuits-Saint-Georges, Clos des Forêts Saint-Georges, Domaine de l'Arlot From 2018 16.0
Fullish colour. Plump nose. Just a little reduced. Medium to medium-full body. Fruity but a bit astringent at the end. Yet there is class and balance here. Very good—perhaps better.

Nuits-Saint-Georges, Clos de la Maréchale, Domaine J. Frédéric Mugnier From 2019 17.5
This is somewhat of a Nuits in Chambolle clothing: neither the one nor the other. It is nevertheless a most attractive wine. Ripe, quite soft. Medium-full bodied. Succulently fruity and quite fresh. It lacks just a bit of vigour and grip.

Nuits-Saint-Georges, Clos-Saint-Marc, Domaine Michèle et Patrice Rion From 2019 17.5
Fullish colour. Some oak on the nose, but otherwise a little rigid. Softened in the glass. Medium-full body. Some oak. Ample and succulent. Attractive and vigorous. Good positive follow-through.

Nuits-Saint-Georges, Les Cras, Domaine du Vicomte de Liger-Belair From 2020 17.5
Medium-full colour. Ripe, medium weight, balanced nose. Not a blockbuster. Medium-full body. Good grip. Ripe tannins. Long and stylish and complex. Fine.

Nuits-Saint-Georges, Les Damodes, Domaine Jean Chauvenet From 2021 18.0
Fullish colour. Good firm, ripe nose with a touch of spice. Medium-full body. Ample attack.

Rich and succulent. Ripe and abundant. Very fine after taste. Long and pure and complex.

Nuits-Saint-Georges, Les Damodes, Domaine Faiveley From 2021 18.5
This is fullish, rich, and concentrated. Very lovely fruit. Lots of personality and very good grip. Very fine for what it is.

Nuits-Saint-Georges, Les Damodes, Domaine de la Vougeraie From 2019 17.0
Medium-full colour. Ripe, stylish, composed nose. But a little weak. This is only medium-bodied. Very ripe and seductive and not a bit short. Yet a bit of energy is missing.

Nuits-Saint-Georges, Les Murgers, Domaine Alain Hudelot-Noëllat From 2020 18.0
Medium to medium-full colour. Quite concentrated and very well-balanced on the nose. Plenty of stylish fruit. Medium-full body. Ripe, vigorous, elegant, and composed. Very seductive. Fine plus.

Nuits-Saint-Georges, Les Murgers; Domaine Méo-Camuzet From 2020 17.5
Medium-full colour. Very ripe, almost jammy-creamy on the nose. More austere on the palate. Medium-full body. Rich and ripe. Good grip. Not the greatest vigour but a fine wine.

Nuits-Saint-Georges, Les Perrières, Domaine Jean Chauvenet From 2019 17.0
Fullish colour. Fresh nose. Good substance and very pure fruit. Good acidity. Fullish body. Ample, oaky, plump, and succulent. Good tannins. Good grip. The aftertaste is long and satisfying. Very good indeed.

Nuits-Saint-Georges, Clos des Porrets Saint-Georges, Domaine Henri Gouges From 2020 17.0
Medium colour. Some evolution. Vigorous, ripe, balanced, and classy on the nose. Medium-full body. Ripe, rich, and energetic on the palate. A bit closed. Lots of wine but a bit solid at present.

Nuits-Saint-Georges,
Les Porrets Saint-Georges,
Domaine Faiveley From 2022 18.0
Medium colour. Some evolution. Soft, aromatic, but balanced and elegant on the nose. Medium-full body. Lots of lovely succulent fruit. Not a blockbuster. But ripe and stylish. Balanced and long on the palate.

Nuits-Saint-Georges, Les Pruliers,
Domaine Henri Gouges From 2023 18.0
Lots of style and energy. Fullish body. Vigorous, profound, and intense. Very lovely fruit and a fine finish. Fine plus.

Nuits-Saint-Georges, Les Pruliers,
Domaine Robert Chevillon From 2020 18.0
Fullish colour. Ripe, rich, vigorous nose. Quite closed. Medium-full body. Some tannin. At first a touch four-square but the follow-through is ample and succulent. Profound and lovely.

Nuits-Saint-Georges, Les Pruliers,
Domaine Grivot From 2021 18.0
Medium-full colour. Ample, quite rich, succulent nose. Medium-full body. Very good tannins and very good grip. Lots of quality. Lots of class. Very good energy. Fine plus.

Nuits-Saint-Georges,
Les Saint-Georges,
Domaine Robert Chevillon From 2021 18.5
Medium-full colour. Quite a high-toned nose. Good grip. But the acidity is quite pronounced. Very classy and very well-balanced. Medium-full body. Very lovely, ample, rich fruit. Lovely finish. Very fine.

Nuits-Saint-Georges,
Les Saint-Georges,
Domaine Henri Gouges From 2024 18.5
This is excellent. Splendidly rich and concentrated. Real class. Not too severe. Long and lovely.

Nuits-Saint-Georges,
Les Saint-Georges,
Domaine Thibault Liger-Belair From 2020 17.5
Fullish colour. Rich, aromatic, oaky nose. Some evolution. A touch reduced. Fullish body. Rich and with very good grip. Lots of fruit. Long on the palate. Fine.

Nuits-Saint-Georges,
Aux Thorey,
Maison Benjamin Leroux From 2019 17.0
Medium-full colour. A little sweaty on the nose, and slightly reduced. Better on the palate. Medium-full body. Good grip. Ripe and fresh. Ample and positive.

Nuits-Saint-Georges,
Les Vaucrains,
Domaine Jean Chauvenet From 2020 17.5
Medium-full colour. A bit ungainly on the nose, but rather better on the palate. Medium-full body. Rich and ripe and balanced. Indeed, complex and classy. The fruit is very seductive.

Nuits-Saint-Georges,
Les Vaucrains,
Domaine Henri Gouges From 2022 17.0
The nose is a bit closed. Full body. Good tannins. Sweet and rich. But, like the Porrets, the sample was a bit warm. Probably a lot better than the note I give it here.

Nuits-Saint-Georges,
Les Vignes Rondes,
Domaine Leroy From 2020 17.0
Another meaty example from Madame Leroy. The tannins are more middle Nuits-Saint-Georges than from the Vosne side. Fullish body. Vigorous. Youthful.

Vosne-Romanée, Domaine
Dr. Georges Mugneret-Gibourg From 2019 16.5
Medium colour. Good substance on the nose. Slightly closed-in. Firm and tannic. Just a bit four-square. But rich as it evolved. Medium-full body. Some oak. Good grip. Balanced and classy. Plenty of intensity. Long. Very good plus.

Vosne-Romanée, Alliance de Terroirs,
Domaine Dominique Mugneret From 2017 16.0
Good colour. Ample, classy nose, fine fruit. Lovely for a village example. Medium to medium-full body. Ample, balanced, ripe, very good grip. Long and complex. Profound for a village wine. Very good indeed for what it is.

Vosne-Romanée, Les Bossières,
Domaine Grivot From 2019 15.5
Good colour. Still a bit closed on the nose. Ripe, gentle, but good vigour. Rich, balanced, and stylish. Quite forward. Good plus.

Vosne-Romanée, Aux Réas,
Domaine A. F. Gros From 2019 15.5
Medium to medium-full colour. Earthy nose. Fullish body. Good substance and richness. Medium to medium-full body. Good acidity but a slight lack of succulence. A little austere. Could have been more generous.

Vosne-Romanée, *Premier Cru*,
Cuvée Duvault-Blochet, Domaine
de la Romanée-Conti From 2019 17.5
Medium colour. Soft, ripe, supple nose. Very stylish without being a blockbuster. It seems quite forward compared to the rest of the range. Medium to medium-full body. Intense and elegant. Balanced and long and lovely.

Vosne-Romanée, Les Beaumonts,
Domaine Bertagna From 2020 17.5
Fullish colour. Classy nose. Very good pure fruit. Balanced and stylish. Intense and energetic. Fullish body. Still a bit closed. Ripe and rich. Long on the palate. Fine.

Vosne-Romanée, Les Beaux Monts,
Domaine Grivot From 2021 18.5
Good colour. Still quite closed on the nose. But a lot of depth here. Fullish body. Quite firm and youthful. A bit of tannin sticks out. Rich and energetic. Lots of dimension. Very fine.

Vosne-Romanée,
Les Beaumonts, Domaine
Alain Hudelot-Noëllat From 2020 16.0
Medium-full colour. Ample, spicy nose. A meaty wine. Fullish body. Quite robust. But there is good depth and energy here. Quite tannic on the attack. Fresh and juicy follow-through. Very good.

Vosne-Romanée, Aux Beaux Monts,
Domaine Leroy From 2019 17.5
Medium-full colour. This is fine. Very elegant. Perhaps not quite the grip of her Brulées. Nor

the sheer concentration or volume. But lovely fruit.

Vosne-Romanée, Les Brulées,
Domaine Eugenie From 2021 18.5
Medium-full colour. Closed-in on the nose, but shows very pure, if a little tight, Pinot Noir fruit. Medium-full body. Some tannin. Very good grip. Ripe and generous and quite oaky as it evolved. Stylish, very intense. Long on the palate. Very fine.

Vosne-Romanée, Les Brulées,
Domaine Grivot From 2022 19.0
Medium-full colour. A little closed-in. But ripe and profound on the nose. Fullish body. Ripe, youthful, energetic, and multidimensional. Very long and vigorous at the end. Lovely.

Vosne-Romanée, Les Brulées,
Domaine Michel Gros From 2021 18.5
Medium-full colour. Quite firm and tannic on the nose. But good depth underneath. Very lovely fruit as it evolved. Medium-full body. Ripe and succulent. Fresh and stylish. Long and complex. Very fine.

Vosne-Romanée, Aux Brulées,
Domaine Leroy From 2021 18.5
This is very fine. Splendidly profound fruit. Full body. Vigorous. Lots of depth. Very high-class. Excellent grip. Very lovely.

Vosne-Romanée, Aux Brulées,
Domaine Méo-Camuzet From 2021 18.5
Full colour. Very lovely, rich, succulent nose. Generous, ripe, and profound. Good backbone. Fullish body. Lovely fruit. Very classy. Harmonious, long, and very fine.

Vosne-Romanée, Les Brulées,
Domaine Gerard Mugneret From 2020 17.5
Medium-full colour. Expansive nose. High-toned in a slightly vegetal way. Cleaner and more stylish as it evolved. On the palate, medium to medium-full body. Doesn't have quite the intensity and grip of the Méo or the Grivot, but positive and classy. Fine.

Vosne-Romanée, Les Chaumes,
Domaine Lamarche   From 2019   17.0
Medium-full colour. Quite accessible on the nose. Medium-full body. No lack of grip. Indeed, quite concentrated, intense, and stylish. Good substance. Firm and tannic. Very good indeed.

Vosne-Romanée, Les Chaumes,
Domaine Méo-Camuzet   From 2020   17.5
Rich, fat, and concentrated. Nicely succulent. Fullish body. Balanced, stylish, and long on the palate. Fine.

Vosne-Romanée, Clos des Réas,
Domaine Michel Gros   From 2020   17.5
Medium-full colour. Lovely nose. Rich and chocolaty. A touch of oak. Medium-full body. Rich and balanced on the palate. Intense and very composed. Real elegance. Lovely finish. Fine.

Vosne-Romanée, Aux Malconsorts,
Domaine Dujac   From 2022   18.5
Delicious fruit. Lots of depth and energy. Fullish body. Very harmonious. Great style. Very fine.

Vosne-Romanée, Les Malconsorts,
Domaine du Clos Frantin
(Albert Bichot)   From 2020   17.5
Medium-full colour. Fine nose. Rich, concentrated, and stylish. Medium-full body. Lots of energy and grip. Very stylish fruit. Harmonious. Long. Profound. Fine.

Vosne-Romanée, Les Malconsorts,
Domaine Alain Hudelot-Noëllat From 2019   15.0
Medium to medium-full colour. Fat, meaty, spicy nose. Decent acidity. Medium-full body. The finish is round, yet the wine is firm and quite tannic. But it lacks a little real class.

Vosne-Romanée, Les Malconsorts,
Domaine Lamarche   From 2020   17.5
Medium-full colour. Classy fruit here. Lots of depth. Harmonious and intense. Medium-full body. Some tannin. Good fruit. Quite backward. Classy, profound, and long on the palate. Fine.

Vosne-Romanée, Les Malconsorts,
Domaine de Montille   From 2022   18.5
Rich and concentrated. Lots of style and dimension. Very good grip. Long and lovely. Very fine.

Vosne-Romanée, Les Malconsorts,
Maison Roche de Bellène   From 2020   16.5
Medium-full colour. Lovely nose. Rich and ripe and generous and elegant. Medium-full body. Slightly austere on the attack. Rich and meaty. Plenty of depth and style. Very good plus.

Vosne-Romanée,
Les Petits Monts, Domaine du
Vicomte de Liger-Belair   From 2020   17.5
Medium-full colour. Ripe, aromatic nose. Accessible and balanced. Medium-full body. Harmonious, ripe fruit. Plenty of dimension. A touch of oak. Fresh and classy. Fine.

Vosne-Romanée,
Les Petits Monts,
Maison Roche de Bellène   From 2020   17.0
Medium-full colour. Slightly perfumed nose. Good fruit. Good balance. Medium-full body. Very good fresh, ripe fruit. A touch of oak. Good depth and energy. This is not a blockbuster but very good indeed.

Vosne-Romanée,
Aux Reignots, Domaine du
Vicomte de Liger-Belair   From 2019   15.0
Medium-full colour. Ripe, spicy nose. Not a lot of distinction here. Medium to medium-full body. Quite sweet. Not a lot of grip. A bit astringent. Unexciting.

Vosne-Romanée, Les Rouges,
Maison Alain Burguet   From 2020   16.5
Medium-full colour. Some oak on the nose. A touch reduced as well. But ample and vigorous. Medium-full body. Ripe and succulent. Good grip. Good energy. Finishes long and positively. Very good plus.

Vosne-Romanée, Les Suchots,
Domaine de l'Arlot   From 2019   14.0
Medium to medium-full colour. Some stems and a little edgy on the nose. A touch common

and a bit astringent on the palate. Medium to medium-full body. Decent fruit but no flair.

Vosne-Romanée, Les Suchots, Domaine de Bellène   From 2021 18.5

Medium-full colour. Laid-back, discreet nose. But lots of dimension. Impressive, indeed. Medium-full body. Very harmonious. Excellent grip. Intense and profound and classy. Very lovely finish. Very fine.

Vosne-Romanée, Les Suchots, Domaine Grivot   From 2021 18.0

Medium-full colour. Fragrant nose. Not a blockbuster. Ripe, elegant, and harmonious. A touch of oak. Medium-full body. Rich and ripe and balanced and positive. Classy, complex, and long on the palate. Indeed, very impressive at the end. Fine plus.

Vosne-Romanée, Les Suchots, Domaine Alain Hudelot-Noëllat   From 2019 15.5

Medium to medium-full colour. Closed-in, firm quite profound and classy nose. On the palate, just a bit astringent on the attack. Medium to medium-full body. Good plus.

Vosne-Romanée, Les Suchots, Domaine du Vicomte de Liger-Belair   From 2019 17.0

Medium-full colour. Spicy nose. But in a balanced, seductive sense. Some new oak. Medium to medium-full body. Accessible, plump, and well-balanced. Lacks just a bit of depth and backbone.

Vosne-Romanée, Les Suchots, Domaine Gerard Mugneret   From 2020 17.5

Fullish colour. Ripe, accessible, plump, fruity nose. Attractive, balanced fruit here. Medium-full body. Ample, harmonious, very good grip. Long and classy and intense. Lovely finish.

Vougeot, Clos de la Perrière, Domaine Bertagna   From 2018 16.5

Medium colour. Some development. Soft, forward, oaky nose. Lacking grip and depth. Better on the palate if only medium-bodied. What there is, is classy and balanced.

Chambolle-Musigny, Domaine Jacques-Frédéric Mugnier   From 2017 16.0

Splendid concentration and depth for a village wine. Great style too.

Chambolle-Musigny, Domaine de la Pousse d'Or   From 2017 16.0

Fine colour. Still very youthful. Medium-full body. Good grip. Pure, slightly austere fruit. Very good indeed for a village wine. Lovely positive finish.

Chambolle-Musigny, Domaine Georges Roumier   From 2017 16.0

Ripe, quite firm attack. Finely shaped tannins. Medium to medium-full body. Lovely fruit. Fine for a village example.

Chambolle-Musigny, *Premier Cru*, Domaine Joseph Drouhin   From 2020 18.0

Medium-full colour. Quite oaky on the nose. But rich and concentrated and classy. Medium-full body. Vigorous and intense. Ample and succulent. Very good grip. Long and complex and energetic. Fine plus.

Chambolle-Musigny, Les Amoureuses, Domaine Francois Bertheau   From 2018 15.0

Medium colour. Some development. Curious nose. There is a touch of pineapple here. Soft, rich, medium-bodied. Good acidity. But rather weedy as it developed in the glass. Yet the finish wasn't too bad.

Chambolle-Musigny, Les Amoureuses, Domaine J. Frédéric Mugnier   From 2021 19.0

Medium-full colour. Lovely fragrant nose. Excellent harmonious fruit. And great class. Accessible on the palate. Medium-full body. Very ripe and intense. Very good grip. Long and classy and delicious. Very fine indeed.

Chambolle-Musigny, Les Amoureuses, Domaine Georges Roumier   From 2022 18.5

Fullish colour. Quite a closed-in nose. Full and meaty for an Amoureuses. But there is depth and class here. Quite high-toned. Medium-full body. Generous, rich, round, and excellently balanced. Very fine.

Chambolle-Musigny, Les Amoureuses, Domaine Comte Georges de Vogüé   From 2022 19.5

Full colour. Quite a high-toned nose. Lovely pure fruit. Class and depth too. Medium-full body. Lots of lovely ripe fruit and no undue oak. Intense and quite powerful but less ungainly than the other two Vogüé wines. Showing better today.

Chambolle-Musigny, Les Baudes, Domaine Christian Serafin   From 2020 17.5

Medium to medium-full colour. Good style on the nose. Medium weight. Oaky. But a little tight at first. Lots of lovely slightly spicy, plump fruit. Very good grip. Long finish. This is fine.

Chambolle-Musigny, Les Charmes, Domaine Ghislaine Barthod   From 2020 18.5

Fullish colour. Fragrant, quite high-toned, balanced, fresh, youthful nose, with no lack of depth. Fullish body. Good grip. Ample, succulent. Good structure and grip. Long. Very fine.

Chambolle-Musigny, Les Charmes, Domaine Francois Bertheau   See note

Fullish colour. Very lovely cassis-blackberry fruit on the nose. Full body. Youthful. Very promising at first but then it collapsed in the glass. To be reviewed.

Chambolle-Musigny, Les Charmes, Domaine Chezeaux (Ponsot)   From 2020 18.0

Fullish colour. Ample, ripe, quite meaty nose. Very lovely, slightly austere Chambolle fruit. Full-bodied, generous, really rich, but very fresh. Splendid depth and a fine, long finish. Fine plus.

Chambolle-Musigny, Les Charmes, Domaine Alain Hudelot-Noëllat   From 2019 17.5

Medium to medium-full colour. Some development. A bit closed-in but fresh and rich on the nose. Medium body. Cool and composed. Lovely laid-back fruit. Long and stylish. Quite forward.

Chambolle-Musigny, Les Charmes, Domaine Leroy   From 2017 16.0

This is a bit reduced on the nose. Medium body. Good harmonious fruit, but a slight lack of depth. Very good at best.

Chambolle-Musigny, Les Charmes, Domaine de la Pousse d'Or   From 2020 18.0

Fullish colour. Ample, rich, generous, aromatic, slightly spicy nose. Good substance here. Medium-full body. Composed. Balanced. Long. Complex and subtle. Fine plus.

Chambolle-Musigny, Les Charmes, Domaine Michèle et Patrick Rion   From 2019 18.0

Medium colour. Some development. Ripe, rich, concentrated, composed nose. Lots of class. Fullish body. Ample, round, very good grip. Good intensity and balance. Finishes long and vigorous. Fine plus.

Chambolle-Musigny, Les Cras, Domaine Ghislaine Barthod   From 2020 17.5

Medium-full colour. Fragrant, high-toned nose. Good stylish fruit. Soft, ample. Medium to medium-full body. A touch of astringency at present, but the follow-through is rich and positive. Fine.

Chambolle-Musigny, Les Cras, Domaine Antonin Guyon   From 2015 14.0

Good colour. Slightly pinched on the nose. Ripe underneath. Medium-full body. Decent balance but not very stylish. Finishes awkwardly. Quite good at best.

Chambolle-Musigny, Les Cras, Domaine Georges Roumier   From 2022 18.5

Medium-full colour. Still quite closed. Lovely firm, rich fruit. Very fine grip. Medium-full body. Great class. Very fine.

Chambolle-Musigny, Les Feusselottes, Domaine de la Pousse d'Or   From 2020 17.5

Medium-full colour. A slight whiff or reduction at first, but fullish, fat, and quite concentrated on the nose. Medium-full body. Firm and fresh. Good depth and vigour. Just a touch of astringency which makes it a little ungainly today. But fine.

Chambolle-Musigny,
Les Feusselottes,
Domaine Cecile Tremblay   From 2020 18.0

Medium-full colour. Quite a succulent, oaky nose. Quite substantial. Medium-full body. Accessible, balanced, fresh, and most attractive. Long and positive and classy at the end. Fine plus.

Chambolle-Musigny, Les Fremières,
Domaine Digioia-Royer   From 2019 17.5

Medium-full colour. Ripe, fragrant, stylish, balanced nose with a touch of oak. Medium to medium-full body. Ripe, round, succulent, classy, and quite intense. Lots of style. Long and fragrant at the end. Fine.

Chambolle-Musigny, Les Fuées,
Domaine Ghislaine Barthod   From 2020 18.0

Medium-full colour. Quite a high-toned nose. Ripe. Good acidity. Very fresh. Good class. Subtle and harmonious. Medium to medium-full body. Very, very ripe on the palate. Yet excellent intensity and grip. Fine plus.

Chambolle-Musigny, Les Fuées,
Domaine J. Fréderick Mugnier   From 2020 16.5

Fullish colour. Ripe, concentrated, succulent, spicy nose. Good substance here. But almost over-ripe. Medium-full body. A little astringency. Very, very rich on the palate. Just a little heavy at the end.

Chambolle-Musigny, Les Groseilles,
Domaine Digioia-Royer   From 2019 16.5

Medium-full colour. Fresh, ripe, classy nose. Quite firm. Fullish body. A little closed on the attack. There is plump attractive fruit here. But not quite the grip of the best. But by no means short.

Chambolle-Musigny, Les Groseilles,
Domaine de la Pousse d'Or   From 2020 18.0

Medium-full colour. Plump and ripe. Good depth, grip, and class here. Medium-full body. Quite oaky. Ripe and pump and succulent. Long and intense at the end. Fine plus.

Chambolle-Musigny, Les Gruenchers,
Domaine Digioia-Royer   From 2018 16.0

Medium to medium-full colour. Attractive fruit on the nose. Medium to medium-full body. Just a bit loose-knit compared with some. Plump, balanced, and attractive nevertheless.

Chambolle-Musigny,
Les Hauts Doits,
Domaine Robert Groffier   From 2022 18.0

Medium-full colour. Quite an intense, mocha nose. Good style and plenty of fruit. Fullish body. Ripe, ample, balanced, and stylish. Fine plus.

Morey-Saint-Denis,
Domaine Dujac   From 2016 15.0

Ripe soft, plump, and stylish. Medium to medium-full body. Very good for a village wine.

Morey-Saint-Denis, *Premier Cru*,
Domaine Dujac   From 2019 15.5

Medium to medium-full colour. Full and quite firm on the nose. Good fruit and depth and class. Medium-full body. A touch of astringency? But good acidity. Decent succulence but could have had more. Long. Good plus.

Morey-Saint-Denis, Les Chaffots,
Domaine Hubert Lignier   From 2017 15.0

Medium-full colour. High-toned, perfumed nose. Medium to medium-full body. Balanced and quite elegant. But not enough weight and depth for *premier cru*.

Morey-Saint-Denis,
Clos de la Bussière,
Domaine Georges Roumier   From 2020 17.0

Quite structured. Rich and meaty. Plenty of depth. Lovely fruit. Very good indeed.

Morey-Saint-Denis,
Clos des Rosiers,
Domaine Chantal Remy   From 2019 16.5

Village *appellation contrôlée* (AC). Medium to medium-full colour. Some development. Plump, fruity, fresh, attractive nose. Some oak. Medium-full body. Good grip. Ample fruity attack. Good follow-through. No lack of energy. Very good plus.

**Morey-Saint-Denis,
Les Faconnières,
Domaine Lignier-Michelot**   From 2019   17.0
Medium-full colour. Still youthful. Quite soft already on the nose. Medium-full body. Vigorous. The tannins now well absorbed. Stylish and full of fruit. Long. Classy. Very good indeed.

**Morey-Saint-Denis,
Les Millandes,
Domaine Christian Serafin**   From 2019   17.0
Medium-full colour. Good depth on the nose. Rich and substantial. Still young. Medium-full body. Just a little four-square on the attack. But good depth and grip. The finish is long and expansive. Very good indeed.

**Morey-Saint-Denis, La Riotte,
Olivier Jouan**   From 2019   17.5
Fullish colour. Rich, concentrated nose. Good depth. Still quite closed. Medium-full body. Stylish and quite profound. A touch of new oak. Long at the end. This is fine.

**Morey-Saint-Denis, Les Ruchots,
Domaine Olivier Jouan**   From 2019   17.0
Fullish colour. Slightly earthy on the nose. But good grip, balance, and substance. Medium-full body. Some oak. The finish is long and classy. Very good indeed.

**Gevrey-Chambertin,
Domaine Armand Rousseau**   From 2018   16.0
Medium to medium-full body. Ripe. Cool. Plump. Stylish and delicious for a village example.

**Gevrey-Chambertin,
Domaine Trapet Père et Fils**   From 2015   15.0
This is the lesser of their two village *cuvées*. Medium to medium-full weight. Ripe. Fruity. A good basic. Lots of charm.

**Gevrey-Chambertin, *Premier Cru*,
Domaine Denis Mortet**   From 2021   18.0
Medium-full colour. Quite substantial. Quite concentrated. A bit closed on the nose, showing new oak. Fullish body. Rich and profound. Lovely fruit. Lots of dimension. Lovely.

**Gevrey-Chambertin, *Premier Cru*,
Domaine Trapet Père et Fils**   From 2017   14.5
Medium colour. Not a very rich or concentrated nose. Quite forward. Medium to medium-full body. A touch of oak. Good acidity. But it lacks a bit of vigour and class. Quite good plus.

**Gevrey-Chambertin, Les Cazetiers,
Domaine Chezeaux (Berthaut)**   From 2018   17.5
Fullish colour. Ample, rich but slightly pinched on the nose at first. Better as it evolved. Fullish body. Ripe. Stylish. Good tannins. Very good acidity. Nice and fresh. Long. Fine.

**Gevrey-Chambertin, Les Cazetiers,
Maison Bernstein**   From 2020   17.5
Medium-full colour. Good depth, concentration, class, and oak on the nose. Medium-full body. Quite firm at first. Some tannin. Rich and ripe and very good grip. Plenty of depth. Fine.

**Gevrey-Chambertin, Les Cazetiers,
Domaine Bruno Clair**   From 2019   16.0
Medium-full colour. Quite oaky nose. Good personality and style. Medium body. Does not have the grip and depth of some. Slightly loose-knit by comparison. Ripe and stylish nevertheless.

**Gevrey-Chambertin, Les Cazetiers,
Domaine Christian Serafin**   From 2020   17.5
Medium colour. Some development. Ample, soft nose. Easy to appreciate. Stylish fruit. But quite forward. More to it on the palate. Medium to medium-full body. Some oak. Very good fruit. Very fresh. Ripe. Balanced. Long and fine.

**Gevrey-Chambertin, Les Cazetiers,
Domaine Armand Rousseau**   From 2018   15.0
Medium-full colour. A touch of chocolate on the nose. Oak too. A bit reduced. This exaggerates the astringency. Good grip. Medium to medium-full body.

**Gevrey-Chambertin, Les Cherbaudes,
Domaine Louis Boillot**   From 2017   14.0
Medium colour. Good substance and even richness on the nose. Medium body. Reasonably fresh but not much here. Forward.

**Gevrey-Chambertin,
Clos-Saint-Jacques,
Domaine Bruno Clair**   From 2020   18.5
Concentrated. Rich. Fat. Profound. Very fine fruit. This is high-class. Fullish body. Very fine.

**Gevrey-Chambertin,
Clos-Saint-Jacques,
Domaine Sylvie Esmonin**   From 2020   18.5
Fullish colour. Cool, classy, very concentrated nose. No over-oaking here. Fullish body. Some tannin. Very lovely fruit. Lots of vigour and depth. Very fine.

**Gevrey-Chambertin,
Clos-Saint-Jacques,
Domaine Jadot**   From 2019   17.5
Medium colour. Some development. Lovely fruit on the nose. And not too much oak. Balanced and profound. Medium to medium-full body. Not the vigour and grip of the other Clos-Saint-Jacques, but certainly fine.

**Gevrey-Chambertin,
Clos-Saint-Jacques,
Domaine Armand Rousseau**   From 2020   18.5
A little slighter, it seems, than the Bruno Clair example. But excellent fruit and grip. And very stylish too. But is there enough weight for great?

**Gevrey-Chambertin, Combes
aux Moines, Domaine Faiveley**   From 2020   16.5
Medium-full colour. Rich nose with a slight touch of caramel. Medium-full body. Good tannins. This has depth and personality. Even concentration and vigour. Long classy finish. Very good plus.

**Gevrey-Chambertin, Aux
Combottes, Domaine Dujac**   From 2017   14.0
Medium-full colour. Ripe but earthy nose. Medium body. Some fruit. Decent balance. But lacks depth.

**Gevrey-Chambertin, Aux
Combottes, Domaine Leroy**   From 2021   18.5
Profound and classy on the nose. Very finely balanced fruit. Medium-full body. Pure and delicious. Very lovely follow-through.

**Gevrey-Chambertin,
Les Corbeaux, Domaine
Denis Bachelet**   From 2019   See note
Medium-full colour. Some substance. But a bit dry. Medium-full body. Good grip. Doesn't sing. Apparently the bottle showed fine the day after. Bachelet is normally a brilliant winemaker.

**Gevrey-Chambertin, Les Corbeaux,
Domaine Christian Serafin**   From 2018   15.0
Medium to medium-full colour. Fresh and balanced on the nose, but not much flair. Medium body. Fresh and fruity and balanced on the palate. Finishes positively. Good.

**Gevrey-Chambertin, Le Crapillot,
Domaine Humbert Frères**   From 2017   14.0
Medium-full colour. A touch reduced on the nose. A bit rustic too. Medium body. A touch astringent. Decent grip but a touch one-dimensional.

**Gevrey-Chambertin,
Estournelles Saint-Jacques,
Domaine Duroché**   From 2019   16.0
Medium to medium-full colour. Ample nose. Quite rich. Good grip. Medium-full body. Good energy and concentration. Positive and vigorous. Long. Very good.

**Gevrey-Chambertin,
Estournelles Saint-Jacques,
Domaine Humbert Frères**   From 2020   17.0
Medium-full colour. Ripe, balanced nose. Quite stylish. Still a bit closed. Fullish body. Rich and vigorous. Some new oak. Plenty of class and depth. Long finish. Very good indeed.

**Gevrey-Chambertin, Le Fonteny,
Domaine Christian Serafin**   From 2017   14.0
Medium to medium-full colour. Fresh and balanced on the nose but not much flair. Medium body. Pleasantly made but lacks a little personality. Finishes positively though.

**Gevrey-Chambertin,
Clos du Fonteny,
Domaine Bruno Clair**   From 2017   14.0
Medium to medium-full colour. Fresh and fruity on the nose but a bit neutral. Medium

body. Not a great deal of depth and dimension, like so many of these second division Gevrey *premières crus*.

**Gevrey-Chambertin,
Lavaux Saint-Jacques,
Domaine Drouhin-Laroze**   From 2017   13.5
Medium-full colour. Ripe nose. Some structure. A touch of oak. On the palate, fruity but a little pinched. Medium to medium-full body. Lacks style. Only fair.

**Gevrey-Chambertin,
Lavaux Saint-Jacques,
Domaine Humbert Frères**   From 2017   13.5
Medium-full colour. Rather pinched and rustic on the nose. Medium weight. Slightly astringent. Ripe underneath but it lacks style.

**Gevrey-Chambertin,
Lavaux Saint-Jacques,
Domaine Maume**   From 2017   14.5
Medium to medium-full colour. Open, somewhat lightweight nose. Clean and fresh and fruity on the palate. Has charm, even some style, and it finishes positively.

**Gevrey-Chambertin,
Lavaux-Saint-Jacques,
Domaine Gerard Raphet**   From 2017   16.0
Medium-full colour. Lovely ripe nose. Medium to medium-full body. Quite forward. Just a little tannin. Very good fruit. Balanced and stylish and positive at the end. Very good.

**Gevrey-Chambertin,
Lavaux Saint-Jacques,
Domaine Armand Rousseau**   From 2019   15.5
Medium-full colour. Discreet nose. Personality and fruit on the palate. Medium-full body. Balanced, but quite forward. Good fruit and style and a positive finish.

**Gevrey-Chambertin,
La Petite Chapelle,
Domaine Humbert Frères**   From 2017   14.0
Medium-full colour. Rather reduced on the nose. Medium body. Forward. Decently balanced fruit but a little neutral. Clean though.

**Gevrey-Chambertin,
Le Petite Chapelle,
Domaine Rossignol-Trapet**   From 2018   15.0
Medium-full colour. A bit earthy on the nose. Better fruit and personality on the palate. A touch of oak. Medium-full body. Good grip. Decent energy. Good.

**Gevrey-Chambertin, Le Poissenot,
Domaine Humbert Frères**   From 2020   17.5
Fullish colour. Youthful nose. Good depth. Medium-full body. Quite concentrated and oaky. Rich and vigorous. A touch of spice. Ample, harmonious, long, and powerful. Needs time. Fine.

Grands Crus

**Corton,
Domaine Follin-Arvelet**   From 2019   17.5
Medium colour. Rich, ample, oaky nose. Essentially quite soft. Medium-full body. Good grip. Classy tannins. Plenty of rich fruit. Fine.

**Corton, Domaine
Bonneaux du Martray**   From 2020   18.0
A subtle wine. Soft at the beginning. Intense and stylish on the follow-through. Rich, concentrated, and profound. Fullish body. Lovely fruit. Fine plus.

**Corton, Cuvée des Bourdons,
Domaine Ponsot**   From 2020   17.5
Good colour. Ripe, quite firm, succulent nose. Lots of personality, class, and vigour. Very good tannins. Full body. A sturdy wine, but a lot of richness underneath. Good energetic finish.

**Corton, Domaine de
la Romanée-Conti**   From 2022   18.0
Splendid colour. Ample, fat, black cherries and chocolate flavours on the nose. Full body. Quite structured and tannic. Very good grip. Just a little four-square on the follow-through. But good richness and depth. Needs time.

**Corton, Bressandes,
Domaine Chandon de Briailles**   From 2017   15.5
Ripe stylish and suave. Quite concentrated but lacking the vigour of a *grand cru*.

Corton, Bressandes,

Domaine Follin-Arvelet   From 2018 16.0

Medium to medium-full colour. Some development. Ripe, quite soft, oaky nose. Plump and ample. Medium-full body. Lots of fruit but it lacks a little zip and freshness. Not short though. Lovely.

Corton, Bressandes,

Domaine de la Pousse d'Or   From 2020 17.5

Fullish colour. Youthful nose. Rich and firm and abundant. Still closed. Fullish body. Good grip. Ripe tannins. Lots of energy and lots of fruit. Vigorous follow-through. Fine.

Corton, Bressandes,

Domaine Tollot-Beaut   From 2020 17.0

Good depth here if a slight absence of elegance. Fullish body. Good grip. Ripe fruit and thankfully less sweet than their Beaune Grèves. Long. Very good indeed.

Corton, Clos des Cortons,

Domaine Faiveley   From 2022 18.5

Very fine rich, ripe nose. Very stylish tannins. Rich and fat and concentrated. Full body. Fine, long, subtle finish. Really classy. Very fine.

Corton, Clos de Meix,

Domaine Comte Senard   From 2018 16.5

Ripe, soft, stylish, and with good grip. More to it than usual. Not fine, but then the land is more *premier* than *grand cru*. But attractive.

Corton, Clos du Roi,

Domaine de Montille   From 2018 15.5

Medium-full colour. Open, fruity nose. Some substance. Quite sweet. Quite evolved. A pleasant, medium to medium-full bodied, balanced fruity wine. But not *grand cru* standard.

Corton, Clos du Roi,

Domaine de la Pousse d'Or   From 2022 18.5

Fullish colour. Firm, youthful, concentrated nose. Very classy. This is a wine for the long term. Full body. Good tannins. Plenty of structure, depth, grip, and energy. Lots of finesse. Very fine.

Corton, Clos du Roi,

Domaine Comte Senard   From 2020 17.5

Fullish body, rich and very stylish. Lovely fruit and just a touch of oak. Lots of charm. Long and fine.

Corton, Clos du Roi,

Domaine de la Vougeraie   From 2020 18.5

Medium-full colour. Ripe, rich, firm, succulent nose. Fullish body. Rich, oaky, and succulent on the palate. Lots of wine here. Creamy and vigorous. Long and classy. Very fine.

Corton, Grèves,

Domaine des Croix   From 2019 17.0

Medium-full colour. Fresh, youthful, classy fruit on the nose. Quite concentrated on the palate. Medium-full body. Lacks just a bit of grip and finesse. Very good indeed.

Corton, Pougets,

Domaine Louis Jadot   From 2019 16.5

Medium colour. Quite a firm nose. Good depth. Medium-full body. Good fruit but not quite the concentration and grip of the best. Good class and a positive finish. Could well turn out better than it showed today.

Corton, Renardes,

Domaine Michel Gaunoux   From 2020 18.0

Full body. Ripe, classy, and intense. Rich and positive. Harmonious. Lovely finish. Fine plus.

Corton, Renardes,

Domaine Leroy   From 2021 17.5

Medium-full colour. Rich, fat, full-bodied, and oaky. Good grip. Plenty of energy. Fine, but not the sheer class for great.

Corton, Renardes, Maison

Thibault Liger-Belair   From 2020 17.5

Medium-full colour. A bit of reduction on the nose. Medium-full body. Ripe and succulent. Good grip. Good energy. Long finish.

Corton, La Vigne au Saint,

Domaine des Croix   From 2020 18.0

Medium-full colour. Full, rich, classy nose with a touch of oak. Lovely, rich, succulent fruit.

Fullish body. Very good grip. This is ripe and ample and long on the palate. Fine plus.

Corton, Clos de la Vigne au Saint, Domaine Louis Latour   From 2019   17.5
Medium colour. Some evolution. Soft, aromatic nose. Ripe and balanced. Good grip. Plenty of depth and a classy follow-through. Fine.

Echézeaux, Domaine du Clos Frantin (Albert Bichot)   From 2022   17.5
Good colour. Rich, concentrated nose. Nicely cool. Ripe, spicy, and fullish on the palate. Very composed fruit. Very ripe tannins. Quite concentrated. Fine.

Echézeaux, Domaine Eugenie   From 2020   17.0
Medium to medium-full colour. A little tight on the nose. But the fruit seems good. Medium-full body. Ample fruit on the palate. Very good intensity. Not the greatest character but very good indeed.

Echézeaux, Domaine A. F. Gros   From 2021   18.5
Medium-full colour. Rich, full, concentrated nose. Good depth. This is very classy. Medium-full body. Lovely fruit. Lots of energy and intensity. Lots of dimension. Very fine.

Echézeaux, Domaine Gros Frère et Soeur   From 2019   16.5
Medium-full colour. High-toned fruit on the nose. Medium to medium-full body. A charming, fragrant, gently oaky example. Evolving quite soon. Most attractive. But not really serious.

Echézeaux, Domaine Lamarche   From 2020   17.5
Medium-full colour. Plump, ripe, accessible, quite stylish nose. Medium-full body. Good tannins. Round, ripe fruit balanced by very good acidity. Long. Classy. Fine.

Echézeaux, Domaine du Vicomte de Liger-Belair   From 2020   17.5
Medium to medium-full colour. Some development. Very ripe on the attck. Lovely, seductive, harmonious fruit. Medium-full body. Very good grip. Fine.

Echézeaux, Domaine Dr. Georges Mugneret-Gibourg   From 2020   15.0
Medium to medium-full colour. Quite a firm nose. Good fruit. Ripe and oaky. But a little lean as it evolved. Medium-full body. Lacks a bit of richness and generosity.

Echézeaux, Domaine Gerard Mugneret   See note
Medium-full colour. Plump and fruity but somewhat corked. Yet one could see a wine with medium to medium-full body, good acidity, and attractive intense fruit. Certainly a success.

Echézeaux, Domaine de la Romanée-Conti   From 2020   17.5
Medium-full colour. Quite a traditional youthful DRC nose, showing evidence of the stems. Soft and ripe and fresh and spicy. Medium to medium-full weight. Ripe and fragrant, but good grip and intensity. Easy to appreciate. Fine.

Echézeaux du Dessus, Domaine Cécile Tremblay   From 2020   17.0
Medium to medium-full colour. Fragrant and lots of fruit on the nose. Fullish body. Oaky, very ripe. Very good intensity. Good grip. Not quite the personality for great but very good indeed.

Grands-Echézeaux, Domaine du Clos Frantin (Albert Bichot)   From 2020   17.5
Medium to medium-full body. Quite a firm nose. But lots of depth and dimension. On the palate this is medium to medium-full bodied. Abundant. But it lacks a bit of intensity. Fine, though.

Grands-Echézeaux, Domaine Drouhin   From 2022   18.5
Lovely nose. Very classy, balanced fruit. Intense and rich. Lots of energy. Lovely Pinot fruit. Very fine.

Grands-Echézeaux, Domaine Eugenie   From 2022   19.0
Medium-full colour. Firm, full, fat, slightly oaky nose. Very classy and profound. Still a little reserved. But very concentrated and

classy. Fullish body. Excellent fruit. Splendid follow-through.

Grands-Echézeaux,
Domaine Gros Frère et Soeur   From 2020   18.5

Medium to medium-full colour. Some development. Fresh, ripe, succulent, and attractive on the nose. Similar on the palate. Medium-full body. Lots of depth and dimension. A little oak. Intense, long finish. Very fine.

Grands-Echézeaux,
Domaine Lamarche   From 2020   17.5

Medium to medium-full colour. Ripe, succulent nose. Accessible, attractive, and classy. Medium to medium-full body. Good plump attack. Not quite the intensity and concentration on the follow-through for great but very seductive.

Grands-Echézeaux, Domaine
de la Romanée-Conti   From 2024   18.5

Rather a deeper colour than the Echézeaux. Fuller, richer, and more closed-in. Fullish body. Very concentrated. Some tannin. This is a considerable step up. Lots of power and depth and very lovely fruit. Needs time. Very fine.

Clos de Vougeot,
Domaine Bertagna   From 2020   18.5

Medium-full colour. Rich, ample, ripe, classy, and composed on the nose. Medium-full body. Ripe. Complete. Very classy fruit on the palate. Ripe, sophisticated tannins. Long and complex. Very subtle at the end. A lovely wine.

Clos de Vougeot,
Domaine Eugenie   From 2021   18.5

Medium-full colour. Rich, slightly spicy nose. Plenty of grip and depth underneath. Fullish body. Splendidly harmonious. Lots of energy. Very abundant fruit. The finish is long, rich, and multidimensional. Very classy indeed.

Clos de Vougeot, Domaine du
Clos Frantin (Albert Bichot)   From 2024   18.5

Very good colour. Splendid nose. Very classy concentrated fruit. Very well-balanced. Lots of depth, energy, and class. Concentrated, complex finish. Very fine.

Clos de Vougeot,
Domaine Grivot   From 2024   18.5

Full colour. Still very closed. Very good structure. Rich and concentrated. Lots of dimension and class. Lovely fruit. Very fine.

Clos de Vougeot,
Le Grand Maupertuis,
Domaine Anne Gros   From 2024   19.0

Fullish colour. Brilliant, concentrated, very high-class nose. Very lovely fruit. Full body. Rich. Profound. Excellent fruit. Very, very complex and multidimensional. Very special.

Clos de Vougeot, Maupertuis,
Domaine Michel Gros   From 2020   18.5

Medium-full colour. Ample, fruity, oaky nose. Bigger and more backward and more serious as it evolved. Fullish body. Some tannin. Very good grip. Intense and classy. This needs time. Very fine.

Clos de Vougeot, Le Musigni,
Domaine Gros Frère et Soeur   From 2020   17.5

Medium-full colour. Fullish nose. Plenty of depth and classy fruit. The oak is absorbed by the concentration of the wine. Fullish body. Quite pronounced oak on the palate. Very good acidity though. This needs time.

Clos de Vougeot, Domaine
Alain Hudelot-Noëllat   From 2020   17.5

Medium colour. Some development. Soft, oaky nose. Slightly lumpy. Medium to medium-full body. Good grip. Fresh and elegant. Very good follow-through. Good intensity. Fine.

Clos de Vougeot,
Domaine Louis Jadot   From 2022   18.5

Medium to medium-full colour. Very lovely nose. Very classy, harmonious fruit. Fullish body. Lots of dimension. Very good tannins. Splendidly profound and harmonious. Very long. Still very young. Lovely.

Clos de Vougeot,
Domaine Lamarche   From 2020   17.5

Medium-full colour. Ample nose. Good fruit. Nice and fresh. Medium-full body. Good tannins. Good grip. Succulent fruit. Good energy. Classy. Fine.

Clos de Vougeot,
Domaine Leroy   From 2021   18.5
Closed-in but very fine on the nose. Full-bodied, rich, vigorous, and concentrated on the palate. Excellent grip. Very lovely, complex, classy fruit. Lots of depth. Very fine finish.

Clos de Vougeot, Domaine
Thibault Liger-Belair   From 2020   18.0
Full colour. Rich, ripe, and with good grip on the nose, if a shade adolescent at present. Fullish body. Very ripe. Very good acidity. Classy and impressive. Finishes long. Fine plus.

Clos de Vougeot,
Domaine Loichet   From 2018   15.5
Fullish colour. A touch reduced but ample and plump on the nose. A slight touch of astringency on the palate. The attack is okay but then it tails of a bit.

Clos de Vougeot,
Domaine Méo-Camuzet   From 2020   17.5
Fullish body. Rich and oaky on the nose. Medium-full body. Ripe and plump. Good style and balance. But it lacks a bit of sparkle.

Clos de Vougeot,
Domaine Château de la Tour   From 2020   17.5
Rich, fat, and concentrated. Good energy. Good tannins. Fullish body. Lots of depth at the end. Fine.

Clos de Vougeot,
Cuvée Vieilles Vignes,
Domaine Château de la Tour   From 2023   18.5
Very lovely nose. Lots of depth and concentration. Very classy fruit. Excellent finish. This is very fine.

Clos de Vougeot,
Domaine de la Vougeraie   From 2020   17.5
Medium to medium-full colour. Some oak on the nose, but a bit tight at present. Better as it evolved. Medium-full body. Good grip. Ripe tannins. Fresh, intense, and classy. Fine finish.

Romanée-Saint-Vivant,
Domaine de l'Arlot   From 2022   17.0
Medium-full colour. Ripe, accessible, stemmy, sweet nose. But there is backbone here. Fullish body. Very good grip but at the same time a little astringency. Quite intense but a bit clumsy.

Romanée-Saint-Vivant,
Domaine Follin-Arvelet   From 2022   18.5
Medium to medium-full colour. Quite a firm, unresolved nose. A bit raw and closed at first. Quite perfumed as it evolved. More and more classy. Fullish body. Some tannin. Lots of finesse and intensity. Lots of grip. The finish is lovely. Most impressive.

Romanée-Saint-Vivant, Domaine
Alain Hudelot-Noëllat   From 2022   19.0
Medium to medium-full body. Quite fresh, firm, high-quality nose. Quite high-toned. This is really fine on the palate. Medium-full bodied. Splendid ripe fruit. Creamy-rich. Very intense. Lots of class. Brilliant.

Romanée-Saint-Vivant,
Les Quatre Journaux,
Domaine Louis Latour   From 2022   17.0
Medium-full colour. Hidden nose. But no lack of personality. Good depth. Medium-full body. At first this showed very lovely fruit on the palate. Ripe and with no lack of grip. But it evolved fast in the glass. Much less impressive at the end.

Romanée-Saint-Vivant,
Domaine Leroy   From 2021   19.5
Very lovely, perfumed, Chambolle-ish nose. Fullish body. Very complex. Lovely harmony. Very high-class fruit. Splendid, long, lingering finish. Excellent.

Romanée-Saint-Vivant,
Domaine de la Romanée-Conti   From 2019   18.0
Good colour. Soft, fragrant nose. As always at the DRC, a touch of the feminine here. His isn't singing today. There is something a little astringent at the end. Good balance and stylish fruit, but it doesn't seem as complete as the Grands-Echézeaux or the Richebourg.

Richebourg, Domaine du
Clos Frantin (Albert Bichot)   From 2022   19.5
Medium-full colour. Full-flavoured, aromatic nose. Slightly four-square at first. Full-bodied, concentrated, and vigorous. Generous, very fine grip and intensity. Lots of dimension and a touch of spice. Very fine indeed.

Richebourg, Domaine
Alain Hudelot-Noëllat   From 2022   20.0
Medium to medium-full colour. Aromatic, rich nose. Very lovely fruit. Lots of class. Fullish body. This is really very stylish. Excellent grip. Very, very pure and intense. A great wine.

Richebourg,
Domaine Anne Gros   From 2022   20.0
Medium-full colour. Vibrant, profound nose. Fresh and plump and delicious. Even better on the palate. Medium-full body. Not a blockbuster but essence of high-class Pinot. Very, very complex and intense. Very subtle. Marvelous finesse. A great wine.

Richebourg,
Domaine A. F. Gros   From 2022   18.5
Medium-full colour. Discreet, classy, balanced, and very fresh. This is subtle and brilliant on the nose. Medium-full body. Very lovely plump fruit. But not quite the grip and intensity at the end. Very fine nevertheless.

Richebourg,
Domaine Gros Frère et Soeur   From 2022   18.5
Medium-full colour. Slightly gamey on the nose. Fullish, some tannin, some oak. Medium-full body. Aromatic, rich, voluptuous, and seductive. A meaty wine. Very fine.

Richebourg, Domaine Leroy   From 2022   19.0
A bigger wine than the Romanée-Saint-Vivant. And because it is slightly reduced, it's a bit clumsy today on the attack. But there is very promising fruit on the follow-through. Long. Multidimensional. Very fine indeed.

Richebourg, Domaine
Thibault Liger-Belair   From 2021   18.5
Medium-full colour. Fat, slightly animal/gamey nose. But rich and substantial. As it evolved, it showed very good class, grip, and depth. Fullish body. Firm. Lots of concentration. Powerful at first, but very impressive at the end.

Richebourg, Domaine
de la Romanée-Conti   From 2025   19.5
Fine colour. Rich, closed, powerful, and concentrated on the nose. Lots of wine here. Full-bodied. Very good tannins. Profound and multidimensional. Excellent fruit. Splendid grip. This is really most impressive.

La Grande Rue,
Domaine Lamarche   From 2022   19.0
Medium to medium-full colour. Firm nose. Very classy. Excellent harmony. Lovely fruit. Fullish body. Backward. Some tannin. Lots of generous stylish fruit. Very, very fine elegant finish. Splendid quality.

La Romanée, Domaine
du Vicomte Liger-Belair   See note
Medium-full colour. Somewhat spicy and reduced on the nose. Very good grip, though. Medium-full body. Lots of wine here and of very high quality. But is is difficult to discern how high. If not reduced, I noted at the time, perhaps the best of the flight (of Romanée-Saint-Vivants and neighbouring monopolies).

La Tâche, Domaine de
la Romanée-Conti   From 2027   20.0
Fine colour. Really quite closed on the nose, even more so than the Richebourg. Lovely perfumed cassis nose. A big, backward, quite tannic wine with excellent grip. More austere than the Richbourg. But it has even more depth and intensity. Very lovely.

Romanée-Conti, Domaine de
la Romanée-Conti   From 2024   20.0
Just a little less colour than the Tâche. Not a lot on the nose at present. You have to go searching for it. What there is, is very poised and very harmonious as well as being very complex and classy. The fruit is more red-flavoured than the Tâche. Marvelously fine and intense. Really quite excellent.

Le Musigny, Domaine Leroy   From 2021   19.5
Still very, very closed. Fat, rich, and concentrated on the nose. Very lovely, balanced, fragrant fruit. This is very complex and the finish is excellent.

**Le Musigny, Domaine
Jacques-Frédéric Mugnier**   From 2023   19.5
Full colour. Very lovely fruit on the nose. Fullish body. A touch of oak. Rich, multidimensional fruit. Very fine balance. Great class. Excellent.

**Le Musigny, Domaine
Comte Georges de Vogüé**   From 2023   18.5
Fullish colour. Fragrant nose. High-toned. Some oak. Medium-full body. Ripe, balanced, classy, and lovely. A rather bigger wine than Mugnier or Vougeraie, and without quite the finesse. But it is rather less developed.

**Le Musigny, Domaine
de la Vougeraie**   From 2022   19.5
Medium-full colour. Very lovely subtle, gently oaky nose. Laid-back. Discreet and very high-class. This is quite brilliant. Fullish body. Marvellously concentrated, harmonious fruit. Splendid finish. A great wine.

**Bonnes-Mares,
Domaine Francois Bertheau**   From 2021   18.0
Medium-full colour. Rich, full, abundant nose. Very fresh acidity so very elegant on the nose. Profound and concentrated as well. Fullish body. Plenty of energy. Not quite the finesse evident on the nose but fine plus.

**Bonnes-Mares,
Domaine Bruno Clair**   From 2023   19.0
Full colour. Ripe, concentrated, masculine nose. Some oak. Good depth here as well as class. Fullish body. Lots of concentration and depth. Very fine, very fresh fruit with excellent grip. Quite powerful. This very fine indeed.

**Bonnes-Mares,
Domaine Drouhin-Laroze**   From 2022   19.0
Fullish colour. Closed-in on the nose. But profound and classy. The fruit is ripe and succulent. Medium-full body. Very good grip. Not a

blockbuster but ripe and balanced and fresh and very stylish. Very harmonious. Very lovely.

**Bonnes-Mares,
Domaine Georges Roumier**   From 2021   17.5
Good colour. Very subtle. The wine seems to lack its usual volume. There is a slight absence of fat and concentration and on this occasion it was eclipsed by his Cras. We'll see. (At the three-year-on tasting, the wine was also a little disappointing.)

**Bonnes-Mares, Domaine
Comte Georges de Vogüé**   From 2021   17.5
Fullish colour. Rich, profound nose. Very high-class. Long and lovely. Lots of energy and very good grip. Fullish body. The attack was intense and very promising but the follow-through showed rather less energy.

**Bonnes-Mares,
Domaine de la Vougeraie**   From 2016   13.0
Medium-full body. Soft, slightly rustic nose. For a Bonnes-Mares this is cheap stuff. Medium body. A little sweet. (How can they make something as bad as this when their Musigny and other wines are so good?)

**Clos-Saint-Denis, Très Vieilles
Vignes, Domaine Ponsot**   From 2020   18.5
Medium-full colour. Still rather reticent on the nose. Touches of spice. Medium-full body. This doesn't sing today. It's all a bit closed-in and ungenerous. But very good ripe fruit, good tannins, and good grip. Long and certainly very fine.

**Clos des Lambrays,
Domaine des Lambrays**   From 2018   17.5
Medium-full colour. Soft nose. Some of the stems evident. Not a blockbuster. Medium to medium-full body. A slight touch of astringence. Ripe but not complete. Quite forward. Is this a bad bottle?

**Clos de la Roche,
Maison Bichot**   From 2020   18.0
Medium-full colour. Firm, youthful nose. Good depth here. Medium to medium-full body.

Fresh, stylish, ample fruit. Finishes long and positively. Fine.

Clos de la Roche,
Domaine Dujac From 2022 18.5
Fullish body. Lots of depth and style. Lots of dimension and very lovely fruit. Rich and flamboyant. Very fine.

Clos de la Roche,
Domaine Louis Jadot From 2025 19.0
Full colour. Rich, concentrated, closed nose. Full body, concentrated, tannic, backward, and very profound on the nose. Very lovely fruit. Lots of energy. Splendid finish. Very fine plus.

Clos de la Roche,
Domaine Leroy From 2018 17.5
Black cherries and oak on the nose. Medium-full body. Minerally. Stylish. Good acidity. The most forward of the Leroy *grands crus*. Fine quality.

Clos de la Roche,
Domaine Hubert Lignier From 2019 17.5
Medium-full colour. High-toned, juicy nose. Good grip. Medium-full body. A touch of new oak. Quite forward, but subtle, long, and balanced. Fine.

Clos de la Roche,
Domaine Ponsot From 2020 19.5
Fine colour. Fabulous concentrated, subtle, classy nose. Marvelous fruit. Fullish body. Vigorous. Multidimensional. Complex and very, very long. This is excellent.

Clos de la Roche,
Domaine de la Pousse d'Or From 2020 18.5
Fullish colour. Round and ripe and spicy on the nose. Good weight behind it. Medium-full body. Concentrated and intense. Very lovely fruit. Very long. Very fine.

Clos de la Roche,
Domaine Chantal Rémy From 2019 17.0
Medium-full colour. Good fruit. Quite closed and youthful. Quite structured. Medium to medium-full body. Ripe, fresh, and succulent. No great backbone but long and positive.

Clos de la Roche,
Maison Roche de Bellène From 2019 17.5
Fullish colour. Fat and rich and expansive. Good grip on the nose. But not the greatest of class. Medium to medium-full body. Soft and ripe and succulent. Good follow-through. Finishes better than it starts.

Clos de la Roche,
Domaine Armand Rousseau From 2018 18.0
Good colour. Soft, but vigorous nose. Lots of ample fruit. Fullish body. Very good grip. Rather more bite and personality than this wine has had in the past. Indeed, very delicious. Lovely plump, balanced fruit. Long on the palate and plenty of class.

Clos de Tart,
Domaine Mommessin From 2022 18.5
Fullish colour. Round, ripe, aromatic nose. Fullish body. Rich and concentrated. Plenty of grip and depth. Lots of dimension. This is very fine.

Chapelle-Chambertin,
Domaine Louis Jadot From 2020 17.5
Medium-full body. A little development. Unaggressive, stylish, balanced nose. Very lovely fruit. Almost perfumed as it evolved. Medium-full body. A little tannin. Very good grip. Balanced and intense and vigorous. Youthful. Fine.

Chapelle-Chambertin,
Domaine Ponsot From 2022 18.5
Good colour. Firm nose, but rich as well as masculine underneath. Very lovely, black cherry fruit. Full body. Still youthful but potentially very delicious. Splendidly ripe at the end.

Chapelle-Chambertin,
Domaine Rossignol-Trapet From 2019 18.5
Medium-full colour. A little development. A touch of new oak. Very classy fruit. Plenty of energy. Fullish body. Ample, rich, and ripe. Some tannin. Still closed. Lots of wine on the follow-through. Very fine.

Chapelle-Chambertin,
Domaine Trapet Père et Fils From 2021 18.0
Rich and concentrated. Very good grip. Stylish and individual. Fullish body. Long. Fine plus.

Charmes-Chambertin,
Domaine Denis Bachelet   From 2023 18.5
Fullish colour. Still a little closed on the nose. Good fruit and good grip. An exotic wine. Medium-full body. Fresh, gently oaky, rich, and profound. Very lovely fruit and real class. Splendid finish.

Charmes-Chambertin,
Domaine Claude Dugat   From 2022 18.5
Medium-full colour. Firm, profound nose. Still closed. Good grip. Medium-full body. Oaky. Ripe, concentrated, and full of fruit. Complex, intense, and very fine.

Charmes-Chambertin,
Domaine Humbert Frères   From 2022 18.5
Fullish colour. Rich, full, concentrated, oaky nose. Plenty of wine here. Fullish body. Some tannin. Rich and meaty. Very good grip. This has a lot of depth. Long and vigorous. Very fine.

Charmes-Chambertin,
Domaine Olivier Jouan   From 2020 17.0
Medium-full colour. Slightly tight on the nose, but good fruit underneath. Medium to medium-full body. Somewhat closed but good grip. Good energy. Stylish. Finishes well.

Charmes-Chambertin,
Domaine Armand Rousseau   From 2018 15.0
Medium to medium-full colour. Some development. Pretty nose. Flowery and fruity. Fresh. But only medium-bodied. Decent fruit but no real depth and class. Tails off a bit at the end.

Charmes-Chambertin,
Domaine Christian Serafin   From 2019 16.0
Medium-full colour. Soft, spicy, smoky nose. Medium to medium-full body. Decent plump, fresh, fruity attack. Balanced and stylish. But a bit lightweight and forward.

Griotte-Chambertin,
Domaine Ponsot   From 2020 18.5
Medium-full colour. Somewhat tight on the nose still. Very good grip. Lacks a little sex appeal. Medium-full body. Very ripe on the palate. Nicely smooth. Very good tannins and very

good grip. Potentially velvety and very classy. Lovely long finish.

Latricières-Chambertin,
Domaine Drouhin-Laroze   From 2025 17.5
Very full colour. Rich, full, slightly spicy, closed-in nose. Similar on the palate. Very good grip. But it lacks a bit of richness. So fine rather than great. Needs time.

Latricières-Chambertin,
Domaine Duroché   From 2018 14.0
Medium-full colour. Good full, meaty nose. Still youthful. Medium body. Ripe. But merely pretty. Lacks intensity and grip.

Latricières-Chambertin,
Maison Camille Giroud   From 2018 15.0
Medium-full colour. Good nose. Accessible, fragrant, and quite intense and balanced. On the palate I find this a little superficial. It lacks zip and concentration. Good at best.

Latricières-Chambertin,
Domaine Leroy   From 2021 18.0
A remarkably different wine from their Clos de la Roche and the Combottes. Rich, juicy, succulent, fat, and spicy. Fullish body. Very good grip. Fine plus.

Latricières-Chambertin,
Domaine Chantal Rémy   From 2018 15.0
Medium colour. Some development. Soft nose. Slightly pinched. No real concentration or succulence. Medium weight. Lacks depth and real flair. Good at best.

Latricières-Chambertin,
Domaine Rossignol-Trapet   From 2020 18.0
Medium-full colour. Some development. Rich, fat, quite concentrated nose. Good grip and good depth. Medium-full body. Composed, harmonious, and classy. Fine plus.

Latricières-Chambertin,
Domaine Trapet Père et Fils   From 2023 18.5
Rather more closed than their Chapelle. A bigger wine with more backbone. Fine grip though. Lovely long finish. Even better.

Mazis-Chambertin,

Maison Bernstein   From 2020   15.0

Medium-full colour. Rich, full, quite substantial nose. Good grip. Still youthful. But somewhat four-square and astringent. Plenty of fruit but lacks a bit of grace.

Mazis-Chambertin,

Domaine Faiveley   From 2020   16.0

Medium to medium-full colour. Some development. A suggestion of reduction on the nose. Underneath there is class if without a lot of power or oak. Medium-full body. A little dry at the end. Ripe, accessible, and seductive though. At least very good.

Mazis-Chambertin,

Domaine Maume   From 2020   17.5

Medium-full colour. Good substance. Good grip. A touch of oak. Medium to medium-full body. Classy fruit. Fresh and juicy. Fragrant and stylish. Reasonably forward. Fine.

Mazoyères-Chambertin,

Domaine de la Vougeraie   From 2020   17.5

Medium to medium-full colour. Ample, rich, gently oaky nose. Good depth and style. Medium-full body. Accessible, rich, ripe, and abundant. Good grip. Very seductive. Fine.

Chambertin, Clos de Bèze,

Domaine Bruno Clair   From 2023   19.0

Full body. Closed. Very concentrated. Excellent grip. Lots of vigour and depth. Really disitinguished. Very fine plus.

Chambertin, Clos de Bèze,

Domaine Drouhin-Laroze   From 2022   19.0

Medium-full colour. Lovely ripe, rich, fragrant fruit on the nose. Quite oaky. Fullish body. Lush, aromatic, and succulent. Very good acidity. Lots of intensity and grip. A fine future ahead of it.

Chambertin, Clos de Bèze,

Domaine Louis Jadot   From 2022   18.5

Medium to medium-full colour. Youthful nose. Just a little rigid at present. But rich and concentrated. Medium-full body. Very ripe, lush fruit. A very lovely wine with an impressive follow-through.

Chambertin, Clos de Bèze,

Domaine Armand Rousseau   From 2022   19.5

Medium-full colour. Slightly closed but good vigour and concentration on the nose. This is full-bodied and very profound, with very fine grip and quite beautiful fruit. Very long on the palate. Quite splendid.

Chambertin, Domaine

du Clos Frantin (Albert Bichot)   From 2022   17.5

Medium to medium-full colour. This has concentration and dimension on the nose. Quite spicy. Fullish body. Lush and harmonious. But a slight lack of intensity. Fine though.

Chambertin,

Maison Camille Giroud   From 2022   19.0

Medium to medium-full colour. Closed-in on the nose. But a profound wine here. Lots of depth. Lots of concentration. And very good grip. Fullish body. Excellent fruit. Very, very classy indeed. Balanced and succulent and almost sweet. Very lovely.

Chambertin, Domaine

Heritiers Louis Latour   From 2020   17.5

Medium colour. Somewhat earthy nose. Good fresh, balanced fruit, but no real Chambertin concentration. Fullish body. Still hidden. On the palate we have lots of dimension and intensity, good grip, and quite an aggressive follow-through.

Chambertin, Domaine Leroy   From 2023   19.5

Very closed-in but very profound and promising. Rich, meaty in the best sense. Full-bodied. Abundant. Lots of wine here. Very, very ripe; but with excellent grip. Long and very lovely indeed. Excellent.

Chambertin,

Domaine Rossignol-Trapet   From 2022   17.5

Medium colour. Smoky-bonfirey nose. A bit rustic on the palate. Full body. Closed and youthful. Ample and vigorous. Very good grip and intensity. Understated. Fine.

Chambertin,
Domaine Armand Rousseau   From 2025 20.0
This is very lovely indeed. Lots of depth and
energy. Excellent fruit. A really profound, vigorous, and classy wine. Beautiful!

Chambertin,
Domaine Trapet Père et Fils   From 2020 17.5
Medium to medium-full colour. Closed-in
nose. Quite high-toned though. No over-oaking. Medium-full body. Attractive fruit. But not
the grip and intensity of the very best. Classy
and positive though. Fine.

SAVIGNY-LÈS-BEAUNE,
PREMIER CRU, 2008

Over the last couple of decades I have written
numerous articles on "Burgundy You Can
Afford" or some similar title. It doesn't appear
to have made a great deal of difference. Volnay
premier cru at twice or more seems easier to sell;
Chambolle-Musigny *premier cru* at four or five
times even more sought after. Nevertheless, I
have persevered and extolled the virtues of the
good addresses in the Côte Chalonnaise, in
Santenay, Auxey and Monthelie, and, of course,
in Savigny-Lès-Beaune. Here in 2008 we have a
classic vintage, one where the wines have good
underlying grip, ripe, clean fruit, and plenty of
promise for the future. And they are inexpensive. Don't pass them up!

TASTING NOTES

The following wines were sampled in Savigny,
chez the Domaine Chandon de Briailles, in
May 2011. My thanks to the de Nicolay family for playing host and to all the growers who
attended with their samples.

Champ-Chevry,
Domaine Tollot-Beaut   From 2014 15.0
Good colour. Round, ripe, fresh nose. Medium
body. Attractive fruit. Just a little tannin. Finishes positively. Good.

Clous, Domaine Chenu   From 2014 14.5
Medium to medium-full colour. Not a lot of
concentration on the nose. Light to medium
body. Quite fresh. Good follow-through, and it
finishes better than it starts. Quite good plus.

Dominodes,
Domaine Bruno Clair   From 2015 15.5
Fullish colour. The nose is a bit unforthcoming
at first. Meaty on the attack. Some tannin. Not
exactly rich. But medium-full-bodied and with
good grip. There is depth here. Good plus.

Dominodes,
Domaine Chanson   From 2014 15.5
Medium to medium-full colour. Aromatic nose.
Medium weight. Good ripe fruit. Fresh and
attractive. Long and succulent. Good finish.
Good plus.

Dominodes,
Domaine Louis Jadot   From 2016 17.0
Medium-full colour. Rich, succulent nose.
Plenty of depth here. Fullish body. Good tannins. Very good grip. This has style, dimension,
and the capacity to last in bottle. Very good
indeed.

Dominodes, Domaine
Jean-Marc et Hugues Pavelot   From 2016 16.5
Good colour. Quite a firm nose. Some tannin.
Fullish body. Ripe. Good energy. Quite struc-
tured. Very good grip. A keeper. Very good plus.

Fourneaux, Domaine
Chandon de Briailles   Drink soon 12.5
Lightish, almost orange colour. Rather weak
and attenuated on the nose. Light on the palate. A little sweet. Better on the palate than
on the nose but essentially too feeble a wine.
Disappointing.

Fourneaux,
Domaine Simon Bize   From 2014 14.5
Medium colour. Quite forward on the nose.
But fresh. Medium weight. No great depth or
dimension but crisp and fruity and attractive.
Even elegant. Quite good plus.

Guettes,

Domaine Simon Bize   From 2016   17.0

Medium-full colour. Quite a rich nose; still a little closed-in. Fullish body. Very good grip. Round, ample, succulent, and vigorous. Lots of depth here. Very good indeed.

Guettes, Domaine Doudet   From 2015   15.0

Medium-full colour. Firm, rich, concentrated nose. Very good fruit. Medium-full body. What it lacks is but a freshness and grip. There is a touch of astringency on the palate. The follow-through is better, but the wine lacks a little succulence. Merely good.

Guettes, Domaine Louis Jadot   From 2014   14.0

Medium colour. Fresh, fruity, forward nose. Medium body. A little weak on the attack. Better on the finish but only quite good. Not enough personality. Forward.

Gravins, Domaine

Jean-Michel Giboulot   From 2014   15.5

Light-medium colour. Ripe nose. Quite succulent. Good grip. Medium body. Good energy. Good style. Round and even rich. Finishes well. Good plus.

Haut Jarrons, Domaine Chenu   Drink soon   13.0

Medium colour. Nothing much on the nose. A bit simple on the palate. Only fair.

Lavières,

Domaine Camus-Brochon   From 2016   16.5

Medium-full colour. Rich, ripe, quite profound nose. Good backbone. Fullish body. Good grip. Good energy and depth. The finish is rich and succulent, long and very stylish. Very good plus.

Lavières, Domaine Chenu   From 2014   14.0

Medium colour. Fresh, fruity, forward nose. Medium body. Decent grip. But not a great deal of personality or succulence. Quite good.

Lavières,

Domaine Jean-Jacques Girard   From 2016   16.5

Medium to medium-full colour. Good ripe nose. Good depth here. Fullish body. Very good fruit. Good tannins. Ripe and succulent. Most attractive. Fragrant and full of character and class. Very good plus.

Marconnets,

Domaine Simon Bize   From 2017   17.0

Full colour. Full, rich, backward nose. Plenty of depth here. Full body. Ripe and rich and well-balanced. Lots of dimension. This is a wine of real concentration and high-quality. Very good indeed.

Narbantons,

Domaine Camus-Brochon   From 2017   17.0

Full colour. Very good substance and depth here. Quite backward. But full and rich. Full-bodied. Very good tannins. Lots of depth and concentration. Very good grip. Very good indeed.

Peuillets,

Maison Albert Bichot   From 2015   15.5

Good colour. Ample, plump, fullish nose. Good style and depth. Medium-full body. Ripe on the palate if without a great deal of energy or vigour. But good fresh fruit. Good plus.

Peuillets,

Domaine Michel Ecard   From 2018   17.0

Very good colour. Full, backward nose. Some tannin here. Full-bodied. Rich. Concentrated. Very good energy and depth. Lots of dimension and lots of potential. Very good indeed. Even classy.

Peuillets,

Domaine Lucien Jacob   From 2014   15.0

Medium to medium-full colour. Not a lot of energy on the nose. Medium weight. Attractive and fruity on the palate. Fresh, if with a slight lack of dimension. Yet the finish is positive. Good.

Peuillets,

Domaine Jean-Jacques Girard   From 2014   14.5

Medium to medium-full colour. Quite a spicy nose. Pretty without being serious. Quite forward. Medium body. Lacks a bit of drive. Quite good plus.

Serpentières,
Domaine Simon Bize   From 2014 15.0
Medium-full colour. Pleasant fruity nose without a lot of weight behind it. Similar on the palate. Quite fresh, and positive at the end. Good but forward.

Serpentières,
Domaine Michel Ecard   From 2016 17.0
Good colour. Plump, attractive, fruity nose. Fullish, quite rich, balanced, and stylish. Plenty of wine here. Very good indeed.

Serpentières, Domaine
Jean-Michel Giboulot   Drink soon 13.0
Medium to medium-full colour. Ripe nose. But light, without a lot of energy. Pretty but a bit attenuated. Short. Only fair.

Serpentières,
Domaine Jean-Jacques Girard   From 2015 15.5
Medium colour. Soft nose. Not much energy here, it seems. Better on the palate. Medium to medium-full colour. Good grip. Ripe. No lack of depth or personality. Finishes well. Even elegant. Good plus.

Serpentières,
Domaine Pierre Guillemot   From 2016 16.5
Good colour. Ample, ripe nose. Fresh on the palate. Rich. Good grip. Very good vigour. Medium-full body. Long and stylish. Very good plus.

Talmettes,
Domaine Simon Bize   From 2016 16.0
Medium-full colour. Round, ripe, succulent nose. Medium to medium-full weight. Good grip. Attractive fresh fruit. Good positive follow-through. Fragrant and elegant. Very good.

Vergelesses,
Domaine Simon Bize   From 2016 16.5
Medium-full colour. Ample, ripe, attractive nose. Medium to medium-full body. Fresh. Stylish. Ripe. Good vigour and a good follow-through. Very good plus.

Vergelesses,
Domaine Dubreuil-Fontaine   From 2016 15.5
Good colour. Still a little hidden on the nose. Medium-full body. Ripe and succulent. Slightly adolescent, and currently it seems to lack a little class. But good energy and the fruit is attractive. Good plus.

Vergelesses,
Domaine Lucien Jacob   From 2016 15.5
Good colour. Youthful nose. Fresh, ripe, still unformed. Medium to medium-full body. Good grip. Good energy. Finishes well. This is at least good plus. May turn out even better.

As you will see, I gave equal highest points to the Guettes and the Marconnets by Patrick Bize, the Narbantons by Camus-Brochon, and the Peuillets and the Serpentières by Michel Ecard. The group as a whole—a dozen or more of the local growers—additionally singled out Jadot's Dominodes and Bichot's Peuillets.

2008 BURGUNDY

There are vintages which somehow never manage to live up to early expectations. Happily there have been few of these in recent memory. What has happened, quite frequently, is the reverse: years where if one extrapolated from

⇢ *Rating for the Vintage* ⇠	
Red	17.0
White	17.5

the weather conditions or the growers' initial pessimistic fears one would tend to expect the worst, but in fact after the wines had settled down in cask and finished their malos, and even more after they had had a few months to repose after bottling, one said with no lack of surprise: "Well, these are not bad at all."

Such is 2008. As far down the line as Monday, September 15, the day the harvest began some two weeks late in the Beaujolais, the auguries were unpromising. Burgundy seemed to be doomed. Then the miracle occurred: the wind changed to the north, and the fruit was able to concentrate. It was warm and sunny,

| → Size of the Crop ← | | | |
| (In hectolitres) | | | |
	RED	WHITE	TOTAL
Grands crus	11,529	3,784	15,313
Village and			
premiers crus	160,492	64,591	225,083
TOTAL	172,021	68,375	240,396

with cool nights to lessen the threat of rot. The sugars rose. The acidities fell, but not as proportionately fast. Absolutely what any doctor would have ordered! But there was nevertheless no shortage of substandard fruit which would have to be cut out. Given an already small crop and looming world depression, how conscientious could the *vignerons* afford to be? Three years on—with the wines having had a year or more in bottle—we have the answer, and it is positive. The 2008 is a small vintage but it is better than 2007, and in both colours. The red wines have plenty of character and harmony, and the best have depth and, indeed, richness. It should not be neglected.

Weather Conditions

Up to the middle of June, when the moon was full on June 18, the season had been cool, wet, and miserable. The flowering was late and drawn out, promising a late and uneven harvest. The next six weeks happily saw marked improvement: plenty of sun, not too much rain—and what there was, was sporadic and localised—though it was warm rather than hot. Temperatures rarely exceeded 30°C. Then the weather deteriorated. There was more rain and less sun right through to mid-September. A bleak summer indeed! Overall, there was

less precipitation on the Côte de Nuits than the Côte de Beaune, and less still in the Côte Chalonnaise. Chablis seems to have enjoyed the mildest weather of all. But inevitably, the incidence of mildew, oidium, and botrytis became ever more serious as the weeks progressed. At various times from the beginning of May on, hail damaged the vineyards of Marsannay, Volnay and Meursault, Chassagne, and parts of the southern Mâconnais and northern Beaujolais.

At the last minute, however, more benign conditions returned and continued well into October. The harvest kicked off in the Beaujolais, as I have said, on September 15. A week or more later, the growers began to attack the Mâconnais and to some extent the Côte de Beaune. But many in the Côte d'Or held off until Monday, September 29, or even, in the Côte de Nuits, into October, and were able to profit from natural sugar levels of 13° and higher. It was the latest harvest for some years, requiring 110 or more, not 100, days from flowering to fruition. And, yes, a severe *tri* was essential, but in fact there was less to cut out than there had been twelve months previously.

The 2008s were not easy wines to taste out of cask in the autumn of 2009. There was, as you might expect, a lot of malic acidity, and the malo-lactic fermentations had been slow to complete. Even in October, twelve months on, many wines had not yet finished their malos. Others, not yet racked, were still full of gas. It felt like one was sampling in July, not in the middle of the fall. On the plus side, however, the red wines had good healthy colours, the tannins were unexpectedly sophisticated, and there was good *terroir* definition. They had more substance than 2007, better tannins and grip than 2006, and very good fruit, especially for those who like their wines to have a bit of bite. The highish acidities—but as Michel Gros pointed out: after the malos had finished, he found his wines only a very little higher in acid than normal—will ensure that the wines will keep well. The Côte de Nuits has produced better wine than the Côte de Beaune, but, except in Beaune itself, to a less marked degree than

2006 and 2007. The 2008 is also one of the best of recent vintages in the Côte Chalonnaise.

The Market

Essentially, the 2008s reached the market at a period of price stability. By and large, Burgundy prices seem to rise like a staircase: a jump when there is a vintage much in demand—2005, 2009—and then a flattening out until the next stellar year.

Some in Burgundy had opted for a small, say 5 percent, increase in 2007. These were persuaded to come down again. With one or two others, it was the reverse. And there is always today the odd estate which is "repositioning" itself. But for most, the 2008s were quoted at the same levels as 2005, 2006, and 2007. It would be different in twelve months' time. And by the time the 2008s were put on the market, the growers already knew they had this big one in the bag.

I feared at the time that the response would be cool, but the 2008s sold better than I had expected. And not just to merchants who wished to register a keenness for the 2009s but further down the pipeline. This was despite the fact that in Britain the wines were shown to the trade, the press and the public, as always, in the first weeks of January 2010, and being, as I have said three months younger than usual, did not show well. "Too acid," said some of the inexperienced, those who never venture into the region itself.

The Wines Three Years On

"Liquorice," said Aubert de Villaine, when we tasted the 2008 Domaine de la Romanée-Conti wines together in November 2010. What I like about the best 2008 reds is their freshness, the frequency of sophisticated tannins, and the amount of intensity of fruit in the best. Three years on, it is clear, such are the high standards of winemaking and *élevage* today, that there is a lot of "best," particularly in Nuits-Saint-Georges, Vosne-Romanée, and Chambolle-Musigny.

Elsewhere, especially in the Côte de Beaune, the wines lack a certain amount of energy and intensity. They are fruity and easy to drink, with no excessive acidity, but also with less tannic structure than I had expected (though there are some which are a little over-extracted). Here there is a lack of backbone. The wines have a class and harmony which is admirable, but not the size and energy. There were also, at our tasting three years on, quite a number of wines which had marked amounts of reduction. This, I would suggest, is a result of the very late malos. This makes the red wine vintage overall very good but not better.

But what I would say finally—and this is not to denigrate the 2009s—is that I am convinced that there are some—not many but some—2008s which are every bit as good, in their very different ways, as the same wines produced a year later. And I don't think I am alone in holding this view.

The Best Wines
20/20

Richebourg, Domaine A. F. Gros

La Romanée-Conti, Domaine de la
    Romanée-Conti

Musigny, Domaine J. Frédéric Mugnier

Musigny, Domaine Comte Georges de Vogüé

Chambertin, Domaine Armand Rousseau

19.5

La Tâche, Domaine de la Romanée-Conti

Musigny, Domaine de la Vougeraie

Bonnes-Mares, Domaine Georges Roumier

19.0

Vosne-Romanée, Les Brulées, Domaine
    Eugenie

Vosne-Romanée, Les Brulées, Domaine
    Michel Gros

Vosne-Romanée, Cros Parentoux, Domaine
    Emmanuel Rouget

Vosne-Romanée, Malconsorts, Domaine
    Sylvain Cathiard

Chambolle-Musigny, Les Amoureuses,
    Domaine Georges Roumier

Gevrey-Chambertin, Clos-Saint-Jacques,
    Domaine Jadot

Clos de Vougeot, "Maupertuis," Domaine
    Anne Gros

Clos de Vougeot, Domaine Remoissenet

Romanée-Saint-Vivant, Domaine
    Arnoux-Lachaux

Richebourg, Domaine du Clos Frantin

Richebourg, Domaine Gros Frère et Soeur

Bonnes-Mares, Domaine Bruno Clair

Clos de la Roche, Vieilles Vignes, Domaine
    Ponsot

Chambertin, Clos de Bèze, Domaine Bruno
    Clair

Chambertin, Clos de Bèze, Domaine Faiveley

Chambertin, Clos de Bèze, Maison
    Perrot-Minot

Chambertin, Clos de Bèze, Domaine Armand
    Rousseau

Chambertin, Maison Henri Boillot

Chambertin, Domaine Louis Rémy

Chambertin, Maison Roche de Bellene

TASTING NOTES

The notes that follow are, as usual, an assembly
of, firstly, the Domaine Familiaux presenta-
tion in March 2011 in Paris; secondly, various
tastings I attended on my annual U.S. visit in
April; and thirdly, the group's three-day tasting
at the end of August. Some wines were seen
more than once, so what you read here is a composite note.

Red Wines

CÔTE CHALONNAISE

Bouzeron, La Fortune,
Domaine A et P de Villaine   From 2014   14.0
Mineral, stylish, and ripe and balanced. Very
good for what it is.

Bouzeron, La Digoine,
Domaine A et P de Villaine   From 2015   15.0
This is the *cuvée* from the older vines. Much
more concentrated. Even rich. Medium body.
Lovely balance. Fine for what it is.

Mercurey, Clos Marcilly,
Domaine Michel Briday   From 2016   15.5
Medium to medium-full colour. Soft, ripe, stylish, most agreeable nose. Nice and plump. Balanced and charming. Very good for what it is.

Mercurey, Clos de Myglands,
Domaine Faiveley   From 2015   15.0
Soft, ripe, and stylish, but only light to medium
body.

CÔTE DE BEAUNE

Chorey-Lès-Beaune,
Pièce de la Chapitre,
Domaine Tollot-Beaut   From 2014   14.0
Medium weight. Fresh and juicy. Lovely fruit.
Good grip. Plenty of charm and plenty of
interest.

Aloxe-Corton,
Clos des Marechaudes,
Domaine du Pavillon   From 2015   13.5
Medium body. Fresh and fruity. Reasonable
depth and character but lacks a bit of fat, and
therefore generosity. Finishes somewhat lean.

Pernand-Vergelesses,
Les Vergelesses,
Domaine Chandon de Briailles   From 2016   15.5
On the light side, but fresh and very agreeably
fruity. Good positive finish. Elegant.

Savigny-Lès-Beaune, Les Guettes,
Domaine Simon Bize   From 2018   16.5
Good colour. Rich and meaty but ripe and styl-
ish. Intense and balanced. Medium-full body.
Fine for a Savigny.

Savigny-Lès-Beaune, Les Serpentières,
Domaine Simon Bize   From 2017   16.0
Medium bodied. Fresh. Ripe. Lovely fruit. Lots
of energy. Positive and surprisingly elegant.
Very good plus.

**Beaune, Clos du
Dessus de Marconnets,
Château de la Tour**   From 2016 14.5

Village *appellation contrôlée*. Good colour. Ripe and fat and round and elegant. Good tannins. Medium-full body. Quite elegant. Quite good plus.

**Beaune, *Premier Cru*,
Cuvée Tante Berthe, Domaine
du Château de Chorey**   From 2016 14.0

This is for oak eaters, and is not for me. I find the oak far too dominating. Ripe and rich and medium-full bodied, but not concentrated enough to balance the oak.

**Beaune, Boucherottes,
Domaine A. F. Gros**   From 2015 15.5

Medium to medium-full colour. Some development. Round and ripe but a bit flat on the nose. Medium to medium-full body. Better on the palate. Balanced, stylish, and positive.

**Beaune, Bressandes,
Domaine Chanson**   From 2015 15.0

Medium colour. A touch green but some substance on the nose. Quite an attractive medium-bodied wine. Fresh and fruity and positive at the end.

**Beaune, Bressandes,
Domaine des Croix**   From 2015 14.5

Medium to medium-full colour. Fresh and fruity on the nose. Light to medium body. Fruity but there is astringency lurking underneath. Stylish though.

**Beaune, Clos des Fèves,
Domaine Chanson**   From 2015 14.5

Medium to medium-full colour. Some development. A bit four-square and clumsy on the nose. Medium-full body. Chunky and a bit astringent on the attack, but decent fruit underneath.

**Beaune, Clos des Mouches,
Domaine Chanson**   From 2014 14.5

Medium to medium-full colour. Good depth on the nose. Quite rich. Ripe, almost sweet attack. Medium to medium-full body. I find the fruit a bit spurious. The wine lacks a bit of style.

**Beaune, Clos des Mouches,
Domaine Joseph Drouhin**   From 2016 16.0

Medium-full colour. The nose is still a little closed. Medium-full body. Good tannins. Balanced and fresh. Lacks a little real elegance, but quite rich. Quite meaty. Good finish. Very good.

**Beaune, Clos du Roi,
Domaine Henri Boillot**   From 2015 15.0

Medium colour. Soft, forward, fruity nose. A little reduced at the moment. Medium weight. A bit astringent. Decent fresh fruit though.

**Beaune, Clos du Roi,
Domaine Tollot-Beaut**   Drink soon 11.0

Light to medium colour. Somewhat skinny nose. Thin and weedy. No.

**Beaune, Clos des Ursules
(Vignes Franches),
Domaine Louis Jadot**   From 2015 15.0

Medium-full colour. Pretty but lightweight nose. Ripe. Medium-bodied. Quite elegant. Certainly balanced. But a little less to it than some.

**Beaune, Les Cras, Domaine
du Château de Chorey**   From 2016 17.0

Good colour. Lots of depth here. Rich, slightly oaky. Meaty and succulent. Medium-full body. Lovely fruit. Finishes very well. Very good indeed.

**Beaune, Epenottes,
Domaine Jean-Marc Boillot**   From 2015 15.0

Medium-full colour. Fresh, soft, plump nose. Good fruit-driven style. Medium-full body. Good tannins. Ripe acidity. Long and elegant and very good on the attack, but slightly thin as it evolved.

**Beaune, Grèves,
Domaine de Bellene**   From 2014 14.5

Medium-full colour. Slightly hard on the nose. Medium body. This is a little astringent at present, but the underlying fruit isn't too bad.

**Beaune, Grèves,
Vigne de l'Enfant Jesus,
Domaine Bouchard Père et Fils**   From 2018 16.5

Medium-full colour. Ripe, round, fresh, seductive nose, with a touch of lightly toasted oak underneath. Medium-full body. Good class and intensity. Long on the palate. Very good plus.

Beaune, Grèves,
Domaine Chanson From 2014 15.0
Medium colour. Soft, fruity, forward nose. Decent fruit on the palate. Even reasonable balance. But not a great deal of class.

Beaune, Grèves,
Domaine des Croix From 2016 15.5
Good colour. A bit hidden but good depth on the nose. Perhaps a bit over-extracted but fresh and balanced. A meaty wine. Just lacks a bit of richness.

Beaune, Grèves,
Domaine Michel Lafarge From 2014 14.0
Light, forward nose. More earthy than fruity on the nose. A bit over-extracted. Medium body. Slightly astringent. Slightly lean too. Only quite good.

Beaune, Grèves,
Domaine de Montille From 2017 17.0
Medium-full colour. Nice and ripe. Even meaty. Good tannins and good grip. Medium to medium-full body. Plenty of succulence here. Long and very good indeed.

Beaune, Grèves,
Domaine Remoissenet From 2017 17.0
Good colour. Rich, fat, oaky, voluptuous nose. Fullish body. Concentrated. Elegant. Plenty of wine here. Finishes very well. One of the best of the 2008 Beaunes.

Beaune, Grèves,
Domaine Tollot-Beaut From 2016 16.0
Medium-full body. Ripe, quite fat. Good oaky base. Nice and rich and accessible. Ample. Very good finish. Very good.

Beaune, Marconnets,
Domaine Remoissenet From 2016 16.0
Good colour. Firm, closed, rich nose. Fullish body. Good tannins. Plenty of grip. A little ungainly now but this has a future.

Beaune, Montée Rouge,
Domaine de Bellene From 2015 15.5
Medium colour. Ripe, quite rich nose. Good depth. Medium to medium-full body. Spicy, balanced, and with a good grip. Attractive finish.

Beaune, Pertuisots,
Domaine Jean-Yves Devevey From 2014 14.0
Medium-full colour. Good fruit on the nose. But a touch of astringency as it developed on the palate. Medium body. Slightly ungainly.

Beaune, Pertuisots,
Domaine des Croix From 2015 15.0
Medium to medium-full colour. Quite closed on the nose. Medium to medium-full body. Good grip. Elegant and decent fruit. Good plus.

Beaune, Teurons,
Domaine Bouchard Père et Fils From 2014 13.0
Medium colour. Some development. Somewhat reduced, sweaty nose. Medium body. Rather spuriously sweet. Ungainly and raw at the end.

Beaune, Teurons,
Domaine Rossignol-Trapet Drink soon 11.0
Medium to medium-full colour. A little thin and vegetal on the nose. Similarly lean on the palate. No.

Volnay, Vendanges Selectionées,
Domaine Michel Lafarge From 2018 16.0
Medium weight. Elegant. Lovely balance and very good fruit. Lovely long finish. The essence of Volnay.

Volnay, Les Caillerets,
Domaine Henri Boillot From 2016 16.0
Medium-full colour. Pleasant fruity nose. No great depth or personality but a touch of reduction. Medium to medium-full body. Good grip and attractive fresh fruit on the palate. A little astringent at the end but very good.

Volnay, Les Caillerets,
Domaine Louis Boillot From 2014 13.0
Medium-full colour. Lots of ripe but rather artificial raspberry fruit all the way through this wine. It seems rather concocted.

Volnay, Les Caillerets,

Domaine de la Pousse d'Or   From 2016 17.0

Medium-full colour. A little reduction on the nose. At first a bit inflexible. Medium-full body. On the palate there is no lack of concentration and richness. And class too as it developed.

Volnay, Caillerets des 60 Ouvrées,

Domaine de la Pousse d'Or   From 2018 18.0

Medium-full colour. Classic, concentrated Volnay nose. Good weight and very good grip. Lovely concentrated fruit. Fullish, ripe, rich, and energetic. Lots of vigour and lots of class. Fine plus.

Volnay, Carelle Sous la Chapelle,

Domaine Jean-Marc Boillot   From 2014 13.5

Medium-full colour. Ripe if somewhat clumsy on the nose. Medium body. A hint of astringency and leanness on the palate. One-dimensional.

Volnay, Les Champans,

Domaine Marquis d'Angerville   From 2016 17.5

Medium to medium-full colour. High-toned but classy, balanced nose. Fullish body. Ripe and generous. Long and intense. Very Volnay. Lovely finish.

Volnay, Les Champans,

Domaine des Comtes Lafon   From 2018 17.5

Medium-full colour. Plenty of depth here. Still closed. Rich complex nose. Splendid concentration of fruit. Fullish body. Lots of energy and class. Lots of dimension. Fine.

Volnay, Les Champans,

Domaine de Montille   From 2018 16.5

Round, ripe, and elegant. Medium body. Full of fruit. Long on the palate. Very good plus.

Volnay, Le Chevret,

Domaine Henri Boillot   From 2016 16.5

Medium-full colour. Rich, ripe, concentrated, and classy on the nose. Fullish body. Good tannins. And grip. Still fresh and youthful. Complex, long, and classy.

Volnay, Clos d'Audignac,

Domaine de la Pousse d'Or   From 2015 16.0

Medium-full colour. Round, ripe, rich, and generous on the nose. Summer pudding. Most attractive and easy to enjoy. Medium-full body. Balanced. Fresh. Ripe and seductive. Positive at the end. Very good.

Volnay, Clos de la Bousse d'Or,

Domaine de la Pousse d'Or   From 2018 18.0

Medium-full colour. Full, closed, concentrated, very, very classy fruit. This is most impressive. Full body. Very ripe tannins. Excellent grip. Really concentrated and multidimensional.

Volnay, Clos de la Cave des Ducs,

Maison Benjamin Leroux   From 2016 15.0

Medium-full colour. Reduced nose. Difficult to taste. Slight touch of CO_2. Underneath the wine is fullish. Meaty, ripe, and rich. Good grip. Doesn't sing today but could be good.

Volnay, Clos du Château des Ducs,

Domaine Michel Lafarge   From 2014 14.0

Medium colour. Slightly closed-in on the nose. Somewhat four-square on the palate. Good depth though. But a touch astringent and lean on the palate. It lacks sex appeal.

Volnay, Clos des Chênes,

Domaine Bouchard Père et Fils   From 2016 14.0

Medium-full colour. Some development. Quite pronounced reduction on the nose. Rather astringent on the palate as a result. Medium to medium-full body. Bitter on the finish. Difficult to taste.

Volnay, Clos des Chênes,

Domaine Antonin Guyon   From 2016 15.5

Medium-full colour. This is a bit closed-in on the nose, and seems to lack a little personality. Medium-full body. Ripe. Quite rich. Balanced and positive at the end nevertheless.

Volnay, Clos des Chênes,

Domaine Michel Lafarge   From 2020 18.5

Real depth and class here. This is fullish-bodied. Rich, concentrated, and very elegant. Lovely.

Volnay, Clos des Chênes,

Domaine des Comtes Lafon   From 2016 15.5

Medium colour. Some development. Rich, ripe, concentrated, sturdy nose. Medium-full body.

Good structure and grip. Slightly hard at present. Decent fruit and acidity. Good depth and a positive finish.

Volnay, Clos des Ducs, Domaine du Marquis d'Angerville   From 2019 18.5
Fullish body. Rich, concentrated, and profound. Very harmonious. Really intense at the end. Very lovely.

Volnay, Les Fremiets, Domaine du Marquis d'Angerville   From 2017 17.0
Soft, elegant, medium-bodied. Intense and classy. Very pure fruit. Very long.

Volnay, Les Fremiets, Domaine Henri Boillot   From 2016 15.5
Medium to medium-full colour. Soft, round, not rich but ripe and balanced and stylish on the nose. Medium to medium-full body. Good tannins. Ripe, balanced fruit. Elegant and positive. This has good length, if not real intensity.

Volnay, Les Fremiets, Domaine Francois Parent   From 2016 16.5
Medium-full colour. Good depth, class, and maturity here on the nose. Medium-full body. Quite concentrated. Ripe tannins. Good structure and grip. Long and classy.

Volnay, Les Mitans, Domaine Michel Lafarge   From 2014 14.5
Medium-full colour. A little rigid and unripe at first on the nose. More flexible as it developed. Medium body. Pretty fruit. Ripe and forward, but a lack of depth and concentration.

Volnay, Les Mitans, Domaine de Montille   From 2014 14.0
Medium colour. Some development. Reduced smells on the nose. The stems evident. Somewhat ungainly and astringent on the palate. Medium body. Slightly short. But the fruit is pretty.

Volnay, Les Santenots du Milieu, Domaine des Comtes Lafon   From 2019 18.5
Good colour. Lovely nose. Fresh, vigorous, and very elegant. The fruit is poised and classy.

Medium-full body. Harmonious. Sophisticated tannins. Lovely.

Volnay, Les Taillepieds, Domaine du Marquis d'Angerville   From 2019 18.0
This is quite a substantial wine. Good depth. Lovely classy fruit. Lots of energy. Medium-full body. Fine plus.

Volnay, Les Taillepieds, Domaine Francois Buffet   From 2016 17.5
Medium to medium-full colour. Lightish, high-toned, fresh, fruity nose. Whole clusters? Ripe underneath. Medium-full body. Ripe and rich and intense. Good vigour and plenty of class. Lovely finish.

Volnay, Les Taillepieds, Domaine de Montille   From 2016 17.0
Medium to medium-full colour. A little tight on the nose. Slightly astringent too from the whole-cluster vinification. Softer and more elegant after aeration. Medium to medium-full body. Plenty of ripe fruit. Good grip. Long on the palate. Very good indeed.

Pommard, Clos des Epenots, Domaine du Comte Armand   From 2017 17.0
Medium-full colour. Sturdy, backward, fullish, and good fruit on the nose. Fullish body. Somewhat four-square at present. But rich underneath. Good grip. Plenty of vigour. Very good indeed.

Pommard, Clos des Ursulines, Domaine du Pavillon   From 2016 15.0
A monopoly, but village *appellation contrôlée*. Lots of finesse, and not a bit austere. Good volume. Ripe tannins. No hard edges. Generous and positive. Very good for what it is.

Pommard, Les Epenots, Domaine Francois Parent   From 2017 17.5
Medium-full colour. Some development. Vigorous, rich, and seductive on the nose. Full body. Rich. Meaty. Concentrated. Very good tannins. Very lovely fruit. Intense and classy. Long. Fine.

Pommard, Les Fremiers,
Domaine Louis Boillot   From 2016 16.0
Medium colour. Some development. Ripe, ample, accessible nose. Civilised. Medium-full body. Ripe. Lots of fruit. Fresh and attractive with a nice stylish finish.

Pommard, Les Grands Epenots,
Domaine Michel Gaunoux   From 2018 17.5
Quite full body. Crisp and fresh and elegant. Lovely fruit. Very good follow-through. Fine.

Pommard, Les Jarollières,
Domaine Jean-Marc Boillot   From 2014 12.0
Medium-full colour. Somewhat hard, pinched, and vegetal on the nose. Lacks charm as well as ripeness. Astringent and attenuated on the palate. No.

Pommard, Les Jarollières,
Domaine de la Pousse d'Or   From 2016 15.5
Medium-full colour. Not the greatest of class on the nose. Slightly thin fruit at the end. Better on the palate. Fresh. Medium-full body. Ample. Good grip. Still young. Slightly ungainly but good plus.

Pommard, Les Pezerolles,
Domaine Bouchard Père et Fils From 2017 16.5
Medium colour. Full nose. Rich, sturdy, and a little four-square. Fullish body. Good class. Good intensity. A bit burly but that is Pezerolles. Balanced and positive.

Pommard, Les Pezerolles,
Domaine A. F. Gros   From 2015 16.0
Medium to medium-full colour. Rich, ripe, fullish nose. Good tannins here. Balanced, accessible, attractive. But enough weight here?

Pommard, Les Pezerolles,
Domaine de Montille   From 2018 15.5
Medium to medium-full body. Good fruit. Ripe and stylish, if not as elegant or complex as their Volnay, Champans.

Pommard, Les Rugiens,
Domaine Henri Boillot   From 2016 13.5
Fullish colour. Backward, firm, yet rich and plentiful on the nose. Just needs time. But it didn't develop well in the glass. The finish became rather lean.

Pommard, Les Rugiens,
Domaine Bouchard
Père et Fils   From 2016 14.0
Medium colour. Fullish, backward, rich and intense, but somewhat ungainly. It lacks class. Good vigour though. May turn out better than this mark would suggest.

Pommard, Les Rugiens,
Domaine Francois Buffet   From 2016 13.5
Medium-full colour. Some development. Firm, spicy, meaty nose. Some stems here. Somewhat lean in the background. Medium to medium-full body. Rather thin and astringent. Lacks class.

Pommard, Les Rugiens,
Domaine Michel Gaunoux   From 2019 17.0
Fullish body. Some tannin. Rich and earthy. Succulent and with plenty of depth. A meaty wine. Very good indeed.

Pommard, Les Rugiens,
Domaine de Montille   From 2019 17.0
Fullish, tannic attack. Still a bit closed. Lovely fruit. Very good indeed.

Pommard, Les Rugiens,
Domaine du Pavillon   From 2018 17.5
Medium-full body. Fine, classy, and profound with lots of fruit and plenty of dimension. Lovely finish. Fine.

CÔTE DE NUITS

Marsannay, Les Longerois,
Domaine Bruno Clair   From 2015 15.5
Good colour. Delicious fruit. Fresh. Medium-bodied. Balanced. Unexpected personality and style.

Nuits-Saint-Georges,
Les Chailots, Domaine
Gilbert et Christine Felletig From 2016 16.5
A village wine under Poirets. Elegant, but only medium-bodied for a Nuits-Saints-Georges. But fragrant and stylish. No rude tannins.

Elegant, ample, balanced fruit. Very clean. Very good, long finish.

Nuits-Saint-Georges, Les Saints-Juliens, Domaine de Montille
From 2018 16.5

A village wine in midslope immediately to the north of the town. Good structure and depth. Fullish body. Ripe and meaty. Very good indeed for a village example.

Nuits-Saint-Georges, *Premier Cru*, Domaine Michel Gros
From 2018 16.0

From Aux Murgers and Aux Vignerondes. Medium-full colour. Full nose. Slightly chunky. Some tannin. Yet fresh and balanced and fruity underneath. Fullish body. Some tannin. Typical Nuits-Saint-Georges. Good grip and plenty of energy. Lacks a bit of real class—the tannins are a bit rude—but very good. The finish is long.

Nuits-Saint-Georges, Les Boudots, Domaine Grivot
From 2018 17.5

Good colour. Round, soft, very ripe nose. Medium-full body. Lots of energy. Very good grip. Classy. Fine.

Nuits-Saint-Georges, Les Cailles, Domaine Bouchard Père et Fils
From 2019 18.0

Full colour. Quite a severe nose. Yet there is depth here. Rich, fullish body. Succulent. Very good acidity. Lots of energy. Very classy fruit on the finish.

Nuits-Saint-Georges, Les Cailles, Domaine Robert Chevillon
From 2020 17.5

Medium-full colour. Rich, full, aggressive, chocolaty nose. Full body. Very good tannins. Almost sweet. Good grip. Needs time.

Nuits-Saint-Georges, Aux Chaignots, Domaine Dr. Georges Mugneret-Gibourg
From 2017 16.5

Fullish colour. Cool, classy, balanced, fragrant nose. Medium to medium-full body. Lacks a bit of grip and vigour, so no better than very good plus.

Nuits-Saint-Georges, Clos des Argillières, Domaine Michèle et Patrice Rion
From 2018 18.0

Full colour. Ample, rich, soft, and succulent on the nose. Fullish body. Oaky. Profound. Very good grip. This is very classy. Ample, energetic, and most impressive.

Nuits-Saint-Georges, Clos de la Maréchale, Domaine J. Frédéric Mugnier
From 2018 17.5

Medium-full body. Rich, ripe, concentrated, and intense. Really elegant for a Nuits-Saint-Georges.

Nuits-Saint-Georges, Clos des Porrets Saint-Georges, Domaine Gouges
From 2017 17.0

Quite soft on the nose. Lovely fruit and very good grip. But by no means a blockbuster. Medium body. Elegant.

Nuits-Saint-Georges, Clos-Saint-Marc, Domaine Michèle et Patrice Rion
From 2017 18.0

Medium-full colour. Balanced, classy, cool nose. Full, concentrated, energetic, and complex. Very fine style too. This is very lovely. Class all the way through.

Nuits-Saint-Georges, Les Cras, Domaine Lamarche
From 2018 18.0

Full colour. Rich, ample, oaky, succulent nose. Lots of style and balance and no lack of structure either. Full body. Very fine grip. Youthful but lots of class and lots of energy too.

Nuits-Saint-Georges, Les Cras, Domaine du Vicomte de Liger-Belair
From 2018 16.0

Fullish colour. Robust, ample, gamey, full-bodied nose. Very Nuits-Saint-Georges. Fullish body. Some tannin. Somewhat aggressive on the attack, but good concentration underneath. Plenty of vigour.

Nuits-Saint-Georges, Les Damodes, Domaine Jean Chauvenet
From 2018 18.0

Medium-full colour. Reticent but elegant nose. Attractive succulent fruit. Quite forward. More to it on the palate. Fullish, ample, vigorous. Lots of depth. Fine finish. Fine plus.

Nuits-Saint-Georges, Les Damodes, Domaine de la Vougeraie   From 2016   15.0
Medium colour. Ample, rich, fullish nose, but something a little four-square here. Medium-full body. Slightly clumsy. Good grip and balance though.

Nuits-Saint-Georges, Aux Murgers, Domine Sylvain Cathiard   From 2019   18.5
Full colour. Classy nose. Closed-in. But nothing aggressive about it. This is most impressive. Full body. Fine tannins and grip. Excellent concentration of very classy fruit. Goes on and on at the end. Quite splendid. Very fine.

Nuits-Saint-Georges, Aux Murgers, Domaine Alain Hudelot-Noêllat   From 2016   16.0
Medium to medium-full colour. Fragrant nose. Balanced, stylish, and high-toned. Medium body. Soft, ripe, and forward. Fresh and attractive. Positive and elegant.

Nuits-Saint-Georges, Aux Murgers, Domaine Méo-Camuzet   From 2018   17.5
Medium body. Not a blockbuster. A little new oak. Quite a relaxed, feminine Nuits-Saint-Georges. Balanced, long, and stylish.

Nuits-Saint-Georges, Aux Perdrix, Domaine de Perdrix   From 2018   17.5
Fullish colour. Rich, ripe, stemmy nose. Stylish and balanced. Fullish body. Rich, very good fruit and very good grip. Lots of energy. Very clean. Positive, complex, and fine.

Nuits-Saint-Georges, Les Perrières, Domaine Jean Chauvenet   From 2020   17.5
Full colour. Rich, full, sturdy, concentrated nose. Plenty of wine here. Lots of depth too. Fullish body. Quite tannic. Rich and substantial. What it lacks is a bit of flexibility, but this will come.

Nuits-Saint-Georges, Les Procès, Domaine Drouhin   From 2019   17.5
Medium-full body. A nice touch of new oak here. Round and quite rich. Long and succulent. Elegant. Fine.

Nuits-Saint-Georges, Les Porrets Saint-Georges, Domaine Bouchard Père et Fils   From 2018   17.5
Medium-full colour. A little closed, even hard, but good depth here on the nose. Fullish body. Good definition. Fragrant and balanced. This has good intensity if not the volume of some. Fine.

Nuits-Saint-Georges, Les Porrets Saint-Georges, Domaine Faiveley   From 2018   17.5
Medium-full colour. A bit austere at first, but better on the palate. Medium-full body. Good grip. Good structure. This has class and dimension. Finishes stylishly too. Fine.

Nuits-Saint-Georges, Les Pruliers, Domaine Robert Chevillon   From 2019   18.0
Medium-full colour. Rich, ample, slightly gamey nose. But attractive and accessible. Fullish body. Very abundant, rich, and ripe. Very good grip. Classy and long on the palate. Most impressive.

Nuits-Saint-Georges, Les Pruliers, Domaine Gouges   From 2019   17.5
Fullish, very rich. Good tannins. Lovely depth and style here. Very good fruit. Fine.

Nuits-Saint-Georges, Les Pruliers, Domaine Grivot   From 2020   17.5
Medium to medium-full colour. Gamey nose, but a bit closed. Fullish body. Some tannin. This is a touch hard at present, but there is no lack of depth and concentration here. It just needs time.

Nuits-Saint-Georges, Les Pruliers, Domaine Taupenot-Merme   From 2019   17.5
Fullish colour. Full, firm, slightly solid nose. A little hard at first. But better on the palate. Ample, fullish-bodied, generous, and even fat on the palate. Very good grip. This has plenty of energy and a fine classy finish.

Nuits-Saint-Georges, Les Saint-Georges, Domaine Gouges   From 2020   18.0
Fullish colour. Closed-in but classic middle Nuits-Saint-Georges nose. Full, rich, but some-

what hard at present. Needs time. Fullish body. Youthful and energetic. Rich and ripe and with very good grip. Long finish. Fine plus.

Nuits-Saint-Georges, Les Saint-Georges, Domaine Thibault Liger-Belair From 2018 17.5

Full colour. Quite a civilised nose for this sector. Even round. Full body. Rich. Ample. Balanced and stylish. Long and complex. Good class.

Nuits-Saint-Georges, Les Terres Blanches, Domaine de Perdrix From 2018 16.0

A "new" vineyard carved out of the land upslope from Aux Perdrix, and promoted directly to *premier cru* in recent years. The vines are still young. Full, vigorous colour. Rich, opulent, oaky nose. Accessible, ripe, and very seductive on the attack. But on the follow-through the wine tails off a bit. Only very good.

Nuits-Saint-Georges, Aux Thorey, Maison Benjamin Leroux From 2017 15.5

Medium-full colour. Just a bit sweaty on the nose. Yet plenty of ample fruit here. Medium body. Ripe. Decent class. Good grip. Not brilliant but an attractive fruity bottle.

Nuits-Saint-Georges, Les Vaucrains, Domaine Jean Chauvenet From 2020 17.5

Full colour. Ample, rich, tannic nose. But not too aggressive. Good grip and plenty of depth. Full body. A big tannic monster. Somewhat four-square. But rich and balanced. All it needs is time.

Nuits-Saint-Georges, Les Vaucrains, Domaine Robert Chevillon From 2016 15.0

Full colour. Rich, full, tannic nose, a little raw. Medium weight. Decent attack but then it tails off. A bit short.

Nuits-Saint-Georges, Les Vaucrains, Maison Camille Giroud From 2016 17.0

Medium-full colour. Quite a solid nose. Some tannin. But these are ripe. Medium to medium-full body. On the palate this is already soft and succulent. It is very good indeed but lacks the backbone for long-term keeping.

Nuits-Saint-Georges, Les Vaucrains, Domaine Gouges From 2020 18.0

This is really quite substantial. Good tannins. Very rich and concentrated. Lovely finish. Fine plus.

Vosne-Romanée, Les Bossières, Domaine Grivot From 2016 16.5

Village *appellation contrôlée*. Pure, mineral, positive nose. Medium body. Slightly austere but classy and complex.

Vosne-Romanée, *Premier Cru*, Cuvée Duvault-Blochet, Domaine de la Romanée-Conti From 2016 16.0

Medium colour. Attractive fruit but a little lightweight on the nose. Medium body. Quite intense if without great tannic structure. Balanced and fresh and stylish. Good length, but by no means a blockbuster.

Vosne-Romanée, *Premier Cru*, Domaine Gros Frère et Soeur From 2017 15.5

From the younger vines in their *grand cru* vineyards. Medium to medium-full colour. Some development. Ripe, fresh, balanced nose. Medium to medium-full weight. Gently oaky. Stylish and balanced. But no great depth or concentration.

Vosne-Romanée, Les Beaumonts, Domaine Dujac From 2017 16.0

Medium-full colour. Somewhat raw on the nose. Good size but currently ungainly. Medium-full body. A little astringent. Yet very good fruit underneath.

Vosne-Romanée, Les Beaux Monts, Domaine Grivot From 2020 18.5

Good colour. Sumptuous nose. Rich, full, vigorous, and profound. A really very concentrated, multidimensional wine. Full body. Great class too.

Vosne-Romanée, Les Beaumonts, Domaine Alain Hudelot-Noëllat From 2018 17.0

Medium to medium-full colour. Ripe, fresh, balanced, and stylish on the nose. Good minerality. Cool and classy. Backward but fine depth and class. What it lacks is just a bit of energy at the end.

Vosne-Romanée, Les Brulées,
Domaine Eugenie From 2019 19.0
Medium-full colour. Ripe, gently oaky. Concentrated and delicious on the nose. Medium-full body. Ripe. Even sweet. But very good grip and harmony. Very intense. Excellent.

Vosne-Romanée, Les Brulées,
Domaine Grivot From 2018 17.5
Medium to medium-full colour. Some development. Ripe and accessible. Balanced and elegant. Fullish body. Soft, yet intense and concentrated. Good grip. Long. Fine.

Vosne-Romanée, Les Brulées,
Domaine Michel Gros From 2019 19.0
Medium-full colour. Rich, concentrated, backward, classy nose. Lots of depth here. Really stylish. Lovely harmony. Fullish body. Splendid fruit. Excellent finish.

Vosne-Romanée, Les Brulées,
Domaine Méo-Camuzet From 2019 18.5
Medium-full colour. Ripe, rich, profound, and very good intensity. Fullish. Backward. Lots of energy and class. Quite oaky. Very long. Very fine.

Vosne-Romanée, Les Brulées,
Domaine Gerard Mugneret From 2019 18.5
Fullish colour. Very lovely nose. Very aristocratic. Lots of dimension. Fullish body. Cool. Mineral. Harmonious. Complex. Lots of intensity. Very lovely.

Vosne-Romanée, La Croix Rameau,
Domaine Lamarche From 2017 14.0
Medium to medium-full colour. Rich, fullish, quite closed-in nose. Medium weight. The tannins are a little extracted though, and there is some astringency on the palate. Only an adequate amount of grip and richness.

Vosne-Romanée, Les Chaumes,
Domaine Arnoux-Lachaux From 2018 17.0
Medium-full colour. Good depth and style on the nose. Medium-full body. Ample. Round.

Succulent. Some tannin. Very stylish and very good grip. Very good indeed.

Vosne-Romanée, Les Chaumes,
Domaine Gros Frère et Soeur From 2018 16.5
Medium-full colour. Soft, ripe, fruity nose. Ripe and rich on the palate. Medium-full body. Balanced. Good depth. Finishes well.

Vosne-Romanée, Les Chaumes,
Domaine Lamarche From 2018 16.5
Medium-full colour. Plenty of substance but quite hidden on the nose. Medium-full body. Not a blockbuster but stylish and complex. Positive finish. Very good plus.

Vosne-Romanée, Clos des Réas,
Domaine Michel Gros From 2019 18.0
Medium colour. Good fruit on the nose but a little closed. Medium-full body. Subtle, harmonious, concentrated, and intense. Very elegant. Lovely finish.

Vosne-Romanée, Cros Parentoux,
Domaine Emmanuel Rouget From 2019 19.0
Fullish colour. Lovely nose. Very classy, intense fruit. Some oak. Impressively aristocratic. Excellent fruit and harmony. Long and complex and vigorous. Lovely finish.

Vosne-Romanée, Les Malconsorts,
Domaine Sylvain Cathiard From 2020 19.0
Medium-full colour. Lots of concentration and lots of very fine fruit on the nose. Fullish body. This is really elegant and profound. Very good grip and concentration. Multidimensional. Very fine plus.

Vosne-Romanée, Les Malconsorts,
Domaine Dujac From 2016 16.0
Medium colour. Ripe on the nose and with good grip, but not a great deal of concentration or substance. Positive at the end, but overall a bit slight.

Vosne-Romanée, Les Malconsorts,
Domaine du Clos Frantin From 2018 18.0
Quite soft, but ripe and succulent. Balanced and classy. Not a huge wine, but lots of depth. Still a bit austere at the end. Good energy. Fine plus.

**Vosne-Romanée,
Les Malconsorts, Domaine
Alain Hudelot-Noëllat**   From 2022 18.0

Fullish colour. Fine, classy, quite rich, quite accessible nose. Lots of nuance. Not a block-buster. Very ripe on the palate. Pure and lovely. Delicate for a Vosne-Romanée. Fullish, harmonious, at present with the acidity showing a little. But very long. Fine plus.

**Vosne-Romanée, Les Malconsorts,
Domaine Lamarche**   From 2018 18.0

Medium-full colour. Slightly closed-in but very classy and well-balanced on the nose. Fullish body. Backward. Ripe and rich and energetic. Classy too. Fine finish.

**Vosne-Romanée, Les Malconsorts,
Domaine de Montille**   From 2019 17.5

This is very elegant. Lovely fruit. Rich and succulent. Balanced and profound. Fullish body. Fine.

**Vosne-Romanée,
En Orveaux, Domaine
Mongeard-Mugneret**   Now to 2018 15.0

Medium to medium-full colour. The fruit is better than I expected. Soft, succulent, and ripe, if without any great distinction. Medium to medium-full body. Good energy. Good grip. Quite soft tannins. But slightly pinched. Lacks class.

**Vosne-Romanée,
Les Petits Monts, Domaine
du Vicomte de Liger-Belair**   From 2019 18.0

Medium-full colour. Elegant, balanced nose. Slightly closed-in. Fullish body. Harmonious. Profound. Complex. Classy. Very long finish. Very good energy. Fine plus.

**Vosne-Romanée, Les Petits Monts,
Maison Roche de Bellene**   From 2018 17.5

Medium-full colour. Good depth, concentration, and class here on the nose. Medium-full body. Ripe and balanced, with good depth and concentration. Good intensity and finesse. Fine fruit on the finish.

**Vosne-Romanée,
Aux Reignots, Domaine
du Vicomte de Liger-Belair**   From 2018 16.0

Medium-full colour. Some development. Rich, full meaty nose. There is fat here, but also a little reduction. Medium-full body. Good acidity. A touch raw and astringent at present. But it needs time.

**Vosne-Romanée,
Les Suchots, Domaine
Alain Hudelot-Noëllat**   From 2018 18.5

Medium colour. Some develoment. Lovely ripe fruit on the nose. Medium-full body. Balanced. Classy and intense. Lovely finish. Very long. Very fine.

**Vosne-Romanée, Les Suchots,
Domaine Arnoux-Lachaux**   From 2017 16.0

Fullish colour. Rich, composed, concentrated nose. Lots of depth here. Fullish body. Almost over-ripe. Good depth and concentration but it lacks a little grip. Finishes sweet but slightly bland.

**Vosne-Romanée, Les Suchots,
Domaine Grivot**   From 2018 17.0

Medium to medium-full colour. Some development. A bit of reduction at first on the nose. Fullish body. Good concentration. Good grip and good tannins. Very ripe. Almost voluptuous. Long. Very good indeed.

**Vosne-Romanée,
Les Suchots, Domaine
du Vicomte de Liger-Belair**   From 2018 18.0

Medium-full colour. Rich and ample on the nose. Ripe. Laid-back. Medium-full bodied. Lots of harmony and subtlety. Very long and very classy. Fine plus.

**Vosne-Romanée, Les Suchots,
Domaine Gerard Mugneret**   From 2018 17.5

Medium to medium-full colour. Somewhat raw on the nose. But ripe and fresh. Fullish body. Some new oak. Concentrated. Plenty of intensity and energy. Lovely finish. This is fine.

Vougeot, Clos de la Perrière,
Domaine Bertagna   From 2016 14.0

Medium to medium-full colour. Ripe nose, but a little feeble and even hollow, which makes it show an astringent touch. Medium body. Lacks a bit of fruit. Only quite good.

Chambolle-Musigny,
Premier Cru, **Cuvée Jules,**
Domaine Lignier-Michelot   From 2018 18.0

Medium to medium-full colour. Some development. Round, ripe, balanced, stylish nose. Lovely laid-back fruit. Fullish body. Concentrated. Complex. Intense and long on the palate. Excellent grip and energy. Delicious.

Chambolle-Musigny,
Les Amoureuses,
Domaine Bertheau   From 2018 15.0

Medium colour. Some maturity. Lovely nose. Ripe, profound, and balanced. Good energy. But it's a bit hard on the palate. Medium-full body. There is a lack of generosity.

Chambolle-Musigny,
Les Amoureuses,
Domaine Robert Groffier   From 2025 17.5

Medium-full colour. Ripe, slightly spicy, with a touch of oak on the nose. Lovely concentrated fruit. Fullish body. Some tannin. Rich and profound. Very good class, if not great. Finishes well. Fine.

Chambolle-Musigny,
Les Amoureuses,
Domaine J. Frédéric Mugnier   From 2020 18.0

Medium-full colour. Some maturity. Soft, ripe, and fragrant on the nose. Full and rich underneath. Full body. Rich and meaty and oaky on the palate. Lots of energy. Currently it is not quite together, but it will be.

Chambolle-Musigny,
Les Amoureuses,
Domaine Georges Roumier   From 2020 19.0

Medium colour. Some maturity. On the nose intense, stylish, finely balanced, and profound. Delicate, sweet, fragrant fruit. Lovely depth and harmony. Very fine indeed.

Chambolle-Musigny,
Les Amoureuses, Domaine
Comte Georges de Vogüé   From 2018 17.0

Medium-full colour. Ripe, oaky, intense but a little tough at first on the nose. Quite a chunky wine on the palate. Fullish. Some tannin. The wine is long. But it's a bit solid.

Chambolle-Musigny,
Les Beaux Bruns,
Domaine Ghislaine Barthod   From 2018 15.0

Medium-full colour. A little pinched on the nose. Rich and minty as it evolved. Fullish body. Very ripe. Meaty for a Chambolle. Good depth, but still youthful. It will get less ungainly as it rounds off.

Chambolle-Musigny,
Les Carrières, Domaine
Gilbert et Christine Felletig   From 2016 16.5

This is the only estate I know which declares this wine. It lies between Feusselottes and Greunchers. Soft and fragrant with lovely elegant fruit. Ripe and succulent. Decent length. Very good plus.

Chambolle-Musigny, Les Charmes,
Domaine Ghislaine Barthod   From 2017 17.5

Fullish colour. Rich, concentrated nose. Ripe, profound, and succulent. Very good depth and class. Fullish. Meaty. Fresh and clean. Lovely fruit. Harmonious. Complex and fine.

Chambolle-Musigny, Les Charmes,
Domaine Bertheau   From 2016 16.0

Medium colour. Some development. Some stems. Ample, rich, and succulent on the nose. Lovely balance. Medium body. Decent grip. But a little sweet. This doesn't really have the energy I'm looking for.

Chambolle-Musigny, Les Charmes,
Domaine Hudelot-Noëllat   From 2016 16.5

Fullish colour. Ample, rich, ripe, and fullish on the nose. Plenty of depth and dimension. It doesn't have the grip and concentration of some of the other Charmes, but there is very good fresh fruit, and it is long and classy.

**Chambolle-Musigny,
Les Charmes, Domaine
Michèle et Patrice Rion**   From 2017   17.5
Medium to medium-full colour. Some development. High-toned nose. Good fruit. Some stems. But cool and succulent. Medium-full body. Fresh, balanced, classy, ripe, and fine quality.

**Chambolle-Musigny,
La Combe d'Orveau,
Domaine Taupenot-Merme**   From 2018   14.0
Medium to medium-full colour. Gamey nose. Not exactly stylish. A bit lean and vegetal in the background. Fullish body. Ripe. Good grip. But a bit clumsy and astringent.

**Chambolle-Musigny, Les Cras,
Domaine Ghislaine Barthod**   From 2018   17.0
Medium-full colour. Ripe, classy, high-toned nose. Rich, ripe, ample, fat, and very lovely on the attack. Medium weight. Harmonious and seductive. Perhaps a slight lack of grip.

**Chambolle-Musigny, Les Cras,
Domaine Georges Roumier**   From 2019   18.5
Fullish colour. Still closed. Rich and concentrated. Fullish body. Lots of depth here. This is really very classy. Lovely.

**Chambolle-Musigny, Les Echanges,
Maison Roland Remoissenet**   From 2019   18.0
Full colour. Ripe and round, fullish and succulent on the nose. Medium-full body. Very lovely harmonious, profound, classy fruit on the palate. Very pure. Fine plus.

**Chambolle-Musigny,
Les Feusselottes, Domaine
Gilbert et Christine Felletig**   From 2018   16.5
Very gently oaky and succulent on the nose. Medium to medium-full body. Juicy, fresh, balanced, and stylish. Long. Very good plus.

**Chambolle-Musigny,
Les Feusselottes,
Domaine Cecile Tremblay**   From 2015   14.0
Fullish colour. Fullish nose. Quite sturdy. Good grip and fruit underneath. Medium-full body.

Ripe and sweet. On the palate, a little short and a bit coarse at the end. Quite good at best.

**Chambolle-Musigny, Les Fuées,
Domaine Ghislaine Barthod**   From 2019   17.5
Full colour. Full nose. Quite firm. Lots of energy. Fullish on the palate. The tannins are very ripe. This is pure and profound and complex and very lovely, if not as impressive as what turned out to be the Mugnier sample.

**Chambolle-Musigny,
Les Fuées, Domaine
Gilbert et Christine Felletig**   From 2019   17.0
Rich and full, with a little new oak. Good tannins. Ample and energetic. Quite structured. Good positive, stylish finish. Very good indeed.

**Chambolle-Musigny, Les Fuées,
Domaine J. Frédéric Mugnier**   From 2020   18.0
Medium-full colour. Some development. Still a little closed, but an impressive amount of class and depth and dimension here. Fullish body. Excellent grip. A generous profound wine with a very long finish.

**Chambolle-Musigny, Les Groseilles,
Domaine Digioia-Royer**   From 2018   17.5
Full colour. Round, ripe, oaky, and attractive on the nose. Fullish body on the palate. Ample, vigorous, and balanced. Plenty of depth and energy. Long. Fine.

**Chambolle-Musigny, Les Gruenchers,
Domaine Digioia-Royer**   From 2018   16.5
Fullish colour. High-toned nose. Cool and fragrant. But classy. Medium-full body. The attack is intense and concentrated, showing very lovely fruit, but the finish is a bit sweet.

**Morey-Saint-Denis, *Premier Cru*,
Domaine Dujac**   From 2017   16.5
Medium-colour. Some development. Stylish fruit. Not a blockbuster. Balanced and accessible. Medium-full body. Good grip and intensity. Classy too. A harmonious wine which finishes well. Very good plus.

Morey-Saint-Denis, Les Blanchards,
Domaine Hubert Lignier   From 2017 16.0
Medium-full colour. Fresh and stylish and balanced on the nose. Medium-full weight. Quite forward. Yet with good depth and vigour. Good concentration. Positive at the end. Very good.

Morey-Saint-Denis, Aux Charmes,
Domaine Lignier-Michelot   From 2018 15.5
Fullish colour. Ripe nose, the stems evident. Medium to medium-full weight. Good depth and class, but rather unformed and less stylish than most of these Moreys.

Morey-Saint-Denis, Aux Chezeaux,
Domaine Lignier-Michelot   From 2018 16.0
Medium-full colour. Fresh, flowery, stylish, and fragrant on the nose. Medium-full. Ripe, balanced, and attractive at first on the palate. But the finish is a little bland.

Morey-Saint-Denis, Le Chenevry,
Domaine Lignier-Michelot   From 2019 17.0
Medium-full colour. Some development. Ripe nose. Some stems. Good vigour. Good grip. Medium to medium-full body. Ripe; even rich. Good intensity.

Morey-Saint-Denis,
Clos de la Bussière,
Domaine Georges Roumier   From 2018 17.0
Rich and meaty. This wine has got more and more sophisticated over the past decade. Ripe, fullish-bodied, and succulent. Very good grip. Long and stylish. Very good indeed.

Morey-Saint-Denis,
Les Faconnières,
Domaine Lignier-Michelot   From 2018 16.0
Fullish colour. Rich and oaky on the nose. Similar on the palate. Ripe. Fullish. Good energy. Rich and succulent. Good depth. Good grip. Very good quality.

Morey-Saint-Denis, Les Millandes,
Domaine Christian Serafin   From 2018 16.0
Medium-full colour. Rich, ripe, meaty, and tannic on the nose. A touch sweet on the palate. A beefy wine with a good grip and a long, lingering finish. Very good.

Morey-Saint-Denis, La Riotte,
Domaine Olivier Jouan   From 2018 16.5
Fullish colour. Rich and oaky on the nose. But a bit closed-in. On the palate, fullish body. Lots of fruit. Very ripe and very good grip. A touch astringent at the end, but I think this is just a stage in the wine's development. Very good plus.

Morey-Saint-Denis, La Riotte,
Domaine Taupenot-Merme   From 2017 15.5
Medium-full colour. Some fruit on the nose, if without a great deal of finesse. A touch sweaty. Medium-full body. Slightly raw and the acidity is a bit aggressive. A meaty example, but I think it will get better as it rounds off.

Morey-Saint-Denis, Les Ruchots,
Domaine Olivier Jouan   From 2018 17.5
Full colour. Rich, oaky, fat, and succulent on the nose. Good grip. Fullish body. Vigorous. Quite concentrated. Ripe and positive. Very good follow-through. Fine.

Gevrey-Chambertin, Les Cazetiers,
Maison Olivier Bernstein   From 2018 17.5
Medium-full colour. High-toned nose. Full body. Rich. Concentrated. Oaky. A very complex and abundant follow-through. The amount of oak puts me off rather, but the wine is fine.

Gevrey-Chambertin, Les Cazetiers,
Domaine Bruno Clair   From 2018 18.5
Full colour. Rich, concentrated, and profound. Full body. Very good tannins. Excellent depth and grip. This is vigorous, long, complex, and very fine.

Gevrey-Chambertin, Les Cazetiers,
Domaine Christian Serafin   From 2018 17.5
Medium to medium-full colour. Supple, stylish nose. Good fruit and class here. Fullish body. Very good grip. Quite concentrated. Lots of fruit and vigour. Long and positive and complex. Very elegant. Fine.

Gevrey-Chambertin, Les Cazetiers,
Domaine Faiveley   From 2019 17.5
Medium to medium-full body. Some tannin. Still a bit closed. Better at the end than on the attack. Ripe, balanced, stylish, good depth. Fine.

Gevrey-Chambertin, Les Cazetiers,
Domaine Armand Rousseau   From 2017   16.5
Medium-full colour. A bit reduced on the nose. Fullish body. Ample. Fresh and fruity on the palate. Nicely pure and concentrated fruit on the follow-through. And good concentration.

Gevrey-Chambertin, Les Champeaux,
Domaine Denis Mortet   From 2019   17.5
Fullish colour. Stylish, balanced, civilised nose. Fullish-bodied, quite oaky, rich, and concentrated. Lots of fruit. Very good grip. Some tannin. But lots of depth. Fine.

Gevrey-Chambertin, Les Cherbaudes,
Domaine Louis Boillot   From 2016   16.0
Medium to medium-full colour. Elegant, fruity, balanced nose. Medium to medium-full weight. Good fruit and grip. Quite stylish. Positive at the end, with a persistent finish. Very good.

Gevrey-Chambertin, Clos du
Fonteny, Domaine Bruno Clair   From 2016   15.0
Fullish colour. Ripe, rich, and concentrated on the nose. Very ripe on the palate. Voluptuous, even. Full and tannic on the palate. Good acidity underneath, but the net effect is a little bland. It lacks bite.

Gevrey-Chambertin, Clos Prieur,
Domaine Rossignol-Trapet   From 2016   14.0
Medium-full colour. Somewhat lightweight nose. But quite stylish and fruity. Medium weight. Lacks a little fruit and generosity. Quite high acidity. Slightly astringent at the end.

Gevrey-Chambertin,
Clos Prieur, Domaine
Jean et Jean-Louis Trapet   From 2015   13.5
Medium to medium-full colour. Lacks a bit of fruit on the nose. Light to medium weight. Somewhat unripe and charmless.

Gevrey-Chambertin,
Clos-Saint-Jacques,
Domaine Bruno Clair   From 2018   18.5
Lush and opulent on the nose, especially for a 2008. Rich, ripe, and seductive. Very lovely stylish, complex finish. Very fine.

Gevrey-Chambertin,
Clos-Saint-Jacques,
Domaine Sylvie Esmonin   From 2018   18.5
Medium-full colour. Quite closed and concentrated on the nose. Full-bodied. Rich. Abundant and some tannin on the palate. A backward wine. But a great deal of depth here. Very fine.

Gevrey-Chambertin,
Clos-Saint-Jacques,
Domaine Louis Jadot   From 2020   19.0
Medium to medium-full colour. Lots of depth and dimension on the nose here. Fullish body. Rich. Oaky. Not a blockbuster but great intensity, splendid fruit, and impressive class. A beauty.

Gevrey-Chambertin,
Clos-Saint-Jacques,
Domaine Armand Rousseau   From 2018   18.5
An impressive wine. Fullish body. Rich, classy, and concentrated. Very lovely fruit. Lots of depth. Very very long and lovely.

Gevrey-Chambertin, Le Closeau,
Domaine Drouhin-Laroze   From 2016   14.0
Light, evolved colour. Soft nose. Some stems. Ripe. Medium-full body. A little astringent. Somewhat ungainly. Yet there is substance here.

Gevrey-Chambertin, Les Combottes,
Domaine Arlaud   From 2015   14.0
Medium-full colour. Some reduction on the nose. Medium weight. Decently balanced fruit. But difficult to judge.

Gevrey-Chambertin, Les Corbeaux,
Domaine Denis Bachelet   From 2019   16.5
Medium-full colour. Rich nose. Balanced and elegant. Fullish. Backward. Very good grip. The follow-through is profound and complex. Quite tannic though. Very good plus.

Gevrey-Chambertin, Le Crapillot,
Domaine Humbert Frères   From 2017   16.0
Medium-full colour. Quite full and rich on the nose. Good style and depth. Fullish body. Good concentration. Good grip. Somewhat raw at present, but there is good potential here.

**Gevrey-Chambertin,
Estournelles-Saint-Jacques,
Domaine Humbert Frères**   From 2017   15.0
Medium-full colour. Backward nose. Just a little
pinched. Better on the palate. A bit astringent,
but ripe and with good grip. Not exactly rich
but a good wine.

**Gevrey-Chambertin, Le Fonteny,
Domaine Christian Serafin**   From 2018   17.0
Medium-full colour. Quite closed on the nose
at first. But good fruit and concentration. Full-
bodied, rich, and masculine. Good tannins. A
backward wine, but very good indeed. Elegant
and positive all the way through.

**Gevrey-Chambertin,
Lavaux-Saint-Jacques,
Domaine Drouhin-Laroze**   From 2015   13.5
Light to medium colour. Slightly raw and
charmless on the nose. Medium weight. Some-
what thin, astringent, and attenuated.

**Gevrey-Chambertin,
Lavaux-Saint-Jacques,
Domaine Claude Dugat**   From 2019   17.5
Full colour. Backward nose, but plenty of depth
and concentration here. Oaky. Fullish. The tannins are nice and ripe. Good grip. Round and
splendidly vigorous at the end. Fine.

**Gevrey-Chambertin,
Lavaux-Saint-Jacques,
Domaine Maume**   From 2018   16.5
Medium-full colour. Some development. Quite
closed on the nose. A bit dense, even. On the
palate, more accessible. Medium-full body.
Balanced, stylish. Long. Elegant. Very good
plus.

**Gevrey-Chambertin,
Lavaux-Saint-Jacques,**   From 2018
Domaine Denis Mortet   See note
Full colour. Ample nose, rich and oaky. But
somewhat corked. Medium-full body. There is
richness, balance, and depth here. Could be
very good indeed.

**Gevrey-Chambertin,
Lavaux-Saint-Jacques,
Domaine Armand Rousseau**   From 2017   16.5
Medium colour. Some development. Ripe,
plump nose. Good style. Good fruit. Medium-
full body. Harmonious. Good energy. Attractive
plump fruit. Finishes well.

**Gevrey-Chambertin, Les Perrières,
Domaine Hubert Lignier**   From 2016   15.0
Medium to medium-full colour. Some develop-
ment. Slightly earthy and tannic on the nose.
Medium-full weight. Fresh and fruity. Bal-
anced. Quite stylish. Finishes positively.

**Gevrey-Chambertin,
La Petite Chapelle,
Domaine Humbert Frères**   From 2016   15.5
Fullish colur. Rich, ample, fruity, oaky nose.
Medium to medium-full body. Good grip. Good
depth. Will get more attractive as it rounds off.

**Gevrey-Chambertin,
La Petite Chapelle,
Domaine Rossignol-Trapet**   From 2015   14.0
Medium-full colour. Somewhat pinched and
attenuated on the nose. Medium weight. Decent
fruit. But a lack of personality and richness.

**Gevrey-Chambertin, Les Poissenots,
Domaine Humbert Frères**   From 2016   16.0
Medium to medium-full colour. Ripe, accessible, medium weight, fruity-oaky nose. Good
style. Medium body. Fresh. Balanced and stylish. Not a blockbuster by any means but positive and attractive.

Grands Crus

**Corton, Domaine
Bonneau du Martray**   From 2018   18.5
Good colour. Rich nose. Quite meaty. Good
fat and succulence. This has depth and class.
Harmonious and very lovely. Long at the end.
Very fine.

Corton, Domaine Follin-Arvelet   From 2017   17.5
Medium colour. Good depth and class on the
nose. Some development. Balanced and fruity.

Fullish body. An ample wine. Good grip. Plenty of potential for the future. Ripe and positive and more and more classy as it developed.

Le Corton, Domaine
Bouchard Père et Fils   From 2017   17.0
Medium to medium-full colour. Quite firm and rich on the nose. Good finesse. Fullish body. Ripe and succulent. Good tannins. Good grip. Plenty of energy. Long and classy at first but somewhat less so as it developed.

Corton, Les Bressandes,
Domaine Chandon de Briailles   From 2016   15.0
This seems rather dry, feeble, and astringent for a *grand cru*. We'll see.

Corton, Les Bressandes,
Domaine du Comte Senard   From 2016   15.0
Medium to medium-full body. Ripe and quite fresh. But a bit lightweight. Not short though.

Corton, Les Bressandes,
Domaine Follin-Arvelet   From 2017   17.5
Medium to medium-full colour. Some development. Quite closed on the nose. Rich and full but with a lack of real succulence. Ample. Fullish body. Plenty of fruit and richness as it opened up in the glass. Long and classy.

Corton, Les Bressandes,
Domaine de la Pousse d'Or   From 2017   15.5
Medium-full colour. A touch of oak and caramel on the nose. Rich and abundant. Medium-full weight. Good fruit. The grip is quite good, but there is something a bit raw and tight here.

Corton, Les Bressandes,
Domaine Tollot-Beaut   From 2018   16.0
Medium-full body. Ripe and fresh. Ample and fruity if not quite the elegance and intensity it could have.

Corton, Clos des Cortons,
Domaine Faiveley   From 2022   18.0
Rich, concentrated, closed-in, but fine quality here. A backward wine which is still quite austere. Big and tannic. Just needs time.

Corton, Clos des Maréchaudes,
Domaine du Pavillon   From 2018   17.5
Here we have the richness and volume missing in the Aloxe. Very good grip. Long classy finish. Fine.

Corton, Clos des Meix,
Domaine du Comte Senard   From 2016   15.0
Medium to medium-full body. Elegant and balanced. Ripe and not astringent, but a little slight.

Corton, Clos du Roi,
Maison Camille Giroud   From 2018   18.0
Medium-full colour. Opulent, balanced, cool, classy nose. Rich and full-bodied. Abundant, oaky, and energetic. There is a lot of depth here. Splendid follow-through and finish. Fine plus.

Corton, Clos du Roi,
Domaine de Montille   From 2020   18.0
Quite closed-in at present. Fullish body. Very good tannins. Quite austere at present but very good depth. Long and potentially lovely.

Corton, Clos du Roi,
Domaine du Comte Senard   From 2017   17.5
This is a lot better than the other two Senard wines. Medium-full body. Ripe, rich, and fruity. Good positive finish. Stylish too.

Corton, Clos du Roi,
Domaine de la Pousse d'Or   From 2018   17.5
Fullish colour. Full, firm, rich nose. Lots of complexity and concentration. Fresh and vigorous. Fullish body. Ripe, rich, and good tannins. Lots of depth at the end. Fine.

Corton, Clos du Roi,
Domaine de la Vougeraie   From 2018   18.0
Medium-full colour. Some development. Closed-in nose, but stylish fruit and very good balance. Fat, rich, oaky, and vigorous. Fine fruit and lots of depth. Fine plus.

Corton, Les Maréchaudes,
Domaine Chandon de Briailles   From 2017   17.5
Medium-full body. Rich, fat. Good energy and depth. Classy too. Lovely finish. Fine.

Corton, Les Pougets,
Domaine Louis Jadot   From 2019   17.5
Medium-full colour. A little development. Ample, full, and rich on the nose. Fullish body. Fragrant. Oaky. And concentrated on the palate. Very good grip. Good depth and vigour. Fine.

Corton, Les Renardes,
Domaine Michel Gaunoux   From 2018   17.5
Medium-full body. Classy. Ripe. Balanced. Lovely freshness. Good tannins. Fine.

Corton, Les Renardes,
Domaine Thibault Liger-Belair   From 2017   16.5
Medium-full colour. A slight touch of reduction on the nose. But good, classy fruit underneath. Medium-full body. Quite rich. Good energy. This has depth and class. Very good plus, but not as fine as some of the others.

Corton, Les Rognets,
Maison Camille Giroud   From 2017   17.5
Fullish colour. Firm, rich, concentrated, classy nose. Fullish body. Succulent. Lots of energy. Very good grip. Lovely fruit. Still youthful. High-class.

Corton, Les Rognets,
Domaine Taupenot-Merme   From 2015   14.5
Medium-full colour. A little pinched and attenuated on the nose. Lacks charm. The attack is rather better but the follow-through is less agreeable. Slightly astringent at the end.

Echézeaux,
Domaine Arnoux-Lachaux   From 2019   18.0
Full colour. Ripe, opulent, and quite substantial on the nose. Rich, pure, fragrant, and quite austere. Very good grip. Full body. Some tannin. A bit closed at present but profound and high-class. Lovely finish. Fine plus.

Echézeaux,
Domaine Joseph Drouhin   From 2019   17.5
Medium-full colour. Lovely fragrant nose. Fullish body. Rich, ripe, stylish, and aromatic. Lots of energy. Complex and classy. Fine.

Echézeaux,
Domaine Eugenie   From 2018   17.5
Medium-full colour. Round and ripe and quite rich and concentrated on the nose. Medium-full body. Oaky. Very ripe, round, luscious fruit. Very good attack. Plenty of length. Balanced and energetic. Fine.

Echézeaux, Domaine
Gilbert et Christine Felletig   From 2016   17.0
Rich, high-toned nose. Medium-full body. A bit closed. Ripe, stylish, and succulent. Not a big wine, but it has charm.

Echézeaux,
Domaine du Clos Frantin   From 2019   18.0
Soft, ripe, and generous on the nose. Fullish body. Rich. Very well-balanced. Intense, classy, and long on the palate. Lots of dimension. This is most impressive.

Echézeaux, Domaine Grivot   From 2017   16.0
Medium-full colour. Somewhat herbal, though not green on the nose. Cool and balanced. Medium to medium-full weight. Good grip. But a lack of real style and richness.

Echézeaux, "Loachausses,"
Domaine Anne Gros   From 2019   18.0
Medium-full colour. Closed-in nose. Fullish body. This is a bit hidden, but there is a lot of depth and quality here. Very pure fruit. Finely balanced. Long, rich, and succulent at the end.

Echézeaux,
Domaine A. F. Gros   From 2019   17.5
Medium-full colour. Ripe, rich, fresh, and classy on the nose. Medium-full body. Good grip. This is profound and harmonious. Ripe and complex. Stylish follow-through. Fine.

Echézeaux,
Domaine Gros Frère et Soeur   From 2019   18.0
Medium-full colour. Spicy, oaky nose. A slight hint of gingerbread. Nice austerity here on the palate. Fullish body. Very luscious ripe fruit. Lots of class and energy. Fine plus.

Echézeaux,
Domaine Lamarche From 2017 17.5
Medium-full colour. Ripe, voluptuous, gamey nose. A touch of oak. Medium-full weight. Plump and plummy. Fresh and attractive. Balanced. Finishes long. Not great but fine.

Echézeaux, Domaine du
Vicomte de Liger-Belair From 2017 16.0
Medium-full colour. Fresh, ripe stylish nose. But less impressive as it developed. There is a sort of farmyardy reduction here. Good energy though. Perhaps just going through a phase.

Echézeaux,
Domaine Gerard Mugneret From 2018 18.0
Medium to medium-full colour. Full, firm, rich nose. Good class. Good depth. Fullish body. Ripe and harmonious. Lovely fruit. Fine plus.

Echézeaux, Domaine
Dr. Georges Mugneret-Gibourg From 2017 16.0
Fullish colour. Full, firm, tannic nose. Backward but classic. Fullish body. Ripe. A touch clumsy at present. But there is good fruit here. Should turn out better than the mark I have given it.

Echézeaux, Domaine
de la Romanée-Conti From 2018 18.0
Good colour and good weight on the nose. Good richness and style too. Medium to medium-full body. Quite a lot better than the Vosne-Romanée *premier cru*. Intense and succulent. Lovely fresh acidity and very elegant.

Echézeaux,
Domaine du Perdrix From 2015 15.0
Fullish colour. High-toned nose. Somewhat ungainly. Fruity but seems a little short. The fruit is a bit artificial. Here's another Echézeaux which is not on form.

Echézeaux,
Domaine Rouget From 2019 18.5
Medium-full colour. Laid-back, classy nose. Profound. Fullish body. Very classy. Multidimensional. Excellent fruit and lovely harmony. Splendid vigour at the end. Very fine.

Grands-Echézeaux,
Domaine Drouhin From 2020 18.0
Medium-full colour. Splendid nose. Super-concentrated. Great depth and class. Full body. Vigorous, profound, and very harmonious. Intense and lovely. Fine plus.

Grands-Echézeaux,
Domaine du Clos Frantin From 2018 17.5
A more mineral wine—slightly more austere—than the Echézeaux. Very pure. Somewhat more astringent and less fat at the moment. Cool and classy underneath. Medium-full body. But is it better?

Grands-Echézeaux,
Domaine Gros Frère et Soeur From 2019 17.5
Medium to medium-full colour. Some development. Attractive spicy, fruit-cakey nose. Round and ripe. Quite firm. Good vigour. Fullish body. Plenty of volume. Good grip and good tannins. Lots of energy. Needs time. Perhaps not the class of the very best.

Grands-Echézeaux,
Domaine Lamarche From 2018 17.0
Medium to medium-full colour. Firm nose. Slightly austere. Good depth and class. Harmonious and promising. Fullish body. Rich and concentrated. Not quite the finesse of the very best, but very good indeed.

Grands-Echézeaux,
Maison Roche de Bellene From 2018 17.5
Medium-full colour. Rich, full, concentrated, backward nose. Fullish, ripe, and high-quality. On the palate this is rather closed and unforthcoming, but the ingredients are there. Fullish body. Long. Fine.

Grands-Echézeaux,
Domaine de la Romanée-Conti From 2019 18.5
Good colour. Firmer and spicier than the Echézeaux and slightly more weight. Both more closed and more concentrated. The tannins show a bit more. Lots of depth and a fine finish. This needs time.

Clos de Vougeot,

Domaine Arnoux-Lachaux   From 2018   18.5

Medium-full colour. Round and ripe but rather hidden at first on the nose. Ample, succulent, full-bodied, ripe, rich, and even exotic on the palate. Good tannins. Very good grip. This is most impressive.

Clos de Vougeot,

Maison Olivier Bernstein   From 2017   17.5

Medium-full colour. Lightweight nose. Pretty fruit. But understated. Medium-full body. Balanced. Stylish. Ripe and with good cool intensity. Fine.

Clos de Vougeot,

Bouchard Père et Fils   From 2017   18.0

Medium colour. Ripe, rich, ample, and oaky on the nose. Attractive, fullish body, balanced. Good ripe tannins. Plenty of energy. Good style too. Fine plus.

Clos de Vougeot,

Domaine Eugenie   From 2017   17.5

Medium-full colour. Quite closed at first but fine fragrant flowers (violets) and fruit on the nose. Good high tones. Good acidity. Medium-full body. Rich and very ripe. Lots of energy. Fine.

Clos de Vougeot,

Domaine du Clos Frantin   From 2017   17.0

Ripe, generous, spicy, and seductive. Medium to medium-full body. Balanced and fresh and not austere.

Clos de Vougeot,

Domaine Grivot   From 2020   18.5

Good colour. Still a bit closed-in on the nose. Good weight here and lots of energy. Rich, fullish body. Very good tannins. Balanced and vigorous and classy. Lovely finish.

Clos de Vougeot, "Maupertuis,"

Domaine Anne Gros   From 2025   19.0

Fullish colour. Still closed on the nose. Very, very concentrated. Excellent depth. Very splendid fruit. Full body. Great style. Very profound. Lovely finish. Excellent.

Clos de Vougeot, "Maupertuis,"

Domaine Michel Gros   From 2017   17.5

Medium colour. Some development. Ripe, abundant, soft, oaky nose. Medium-full body. A luscious wine. Good acidity. The attack is plump. The finish shows the grip. Fine.

Clos de Vougeot, "Le Musigni,"

Domaine Gros Frère et Soeur   From 2017   15.0

Medium-full colour. Some development. Rich coffee-chocolate nose. Good balance and good grip. Medium-full body. A little burly and ungainly on the attack. Good acidity. But overall it doesn't really sing.

Clos de Vougeot, Domaine

Alain Hudelot-Noëllat   From 2017   17.5

Medium to medium-full colour. Fresh, fragrant nose. Good balance. Currently a little rigid and closed on the palate. Medium-full body. But good depth and richness underneath.

Clos de Vougeot,

Domaine Louis Jadot   From 2017   16.0

Medium-full colour. Firm nose. Backward. Fresh. Youthful. Intense. Slightly aggressive on the attack. Fullish body. Ripe but a bit lumpy. Good grip. But a little ungainly at present.

Clos de Vougeot,

Domaine Lamarche   From 2018   17.5

Medium-full body. Plenty of depth and volume here without being aggressive. Nice and rich. Backward. Full-bodied. Lots of grip. Some tannin. Still very young. Needs time. Promising finish. Fine.

Clos de Vougeot,

Domaine Thibault Liger-Belair   From 2018   18.0

Medium-full colour. Ripe, quite firm, youthful nose. No lack of depth here. But a little ungainly at present. On the palate the wine is full-bodied. Rich, ripe, and has some tannin. Plenty of depth and class. Needs time but impressive pure fruit at the end.

Clos de Vougeot,

Domaine Loichet   From 2017 16.0?

Full colour. Some reduction on the nose. Fullish body on the palate. Seems rich and balanced. Full body. Spicy and abundant. But difficult to judge.

Clos de Vougeot,
Domaine Méo-Camuzet   From 2016   16.0
Slight astringency here on the attack. The finish is better but the wine seems rather insubstantial.

Clos de Vougeot,
Domaine Remoissenet   From 2018   19.0
Medium-full colour. Firm, full, very classy nose. Lovely fruit and very fine balance. This is continued on the palate. Fullish body. Splendid intensity. Cool and laid-back. Marvelous finish.

Clos de Vougeot,
Maison Roche de Bellene   From 2017   17.0
Fullish colour. Ample, full, rich nose. Quite fat. Still closed. Lots of depth. Full body. At first I found it a little tough and I wondered about the level of acidity. But as it evolved, I was sure there was enough grip. Nice abundant fruit underneath.

Clos de Vougeot,
Château de la Tour   From 2019   17.5
Good colour. This is quite a meaty example. Fullish body. Good depth. Good tannic structure. Plenty of wine here. Fine.

Clos de Vougeot, Vieilles Vignes,
Château de la Tour   From 2022   18.5
This is delicious. Full, rich, and concentrated. Lots of vigour and depth. Very lovely long finish. Very fine.

Clos de Vougeot,
Domaine de la Vougeraie   From 2015   13.5
Medium colour. Some development. A little weedy on the nose and there are notes of reduction here, especially as it evolved in the glass. Medium body. Fruity but lacks class.

Romanée-Saint-Vivant,
Domaine Arnoux-Lachaux   From 2019   19.0
Medium-full colour. Some development. Ample, slightly gingerbread-spicy nose. Fullish body. Good depth and vigour. A bit closed but not at all clumsy. Ripe, youthful, and very classy.

Romanée-Saint-Vivant,
Domaine Follin-Arvelet   From 2019   18.5
Medium colour. Some development. Rich, ripe, fresh, high-quality nose. Fullish body. Very good depth. Lovely ripe fruit. Lots of energy. Pure, concentrated, vigorous, and classy. Lovely finish.

Romanée-Saint-Vivant,
Domaine Alain Hudelot-Noëllat   From 2019   18.5
Medium-full colour. Full, youthful, austere—in the best sense—on the nose. Fresh and complex. Medium-full body. Balanced and classy. Good intensity on the follow-through. Very fine.

Romanée-Saint-Vivant,
Domaine de la Romanée-Conti   From 2018   18.5
Lovely fragrant nose, but lighter than the Grands-Echézeaux. Softer but very stylish. This has particularly lovely cool, composed fruit. Fresh, long, complex, and classy. Very fine.

Richebourg,
Domaine du Clos Frantin   From 2020   19.0
Fine colour. Full nose. Still closed. Rich and concentrated and with lots of breed. Full body. Splendid balance. A profound, multidimensional wine with lovely harmony and class. Excellent.

Richebourg, Domaine Grivot   From 2020   18.5
Medium to medium-full colour. Classy and concentrated on the nose. Very lovely fruit. Harmonious and laid back. Not a blockbuster but fullish bodied, ripe, vigorous and concentrated on the palate. Lots of finesse here. Very fine.

Richebourg,
Domaine Anne Gros   From 2020   18.5
Medium to medium-full colour. Some development. High-toned nose. Vigorous. Still closed. On the palate, fullish body. Still very youthful. Abundantly fruity. Ripe, fragrant, subtle, and seductive. Very classy at the end and improved considerably in the glass.

Richebourg,

Domaine A. F. Gros   From 2020 20.0

Fullish colour. High-toned, oaky nose. Youthful. Good energy. Very harmonious. Splendid ripe fruit. Full body. Fine tannins. Really classy, concentrated fruit. And a very lovely long finish. Excellent.

Richebourg,

Domaine Gros Frère et Soeur   From 2020 19.0

Medium-full colour. Rich. Somewhat biscuit-spicy on the nose. Lots of depth and interest. This is very, very lovely. Full-bodied, rich, and concentrated. Lots of vigour. Lots of depth. Harmonious; backward and mouth-filling.

Richebourg,

Domaine Thibault Liger-Belair   From 2019 17.0

Medium to medium-full colour. Some development. A little reduced and sweaty on the nose. Ripe and ample underneath. Fullish body. Meaty. Balanced but not exactly classy at present. Give it time.

Richebourg,

Domaine de la Romanée-Conti   From 2022 18.5

A big, tannic, quite aggressive example. The stems show more here than in the other DRC wines. Rich, fat, full-bodied, and generous, but rather ungainly at present.

La Grande Rue,

Domaine Lamarche   From 2019 18.0

Medium-full colour. Just a little four-square on the nose. Good volume. Very good fruit. Fullish body. Rich. Even slightly solid at present. Plenty of depth and energy. Fine plus.

La Tâche, Domaine de

la Romanée-Conti   From 2022 19.5

Full colour. Splendidly opulent nose. Rich and succulent. Very good tannins. Rather more integrated and sophisticated than the Richebourg. Very lovely fruit, and very finely balanced. A slight touch of mint at the end. Very long. Very fine indeed.

La Romanée, Domaine du

Vicomte de Liger-Belair   From 2019 18.5

Medium to medium-full colour. Some development. Fullish, rich, yet essentially delicate. Medium-full body. Balanced and abundantly fruity. It is a bit difficult to see quite how classy this is as there is some reduction here. Very fine at least.

La Romanée-Conti, Domaine de

la Romanée-Conti   From 2020 20.0

Good colour. Very fragrant, intense, delicate but classy nose. Creamy-rich. Very fine tannins. Lots of concentration here. Heaps of finesse. Brilliant.

Musigny,

Domaine Joesph Drouhin   From 2020 18.5

Medium-full colour. Still a bit closed on the nose. Ripe and sweet. But really quite delicate. Lovely fragrance. Long, complex, and very classy. But is it intense enough?

Musigny,

Domaine J. Frédéric Mugnier   From 2020 20.0

Good colour. Very lovely nose. Rich and concentrated, laid-back, and very, very classy and intense. Marvelous purity, dimension, and vigour on the palate. A great wine.

Musigny,

Domaine de la Vougeraie   From 2020 19.5

Medium to medium-full colour. Ripe, full, fat vigorous nose. Lots of depth. Soft, sweet, gentle yet very intense on the palate. Marvelous classy fruit. Lots and lots of dimension. Quite delicious.

Musigny, Domaine

Comte Georges de Vogüé   From 2022 20.0

Medium-full colour. Lovely complex, fragrant nose. Very fine attack with a follow-through that is profound, energetic, and multidimensional. Fullish body. Abundant fruit. Excellent harmony. This is quite special.

Bonnes-Mares,

Maison Olivier Bernstein   From 2019 18.0

Full colour. Rich, ample fruit on the nose. Succulent and lovely. Fullish body. Quite firm. Ripe, classy, profound, and complex. Very fine.

Bonnes-Mares,

Domaine Bertheau   From 2019   17.0

Fullish colour. Ample, lush, and succulent. But poised, elegant, and classy. Fullish body; quite firm, good grip. Needs time but the elements are here. Very good indeed but not fine.

Bonnes-Mares,

Domaine Bruno Clair   From 2019   19.0

Very full colour. At first a bit inflexible, if not tough on the nose. But lots of richness and succulence in the background. Splendidly fat and lush and concentrated. Excellent class and grip. This is very special.

Bonnes-Mares,

Domaine Drouhin-Laroze   From 2018   17.0

Medium to medium-full colour. Clean, pure nose. Good style if no real substance. Medium body. Ripe and soft. Sweet and balanced. But a slight lack of volume and energy. Elegant at the end though.

Bonnes-Mares,

Maison Benjamin Leroux   From 2017   15.0

Fullish colour. Not exactly clean on the nose. There seems to be a whiff of chlorine here. Better as it evolved. Good acidity and ripeness. But it lacks a bit of grip, and there is some astringency here.

Bonnes-Mares,

Domaine Georges Roumier   From 2022   19.5

Full colour. Rich and concentrated on the nose. This is a really profound wine. Full-bodied. Backward. Very distinguished. Brilliant.

Bonnes-Mares, Domaine

Comte Georges de Vogüé   From 2017   16.5

Medium to medium-full body. Some development. Rich, ripe, firm, oaky nose. Medium body. An attractive and well-balanced wine, even classy, if you don't mind so much oak. But there is a lack of energy and bite at the end.

Bonnes-Mares,

Domaine de la Vougeraie   From 2019   18.5

Fullish colour. At first a bit rude and ungainly on the nose. But that's just the stems. Ripe and balanced underneath. Fullish, closed-in. Cool. Lots of depth and energy, but still quite young. Quite a lot of power here. This I like. Very fine.

Clos des Lambrays,

Domaine des Lambrays   From 2020   17.5

Medium-full colour. Lots of depth here. A bit adolescent. Medium-full body. Not showing well. There is a touch of astringency. Behind there is a medium-full bodied wine with very promising intensity and very classy fruit. Fine (plus). (Seen twice: identical comment.)

Clos-Saint-Denis,

Domaine Dujac   From 2020   18.0

Fullish colour. Exotic, intense, and some stems on the nose. Lovely balancing acidity. Medium-full body. Very ripe tannins. Excellent fruit. Pure, intense, long, complex, and delicious. Fine plus.

Clos de la Roche,

Domaine Arlaud   From 2016   15.5

Medium to medium-full colour. Some development. A little reduced on the nose. Fullish body. Ripe. Ample. Slight touch of the stems. A bit ungainly at present but certainly good plus at the very least.

Clos de la Roche,

Domaine du Clos Frantin   From 2018   18.5

Medium-full colour. Good depth and vigour here. Ripe and balanced and classy. Fullish body. Ample and profound. Very good grip. Backward. Very fine.

Clos de la Roche,

Domaine Dujac   From 2016   16.5

Medium to medium-full colour. Fresh, ripe, and fruity on the nose. Medium to medium-full body. A wine of charm, but somewhat deficient in vigour and backbone.

Clos de la Roche,

Domaine Louis Jadot   From 2020   18.0

Full colour. Lovely plummy nose. Cool and concentrated. Medium-full body. Intense, vigorous, medium-full bodied, and splendidly classy. Fine plus.

Clos de la Roche,
Domaine Lignier-Michelot From 2018 16.0
Fullish colour. Full, ample, ripe, and rich on the nose. Quite evolved. Medium-full body. The fruit is almost sweet and the finish a bit tarty and astringent. But very good.

Clos de la Roche,
Vieille Vignes,
Domaine Ponsot From 2020 19.0
Full colour. Very complex, classy, multidimensional nose. Great concentration and intensity. Splendid depth and class. Brilliant fruit. Very lovely.

Clos de la Roche,
Domaine Louis Rémy From 2018 17.5
Full colour. Rich, concentrated, profound nose. Lots of dimension. Lots of energy. Medium-full body. Ripe, ample, balanced, and stylish. Perhaps just a little too straightforward for very fine.

Clos de Tart,
Domaine Mommessin From 2020 18.0
Full colour. Full, very concentrated, very complex, fat, and vigorous on the nose. Good energy on the palate. Full body, ripe, almost sweet. Balanced. Could it have done with a bit more class?

Chapelle-Chambertin,
Domaine Louis Jadot From 2018 18.0
Medium-full colour. Ripe, abundant, high-toned, classy nose. Medium-full body. Ample, oaky attack. Good grip. Fresh at the end. Long. Fine plus.

Chapelle-Chambertin,
Domaine Perrot-Minot From 2019 18.5
Fullish colour. Rich, full, abundant nose. Still a bit closed. Fullish body. A lot of energy here. Profound. Still a bit hidden. But very fine.

Chapelle-Chambertin,
Domaine Rossignol-Trapet From 2018 17.5
Fullish colour. Abundant, rich, vigorous nose. Fullish body. Rich. Succulent and very ripe. The finish is fine. Closed-in and concentrated.

Chapelle-Chambertin, Domaine
Jean et Jean-Louis Trapet From 2018 17.5
Good colour. Clean, mineral nose. Very stylish. Medium-full body. Lots of depth. Harmonious and full of fruit. Fine.

Chapelle-Chambertin,
Domaine Cécile Tremblay From 2016 15.5
Fullish colour. Full, oaky, somewhat earthy, gamey nose. Plenty of depth. Medium to medium-full body. Lacks a little grip. An attractive example but slightly bland.

Charmes-Chambertin, Mazoyères,
Domaine de la Vougeraie From 2017 17.5
Medium colour. Soft and fruity on the nose. Not aggressive. Medium-full body. Good grip. Fresh and stylish. Quite complex. Fragrant. Long. Fine.

Charmes-Chambertin,
Domaine Arlaud From 2016 14.0
Medium colour. Slight touch of reduction on the nose. On the palate fullish body. The attack is quite fruity and stylish, but there is also some astringency, and the follow-through is less distinguished. (Note: Others liked this more than I did. Indeed, by some way it was voted the best of the Charmes.)

Charmes-Chambertin,
Domaine Denis Bachelet From 2019 17.5
Medium-full colour. Some substance here on the nose. But a backward wine which is rather closed-in at present. Fullish weight. Fresh. Ample. Balanced and abundant. Very well-balanced, vigorous fruit. Tannic yet not a bit too dense. Fine at the very least.

Charmes-Chambertin,
Maison Henri Boillot From 2016 16.0
Medium to medium-full colour. Ripe and oaky on the nose. Not a blockbuster. Medium weight. Attractive, fresh, juicy wine. Balanced, stylish, and long.

Charmes-Chambertin,
Domaine Claude Dugat From 2016 16.0
Medium to medium-full colour. Gentle oaky nose. Soft and forward. Medium weight. Fresh

and fruity. Not a blockbuster but neat and balanced and positive.

Charmes-Chambertin,
Maison Camille Giroud   From 2016   15.0
Medium-full colour. Good high-toned fruit on the nose. Medium body. Only of medium interest on the palate. Fresh and fruity. Ripe and decently balanced. But a little one-dimensional.

Charmes-Chambertin,
Domaine Humbert Frères   From 2017   17.5
Fullish colour. Rich, full, concentrated nose. Fullish body. Very good grip. Very classy and very intense. Fine.

Charmes-Chambertin,
Domaine Olivier Jouan   From 2018   18.5
Fullish colour. Very, very rich and concentrated. Yet not a bit too closed on the nose. Backward. This is very fine. Fullish body. Profound and abundant. Lots of dimension.

Charmes-Chambertin,
Domaine Maume   From 2017   17.0
Fullish colour. Ripe, rich, full-bodied, and concentrated. Classy too. Very good fruit. Energetic and stylish. Fragrant, vigorous, and long on the palate.

Charmes-Chambertin,
Domaine Perrot-Minot   From 2017   17.5
Medium-full colour. Ripe, abundant, fresh, and accessible on the nose. Classy too. Medium-full body. Very good grip. Very ripe. Good energy. Fine long finish.

Charmes-Chambertin,
Maison Roland Remoissenet   From 2015   15.0
Medium-full colour. Soft and fruity but essentially gentle and of lightish weight, both on the nose and on the palate. A little too loose-knit to take seriously.

Charmes-Chambertin,
Maison Roche de Bellene   From 2017   17.5
Medium-full colour. Rich, quite concentrated, splendidly fruity nose. Lots of depth and style. Medium-full body. Ripe, rich, and oaky. Good

grip. Open and abundant and quite accessible. Lovely finish.

Charmes-Chambertin,
Domaine Armand Rousseau   From 2016   15.5
Medium to medium-full body. A touch astringent on the palate. Good at the end though.

Charmes-Chambertin,
Domaine Taupenot-Merme   From 2015   13.0
Medium to medium-full colour. Some development. Somewhat thin and weedy on both the nose and the palate. And astringent at the end.

Griotte-Chambertin,
Domaine Joseph Drouhin   From 2018   18.0
Fullish colour. Round, ripe, succulent, and full of fruit on the nose. Perhaps it lacks a little intensity and vigour. Better as it evolved. Very Chambolle-ish. Sweet, long, and lovely. Fine plus.

Latricières-Chambertin,
Domaine Arnoux-Lachaux   From 2018   17.5
Fullish colour. Fine cassis-flavoured nose. Rich and full-bodied. Oaky. Some tannin. Quite a powerful wine, especially on the follow-through. Lots of energy. Fine.

Latricières-Chambertin,
Domaine Drouhin-Laroze   From 2020   17.5
Medium-full colour. Soft, aromatic nose. Medium to medium-full body. Clean and balanced. Not rich or complex or classy enough for great, but long and very satisfactory nonetheless. Fine.

Latricières-Chambertin,
Domaine Faiveley   From 2018   18.0
Medium-full colour. Gamey nose. Spicy and animal. Balanced, rich, oaky, and vigorous. Medium-full body. Vigorous, profound, and elegant. Very long and luxurious.

Latricières-Chambertin,
Domaine Louis Rémy   From 2018   17.0
Medium to medium-full colour. Some development. Slightly sweaty, gamey nose, but good balance and depth. Medium-full body. Fresh

and fruity. Ripe and attractive. But very good indeed rather than fine.

Latricières-Chambertin,
Domaine Rossignol-Trapet   From 2019 18.0
Medium-full colour. Some development. Closed-in nose. Fullish body. Rich and concentrated. Lush, ample, abundant, and with very good acidity. Lots of vigour. Lots of class.

Latricières-Chambertin, Domaine
Jean et Jean-Louis Trapet   From 2018 17.0
Good colour. A rich wine with no lack of backbone. Fullish body. I find it less elegant and less mineral than their Chapelle, but this is ample and satisfying. Very good indeed.

Mazis-Chambertin,
Domaine Faiveley   From 2020 18.5
Closed on the nose. Fullish body. Vigorous. Very good grip. Lots of style and complexity. Lots of class and depth. Very fine.

Mazis-Chambertin,
Domaine Maume   From 2018 18.0
Medium-full body. High-toned, oaky-caramel nose. Fullish body underneath. Very rich, ample wine. Heaps of voluptuous fruit. Lots of energy and very seductive.

Mazoyères-Chambertin,
Domaine Perrot-Minot   From 2018 17.5
Medium-full colour. Good clean, pure, concentrated fruit on the nose. Fullish body. Ripe and energetic. Very good grip. Lots of dimension. Fine.

Mazoyères-Chambertin,
Domaine Taupenot-Merme   From 2015 13.0
Medium-full colour. Very pinched and vegetal on the nose. Thin and attenuated. Highish acidity.

Ruchotte-Chambertin, Domaine
Dr. Georges Mugneret-Gibourg   From 2019 19.0
Medium-full colour. Splendid concentration and class on the nose. Full body. Some oak. Very harmonious. Very lovely balanced fruit. Profound and multidimensional. This is really very fine plus.

Ruchottes-Chambertin,
Domaine Christophe Roumier   From 2018 18.0
Medium to medium-full colour. Fresh, quite minty nose. Good depth and generosity. Some stems. Fullish body. Rich and energetic on the palate. Lots of depth. This is less developed than most. Fine plus.

Chambertin, Clos de Bèze,
Domaine Bruno Clair   From 2020 19.0
Full colour. Very good tannins. Excellent fruit. Really elegant. Vigorous and complex. A profound wine. Very long and very lovely.

Chambertin, Clos de Bèze,
Domaine Drouhin-Laroze   From 2018 17.0
Medium colour. There is something a little herbal which puts me off in the nose. Fullish body. A little astringency. Good fruit and very good grip though. And a long vigorous finish, but it doesn't add up to any more than very good indeed.

Chambertin, Clos de Bèze,
Domaine Faiveley   From 2020 19.0
Medium-full colour. Firm, rich, full, well-balanced, and very classy and profound on the nose. Very complex. Most imprssive. On the palate, still rather youthful and closed-in. Full body. There is a lot of flair here but it's all in potential. Very lovely fruit as it developed.

Chambertin, Clos de Bèze,
Domaine Louis Jadot   From 2018 18.0
Medium-full colour. Soft, fruity, generous, harmonious nose. Quite closed. Fullish body. Ample, fruity attack. Plenty of depth. Very good energy. Fine plus.

Chambertin, Clos de Bèze,
Maison Perrot-Minot   From 2020 19.0
Medium-full colour. Lots of abundant ripe fruit on the nose. Just a faint trace of reduction. On the palate this is very lovely. Full-bodied. Rich. Ripe and harmonious. Lots of depth and energy. Very classy. Still very young. Excellent.

Chambertin, Clos de Bèze,

Domaine Armand Rousseau   From 2020   19.0

This is profound and intense and very lovely. Ripe, rich, concentrated, and classy. Multidimensional. Lovely finish. Excellent.

Chambertin,

Domaine Bertagna   From 2018   16.5

Medium-full colour. Soft and quite oaky on the nose. Rather too much new wood for this size of wine. For it is only medium-full bodied, if that. Pretty fruit and reasonable grip. But it lacks energy and intensity. Very good plus at best.

Chambertin,

Maison Henri Boillot   From 2020   19.0

Medium to medium-full colour. Rich, fullish, oaky, and profound on the nose. Fullish body. Ripe, vigorous, balanced, and classy. Cool. Very long. Excellent.

Chambertin,

Domaine du Clos Frantin   From 2018   17.5

Medium-full colour. Just a little four-square on the nose. Rather hidden at present. There is very good fruit underneath. Medium to medium-full body. But quite enough energy, grip, and depth for a Chambertin. Plus the fruit is ripe and seductive.

Chambertin,

Maison Camille Giroud   From 2018   17.5

Medium to medium-full colour. Rich, ample, slightly stemmy nose. Spicy and gamey. Fullish body. Rich, fat, and abundant. Good follow-through. Good depth. But not great. It lacks a bit of grip and intensity.

Chambertin, Domaine Rémy   From 2020   19.0

Medium colour. High-toned nose. Lovely ample, complex fruit. But essentially quite delicate. Fullish body. Very, very rich and succulent. Splendid vigorous fruit. Lovely finish. Very fine indeed.

Chambertin,

Maison Roche de Bellene   From 2020   19.0

Medium-full colour. Fine nose. Still a bit hidden. Rich, profound, and austere. Full body.

Very vigorous. Excellent ripe concentrated fruit. Very fine classy wine here.

Chambertin,

Domaine Rossignol-Trapet   From 2019   17.5

Medium colour. Ripe, stylish, generous, medium-weight nose. A slight echo of the lean and vegetal on the palate, but otherwise fullish-bodied, rich, abundant, and vigorous. Still young.

Chambertin,

Domaine Armand Rousseau   From 2020   20.0

Medium-full colour. Splendid nose. Full and profound, very concentrated, quite oaky, yet understated and still very youthful. Fullish body. Harmonious, multidimensional fruit. Excellent grip. Really impressive. Very lovely follow-through. Splendid.

Chambertin, Domaine

Jean et Jean-Louis Trapet   From 2020   18.5

Good colour. A fullish, rich wine, but a little closed-in at present. There is plenty of depth, but not quite the purity and profundity I was hoping for. Yet the finish is concentrated and persistent. (Note: I marked the sample at our three-year-on tasting 19.5.)

2007 BURGUNDY

Putting it brutally, 2007 is the least good red wine Burgundian vintage in the 2005–2009 period. Having said that, it must not be assumed that it should be considered beneath contempt. Far from it. While there are few

⇢ *Rating for the Vintage* ⇠	
Red	14.5
White	15.5

wines, even at the very top levels, with the depth, concentration, and intensity one would like to find, there is no shortage of very pleasant, fresh, fruity bottles for drinking in the relatively short term. Indeed, many village Côte de Beaunes are already soft and palatable, and it will not be long before most of the rest are equally *gouleyant*. They arrived onto a market which was in a state of economic shock. And

Size of the Crop
(In hectolitres)

	RED	WHITE	TOTAL
Grand cru	12,230	4,126	16,356
Village and			
premier cru	168,721	70,884	239,605
TOTAL	180,951	75,010	255,961

for this reason, as well as their perceived quality as only *moyen*, their take-up was only minimal. One merchant friend was candid: "I'm pleasantly surprised we have sold any," he told me in January 2009, in the aftermath of the annual London Burgundy *en primeur* tastings.

But this means that there were a lot of bottles left unwanted in Burgundian cellars. To shift those, with better 2008s to hand a year later, plus what then became very clear: an even finer, if not very fine 2009 in the pipeline, required a face-up to reality and acts of generosity on the part of the Burgundian trade. I suspect there are still some bargains to be had. If you know where to look.

Weather Conditions

Climatically it was a very curious year. After a mild, dry winter—only one serious frost at the end of January—Burgundy enjoyed its summer in April, with temperatures as high as the thirties (85-plus Farenheit) and four weeks of abundant sun. This ensured an early start to the vegetative cycle, and, despite inclement conditions to follow, 2007 would result in an early harvest. Thereafter, apart from a week in mid-May, when the vines flowered some three weeks in advance of the average, the weather remained cold, wet, and miserable for two and

a half months. Even after July 14, the date most of the French consider summer has begun, it continued patchy, with more days of cloud and rain than sun. Unsettled weather persisted until the last week of August, when, right at the last minute, the clouds cleared and temperatures improved. Overall, it was a very wet summer indeed. Mildew, oidium, and rot remained a constant threat. Good husbandry in the vineyard, constant vigilance, and a crop reduced to the minimum were essential.

The vintage began first in the Côte de Beaune, around Monday, September 3. This was followed a week later by the Côte de Nuits, Chablis, and the Mâconnais and Beaujolais. Usually these last two regions pick a full ten days or more ahead of the Côte d'Or. The latest to pick, the Côte Chalonnaise and the Hautes Côtes, had the best of it, being able to profit more from the return to fine weather. Sadly, 2007 could not, like 2008 would be, claim to be a "saved at the last minute" vintage. By mid-September the Côte d'Or fruit was ready. If left it would simply rot on the vine. In retrospect, this was doubly tragic, for the autumn of 2007 was quite glorious, with leaf colour to rival Vermont at its best—and for a month or more.

It was, it hardly needs to be said, essential to *tri*, to eliminate substandard fruit before vinification. As a result, most top estates have produced a reduced crop, some announcing 25 percent less than 2006 (which was by no means large). In total, the Côte d'Or crop was 4.2 percent less that 2006 in red, but 18.6 percent larger in white wine.

The Wines

The Chablis results are variable. Alcohol levels are reasonable but acidities are low. Many wines are rather soft and ephemeral. There is a lack of minerality and breed. At the other end of Burgundy, the Beaujolais and Mâconnais are again good but not great. Where there are some unexpectedly nice wines, as in 2008, where they are even better, is in the Côte Chalonnaise.

The white wines of the Côte de Beaune

started off sultry, hiding whatever merit they might have had. Then, a year after production, one could see relatively soft-centred wines, with at the very least a refreshing acidity and ripe and racy fruit. While rather better in Meursault and Puligny than in Chassagne, they were otherwise more consistent though rather lighter than the 2006s, where there are some lovely wines but some horrors as well.

As far as the red wines are concerned, once again, as so often, the Côte de Nuits has produced proportionally better wines than the Côte de Beaune. The skins were fragile, so this was a vintage to avoid subjecting the musts to too prolonged an extraction. In general, the red wines are of medium weight, less than medium strength, but at their best supple, juicy, soft, and full of most agreeable fruit. In some cases, especially in the Côte de Beaune, they are too *tendre*. In more cases, while not too feeble, what you get on the attack is all there is, there is no extra dimension on the follow-through. Only at the very top levels have we wines of intensity. But at the very least there is a pleasant supporting acidity. This is the saving grace of the 2007 vintage. So we have something between 2000 and 2001, but better in the Côte de Beaune than in these two years. And the best of these are charming and satisfying bottles to drink— if not today, very soon.

Where are the best wines? The most consistent and satisfactory commune is certainly Nuits-Saint-Georges. The somewhat burly tendency of the wines has been softened by the style of the vintage. The Gevreys are also good, as are the Cortons, for much of the same reason. This is not to say that there are not some delicious wines in Vosne and Chambolle, but often there is a lack of the third dimension of concentration and vigour at the end of the palate. Too many wines are charming but soft-centred.

When will the 2007s be at their best? The vast majority of the red 2007s will be at their summit by 2014 or so: some of the weaker Côte de Beaunes are indeed already at their peak. Very few will need extra cellaring after 2016, and for the most part, few will endure much

beyond 2020. To get most enjoyment out of the 2007s, drink the vintage while it is still fresh, as soon as it has softened up.

The Best Wines

19.5/20

La Romanée, Domaine du Vicomte de Liger-Belair

Musigny, Domaine J. F. Mugnier

Chambertin, Domaine Leroy

Chambertin, Domaine Armand Rousseau

19.0

Chambolle-Musigny, Les Amoureuses, Domaine J. F. Mugnier

Romanée-Saint-Vivant, Domaine Alain Hudelot-Noëllat

Romanée-Saint-Vivant, Domaine Leroy

La Tâche, Domaine de la Romanée-Conti

Bonnes-Mares, Domaine Georges Roumier

Bonnes-Mares, Domaine Comte Georges de Vogüé

Chambertin, Domaine Louis Rémy

18.5

Volnay, Clos des Ducs, Domaine Marquie d'Angerville

Nuits-Saint-Georges, Clos des Porrets, Domaine Henri Gouges

Nuits-Saint-Georges, Les Saint-Georges, Domaine Henri Gouges

Chambolle-Musigny, Les Amoureuses, Domaine Georges Roumier

Gevrey-Chambertin, Clos-Saint-Jacques, Domaine Bruno Clair

Corton, Bressandes, Domaine Comte Senard

Corton, Renardes, Domaine Michel Gaunoux

Corton, Clos du Roi, Domaine Conte Senard

Clos de Vougeot, Domaine Grivot

Clos de Vougeot, Domaine Leroy

Clos de Vougeot, Vieille Vignes, Château de la Tour

Echézeaux, Domaine Gérard Mugneret

Echézeaux, Emmanuel Rouget

Grands-Echézeaux, Domaine du Clos Frantin

La Grande Rue, Domaine Lamarche

Romanée-Saint-Vivant, Domaine
Follin-Arbelet

Romanée-Saint-Vivant, Domaine de la
Romanée-Conti

Richebourg, Domaine Grivot

Richebourg, Domaine Leroy

Romanée-Conti, Domaine de la
Romanée-Conti

Musigny, Domaine Comte Georges de Vogüé

Chapelle-Chambertin, Domaine
Rossignol-Trapet

Chambertin, Clos de Bèze, Domaine du Clos
Frantin

Chambertin, Clos de Bèze, Domaine Bruno
Clair

Chambertin, Domaine Bertagna

Chambertin, Maison Henri Boillot

Chambertin, Maison Camille Giroud

Chambertin, Domaine Jean et Jean-Louis
Trapet

TASTING NOTES

The vast majority of the following wines were sampled at the Annual Domaines Familieux tasting in Paris in March 2010 and the group's annual tasting at the end of August 2010. I have added others, tasted for the most part on my annual visit to the United States in April 2010. Most of the Domaine Leroy wines and those of the Domaine de la Romanée-Conti were sampled in situ.

White Wines

Corton-Charlemagne,
Domaine Faiveley   Now to 2020   17.5
Medium colour. A suggestion of development. Aromatic nose. The oak comes across as a sug-

gestion of digestive biscuits. Plus a gentle caramelly touch. On the palate, dry but soft. Good grip. Better energy and dimension at the end than the attack would suggest. Long, positive finish. Fine.

Red Wines
CÔTE DE BEAUNE

Santenay, Beauregard,
Domaine Chanson   Now to 2016   14.0
Medium colour. Light, fruity; slightly earthy nose. Light to medium body. Ripe and fruity. Quite good. Just about ready.

Santenay, Beaurepaire,
Domaine Vincent Morey   Now to 2016   13.0
Medium colour. Soft nose. Somewhat thin and one-dimensional. Not a great deal of style either. Not bad at best.

Santenay, Beaurepaire,
Domaine Anne-Marie et
Jean-Marc Vincent   Now to 2016   13.0
Light, soft, easy to drink. No great weight at all. And not much style either. Only fair.

Santenay, Gravières,
Domaine Anne-Marie et
Jean-Marc Vincent   From 2013   15.0
This is rather better than their Beaurepaire. Fresher, more depth, more future. In fact, a most attractive example.

Santenay, Passe-Temps,
Domaine Anne-Marie et
Jean-Marc Vincent   From 2013   14.5
A little lighter than their Gravières, but generous and succulent. Fresh enough. But I prefer the Gravières.

Monthelie, Sur la Velle,
Domaine Eric de Suremain   From 2014   15.5
Medium to medium-full body. Sophisticated and positive. Good tannins. Very good fruit. Positive and promising. There have been improvements here. (And the village wine can also be recommended.)

Savigny-Lès-Beaune, La Dominode,
Domaine Chanson   Now to 2016   12.5
Medium colour. Thin on the nose. A bit cheap.
Light, rustic, and already a bit astringent.

Savigny-Lès-Beaune, Les Godeaux,
Maison Seguin-Manuel   From 2013   14.0
Medium colour. Soft, fruity, charming nose.
No great backbone but the fruit is stylish and
the wine fresh and balanced. Good depth here.
Good for what it is.

Savigny-Lès-Beaune, Les Lavières,
Domaine Camus-Brochon   Now to 2016   13.0
Medium colour. Soft nose. Rather thin and
one-dimensional, but not bad.

Savigny-Lès-Beaune, Les Lavières,
Domaine Chandon de Briailles   From 2013   13.5
Lightish, but interesting nevertheless. Good
attack, but it lacks a bit of grip. Not bad plus.

Savigny-Lès-Beaune, Les Lavières,
Maison Seguin-Manuel   From 2013   14.0
A similar wine to the Godeaux, but with just
a little bit more to it, especially on the follow-
through. An attractive if unpretentious wine
for early drinking.

Savigny-Lès-Beaune,
Les Narbantons,
Domaine Camus-Brochon   Now to 2015   12.5
Medium colour. Not much on the nose. Thin,
short, and cheap on the palate. Unexciting.

Savigny-Lès-Beaune,
Les Narbantons,
Domaine Leroy   From 2014   14.5
Firm for a 2007 on both the nose and the pal-
ate. Slightly hard at present on the attack. Good
follow-through though. No lack of wine here.

Savigny-Lès-Beaune, Les Peuillets,
Domaine Nicky Potel   Now to 2015   12.0
Medium colour. A hint of volatile acidity on
the nose. Thin and astringent on the palate.
Unexciting.

Savigny-Lès-Beaune,
Les Vergelesses,
Domaine Simon Bize   From 2014   16.0
Good colour. Stylish nose. Nice plummy fruit.
Good depth and tannins for a 2007 and plenty
of class. Positive at the end. Very good.

Pernand-Vergelesses,
Les Vergelesses,
Domaine Chanson   From 2013   14.5
Medium colour. Good fruit on the nose. Good
weight on the palate. Will still improve positive
and stylish.

Pernand-Vergelesses,
Ile de Vergelesses,
Domaine Chandon de Briailles   From 2014   17.5
Medium colour. Plenty of depth and personality on the nose. Lovely supple fruit. Medium to
medium-full body. Good tannins. Nice and rich
and fresh and complex. Plenty of energy. Lovely.

Pernand-Vergelesses,
Ile de Vergelesses,
Domaine Rollin   Now to 2015   13.0
Medium colour. Earthy nose. Light and thin
and lacks fruit. Not special.

Aloxe-Corton, Les Suchots,
Domaine Simon Bize   Now to 2015   12.0
A bit light and thin. Forward. Uninspiring.

Beaune, Aigrots,
Domaine Michel Lafarge   From 2014   16.0
Fragrant nose. Stylish, ripe, and medium-bod-
ied. Lacks a little energy but long and lovely.
Very good.

Beaune, Boucherottes,
Domaine A. F. Gros   From 2013   14.0
Medium to medium-full colour. Lightish nose
but elegant and fruity. Medium body. Decent
class, fruit, and balance. Quite good.

Beaune, Bressandes,
Domaine Chanson   From 2013   14.0
Medium colour. Quite fruity and fragrant on
the nose. Not a lot of weight and grip but a
pleasant forward bottle.

Beaune, Bressandes,
Domaine des Croix From 2013 13.5
Medium body. I don't think this is the best of bottles, but it improved in the glass. At first very herbaceous. Underneath medium body, some decent fruit and at least some grip.

Beaune, Champ Pimont,
Domaine Chanson From 2013 15.5
Medium full colour. Round, ripe, and fruity on the nose. Ample, juicy, medium to medium-full bodied on the palate. Good grip. Good plus.

Beaune, Cras, Domaine
du Château de Chorey From 2013 16.0
Medium colour. Good, ripe, positive nose. Rich, fullish-bodied and ample. Plenty of energy and dimension. Very good.

Beaune, Coucherias,
Domaine Francois Labet From 2014 15.5
Medium body. Youthful, fruity, ripe, balanced, and stylish. Rather better than it used to be. Good plus.

Beaune, Epenottes,
Domaine Jean-Marc Boillot From 2015 16.0
Medium to medium-full colour. Good class and weight on the nose. Medium to medium-full body. Good grip. Positive. Elegant. Long. Very good.

Beaune, Clos des Fèves,
Domaine Chanson From 2013 14.5
Medium colour. Pleasantly fruity, if somewhat earthy nose. Positive. Medium-bodied. Quite good plus.

Beaune, Grèves,
Vigne de l'Enfant Jesus,
Domaine Bouchard Père et Fils From 2013 14.0
Medium colour. A touch of reduction at first. Fresher on the palate. Medium weight. Quite fresh, fruity, and positive at the end. Quite good.

Beaune, Grèves,
Domaine Chanson From 2013 13.5
Medium colour. Medium weight on the nose, but fragrant and elegant. Medium body. Fresh at the end. Lacks a bit of bite but not bad plus.

Beaune, Grèves,
Domaine des Croix From 2013 14.0
Medium colour. Fruity nose. Juicy and agreeable. Medium body. Positive finish. Quite good.

Beaune, Grèves,
Domaine de Montille From 2013 16.0
Medium to medium-full body. Quite rich. Plump and ripe. Good backbone and grip. Crisp and stylish. Long and positive. Very good.

Beaune, Grèves,
Domaine Nicky Potel From 2014 16.0
Medium to medium-full colour. Rich, fat, and ample on the nose. Very good fruit here. Medium to medium-full body. Good structure. Good drip. Positive at the end. Very good.

Beaune, Grèves,
Domaine Tollot-Beaut From 2013 14.0
Medium colour. Earthy nose. A bit reduced at first. But this soon blew off. Positive and balanced. Some substance. Quite good.

Beaune, Clos des Marconnets,
Domaine Chanson From 2013 13.0
Medium colour. Some weight but not much style on the nose. A bit cheap on the palate.

Beaune, Marconnets,
Domaine Bouchard Père et Fils From 2013 13.5
Medium colour. Light nose, lacking weight and grip. Ripe but slight on the palate. Some style though.

Beaune, Clos des Mouches,
Domaine Joseph Drouhin From 2013 17.0
Medium to medium-full body. Quiet attack. But a good positive follow-through. Ripe and vigorous. Long and classy. Lovely fruit. Very good indeed.

Beaune, Pertuisots,
Domaine des Croix From 2013 13.0
Medium colour. A little thin on the nose. Pretty but light and forward. Will it get astringent? Only fair.

Beaune, Pertuisots,
Domaine Jean-Yves Devevey From 2013 13.0
Medium colour. Not a lot on the nose. Medium body. Lacks a bit of fruit. Some astringency already. Only fair.

Beaune, Pertuisots,
Domaine Nicky Potel From 2013 13.5
Medium colour. Ripe nose, but a bit rustic. Medium to medium-full body. Slightly dry on the follow-through. Decent fruit and grip, but not exciting.

Beaune, Clos du Roi,
Domaine Tollot-Beaut From 2013 16.5
Medium colour. Ripe, stylish, creamy nose. Medium to medium-full body. Good depth. Ample fruit. Lovely.

Beaune, Les Sizies,
Domaine de Montille From 2013 14.0
Medium weight. Not really very much depth. Pretty fruit. Decent balance. But a bit superficial. Quite good.

Beaune, Teurons,
Domaine Bouchard Père et Fils From 2013 14.5
Medium colour. Soft and fruity on the nose. But not much depth. Medium weight. Fresh and easy to drink.

Beaune, Teurons,
Domaine Chanson From 2013 14.5
Medium colour. Ripe but just a little thin on the nose. Fresh and easy to enjoy on the palate. Medium weight. Positive at the end.

Beaune, Teurons, Domaine
de Château du Chorey Drink soon 12.0
Medium colour. High-toned and rather thin on the nose. Weedy and short.

Beaune, Teurons,
Domaine Rossignol-Trapet From 2013 14.0
Medium colour. Spicy nose. Some substance. Medium body. Decent fruit. No great distinction but quite good.

Beaune, Vignes Franches,
Domaine du Château de Chorey From 2013 15.5
Medium-full colour. Not much on the nose. Fresh, ripe, and stylish on the palate. Medium to medium-full body. Good grip. Positive at the end. Good plus.

Volnay, Vendanges Selectionées,
Domaine Michel Lafarge From 2014 15.5
Soft, but ripe and concentrated, with good tannins. Very good grip. This has no lack of volume and depth. Nor style. Good plus.

Volnay, Clos de la Bousse d'Or,
Domaine de la Pousse d'Or From 2013 15.5
Medium to medium-full colour. Forward, fruity, and a bit loose-knit on the nose. On the palate, decent grip, and very nice ripe fruit. Medium body. Good grip. Good plus.

Volnay, Caillerets,
Domaine Henri Boillot From 2014 17.5
Medium-full colour. Rich, full, concentrated nose. Very cassis. Lots of depth. High-quality. Fullish body. Still youthful. Very good grip. Fine.

Volnay, Domaine Louis Boillot Drink soon 12.0
Medium-full colour. Rather attenuated and weedy on both the nose and the palate. Disappointing.

Volnay, Caillerets, Domaine
Bouchard Père et Fils From 2013 17.5
Medium-full colour. Soft, fragrant, stylish but quite forward nose. Good grip. Quite intense. Classy fruit. Long. Fine.

Volnay, Caillerets,
Domaine de Montille From 2013 13.0
Medium colour. Not much depth or substance on the nose. Medium body. Rather nondescript.

Volnay, Caillerets,
Clos des 60 Ouvrées,
Domaine de la Pousse d'Or From 2013 15.0
Medium colour. Decent substance if a bit foursquare on the nose. Good grip. Youthful. Good fruit and grip. Good.

Volnay, Caillerets,

Domaine Nicolas Rossignol   From 2013   17.5
Softer-centered than his Taillepieds but equally intense. Medium-full body. Less reserved. Quite round already. Lovely fruit. Very good style. Fine too.

Volnay, Carelle sous la Chapelle,

Domaine Henri Boillot   From 2013   16.5
Medium to medium-full colour. Slightly reduced at first but good depth and balance. Medium to medium-full body. Positive, stylish, and fragrant. Good grip. Very good fruit.

Volnay, Clos de la Cave des Ducs,

Maison Leroux   From 2013   17.5
Medium colour. Soft but ripe on the nose. Balanced and fragrant. Medium to medium-full body. Intense. Harmonious. Classy and complex. Lovely.

Volnay, Champans, Domaine

Marquis d'Angerville   From 2014   17.0
A bigger and today more astringent wine than the Fremiets. But this is just on the attack. The follow-through is elegant and ample. Long and fragrant. Very good indeed.

Volnay, Champans,

Domaine des Comtes Lafon   From 2014   17.0
Medium-full colour. Quite profound and substantial on the nose. Good depth and complexity and an attractive personality. Balanced. Even sturdy. Some tannin. Very good indeed.

Volnay, Clos du Château des Ducs,

Domaine Lafarge   From 2013   14.5
Medium colour. Some fragrance and interest on the nose. But not a great deal of character. Medium body. Balanced and fresh. Quite forward. Quite good plus.

Volnay, Chevret,

Domaine Nicolas Rossignol   From 2013   15.5
Medium to medium-full weight. Good balance. Charming fruit. An attractive wine if without the depth and flair of his Caillerets. Good plus.

Volnay, Chevret,

Domaine Henri Boillot   From 2014   17.5
Medium-full colour. Good depth and substance on the nose. Ripe and rich. Some tannin. Good grip. Still a bit closed. Medium-full body. Concentrated. Lots of style. Complex and long on the palate. Fine.

Volnay, Clos des Chênes,

Domaine Bouchard Père et Fils   From 2013   15.0
Medium-full colour. Soft, round, slightly overripe, spicy nose. Medium body. Almost exotic. Certainly a little sweet. But no lack of grip. Finishes positively. Good.

Volnay, Clos des Chênes,

Domaine Francois Buffet   Drink soon   12.0
Light nose. Straightforward fruity nose. Light and rather too evolved.

Volnay, Clos des Chênes,

Domaine Michel Lafarge   From 2015   17.5
Medium-full body. Ripe, intense, concentrated, and very classy. By no means a blockbuster, even in 2007 terms. But very lovely fresh fruit and very long. Fine.

Volnay, Clos de Chênes,

Domaine des Comtes Lafon   From 2013   15.5
Medium colour. Ripe nose. Balanced. Soft. Decent style if no great weight. Quite fresh. Positive and charming. Good plus.

Volnay, Clos des Chênes,

Domaine René Monnier   From 2013   14.0
Medium colour. Soft, fruity, pleasant nose, if no real depth or distiction. Medium body. Not a lot of tannin. But decent balance. Quite good.

Volnay, Clos des Ducs,

Domaine Marquis d'Angerville   From 2015   18.5
Full-bodied, rich, and fat. This is very lovely. Excellent fruit and depth. Lovely complex, multidimensional wine. Very fine.

Volnay, Fremiets,

Domaine Marquis d'Angerville   From 2014   17.5
Refined, fragrant, nose. Intense, backward, concentrated, and fullish for a 2007 on the

palate. Lots of vigour. Surprisingly fine. This is normally eclipsed by the other Angerville Volnays.

Volnay, Fremiets;
Domaine Comte Armand   From 2013 16.0

Medium to medium-full colour. Ripe, fresh, quite substantial nose. Good depth and grip. Medium to medium-full body. Ample, balanced, and positive. Still a bit adolescent. Very good.

Volnay, Fremiets,
Domaine Henri Boillot   From 2013 16.5

Medium to medium-full colour. A bit stiff and unforthcoming on the nose at first. Better as it developed. Good substance and balance. Medium to medium-full body. Quite concentrated. Good grip. Long. Very good plus.

Volnay, Fremiets,
Domaine Faiveley   Now to 2016 12.0

Medium to medium-full colour. Tarty, attenuated nose. Thin and cheap. Unstylish.

Volnay, Mitans,
Domaine Lafarge   Now to 2016 12.5

Medium to medium-full colour. Forward. Already a bit astringent. Loose-knit and undistinguished.

Volnay, Mitans,
Domaine de Montille   Now to 2016 12.5

Rather weak and neutral. Lacks grip. Already a bit astringent.

Volnay, Ronceret,
Domaine Nicolas Rossignol   From 2012 14.0

Very blackberry in flavour. Rich, almost exotic. Not quite the grip of Rossignol's other Volnays, though. I find this a little dry at the end. Will it resolve itself?

Volnay, Clos de la Rougeotte,
Domaine Henri Boillot   From 2013 16.0

Medium to medium-full colour. Quite a forward nose. Ripe and fragrant. No great weight but elegant and balanced. Really quite concentrated. Very good fruit.

Volnay, Santenots, Domaine
du Pavillon (Albert Bichot)   From 2013 14.0

Medium-full colour. Soft, fragrant, and fruity on the nose. Quite forward. Medium body. Decent balance but a little one-dimensional. Quite good.

Volnay, Santenots du Milieu,
Domaine des Comtes Lafon   From 2016 17.5

Good colour. Quite a bit more profound and vigorous than the Champans. Medium-full body. Vigorous and classy. Very good tannins and plenty of length and dimension. Fine.

Volnay, Santenots du Milieu,
Domaine Leroy   From 2013 15.5

Forward but a good ample, stylish attack. Then it tails off. Medium body. Ripe but no great concentration. Good plus.

Volnay, Santenots,
Maison Roche de Bellene   From 2013 13.0

Nicolas Potel's *negocaint*'s business. Medium-colour. Smoky nose. Slightly astringent. Medium to medium-full body. Lacks style and dimension. Only fair.

Volnay, Taillepieds,
Domaine de Montille   From 2014 14.5

Better than their Mitans, but also a little weak and short. Decent fruit. Quite fresh. Quite good plus.

Volnay, Taillepieds,
Domaine Nicolas Rossignol   From 2014 17.5

Medium-full body. Quite firm for the vintage. Minerally and nicely austere. Good grip. Very classy fruit. Fine.

Pommard, *Premier Cru*,
Domaine Michel Gaunoux   From 2014 16.5

Fullish body. Plump, ripe, very good grip. Rather more style here than in the past. Long on the palate. Very good plus.

Pommard, Clos des Epeneaux,
Domaine Comte Armand   From 2015 17.5

Medium-full colour. A good, full, meaty wine on the nose. Oaky too. Medium-full body. Some tannin. Classy fruit. Very good grip. Harmonious. Fine. Needs time.

Pommard, Les Grands Epenots,
Domaine Michel Gaunoux   From 2014   17.5
Even more stylish and complete than their *premier cru*, if slightly less weight. Lovely balanced fruit. Long. Fine.

Pommard, Epenots,
Maison Camille Giroud   From 2013   11.0
Medium colour. High-toned nose. Both reduced and attenuated. Rather stewed and soupy. No.

Pommard, Epenots,
Domaine Francois Parent   From 2014   16.0
Medium to medium-full colour. Quite soft and ripe on the nose. Medium body. Ripe and smooth, balanced and attractive and easy to enjoy. Good grip. Well-made. Balanced and very good.

Pommard, Fremiers,
Domaine Louis Boillot   Drink soon   11.0
Medium-full colour. High-toned nose. High volatile acidity. Thin and astringent on the palate. No.

Pommard, Jarollières,
Domaine Jean-Marc Boillot   From 2013   12.0
Medium-full colour. A bit sweaty on the nose. Medium weight. Somewhat attenuated and astringent. Lacks style.

Pommard, Jarollières,
Domaine de la Pousse d'Or   From 2014   17.5
Medium to medium-full colour. Fresh nose. Quite sturdy and substantial. Good weight and good grip. This has depth. A little adolescent at present but I think it's going to be fine.

Pommard, Pezerolles,
Domaine Bouchard Père et Fils   From 2013   14.5
Medium to medium-full colour. Ripe—very ripe; almost sweet—on the nose. Decent substance if no real personality. Medium-full body. Slightly rigid at present. But good grip. Quite good plus.

Pommard, Pezerolles,
Domaine A. F. Gros   From 2013   13.0
Medium to medium-full colour. Some substance on the nose. But a bit sturdy, even slightly stewed. Good acidity. But a lack of style.

Pommard, Rugiens, Domaine
du Pavillon (Albert Bichot)   From 2014   16.5
Medium to medium-full colour. Lots of new oak here on the nose. There is substance and fruit but it is a bit smothered. Medium-full body. Ample. Good grip. Good style. Very good plus.

Pommard, Rugiens, Domaine
Bouchard Père et Fils   From 2014   15.0
Medium-full colour. Closed-in nose. Ripe. Good depth and substance. Needs time. High-toned fruit on the palate. Lacks a little fat but decent length and a positive finish. Good.

Pommard, Rugiens,
Domaine Faiveley   From 2015   17.5
Medium-full colour. Round, ripe, harmonious nose. Fullish body. Very good class and intensity. This is admirable. Long and subtle. Needs time. Lovely.

Pommard, Rugiens,
Domaine de Montille   From 2014   17.0
Medium colour. Rich, closed-in, ripe nose. Good style here. Medium-full body. Ripe and balanced. Well-made. Good grip. Long and positive at the end. Classy too. Fine.

CÔTE DE NUITS

Marsannay, Les Longerois,
Domaine Bruno Clair   Now to 2016   13.0
Medium colour. Not a lot of weight and energy. Indeed a little hollow. Only fair.

Nuits-Saint-Georges,
Domaine Gouges   From 2014   16.0
Rather more weight and depth than some. Medium to medium-full body. Good grip. Plump and ample. Long and positive. Very good indeed for a village wine.

**Nuits-Saint-Georges,
Domaine Méo-Camuzet**   From 2013   14.0

Soft, balanced, oaky, attractive nose. Lacks a little ripeness and richness on the palate. So not much charm. And the oak is a bit too excessive at the end. Quite good at best.

**Nuits-Saint-Georges, Clos
des Argillières, Domaine
Michèle et Patrice Rion**   From 2013   15.5

Medium to medium-full colour. Ample nose. Quite fresh and stylish. Medium body. Good acidity. A touch of oak. Good follow-through. Positive if without the greatest distinction. Good plus.

**Nuits-Saint-Georges, Clos
de l'Arlot, Domaine de l'Arlot**   From 2013   14.5

Medium colour. Fresh, charming, fruity, and stylish nose. Medium body. No undue stems. Not much tannin. Decent fruit. Somewhat one-dimensional but a pleasant drink. The finish is positive. Quite forward. Good.

**Nuits-Saint-Georges,
Aux Boudots, Domaine Grivot**   From 2014   16.5

Medium-full body. Soft, round, aromatic, balanced, and stylish, but could have done with a little more concentration and grip. Very elegant at the end. Very good plus.

**Nuits-Saint-Georges, Aux
Boudots, Domaine Leroy**   From 2013   13.0

Fragrant, but rather weak at the end. I prefer the Vignerondes. This is pretty but a little short. Disappointing.

**Nuits-Saint-Georges, Les Cailles,
Domaine Robert Chevillon**   From 2014   16.0

Medium-full colour. Open, quite evolved, fruity nose. Somewhat loose-knit. Medium to medium-full body. Good grip. Ample. Almost sweet. Good follow-through. Quite classy. Very good.

**Nuits-Saint-Georges, Les Chaignots,
Domaine Gouges**   From 2014   16.5

Not the greatest of weight and energy. But ripe and balanced, stylish and intense. Long and very good plus.

**Nuits-Saint-Georges,
Les Chaignots, Domaine
Dr. Georges Mugneret-Gibourg**   From 2014   17.0

Medium-full colour. Somewhat closed but good depth and style here on the nose. Medium-full body. Good grip. Balanced, energetic, and elegant. Finishes well. Very good indeed.

**Nuits-Saint-Georges,
Clos des Corvées,
Domaine Prieuré-Roch**   From 2013   15.0

Good colour. Soft, spicy, stemmy nose. Medium weight. Very ripe on the palate. A certain astringency, but not weak. Nor rustic. Decent balance and grip. Good.

**Nuits-Saint-Georges, Les Cras,
Domaine Lamarche**   From 2013   13.0

Fullish colour. Odd nose. Somewhat malic. Better on the palate, but there is nevertheless a certain astringency. I'd like to see another bottle.

**Nuits-Saint-Georges,
Les Cras, Domaine du
Vicomte de Liger-Belair**   From 2014   16.0

Medium-full colour. Gentle, poised, delicately oaky nose. Very complex. Medium weight. Ample and rich. Most attractive if quite forward.

**Nuits-Saint-Georges, Les Damodes,
Domaine Jean Chauvenet**   From 2014   17.5

Medium-full colour. Very ripe nose. A touch of oak. Ample. Austere as it developed. But fullish and concentrated. Good energy. Lots of depth. Fine.

**Nuits-Saint-Georges, Les Damodes,
Domaine de la Vougeraie**   From 2014   15.5

Medium-full colour. Soft, ample oaky nose. Medium body. Ripe and enjoyable. Balanced and stylish, if not very profound. Good plus.

**Nuits-Saint-Georges,
Les Didiers, Domaine
des Hospices de Nuits**   From 2014   17.0

Good colour. Nice and vigorous on the nose. Plenty of substance. Ripe, good tannins, very good grip. This has lovely fruit. Nothing weak about it. Very good indeed.

Nuits-Saint-Georges, Clos des Forêts, Domaine de l'Arlot From 2013 15.0
Medium colour. Soft nose. Ripe and not too stemmy. Medium to medium-full weight. A little tannin. Decent fruit, but a touch of astringency on the follow-through. But the finish is positive. Good.

Nuits-Saint-Georges, Clos des Grandes Vignes, Domaine du Château de Puligny-Montrachet From 2014 16.0
Medium colour. Fresh, ripe; stylish, fragrant nose. Medium to medium-full body. Good grip and intensity. I would have liked a bit more weight and concentration. But this has plenty of depth and personality. Very good.

Nuits-Saint-Georges, Clos-Saint-Marc, Domaine Michèle et Patrice Rion From 2014 15.5
Medium colour. Light but fragrant nose. Medium body. Attractive fruity attack but then it tails off a bit. Fresh and stylish at the end though. And decent length. Good plus.

Nuits-Saint-Georges, Clos de la Maréchale, Domaine J. F. Mugnier From 2014 16.5
Medium colour. Lovely fragrant nose. Unexpectedly elegant. Chambolle-ish too. Medium body. Very intense. More concentrated than it seems at first. Lovely fruit. Long and complex. Very good plus.

Nuits-Saint-Georges, Les Murgers, Domaine Sylvain Cathiard From 2014 17.0
Medium-full colour. Fullish, rich, vigorous, intense, and very classy on the nose. Finely tuned. Fullish body. Very concentrated. Very well-balanced. Very good indeed.

Nuits-Saint-Georges, Les Murgers, Domaine Alain Hudelot-Noëllat From 2014 14.5
Medium to medium-full colour. Slightly reserved at first, but clean, classy, and balanced. Forward on the palate. Medium body. Attractive but lacks a little depth. Quite good plus.

Nuits-Saint-Georges, Les Murgers, Domaine Méo-Camuzet From 2015 17.5
Medium-full colour. Soft, plump, gently oaky nose. No great weight but balanced and very seductive. Medium-full body. More vigour than it seemed at first. Complex and stylish and long on the finish. Fine.

Nuits-Saint-Georges, Aux Perdrix, Domaine de Perdrix From 2014 15.5
Medium colour. Fresh nose, but not the backbone of the Huit Ouvrées. Medium to medium-full body. Ripe and stylish. Forward and fragrant and elegant. Nice balance. Good plus.

Nuits-Saint-Georges, Aux Perdrix, Les Huit Ouvrées, Domaine de Perdrix From 2016 17.5
From vines planted in 1922. Good colour. Splendidly ripe, concentrated nose, with a touch of new oak. Fullish body. Good tannins. Very good grip. This is youthful and profound. Fine.

Nuits-Saint-Georges, Les Perrières, Domaine Jean Chauvenet From 2014 15.0
Fullish colour. An odd nose. Not really together. Not much Pinot fruit. Ungainly on the palate. Medium-full body. Ripe. Good grip. A bit foursquare. Improved in the glass. But good at best.

Nuits-Saint-Georges, Clos des Porrets-Saint-Georges, Domaine Gouges From 2015 18.5
Medium-full colour. Ripe, rich, masculine, balanced, and classy on the nose. Backward, but multidimensional. Full-bodied. Splendid fruit. Very long and very lovely.

Nuits-Saint-Georges, Les Proces, Domaine Joseph Drouhin From 2014 16.0
Medium to medium-full body. Soft on the attack. Balanced and elegant, but it is more 2007 than Nuits-Saint-Georges. What it lacks is virility. Very good though.

Nuits-Saint-Georges, Les Pruliers, Domaine Robert Chevillon From 2014 17.0
Medium-full colour. Just a touch *sauvage* on the nose at first. But fullish and fleshy. Medium-

full body. Good grip. Very good fruit and energy. Lots of depth. Very good indeed.

Nuits-Saint-Georges, Les Pruliers, Domaine Gouges
From 2015   17.0

Medium-full colour. Fullish but closed-in on the nose. Fresh. Fullish body. Good grip and tannins. Plenty of wine here. Rich and energetic. Very good indeed.

Nuits-Saint-Georges, Les Pruliers, Domaine Grivot
From 2015   17.5

Medium-full colour. Firm, rich, profound nose. Good grip. Lots of intensity. Lovely fruit. Fine.

Nuits-Saint-Georges, Les Pruliers, Domaine Taupenot-Merme
From 2015   18.0

Fullish colour. Closed-in nose. Firm, full-bodied, and profound. Rich, ample, and oaky. Succulent fruit. Profound and balanced. Long and lovely. Fine plus.

Nuits-Saint-Georges, La Richemone, Domaine Perrot-Minot
From 2015   17.0

Medium-full colour. Just a touch reduced at first. But medium-full body. Ample, rich, concentrated, and well-balanced. Lovely finish. Very good indeed, even fine.

Nuits-Saint-Georges, Les Saint-Georges, Domaine Gouges
From 2016   18.5

Full-bodied, rich, complete, and very concentrated. This is very lovely. Lots of depth and energy. Long. Very fine.

Nuits-Saint-Georges, Les Saint-Georges, Domaine Thibaut Liger-Belair
From 2015   17.0

Medium-full colour. Good rich, meaty, fullish nose. Class too. Full body. Some tannin. Quite structured. Good grip and energy. Very good fruit. Very good indeed/fine.

Nuits-Saint-Georges, Aux Thorey, Maison Leroux
From 2013   16.0

Medium-full colour. Rich, ripe, soft, gently oaky nose. Stylish. Medium body. Quite forward. Round, elegant, balanced, and quite complex. Good class. Very good.

Nuits-Saint-Georges, Les Vaucrains, Domaine Jean Chauvenet
From 2015   17.0

Medium-full colour. Rich, ripe, almost perfumed nose. Is it a bit sweet? Better on the palate. Fresh. Medium-full body. Balanced and a lot more classy than appeared at first. Long on the palate.

Nuits-Saint-Georges, Les Vaucrains, Maison Camille Giroud
From 2015   18.0

Medium-full colour. Closed-in, backward nose. But plenty of class, depth, and fruit. This is very lovely. Fullish body. Very good grip. Ample, concentrated, and very profound. Fine plus.

Nuits-Saint-Georges, Les Vaucrains, Domaine Robert Chevillon
From 2013   15.5

Medium-full colour. Not a great deal of weight and concentration on the nose. Medium weight. Ripe and fruity. Fresh and attractive. But a little loose-knit for what it is. Good plus at best.

Nuits-Saint-Georges, Aux Vignerondes, Domaine Leroy
From 2013   16.0

Soft but ripe, ample, and seductive. Good freshness. Medium body. Quite oaky, but round and positive at the end. Long. Charming. Very good.

Vosne-Romanée, *Premier Cru*, Domaine Gros Frère et Soeur
From 2014   16.0

Medium-full colour. Quite a burly, oaky wine on the nose. At first a bit four-square. But it improved in the glass. Good rich fruit and good grip. Medium-full body. Very good.

Vosne-Romanée, Aux Beaux Monts, Domaine Bertagna
From 2014   16.5

Medium-full colour. A bit closed-in at first. But rich and balanced as it evolved. Medium-full body. Ripe Pinot fruit. Attractive and harmonious. Good depth. Very good.

Vosne-Romanée, Aux Beaux Monts, Domaine Grivot
From 2016   18.0

Full body. Very rich and concentrated. Ripe and profound. Very fine tannins. A wine of great quality and distinction.

Vosne-Romanée, Aux Beaux Monts,
Domaine Leroy From 2015 17.5
A bit reduced so a touch astringent. But ripe
and rich enough underneath. And I think it has
the elegance. Medium-full body. Good grip and
tannic structure. Plenty of depth here. Fine.

Vosne-Romanée, Les Bossières,
Domaine Grivot From 2014 16.0
Compared with many village wines this is a great
success. Fullish, ample, rich, and full of fruit.
Very good grip. Long and positive. Very good.

Vosne-Romanée, Aux Brulées,
Domaine Eugenie From 2014 16.0
Ripe rich, some new oak. Good substance. A
little tannin. Good concentration and depth,
but the oaky-ness is a bit aggressive.

Vosne-Romanée, Aux Brulées,
Domaine Grivot From 2015 17.0
Medium-full colour. A bit four-square on the
nose. Fullish body. Very good grip. Still a bit
austere. But underneath very promising concentrated fruit. Very good indeed.

Vosne-Romanée, Aux Brulées,
Domaine Michel Gros From 2014 17.5
Medium-full colour. Rich, aromatic, even spicy
nose. Fullish body. Good energy and depth.
Plenty of richness. Lovely finish. Fine.

Vosne-Romanée, Aux Brulées,
Domaine Leroy From 2015 17.0
Quite full body for a 2007. Some tannin. Less
evolved than most. Better grip. Still currently a
bit austere. But good depth and rich at the end.
Very good indeed.

Vosne-Romanée, Aux Brulées,
Domaine Méo-Camuzet From 2014 15.5
Medium-full colour. A bit austere at first on the
nose. Better on the palate. Some tannin. Good
grip. Plenty of fruit. Lacks a bit of charm and
succulence perhaps.

Vosne-Romanée, Aux Brulées,
Domaine Gérard Mugneret From 2014 16.5
Medium-full colour. Good fruit and personality
here. Medium-full body. Ripe. Balanced. Good

energy and class. Long and vigorous. Very good
plus.

Vosne-Romanée, Les Chaumes,
Domaine Lamarche From 2014 16.0
Medium-full colour. Fresh ripe nose. Medium-
full body. Attractive fruit, balanced, quite
classy. Good depth. Very good.

Vosne-Romanée,
Les Chaumes, Domaine du
Vicomte de Liger-Belair From 2014 17.0
Medium-full colour. Open, juicy, elegant, very
poised nose. Very good accessible fruit. Harmo-
nious and subtle if by no means a blockbuster.
Very good indeed.

Vosne-Romanée, La Croix Rameau,
Domaine Lamarche From 2014 15.0
Medium-full colour. Soft, ripe, quite forward
nose. Medium body. Juicy and succulent.
Almost sweet. An attractive wine. If a little
slight. Good.

Vosne-Romanée, Cros Parantoux,
Domaine Emmanuel Rouget From 2015 18.5
Medium-full colour. Rich, fresh, quite concen-
trated nose. Lots of fruit and style. Medium-full
body. Oaky and succulent. Profound and classy.
Long and classic. Very lovely.

Vosne-Romanée, Aux Malconsorts,
Domaine du Clos Frantin,
Albert Bichot From 2015 18.0
Medium-full colour. Good vigorous nose.
Medium-full body. Good concentration. Oaky.
Good grip and tannins. Above all, lots of ele-
gant Pinot fruit. Long on the palate. Fine plus.

Vosne-Romanée, Aux Malconsorts,
Domaine Lamarche From 2015 17.5
Medium-full colour. Ripe, attractive nose. This
is fine. Medium-full body. Rich. Some con-
centration. Positive and complex. High-class.
Lovely finish.

Vosne-Romanée, Les Petits Monts,
Domaine Drouhin From 2014 16.5
Medium-full colour. A little closed-in at first.
As it evolved, it became a quite firm, fullish

wine with good fruit and grip. Positive on the follow-through. Good class. Very good plus.

Vosne-Romanée, Les Petits Monts, Domaine du Vicomte de Liger-Belair   From 2014   16.0

Medium-full colour. Good depth on the nose. Easy to enjoy. Medium-full body. Gently oaky. Balanced. Finishes well. Very good.

Vosne-Romanée, Clos des Réas, Domaine Michel Gros   From 2014   17.0

Medium-full colour. Some depth and class here on the nose, but it is less developed than some. Medium-full body. Some tannin. Good grip. Lovely fruit underneath and very well put together. Very good indeed.

Vosne-Romanée, Aux Reignots, Domaine Cathiard   From 2014   17.5

Medium-full colour. Ample, oaky nose. Medium-full body. Ripe. Succulent. Complex. Long on the palate. Very lovely fruit and an equally lovely finish. Fine.

Vosne-Romanée, Aux Reignots, Domaine du Vicomte de Liger-Belair   From 2014   17.0

Medium-full colour. Rich, succulent nose. Some oak. Medium-full body. Fresh. Fragrant. Balanced and stylish. Finishes well. Very good indeed.

Vosne-Romanée, Les Suchote, Domaine de l'Arlot   From 2014   15.5

Medium-full colour. The wine seems quite evolved on the nose. Soft, forward, and pretty. Good acidity. Quite intense. And, of course, the taste of the stems. Good plus.

Vosne-Romanée, Les Suchots, Maison Bernstein   From 2014   14.0

Medium-full colour. Odd spices and flavours on the nose. Medium to medium-full body. Decent energy and grip. Ripe fruit. Good length. But I find it lacks style.

Vosne-Romanée, Les Suchots, Domaine Grivot   From 2015   18.0

Medium-full colour. Expansive nose with a touch of oak. Very stylish ripe fruit. Medium-

full body. Good grip. Elegant, intense, and energetic. Long on the palate. Fine plus.

Vosne-Romanée, Les Suchots, Domaine du Vicomte de Liger-Belair   From 2014   17.5

Medium-full colour. Quite a delicate, if intense nose. Medium-full body. Very elegant, ample, harmonious fruit. Very good length. Fine.

Vosne-Romanée, Les Suchots, Domaine Gérard Mugneret   From 2015   18.0

Medium-full body. Quite exotically perfumed on the nose. Some oak. Ripe and succulent on the palate. Lush. Medium-full body. Good grip. Very seductive. Very long and complex. Fine plus.

Vougeot, Les Petits Vougeots, Domaine Alain Hudelot-Noëllat   From 2014   14.5

Evolved colour. Rather a weak nose. Ripe but lacking energy and not as sophisticated as it should be. A touch of new oak. Medium body. Quite fresh on the palate. But it lacks a bit of dimension. Quite good plus.

Chambolle-Musigny, Domaine J. F. Mugnier   From 2014   16.5

Typically elegant, fragrant, composed, Chambolle fruit here. Medium to medium-full body. Very fine energy. This is very lovely for a village wine. Real elegance and a very impressive complex finish.

Chambolle-Musigny, Domaine Georges Roumier   From 2014   16.0

Very ripe and rich on the nose. Crammed with fruit. Medium-full body. Lots of energy here. Not a bit weak. Long and vigorous and very good indeed, especially for a village wine.

Chambolle-Musigny, Les Amoureuses, Domaine Francois Bertheau   From 2015   17.5

Medium-full colour. Quite a lot of new oak on the nose, over a wine which is by no means a blockbuster. Will this dominate? Otherwise, balanced, fruity, and elegant enough. Fine.

Chambolle-Musigny,
Les Amoureuses,
Domaine Drouhin   From 2015   17.5
Medium-full colour. A little tight on the nose at first. But better on the palate. Ample, balanced, very stylish fruit. Evolved to become rich and ample. Fine.

Chambolle-Musigny,
Les Amoureuses,
Domaine Robert Groffier   From 2015   17.5
Medium-full colour. Rich, closed-in nose. Backward. Quite a substantial wine on the palate. Ample, balanced, succulent attack. On the follow-through, good energy but not quite the class for better than fine.

Chambolle-Musigny,
Les Amoureuses,
Domaine J. F. Mugnier   From 2015   19.0
Medium-full colour. Soft, aromatic, elegant, subtle nose. Very lovely. Medium-full body. Very rich, ripe, quite delicious fruit. Very ample. Excellent balancing acidity. Intense, complex, and very classy. Brilliant.

Chambolle-Musigny,
Les Amoureuses,
Domaine Georges Roumier   From 2015   18.5
Medium-full colour. A touch of new oak on the nose. Ripe, subtle nose. Lots of class. Medium-full body. Cool. Stylish. Lots of energy. A lovely, fresh, balanced wine. Very long. Very fine.

Chambolle-Musigny,
Les Amoureuses, Domaine
Comte Georges de Vogüé   From 2014   16.5
Medium-full colour. A bit tight on the nose at first, but good quality underneath. Just a suggestion of attenuation, however. Medium-full body. Good attack, but then it tails off a bit. It's no more elegant or profound than very good plus.

Chambolle-Musigny, Les Charmes,
Domaine Ghislaine Barthod   From 2014   17.5
Medium-full colour. Good depth on the nose. More backward than most. Medium-full body. Rich, concentrated, and substantial on the pal-

ate. Lots of depth and fine classy fruit. Fine quality.

Chambolle-Musigny, Les Charmes,
Domaine Francois Bertheau   From 2014   17.5
Medium-full colour. Good weight on the nose. Concentrated and with no lack of new oak. Medium-full body. Ample, rich, and profound. Long. Fine quality.

Chambolle-Musigny, Les Charmes,
Domaine Leroy   From 2014   17.0
Medium weight. Fragrant and elegant. Soft. Good acidity but no hard edges. Long and positive. Very good indeed.

Chambolle-Musigny, Les Charmes,
Domaine Ponsot   From 2014   17.0
Medium body. Warm, soft but classy and intense on the nose. Very lovely ripe fruit. Very good *terroir* definition. Long. Very good indeed.

Chambolle-Musigny,
Les Charmes, Domaine
Michèle et Patrice Rion   From 2014   17.0
Medium-full colour. Lovely soft Chambolle fruit on the nose. Medium-full body. Fresh and ripe and stylish. Complex, long, and classy. Very good indeed.

Chambolle-Musigny, Les Chatelots,
Domaine Ghislaine Barthod   From 2014   15.5
Medium colour. Fresh, quite firm nose. Medium-full body. Good fruit and grip. An attractive wine.

Chambolle-Musigny,
La Combe d'Orveaux,
Domaine Perrot-Minot   From 2015   17.5
Medium-full colour. A little tight on the nose at the start. But very good depth underneath. Fullish body. Backward. Very good grip. Fresh and positive. Lovely fruit. Long. Impressive.

Chambolle-Musigny,
La Combe d'Orveaux,
Domaine Taupenot-Merme   From 2014   16.0
Medium-full colour. Fullish, quite firm nose. Still youthful. Fullish body. Very good grip.

Could have done with a bit more elegance but very good.

Chambolle-Musigny, Les Cras,
Domaine Ghislaine Barthod   From 2015   17.5
Medium-full colour. Ripe nose with a touch of caramel. Medium-full body. Good fresh, ripe attack. Good grip. Plenty of depth. Still a bit closed. Fine.

Chambolle-Musigny, Les Cras,
Domaine Georges Roumier   From 2015   18.0
Rich, full, energetic nose. Fullish. Concentrated. Very good grip. Noble and distinguished. Very long and very lovely. Fine plus.

Chambolle-Musigny, Les Fuées,
Domaine Ghislaine Barthod   From 2015   17.0
Medium-full colour. Round, ripe, almost sweet, fruity nose. Very luscious. Medium-full body. Rich, ripe, and abundant on the palate. Plenty of depth. Very good indeed.

Chambolle-Musigny, Les Fuées,
Domaine J. F. Mugnier   From 2015   18.0
Medium-full colour. Firm, backward nose. Very good depth here. Medium-full body. Some tannin. Still youthful. Lots of energy. Above everything, this has very lovely, complex fruit. Very long on the palate. Fine plus.

Chambolle-Musigny, Les Groseilles,
Domaine Digioia-Royer   From 2014   17.0
Medium-full colour. Plump and fruity, ample and balanced. Medium-full weight. Good grip. Good energy. Long. Very good indeed.

Chambolle-Musigny, Les Gruenchers,
Domaine Digioia-Royer   From 2014   16.5
Medium-full colour. Ripe nose. Good depth. Cool, classy, and well-balanced. Very good fruit. A slight touch of volatile acidity, but long and complex and very good plus.

Chambolle-Musigny, Les Hauts-Doix,
Domaine Robert Groffier   From 2014   14.5
Medium to medium-full colour. A little rustic on the nose. Better on the palate. Good freshness. Quite fruity. Quite good plus.

Chambolle-Musigny, Les Noirots,
Domaine Arlaud   From 2014   15.5
Medium colour. Fresh, plump, attractive nose. Medium to medium-full body. Good succulent fruit. Good but not great finesse. Good plus.

Chambolle-Musigny, Les Sentiers,
Domaine Robert Groffier   From 2014   14.5
Medium to medium-full colour. A bit attenuated on the nose, but the palate is better. The attack is fresh, balanced, and fruity. Medium weight. Quite good plus.

Morey-Saint-Denis,
Domaine Dujac   From 2013   15.0
Soft, round, very ripe nose. But forward and quite delicate. Lovely fruit on the attack, but then it tails off a bit. Elegant though. Good quality.

Morey-Saint-Denis, *Premier Cru*,
Domaine Dujac   From 2014   16.0
Medium colour. There is depth as well as the usual taste of the stems on the nose, but it's a bit adolescent at present. Medium weight. Good grip. Ripe and intense. Very good.

Morey-Saint-Denis, *Premier Cru*,
Cuvée du Pâpe Jean-Paul II,
Domaine Bryczek   From 2014   16.5
Good colour. Quite a firm nose. But ripe and generous. Good energy and very good tannins. Long and satisfying. Very good plus.

Morey-Saint-Denis,
Clos de la Bussière,
Domaine Georges Roumier   From 2014   15.5
Medium-full colour. Fresh nose. Stylish but still a bit hidden. Medium-full body. Good grip. Fruity and with good dimension. Balanced. Good plus.

Morey-Saint-Denis, Les Chaffots,
Domaine Hubert Lignier   From 2014   13.5
Medium-full colour. A little rustic on the nose. Medium weight. Decent fruit, but lacks a bit of style.

Morey-Saint-Denis, La Riotte,
Domaine Taupenot-Merme   From 2014   14.5
Medium-full colour. Ripe, forward nose.
Medium weight. Fresh and fruity, but not a lot
on the follow-through. Quite good plus.

Morey-Saint-Denis, Les Ruchots,
Domaine Arlaud   From 2014   14.5
Medium-full colour. Light, fruity but stylish
nose. Not a great deal to it on the palate but
quite good plus.

Gevrey-Chambertin, Domaine
Jean et Jean-Louis Trapet   From 2014   16.0
Medium body. But fresh, balanced, stylish,
and charming. No great structure but plenty of
dimension. Very good.

Gevrey-Chambertin, Belair,
Domaine Taupenot-Merme   From 2015   17.0
Medium-full colour. Ripe nose. Good substance
but a little four-square. Fullish body. Ripe. bal-
anced and more elegant than seemed at first.
Good class. Very good indeed.

Gevrey-Chambertin, Les Cazetiers,
Domaine Bruno Clair   From 2015   17.5
Slightly cool as always. But fullish body, rich,
balanced, and classy. Lots of depth. Fine at the
end.

Gevrey-Chambertin, Les Cazetiers,
Maison Camille Giroud   From 2015   17.0
Medium-full colour. The nose is a bit closed
at first. Medium-full body. Ample and fruity.
Fresh and well-mannered. Plenty of vigour.
Very good indeed.

Gevrey-Chambertin, Les Cazetiers,
Domaine Faiveley   From 2016   18.0
Full colour. Rich, profound, high-quality fruit
on the nose. Full body. Meaty. Very good grip
and very good tannins. Quite firm for a 2007.
Fine plus.

Gevrey-Chambertin, Les Cazetiers,
Domaine Serafin   From 2015   18.0
Medium-full colour. Lovely nose. Soft, rich,
ripe, and gently oaky. Fullish body. Ripe. Suc-

culent. Very good grip. Lots of style. Very fresh.
Lovely long, seductive finish. Fine plus.

Gevrey-Chambertin, Les Champeaux,
Domaine Denis Mortet   From 2015   17.5
Fullish colour. Fullish nose. Plenty of new oak.
Ripe and stylish. Medium-full body. Good grip
and intensity. Ripe, complex, long, and elegant.
Lovely.

Gevrey-Chambertin, Les Cherbaudes,
Domaine Louis Boillot   From 2013   13.5
Medium-full colour. High-toned nose. A bit
short and attenuated on the palate. Not much
here. Disappointing.

Gevrey-Chambertin, Les Cherbaudes,
Domaine Fourrier   From 2015   17.5
Fullish colour. Fullish nose. Ample, ripe, vigorous, and quite substantial on the palate. Lots of
depth here. Currently a bit adolescent but fine
quality.

Gevrey-Chambertin, Les Cherbaudes,
Domaine Rossignol-Trapet   From 2013   13.5
Medium-full colour. Somewhat ungainly on
the nose. Sweaty, animal aromas. Medium to
medium-full body. Unexciting.

Gevrey-Chambertin, Clos du Fonteny,
Domaine Bruno Clair   From 2014   15.0
Fullish colour. Ripe and gently oaky on the
nose. Medium to medium-full body. Decent
attack, but a bit unforthcoming. At least good.

Gevrey-Chambertin,
Clos-Saint-Jacques,
Domaine Bruno Clair   From 2016   18.5
Fine colour. Full body, tannic and vigorous.
Good oaky base. Splendid depth and a very
lovely abundant finish. Very fine.

Gevrey-Chambertin,
Clos-Saint-Jacques,
Domaine Sylvie Esmonin   From 2015   18.0
Medium-full colour. Rich, full, concentrated,
and oaky on the nose. Still youthful. Medium-
full body. Elegant, balanced, classy, and cool on
the palate. Very good tannins. Lovely finish.
Fine plus.

Gevrey-Chambertin,
Clos-Saint-Jacques,
Domaine Fourrier From 2016 18.0
Fullish colour. Ample nose. Plenty of distinction. On the palate, the complete wine. Lots of
energy. Full-bodied. Rich. Gently oaky. Very
lovely profound fruit. Fine plus.

Gevrey-Chambertin,
Clos-Saint-Jacques,
Domaine Armand Rousseau From 2015 17.5
This is a great deal better than his Ruchottes,
but it is really quite oaky. Some volume.
Rich and ripe, quite concentrated. And well-
balanced. Fine. Against the Clos-Saint-Jacques
above, I gave it a marginally lower score. But the
group as a whole voted it the best of the four.
And it usually is the best.

Gevrey-Chambertin, Le Closeau,
Domaine Drouhin-Laroze From 2015 16.5
Medium-full colour. Soft, agreeable, gently
oaky nose. Good style. A fullish, meaty wine.
Good grip. Plenty of energy. At the moment a
bit adolescent. But long and very good plus.

Gevrey-Chambertin,
Les Combottes,
Domaine Arlaud From 2014 17.0
Medium-full colour. Rich, ample; sweet and
seductive nose. Medium-full body. Ripe, round,
succulent, and balanced. Full of fruit. Elegant
too.

Gevrey-Chambertin,
Les Combottes,
Domaine Dujac From 2015 17.5
Medium to medium-full colour. Soft, stylish
nose. A touch of the stems. Medium-full body.
Ripe, fresh, intense, balanced, and elegant.
This is very lovely.

Gevrey-Chambertin,
Les Combottes,
Domaine Leroy From 2015 18.0
Ripe and positive on the nose, wth delicious
summer pudding fruit. Fat and ample, with a
very good follow-through. This is clearly the
best of the Leroy first growths.

Gevrey-Chambertin, Les Combottes,
Domaine Hubert Lignier From 2014 16.5
Full colour. Quite an extracted, oaky nose. Fullish body. Very rich if a touch ungainly. But the
finish is positive.

Gevrey-Chambertin, Les Combottes,
Domaine Rossignol-Trapet From 2014 15.5
Medium-full colour. Strange, toffee-flavoured
nose. Medium-full body. Good grip. A little raw
and unresolved at first on the attack. But the
finish is better. Good plus.

Gevrey-Chambertin, Les Corbeaux,
Domaine Denis Bachelet From 2016 17.5
Medium-full colour. Soft, gently oaky nose.
Medium-full body. Good grip and concentra-
tion. Fresh, elegant, and complex. Lovely fol-
low-through. Fine.

Gevrey-Chambertin, Les Corbeaux,
Domaine Serafin From 2014 16.0
Medium-full colour. Not a lot on the nose at
first, but what there is, is stylish and balanced.
Medium to medium-full body. Spicy, earthy,
gently oaky flavours. Good grip. Very good, but
lacks a bit of power.

Gevrey-Chambertin, Le Craipillot,
Domaine Humbert Frères From 2016 17.5
Fullish colour. Decent substance. Fresh. Good
depth and ripeness on the nose. Medium-full
body. Fragrant, ripe, and harmonious. Stylish
and long. This is fine.

Gevrey-Chambertin,
Estournelles-Saint-Jacques,
Domaine Humbert Frères From 2015 17.5
Full colour. Good class and depth here. Still
youthful. Full-bodied. Voluptuous, ample, rich,
and full of fruit. Very good grip. A very seductive example. Long and vigorous. Fine.

Gevrey-Chambertin, Le Fonteny,
Domaine Serafin From 2015 17.5
Fullish colour. Fresh, elegant, quite substantial
nose. Similar palate. Lots of ripe, rich fruit.
Some tannin. This will develop. The finish is
long. Fine.

Gevrey-Chambertin, Les Goulots,
Domaine Fourrier   From 2014   16.0

Medium-full colour. Soft, ripe, ample nose. Good style. Some development. Medium to medium-full body. Balanced. Stylish. Good fruit. Positive at the end.

Gevrey-Chambertin,
Lavaux-Saint-Jacques,
Domaine du Clos Frantin,
Albert Bichot   From 2014   16.5

Medium-full colour. A bit closed on the nose. But no lack of style. Fullish on the palate. Nice and fresh. Good attack. Slightly less strength on the follow-through but very good plus.

Gevrey-Chambertin,
Lavaux-Saint-Jacques,
Maison Chanson   From 2014   17.0

Medium to medium-full colour. Soft, ample, crème caramel nose. Medium-full body. Balanced and stylish. A little rigid on the follow-through. But a very good wine here. Long on the palate.

Gevrey-Chambertin,
Lavaux-Saint-Jacques,
Domaine Drouhin Laroze   From 2014   14.5

Medium-full colour. Not a great deal on the nose. Medium to medium-full body. Clean but dull, lacking a bit of freshness. Reasonable follow-through. But nothing special.

Gevrey-Chambertin,
Lavaux-Saint-Jacques,
Domaine Humbert Frères   From 2015   17.5

Fullish colour. Ample, soft oaky nose. Good ripe fruit. This is fullish, fresh, round, and very well-balanced. Good vigorous fruit. Lots of depth. Classy too. Fine.

Gevrey-Chambertin,
Lavaux-Saint-Jacques,
Domaine Maume   From 2013   11.0

Medium-full colour. Rather crude, vegetal nose. And quite over-ripe vegetal at that. Similar on the palate. Barely drinkable.

Gevrey-Chambertin,
Lavaux-Saint-Jacques,
Domaine Denis Mortet   From 2015   17.5

Medium-full colour. Youthful, balanced, stylish nose. Medium-full body. Ripe. Good intensity. Harmonious and vigorous. Fine.

Gevrey-Chambertin,
Lavaux-Saint-Jacques,
Domaine Armand Rousseau   From 2015   18.0

Medium-full colour. Firm, full, vigorous, classy nose. Youthful but lovely fruit and balance. Full body. Ample. Rich. Very good grip. Lots of depth here. Very long. Lovely.

Gevrey-Chambertin,
Le Petite Chapelle,
Domaine Humbert Frères   From 2014   17.5

Fullish colour. Fresh, stylish, substantial nose. Lovely ripe fruit on the palate. Good grip and plenty of dimension. Fine.

Gevrey-Chambertin, Le Poissenot,
Domaine Humbert Frères   From 2015   16.0

Fullish colour. Ripe, quite chunky nose. Needs time. Medium-full body. Ripe and fruity. Good grip. Good tannins. Not the dimension of fine but very good.

Grands Crus

Corton,
Domaine Bonneau du Martray   From 2015   17.5

Medium to medium-full colour. Fresh nose. Good weight and ripeness. An attractive bottle with a touch of spice. Good grip. Persistent and classy at the end. Fine.

Corton, Domaine Follin-Arbelet   From 2015   17.5

Medium-full colour. Still youthful. Rich, spicy nose. Some tannin. Medium-full body. Good grip. This has plenty of future. Ripe and complex. Needs time. Fine.

Le Corton,
Domaine Bouchard Père et Fils   From 2013   16.0

Medium colour. Not much nose. It seems a bit lightweight. Medium body. Ripe and balanced.

No great depth, but an attractive, harmonious wine. Positive at the end. Very good.

Corton, Bressandes,
Domaine Chandon de Briailles   From 2013   16.0
Medium colour. I expected more after the Ile. Not a lot on the nose. And though not lacking fruit, nor an attractive and balanced follow-through, it lacks a bit on the attack.

Corton, Bressandes,
Domaine du
Château de Chorey   From 2014   17.5
Medium-full colour. Ripe and really quite concentrated on the nose. Lovely fruit. This is intense and very classy. Fullish body. Very good tannins. Excellent grip. Still closed. Fine quality.

Corton, Bressandes,
Domaine Follin-Arbelet   From 2015   17.5
Medium-full colour. Soft, elegant, fresh, gently oaky nose. Delicious ripe fruit. Medium-full body. Good energy. Good tannins and grip. Lots of concentrated fruit well supported by the oak. Fine.

Corton, Bressandes,
Domaine de la Pousse d'Or   From 2015   18.0
Medium-full colour. Fresh, ripe, stylish, and balanced on the nose. Very good fruit. Medium-full body. Rich, intense, and very good grip. Very elegant and with a lovely follow-through. Just gently oaky. Lots of class. Fine plus.

Corton, Bressandes,
Domaine Comte Senard   From 2015   18.5
Fullish, quite firm nose. Very good depth and grip. Fullish, good tannins. This has more backbone, vigour, and intensity than most. Lots of future. Very classy. Very fine.

Corton, Bressandes,
Domaine Tollot-Beaut   From 2013   14.0
Medium colour. Slightly reduced at first on the nose. Medium weight. Decent fruit. The reduction, which didn't seem to move, made this wine a little dry at the end. Decent fruit and acidity otherwise.

Corton, En Charlemagne,
Domaine Comte Senard   From 2013   16.5
Good colour. Softer on the nose than the Clos de Meix. Good fruit but less vigour. Pleasant and fresh. Positive. But very good plus rather than fine.

Corton, Clos des
Cortons Faiveley,
Domaine Faiveley   Now to 2020 plus   17.5
Medium colour. Lovely rich, fragrant, oaky nose. Medium to medium-full body. Balanced, ripe, and harmonious. Intense at the end. Fine.

Corton, Clos de la Maréchale,
Domaine Bichot   From 2015   17.0
Medium-full colour. Soft, elegant, ripe nose. Quite forward. Medium-full body. Good tannins. Good grip. Stylish and quite intense. Balanced. Good energy. Very good indeed.

Corton, Clos des Meix,
Domaine Comte Senard   From 2015   18.0
Good colour. Very good succulent fruit. No lack of depth or backbone here. Good grip. Ripe and enticing. Much more to it than most 2007s. Good energy and intensity. Fine plus.

Corton, Paulands,
Domaine Comte Senard   From 2014   16.5
Good colour. Rich nose. Good depth; quite muscular. Good acidity and backbone. But not the class of the Clos de Meix, let alone the distinction of the Bressandes.

Corton, Pougets,
Domaine Louis Jadot   From 2014   15.5
Medium colour. Ample nose. But quite soft and forward. Medium weight. Well-balanced and stylish. Good fruit. Not the depth of some but good plus.

Corton, Renardes,
Domaine Michel Gaunoux   From 2016   18.5
Fullish body. Concentrated. Lots of depth. Lovely balance. Absolutely no weakness here. Very lovely finish. Very fine.

Corton, Renardes,

Domaine Leroy From 2015 18.0

Fresh nose. Attractive fruit. Medium-full body. Ripe, quite oaky, and with good acidity. Good length. Not *sauvage*. Fine plus.

Corton, Renardes,

Domaine Thibault Liger-Belair From 2014 15.0

Medium to medium-full colour. Caramel and oak on the nose. Somewhat ungainly and unstylish, but adolescent at first. Balanced and vigorous on the follow-through. But it lacks a bit of breed. Merely good.

Corton, Rognets,

Domaine Méo-Camuzet From 2014 15.5

Medium-full body. Rich, quite oaky nose. A touch astringent on the palate. Lacks freshness. Unexciting.

Corton, Clos du Roi,

Maison Camille Giroud From 2014 16.0

Medium-full colour. Rich, backward, concentrated, classy nose. Some oak. Medium-full body. Fat and voluptuous. Good grip. Quite forward though.

Corton, Clos du Roi,

Domaine de Montille From 2015 17.5

Medium-full colour. Evidence of vinification with the stems. Medium body. Very luscious, almost sweet fruit. Balanced and stylish. Fine.

Corton, Clos du Roi,

Domaine de la Pousse d'Or From 2015 17.5

Medium-full colour. Closed-in at first on the nose. Slightly inflexible. Rather hard. Better on the palate. Fullish body. Good grip of acidity. Ample rich fruit, if slightly austere at present. Fine.

Corton, Clos du Roi,

Domaine Comte Senard From 2015 18.5

Medium-full colour. Lots of class here. Quite full body. Firm. Impressively profound fruit. Very good tannins. Just a touch of oak. Long, complex, and very lovely.

Corton, Clos du Roi,

Domaine de la Vougeraie From 2013 13.0

Medium-full colour. Rather hard and tight on the nose. But good fruit and balance underneath. But as it evolved, it became very vegetal. A bad bottle?

Clos de Vougeot, Domaine

du Clos Frantin, Albert Bichot From 2013 13.5

Medium-full colour. Ample nose, but a touch of reduction. This made it rather astringent on the palate. Medium-full body. I'd like to see this again.

Clos de Vougeot,

Domaine Drouhin From 2014 13.5

Medium-full colour. Quite a fresh nose, but a little four-square. Medium to medium-full body. Somewhat lumpy on the palate. Lacks grace.

Clos de Vougeot,

Domaine Eugenie From 2015 17.0

There were originally two *cuvées*. One de-stemmed, the other from whole clusters. Blended together later. Round, rich, fat, and spicy. Very good grip. Good structure and intensity. Less volume and quite different from the Grands-Echézeaux.

Clos de Vougeot,

Domaine Grivot From 2016 18.5

Fullish body. Good depth. Very good style. Lovely fruit. Some tannin to resolve. Lots of class and energy and a very lovely finish. Very fine.

Clos de Vougeot,

Domaine Anne Gros From 2015 18.0

Medium-full colour. Soft, sweet, and succulent on the nose and the palate. Classy. Medium-full body. Fresh and balanced. This is concentrated, rich, and very attractive. Fine plus.

Clos de Vougeot,

Domaine Michel Gros From 2016 17.5

Medium-full colour. A good, meaty wine on the nose, but a little rigid at first on the palate. Fullish body. Ample as it evolved. Good grip. Fresh and classy at the end. Fine.

Clos de Vougeot,

Domaine Gros Frère et Soeur   From 2013 13.0

Medium-full colour. Somewhat lumpy on the nose. Medium to medium-full body. Marked acidity. Unbalanced. Lacks charm.

Clos de Vougeot, Domaine

Alain Hudelot-Noëllat   From 2014 16.0

Medium colour. Fresh, youthful, fragrant nose. There is a touch of reduction here. But underneath the wine is medium-full bodied and meaty, with good fruit. Very good.

Clos de Vougeot,

Domaine Louis Jadot   From 2014 15.0

Medium-full colour. Rather evolved nose with a touch of reduction. Medium-full body. Decent fruit and grip. But slightly rigid at present. But good stuff.

Clos de Vougeot,

Domaine Lamarche   From 2014 16.5

Medium-full colour. Ample, ripe, cool, and vigorous on the nose. Very good fruit here. Rich. Fullish body. Balanced. Vigorous. Positive. Very good plus.

Clos de Vougeot,

Domaine Leroy   From 2016 18.5

Lots of depth and style on the nose. Rich, profound, and harmonious. This is a serious Clos de Vougeot. Fullish body. Very good grip. Lots of energy and a very lovely finish. Very fine.

Clos de Vougeot,

Domaine Thibault Liger-Belair   From 2016 18.0

Medium-full colour. Good depth and concentration here on the nose. Balanced and intense. Fresh and vigorous. Complex and classy. Lovely finish. Fine plus.

Clos de Vougeot,

Domaine Loichet   From 2014 14.5

Medium-full colour. Plump nose. Good grip. Medium to medium-full body. Good acidity. The follow-through is slightly raw. And I don't get a great deal of class here. Quite good plus.

Clos de Vougeot,

Domaine Méo-Camuzet   From 2014 16.0

Medium weight. Ripe and pretty. Some oak. Quite sweet. But there is a lack of grip: nothing to hold the wine together or add on the follow-through.

Clos de Vougeot,

Domaine Denis Mortet   From 2015 17.0

Fullish colour. Rich, oaky, plump, attractive nose. Fullish body. Gently oaky on the palate. Fresh. Succulent. Balanced, classy, and positive. Very good indeed.

Clos de Vougeot,

Maison Roche de Bellene   From 2015 15.5

Fullish colour. Vigorous nose. Good fruit. Good class. Good depth. Fullish body. Ripe and ample. Good grip. Not as classy as it evolved as I thought at first. But good stuff nevertheless.

Clos de Vougeot,

Château de la Tour   From 2016 18.0

Good colour. A meaty wine. But styish, concentrated, ripe, and succulent. Very good grip and a very good follow-through. Fine plus.

Clos de Vougeot,

Château de la Tour,

Vieilles Vignes   From 2017 18.5

Full body. Ripe, very concetrated, fat, and rich. Profound and classy. Excellent grip. Very lovely.

Clos de Vougeot,

Domaine de la Vougeraie   From 2014 17.0

Medium-full colour. Fragrant nose. Plump, relaxed fruit. Quite classy. Some evolution. But ripe and intense. Good energy. Long. Very good indeed.

Echézeaux,

Domaine Daniel Bocquenet   From 2016 18.0

Good colour. Soft, supple nose. But not a bit weak. Concentrated and stylish. Rich and succulent. Clean and crisp. Medium-full body. Good oaky support. Very good grip. Lovely. Fine plus.

Echézeaux, Domaine Eugenie   From 2015 16.0
Medium-full colour. Fresh, stylish, quite oaky nose. Soft and harmonious. By no means a blockbuster but plenty of charm. Very good.

**Echézeaux, Domaine du
Clos Frantin, Albert Bichot**   From 2015 18.0
Medium-full colour. Plump, gently oaky nose. Medium-full body. Quite firm. Good grip. Very good, intense fruit. Long on the palate. Plenty of dimension. Fine plus.

Echézeaux, Domaine Grivot   From 2015 17.5
Medium to medium-full weight. This is a more mineral wine than their Clos de Vougeot. Attractive, lush, but very pure nose. Lovely fruit. Harmonious and intense and classy. Fine.

**Echézeaux,
Domaine Anne Gros**   From 2014 17.0
Medium colour. Sweet, fragrant nose. Balanced, elegant, and intense. Medium body. Ripe, fresh, and succulent. By no means a blockbuster. Long and very charming. Perhaps not serious but very good indeed.

Echézeaux, Domaine A. F. Gros   From 2014 16.0
Medium-full colour. Good stylish, quite forward fruit on the nose. Reasonably fresh. Good balance and quite elegant. Very good.

**Echézeaux,
Domaine Gros Frère et Soeur**   From 2015 16.5
Medium-full colour. Ample nose, ripe and spicy. Medium-full body. Good grip. Not too sweet and all the better as a result. Long. Very good plus.

Echézeaux, Domaine Lamarche   From 2015 17.5
Medium-full colour. Soft, ripe, fruity nose. Medium-full body. Good grip. Lovely succulent, very well-balanced, ripe fruit. A real cornucopia. Very seductive. Fine.

**Echézeaux, Domaine
du Vicomte de Liger-Belair**   From 2015 16.5
Medium-full colour. Good classy fruit on the nose. Medium-full body. Ripe on the attack. Slightly closed-in. A good ample, intense, well-balanced example. Very good indeed.

**Echézeaux,
Domaine Dr. Georges
Mugneret-Gibourg**   From 2015   17.5
Medium-full colour. Fragrant, soft, accessible nose. Medium-full body. Lovely pure fruit. Very elegant and composed. Fine.

**Echézeaux,
Domaine Gérard Mugneret**   From 2015 18.5
Medium-full colour. Fresh, youthful nose. Ample, balanced, and stylish. Medium-full body. Long and complex. Lovely fruit. Lots of dimension. Very fine.

**Echézeaux,
Domaine Jacques Prieur**   From 2013 14.5
Medium-full colour. Soft, gentle, forward, slightly spicy. Decent freshness but nothing very exciting.

**Echézeaux,
Domaine de la Romanée-Conti**   From 2015 17.5
Good colour. Ample, round, ripe nose. Gingerbread touches. Medium-full body. Good vigour and backbone. Good depth. Harmonious, long, stylish, and complex. Fine.

**Echézeaux,
Domaine Emmanuel Rouget**   From 2015 18.5
Medium-full colour. Ample, succulent, oaky nose. Fullish body. Oaky on the palate. Balanced and very classy. Splendid long finish. This is very lovely. Very fine.

**Echézeaux,
Domaine Cecile Tremblay**   From 2014 17.0
Medium-full colour. I hate to say it, but there is a feminine touch here (and I wrote this before I knew the wine's provenance). Medium-full body. Delicate and intense. Very pure fruit. Stylish and persistent. Very good indeed.

**Grands-Echézeaux,
Domaine du Clos Frantin,
Albert Bichot**   From 2015 18.5
Medium-full colour. Ample, rich, succulent, oaky nose. Medium-full body. Cool, stylish fruit. Quite concentrated. Good positive, energetic follow-through. Very fine.

Grands-Echézeaux,
Domaine Drouhin   From 2014 16.0
Medium-full colour. Some evolution. Soft, fruity nose. Has charm if not a great deal of energy. Medium to medium-full weight. Ripe and charming. But no more than very good.

Grands-Echézeaux,
Domaine Eugenie   From 2016 17.5
Medium-full colour. Plummy nose. Ample fruit. Succulent, full-bodied, fat, and ripe. Very good grip. Distinctly better than the Echézeaux. But again the oak is a bit too much. (100 percent for the *grands crus*.)

Grands-Echézeaux,
Domaine Lamarche   From 2015 17.5
Medium-full colour. Firm, fresh, succulent nose. Medium-full body. Good attack. Very good fruit. Lush and ripe but with very good grip. Long. Fine.

Grands-Echézeaux,
Domaine de
la Romanée-Conti   From 2014 17.0
Medium colour. Very soft nose. Less grip than the Echézeaux it seems. Medium body. Good ripe fruit, but a touch of astringency on the attack. Better on the follow-through; ample and quite fat. But not as impressive for what it is as the Echézeaux.

La Grande Rue,
Domaine Lamarche   From 2016 18.5
Medium-full colour. Oaky nose with a hint of caramel. Medium-full body. Good grip. Plenty of energy. Lots of dimension. A lot of class too. Lush, ripe fruit. Very fine.

Romanée-Saint-Vivant,
Domaine de l'Arlot   From 2015 16.0
Medium-full colour. Closed-in on the nose. Some tannic dryness plus the stems. No lack of richness and dimension underneath. Medium-full body. Rich. Good structure. Very good grip. Ripe at the end. I marked this highly at first, but it evolved rather too fast in the glass.

Romanée-Saint-Vivant,
Domaine Follin-Arbelet   From 2016 18.5
Medium-full colour. Discreet, classy nose. Lovely balanced, high-quality fruit here. Medium-full body. Lush, ripe, quite concentrated, and very intense. Very fine.

Romanée-Saint-Vivant,
Domaine Alain Hudelot-Noëllat From 2016 19.0
Medium-full colour. Classy fruit on the nose. Still a bit reticent. Intense and rich on the palate. Medium-full body. Lush and voluptuous. Lots of energy. Very lovely.

Romanée-Saint-Vivant,
Domaine Leroy   From 2017 19.0
This is very, very lovely. Splendidly concentrated, poised fruit. Very good grip. Only medium-full body, but intense and elegant, long and complex. Very fine indeed.

Romanée-Saint-Vivant,
Domaine de la Romanée-Conti   From 2016 18.5
Good colour. Better than the Richebourg. Lovely nose. Pure and succulent. Ripe and round but fresh and vigorous for a 2007. Fullish body, ample and velvety on the palate. Good grip. This is complex and very elegant. Lovely finish. Very fine.

Richebourg, Domaine Grivot   From 2016 18.5
Medium-full colour. Quite an austere nose. But high-quality underneath. Medium-full body. Ripe. Intense. Splendid, really profound, concentrated fruit. Long and complex and very classy. Very fine.

Richebourg, Domaine A. F. Gros From 2016 18.0
Medium-full colour. Rich, ample, silky-smooth, and voluptuous on the nose. Fullish body. Youthful. Very good grip. Ripe and intense. Fat and very seductive. Fine plus.

Richebourg, Domaine Leroy   From 2017 18.5
More reticent on the attack than the Romanée-Saint-Vivant. Slightly less advanced, but not as complete. Medium-full body. Good grip. Very lovely fruit. Very fine.

Richebourg,

Domaine Thibault Liger-Belair   From 2016   17.5
Medium-full colour. Closed-in nose. Somewhat adolescent at present. But lots of vigour and richness. Medium-full body. A little oak. Rich if a bit sturdy at present. Fine, surely.

Richebourg,

Domaine de la Romanée-Conti   From 2016   17.5
Medium colour. Less to it than the Romanée-Saint-Vivant. Pleasant fruity nose. No great depth or vigour. Medium body. Gentle, ripe, round, soft, and stylish. But it lacks intensity, especially for a Richebourg.

La Tâche,

Domaine de la Romanée-Conti   From 2017   19.0
Good colour. Rich, ample, concentrated nose. Plenty of wine here. Fullish body. Good grip. Plenty of depth. Nice and fresh and positive. Classy and profound. Lovely finish. Very fine plus.

La Romanée, Domaine du

Vicomte de Liger-Belair   From 2016   19.5
Medium-full colour. Very fine class and concentration on the nose. On the palate the wine is fullish and has glorious, multidimensional fruit. A really profound, complex, and aristocratic wine. Brilliant.

Romanée-Conti,

Domaine de la Romanée-Conti   From 2015   18.5
Good colour. Delicate but intense nose. No weakness here. Very complex and subtle. Very lovely fruit. La Tâche gains by having more volume. This tails off just a touch at the end. Very fine nevertheless.

Bonnes-Mares,

Domaine Francois Bertheau   From 2015   18.0
Medium-full colour. Quite new oaky. But rich and ample on the nose. Fullish body. Lovely fruit. Nice and cool and balanced. But the oak is a bit dominant. Fine plus.

Bonnes-Mares,

Domaine Bruno Clair   From 2016   17.5
Medium-full colour. Full, fresh, youthful nose. Medium-full body. Rich. Fresh. Not quite the concentration and intensity but no lack of class and depth. Fine.

Bonnes-Mares,

Domaine Drouhin-Laroze   From 2016   18.0
Medium-full colour. Youthful nose. Sturdy and fresh. Lots of class and depth on the palate. Full body. Very energetic. Very good grip. Fine tannins. This is impressive. Needs time. Fine plus.

Bonnes-Mares,

Domaine Robert Groffier   From 2014   14.0
Medium-full colour. This is a bit of a disappointment. Somewhat rustic and reduced on the nose. Only medium body. Lacks grip. Some fruit at the end. I'd like to see this again.

Bonnes-Mares,

Domaine Georges Roumier   From 2016   19.0
Medium-full colour. Very closed-in on the nose. Needs time. Some new oak evident. Full body. Backward. Some tannin. Lots of grip and energy. Lovely ample, rich follow-through. Very long on the palate, high-class. Very fine indeed.

Bonnes-Mares, Domaine

Comte Georges de Vogüé   From 2016   19.0
Medium-full colour. Youthful, closed-in, but very classy nose. Medium-full body. Very ripe, succulent fruit. Ripe tannins and very good grip. Classy, long, complex, and very lovely. Splendid long finish. But by no means a blockbuster. Very fine indeed.

Bonnes-Mares,

Domaine de la Vougeraie   From 2015   16.0
Medium-full colour. Spicy nose. Some elements of reduction. Medium-full body. There is some very good fruit here and no lack of grip. But at this stage I have a question mark over the class.

Musigny, Domaine Leroy   From 2014   See note
Slightly reduced, but it doesn't seem to have a great deal to it. Decent acidity. But a lack of depth and richness. Disappointing. To be seen again.

Musigny,

Domaine J. F. Mugnier   From 2017   19.5

Good colour. Lovely nose: rich, harmonious, ripe, and concentrated. Classy and complex. Fullish body. Intense. Crammed with fruit. Lots of energy and depth. Great finesse. Very fine indeed.

Musigny,

Domaine de la Vougeraie   From 2016   17.5

Good colour. Full, rich, and concentrated on the nose. Fullish body. Somewhat adolescent at present. Good grip and intensity. Abundant succulent fruit. Very fine grip. Fine but not great.

Musigny, Domaine

Comte Georges de Vogûé   From 2016   18.5

Good colour. Subtle, complex, very laid-back, very lovely fruit on the nose. Fullish body. Some new oak. This is certainly very fine, if without the complexity and intensity of great.

Clos des Lambrays,

Domaine des Lambrays   From 2014   15.0

Medium-full colour. Elegant but delicate on the nose. Medium to medium-full body. Stylish and fruity. Good intensity. Quite forward.

In view of the note I took at the Clos des Lambrays six months or so later, we either had a bad bottle here, or I just simply wasn't tasting correctly. My note of February 2011 was much more complimentary.

Clos-Saint-Denis,

Domaine Bertagna   From 2015   16.0

Medium-full colour. Good depth here. Good style and balance too. Medium-full body. Good grip. Fresh and elegant. Positive. Very good.

Clos de la Roche,

Domaine Dujac   From 2014   15.5

Essentially a soft-centred wine. Ripe. Even sweet. Balanced and classy. But not really enough backbone and energy. Good plus.

Clos de la Roche,

Domaine Leroy   From 2014   16.0

Medium weight. Ample, pretty, fresh, and fruity. But it lacks real grip and energy. Very good at best.

Clos de la Roche,

Domaine Hubert Lignier   From 2014   14.5

Medium-full colour. Ripe nose. Quite sturdy. Medium-full body. Good grip. A little adolescent at present.

Clos de la Roche,

Domaine Louis Rémy   From 2014   14.5

Medium colour. Fresh, quite stylish but forward nose. On the palate this shows good fruit, if not a lot of depth. Quite good plus.

Clos de Tart,

Domaine du Clos de Tart   From 2015   17.0

Medium-full colour. Ample and fruity on the nose, with good depth and dimension. Medium-full body. No lack of wine here. A touch of new oak. Good grip. Ripe and positive. Very good indeed.

Chapelle-Chambertin,

Domaine Jadot   From 2016   18.0

Medium-full colour. Vigorous on both the nose and the palate. Fat, rich, and concentrated. Medium-full body. This is fine plus. It has more to it than most.

Chapelle-Chambertin,

Domaine Perrot-Minot   From 2015   18.0

Fullish colour. Rich, ample, fat, concentrated nose. Fullish body. Ripe, vigorous, and seductive. Classy and energetic. Fine plus.

Chapelle-Chambertin,

Domaine Ponsot   From 2016   18.0

Fullish structure. This has a bit more backbone than his Griotte. And doesn't show as well today. Good grip. Fine ripe tannins. Very good vigour. Will be lovely.

Chapelle-Chambertin,

Domaine Rossignol-Trapet   From 2015   18.5

Medium-full colour. High-toned nose. Gentle oaky background. Medium-full body. Rich, succulent, complex, and complete. High-class. Very long and very lovely.

Chapelle-Chambertin,

Domaine Cecile Tremblay   From 2015   16.0

Medium-full colour. Ripe, ample, slightly earthy nose. Soft, ample, sweet, and succulent on the palate. Medium-full body. Good vigour, but just a little astringency detracts from the enjoyment.

Chapelle-Chambertin, Domaine
Jean et Jean-Louis Trapet   From 2016   18.0

Soft, ripe, vigorous but understated. Very classy. Lots of dimension. Very classy and a lovely finish. Fine plus.

Charmes-Chambertin,
Domaine Arlaud   From 2015   17.0

Medium-full colour. Fresh, gently oaky nose. Stylish. Very good grip. Medium-full body. Round, ripe, vigorous fruit. Juicy and succulent. Lots of energy. Long and complex. Very good indeed.

Charmes-Chambertin,
Domaine Denis Bachelet   From 2015   18.0

Fullish colour. A ripe, rich, concentrated wine with a lot of depth. Very classy. Medium-full body. As ever, it is a cut above most of the Charmes-Chambertins. But it is very 2007, in that it lacks real dimension and energy.

Charmes-Chambertin,
Maison Henri Boillot   From 2015   16.5

Medium-full colour. Rich, fat, concentrated, oaky nose. Very pure Pinot fruit. Medium-full body. Fresh and harmonious. Good length and depth. Long. Very good plus.

Charmes-Chambertin,
Maison Chanson   From 2014   14.0

Medium to medium-full colour. Fresh, ample, balanced nose. Good fruit. Medium-full body. On the palate this is ripe but a little uncouth. The finish is a touch astringent.

Charmes-Chambertin,
Domaine Drouhin   From 2014   16.0

Medium-full colour. Ripe, somewhat new-oaky on the nose. Medium to medium-full body. Good grip. Once again a little soft-centred but there is style here. Very good.

Charmes-Chambertin,
Humbert Frères   From 2014   15.5

Medium-full colour. Rather adolescent at present. But good substance and grip. No lack of ripe, if at the moment somewhat burly, fruit. Good plus.

Charmes-Chambertin,
Maison Camille Giroud   From 2014   15.0

Medium-full colour. Ripe, soft nose. Good depth if no great backbone. Soft, plump, and easy to drink.

Charmes-Chambertin,
Domaine Perrot-Minot   From 2014   16.0

Medium-full colour. Soft, ripe nose. Abundant and round and easy to drink. Medium to medium-full body. Stylish and balanced if a little soft-centred.

Charmes-Chambertin,
Maison Roche de Bellene   From 2014   14.0

Medium-full colour. Fresh, ample, ripe, fruity nose. Medium-full weight. Good grip. A little weak on the follow-through. Only quite good.

Charmes-Chambertin,
Domaine Armand Rousseau   From 2014   15.0

Medium-full colour. Rich, ample, vigorous nose. Good style. Medium-full body. Good but some brettanomyces flavours on the palate.

Charmes-Chambertin,
Domaine Serafin   From 2015   17.5

Medium-full colour. Gently oaky, quite intense, very ripe nose. Medium-full body. Lovely balanced, poised Pinot fruit here. Very succulent. Very seductive. Fine.

Charmes-Chambertin,
Domaine Taupenot-Merme   From 2014   17.0

Medium-full colour. Soft, fresh, elegant nose. No great depth but balanced and stylish. Medium to medium-full body. Ripe and luscious. Attractive finish.

Charmes-Chambertin,
Mazoyères,
Domaine de la Vougeraie   From 2014   16.0

Medium-full colour. Soft and fruity on the nose, if a little loose-knit. Medium to medium-full body. Ripe and oaky and attractive. Good balance. Quite vigorous at the end. Very good if not great.

Griotte-Chambertin,

Domaine Drouhin From 2014 17.0

Medium-full colour. A little raw on the nose at present, but ample and vigorous. Ripe and stylish. Good acidity. Medium-full body. Lovely complex fruit. Very good indeed, but very 2007.

Griotte-Chambertin,

Domaine Ponsot From 2015 18.0

Medium-full body. Very pure, splendidly intense fruit. Very classy. Balanced and fragrant and lovely.

Latricières-Chambertin,

Domaine Simon Bize From 2015 17.5

Medium colour. Soft and quite markedly oaky on the nose. Ripe, balanced, and stylish. Rich and concentrated on the palate. Lots of energy and a fine long finish. Fine.

Latricières-Chambertin,

Domaine Drouhin-Laroze From 2014 16.0

Medium-full colour. Soft nose. Fresh but on the light side. A most attractive, well-balanced, juicy wine, but without *grand cru* concentration.

Latricières-Chambertin,

Domaine Faiveley From 2015 15.5

Medium colour. Some development. Somewhat diffuse on the nose. Here is a lack of grip and flair here. Medium to medium-full body. Quite fruity and the tannins are ripe. But it lacks vigour.

Latricières-Chambertin,

Domaine Leroy From 2014 13.5

Somewhat raw. But not much backbone here. Unexciting.

Latricières-Chambertin,

Domaine Louis Rèmy From 2016 18.0

Medium-full colour. Super-concentrated fruit here on the nose. Very lovely indeed. Long, complex, and laid-back. Velvety. Very fine fruit. Medium-full body. This is really classy.

Latricières-Chambertin,

Domaine Rossignol-Trapet From 2016 18.0

Medium-full colour. Rich, full, spicy nose. Fullish body. Concentrated. Very good grip. Full of fruit. Good style and still youthful. Fine plus.

Latricières-Chambertin, Domaine

Jean et Jean-Louis Trapet From 2016 17.0

A bigger wine than their Chapelle. But more rustic as well as more tannic. Not as much elegance and flair. But very good indeed nevertheless.

Mazis-Chambertin,

Maison Bernstein From 2014 16.0

Good colour. Rich, ample, and a little fleshy on the nose. Some oak if not a great deal of dimension. Medium body. Finishes a little short. Very good at best.

Mazis-Chambertin,

Domaine Faiveley From 2016 17.5

Full colour. Backward on the nose. Firm and concentrated. Very good grip. A fragrant wine. Today it is their Cazetiers which seems the bigger and the more profound. But this has lovely, balanced, elegant fruit and a lovely finish.

Mazis-Chambertin,

Domaine Maume From 2015 16.5

Medium-full colour. Soft, gently oaky, fruity nose. Fullish body. Just a little hard. The tannins are a bit rigid. But there is plenty of grip here. Good concentrated fruit. Very good plus.

Mazoyères-Chambertin,

Domaine Perrot-Minot From 2014 17.5

Medium-full colour. Firm, vigorous, youthful, very lovely nose. Good grip. Quite structured and at present a bit austere. Some tannin. But very good fruit. The finish is fine.

Mazoyères-Chambertin,

Domaine Taupenot-Merme From 2014 17.0

Medium-full colour. Ripe, succulent nose. Stylish and well-balanced. Medium-full body. Good grip. Finishes positively. Very good indeed.

Ruchottes-Chambertin,

Dr. Georges Mugneret-Gibourg From 2015 18.0

Medium-full colour. Rich, ample concentrated fruit on the nose. Fullish, balanced, and complex. Lots of grip. Very good acidity. High-class.

Ruchottes-Chambertin,
Clos des Ruchottes,
Domaine Armand Rousseau   From 2014   15.0
Not really very much here, and an absence of freshness. Some astringency. Not enough fruit.

Ruchottes-Chambertin,
Domaine Christophe Roumier   From 2016   18.0
Medium-full colour. Lots of class here. Very lovely, virile fruit on the nose. Medium-full body. Lots of dimension on the palate. Very good grip. Very lovely subtle fruit. Very fine.

Chambertin, Clos de Bèze,
Domaine du Clos Frantin,
Albert Bichot   From 2016   18.5
Medium-full colour. Rich, oaky nose. Fullish body. Very lovely fruit. Harmonious and classy. Long and complex. Succulent and oaky. Very fine.

Chambertin, Clos de Bèze,
Domaine Bouchard Père et Fils   From 2016   18.0
Good colour. Ripe and ample on the nose. Not a bit weak-kneed. Fullish body. Good tannins. Good grip. Very stylish fruit. Lots of depth and class. Fine plus.

Chambertin, Clos de Bèze,
Domaine Bruno Clair   From 2017   18.5
Full colour. Very closed-in on the nose. Still very young. Fullish body. Rich, fat, very concentrated. Excellent grip. This is very fine.

Chambertin, Clos de Bèze,
Domaine Pierre Damoy   From 2014   17.5
Medium colour. Soft, fragrant, elegant nose. Not a lot of backbone but ripe and stylish. Medium body. Good length. Quite forward.

Chambertin, Clos de Bèze,
Domaine Drouhin-Laroze   From 2013   16.5
Medium to medium-full colour for the vintage. Soft, fragrant nose. Not a blockbuster. Indeed, rather on the light side. Yet decent grip and intensity. And a good, positive, fresh, elegant finish.

Chambertin, Clos de Bèze,
Domaine Louis Jadot   From 2016   18.0
Medium weight. Fresh. Good grip. Ripe and succulent. Lots of style. Complex and really quite intense for a 2007. No great substance or tannic structure of course. But good character.

Chambertin, Clos de Bèze,
Domaine Armand Rousseau   From 2016   18.0
Medium-full colour. Soft, quite oaky nose. Medium-full body. Good rich fruit. Quite oaky. Balanced and quite profound. Fine plus.

Chambertin,
Domaine Bertagna   From 2016   18.5
Good colour for the vintage. Good fat, ample, slightly spicy nose. Very good size and depth and vigour for the vintage. Class too. Ripe and succulent. Good energy. One of the very best Chambertins this year. Very fine.

Chambertin,
Maison Henri Boillot   From 2016   18.5
Fullish colour. Firm nose. Quite closed; fullish body. Good grip. A little austere at present. Some tannin. Plenty of weight and depth. Very good fruit underneath. Will get more charming as it evolves. Very fine.

Chambertin, Domaine du
Clos Frantin, Albert Bichot   From 2014   17.5
Medium-full colour. Soft nose. No great depth or weight. Medium body. Not a great deal of tannin. Nor dimension. Yet an attractive wine for quite early drinking. Not short, nor does it lack charm.

Chambertin,
Maison Camille Giroud   From 2015   18.5
Medium-full colour. Ripe, fullish nose. Fullish body. Lots of succulent fruit here. Rich. Very good grip. Lovely finish. Very fine.

Chambertin, Domaine Leroy   From 2018   19.5
Good nose. Rich and full, profound and classy. A lot of wine here for a 2007. Splendid fruit and a lot of depth and concentration. Lovely, long, intense finish. Very fine indeed.

Chambertin,
Domaine Jacques Prieur   From 2015 18.0
Medium colour. Gentle nose. Roasted nuts and bacon. More impressive on the palate. Good grip. This has vigour, freshness, and a positive finish. Quite ample. This has got more to it than most.

Chambertin,
Domaine Louis Rémy   From 2016 19.0
Fullish colour. Quite full and concentrated on the nose. Full body. This is very lovely. Concentrated and harmonious. Very splendid fruit. Oaky and multidimensional. Very impressive.

Chambertin,
Domaine Rossignol-Trapet   From 2015 17.5
Medium-full colour. Ripe, succulent soft fruit, more red than black, on the nose. A gentle wine. No great strength, but it has good depth and grip and is very stylish. Fine but not great.

Chambertin,
Domaine Armand Rousseau   From 2014 19.5
Good colour. Not very forthcoming at first on the nose. Fullish body. Rich and oaky. Lots of depth. Very good grip. Plenty of wine here and plenty of class. Excellent.

Chambertin, Domaine
Jean et Jean-Louis Trapet   From 2015 18.5
Medium-full colour. Classy nose. Lots of depth. Concentrated and very harmonious. Fullish body. Ample. Rich. Lots of grip. Lots of finesse. Very fine.

2006 BURGUNDY

The 2006 is a good but not great Burgundy vintage. If we look over the last decade or so, we have better years in 1998, 1999, 2002, 2005,

☞ *Rating for the Vintage* ☜	
Red	14.0 (Côte de Beaune)
White	17.0
	16.0 (Côte de Nuits)

☞ *Size of the Crop* ☜ (In hectolitres)			
	RED	WHITE	TOTAL
Grands crus	12,738	4,004	16,742
Village and premiers crus	165,281	63,527	228,808
TOTAL	178,019	67,531	245,550

2006, and 2009, but less successful outcomes in 2000, 2001, 2003, 2004, and 2007. The white 2006s are very good, especially in Chablis and the Côte Chalonnaise—they are somewhat more irregular in the Côte de Beaune but better than the reds—while overall the red 2006s are charming, fruity, and soft-centred, riper than the 2004s but without the depth, vigour, and concentration of 2002, let alone the 2005s.

Weather Conditions

Winter 2005–2006 was cool rather than cold, but dry, and this was followed by a late spring. Thereafter the summer was largely unexceptional, average in May and June, very hot in July, but cold and miserable in August. September began as an improvement but then proved patchy. The skins were fragile after the August rains, and the vintage was forced upon the growers before the fruit deteriorated. Some vintages favour the late-pickers. The 2006 was not one of them.

There had been hail in the spring in Gevrey. This did not affect the quality. It merely reduced the crop. Later there was hail in Chambolle and in Volnay. Here I fear the quality *has* been compromised. Overall, there was less precipitation in the Côte de Nuits than in the Côte de Beaune. So it is in Nuits Saint-Georges and Vosne-Romanée that we find the best wines. I was also impressed by the Cortons.

At the outset, no one was very enthusiastic about the 2006 reds. They appeared a little inconsequential. But they seemed to improve after the malos had completed and after the autumn 2007 rackings. Once they had settled down after bottling, it was clear that this was a vintage with no lack of merit. These 2006s are medium-bodied, plump, fresh, fruity, and pleasant. The very best are in addition ripe and stylish. Acidities are not aggressive; indeed, some of the less-successful bottles already show signs of astringency because there is a lack of grip. They will evolve in the medium term. There are plenty of attractive bottles for the mid-2010s.

Where are the best wines? The best 2006s will be found in Nuits-Saint-Georges, Vosne-Romanée, and Gevrey-Chambertin. There are also some good Cortons. By contrast, the Chambolle-Musignys and Morey-Saint-Denis are more irregular, while the Côte de Beaunes are often a bit feeble. When should you drink your 2006 red Burgundies? Much of the Côte de Beaune will be ready fairly soon: by 2013 or 2014. Some indeed are already at their best. The Côte de Nuits, on the other hand, should still be kept a few years. Don't pull any corks until 2015 or so. While the Côte de Beaunes are for the short term, and few will survive after 2020, there is no hurry with their northern neighbours. Here we do have wines which will last into the mid-2020s.

The Best Wines of the Vintage

20/20

La Romanée-Conti, Domaine de la
    Romanée-Conti

Musigny, Domaine J. F. Mugnier

19.5

Richebourg, Jean Grivot

Chambertin, Armand Rousseau

19.0

Vosne-Romanée, Malconsorts, Sylvain Cathiard

Chambolle-Musigny, Amoureuses,
    J. F. Mugnier

La Grande Rue, Lamarche.

La Tâche, Domaine de la Romanée-Conti

Clos des Lambrays

Chambertin, Clos de Bèze, Bruno Clair

Chambertin, Clos de Bèze, Armand Rousseau

Chambertin, Rossignol-Trapet

18.5

Nuits-Saint-Georges, Cras, Vicomte de
    Liger-Belair

Nuits-Saint-Georges, Saint-Georges, Robert
    Chevillon

Vosne-Romanée, Beaux Monts, Jean Grivot

Vosne-Romanée, Malconsorts, Dujac

Vosne-Romanée, Malconsorts, Lamarche

Vosne-Romanée, Reignots, Sylvain Cathiard

Vosne-Romanée, Suchots, Hudelot-Noëllat

Gevrey-Chambertin, Clos-Saint-Jacques,
    Bruno Clair

Gevrey-Chambertin, Clos-Saint-Jacques,
    Armand Rousseau

Clos de Vougeot, Robert Arnoux

Romanée-Saint-Vivant, Robert Arnoux

Bonnes-Mares, Drouhin-Laroze

Latricières-Chambertin, Jean et Jean-Louis
    Trapet

Two wines from the Côte de Beaune scored 18/20, both from Bouchard Père et Fils: Volnay, Caillerets and Le Corton. One or two wines escaped us, which I am fairly confident would have found their way onto the above list. I immediately think of Anne Gros's Richebourg and Sylvain Cathiard's Romanée-Saint-Vivant. There are others.

TASTING NOTES

As usual, the notes which follow come from several tasting sessions. The first was in March 2009 at the Domaines Familiaux/Masters of Wine tasting in London. The last was our annual group tasting held in Beaune at the end of August. Additional notes come from my visit to the United States in April. The Domaine de la Romanée-Conti wines were sampled seperately in Vosne-Romanée.

White Wines

Chablis, Les Clos,
Domaine Joseph Drouhin   Now to 2018   18.0
Very lovely nose: crisp, racy, and youthful. Very fine fruit. Poised and profound. Still very youthful.

Rully, *Premier Cru*,
Domaine Eric de Suremain   Drink soon   16.0
À point. Clean and pure and fresh. Fine for what it is. There have been inprovements here, quite obviously. And from now on, the Domaine Leflaive will be looking after the estate.

Savigny-Lès-Beaune,
Les Vergelesses,
Domaine Simon Bize   Drink soon   16.0
Ample, seductive, long, and stylish. Very ripe underneath, yet good grip. Very good.

Pernand-Vergelesses,
Le Clos du Village,
Domaine Rapet Père et Fils   Drink soon   16.0
Crisp, neat, medium-full body, and very stylish. Lovely peachy fruit. From 2010.

Pernand-Vergelesses,
Les Combottes, Domaine
du Château de Chorey   Drink soon   15.5
Crisp, classy, racy, and cool. Lovely style. Medium body.

Beaune, Clos des Mouches,
Domaine Joseph Drouhin   Now to 2017   16.0
Rich, full, and backward: indeed, still a bit closed. Surprisingly concentrated. Just a bit four-square perhaps, because it lacks high tones. Very good though.

Meursault, Blagny, Domaine
Thierry et Pascale Matrot   Now to 2017   16.5
Very lovely. Pure, elegant, balanced, and peachy. Very composed. Medium-full body. Lovely white flowery fruit. Very good plus.

Meursault, Clos de la Barre,
Domaine des Comtes Lafon   Now to 2017   16.5
Full, quite firm, profound nose. Very good grip. Lovely fruit. Still youthful. On the palate softer. But still good volume. A touch of the exotic on the mid-palate. Good long finish. Very good plus.

Meursault, Charmes,
Domaine des Comtes Lafon   2014 to 2024   18.0
Two notes. Lovely pure, minerally-flowery nose. A wine of considerable enegy and potential. Fullish, concentrated, intense, and vigorous. Very lovely fruit and excellent grip. Very long on the palate. This is is still very young. Really very fine.

Meursault, Genevrières,
Jean-Francois
Coche-Dury   Now to 2020 plus   19.0
This is very excellent. Very youthful. Full, rich, and vigorous. Excellent grip. Splendid dimension of fruit. Very ripe, but nothing too exotic here. Marvelous concentration and depth. This is very fine indeed, and would serve as a splendid introduction to anyone as yet doubtful about all the ballyhoo surrounding Coche-Dury's wine.

Meursault, Genévrières,
Maison Olivier Leflaive Frères   Drink soon   15.0
Good substance, but not a lot in the way of depth and interest. Merely good.

Meursault, Perrières,
Domaine Ballot-Millot   Now to 2020   17.5
Still quite closed, but full-bodied, rich, backward, and concentrated. Very lovely fruit. Mineral and intense. Lovely long finish. Fine.

Meursault, Perrières,
Domaine Bitouzet-Prieur   Now to 2020   18.0
Splendid minerality. Very concentrated. Lovely fruit. Still very young but potentially very fine. Very intense and with great class.

Meursault, Perrières,
Domaine Albert Grivault   Now to 2020   18.0
Lovely nose; more pronounced and individual than their Clos des Perrières. Quite full; bal-

anced, and stylish and very lovely. The oak is very discreet. Profound and very fine.

Meursault, Clos des Perrières,
Domaine Albert Grivault   Now to 2018   17.5
Ripe nose, broad-flavoured but nevertheless very Perrières. Fullish body. Ample, a litle richer than the above. Not quite the same *élan* but lovely all the same. Fine follow-through.

Puligny-Montrachet,
Les Champs-Gain, Maison
Olivier Leflaive Frères   Now to 2018   16.5
Delicate and poised, with lovely ripe fruit. Balanced, long, but without a great deal of backbone. For quite early drinking. Very good plus.

Puligny-Montrachet,
Le Clavoillon,
Domaine Leflaive   Now to 2017   16.0
Quite rich, full, and ample on the nose. Similar on the palate, though perhaps it lacks just a bit of concentration and grip. But very good fruit and long enough.

Puligny-Montrachet,
Les Folatières,
Domaine Vincent Bouzereau   Now to 2016   17.0
Youthful colour. Ripe, succulent, fruity, balanced, and still very fresh on the nose. Now *à point*. Medium-full body. Good grip. Peachy and fruit-salady. Finishes well. Very good indeed.

Puligny-Montrachet;
Les Perrières,
Domaine Louis Carillon   Now to 2019   17.5
Very concentrated. Lovely style. Mineral and racy. Very gently oaky. This is still very young. Very long and elegant on the palate. Fine.

Chassagne-Montrachet,
Les Blanchots Dessus,
Domaine Darviot-Perrin   Drink soon   15.5
This is almost too exotic, and I don't think it will last well, but it is most enjoyable now. Medium-full body. Good depth of fruit. Very ripe. No lack of freshness. Would go well with Chinese food.

Chassagne-Montrachet,
Les Grandes Ruchottes, Domaine
Fernand et Laurent Pillot   Now to 2020   18.0
Youthful colour. Very fresh on the nose. Full-bodied. Rich, classy, and concentrated. A wine of real class and depth here. Very lovely fruit Fine plus.

Chassagne-Montrachet,
Les Macharelles,
Maison Jean-Yves Devevey   Now to 2017   16.0
Ripe, luscious, and medium-full bodied, but very good depth and grip. Good fruit. Very good.

Chassagne-Montrachet, Morgeot,
Clos de la Chapelle, Domaine
Magenta/Louis Jadot   Now to 2016   16.0
Quite a closed-in nose. Fresh, full, and firm. A little unyielding at present. A meaty wine, but with good grip and not four-square. Lacks a little nuance, but very good.

Chassagne-Montachet, Les Vergers,
Domaine Michel Niellon   Now to 2016   16.0
A whiff of sulphur at first. Fullish, round, profound, and spicy. Not the greatest class, but that is Vergers. Good grip. Very gently oaky. Really quite rich. Very good.

Corton Blanc,
Domaine Senard   Now to 2018   17.5
Very individual fruit. Not Charlemagne but very lovely. A touch of oak. Original. Balanced. Medium-full body. Long fine plus.

Corton-Charlemagne, Domaine
Bonneau du Martray   2014 to 2024   19.0
Bottled April 2008. The first bottle was a little reduced and didn't show well, but I then sampled an example which had been opened the previous day. This was as it should be. Full-bodied. Backward. Very concentrated and very classy. Very lovely steely, complex fruit. High-class.

Corton-Charlemagne,
Maison Olivier Leflaive Frères   Now to 2018   16.5
Clean and crisp, but lacks dimension. Medium-full body. Starts well but then it finishes with

an absence of vigour. Only good in *grand cru* terms.

Bâtard-Montrachet,
Domaine Leflaive   Now to 2018   17.5

Like a bigger, sturdier example of their Clavoillon. On the nose a little four-square. Better on the palate. Fresher, good grip, no lack of nuance. This is very fine.

Le Montrachet, Domaine
de la Romanée-Conti   2016 to 2028   19.0

Rich, fat, oaky, and quite exotic. Sumptuous and vanilla-y, yet very good grip. Underneath, very minerally. Full-bodied. Very ripe fruit. Honeyed and opulent and very classy. Very fine indeed. Lovely.

Red Wines

CÔTE DE BEAUNE

Monthelie,
Domaine Pierre Morey   Drink soon   14.0

Soft, light, balanced, and fruity. Forward but lots of charm.

Château de Monthelie,
Domaine Eric de Suremain   Drink soon   13.5

Some tannins, and these are a bit rustic. Good ripeness. Somewhat *sauvage* but also rather soupy fruit. Quite good.

Château de Monthelie, Sur La Velle,
Domaine Eric de Suremain   Drink soon   13.5

A bit more depth and interest, but soupy nevertheless.

Pernand-Vergelesses,
Ile de Vergelesses, Domaine
Chandon de Briailles   Now to 2018   17.0

Lovely elegant nose. Medium weight. Stylish and intense and concentrated. Just a little tannin. Long. Very good indeed.

Savigny-Lès-Beaune,
Les Marconnets,
Domaine Simon Bize   Now to 2018   16.5

Medium weight. Ripe, spicy, succulent, and full of interest. Balanced and fresh. Lovely fruit. Very good indeed for what it is.

Aloxe-Corton, *Premier Cru,*
Domaine Prince
Florent de Mérode   Drink soon   15.0

Medium colour. Soft, ripe, medium-bodied. Stylish and generous. Lots of charm. Good. Ready now.

Aloxe-Corton, Clos du Chapitre,
Domaine Follin-Arbelet   Drink soon   14.0

Medium colour. Quite a firm nose, if no grace. Medium body. Some fruit and decent acidity. But no real flair.

Aloxe-Corton, Les Fournières,
Domaine Tollot-Beaut   Now to 2017   16.0

Medium-full colour. Some fruit and depth on the nose. Even vigour. Medium body. Ripe and fresh and fruity and positive. A plump wine, and elegant for Aloxe-Corton. Very good.

Aloxe-Corton, Les Valozières,
Domaine Senard   Drink soon   12.0

Medium colour. Weedy, stemmy nose. Slightly reduced on the palate. Dry and astringent.

Aloxe-Corton, Les Vercots,
Domaine Follin-Arbelet   Now to 2018   15.0

Medium-full colour. Quite rich fruit on the nose. Good substance and depth on the palate. Positive and fresh. Good.

Aloxe-Corton, Les Vercots,
Domaine Tollot-Beaut   Drink soon   13.0

Medium to medium-full colour. Soft, quite oaky, weedy, and tarty. Forward.

Beaune du Château,
Premier Cru, Domaine
Bouchard Père et Fils   Now to 2017   14.0

Medium colour. Soft, ripe, forward nose. No great weight here. But fruity and balanced, with a positive finish. Quite good.

Beaune, Aigrots,
Domaine Michel Lafarge   Now to 2017   14.0

Medium colour. Soft, fruity, forward nose. Decent weight on the palate. There is even a little backbone. Decent grip too. Quite positive. Quite good.

Beaune, Bressandes,

Domaine Chanson Now to 2017 14.0

Medium to medium-full colour. Plump. Decent grip and substance. Cool and stylish. Quite good.

Beaune, Bressandes,

Domaine des Croix Now to 2016 13.5

Medium to medium-full colour. Decent Pinot fruit on the nose. Fruity attack but a little astringent at the end. Okay at best.

Beaune, Champ Pimont,

Domaine Chanson Now to 2016 13.0

Medium to medium-full colour. Forward nose. Medium weight. Some fruit but no real grip. A little astringent at the end. Not bad.

Beaune, Clos des Avaux,

Domaine Newman Now to 2016 13.0

Medium to medium-full colour. Not a lot on the nose. Medium weight. Fresh and fruity. Slightly astringent at the end. But decent stuff.

Beaune, Clos des Fèves,

Domaine Chanson Now to 2017 14.0

Medium colour. Lightweight nose. Pleasant and fruity. Decently fresh. Medium weight. Quite good.

Beaune, Clos de Marconnets,

Domaine Chanson Now to 2016 13.5

Medium to medium-full colour. Pleasant fruit but a bit dilute on the nose. Ripe but not enough grip. Medium weight. Yet a decent finish. Not bad plus.

Beaune, Clos de
la Mousse, Domaine

Bouchard Père et Fils Drink soon 11.5

Medium-full colour. Quite rich but a bit subdued on the nose. Light, forward, not entirely pure, and a bit thin on the palate. Just about ready.

Beaune, Clos du Roi,

Domaine Rapet Père et Fils Now to 2018 14.5

Good colour. Ripe but a little raw on the nose. But good fruit and medium to medium-full weight on the palate. Lacks a little distinction, but that is the *climat*. Only a little tannin. Fresh. Good.

Beaune, Clos du Roi,

Domaine Tollot-Beaut Now to 2016 13.5

Medium to medium-full colour. Plump, spicy nose. Decent attack, but then it loses its grip and finishes a bit astringent. Only fair.

Beaune, Clos des Ursules,

Domaine Louis Jadot From 2015 17.0

Medium-full body. Rich, fat nose. Lots of depth. Good definition and style. Lots of concentration. Still youthful. Good vigour. Lovely. Needs time.

Beaune, Couchereaux,

Domaine Louis Jadot Drink soon 13.0

Medium colour. Decent fruit but not much character on the nose. Rather dilute on the palate. One-dimensional. Decent freshness so not bad. Forward.

Beaune, Cras, Domaine
du Château de Chorey From 2014 16.5

Full, rich, abundant nose. Medium-full body. Balanced, concentrated, and composed. Long and subtle. Very good plus.

Beaune, Epenottes,

Domaine Jean-Marc Boillot Drink soon 12.0

Good colour. Rich, plump nose. Good ripe fruit. Yet somewhat thin and weedy elements on the palate. Somewhat astringent.

Beaune, Grèves, Vigne de
L'Enfant Jesus, Domaine

Bouchard Père et Fils Now to 2018 15.0

Medium colour. Lightweight but plump and fruity. Decent weight on the palate. Positive finish. Good.

Beaune, Grèves,

Domaine Chanson Drink soon 13.0

Medium to medium-full colour. Round nose with a touch of spice. A bit light and astringent on the palate. Only fair.

Beaune, Grèves,

Domaine des Croix Drink soon 13.5

Medium to medium-full colour. Fresh nose if a little lightweight. Decent fruit, but not a lot of weight on the palate. Pleasant.

Beaune, Grèves,
Domaine de Montille   Drink soon   12.5
Medium colour. Fresh, fruity, and forward on
the nose. Rather too light and weedy on the palate. Thin finish.

Beaune, Grèves,
Domaine Newman   Now to 2018   15.5
Medium to medium-full colour. Decent persistence and intensity on the nose. Ripe. A touch
of oak. Good grip. Medium to medium-full
colour. Positive at the end, even long. Good
plus.

Beaune, Grèves,
Domaine Tollot-Beaut   Drink soon   12.5
Medium colour. Round, soft, plump, forward nose. A bit dilute on the palate. Finishes
astringently.

Beaune, Pertuisots,
Domaine des Croix   Drink soon   13.5
Medium to medium-full colour. Not much on
the nose, but a pleasant, fruity, forward wine.
Quite harmonious. Not bad.

Beaune, Pertuisots,
Domaine Jean-Yves Devevey   Drink soon   14.5
Medium body. Good fruit underneath, but currently a little bit rigid on the attack. Otherwise
the balance is correct. Good.

Beaune, Teurons, Domaine
Bouchard Père et Fils   Now to 2017   15.0
Medium to medium-full colour. Fresh, fruity
but lightweight nose. But good fruity consis-
tency on the palate. Good grip. Finishes well.
Stylish. Good.

Beaune, Teurons,
Domaine Chanson   Now to 2017   14.5
Medium to medium-full colour. Ripe, stylish
nose and attack. Medium body. Fresh and positive. Forward. Quite good plus.

Pommard, Charmots,
Domaine Gabriel Billard   Now to 2018   16.0
Good substance and depth. Ripe tannins.
Plenty of style. Medium to medium-full body.
Good grip. This is elegant for a Pommard, and

it has good energy and a long positive finish.
Very good.

Pommard, Clos des Epeneaux,
Domaine du Comte Armand   Now to 2019   15.0
Medium-full colour. Some extraction on the
nose. Firm but slightly bitter. A bit stewed at
the end, though the attack is not bad. It lacks
a bit of charm, but there is grip here. It will
improve. Good.

Pommard, Fremiers,
Domaine Louis Boillot   Drink soon   12.5
Medium colour. Fruity but a bit weak on the
nose. Light, forward, a bit weedy, and astringent on the palate.

Pommard, Grands Epenots,
Domaine Michel Gaunoux   Now to 2017   13.5
Slightly bland, vegetal nose. Fresher on the palate. Medium to medium-full body. Decent acidity. But overall only quite good.

Pommard, Jarollières,
Domaine Jean-Marc Boillot   Now to 2016   13.5
Medium-full colour. Rich and ripe on the nose,
but slightly attenuated and astringent on the
palate. Decent fruit but an ungainly finish. Not
bad plus.

Pommard, Jarollières,
Domaine de la Pousse d'Or   Now to 2018   15.5
Medium-full colour. Aromatic, plump nose.
Good freshness. Medium body. Attractive
attack. There is good fruit here, if no great
depth. Positive finish. Good plus.

Pommard, Pezerolles, Domaine
Bouchard Père et Fils   Drink soon   14.0
Medium colour. Ripe, even a little sweet on
the nose. Medium body. Decent fruit if no real
depth. Neither short nor dry though. Quite
good.

Pommard, Rugiens, Domaine
Bouchard Père et Fils   Now to 2019   17.0
Medium-full colour. Good substance, fruit, and
depth on the nose. Decent volume. Good grip.
Plump, ripe, and balanced. This even has class.
Long and positive at the end.

Pommard, Rugiens,
Domaine Michel Gaunoux   Now to 2018   14.0
Slight attenuation on the nose. But not as vegetal as the Epenots. Richer, fatter, and fresher. More style and better balanced. Quite good.

Pommard, Rugiens,
Domaine Louis Jadot   Drink soon   13.0
Medium colour. Feeble on the nose. Light, fruity, forward. Rather one-dimensional.

Pommard, Rugiens,
Domaine de Montille   Drink soon   12.5
Medium colour. Weak and weedy on the nose. Some fruit on the attack but dry and attenuated on the follow-through.

Pommard, Rugiens, Domaine
du Pavillon (Albert Bichot)   Now to 2019   16.0
Medium-full colour. Round, ripe, and fruity on the nose. Good depth here. Good grip. Positive and energetic. Very good.

Volnay, Brouillard,
Domaine Louis Boillot   Drink soon   12.5
Medium-full colour. Thin and weedy on the nose. And on the palate too. Decent fruit on the attack, but then it tails off.

Volnay, Caillerets,
Domaine Henri Boillot   Now to 2017   15.0
Medium-full colour. Some substance but a hint of attenuation on the nose. Medium body. Decent fruity attack. Even fresh. But it tails off. Good though.

Volnay, Caillerets,
Domaine Bouchard Père et Fils   From 2015   18.0
Medium colour. Fresh nose. Good style and depth. This is even a little closed. Here is a wine with potential. Fullish in 2006 terms. Concentrated, vigorous, classy, and profound. Lovely finish. Fine plus.

Volnay, Caillerets,
Clos des 60 Ouvrées,
Domaine de la Pousse d'Or   From 2015   17.5
Medium-full colour. A little closed on the nose. But firm and rich and quite substantial. Fullish body. Rich. Good grip. Some tannin.

Plenty of vigour and dimension. This will keep well. I did not find it had quite the flair of the Bouchard example, which it followed, but certainly fine.

Volnay,
Carelle Sous La Chapelle,
Domaine Jean-Marc Boillot   Drink soon   12.5
Medium-full colour. Plump but a little weedy on the nose. Light and a bit too dry and thin on the palate.

Volnay, Champans, Domaine
du Marquis d'Angerville   See note
Medium to medium-full colour. Seems to have decent substance but very reduced. Difficult to taste. Judgment deferred.

Volnay, Champans,
Domaine des Comtes Lafon   Now to 2017   14.0
Medium-full colour. Ripe, fresh nose, if a little one-dimensional. Decent juicy fruit on the palate. But not enough grip and depth. Quite good.

Volnay, Chevret,
Domaine Henri Boillot   Drink soon   13.5
Medium-full colour. Some substance on the nose, but a bit weedy at the same time. Medium body. Decent fruit on the attack. But a little attenuated, even astringent on the follow-through. Only fair.

Volnay, Chevret,
Domaine Louis Latour   Now to 2016   14.5
Medium colour. Slightly cooked nose. But there is depth underneath. Rich, ripe, and spicy. Not very Volnay, nor very elegant. But decent grip at first, though it got weedy later. Quite good plus.

Volnay, Clos de la Bousse d'Or,
Domaine de la Pousse d'Or   Now to 2019   16.5
Medium-full colour. Nicely plump, fruity nose. Medium to medium-full weight. Good fruit here, even concentration. Good grip, even some backbone. Lovely finish. This is very good plus.

Volnay, Clos du Château des Ducs,
Domaine Michel Lafarge   Now to 2018   15.5
Medium colour. Ripe, fresh, positive nose, if no great weight. Forward. Juicy and reasonably

fresh on the palate. Finishes well. Above all, stylish.

Volnay Clos des Chênes, Domaine Bouchard Père et Fils   Now to 2019 17.5

Medium to medium-full colour. Fresh, high-toned nose if without much backbone. On the palate, silky-smooth. Medium to medium-full body. Ripe and stylish. Long and positive. Impressive follow-through. This is very elegant and very long. Fine.

Volnay, Clos des Chênes, Domaine Louis Jadot   Drink soon 14.5

Medium to medium-full colour. Ripe, plump, and fruity, but an absence of real grip. Medium body. Fresh, fruity, and pleasant at first, but then it tails off. Drink early.

Volnay, Clos des Chênes, Domaine Michel Lafarge   From 2015 16.5

Lovely nose. Splendid concentrated fruit. Ripe and stylish and succulent. On the palate this has good structure and is a little bit in its shell. Best at the end. Long. Very good plus. This was at the Domaines Familiaux tasting (not blind). At the group tasting, the sample did not show as well and was marked by others, as well as me, lower than his Clos du Château des Ducs.

Volnay, Clos des Chênes, Domaine des Comtes Lafon   Now to 2018 16.5

Medium to medium-full colour. Ripe, plump nose. Good depth here. No weakness. Positive, firm, and elegant. Not a blockbuster but good substance for a 2006 Volnay. Fresh and stylish all the way through. Very good plus.

Volnay, Clos des Ducs, Domaine Marquis d'Angerville   Now to 2018 15.0

Medium-full colour. Round, fruity nose. Good weight. Positive. Medium to medium-full body. Plump and ample. Not much tannin but good grip and depth. Lacks a little elegance. Finishes well though.

Volnay, Clos de la Rougeotte, Domaine Henri Boillot   Drink soon 13.5

Medium colour. Stylish, plump, silky nose. Good Pinot fruit. Medium body. Not a great

deal of grip and personality on the palate. The wine finishes a bit weedy. But not bad.

Volnay, Fremiets, Domaine du Comte Armand   Now to 2018 15.5

Medium-full colour. A little dry on the nose. Better on the palate. Decent length and some grip. Good follow-through. This is more positive and energetic than most. Good plus.

Volnay, Mitans, Domaine Michel Lafarge   Drink soon 12.0

Medium-full colour. Light nose. Perhaps a bit empty, but quite fruity. A bit hard at the end, as well as astringent.

Volnay, Santenots du Milieu. Domaine des Comes Lafon   From 2015 17.5

Good colour. Firm nose. More austere than Lafarge's Clos des Chênes. Still closed-in. But good tannin. Lots of fruit and very good grip. Rich on the palate. Needs time. Fine.

CÔTE DE NUITS

Côte de Nuits Villages, La Robignotte, Domaine Gilles Jourdan   Drink soon 14.0

Soft, ripe, succulent. Seems to have a little less substance than the 2007, and the oak is a bit more noticable. Not as fine or as profound, but delicious everyday drinking.

Nuits-Saint-Georges, *Premier Cru*, Domaine Michel Gros   Now to 2020 16.0

Medium-full colour. Rich, full, quite firm but essentially juicy on the nose. Medium-full body. Some tannin. Rich. A little closed-in at present but good potential. Finishes well. Very good.

Nuits-Saint-Georges, Les Boudots, Domaine Jean Grivot   From 2015 17.5

Medium-full body. Ripe and rich. Balanced, vigorous, and stylish. Lovely fruit. Not the sheer brilliance of their Beaumonts but fine.

Nuits-Saint-Georges, Les Boudots, Domaine Louis Jadot   Now to 2020 15.0

Medium-full colour. Slightly flat on the nose. Medium body. A relatively simple wine. Reasonably fresh despite the nose. Decent fruit and a positive finish. But merely good.

Nuits-Saint-Georges, Les Boudots, Domaine Leroy From 2015 17.0
Fullish colour. Rich, ripe, very concentrated nose. Some stems here. Medium-full body. Ripe, intense, still youthful but long and vigorous. Very good indeed.

Nuits-Saint-Georges, Les Cailles, Domaine Bouchard Père et Fils From 2016 18.0
Medium-full colour. Rich, full, and elegant on the nose. Concentrated, intense, and harmonious. Stylish too. Fullish body. Very rich on the palate. Fine plus.

Nuits-Saint-Georges, Les Cailles, Domaine Robert Chevillon From 2016 16.5
Fullish colour. Muscular and slightly dense on the nose. On the palate, more civilized. Fullish body, rich, very good grip. Plenty of ripe tannin. Vigorous, meaty, very typical. Very good plus.

Nuits-Saint-Georges, Les Chaignots, Domaine Robert Chevillon From 2015 16.0
Full colour. High-toned nose with a little more development than most. Medium-full body. Very ripe. Decent grip. Very good but not fine.

Nuits-Saint-Georges, Les Chaignots, Domaine Faiveley From 2015 17.5
Fullish colour. Fresh, ripe, quite delicate nose. Soft and balanced. An elegant wine. Intense but not aggressive. Long, satisfying rich fruit. Fine.

Nuits-Saint-Georges, Les Chaignots, Domaine Henri Gouges From 2016 15.0
Fullish colour. Ripe, open, but not a great deal of class on the nose. Medium-full body. Good grip. But a bit too sturdy for its own good. Good at best.

Nuits-Saint-Georges, Les Chaignots, Domaine Mugneret-Gibourg From 2016 18.0
Full colour. Lovely ample, elegant fruit on the nose. Medium-full body. Intense. Concentrated. Structured. Lovely rich, elegant finish. Fine plus.

Nuits-Saint-Georges, Clos des Argillières, Domaine Michèle et Patrice Rion From 2015 17.0
Medium-full colour. Firm, tannin, meaty nose. Some tannin to resolve. Fullish body. Good grip. Good richness here. Backward but very good potential. Long, complex, and even classy. Very good indeed.

Nuits-Saint-Georges, Clos de l'Arlot, Domaine de l'Arlot From 2015 15.0
Medium-full colour. Soft, ripe nose. Evidence of the stems. Medium body. Full of fruit, but slightly loose-knit. Balanced. Good but not great.

Nuits-Saint-Georges, Clos des Corvées-Pagets, Domaine Robert Arnoux From 2016 17.5
Full colour. Rich, full, and very concentrated on the nose. Backward and structured. A rich, full wine with very impressive fruit and depth. Long, complex, and elegant. Fine quality.

Nuits-Saint-Georges, Clos des Forêts, Domaine de l'Arlot From 2015 17.0
Medium-full colour. Quite a rich, firm nose. Evidence of the stems. Medium-full body. Rich, fat, but quite tannic. This will resolve itself. Complex at the end. Very good indeed.

Nuits-Saint-Georges, Clos de la Maréchale, Domaine Frédéric Mugnier From 2015 17.0
Very good colour. Rich, fat, succulent, yet with an underlying Prémeaux backbone and touch of the rustic. Fullish body. Meaty. Stylish and balanced nonetheless. Long and very good indeed.

Nuits-Saint-Geoges, Clos des Perrières, Domaine Guy et Yvan Dufouleur From 2015 15.5
Medium-full colour. Rich, full, firm nose. Medium-full body. Some tannin. Good succulent fruit. Well-balanced. Good plus.

Nuits-Saint-Georges, Clos des Porrets, Domaine Henri Gouges From 2015 17.5
Good colour. Fresh, rich nose. Good backbone. Good depth. Fullish body. Good tannins. Very good depth and grip. Needs time. Fine.

Nuits-Saint-Georges,
Clos-Saint-Marc, Domaine
Michèle et Patrice Rion From 2016 18.0

Fullish colour. Lovely plump, ripe, black-fruit nose. Full, firm, and stylish on the palate. Medium-full body. Succulent, old-viney concentration, and fat. Long. Lovely.

Nuits-Saint-Georges,
Les Cras,
Domaine Lamarche From 2015 18.0

Fullish colour. High-toned but fresh and classy on the nose. Mocha and oak as it developed. Medium-full body. Open. Accessible. Plump and attractive. Fresh and balanced and long at the end. Fine plus.

Nuits-Saint-Georges,
Les Cras, Domaine du
Vicomte de Liger-Belair From 2015 18.5

Full colour. Spendidly concentrated nose. Very lovely fruit. This has impressive depth and style. Soft, round, but intense on the palate. Medium-full body. Very pure fruit. Very classy. Very fine.

Nuits-Saint-Georges,
Les Damodes, Domaine
Bouchard Père et Fils From 2015 17.5

Medium-full colour. Ripe, abundant fruit on the nose. Medium to medium-full body. Good grip. Clean and stylish. Long. Fine.

Nuits-Saint-Georges,
Les Damodes,
Domaine Chauvenet From 2015 18.0

Fullish colour. Ripe nose. Quite closed. Good freshness. Very good fruit. Some oak. Medium-full body. Good grip. Elegant and succulent. Long on the palate. Fine plus.

Nuits-Saint-Georges,
Les Damodes,
Domaine Faiveley From 2014 See note

Fullish colour. Medium-full body. Ample. Good fruit and balance. The sample was corked, but one could see a serious wine.

Nuits-Saint-Georges, Les Murgers,
Domaine Hudelot-Noëllat From 2015 17.5

Medium-full colour. Rich, fat, ample, succulent nose. Almost sweet. Medium-full body. Rich. Good tannins. Very good acidity. Long and vigorous and most enticing. Fine.

Nuits-Saint-Georges, Les Perrières,
Domaine Chauvenet From 2015 18.0

Full colour. Firm, full, fresh, and fine on the nose. Backward. Full body. Oaky. Very rich and concentrated. Excellent vigour and grip. No lack of tannin, but these tannins are nice and ripe. Lovely. Fine plus.

Nuits-Saint-Georges, Les Porrets,
Maison Bouchard Père et Fils From 2015 16.0

Fullish colour. Soft, round, ripe nose, with a touch of toffee. Medium-full body. Ripe and succulent. Balanced. Rich. Good follow-through. Very good.

Nuits-Saint-Georges, Les Porrets,
Maison Chanson From 2014 14.0

Fullish colour. A little weak on the nose but better on the palate. Medium body. Quite fresh and vigorous. But not very classy. Quite good.

Nuits-Saint-Georges, Les Porrets,
Domaine Faiveley From 2015 16.0

Fullish colour. Fullish on the nose. Good concentration and depth. Good class too. Medium-full body. Balanced. Good grip. The typical middle-Nuits burliness. But long and satisfying. Very good.

Nuits-Saint-Georges,
Les Poulettes, Domaine
Guy et Yvan Dufouleur From 2015 16.5

Medium-full colour. Rich, ample if slightly reduced nose. Fullish body, fat, and with good tannins on the palate. Quite backward. Good vigour and energy. Long. Very good plus.

Nuits-Saint-Georges, Les Pruliers,
Domaine Robert Chevillon From 2015 17.0

Good colour. Fullish, quite backward nose. Medium-full body. Some tannin. Elegant and intense and full of fruit. Cool, long, and complex. Very good indeed.

Nuits-Saint-Georges, Les Pruliers,

Domaine Henri Gouges   From 2015   16.5

A little less firm than the Porrets; but slightly richer, more succulent, and more exotic. Abundant, rich, and very well-balanced. Very lovely. Will be a seductive wine.

Nuits-Saint-Georges, Les Pruliers,

Domaine Jean Grivot   From 2015   16.0

Fullish colour. Plump and balanced and quite forward on the nose. Not a blockbuster. Medium-full body. Fresh. Elegant. Very good.

Nuits-Saint-Georges, Les Pruliers,

Domaine Taupenot-Merme   From 2015   14.0

Fullish colour. Round, ripe nose. Medium weight. Plenty of fruit but a little diffuse. Quite good.

Nuits-Saint-Georges, Les Roncières,

Domaine Jean Grivot   From 2015   14.0

Medium-full colour. A little thin on the nose. Ripe, medium bodied, and high-toned on the palate. Decent acidity. But I don't find it very stylish. Quite good at best.

Nuits-Saint-Georges, La Rue de Chaux, Domaine Chauvenet   From 2014   15.0

Medium-full colour. Ripe but slightly dry on the nose. Medium to medium-full body. Quite fresh and elegant but a hint of astringency. Good at best.

Nuits-Saint-Georges,

Les Saint-Georges,

Domaine Robert Chevillon   From 2016   18.5

Full colour. Firm, full, rich, tannic, and backward on the nose. Fullish body. Cool and composed. A big wine in every way. But everything in place. Very lovely rich fruit and splendid balance. Very fine.

Nuits-Saint-Georges,

Les Saint-Georges,

Domaine Henri Gouges   See note

Very full colour. Fresh nose. High-toned and rather closed. Fullish, ample, and rich. Good attack but rather adolescent. Needs time. It didn't show well at the group tasting, the only time I have sampled the wine recently. Judgment deferred.

Nuits-Saint-Georges,

Les Saint-Georges,

Domaine Thibault Liger-Belair   From 2015   16.5

A soft, supple wine, which is out of place in Les Saint-Georges. Medium weight. Balanced, stylish, and succulent. Good depth and vigour. Long on the palate. Very good plus.

Nuits-Saint-Georges,

Les Vaucrains,

Domaine Chauvenet   From 2016   17.5

Fullish colour. Attractive fruit on the nose. Not too tannic or aggressive. Medium-full body. Nicely balanced plummy fruit supported by ripe tannins and very good grip. Stylish. Still youthful. Fine.

Nuits-Saint-Georges,

Les Vaucrains,

Maison Camille Giroud   From 2015   16.0

Medium-full colour. Rich, spicy, aromatic, quite fat nose. Medium-full body. More forward than the rest of these top middle Nuits wines. Ripe but a little sweet. Decent balance and follow-through. Easy to enjoy. Very good.

Nuits-Saint-Georges, Les Vaucrains,

Domaine Henri Gouges   See note

A corked bottle but full, ample, and generous, with plenty of tannin and backbone. Needs time.

Nuits-Saint-Georges,

Les Vignerondes,

Domaine Faiveley   From 2014   15.0

Medium-full colour. Quite closed-in on the nose, but good grip. On the palate, a little hard and astringent. Decent attack but then it tails off. Good at best.

Vosne-Romanée, Domaine

Richard Manière-Noirot   From 2014   15.0

Medium colour. A hint of mint on the nose. Medum body. Fruity, elegant, and balanced, but a lack of depth on the middle palate. More to it at the end. Good.

Vosne-Romanée, Vieilles Vignes,
Domaine Cécile Tremblay   From 2014 16.0

A lovely example. Medium-full body. Very stylish, harmonious, ample fruit. Long and elegant.

Vosne-Romanée, *Premier Cru*,
Cuvée Duvault-Blochet, Domaine
de la Romanée-Conti   From 2015 16.0

Not just young vines, as I have mistakenly said in *The Wines of Burgundy*, as much as the results of a second, later *passage* through the vines. Medium weight. The attack is soft, but there is a lot more to this on the follow-through. Very stylish, quite concentrated fruit. A little tannin. But good grip and depth. Very good.

Vosne-Romanée,
Les Beaux Monts,
Domaine Jean Grivot   From 2016 18.5

Good colour. Very lovely nose. Rich, full, and concentrated. Lots of elegance and definition. Vigorous and intense. Very good grip. Excellent. Less good at the group tasting.

Vosne-Romanée,
Les Beaux Monts,
Domaine Hudelot-Noëllat   From 2015 17.5

Fullish colour. Round, ample, succulent nose. Medium-full body. Some tannin. Lovely fruit. Ripe and vigorous. This has a lot of style and is harmonious and promising. Lovely finish. Fine.

Vosne-Romanée, Les Brulées,
Domaine Eugenie   From 2016 17.5

Domaine Engel as was. Medium-full colour. Rich and concentrated. Fat and energetic on the nose. Firm, rich, and full-bodied on the palate. Tannic, chocolaty, and with black cherry–flavoured fruit. Complex and impressive. Needs time. Fine.

Vosne-Romanée, Les Brulées,
Domaine Jean Grivot   From 2016 16.5

Medium-full colour. Ample, ripe, fresh nose. Medium-full colour. Still a little closed-in. Plump, attractive, and harmonious. Long finish. This will develop. Very good plus at least.

Vosne-Romanée, Les Brulées,
Domaine Michel Gros   From 2015 17.5

Fullish colour. Plenty of wine here. But it needs time. Fullish body. Lovely intense, ripe, concentrated fruit. Lots of energy. This is fine.

Vosne-Romanée, Les Brulées,
Domaine Gérard Mugneret   See note

Medium-full body. Ample, ripe, medium-full bodied wine with no lack of rich fruit. But corked.

Vosne-Romanée, Les Chaumes,
Domaine Robert Arnoux   From 2015 16.5

Fullish colour. Ample, fruity nose but no real backbone. More to it on the palate. Medium to medium-full body. Good grip. There is some energy here. And the fruit is stylish and quite long.

Vosne-Romanée, Les Chaumes,
Domaine Lamarche   From 2015 16.5

Medium-full colour. Soft nose. No great weight. But elegant. Medium body. Crisp and full of fruit. Good balance, if no great grip or concentration. Quite forward. Classy though. Very good plus.

Vosne-Romanée, Les Chaumes,
Domaine Méo-Camuzet   From 2015 15.0

Full colour. A little reduced and rustic on the nose. Medium-full body. Some tannin. Decent fruit but a little four-square. Good grip. Developed in the glass. But no better than good.

Vosne-Romanée, Clos des Réas,
Domaine Michel Gros   From 2015 17.5

A bad bottle at the group tasting. In the April round, concentrated, graceful, and splendidly intense and balanced, without being a blockbuster.

Vosne-Romanée,
La Croix Rameau,
Domaine Lamarche   From 2015 16.0

Medium-full colour. Stylish, ripe, gently oaky nose; with a touch of mocha as it developed. Good vigour. Not the greatest depth but elegant and balanced. Quite forward.

Vosne-Romanée, Cros Parantoux,
Domaine Méo-Camuzet   From 2015   16.5
Fullish colour. Fullish, very new oaky nose. But rich underneath. Medium-full weight. Fat, fruity, and oaky on the palate. Good follow-through. Fresh and complex. Very good plus.

Vosne-Romanée, Cros Parantoux,
Domaine Emmanuel Rouget   From 2012   15.0
Medium-full colour. Quite fresh on the nose but no real depth. Medium-full body. Soft. Supple, ripe, fruity but quite forward. A pleasant wine for quite early drinking.

Vosne-Romanée, Aux Malconsorts,
Domaine du Clos Frantin
(Albert Bichot)   From 2016   18.0
Full colour. Firm and full with beautiful fruit and harmony on the nose. Ample, ripe, soft, silky, and medium-full bodied on the palate. Good acidity. Long. Fine plus.

Vosne-Romanée, Aux Malconsorts,
Domaine Cathiard   From 2016   19.0
Medium-full colour. Rich, full, ample, vigorous, and energetic on the nose. Lovely style here. Medium-full body. Ripe, generous, fresh, and harmonious on the palate. Long and very lovely. Lots of class. The best of the Vosne-Romanée *premiers crus*.

Vosne-Romanée, Aux Malconsorts,
Domaine Dujac   From 2016   18.5
This is very lovely. Rich, concentrated, and old-viney. Fat and profound. Fullish body. Lovely long finish. Real class. A classic. Very fine.

Vosne-Romanée, Aux Malconsorts,
Domaine Lamarche   From 2016   18.5
Medium-full colour. Full, firm, cool, balanced, and vigorous on the nose. Fullish body. Very high-quality. Very intense. Super-concentrated. Full body and excellent balance. Very fine.

Vosne-Romanée, Aux Malconsorts,
Domaine de Montille   From 2015   16.5
Fullish colour. Closed-in nose. Some tannin. Just a little ungainly at present, but this will sort itself out. Fullish body. Round, ripe, plenty

of fruit. Not quite the class of the best, but long on the palate and very good plus.

Vosne-Romanée, Les Petits Monts,
Domaine Véronique Drouhin   From 2015   16.0
Medium to medium-full colour. Ripe, mocha-ish nose. Medium body. No great weight here but some very elegant, balanced, quite intense fruit. Long on the palate. Perhaps a little too forward.

Vosne-Romanée, Les Petits Monts,
Domaine Thibaut Liger-Belair   From 2015   18.0
Medium-full colour. Fine, rich, concentrated nose. Good substance. Some tannin. Rich, meaty, and vigorous on the palate. Nicely cool but very good black fruit character. Long. Fine plus.

Vosne-Romanée, En Orveaux,
Domaine Sylvain Cathiard   From 2015   17.5
Fullish colour. A little closed-in on the nose, but good ripe fruit and plenty of complexity in a high-toned sort of way. Ripe and sweet and vigorous on the palate. Medium-full body. Ample and succulent. Fine.

Vosne-Romanée, Les Reignots,
Domaine Sylvain Cathiard   From 2016   18.5
Full colour. Rich, ripe nose. Still youthful. Full body. Firm, intense, and high-class. Good tannins. An understated wine with a lot of depth. Very fine. (And yet the vines are much younger.)

Vosne-Romanée, Les Reignots,
Domaine Jean Grivot   From 2014   15.0
Medium-full colour. A little more diffuse than Cathiard's example. Medium-full body. Soft. Quite fresh. Finishes positively. But good rather than fine.

Vosne-Romanée,
Les Reignots, Domaine
du Vicomte de Liger-Belair   From 2015   16.0
Fullish colour. Fullish, ample but lacking just a little elegance on the nose. Quite vigorous though. Decent ripe fruit. Medium-full body. Good grip. Very good if not great.

Vosne-Romanée, Les Rouges,
Domaine Jean Grivot   From 2014   15.5
Medium colour. Fresh nose. Vigorous and ripe and elegant, if by no means a blockbuster. Medium body. Fresh. Ample. Fruity. And with decent acidity. Perhaps a slight lack of definition. Good plus.

Vosne-Romanée, Les Suchots,
Domaine de l'Arlot   From 2014   15.0
Medium-full colour. An open, gingerbready nose, with evidence of the stems. A little sweet on the palate. Medium-full body. Fresh but not a lot of dimension. Merely good.

Vosne-Romanée, Les Suchots,
Domaine Robert Arnoux   From 2016   18.0
Fullish colour. Firm nose, but not without sex appeal. Rich, sweet, fullish-bodied, and vigorous on the palate. Very good class and balance. Fresh and profound on the finish. Fine plus.

Vosne-Romanée,
Les Suchots, Domaine
Bouchard Père et Fils   From 2016   18.0
Fullish colour. The nose is a bit hidden. But plenty of wine on the palate. Full-bodied, rich, tannic, and meaty. Good depth and vigour. Long and satisfying. Fine plus.

Vosne-Romanée, Les Suchots,
Domaine Jean Grivot   From 2015   17.5
Medium-full colour. A slight touch of reduction on the nose at first. Ripe and fruity, succulent and exotic nevertheless. No lack of energy or richness. Medium-full body. All a bit mixed up at present, but fine once it sorts itself out.

Vosne-Romanée, Les Suchots,
Domaine Hudelot-Noëllat   From 2015   18.5
Fullish colour. Firm, oaky, but cool nose. Lots of depth. Lovely smooth; fresh, vigorous fruit. Medium-full body. Lots of dimension and class and a splendid finish. Very fine.

Vosne-Romanée, Les Suchots,
Domaine Louis Jadot   From 2015   16.5
Fullish colour. Rich, ripe, meaty nose. Not a bit aggressive. Round, ripe, fruity, sweet, and rich on the palate, with a touch of new oak. Fullish body. Quite perfumed.

Vosne-Romanée, Les Suchots,
Domaine Lamarche   From 2016   17.5
Medium-full colour. Soft nose. Elegant and ripe but no great backbone. Fullish body. Energetic, rich, and ripe. Good grip. Lots of dimension and vigour. Quite oaky. Fine.

Vosne-Romanée,
Les Suchots, Domaine
du Vicomte de Liger-Belair   From 2015   17.0
Fullish colour. Fullish, ample nose. A lush, medium-full bodied wine with no hard edges. Soft and harmonious. Will develop sooner than some. Very good indeed.

Vosne-Romanée, Les Suchots,
Domaine Jean-Marc Millot   From 2014   15.5
Fullish colour. A little diffuse on the nose. Medium-full body. Ample soft fruit, if no great grip or depth underneath. But a pleasant wine for quite early drinking.

Vosne-Romanée, Les Suchots,
Domaine Gérard Mugneret   From 2015   17.0
Fullish colour. Ample, rich, open nose. On the palate, medium-full body. Ripe and soft and succulent. Lovely fruit and style. Very good indeed.

Vougeot, Les Petits Vougeots,
Domaine Hudelot-Noëllat   From 2015   17.0
Medium to medium-full colour. Fresh, medium-weight nose. Decent fruit. Medium-full body. Stylish, balanced, and rich. Good depth. Finishes well. An attractive wine.

Chambolle-Musigny, Vieilles Vignes,
Domaine Digioia-Royer   From 2014   15.5
Very good colour. At present a bit hidden on the nose. Full-bodied, rich, ample, and even concentrated underneath. Plenty of energy. Good tannins and lovely fruit. Good plus.

Chambolle-Musigny, Les Amoureuses,
Domaine Francois Bertheau   From 2015   18.0
Fullish colour. Soft, forward, understated, subtle but most attractive nose. Some oak on the

palate. Medium-full body. Intense and classy. Ripe. Very long. Fine plus.

Chambolle-Musigny, Les Amoureuses, Domaine Joseph Drouhin
From 2014   14.5

Medium-full colour. The nose is a bit closed-in at present. Gentle and classy on the palate. Medium to medium-full body. It lacks grip and intensity. It is merely pretty. Quite good plus.

Chambolle-Musigny, Les Amoureuses, Domaine J. F. Mugnier
From 2015   19.0

Fullish colour. Understated but very classy on the nose. Very beautiful. Medium-full body. Very harmonious and lots of finesse. Splendid fruit. Totally captivating.

Chambolle-Musigny, Les Amoureuses, Domaine Georges Roumier
From 2016   17.5

Fullish colour. Quite high-toned on the nose. Quite full-bodied. Ripe and very fresh. Some tannin. Lots of vigour and energy. Lots of depth. Very youthful still. Needs time. Fine.

Chambolle-Musigny, Les Amoureuses, Domaine Comte Georges de Vogüé
From 2016   16.0

Fullish colour. Oaky and really quite jammy fruit on the nose. Larger than life. Fullish. Some tannin. Very oaky on the palate too. Plenty of ripe fruit. But is it all a bit too obvious?

Chambolle-Musigny, Les Baudes, Domaine Ghislaine Barthod
From 2015   16.0

Good colour. Ripe, soft nose. Medium-full body. Gently oaky. Succulent and nicely concentrated. Ripe tannins. Good structure and grip. Tails off just a little at the end. Very good.

Chambolle-Musigny, Les Baudes, Domaine Christain Serafin
From 2015   15.0

Medium-full colour. Quite oaky on the nose. But high-toned and with ripe fruit. Medium to medium-full body. Abundant fruit. Just a little dry at the end. Good.

Chambolle-Musigny, Les Charmes, Domaine Ghislaine Barthod
From 2015   17.5

Medium-full colour. Still a little hard and closed on the nose. Fullish body, firm, rich, profound,

and with very good grip. This has a lot of depth. Lovely rich finish. Fine.

Chambolle-Musigny, Les Charmes, Domaine Francois Bertheau
From 2015   17.0

Medium-full colour. Nicely spicy, round, meaty nose. Good substance. Medium-full body. Good depth and grip. Lovely finish. Very good indeed.

Chambolle-Musigny, Les Charmes, Domaine Hudelot-Noëllat
From 2015   17.5

Medium-full colour. Fat, quite rich nose. Fullish body. Firm, rich, and oaky on the palate. An abundant medium-full bodied wine. Lots of fruit and no lack of class. Fine.

Chambolle-Musigny, Les Charmes, Domaine Ponsot
See note

One can see a wine which is medium-bodied rather than substantial. But it's corked. To be seen again.

Chambolle-Musigny, Les Charmes, Domaine Michèle et Patrice Rion
From 2014   16.0

Medium-full colour. Soft, charming, fruity nose. Good style. A gentle very typical Chambolle. Round, ripe, sweet. Medium to medium-full body. Good grip. Quite accessible already.

Chambolle-Musigny, Les Chatelots, Domaine Ghislaine Barthod
From 2014   15.0

Medium-full colour. Lightish, high-toned nose. Medium body. A touch dry at the end and not enough fat and backbone in the middle. Yet stylish and positive nonetheless. Good.

Chambolle-Musigny, La Combe d'Orvaux, Domaine Taupenot-Merme
From 2014   14.0

Medium-full colour. A little bland on the nose. Medium body. Quite a forward example. But with decent fruit and style. But only quite good.

Chambolle-Musigny, Les Cras, Domaine Georges Roumier
From 2016   18.0

Medium colour. Ripe, fresh, stylish nose. Attractive fruit here. Fullish body. Good backbone. Lots of depth and quality. Lovely fruit. Delicious.

**Chambolle-Musigny,
Les Feusselottes,
Domaine Mugneret-Gibourg**   From 2015   17.5
Medium-full colour. Rich, ripe, quite opulent nose. Lovely lush fruit and very good grip. Medium-full body. Good ripe tannins. A concentrated, succulent example. Fine.

**Chambolle-Musigny,
Les Feusselottes,
Domaine Cécile Tremblay**   From 2013   14.0
Medium-full colour. Quite substantial on the nose. If a slight absence of class. Medium to medium-full body. Decent fruit. Quite good.

**Chambolle-Musigny, Les Fuées,
Domaine Louis Jadot**   From 2015   16.5
Medium to medium-full colour. Not the greatest depth or dimension, but what there is, is attractive. Soft, consistent, gently oaky. Medium to medium-full body. Fresh and balanced. Long and positive. Very good plus.

**Chambolle-Musigny, Les Fuées,
Domaine J. F. Mugnier**   See note
Fullish colour. Good structure on the nose. Lovely fresh fruit. Started off well on the palate. Medium-full body. But it tailed off in the glass. So I marked it down to quite good only. A bad bottle?

**Chambolle-Musigny, Les Fuées,
Domaine Ghislaine Barthod**   From 2015   17.5
Very good colour. Lovely nose. Lots of vigour. Classy balanced fruit. Fullish body. Good tannins. Rather more grip and concentration than the Baudes. Vigorous, classy, long, and fine.

**Chambolle-Musigny,
Les Groseilles,
Domaine Digioia-Royer**   From 2014   16.0
Medium colour. Soft, charming, Chambolle nose with a touch of new wood. Medium to medium-full body. Succulent and balanced. Long and positive. Good style too. Long finish. Very good.

**Chambolle-Musigny, Les Gruenchers,
Domaine Digioia-Royer**   From 2015   16.5
Medium-full colour. Good depth and plenty of clean fruit on the nose. Fullish. Quite firm. But good ripe tannins and plenty of fruit on the palate. This is long and positive and will keep better than most.

**Chambolle-Musigny, Les Gruenchers,
Domaine Fourrier**   From 2015   16.0
Medium to medium-full colour. Elegant nose. Lovely Chambolle fruit. Balanced and positively silky. Medium to medium-full body. Ripe and soft. Good grip. Quite forward but stylish and harmonious. Good long finish.

**Chambolle-Musigny, Les Sentiers,
Domaine Arlaud**   From 2014   16.0
Medium-full colour. Good slightly austere nose. Medium to medium-full body. Good grip. Ripe tannins and plenty of fruit. Long and stylish, if not very profound. But very good.

**Morey-Saint-Denis, *Premier Cru*,
Domaine Dujac**   From 2014   16.0
Medium colour. Quite a firm nose. Backward but good style and grip. Medium-full body. Fresh, ripe, no lack of depth. Some tannin. Good positive follow-through. Very good.

**Morey-Saint-Denis, Les Chaffots,
Domaine Hubert Lignier**   From 2016   16.0
Medium-full colour. Good depth on the nose, plus a touch of new wood. Medium-full body. Fresh. Balanced. Good dimension. Ripe tannins. Finishes well. Youthful but very good.

**Morey-Saint-Denis, Clos de la Bussière,
Domaine Georges Roumier**   From 2015   16.0
Good colour. Fullish body, rich, and fat with good acidity. Ripe. Still slightly austere. But good tannins and vigorous at the end. Very good.

**Morey-Saint-Denis, La Forge,
Domaine du Clos de Tart**   From 2014   14.5
This is the second wine. Medium-full colour. A bit austere on the nose. Medium-full body. Good fruit and balance but a bit ungainly at present. Quite good plus.

Morey-Saint-Denis, Les Millandes,
Domaine Arlaud   From 2014 16.0
Medium-full colour. Rich nose, with a touch of new oak. Good class and depth on the palate. Medium-full body. Ample, balanced, and stylish. Good grip and good follow-through.

Morey-Saint-Denis, Les Millandes,
Domaine Christian Serafin   See note
Fullish colour. Some new oak but rather too much volatile acidity. To be seen again.

Morey-Saint-Denis, La Riotte,
Domaine Taupenot-Merme   Now to 2017 13.5
Medium-full colour. Some oak but a little bland on the nose. Medium to medium-full body. Finishes a bit astringent. Lacks style. Only fair.

Morey-Saint-Denis,
Les Ruchots,
Domaine Arlaud   Now to 2018 15.0
Medium-full colour. Good nose, ripe and substantial. Medium to medium-full body. Plump, attractive, fresh, and positive. Will evolve reasonably soon. Good.

Gevrey-Chambertin, Bel-Air,
Domaine Taupenot-Merme   From 2014 15.5
Medium colour. Light, forward, oaky nose. Has charm if not much depth. Decently positive on the palate. Plump, fresh, medium-bodied. Good fruit. An attractive wine. Good plus.

Gevrey-Chambertin,
Les Cazetiers, Domaine
Bouchard Père et Fils   From 2016 18.0
Fullish colour. Rich, gently oaky, mocha-flavoured nose. Fullish body. Ample, succulent fruit. Very good grip and lots of dimension. Classy, long, and harmonious. Fine plus.

Gevrey-Chambertin,
Les Cazetiers,
Domaine Bruno Clair   From 2015 17.5
Fullish nose. Nicely backward and a little austere. Very good fruit and excellent grip. Medium-full body. Balanced, poised, complex, and elegant. Lovely. Fine.

Gevrey-Chambertin, Les Cazetiers,
Domaine Faiveley   From 2015 16.0
Slightly rigid on the nose. Fullish, good tannins, good grip. Ripe, quite firm. Good depth. Very good.

Gevrey-Chambertin, Les Cazetiers,
Maison Louis Latour   From 2015 16.5
Medium to medium-full colour. Fresh. Good backbone. Classy fruit of the nose. Medium-full body. Ripe and round and full of energy. Good grip. Long and satisfactory. Very good plus.

Gevrey-Chambertin, Les Cazetiers,
Domaine Armand Rousseau   From 2015 17.5
Medium-full weight. Plump, classy nose. A little closed-in. But splendidly balanced and fresh. Complex, long, and lovely.

Gevrey-Chambertin, Les Cazetiers,
Domaine Christain Serafin   From 2016 17.5
Medium-full colour. Ripe, rich, classy nose. Medium-full body. Good vigour and grip. Very good tannins. This has a lot of depth and classy fruit and a lovely long finish. Fine.

Gevrey-Chambertin,
Les Champeaux,
Domaine Fourrier   From 2014 14.0
Fullish colour. Fresh nose. Good depth and backbone. A keeper, it seems, in 2006 terms. As it evoved, it did not quite live up to its early promise and I marked it down, but overall it scored as well as his Goulots and Cherbaudes.

Gevrey-Chambertin,
Les Champeaux,
Domaine Maume   Now to 2016 13.5
Medium to medium-full colour. Lightish, forward, and unconcentrated. Rather sweet fruit. Despite a decent finish only fair at best.

Gevrey-Chambertin,
Les Champeaux,
Domaine Mortet   From 2015 16.0
Full colour. Somewhat dense on the nose at first. But better on the palate. Quite full body. But ripe tannins and good grip. Not astringent as I feared from the nose. Plenty of energy. Very good.

Gevrey-Chambertin, Les Cherbaudes,
Domaine Louis Boillot   From 2015 16.0
Medium-full colour. Good soft fruit on the nose. Medium to medium-full body. Fresh and charming. Nice and ripe. Positive follow-through. Very good.

Gevrey-Chambertin, Les Cherbaudes,
Domaine Fourrier   From 2015 16.0
Medium-full colour. Quite rich on the nose, with a touch of oxidation at first, but this blew off. Medium-full body. Good grip. Plenty of juicy fruit. Harmonious. Positive. Even classy. Very good.

Gevrey-Chambertin, Les Cherbaudes,
Domaine Rossignol-Trapet   Now to 2016 14.0
Medium-full colour. The nose is a little slight. Medium to medium-full body. Herbal flavours. A lack of real richness and grip. Forward. Quite good.

Gevrey-Chambertin,
Clos-Saint-Jacques,
Domaine Bruno Clair   From 2016 18.5
Medium-full colour. Lovely nose. Rich, slightly spicy, fat, and vigorous. Fullish body. Lots of energy and complexity. Lots of depth and dimension. Very fine grip. Very classy indeed. Impressive.

Gevrey-Chambertin,
Clos-Saint-Jacques,
Domaine Sylvie Esmonin   From 2015 17.5
Medium-full colour. Classy fruit on the nose, in a slightly lean sort of way. Medium-full body. Very poised ripe fruit. Good grip. Good richness underneath. Backward. Fine.

Gevrey-Chambertin,
Clos-Saint-Jacques,
Domaine Fourrier   From 2015 17.0
Medium-full colour. A slim, but elegant wine, better on the palate than on the nose. Medium-full body. Good tannins. Understated. Balanced and classy. Not as exotic as Rousseau or as elegant as Clair. But very good indeed.

Gevrey-Chambertin,
Clos-Saint-Jacques,
Domaine Armand Rousseau   From 2016 18.5
Compared with their Cazetiers, this is richer, riper, more profound, and more succulent. Very impressive on the nose. Quite splendid on the palate. Full and the most backward of all these Clos-Saint-Jacques. Great intensity and complexity. Lots of energy and real finesse. Very fine.

Gevrey-Chambertin, La Combe
Aux Moines, Domaine Faiveley   See note
Medium to medium-full colour. Fresh and fruity on the nose if without the greatest personality—or indeed in the case of this bottle—cleanliness. Medium to medium-full body. To be seen again.

Gevrey-Chambertin, Les Combottes,
Domaine Dujac   From 2015 16.0
Fullish colour. Lovely classy fruit on the nose. Fullish body. Good grip. This is positive and very good, though it lacks a bit of dimension at the end.

Gevrey-Chambertin, Les Combottes,
Domaine Hubert Lignier   From 2015 16.0
Medium-full colour. There is depth and substance here on the nose. Medium-full body. Good attack. Quite rich and with good grip. Nice long finish. Has class. Very good.

Gevrey-Chambertin, Les Combottes,
Domaine Rossignol-Trapet   Now to 2016 14.0
Medium-full colour. Soft nose. Forward. Medium body. Not a great deal of backbone or grip, or indeed richness and vigour. Decent fruit. But it doesn't excite.

Gevrey-Chambertin, Les Corbeaux,
Domaine Denis Bachelet   From 2016 17.0
Fullish colour. Firmish nose. Slightly tight at present. Medium-full body. A little tannin. Good grip and the finish is positive, indeed classy. Long finish. Very good indeed.

Gevrey-Chambertin, Les Corbeaux,
Domaine Christian Serafin   From 2015 16.0
Fullish colour. A little diffuse on the nose at first, but rather better on the palate. Medium-

full body. Some oak. A little tannin. Good grip. No lack of charm. Finishes well. Very good.

Gevrey-Chambertin, Le Craipillot, Domaine Drouhin-Laroze   From 2014   15.0

Medium-full colour. Rich, ample, gentle, and gently oaky on the nose. Full of charm. Medium to medium-full body. Fresh. Quite forward. No great tannin or backbone. Good.

Gevrey-Chambertin, Les Etelois, Domaine Rossignol-Trapet   From 2014   15.5

Soft, fragrant, balanced, and elegant on the nose. Flowery and enticing on the palate, with a nice touch of new oak underneath. Medium body. Fresh and positive. Long at the end. Most attractive. Good plus.

Gevrey-Chambertin, Les Fontenys, Domaine Roty   Now to 2016   15.0

Fullish colour. Quite rich on the nose. Good depth here. On the palate it falls away a bit. Medium-full body. Decent depth and grip. And quite stylish. But good at best.

Gevrey-Chambertin, Les Fontenys, Domaine Christian Serafin   From 2014   15.0

Fullish colour. Some oak on the nose but rather more soft-centred than his Corbeaux. Medium to medium-full body. Gentle and fruity. Fresh but quite forward. Good at best.

Gevrey-Chambertin, Les Goulots, Domaine Fourrier   From 2015   17.0

Fullish colour. Firm, rich, concentrated nose. There is depth here. Fullish body. Rich, concentrated, and classy on the palate. Some tannin. Very good grip. Lovely long finish. This is very good indeed. I preferred it to his Cherbaudes, which preceded it in the lineup.

Gevrey-Chambertin, Lavaux-Saint-Jacques, Domaine du Clos Frantin (Albert Bichot)   From 2015   17.0

Medium-full colour. Fresh, fruity, accessible nose. A well-made wine, every element in harmony. Fullish body. Good tannins. Good grip. Positive and classy. Very good indeed.

Gevrey-Chambertin, Lavaux-Saint-Jacques, Maison Chanson   From 2014   15.5

Medium-full colour. Soft, fruity, oaky nose. Charm here if no great energy. Medium-full body. Fresh. Plump. Quite stylish. Finishes positively. Good plus.

Gevrey-Chambertin, Lavaux-Saint-Jacques, Domaine Drouhin-Laroze   From 2015   16.0

Medium-full colour. Some substance here but not enough nuance on the nose. Medium to medium-full body. Decent fruit and grip and it grew in the glass. Very good.

Gevrey-Chambertin, Lavaux-Saint-Jacques, Domaine Maume   From 2014   14.0

Medium-full colour. Slightly weedy and stemmy on the nose. Medium body. Decent grip. Quite juicy but not very stylish. Forward too. Quite good at best.

Gevrey-Chambertin, Lavaux-Saint-Jacques, Domaine Mortet   From 2015   16.0

Fullish colour. Somewhat dense and closed-in on the nose but, like their Champeaux, not too dense. Medium-full body. Lots of almost over-ripe fruit. Good acidity nevertheless. And ripe tannins. Very good but not the depth and style for better.

Gevrey-Chambertin, En Pallud, Domaine Maume   From 2014   14.0

Medium-full colour. A little artisanal on the nose. Medium to medium-full body. Good tannins. Good grip. More sophisticated than it used to be. Good meaty fruit. Round and succulent. Quite good.

Grands Crus

Corton, Domaine Bonneau du Martray   From 2015   17.5

Two notes. Ripe, ample, and succulent on the nose. This is very classy. A generous wine.

Medium to medium-full bodied. Rich and balanced and sophisticated. Lovely.

Corton, Domaine Follin-Arbelet   From 2015   16.5
Medium-full colour. Fruity nose, if no great grip or backbone at first, but it put on weight in the glass. Some extraction, but good acidity and structure and nice cool fruit. Finishes well. Very good plus.

Corton, Domaine Tollot-Beaut   From 2014   15.5
Medium to medium-full colour. Decent substance on the nose, if no real class. Or personality. Better on the palate. Medium-full body. Good grip. Not unstylish and a good positive finish. Good plus.

**Château Corton-Grancey,
Domaine Louis Latour**   From 2014   15.0
Medium colour. Slightly hard on the nose. Medium-full body. Decent if somewhat cooked fruit, but also grip on the nose. No great finesse or dimension but good.

**Le Corton, Domaine
Bouchard Père et Fils**   From 2015   18.0
Medium-full colour. Rich, ripe, quite firm, substantial nose. Good depth here. Fullish body. Quite backward. Good grip and fine tannins. Long, ripe, and complex at the end. Fine plus.

**Corton, Bressandes,
Domaine Follin-Arbelet**   From 2015   16.5
Medium-full colour. Ripe, quite rich, essentially soft nose. Medium to medium-full body. Stylish fruit. Good acidity. This has good depth and style. And a positive finish. Very good plus.

**Corton, Bressandes,
Domaine Chandon de Briailles**   From 2015   17.0
Very lovely intense, succulent fruit on the nose. Fullish. Very sophisticated. Harmonious and profound. Very good indeed.

**Corton, Bressandes,
Domaine de la Pousse d'Or**   From 2015   16.5
Fullish colour. This has plenty of depth on the nose but it's a bit closed. Medium-full body. Fresh. Elegant. Poised. Long on the palate. Very good plus.

**Corton, Bressandes, Domaine
Prince Florent de Mérode**   From 2014   18.0
The fullest colour of the Prince's *grands crus*. Still a little closed-in on the nose. Full body, oaky, intense, rich, and concentrated. High-quality and lovely fruit.

**Corton, Bressandes,
Domaine Senard**   From 2014   17.0
Good fruit on the nose. Medium-full body. Ripe, rich, fresh, and positive. Good depth and class. Very good indeed.

**Corton, Bressandes,
Domaine Tollot Beaut**   From 2015   17.5
Medium-full colour. Good class and depth here on the nose. Medium-full body. Good ripe tannins. Rich and quite meaty. Good grip. Plenty on the follow-through. Good intensity and class. Fine.

**Corton, Clos des
Cortons-Faiveley,
Domaine Faiveley**   From 2014   14.0
Firm, full, rigid, and not entirely clean on the nose (I tried this on three occasions). Inflexible. A disappointment.

**Corton, Clos de la
Maréchaude, Domaine du
Pavillon (Albert Bichot)**   From 2015   17.5
Medium to medium-full colour. Rich, soft, oaky, toffee-flavoured nose. This is most seductive. Round, ripe, fresh, and balanced. Classy fruit. Long on the palate. Fine.

**Corton, Clos de Meix,
Domaine Senard**   Now to 2017   13.5
Medium colour. Firm nose but good depth. But weedy as it evolved. Medium body. Decent fruit. But a disappointment.

**Corton, Clos du Roi, Domaine
Prince Florent de Mérode**   From 2014   17.0
Full colour. Cool, rich, aromatic nose. Elegant and profound. Fullish body. Still a bit of tannin. Rich and meaty. Plenty of depth and style. Good energy. Very good indeed.

Corton, Clos du Roi,
Domaine de Montille   From 2014 17.5
Medium to medium-full colour. Good rich fruit on the nose. Good grip but high-toned on the palate. Ample, ripe, soft attack. Medium to medium-full body. Plenty of style. Long and complex. Fine.

Corton, Clos du Roi,
Domaine de la Pousse d'Or   From 2014 16.0
Medium colour. Some fruit on the nose but a bit bland. Better on the palate. Medium to medium-full body. Quite fresh. Good fruit. Positive finish. Very good.

Corton, Clos du Roi,
Domaine Senard   From 2014 16.0
Fullish colour. Some substance on the nose. But a bit rustic. Medium to medium-full body. Some tannin to resolve. Good grip. Slightly dry at the end but very good.

Corton, Clos du Roi,
Domaine de la Vougeraie   From 2014 15.5
Fullish colour. Slightly reduced on the nose but quite fat underneath. Medium to medium-full body. Rich and mocha-ish on the palate. Good fruit but it lacks a bit of grip and finishes short. An attractive wine though. Good plus.

Corton, Maréchaudes, Domaine
Prince Florent de Mérode   From 2014 15.5
Medium-full colour. Rich, ripe, spicy nose. Firmer than his Renardes, but not as complete or as elegant. There is a faint touch of rubber here. Better on the palate, if a little sweet. Medium-full body. Good intensity. But, if more to it than the Renardes, less class. Good plus.

Corton, Paulands,
Domaine Senard   From 2014 15.0
Medium colour. Not very expressive on the nose. Medium to medium-full body. Ripe and succulent at first. Slightly boiled-sweety though. And a little astrinent on the follow-through. Tarty but good stuff.

Corton, Pougets,
Domaine Louis Jadot   From 2016 17.0
Medium-full colour. Rich, coffee-chocolate flavours on the nose, with a good base of oak. Medium-full body. Good fruit and grip. On the attack a little dry, but the follow-through is lusher. Needs time.

Corton, Renardes, Domaine
Prince Florent de Mérode   From 2014 16.0
Medium colour. Soft, round nose. Quite a gentle wine. Ripe tannins. Fresh. Good elegance. Balanced and slightly earthy. Very good.

Corton, Rognets,
Domaine Taupenot-Merme   Now to 2016 13.5
Good colour. Somewhat tarty, soft-centred nose. Mocha here at first, boiled sweets later. Will get astringent, I fear.

Echézeaux,
Domaine Robert Arnoux   From 2016 17.5
Full colour. Ample, concentrated, profound nose. Lots of wine here, but not too burly. Medium-full body. Rich and energetic. Plenty of depth. Fine.

Echézeaux, Domaine
du Clos Frantin (Albert Bichot)   From 2015 16.0
Fullish colour. Rich, open, aromatic yet quite sturdy nose. Medium-full body. Lush, ripe, and exotic on the palate. Quite fresh. Attractive for drinking quite soon.

Echézeaux, Domaine
Bouchard Père et Fils   From 2015 16.5
Fullish colour. Ripe, rich, quite sturdy nose. Good class and definition. Decent vigour but not quite enough grip for fine. Medium-full body. Very good plus.

Echézeaux, Domaine Eugenie   From 2015 15.5
This used to be Domaine Engel. Medium-full colour. Silky-smooth, accessible, oaky nose. Quite a pronounced acidity. Ripe and generous on the palate. Medium-full weight. Lacks a little vigour and backbone but good plus.

Echézeaux, Domaine Faiveley   From 2014 15.0
Medium-full colour. Soft, ripe nose. A little diffuse. Medium-full body. A forward example. Lush and fruity. Good but not special.

Echézeaux,
Domaine Jean Grivot   From 2015 16.5
Medium-full colour. A bit hidden, like so many of Grivot's wines at present. But there is depth and quality here. Medium-full body. Balanced. Plenty in reserve. Very good plus.

Echézeaux,
Domaine Lamarche   From 2016 17.5
Medium-full colour. Cool, stylish, aromatic nose. Ripe and medium-full bodied on the palate. Good energy. Stylish, fresh, profound, and long on the palate. Impressive.

Echézeaux, Domaine
du Vicomte de Liger-Belair   From 2015 16.5
Full colour. Firm nose. Some tannin. Still a bit closed. Medium-full body. Cool, good vigour and grip. At present a bit severe but very good plus, at least, I think.

Echézeaux,
Domaine Jean-Marc Millet   From 2015 17.0
Full colour. Rich, ripe, full fat nose. Medium-full body. Plump, succulent, balanced, and vigorous. This is very good indeed.

Echézeaux,
Domaine Gérard Mugneret   From 2015 16.5
Fullish colour. Ripe, quite fat nose with touch of reduction. At the moment this degrades the class. But medium-full body. Good grip. And at least very good plus when it sorts itself out.

Echézeaux,
Domaine Mugneret-Gibourg   From 2015 17.0
Medium-full colour. Rich nose. Fat and vigorous. Quite firm still. Medium-full body. Rich, ripe, and full of fruit. Good grip and backbone. Plenty of vigour. Very good indeed.

Echézeaux,
Domaine de la Romanée-Conti   From 2015 16.5
Medium colour. Ripe, fresh nose. Elegant if not very voluminous. Sweet, spicy, slightly stemmy flavours. Medium weight. Good follow-through. Fresh, balanced, stylish, and with a positive finish. Very good plus.

Echézeaux,
Domaine Emmanuel Rouget   From 2016 18.0
Medium-full colour. Still quite hidden on the nose. Good substance. Good tannins. Just a little rough and ready at present. Good grip. Plenty of depth and richness. Plus a touch, but not excessively so, of oak. Long. Fine plus.

Echézeaux,
Domaine Cécile Tremblay   From 2014 14.5
Fullish colour. Ripe but a little bland on the nose. Medium to medium-full body. Decent fruit and grip. A little ungainly at present and the finish is a bit dry. Only quite good plus at present.

Echézeaux,
Domaine Fabrice Vigot   From 2014 15.5
Stylish and harmonious. Still a little bit raw at the moment. Could have had a bit more substance. But the follow-through is positive enough. Good plus.

Grands-Echézeaux,
Domaine Joseph Drouhin   From 2015 17.5
Medium-full weight. Ripe, balanced, and succulent. Lovely fruit. Not quite the flair and energy for "very fine" but certainly "fine."

Grands-Echézeaux,
Domaine Gros Frère et Soeur   See note
Full colour. Austere nose with high, almost balsamic, volatile acidity. Fullish body. No lack of new wood. To be seen again.

Grands-Echézeaux,
Domaine Lamarche   From 2016 18.0
Medium-full colour. Fresh, new oaky nose. Classy fruit here. Fullish body. Ripe and balanced and with plenty of energy. Lots of depth. Impressive. Fine plus.

Grands-Echézeaux,
Domaine de la Romanée-Conti   From 2015 17.5
This is rather more structured than the Echézeaux. Quite a lot richer too. Medium-full

body. Lots of fruit and concentration. Very well-balanced. Lovely finish. Elegant. Fine.

Clos de Vougeot,
Domaine Robert Arnoux　　From 2016　18.5
Full colour. Some substance on the nose. But a little four-square at first. Evolved well. Fullish. Some tannin. Very good grip. Lovely black fruit. Lots of depth. This is impressive. It needs time, but it will last well.

Clos de Vougeot,
Domaine Bouchard Père et Fils　From 2015　16.0
Medium-full colour. Fresh, ripe, balanced, and stylish on the nose. But not a blockbuster. Medium-full body. Good fruit with a touch of oak. And a long, positive finish. Very good.

Clos de Vougeot,
Maison Chanson　　From 2014　14.5
Medium-full colour. A bit tight on the nose but good depth. Broad-flavoured. No great backbone or grip, so a touch of astringency at the end. The fruit is quite classy though. Quite good plus.

Clos de Vougeot, Domaine
Philippe Charlopin-Parizot　From 2014　15.5
Medium-full colour. Not a lot on the nose, save that it is ripe and plump. Medium-full body. I don't find much personality here, nor *grand cru* finesse. Ample, balanced, and positive at the end, but no better than good plus.

Clos de Vougeot, Domaine
du Clos Frantin (Albert Bichot)　From 2016　18.0
Medium-full colour. Ripe, rich, and quite oaky on the nose. Firm and backward too. Fullish, rich, ample, and new oaky on the palate. Good class and depth. Fresh and harmonious. Fine plus.

Clos de Vougeot,
Domaine Faiveley　　From 2016　17.5
Fullish colour. A big, rich, quite extracted, tannic wine. Is it too big for its boots? Better on the palate. Fullish. Good energy and class. Needs time but fine, I think.

Clos de Vougeot,
Domaine Jean Grivot　　From 2016　18.0
Good colour. Very lovely fruit here. Fullish, concentrated. Excellent grip. Fine tannins. Lots of character and class. Long, subtle, and profound. Fine plus.

Clos de Vougeot, Grand Maupertuis,
Domaine Anne Gros　　From 2016　17.5
Fullish colour. Firm, fresh, oaky nose. Still a bit closed-in. Rich and ripe on the attack. Quite full bosy. Very good grip. Above all this has class. Fine.

Clos de Vougeot, Grand Maupertuis,
Domaine Michel Gros　　From 2015　16.0
Medium-full colour. Stylish nose. Gentle and fruity, oaky and full of charm. Medium-full body. This will evolve quite soon. Most attractive if lacks a little power. Very good.

Clos de Vougeot, Musigni,
Domaine Gros Frère et Soeur　From 2016　18.0
Full colour. Full, rich, concentrated, and backward on the nose. But lots of class and depth here. This is a big, youthful, fine-quality wine. Very lovely fruit. Lots of energy. Fine plus.

Clos de Vougeot,
Domaine Hudelot-Noëllat　　From 2015　18.0
Medium-full colour. Succulent, attractive fruit on the nose. Good class here. Medium-full body. Ripe, concentrated, intense, and classy. A fullish, lush wine with plenty of energy. Long and vigorous. Fine plus.

Clos de Vougeot,
Domaine Lamarche　　From 2015　16.0
Fullish colour. Abundant, quite oaky nose, if no great concentration. Medium-full body. The fruit is classy and the wine well-balanced. Finishes positively. Very good.

Clos de Vougeot,
Domaine Thibaut Liger-Belair　From 2015　16.0
Full colour. The nose is a bit closed. Medium-full body. Quite oaky. Rich and lush on the palate. Decent grip. Very good.

Clos de Vougeot,

Domaine Sylvain Loichet   From 2013   15.5

Full colour. Smooth nose. Decent balance but a slight lack of energy. Medium to medium-full body. Ripe and pretty. Good balance. Quite a forward example. But good stuff.

Clos de Vougeot,

Domaine Méo-Camuzet   From 2015   15.5

Full colour. Quite oaky on the nose and well-structured, if not a little burly as well. Fullish body. Good grip. Rich underneath, but a little ungainly at present. Good plus, perhaps better.

Clos de Vougeot,

Domaine Jean-Marc Millot   From 2014   15.5

Medium-full colour. An open, gentle, spicy nose. Medium to medium-full body. Round and ripe, even succulent. Quite a forward example but good plus.

Clos de Vougeot,

Château de la Tour   Now to 2017   14.0

Fullish colour. Abundant, spicy nose. But no great class here. Medium to medium-full body. A little diffuse. The fruit is a bit one-dimensional and the finish a bit short. Quite good at best.

Clos de Vougeot, Vieilles Vignes,

Château de la Tour   From 2016   17.0

Not weedy on the nose, which this wine has regularly been in the past. Indeed fresh, fruity, and stylish. Medium to medium-full weight. Decent balance. Quite positive. Not brilliant but very good indeed. Obviously an improvement has taken place here.

Clos de Vougeot,

Domaine de la Vougeraie   From 2015   16.0

Full colour. Good firm, rich nose. Lovely fruit. Medium-full body. Perfumed. Lush and succulent and seductive. Very good.

Romanée-Saint-Vivant,

Domaine de l'Arlot   From 2015   17.5

Full colour. Aromatic nose. Some stems. Ripe and high-toned on the attack. Medium-full body. Fresh, fruity, juicy, and succulent. Fine.

Romanée-Saint-Vivant,

Domaine Robert Arnoux   From 2016   18.5

Full colour. Very refined, pure, classy nose. Very lovely. Rich, fat, energetic, and full-bodied on the palate. Good grip. Backward. This has a lot of depth.

Romanée-Saint-Vivant,

Domaine Follin-Arbelet   From 2015   17.5

Full colour. A big, fat, even muscular wine here. Full body. Sweet and rich and ripe on the attack. Plenty of wine here. Fine.

Romanée-Saint-Vivant,

Domaine Hudelot-Noëllat   From 2015   17.0

Full colour. Good class on the nose, but a little pinched. Fullish body. Ample, quite classy fruit. And consistent from start to finish. Could have had a bit more vigour and intensity, but very good indeed.

Romanée-Saint-Vivant,

Domaine de la Romanée-Conti   From 2015   17.5

Fragrant nose. Good acidity. Flowery and elegant. Medium to medium-full body. Quite a delicate wine. But fresh and balanced and stylish. Good positive follow-through. Fine.

Richebourg,

Domaine Jean Grivot   From 2017   19.5

Fullish colour. This was very closed-in at first, but opened up to show something of real beauty. Fullish. Tannic. Ripe, rich, and concentrated. Splendidly profound fruit. Very long and really quite splendid.

Richebourg, Domaine

Gros Frère et Soeur   From 2016   17.5

Full colour. High-toned nose. Another wine which was rather tight at first and then opened up. Fullish body. Very good grip. Oaky and concentrated. Some tannin. Not as spectacular as some, but very good indeed at the very least. Needs time.

Richebourg, Domaine Leroy   From 2016   18.0

Full colour. Rich, aromatic nose, with evidence of the stems. (This is more marked than usual in the Leroy 2006s.) Fullish. Ripe, rich, and attractive. Opened up in the glass. A lush, succulent wine. Fresh and balanced. Lovely. Fine plus.

Richebourg,
Domaine Thibaut Liger-Belair   From 2016   18.0
Fullish colour. Rich, full, concentrated, and classy on the nose. Fullish body. Very good grip. Lovely fruit. Intense and stylish. Not a blockbuster but very lovely.

Richebourg,
Domaine de la Romanée-Conti   From 2016   18.0
Plump, fat, and medium-full bodied. At present a little closed-in. Best on the finish. Very good grip and lovely ample fruit. This is long on the palate and has a lot of dimension and class. Fine plus.

La Grande Rue,
Domaine Lamarche   From 2016   19.0
Full colour. Very pure and very, very classy on the nose. Cool, composed, rich, and concentrated on the palate. Plus a touch of new oak. Medium-full body. Balanced, understated, fresh, and intense.

La Romanée, Domaine
du Vicomte de Liger-Belair   From 2015   18.0
Full colour. Very seductive, aromatic, ripe nose. Rich and succulent. Medium-full body. Very good grip. Subtle and harmonious and very long on the palate. Fine plus.

La Tâche,
Domaine de la Romanée-Conti   From 2018   19.0
Good colour. The nose is a bit hidden. But it is evident that this is a big step up on the Richebourg. More concentration. More volume. More depth. Above all, more class and definition. Very lovely balanced fruit and an excellent long finish. Very fine plus.

La Romanée-Conti,
Domaine de la Romanée-Conti   From 2016   20.0
Medium-full weight. Very lovely, almost Musigny-like fruit here. Complex, concentrated, and intense. Marvelous harmony. Very, very long and multidimensional. This is very special.

Musigny,
Domaine J. F. Mugnier   From 2016   20.0
Very lovely nose. Rich, complex, concentrated, harmonious, and spendidly elegant. Fullish body. Marvelous fruit. Not the vigour of Roumier's Bonnes-Mares but just as intense and pretty well perfect as 2006s go. It has a most lovely long, lingering finish.

Musigny, Domaine
Comte Georges de Vogüé   From 2016   16.0
Fullish colour. Very abundant, mocha-toffee nose. Plus a lot of new oak. On the palate, not the greatest grip or complexity. Indeed, like the Bonnes-Mares, it's a bit tarty. Full body. Balanced. Needs time. Where is the usual Musigny delicacy?

Musigny,
Domaine de la Vougeraie   From 2015   17.5
Medium-full colour. Abundant nose, but not the usual subtlety. Medium-full colour. Good grip. Good stylish fruit. Balanced and long on the palate, and better here than on the nose. Fine.

Bonnes-Mares, Domaine Arlaud   See note
Medium to medium-full colour. Quite evolved on both the nose and the palate. A soft, fruity, quite spicy wine. Rather disappointing. Is this a representative bottle?

Bonnes-Mares,
Domaine Francois Bertheau   From 2016   16.5
Medium-full colour. Very ripe, abundant, succulent fruit on the nose. On the palate, more evolved than the nose would indicate. Quite new oaky. A flamboyant example but it lacks a little class. Very good plus.

Bonnes-Mares,
Domaine Bouchard Père et Fils   From 2016   18.0
Medium-full colour. Rich, full, and oaky on the nose. Fullish body. Very oaky. Very lush fruit. But lots of energy and no lack of class. Lovely finish. Fine plus.

Bonnes-Mares,
Domaine Drouhin-Laroze   From 2016   18.5
Fullish colour. Concentrated, profound, backward nose. Lots of depth here. Full body. Some

tannin. Cool and composed. Understated. Very fine.

Bonnes-Mares,
Domaine Georges Roumier   From 2017   18.5

Good colour. Quite firm on the nose. Rich, concentrated, fullish weight, and very classy indeed. Lots of depth and energy on the palate. Lots of fruit. Complex, vigorous, and very fine.

Bonnes-Mares, Domaine
Comte Georges de Vogüé   From 2016   18.0

Medium-full colour. Fresh, quite firm, attractive nose with a touch of oak and spice. Medium-full body. Good tannins. Nicely abundant fruit. Good grip. This is long on the palate and fine plus.

Bonnes-Mares,
Domaine de la Vougeraie   From 2016   18.0

Fullish colour. Rich, fat, and oaky on the nose. But a little more restrained than some. Full body. Ample. Quite tannic. But very ripe and with very good grip. Backward. Lots of depth. Fine plus.

Clos des Lambrays,
Domaine des Lambrays   From 2016   19.0

Fullish colour. Lovely nose. Rich, profound, high-quality. Fullish body. Complete. Very rich concentrated fruit. Real finesse. Excellent.

Clos de la Roche,
Domaine Dujac   From 2015   17.5

Medium-full colour. Ripe nose, but a little closed at first. Good grip. Medium-full body. On the palate plenty of lush, succulent fruit. Lots of depth. Fine. Just needs time.

Clos de la Roche,
Domaine Hubert Lignier   See note

Fullish colour. Fullish, ample, profound, and new oaky on the nose. Fullish body. This bottle is corked, but the wine is promising. To be seen again.

Clos de la Roche,
Domaine Ponsot   From 2016   16.5

Medium colour. Soft, scented wood on the nose. Medium to medium-full body. Smooth,

ripe tannins, good fruit. Not a blockbuster but good intensity. Finishes well. Very good plus.

Clos de la Roche,
Domaine Louis Rémy   From 2016   17.0

Medium-full colour. Rich, quite new oaky on the nose. Medium-full body. Ample and succulent. Good backbone, vigour, and plenty of depth. Very good grip. Long. Very good indeed.

Clos-Saint-Denis, Domaine
Philippe Charlopin-Parizot   From 2016   17.0

Good colour. Rich, ripe nose, and stylish too. Medium-full body. Quite vigorous and intense on the palate. Good fruit. Good grip. Good vigour. Long and very good indeed.

Clos-Saint-Denis,
Domaine de Chézeaux   From 2015   17.5

Surprisingly accessible. Very fine tannins. Medium to medium-full body. Lovely fresh, elegant fruit. A very composed wine. Ripe, complex, ample but essentially gentle. Long. Fine.

Clos de Tart,
Domaine Mommessin   From 2016   18.0

Medium-full colour. A little closed-in on the nose. But there is class here. Fullish body. Good tannins. Very good grip. Youthful and a bit ungainly at present. But high-class fruit and depth underneath. Fine plus.

Chapelle-Chambertin,
Domaine Bouchard
Père et Fils   From 2016   18.0

Medium-full colour. Fresh, fruity, and classy on the nose. Medium-full body. Some oak. Good grip and intensity. Still quite closed-in. Very lovely, long, cool, composed finish. Fine plus.

Chapelle-Chambertin,
Domaine Drouhin-Laroze   From 2015   16.0

Fullish colour. Nicely rich and meaty on the nose. Something just a little unclean on the nose, which made others mark it down. I ignored this, as I don't think it's a long-term problem. Medium-full body. Ripe and vigorous. Good tannins. Long at the end. Very good.

Chapelle-Chambertin,
Domaine Rossignol-Trapet   From 2016   18.0
Fresh, firm, and showing very good fruit on the nose. Nicely cool and composed. A lot of depth and class. Medium-full body. Good tannins. Long and stylish. Fine plus.

Chapelle-Chambertin,
Domaine Cécile Tremblay   From 2015   15.0
Full colour. This is rather tight at present and it lacks a bit of charm. Yet there is fruit and balance and good grip at the end. Good, perhaps even better.

Charmes-Chambertin,
Domaine Denis Bachelet   From 2016   18.5
Full colour. Rich but closed-in nose. Still a bit austere. Full body. Quite tannic, but by no means overdone. Plenty of fruit and depth. Lots of potential. A profound wine. Very fine.

Charmes-Chambertin,
Maison Henri Boillot   From 2015   16.0
Medium-full colour. Ample, quite soft nose, if no great vigour or depth. Medium to medium-full body. Fruity and pleasant and balanced. Fresh and stylish. Quite forward. Very good.

Charmes-Chambertin,
Maison Chanson   Drink soon   13.0
Medium-full colour. Very rich on the nose. But a bit over the top and a little oxidation. Medium to medium-full body. Tired. Fair at best.

Charmes-Chambertin, Domaine
Philippe Charlopin-Parizot   From 2015   16.0
Medium-full colour. Ample, plump, fruity nose. Medium to medium-full body. Ripe, round, and balanced, but not really *grand cru* depth or finesse. Decent length though. Very good at best.

Charmes-Chambertin,
Maison Camille Giroud   From 2015   16.0
Medium to medium-full colour. Fullish but a little four-square on the nose. Medium-full body. Quite fresh. More interest than that shown on the nose. Good depth. Very good.

Charmes-Chambertin,
Domaine Maume   From 2015   17.0
Medium colour. Some stems on the nose. A bit more developed than most. Medium to medium-full body. Ample, positive, lush, and exotic. Lots of fresh fruit. Good energy. Very good indeed.

Charmes-Chambertin, Très Vieilles
Vignes, Domaine Roty   See note
Medium-full colour. Full and rich on the nose. Sadly this is corked, but one can see a structured, meaty wine with good grip and tannins. Backward. This is at least fine. What a pity!

Charmes-Chambertin,
Domaine Armand Rousseau   From 2015   15.5
Medium colour. Plump nose. Medium to medium-full body. Ripe, balanced, generous, and long on the palate. Lacks a bit of flair but good plus.

Charmes-Chambertin,
Domaine Christian Serafin   From 2016   18.0
Full colour. Ripe, stylish, gently oaky, most attractive nose. Fullish body. Plenty of vigour. Rich. Very good grip. Some tannin. Long, complex finish. Fine plus.

Charmes-Chambertin,
Les Mazoyrères,
Domaine de la Vougeraie   From 2015   17.5
Medium-full colour. Plump, soft, quite aromatic nose. Nicely ripe and fresh. Medium-full body. Good energy. Ample and vigorous. Still needs time. Very good grip. Lots of potential here. Fine.

Mazoyères-Chambertin,
Domaine Taupenot-Merme   From 2015   16.0
Fullish colour. Slightly hard new oak on the nose. A little rigid at first. But good plump, succulent fruit underneath. Medium-full body. Good grip. Very good.

Griotte-Chambertin,
Domaine Ponsot   From 2015   15.5
Fullish colour. A touch of reduction on the nose. Medium-full body. Oaky. Fat and ripe

and with good acidity. But it doesn't add up to anything very classy. There is a positive finish though. Good plus.

Latricières-Chambertin,
Domaine Drouhin-Laroze   From 2016   17.0
Medium-full colour. Fresh, high-toned, fruity nose. Good class and depth. There is a touch of rigid oak here, but basically the wine is balanced. Full-bodied. Concentrated. Good finish. Very good indeed.

Latricières-Chambertin,
Domaine Faiveley   From 2014   15.5
Full colour. Slightly lean, but ripe, balanced, and classy on the nose. Medium-full body. Some oak. Not really enough fat and concentration and grip. I fear it may dry out. Good plus.

Latricières-Chambertin,
Domaine Louis Rémy   From 2015   17.0
Full colour. Ample, voluminous, round, rich nose. Even fat. Just a bit four-square. Yet on the palate the fruit is very ripe and abundant—a real summer pudding. Seductive, but not quite the grip for fine. Very good indeed.

Latricières-Chambertin,
Domaine Rossignol-Trapet   From 2016   18.0
Medium-full colour. Rich, black-fruity, concentrated nose. Fullish body and high-class. Some tannin. Backward. Vigorous. Profound. This has very good grip. Very, very long. Fine plus.

Latricières-Chambertin, Domaine
Jean et Jean-Louis Trapet   From 2016   18.5
Fullish colour. Rich, meaty nose. Fullish body. Quite round, yet good supporting tannins and acidity. Classy fruit. Good intensity. Very ripe and very fine.

Mazis-Chambertin, Domaine
Phillipe Charlopin-Parizot   From 2015   16.0
Good colour. Somewhat overblown on the nose. A touch of new oak here. Medium-full body. The attack is balanced and quite stylish, but then it tails off. No better than his Charmes. Very good at best.

Mazis-Chambertin,
Domaine Faiveley   From 2016   17.0
Fullish colour. Ripe, round, fresh, plump, and vigorous on the nose. Nothing aggressive here. Fullish, still some tannin. Good depth and backbone. Needs time. Very good indeed.

Mazis-Chambertin,
Domaine Maume   From 2015   15.5
Full colour. Some stems but a meaty wine, a little four-square perhaps. Nice and ripe. Vigorous and rich. Quite elegant. Good plus.

Mazis-Chambertin,
Domaine Newman   From 2016   17.5
Medium-full colour. The nose is a little closed but the wine has depth and class. Fullish body. Lovely fruit. Very good tannins. Very good grip. Above all, finesse. Not the intensity for great but a fine wine.

Ruchottes-Chambertin,
Domaine Christophe Roumier   From 2016   15.0
Full colour. Big nose. Quite a long extraction here, quite evidently. Fullish. Quite tannic, even a little astringency on the palate. A little bitter at the end. Good. But better? I expected better when I was told what it was.

Chambertin,
Clos de Bèze, Domaine
Bouchard Père et Fils   See note
Full colour. Somewhat hard on the nose. Very much in its shell still. Medium-full colour. At the moment it lacks a little charm. It was one of the few (if not the only) Bouchard wine I didn't warm to at the group tasting, and others liked it better than I did, though only at a "very good indeed" level. I'll wait until I see it again.

Chambertin,
Clos de Bèze,
Maison Chanson   From 2015   17.5
Full colour. Ripe, rich, and vigorous on the nose, with a touch of the stems. Medium-full body. This does not have quite the intensity of the very best, but it is abundant, long, and complex. Fine.

Chambertin, Clos de Bèze,
Domaine Bruno Clair   From 2017 19.0
Medium-full colour. High-quality on the nose here. Rich, balanced, and vigorous. Full body. Some tannin. Lots of energy. Very harmonious. Profound and very exciting. Quite lovely. Needs time.

Chambertin, Clos de Bèze,
Domaine Drouhin-Laroze   From 2016 18.0
Medium-full colour. Rich and full but slightly earthy nose. Medium-full body on the palate. Very lovely fruit. But not the backbone. Very good grip, but not quite the intensity. Fine plus nevertheless.

Chambertin, Clos de Bèze,
Domaine Faiveley   From 2016 17.5
Full colour. Full, rich, backward, very concentrated nose. This has depth and quality. On the palate, though, it was a bit earthy, like the Drouhin-Laroze wine, but underneath the wine is balanced, vigorous, and has high-class fruit.

Chambertin, Clos de Bèze,
Domaine Armand Rousseau   From 2017 19.0
Fullish colour. Medium-full weight on the nose. High-toned, very classy, very well-balanced nose. Very lovely fruit. Fullish body. Pure and intense. Not the biggest of wines, but with a vigour and a depth of flavour which is hard to beat. Very lovely at the end.

Chambertin, Domaine
Madame Jocelyne Baron, made
by Philippe Charlopin-Parizot   From 2016 17.5
Good colour. Very ripe, if not a bit over-ripe on the nose. Medium-full body. On the palate, also very ripe, even sweet. Yet good acidity, concentration, and depth. What it lacks is real finesse. But fine quality.

Chambertin,
Domaine Louis Remy   From 2015 17.5
Medium-full colour. Ample, round, slightly spicy, sweet nose. Medium-full body. Ample and fruity if without the concentration, grip, and vigour of the very best. Fine, though.

Chambertin,
Domaine Rossignol-Trapet   From 2017 19.0
Not a blockbuster but very subtle, elegant, and concentrated. Very lovely fruit. Medium-full body. Ripe tannins. Very good grip. Lovely, velvety cassis flavours. Long and complex. Very fine plus.

Chambertin,
Domaine Armand Rousseau   From 2017 19.5
Fullish colour. The nose is rather more hidden than his Clos de Bèze. But there is a lot of quality and depth here. On the palate, fullish body. Splendidly concentrated fruit. Rich and fat and complex and high-class. Very, very lovely.

Chambertin, Domaine
Jean et Jean-Louis Trapet   From 2016 18.0
Medium-full colour. Rich, profound, and gently oaky on the nose. Fullish, intense, youthful but not aggressively tannic on the palate. Very good grip. Lots of depth. Classy. Not brilliant but fine plus.

2005 BURGUNDY

A magnificent red wine vintage. This was a dry year, though never particularly hot, save for a heat wave in May. A hailstorm on July 17 devastated the vines between the villages of Santenay and Chassagne-Montrachet. After a mixed

⤖ *Rating for the Vintage* ⤕	
Red	19.0
White	16.5

August, and much-needed rain on September 6, the skies cleared and it became increasingly sunny and warm. The Côte d'Or harvest began in the middle of the month and was all but complete by the weekend of October 1.

Now in bottle, the red wines, though they have begun to shut down a bit, are well deserving of all the ballyhoo they engendered at the outset. The vintage is consistently good (except naturally in Santenay and Chassagne-Montrachet) from Marsannay to Maranges, as

Size of the Crop
(In hectolitres)

	RED	WHITE	TOTAL
Grand cru	13,214	3,692	16,906
Village and premier cru	175,674	58,817	234,491
TOTAL	188,888	62,509	251,397

well as proportionately so from *grand cru* to the humblest generic. Few past vintages come close. Perhaps the nearest is 1999, but this was a very much more generous harvest. The relative shortness of the 2005 crop can be seen in the concentration of the wines. They also have depth, finesse, harmony, and the potential to last. What more do you want? Lay them down and throw away the key.

Where are the best red wines? The simple answer is: just about everywhere. And, as in the really fine vintages, all the way from generic level to *grand cru*. Only in Chassagne and Santenay does one need to select with care.

When will the red 2005s be at their best? This is a vintage which will amply repay patience. Meanwhile, you have other vintages to drink. While you can start drinking the wines sooner (as I have indicated in the tasting notes below), it would be more rewarding not to commence drinking the village Côte de Beaunes until around 2016 and the *premiers crus* not until 2018 and 2019. The village Côte de Nuits should be held until 2019, while many of the top *premiers* and *grands crus* need keeping until the mid-2020s. One of the beauties of red Burgundy is that the wines are so delicious young . . . but they do repay the extra cellar time.

Stars of the Vintage

20/20

La Grande Rue, Domaine Lamarche

Richebourg, Domaine Anne Gros

Romanée-Conti, Domaine de la Romanée-Conti

Musigny, Domaine Comte Georges de Vogüé

Chambertin, Domaine Armand Rousseau

19.5

Richebourg, Domaine Grivot

19.0

La Romanée, Domaine du Vicomte de Liger-Belair

Richebourg, Domaine Gros Frère et Soeur

Bonnes-Mares, Domaine Comte Georges de Vogüé

Musigny, Domaine J. F. Mugnier

Clos de Tart, Domaine du Clos de Tart

Chambertin, Clos de Bèze, Domaine Bruno Clair

Chambertin, Clos de Bèze, Domaine Armand Rousseau

Chambertin, Domaine Rossignol-Trapet

18.5

Vosne-Romanée, Aux Beaux Monts, Domaine Grivot

Vosne-Romanée, Aux Beaux Monts, Domaine Cecile Tremblay

Vosne-Romanée, Aux Brulées, Domaine Méo-Camuzet

Vosne-Romanée, Chaumes, Domaine Lamarche

Vosne-Romanée, Aux Malconsorts, Domaine Cathiard

Vosne-Romanée, Aux Malconsorts, Domaine Lamarche

Vosne-Romanée, Les Suchots, Domaine Grivot

Vosne-Romanée, Les Suchots, Domaine Louis Jadot

Chambolle-Musigny, Les Amoureuses,
Domaine J. F. Mugnier

Chambolle-Musigny, Les Amoureuses,
Domaine Comte Georges de Vogüé

Chambolle-Musigny, Les Cras, Domaine
Ghislaine Barthod

Chambolle-Musingy, Les Cras, Domaine
Georges Roumier

Chambolle-Musigny, Les Fuées, Domaine
Ghislaine Barthod

Gevrey-Chambertin, Clos-Saint-Jacques,
Domaine Bruno Clair

Gevrey-Chambertin, Clos-Saint-Jacques,
Domaine Sylvie Esmonin

Gevrey-Chambertin, Clos-Saint-Jacques,
Domaine Louis Jadot

Gevrey-Chambertin, Clos-Saint-Jacques,
Domaine Armand Rousseau

Corton, Clos du Roi, Domaine de Montille

Grands-Echézeaux, Domaine du Clos Frantin

Clos de Vougeot, Domaine Grivot

Clos de Vougeot, Domaine Lamarche

Richebourg, Domaine Thibault Liger Belair

Bonnes-Mares, Domaine Georges Roumier

Clos des Lambrays, Domaine des Lambrays

Clos de la Roche, Domaine Dujac

Charmes-Chambertin, Domaine Serafin

Latricières-Chambertin, Domaine Faiveley

Mazis-Chambertin, Domaine Faiveley

TASTING NOTES

The following tasting notes come from three comprehensive tastings. Firstly, in January 2008, I invited the Savigny growers to join me in a tasting of their *premiers crus,* as we tend to confine our annual group tasting to Volnay, Pommard, and Beaune, plus Corton, in the Côte de Beaune. They responded magnificently, as you will see. Secondly, there was the annual Masters of Wine/Domaine Familiaux tasting at Vintners Hall in London at the beginning of March. The group tasting was held in Beaune

at the end of August. Thank you to Jasper Morris MW and Roy Richards, who organised it. In addition, while in the United States in April, I participated in a number of sampling sessions of 2005s. I have included all these notes. I saw quite a few wines on more than one occasion, as you can imagine. Here I have provided a composite tasting note. All wines, except where otherwise indicated, are *premier* or *grand cru.*

Savigny-Lès-Beaune

Clous, Domaine d'Ardhuy   Now to 2019   15.5
Good colour. Rich, full, aromatic nose. Full body. Ripe, slightly spicy. Good tannins. Plenty of depth and potential. Very good.

Dominodes,
Domaine Bruno Clair   Now to 2020   16.0
Medium-full colour. Mature tannins. Good concentration. Medium to medium-full body with rich, balanced fruit and a touch of oak. Backward. Very good.

Dominodes,
Domaine Chanson   Now to 2019   15.5
Medium colour. Fragrant nose. Ripe and succulent. Medium body. Not a lot of backbone but harmonious and stylish. Good plus.

Dominodes,
Domaine Louis Jadot   Now to 2020   16.0
Medium colour. Rather more closed-in on the nose than most. This is quite a tannic wine, but rich and concentrated too. Very good grip. Impressive depth at the end. Very good.

Dominodes,
Domaine Pavelot   Now to 2020   16.0
Medium-full colour. Lovely nose. Really quite profound. On the palate, still recovering from the bottling (it was very much better the next day). Medium to medium-full body. Rich and concentrated. Very good.

Fourneaux, Domaine
Chandon de Briailles   Now to 2018   15.5
Medium colour. Fragrant nose. Sophisticated, cool fruit. Medium body. Ripe. Not a lot of tan-

nin. But good depth, intensity, and style. Good plus.

Fourneaux,
Domaine Simon Bize Now to 2020 16.0
Medium colour. Soft, fragrant, ripe, stylish nose. Medium body. Fresh, complex, harmonious, juicy, and delicious. Quite forward.

Fourneaux,
Domaine Nicolas Rossignol Now to 2018 15.0
Medium colour. Ripe nose. Succulent, almost sweet. Medium to medium-full body. Fresh. Balanced. Good.

Gravins,
Domaine Michel Ecard Now to 2019 15.5
Medium colour. Very elegant composed nose. Really stylish and complex. Medium body. As much raw as tannic. Quite forward. Attractive fruity finish. Good plus.

Gravins, Domaine Giboulot Now to 2017 15.0
Medium colour. Lightish, soft, fruity nose. Similar on the palate. Not a lot of backbone here but plenty of jucy, blanced fruit. Forward.

Gravins, Domaine Pavelot Now to 2020 16.0
Good colour. Like their Dominodes, this is a bit adolescent. It was better the next day. Medium-full body. Good balance. Ripe fruit. There is depth here. Very good.

Clos des Guettes,
Domaine André Gagey,
Maison Louis Jadot Now to 2020 16.5
Good colour. Fine rich nose. Quite a substantial wine. Medium-full body. Good tannins. Ripe, rich, and balanced. Very stylish too. Lovely finish. Very good plus.

Guettes, Domaine Pavelot Now to 2020 16.5
Medium-full colour. Rich, fat, concentrated nose. Medium-full body. Lovely complex fruit. Good depth. Very good plus.

Guettes,
Domaine Simon Bize Now to 2020 17.0
From magnum. Good colour. Rich, full, backward, and concentrated. Some tannin. Lots

of depth and class. Very good grip. Very good indeed.

Hauts Jarrons,
Domaine Nicolas Potel Now to 2019 16.0
Good colour. Ripe, rich nose. Very stylish. Medium to medium-full body. Attractive, balanced, fresh, and plump. Nice and pure. Easy to enjoy. Very good.

Lavières, Domaine
Bouchard Père et Fils Now to 2020 16.0
Medium-full colour. A bit closed-in on the nose. But lovely rich fruit on the palate. Good weight. Good grip. Good style. Long. Very good.

Lavières, Domaine
Chandon de Briailles Now to 2019 16.0
Medium colour. Soft, fragrant, spicy nose. Medium body. Ripe tannins. Very good definition. Composed. Harmonious. Very long on the palate. Very good.

Lavières, Domaine
Jean-Jacques Girard Now to 2019 15.0
Medium colour. Good weight on the nose. Medium-full body. Good tannins. Very ripe, fresh, but slightly jammy fruit. Yet attractive and balanced. Good.

Lavières,
Domaine Nicolas Rossignol Now to 2019 16.0
Good colour. Rich, quite concentrated, succulent nose. Medium-full body. Ripe tannins. Good, slightly spicy fruit and fresh and very positive at the end. Very good.

Marconnets,
Domaine Simon Bize Now to 2020 15.5
Meduim colour. Rich, succulent nose. Plenty of complexity and style. Medium to medium-full body. Ripe tannins. But not *that* structured. Vigorous, long, and full of interest nevertheless. Good plus.

Narbantons,
Domaine Giboulot Now to 2016 13.0
Medium colour. Soft, slightly jammy nose. Ripe and juicy but lacks a bit of style as well as backbone and depth. Only fair.

Narbantons, Domaine
Jean-Jacques Girard   Now to 2019   15.5
Medium colour. Fresh, ripe nose, with good style and depth. Medium to medium-full body. Quite a robust touch to the tannins. But balanced, long, and positive. Good plus.

Narbantons,
Domaine Louis Jadot   Now to 2020   17.0
Good colour. Rich, meaty nose. Quite substantial, but ripe tannins. Very harmonious. Good finesse. Very long. Most impressive. Very good indeed.

Narbantons, Domaine Leroy   Now to 2020   17.0
Good colour. Rich, concentrated nose. Lots of class and depth. Medium-full body. Very good grip. Very lovely pure fruit. Fine tannins. This is most impressive. Very good indeed.

Narbantons,
Domaine Pavelot   Now to 2020   16.5
Very good colour. Quite a structured wine on the nose. But all the elegance is in place. Fullish. Very good grip. Ripe tannins. Lovely finish. Slightly adolescent at present but potentially very good plus.

Peuillets,
Domaine Michel Ecard   Now to 2019   15.5
Medium to medium-full colour. Rich, plummy nose. Fresh, succulent, and attractive. Medium body. Not a huge amount of grip, but fresh enough. As much raw as tannic. Positive at the end. Good plus.

Peuillets, Domaine Giboulot   Now to 2017   14.0
Medium colour. Soft nose. Ripe and juicy but no great backbone here. Better than his Narbantons but still a little slight. Yet not unstylish. Quite good.

Peuillets, Domaine
Jean-Jacques Girard   Now to 2020   16.0
Medium to medium-full colour. Good nose: fresh, ripe, positive, and meaty. Medium to medium-full body. Lovely cool fruit. Good tannins. Complex and stylish. Fine finish. Very good.

Peuillets,
Domaine Nicolas Potel   Now to 2020   16.0
Good colour. Velvety rich on the nose. Good substance. Ripe and stylish. Cool fruit. Lovely finish. Very good.

Serpentières,
Domaine Simon Bize   Now to 2020   16.5
Medium colour. Fragrant nose. Balanced. Cool. Complex. Medium body. Already open. Not a lot of tannin. But balanced and intense, elegant and pure. Very good plus.

Serpentières,
Domaine Michel Ecard   Now to 2020   16.0
Medium to medium-full colour. Ripe nose. Quite concentrated, and with a touch of spice. Medium to medium-full body. Balanced, vigorous, and most attractive. Very good.

Serpentières,
Domaine Giboulot   Now to 2018   14.5
Medium colour. Good attack. The nose is nice and fresh and plump. Medium body. Good acidity. But lacks a little vigour and structure. Quite good plus.

Serpentières,
Domaine Jean-Jacques Girard   Now to 2019   16.0
Medium colour. Good meaty wine on the nose, plummy and vigorous. Medium to medium-full body. Ripe, balanced, long, and stylish. Very good.

Serpentières,
Domaine Patrick Javillier   Now to 2019   15.5
Not a lot of colour. Forward, pretty fresh, fruity, and not unstylish. Not a bit short. Lacks a bit of backbone but long and elegant at the end. Good plus.

Vergelesses,
Domaine Simon Bize   Now to 2019   16.0
Medium colour. Soft, ripe, quite forward nose. Medium body. No great structure but a lovely elegant expression of fruit. Complex too. Long. Very good.

Vergelesses,

Domaine Nicolas Potel   Now to 2020   17.0

Good colour. Plump, succulent nose. Very good fruit. Nice and cool. Medium to medium-full body. Ripe, balanced, classy, positive, and vigorous. Long on the palate. Lovely.

Vergelesses,

Domaine des Terregelesses   Now to 2019   16.0

Medium colour. Very ripe and plump on the nose, but not a bit soupy. On the palate it lacks a little structure, but it is balanced, classy, and vigorous. Long too. Very good.

PERNAND-VERGELESSES

Ile de Vergelesses, Domaine

Chandon de Briailles   Now to 2020   16.5

Medium colour. Elegant, slightly spicy nose. Good grip but a little lean. Medium weight. Lovely ripe fruit. Long and intense. Very good plus.

ALOXE-CORTON

Clos du Chapitre,

Domaine Follin Arbelet   Now to 2019   14.0

Medium-full colour. Slightly stewed on the nose. Better on the palate. Medium to medium-full body. Balanced and reasonably fresh, if not very stylish. Quite good.

Clos des Maréchaudes,

Domaine de Pavillon

(Albert Bichot)   Now to 2018   15.5

Good colour. Classy nose; ripe and generous. Just a touch of oak. Medium body. Fresh. Good fruit. Reasonable depth. No hard edges. Perhaps it should have had a bit more stuffing. But good plus.

Vercots,

Domaine Follin Arbelet   Now to 2018   14.0

Medium-full colour. Rich, chocolate-mocha nose. At first attractive, but astringent on the palate. Decent balance and freshness, but rather common. Quite good at best.

Vercots,

Domaine Tollot Beaut   Now to 2016   13.0

Medium colour. Anonymous but pleasantly fresh nose. Medium body. Slighly attenuated. Nothing very exciting here. Thin, mean finish.

BEAUNE

Beaune du Château, Domaine

Bouchard Père et Fils   Now to 2020   16.0

Medium-full colour. Nicely ripe, roasted nose. A touch of oak. Medium-full body. Good tannins, grip, and depth. Ripe and civilised. Very good. (Note: This was the first wine of the group tasting. I said to myself: "Yum yum. If this wine is any indication, I'm going to enjoy this." I did.)

Aigrots,

Domaine Michel Lafarge   Now to 2018   13.0

Medium-full colour. Lightish, round nose without much bite. Light to medium body. Not much depth here and a suggestion of astringency. Only fair. And a disappointment for this domaine.

Avaux,

Domaine Camille Giroud   Now to 2020   15.0

Medium colour. After an initial touch of reduction of the nose (by no means a long-term defect), the wine expanded out of the glass to become ripe, attractive, and nicely succulent. Medium body. Fresh and balanced, finishing positively. Good.

Boucherottes,

Domaine Louis Jadot   Now to 2020   16.0

Medium-full colour. Ripe, succulent balanced nose. Plenty of depth and style. Medium-full body. Good tannins. Rich and vigorous. Lovely fruit. Long. Very good.

Bressandes,

Domaine Chanson   From 2015   17.5

Full colour. Backward, closed-in nose. Fullish body. Good tannins. Lots of depth. Slight touch of oak. Really profound and with lots of class and dimension. Fine.

Bressandes,
Domaine des Croix   From 2015   17.0

Full colour. Backward nose. Profound, full, and oaky on the palate. Lovely classy fruit. Lots of vigour. Balanced, long, and very good indeed.

Clos des Couchereaux,
Domaine Louis Jadot   From 2015   17.5

Good colour. Lovely nose: complex and profound for a Beaune. Medium-full body. Good oaky base. Very classy, well-balanced fruit. Lovely.

Clos de l'Ecu,
Domaine Faiveley   From 2015   16.0

Good colour. Good weight and depth on the nose here. This is very promising. Medium-full body. Lovely fruit. Just a touch rigid at present, but this will go. Very good.

Clos des Fèves,
Domaine Chanson   Now to 2020   14.0

Medium to medium-full colour. Soft nose. A little anonymous. Medium body. Forward. Balanced, fresh, and quite pretty, but a bit one-dimensional. Quite good.

Clos des Marconnets,
Domaine Chanson   From 2015   15.5

Medium to medium-full colour. Nicely rich and firm on the nose. Medium-full body. Good tannins. Good fruit. Fresh and balanced. Good plus.

Clos des Mouches,
Domaine Drouhin   From 2015   14.5

Medium to medium-full colour. Quite firm, even a bit austere on the nose. There is a slight lack of generosity here. Medium-full body. A bit adolescent. The tannins somewhat unsophisticated. Good grip though. May turn out better than it shows today. Quite good plus. (Note: I liked it better in April in the United States; it was not so severe: 16.0.)

Clos de la Mousse, Domaine
Bouchard Père et Fils   Now to 2020   16.0

Medium to medium-full colour. Lovely, soft, succulent, classy nose. A wine of great charm if no great depth and backbone. Medium body. Not a lot of tannin. Fresh and fragrant. Good follow-through and a positive finish. Quite forward. Very good.

Clos des Ursules,
Domaine Louis Jadot   From 2015   17.5

Good colour. Rich, succulent, classy nose. Good depth. Very good grip. Ripe tannins. Medium-full body. Still a little austere but fine quality. Long and complex.

Coucherias,
Domaine Labet-Dechelette   Now to 2018   13.5

Medium colour. Clean but weedy on the nose. Balanced but rather slight on the palate. Better than usual though. Not bad plus at best.

Grèves, Vigne de l'Enfant Jesus,
Domaine Bouchard Père et Fils   From 2015   17.0

Good colour. Lots of depth and quality on the nose. Fullish body. Rich, fat, spicy, and vigorous. Good ripe tannins. Very fresh and complete. Very good indeed.

Grèves, Domaine des Croix   From 2015   17.0

Medium-full colour. Unforthcoming nose. Fullish, ample, quite oaky, and well-balanced on the palate. Plenty of style, depth, and grip. One of the best of these Beaunes. Long on the palate and very good indeed.

Grèves, Domaine de Montille   Now to 2018   13.5

Medium colour. Ripe stylish nose. Good fruit. Medium to medium-full weight. But a little suave and slight on the palate. Quite forward. No better than decent.

Grèves,
Domaine Tollot-Beaut et Fils   Now to 2020   14.0

Good colour. At first a slight touch of reduction on the nose. This blew off to reveal a medium to medium-full bodied, plump wine with decent balance but no real class. Quite good. (Note: I saw this twice and gave it a better note the second time [16.0], but then the sample was not reduced.)

Marconnets,

Bouchard Père et Fils Now to 2020 16.5

Medium to medium-full colour. Ripe, clean, fragrant nose. Very good style for a Marconnets. Not a blockbuster. Medium body. Elegant. Quite forward. But good intensity and depth, and a positive finish. Very good plus.

Perrières,

Domaine de Montille Now to 2018 13.0

Medium to medium-full colour. Slightly attenuated on the nose, and a bit thin and astringent on the palate. But decent fresh fruit underneath. Not bad. Forward though.

Pertuisots, Domaine des Croix From 2015 17.0

Medium-full colour. Fullish, ample, succulent nose with a touch of oak. Quite full for a Beaune. Rich, even concentrated. Very good grip and very good tannins. Lovely follow-through. Very good indeed.

Pertuisots,

Domaine Devevey Now to 2020 15.5

Medium to medium-full colour. Medium weight, balanced, attractive nose. A good basic. Medium-full body. Ripe, harmonious, fresh, and generous. Easy to enjoy. Good plus.

Sizies, Domaine de Montille Now to 2018 13.0

Medium to medium-full colour. Slightly lean on the nose. Light to medium body. Decent fruit, but not much style and depth. One-dimensional. Only fair.

Teurons,

Château de Chorey-lès-Beaune From 2015 15.0

Medium colour. Attractive fragrant nose. Good stylish fruit here. Medium body. Somewhat gamey. But good grip and no lack of personality. Good, but lacks a little class on the follow-through.

Teurons,

Domaine Rossignol-Trapet From 2014 15.0

Medium colour. Soft, fruity nose. Lacks a bit of grip but ripe enough. Medium to medium-full weight. Balanced. Attractive. There is more depth than seems on the nose. Well-made. Good.

Vignes Franches,

Domaine Latour Now to 2020 15.0

Medium colour. Soft nose. A little anodyne. Medium weight. Ripe, even a bit sweet. Could have done with more grip. Decent style and a positive finish. Good.

Hospices de Beaune, *Premier Cru,*
Cuvée Maurice Drouhin,

Seguin-Manuel From 2015 15.0

Good full colour. Rich, concentrated, plummy nose. Fullish body. Some tannin. No exaggerated oak but a little four-square, even clumsy, on the palate. Lacks fragrance. Good at best.

VOLNAY

Angles, Domaine Louis Boillot See note

Medium-full colour. The wine is corked, but one can see something of substance and depth; ready probably in 2013 or so.

Brouillard,

Domaine Roblet-Monnot See note

Medium-full colour. This is thin, reduced, artificially sweet, and unpleasant. Surely this can't be a representative bottle?

Caillerets,

Domaine Henri Boillot From 2015 16.5

Medium-full colour. Smoky nose. Medium-full body. Fresh and fragrant. Yet with the earthy-oaky flavour apparent on the nose. Long, complex. Very good plus.

Caillerets,

Domaine Bouchard Père et Fils From 2015 15.0

Medium-full colour. A slight smell of bonfires here. Decent attack. Medium weight. A slight lack of freshness and zip on the follow-through, but ripe and the finish is not short. Good.

Caillerets, Domaine Lafarge From 2015 17.0

Medium-full colour. Good depth and plenty of style and dimension here. Medium-full body. Some tannin. Ripe and rich. Good grip. Needs time. Lovely finish. Very good indeed.

Carelle sous la Chapelle,
Domaine Jean-Marc Boillot   Now to 2018   13.0
Medium-full colour. Smoky nose. Ripe and spicy. But only medium-bodied on the palate. Short and thin. Forward.

Champans,
Domaine Marquis d'Angerville   From 2015   17.5
Medium to medium-full colour. Quite closed-in on the nose, but good style and depth evident. Medium-full body. Some tannin. Ripe and succulent. Very good grip. Long and positive. Lovely finish. Fine.

Champans,
Domaine des Comtes Lafon   From 2015   18.0
Medium-full colour. Good depth and plenty of substance on the nose. Ripe and generous. Plenty of vigour. Medium-full body. Balanced, fragrant, poised, complex, and multidimensional. Classic. Fine plus.

Champans,
Domaine de Montille   From 2015   16.0
Medium colour. Some depth on the nose and rather more weight than their Beaune, Grèves. Balanced, complex, long, and vigorous. Classy too. Very good.

Chevrets,
Domaine Henri Boillot   From 2015   16.0
Medium-full colour. Fresh, fragrant, and very Volnay on the nose. Medium-full body. Some tannin. Good grip. Not as rich or as generous as some but no lack of style and depth. Very good.

Clos de la Barre, Maison Jadot   From 2014   15.5
Medium to medium-full colour. Soft, oaky, but slightly bland nose. Ripe though and not a bit unstylish. Medium body. Ripe, forward, attractive, and decently balanced. Easy to enjoy. Good plus.

Clos de la Bousse d'Or,
Domaine de la Pousse d'Or   From 2014   16.5
Good colour. A curious smell of soap at first. Better on the palate. Medium to medium-full body. Succulent and ripe and persistent. Lots of fruit. Fresh. Not a lot of backbone, but attractive and stylish, and with a positive finish. Very good plus.

Clos de la Chapelle,
Maison Nicolas Potel   From 2015   15.5
Medium-full colour. Fresh, quite oaky nose. Good substance, concentration, tannins, and acidity. Backward. No lack of depth. Will get more charming as it evolves. Good plus or better.

Clos de Château des Ducs,   From 2015
Domaine Michel Lafarge   See note
Medium to medium-full colour. Round, ripe nose. At first a touch of reduction which hid the fragrance. Better on the palate. Medium to medium-full body. Good fruit and grip. Positive and balanced. I'd like to see a fresher bottle.

Clos des Chênes,
Domaine Michel Lafarge   From 2015   18.0
Good colour. Splendid nose. Fullish, vigorous, rich, and concentrated. Above all, very classy. Full body. A splendid essence of Pinot Noir fruit. Very complete and very fine at the end. Very lovely. Fine plus.

Clos des Chênes,
Domaine des Comtes Lafon   Now to 2020   15.0
Medium to medium-full colour. Fragrant nose: somewhat ungainly, but this is the youth of the wine. Medium body. Good grip and attractive fruit, but a bit unbalanced. Quite forward. Good at best.

Clos des Ducs, Domaine
Marquis d'Angerville   Now to 2019   14.0
Medium-full colour. Plump nose, but the fruit lacks style, and the wine lacks succulence. Medium body. Slight astringency. Lacks charm. (Note: This came as a big surprise after the results were revealed. Perhaps a bad bottle. But none of us was enthusiastic.)

Clos de la Rougeotte,
Domaine Henri Boillot   Now to 2018   13.5
Medium-full colour. Soft, elegant, very Volnay, fragrant, oaky nose. Somewhat thin on the palate though. A little attenuated and a little sweet. Fair at best.

Fremiets, Domaine d'Angerville From 2015 16.0
Medium-full colour. Attractive, succulent fruit on the nose. Full body. Good tannins. Rich, generous, even fat. Very good finish. Long and stylish. Very good.

Fremiets,
Domaine Henri Boillot From 2014 16.5
Medium to medium-full colour. Ripe, fragrant, and very clean and positive on the nose. Medium-full body. Harmonious, classy, and succulent. Long and very promising. Very good plus.

Robardelle,
Domaine Roblet-Monnot Now to 2018 13.0
Medium to medium-full colour. Not much nose. Medium to medium-full body. Some tannin. Decent balance, but there seems to be a lack of succulence and true Volnay character.

Santenots, Maison Champy Now to 2020 16.0
Good colour. Ripe, succulent, balanced nose. Stylish. Good sustance and depth. Slightly earthy, but quite concentrated. Good follow-through. Very good.

Santenots de Milieu,
Domaine des Comtes Lafon From 2015 18.0
Very good colour. Closed-in on the nose, but very rich and concentrated underneath. Still very young but a very promising wine. Full body. Quite tannic, but the tannins are very ripe. Splendid long, satisfying finish. Fine plus.

Santenots,
Domaine Roblet-Monnot Now to 2018 13.0
Medium-full colour. Rather over-evolved. A touch of volatile acidity. Medium weight. Decent fruit. But it tails off. Forward. Only fair.

Taillepieds,
Domaine de Montille From 2014 17.5
Magnum. Medium-full colour. Fragrant nose. Not very forthcoming at first, but with fine, high-toned fruit. Medium to medium-full body. Elegant and delicious on the palate. Very Volnay. Intense, harmonious, and profound. Lovely.

POMMARD

Epenots,
Maison Camille Giroud From 2015 16.0
Medium to medium-full colour. The tannins are a little earthy, but there is very good fruit on the nose. Medium-full body. Good grip. Ripe, succulent, and classy. Lots of depth. Very good.

Fremiers,
Domaine Louis Boillot From 2016 17.5
Fullish colour. Full, rich, firm, and backward on the nose. Full and tannic. Backward but profound on the palate. Very fine grip. Lots of dimension. Fine.

Jarollières,
Domaine Jean-Marc Boillot From 2014 14.5
Medium to medium-full colour. Ripe, plump nose. Fullish but not aggressive. Medium-full body. Attractive balanced fruit, if at the end, a bit crude. Quite good plus.

Grands Epenots,
Domaine Michel Gaunoux From 2014 14.5
Good colour. Full, ample but jammy nose. Fullish body. Seems a bit stewed. Good tannins and decent acidity. But no flair. Quite good plus at best.

Pézerolles,
Domaine de Montille From 2014 17.0
Good colour. Ripe, full, assertive fruit on the nose. Medium to medium-full body. Fragrant on the palate. Good tannins. Very good grip. Long, and stylish and complex for a Pommard. Very good indeed.

Rugiens,
Domaine Bouchard Père et Fils From 2014 14.0
Medium to medium-full colour. Slightly bland, though there is some substance here on the nose. Medium to medium-full body. Decent fruit. Slight astringency. Not unstylish. But it lacks grip. Quite good.

Rugiens,
Domaine Michel Gaunoux From 2015 16.5
Good nose. Richer and more tannic on the nose than their Grands Epenots. Cleaner and rather

better on the palate. Fullish body. Good grip. Plenty of rich fruit and a good, classy follow-through. Very good plus.

Rugiens, Domaine de Montille   From 2015 . 17.5
Good colour. Full, rich, meaty nose. Much more to it than the Pézerolles. Fullish body. Good oak. Some tannin and very well put together. Very good grip. Lots of dimension and class. Fine.

Rugiens, Domaine du Pavillon,
(Albert Bichot)   From 2015   17.0
Medium-full colour. Good depth and class on the nose. Medium-full body. Ripe tannins. Plenty of depth. Lots of style. Long and complex. Very good indeed.

NUITS-SAINT-GEORGES

Argillas,
Domaine Chauvenet-Chopin   From 2014   16.0
Medium colour. Soft, gently oaky, seductive, ripe nose. Medium body. A succulent, charming wine with no hard edges. Quite forward. Very good.

Boudots,
Domaine Jean Grivot   From 2017   18.0
Good colour. Very lovely full, rich, profound nose. Very gently oaky. Fullish body. Elegant, especially for a Nuits-Saint-Georges. Lots and lots of depth and concentration. Fine plus.

Boudots,
Domaine Louis Jadot   From 2015   18.0
Fine colour. Lovely rich, concentrated, classy nose. Fullish. Very ripe tannins. Potentially velvety. Very lovely, rich, harmonious fruit on the palate. Very Vosne-ish. Long. Fine plus.

Boudots,
Domaine Gérard Mugneret   From 2014   15.0
Medium-full colour. Soft, oaky nose. Perhaps a slight lack of grip. Medium body. A bit bland. Pretty fruit, but forward and a little too easy to drink at this stage. It lacks real depth. Good at best.

Bousselottes,
Domaine Jean Chauvenet   From 2017   17.5
Medium-full colour. Firm, rich nose. Really very fine fruit here. Fullish body. Good tannins. Very good grip. This needs time but it has vigour and lots of class. Lovely finish. Fine.

Cailles, Domaine Chevillon   From 2015   17.0
Full colour. Very rich and ripe on the nose. Plenty of substance and depth. Medium-full body. Good fruit and a long positive aftertaste. Very good indeed.

Chaignots, Domaine Faiveley   From 2015   17.5
Fullish colour. Ample, concentrated, quite full nose. Quite firm. Lots of depth. Lots of finesse for a Nuits-Saint-Georges. Fullish. Some tannin. Rich and ripe. Very good grip. Classy and vigorous. Long. Fine.

Chaignots,
Domaine Alain Michelot   From 2015   16.5
Full colour. Still quite tight on the nose. Rich and fullish. A bit adolescent but fragrant, balanced, ripe, and full of fruit. Very good depth and complexity. Classy too. Very good plus.

Chaignots,
Domaine Georges Mugneret   From 2015   18.0
Fine colour. Good firm nose. Rich and full and quite sturdy. Very Nuits-Saint-Georges. Plenty of depth. Medium-full body. Rich, concentrated, and oaky on the palate. Lots of ripe, succulent fruit. Long and harmonious. Most attractive. Very seductive. Fine plus.

Clos des Argillières, Domaine
Michelle et Patrice Rion   From 2015   16.0
Medium colour. Rich, backward nose. Good style. Medium-full body. Ripe tannins. Balanced. Nice and fresh and classy. Good grip. Finishes well.

Clos de l'Arlot,
Domaine de l'Arlot   From 2013   16.0
Medium colour. Some development. Soft and classy on the nose. Medium body. A little tannin. Soft and fragrant on the palate. No hard edges. An attractive wine which will come forward soon.

Clos de Fôrets-Saint-Georges,

Domaine de l'Arlot   From 2015   16.0

Medium to medium-full colour. Chunky nose but no lack of style. Medium-full body. More sophisticated on the palate than on the nose. Some tannin. Good grip. Shows well.

Clos de la Maréchale, Domaine

Jacques Frédéric Mugnier   From 2015   17.0

Full colour. Remarkably stylish, fragrant nose. It really has a Chambolle touch. Medium-full body. Good, plump attack. Not quite the grip and flair on the follow-through for fine, but long and potentially silky-smooth.

Clos des Porrets-Saint-Georges,

Domaine Henri Gouges   From 2017   17.5

Full colour. A little closed-in on the nose at first; not as approachable as their Pruliers. Better on the palate. Medium-full body. Good grip. Attactive, plummy fruit. Long, complex, and classy. Fine.

Damodes,

Domaine Jean Chauvenet   From 2015   17.5

Medium-full colour. Quite firm but good depth on the nose. Medium-full body. Good tannins. Good grip. Meaty and muscular, but classy and quite profound. Very good fruit and a long positive finish. Fine.

Murgers,

Domaine Méo-Camuzet   From 2015   18.0

Medium-full colour. Full, ample, ripe nose, with a touch of oak. Medium-full body. Definitely oaky on the palate. Ripe and succulent. Very fine grip. Not a blockbuster but a very elegant wine with a lovely finish. Fine plus.

Perrières,

Domaine Jean Chauvenet   From 2016   18.0

Full colour. Ripe, very rich, abundant, meaty nose. Full body. Some tannin. Very superior fruit here, pretty well of *grand cru* quality. Needs time, but long, vigorous, and very promising. Fine plus.

Pruliers, Domaine Chevillon   From 2016   18.0

Medium to medium-full colour. Rich, full, and meaty on the nose. Lots of fruit here. Fullish body. Very good tannins. Very fine grip. Vigorous, rich, and opulent. Long on the palate. Fine plus.

Pruliers,

Domaine Henri Gouges   From 2017   18.0

Full colour. Full, ample, rich, and positive on the nose. Very lovely fruit here. Fullish body. This has real depth and concentration and not a bit of the habitual Nuits brutality. Fine plus. (Note: We had a less exciting bottle at the group tasting.)

Pruliers, Domaine Jean Grivot   From 2015   16.5

Medium-full colour. Soft, stylish nose, rather more advanced than some. Medium to medium-full colour. Ripe, balanced, and attractive. Lovely finish. For reasonably early drinking but a most enjoyable wine.

Les Saint-Georges,

Domaine Thibaut Liger-Belair   From 2014   17.5

Medium-full colour. Refined, fragrant, classy nose. Not the volume of some of these middle Nuits-Saint-Georges, but has medium to medium-full body and lovely succulent fruit and very good grip. Fine.

Vaucrains,

Domaine Jean Chauvenet   From 2014   17.0

Fullish colour. Closed-in, oaky nose. Medium-full body. Attractive, succulent, balanced fruit. Not a blockbuster but with plenty of flair.

Vaucrains, Domaine Chevillon   From 2014   17.0

Medium to medium-full colour. Soft, round, balanced, ripe, quite forward nose. Medium-full body. Fragrant, fresh, elegant, and complex. Will evolve sooner than some. Very good indeed.

VOSNE-ROMANÉE

Premier Cru,

Domaine Gros Frère et Soeur   From 2015   15.5

Medium-full colour. Plump balanced nose, but lacks a little class. Medium-full body. Decent fruit. Good grip. Vigorous but not very elegant on the palate. Good plus at best.

Beaux Monts,
Domaine Clavelier From 2015 18.0
Medium-full colour. Good rich, fat, creamy, gently oaky nose. On the palate, medium-full body. No hard edges, potentially. Ripe, round, fresh, and attractive. A seductive wine. Long on the palate. Fine plus.

Beaux Monts,
Domaine Jean Grivot From 2017 18.5
Good colour. Closed-in on the nose, but very elegant and very complex. Full body. Brilliant fruit. Not a blockbuster but all the more subtle as a result. Very harmonious. Real finesse. Very fine indeed.

Beaux Monts,
Domaine Cecile Tremblay From 2015 18.5
Fullish colour. Fresh, firm, closed-in nose. Profound and classy. Fullish body. Very lovely concentrated, vigorous, ripe fruit on the palate. Very good grip. This has length, depth, and high-quality. Very fine.

Brulées,
Domaine Clavelier From 2014 See note
Medium-full colour. Medium-full weight. The wine was somewhat corky but nevertheless, though certainly very good, not up to the standard of his Beaumonts.

Brulées, Domaine Michel Gros From 2014 17.0
Medium-full colour. Accessible, fresh, fruity nose. Not a blockbuster. Medium-full body. Only a modicum of tannin. Crisp and ripe and attractive. But not as profound or as intense as some. Very good indeed.

Brulées,
Domaine Méo-Camuzet From 2015 18.5
Full colour. Rich, oaky, substantial, and profound on the nose. Medium-full weight. Ample, ripe, rich, and harmonious. Complex and classy. Long. Very fine.

Chaumes, Domaine Lamarche From 2015 18.5
Medium-full colour. Ripe, rich, profound, oaky nose. Round, ample, and succulent on the palate. Fullish. Vigorous. A lovely, intense, classy, understated wine. Very fine at the end.

Chaumes,
Domaine Méo-Camuzet From 2017 17.5
Very good colour. Full, rich, ample, oaky nose. Full body. Very good tannins. Lots of grip and energy. Plenty of concentrated, plummy fruit. Like the nose, quite oaky on the palate, but not excessively so. Fine.

Clos des Réas,
Domaine Michel Gros From 2015 18.0
Fine colour. Very lovely, harmonious fruit on nose and palate. Medium-full body. Excellent grip. Concentrated and potentially very smooth and silky. Lots of subtlety and dimension. Very long and very lovely. Fine plus.

Malconsorts,
Domaine Cathiard From 2015 18.5
Fullish colour. High-toned nose. Vibrant, fragrant, and intense. Some oak. Medium-full body. Ripe, rich, ample, and succulent. Long, classy, and very seductive. Very fine.

Malconsorts, Domaine du
Clos Frantin, (Albert Bichot) From 2015 17.5
Medium colour. Most attractive fruit on the nose. Ripe and succulent. Medium to medium-full body. Very good grip. Not a blockbuster but vigorous, intense, very classy, and very harmonious. Fine.

Malconsorts,
Domaine Lamarche From 2015 18.5
Full colour. Rich, profound, classy, gently oaky nose. Fullish body. Firm. Closed-in. Intense, long, and profound. Lovely finish. Very fine.

Malconsorts,
Domaine de Montille From 2013 16.0
Medium colour. Fragrant nose. Ripe and elegant. Soft and subtle. Only medium-bodied. Good fruit, but not the intensity and drive of the wines above. Yet a very attractive stylish wine. Very good.

Orveaux, Domaine Cathiard From 2015 18.0
Full colour. Open, round, rich, oaky nose. Medium-full body. Succulent, ripe, rich, and oaky on the palate. A very seductive wine with good supporting energy. Fine plus.

Reignots, Domaine Cathiard   From 2015 18.0
Medium to medium-full colour. Fresh, succulent, and oaky on the nose. Fullish. Quite meaty. Ample and vigorous. Good intensity and very good grip. Classy. Fine plus.

Reignots, Domaine Grivot   From 2015 17.5
Fullish colour. Firm, rich, backward, profound nose. This is very lovely and very complete. Splendid intense, ripe, multidimensional fruit. Fullish body. Long, complex, and classy. At first I was very complimentary (18.5), but it evolved fast in the glass.

**Reignots, Domaine
du Vicomte de Liger-Belair**   From 2014 17.5
Medium to medium-full colour. Attractive, plump, oaky nose. But only medium weight on the palate. Ripe. Good acidity. Plenty of length and finesse. Not great, but fine.

Suchots, Domaine Grivot   From 2017 18.5
Fullish colour. Firm; backward nose. Rather tight at present. Quite a substantial wine. Good tannins. Very good grip. Plenty of ripe fruit, vigour, and intensity. Got better and better in the glass. Every time I went back to it, I marked it higher and higher.

Suchots, Maison Louis Jadot   From 2016 18.5
Fine colour. Full, backward, and concentrated on nose and palate. A very fine, cool, structured wine. Very long. Very complete. Lots of wine here. Lovely finish. *Grand cru* quality.

CHAMBOLLE-MUSIGNY

**Village AC, Domaine
Comte Georges de Vogüé**   From 2014 17.0
Medium-full colour. Lovely, fullish, fragrant, elegant nose: archetypal Chambolle-Musigny. Splendid fruit on the palate. Medium body. Great charm. Lovely classy finish. Very good indeed.

**Amoureuses,
Domaine Amiot-Servelle**   From 2013 13.5
Full colour. Both oaky and austere on the nose. Medium body. Good, rich but rather artificial fruit, and a lack of grip, concentration, and succulence. There seems to be a hollow in the middle of this wine, and a lack of Pinot flair. Disappointing for what it is.

**Amoureuses,
Domaine Francois Bertheau**   From 2014 16.5
Medium-full colour. Good depth on the nose. Quite firm. A little closed. Medium to medium-full body. Stylish. Good intensity and vigour, but not quite as much as there could have been with this *climat*. Very good plus.

**Amoureuses,
Maison Alex Gambal**   From 2015 17.0
Medium-full colour. Quite full, intense, fragrant nose. This has good depth and high-quality. Fullish body. Not quite as rich, concentrated, and elegant as it could be on the palate, but very good indeed.

**Amoureuses,
Domaine Robert Groffier**   From 2018 18.0
Full colour. Backward, concentrated, intense, and fragrant on the nose. Fullish body. Firm, profound, very lovely, classy fruit. Complex and multidimensional. Not a bit soupy, which Groffier's wines can be sometimes. Lovely finish. Fine plus.

**Amoureuses, Domaine
Jacques-Frédéric Mugnier**   From 2015 18.5
Good colour. Stylish, persistent, and complex on the nose. Very lovely classy fruit here. Medium-full body. Soft; elegant, long, and lovely. Archetypal Amoureuses.

**Amoureuses,
Domaine Georges Roumier**   From 2020 18.5
Firm, youthful colour. Very fine, closed-in, profound nose. Classy fruit. Some oak. Full body. Quite some tannin. Very good acidity. Very fine fruit. Still very much an infant but potentially very fine.

**Amoureuses,
Domaine Hervé Roumier**   From 2014 16.5
Medium-full colour. Fragrant nose. Balanced, fruity, charming, and with good intensity. Medium to medium-full body. Not quite classy or complex enough for a top Amoureuses, but very good plus. Quite forward.

Amoureuses, Domaine

Comte Georges de Vogûé   From 2016   18.5

Full colour. Quite closed-in on the nose, but clearly very profound. Fullish body. Some tannin. Fresh, youthful, vigorous, and classy. Splendid quality. Very fine.

Charmes,

Domaine Ghislaine Barthod   From 2014   16.5

Fullish colour. Backward, but potentially rich and profound on the nose. Medium to medium-full body. Plenty of class. Very good stylish fruit. I would have liked just a little more zip, but this going to be a very seductive wine.

Charmes,

Michelle et Patrice Rion   From 2015   18.0

Fullish colour. Very lovely, slightly austere fruit on the nose. Profound and classy on the palate. Firm and fullish in body. Marvelous, intense fruit. Very long. Fine plus.

Combe d'Orveaux,

Domaine Taupenot-Merme   From 2014   16.0

Medium-full colour. A little bit more protective sulphur here than in most of these wines, which makes it more difficult to taste. Medium to medium-full body. Good fruit. Slightly foursquare at present, but decent grip; even class, and it finishes better than it starts. Very good.

Cras,

Domaine Ghislaine Barthod   From 2015   18.5

Medium-full colour. Soft, ripe, black cherry–flavoured nose. Not a blockbuster. Medium-full body. Rich, round, intense, and very lovely. Really classy. Very long and complex. Very fine.

Cras,

Domaine Georges Roumier   From 2017   18.5

Fullish colour. Ripe, quite firm, fullish, and spicy on the nose. Fullish body. Rich, some tannin, and with very good grip and reserves behind it. Plenty of class. Got better and better in the glass. Very fine.

Fremières,

Domaine Digioia-Royer   From 2015   16.5

Medium-full colour. Succulent, fat, ripe nose. Medium-full body. Very good style. Ripe tan-

nins and very good grip. Long. Fresh. Ample. Very good plus.

Fuées,

Domaine Ghislaine Barthod   From 2015   18.5

Fullish colour. Backward but profound and classy on the nose. Fullish body. This is very lovely. Complex, backward, and oozing with fruit. Very long and seductive at the end. Very fine.

Fuées, Domaine

Jacques Frédéric Mugnier   From 2015   18.0

Fullish colour. Rich, fat, profound, complete, and classy on the nose. A very ample, rich, succulent wine. Fullish body. Very good grip. Stylish and lovely.

Groseilles,

Domaine Digioia-Royer   From 2014   14.5

Medium-full colour. Muscular nose, lacking a little of the class of most of these Chambolles. Medium-full body. Good substance and balance but a little tough and ungainly. Quite good plus.

Gruenchers,

Domaine Digioia-Royer   From 2015   17.0

Medium-full colour. Succulent, ripe, and fruity on the nose. Medium-full body. Ample and plump with good acidity. Very good length, intensity, and style. Very good indeed.

Gruenchers, Domaine Fourrier   From 2015   17.0

Medium-full colour. Firm but classy and balanced on the nose. Medium-full body. Succulent and elegant. Harmonious, long, and classy. Very good indeed.

Noirots, Domaine Arlaud   From 2013   16.0

Medium-full colour. Ripe, abundant nose, but quite open and evolved. Medium body. Soft and forward. Charming and attractive. Fresh at the end. Very good.

MOREY-SAINT-DENIS

***Premier Cru*, Domaine Dujac**   From 2014   17.5

Medium to medium-full colour. Stylish, ample, fragrant, and succulent on the nose. Fullish.

Good tannins. Very good acidity. Ripe and rich. Elegant, long, and complex. Fine.

Blanchards,
Maison Frédéric Magnien   From 2015   16.0

Fullish colour. Not too oaky on the nose. Fresh fruit. Very good acidity. But slightly rigid on the palate. Medium to medium-full body. Ripe, succulent, fresh, and, if it wasn't for the oak, long and stylish. Very good. Better still if it softens up satisfactorily.

Chezeaux, Domaine Arlaud   From 2014   15.5

Fullish colour. Ripe and rich on the nose. Succulent and fat. Medium-full body. It doesn't have the class of the Dujac above, but it is balanced and fruity. Good plus.

Clos de la Bussière,
Domaine Georges Roumier   From 2016   17.0

Medium-full colour. Rich nose: plump and attractive. Medium body. Fresh, ripe, and accessible. No hard edges. Very good, classy finish. Very good indeed.

Millandes, Domaine Arlaud   From 2014   16.0

Medium-full colour. Ripe, soft, and fragrant on the nose. Medium to medium-full body. Fresh, balanced, succulent, and attractive. Long and positive. But very good rather than great.

Millandes, Domaine Serafin   From 2016   16.0

Fullish colour. This is a bit tight and closed-in. On the nose a little four-square. Medium-full body. Some tannin. Good grip. Underneath there is classy fruit. Needs time. Doesn't sing today, but very good, if not better still. All in good time.

Riotte,
Domaine Taupenot-Merme   See note

Medium-full colour. A lot of reduction here. So much so that I couldn't mark it. Some colleagues marked it very good. I'll wait and see.

Ruchots, Jean-Louis et Didier Amiot,
Domaine Pierre Amiot   From 2014   17.0

Medium colour. Ripe, soft, and fragrant on the nose. Medium body. Gently oaky. Balanced and stylish. Good intensity and finesse, if by no means a blockbuster. Forward but not short and very good indeed.

GEVREY-CHAMBERTIN

Village AC, Vieilles Vignes,
Domaine Bernard Dugat-Py   From 2015   16.0

Full colour. Firm, rich nose. Still a bit closed. Lots of depth. A bit austere at present, but the tannins are very ripe. Plenty of fruit. Harmonious and quite concentrated, if without the elegance of a *premier cru*. Very good.

Cazetiers,
Domaine Bruno Clair   From 2016   17.5

Medium to medium-full colour. Fresh nose. Plenty of depth and class here. But quite closed. Medium to medium-full body. Intense. Very good grip. A cerebral rather than an exotic wine. But long and with lots of finesse. Fine.

Cazetiers, Domaine Faiveley   From 2016   17.5

Good colour. Full, slightly closed-in nose. Medium-full body. Very lovely fruit on the palate. Firm and energetic. Quite oaky in a slightly rigid way at present. Very good grip. Rich. Long. Fine.

Cazetiers,
Domaine Armand Rousseau   From 2016   17.0

Medium colour. Balanced, classy nose. Good depth. Attractive fruit. Medium to medium-full body. Ripe, plump. Very good indeed.

Cazetiers, Domaine Serafin   From 2016   17.0

Medium to medium-full colour. Soft, ripe, stylish, gently oaky nose. Medium to medium-full body. Balanced, succulent, long, and complex. Elegant all the way through. Very good indeed.

Champeaux, Domaine Fourrier   From 2015   16.0

Medium to medium-full colour. Not a blockbuster but balanced and stylish on the nose. Medium-full body. Ripe and balanced. Fresh and complex. Long and positive. Very good.

Champeaux,
Domaine Denis Mortet   From 2016   17.0

Medium-full colour. Lovely, plump, classy nose. Gently oaky. Medium-full body. Very rich—it's almost sweet. Very good grip. Long and stylish. Very good indeed.

Cherbaudes,
Domaine Louis Boillot   From 2015   15.5
Medium-full colour. Good fruit if slightly four-square on the nose. Medium-full body. Quite rich. Nicely fresh. Decent grip and class. Finishes positively. Good plus.

Clos Prieur,
Domaine Jean et Jean-Louis Trapet   From 2015   See note
Medium to medium-full colour. Slightly reduced on the nose. Medium to medium-full body. It was difficult to see the class here. No lack of substance and fruit though. The group marked it "quite good plus" (14.5).

Clos-Saint-Jacques,
Domaine Bruno Clair   From 2017   18.5
Very good colour. Very lovely nose: slightly cooler and less seductive as well as marginally less oaky than Rousseau's example. Equally impressive. Full body. Excellent tannins. Lots of finesse and very, very subtle and complex. Marvelous finish. Very fine.

Clos-Saint-Jacques,
Domaine Sylvie Esmonin   From 2016   18.5
Full colour. Very, very rich and concentrated on the nose. Some oak. Lovely fruit. This is hugely seductive. The fruit is almost over-ripe. Fullish body. Excellent grip. Very fine.

Clos-Saint-Jacques,
Domaine Fourrier   From 2015   17.0
Medium to medium-full colour. Rich, gently oaky, velvety nose. Medium to medium-full body. Fresh, attractive, and balanced, if without the volume and intensity of the other Clos-Saint-Jacques. Very good indeed.

Clos-Saint-Jacques,
Domaine Louis Jadot   From 2017   18.5
Medium to medium-full colour. Subtle and classy on the nose. Understated and multidimensional. Medium to medium-full body. Har-

monious, complex, classy, and very long and lovely. *Grand cru* quality. Very fine.

Clos-Saint-Jacques,
Domaine Armand Rousseau   From 2017   18.5
Good colour. Splendid nose. Very lovely rich, concentrated, perfumed fruit. The tannins underneath are very distinguished. Full body. Very complex and classy. The follow-through is ample, vigorous, and very subtle. *Grand cru* quality, unmistakably. Very fine. Note: The group as a whole overwhelmingly (by a good point and more out of 20) scored the Rousseau first among the five Clos-Saint-Jacques.

Clouseau,
Domaine Drouhin-Larose   From 2015   15.5
Medium-full colour. Slightly four-square on the nose. But ripe and fullish. Medium-full body. Spicy and vigorous. Good grip. Not the greatest finesse but the finish is positive. Good plus.

Combottes, Domaine Dujac   From 2015   17.5
Good colour. Lovely nose: ripe and sophisticated and complex. Quite backward and austere. Fullish body. Quite structured. Very good tannins. Lovely fruit. Long. Fine.

Corbeaux, Domaine Clavelier   From 2015   14.0
Medium to medium-full colour. Ripe, abundant, slightly tarty fruit on the nose. Medium to medium-full body. A suggestion of astringency. Plump fruit. Decent balance. But slightly pedestrian. Quite good.

Corbeaux,
Domaine Denis Bachelet   See note
Medium-full colour. Rather reduced on the nose and, as a result, rather astringent on the palate. Medium to medium-full body. Judgment reserved.

Crapillot,
Domaine Humbert Frères   From 2015   15.5
Medium-full colour. Full nose. Rich, fat, and backward, with a touch of mocha. Medium-full body. A muscular wine. But it has good grip and is ripe and vigorous, if not with the greatest class. Positive at the end. Good plus.

Estounelles Saint-Jacques,
Domaine Humbert Frères From 2015 16.0
Medium to medium-full colour. Soft, plump nose. Medium-full body. Ripe, full of fruit, attractive, and well-balanced. Quite forward. Not the greatest depth but very good.

Evocelles,
Domaine de la Vougeraie From 2015 17.5
Very good colour. Lovely nose. Not a bit chunky. Rich and potentially velvety. Very ripe fruit. Fragrant and succulent. Medium-full body. Very juicy and very elegant. Long on the palate. Unexpectedly elegant. Fine.

Fonteny, Domaine Serafin From 2015 14.0
Medium to medium-full colour. Plump nose, without the greatest of class. Medium-full body. Decent balance but the fruit is a little common. Quite good at best. (Note: Others liked it better than I.)

Lavaux Saint-Jacques,
Maison Chanson See note
Medium to medium-full colour. Very reduced on the nose, and virtually undrinkable on the palate. Seems only medium weight. Judgment deferred.

Lavaux Saint-Jacques,
Domaine Maume From 2016 16.0
Medium to medium-full colour. Somewhat four-square on the nose. But with decently plump fruit. Medium to medium-full body. Good fruit, harmony, and depth, and it got classier as it developed. Very good.

Lavaux Saint-Jacques,
Domaine Denis Mortet From 2016 17.0
Medium-full colour. Ripe, rich, gently oaky nose. Most attractive. Medium-full body. Ripe tannins. Good grip. Plenty of fruit. Long and harmonious at the end. Very good indeed.

Petite Chapelle,
Domaine Humbert Frères From 2015 15.0
Medium-full colour. Smells a little of peppermint. Medium to medium-full body. Decent fruit, though it could be richer. And the follow-through is decent. But it's only good at best.

Petite Chapelle,
Domaine Rossignol-Trapet From 2015 16.0
Medium colour. Some development. Soft, plump, elegant nose. Medium body. Ripe, stylish, and harmonious, though by no means a blockbuster. Long on the palate. Very good.

Poissenot,
Domaine Humbert Frères From 2015 15.5
Medium-full colour. Spicy and a bit dry on the nose: the wood tannins to the fore. But good depth underneath. Medium to medium-full body. Slightly four-square on the attack, but better on the follow-through. A burly wine, but that is Gevrey. Good plus.

Grands Crus
CORTON

Corton,
Domaine Bonneau du Martray From 2017 17.5
Good colour. The nose is a little hidden at first. But there is plenty of good wine here. Good weight. Ripe, rich, stylish, and with very good grip. Fine.

Corton, Domaine Follin-Arbelet From 2014 13.0
Medium colour. Good, firm, mocha-flavoured nose. Medium body. A bit confected on the palate. Some grip, but the finish lacks elegance.

Corton, Domaine Tollot Beaut Drink soon 10.0
Medium colour. Earthy, ungainly nose. Medium weight. Coarse and stewed. Not for me. (Note: Others were more enthusiastic.)

Château Corton-Grancey,
Domaine Louis Latour From 2013 13.0
Medium colour. Quite evolved. Soft, fruity nose. Not a lot of substance or depth. Forward. Medium-bodied. Sweet, indeed jammy. An unstylish wine yet quite fresh at the end. Not bad.

Le Corton,
Domaine Bouchard Père et Fils From 2015 15.0
Medium to medium-full colour. Bland but fruity nose. Better on the palate. Decent grip and fragrance. Positive and really quite long.

Good fruit. Yet not the depth and class of a real *grand cru*.

Corton, Bressandes,
Domaine Chandon de Briailles   From 2016   17.5
Medium colour. Lovely nose. Really very classy fruit. Balanced and complex. Medium-full body. Splendid intensity on the palate. Lovely finish. This is most impressive. Fine.

Corton, Bressandes,
Domaine Follin Arbelet   From 2013   13.0
Medium-full colour. Round nose. Good ripe if somewhat anonymous fruit. Medium body. Lacks grip. One-dimensional and very forward, especially for a Corton.

Corton, Bressandes,
Domaine Senard   From 2015   16.5
Just a little more colour than their Paulands. More weight on the nose too, and very good fruit. Ripe, harmonious, classy, and complex, but only medium to medium-full bodied. Finishes well. Very good plus.

Corton, Bressandes,
Domaine Tollot-Beaut et Fils   From 2015   15.0
Good colour. Full, meaty nose, with some oak noticable. Medium to medium-full body. Decent fruit. But a little artisanal for a *grand cru*. Good at best.

Corton, Clos des
Cortons-Faiveley,
Domaine Faiveley   From 2015   17.5
Medium-full colour. Classy nose. Concentration and grip here, and no lack of depth. Medium-full body. Fresh. Very good grip. Profound and classy, complex and vigorous. Fine.

Corton, Clos des
Marechaudes, Domaine du
Pavillon (Albert Bichot)   From 2015   16.0
Very good colour. Rich, concentrated, oaky nose. Lots of dimension here. Medium-full body. Good ripe tannins. A touch earthy but sophisticated enough. Ripe. Good grip. Finishes well. Very good.

Corton, Clos du Roi,
Domaine de Montille   From 2016   18.5
Medium-full colour. Quite a firm nose. Lots of depth and quality. Ripe, succulent, and very rich. Rather more opulent than the Pougets. Full body. Lots of depth. Excellent fruit at the end. Very fine.

Corton, Clos du Roi,
Domaine de Vougeraie   From 2016   18.0
Medium-full colour. Fresh nose. Classy and profound. Medium-full body. This is a serious wine, unlike, sadly, the majority of these Cortons. Rich and concentrated. Very good grip and vigour. But above all classy. Fine plus.

Corton, Hautes-Mourottes,
Domaine d'Ardhuy   From 2015   16.5
Good colour. Ripe, firm, gently oaky nose. Fullish body. Somewhat rough and ready, but fine fruit underneath. Rich, balanced, very good grip. Long. Very good plus.

Corton, Paulands,
Domaine Senard   From 2014   15.5
Lightish colour. Pleasant ripe fruit on the nose. But surely Cortons should be bigger and more concentrated than this? Medium body. Elegant and balanced, classy and stylish nonetheless, with good energy at the end. Good plus.

Corton, Pougets,
Domaine Louis Jadot   From 2017   18.0
Good colour. Closed-in nose. Very fresh, lovely black cherry fruit. Full body, firm, and backward; even quite sturdy. Lots of vigour. Very good tannins and very good grip. This has real depth. Fine plus.

Corton, Pougets,
Domaine de Montille   From 2016   18.0
Medium-full colour. Full, rich, somewhat meaty-earthy nose. Full body. Ripe tannins. Quite a sizeable wine. Still a bit closed. Very good grip. Intense and classy on the follow-through. Long. Fine plus.

Corton, Rognets,

Domaine Taupenot-Merme   From 2014   13.0

Medium-full colour. Some fruit here on the nose, though there is lack of elegance. Medium to medium-full body. A little coarse and stewed. Only fair.

Corton, Rognets,

Maison Camille Giroud   From 2015   15.0

Medium-full colour. Soft, fresh, fruity, and balanced on the nose. Medium-full body. Not the greatest depth and style (for a *grand cru*), but ample, harmonious, and fresh at the end. Good.

Hospices de Beaune, Corton,
Cuvée Dr. Peste,

Pierre-Yves Colin   From 2016   17.5

Full colour. A big, tannic example. Classy fruit and very good grip. Full-bodied. Good tannins. Lots of energy. Fine quality.

ECHÉZEAUX AND GRANDS-ECHÉZEAUX

Echézeaux,

Domaine Robert Arnoux   From 2018   17.5

Full colour. Rich, quite tannic nose. This is going to need time. Fullish body. Lots of depth and energy. High-class fruit. At present a little adolescent but fine quality.

Echézeaux,

Domaine Jacques Cacheux   From 2016   17.0

Full colour. Rich, full, slightly solid nose. Full-bodied and fat on the palate. Some tannin. Some oak. Somewhat four-square but nice and ripe and rich underneath. Lots of energy. Very good indeed.

Echézeaux,

Maison Alex Gambal   From 2016   17.5

Fullish colour. Good cool, rich, classy, Pinot nose. Good energy in a spicy sort of way. Medium-full body. Ripe tannins. Nicely fragrant. Elegant. Long. Fine.

Echézeaux, Domaine Grivot   From 2016   17.0

Full colour. A little reduced on the nose. At first I was not very impressed, but it just got better and better in the glass as the reduction blew off.

Fullish. Very good grip. Ripe tannins. Increasingly classy. Very good indeed, perhaps better.

Echézeaux,

Domaine Lamarche   From 2016   18.0

Medium-full colour. Good vigour and intensity on the nose. Lovely fruit, if not a blockbuster. Round, ripe, succulent, and oaky on the palate. Fruity and abundant. Good grip. Long, complex, and classy. Fine plus.

Echézeaux, Maison Potel   From 2016   17.0

Fullish colour. Soft, elegant, oaky, fruity nose. Not the greatest depth and complexity, but attractive fruit here and quite fresh with it. Positive finish and no lack of finesse. Very good indeed.

Echézeaux,

Domaine Emmanuel Rouget   From 2015   16.5

Medium colour. Soft, rich fruit on the nose. Attractive, if with no real distinction. No undue oak though. Ripe, medium-full body. Soft and sexy. Sweet and seductive. Not a lot of tannin. Fresh. Long on the palate. Quite forward. Very good plus.

Grands-Echézeaux, Domaine
du Clos Frantin (Albert Bichot)   From 2016   18.5

Medium-full colour. Profound nose. Slightly more structured and a little more hidden than their Clos de Vougeot. Fullish body. Excellent fruit. Intense and virile and very, very lovely. Very fine.

Grands-Echézeaux,

Domaine Gros Frère et Soeur   From 2016   15.5

Full colour. Sturdy nose. Full, oaky, and quite high in volatile acidity. Better as it evolved. Not too four-square but somewhat adolescent, even medicinal at present. It lacks the generosity of the vintage. Odd. Very good plus at best.

Grands-Echézeaux,

Domaine Mongeard-Mugneret   From 2014   14.0

Fullish colour. Slightly rustic nose. Medium-full body. Ripe but not much depth, let alone sophistication or concentration. Forward. Quite good at best.

Grands-Echézeaux,

Maison Nicolas Potel   See note

Fullish colour. Rich, fat, and concentrated on the nose. Medium-full body. Some tannin. An altogether bigger wine than his Echézeaux, but as it was a little corked it was difficult to judge definitively. To be retasted.

CLOS DE VOUGEOT

Clos de Vougeot, Domaine

du Clos Frantin (Albert Bichot)   From 2016   18.0

Medium-full colour. Fine, ripe, rich, generous, gently oaky nose. Fullish body. Finely ripe fruit. Excellent grip. Very lovely complexity here. Real class and depth. Lovely finish. Fine plus.

Clos de Vougeot,

Domaine Jean Grivot   From 2020   18.5

Very good colour. Full, classy but backward nose. Similar palate. Some tannin. Very good grip. This is going to need time. Really profound and concentrated though, and with real finesse. Very fine indeed.

Clos de Vougeot,

Domaine Michel Gros   From 2016   18.0

Medium-full colour. Ripe, quite oaky nose. Good depth. Fullish, balanced, vigorous, and classy. Delicious fruit. Lovely finish. Fine plus.

Clos de Vougeot,

Domaine Lamarche   From 2016   18.5

Medium-full colour. Stylish nose. Ripe, oaky, and profound. Medium-full body. Very good grip. Good tannins. Vigorous and long and with lots of potential. Nicely minerally at the end. Very fine.

Clos de Vougeot,

Domaine Sylvain Loichet   From 2015   16.5

Fullish colour. Plump nose, if without the distiction of most. Medium-full body. Some tannin. Good acidity. This is certainly praiseworthy, but the fruit is not sophisticated enough for "fine."

Clos de Vougeot,

Domaine Méo-Camuzet   From 2016   17.0

Full colour. Ample, plump, oaky nose. Medium-full body. Abundant and succulent on the pal-ate. Good acidity. Not quite the vigour and intensity, or even the class of the very best, but very good indeed.

Clos de Vougeot,

Domaine Denis Mortet   From 2016   17.5

Full colour. Firm, rich, profound, oaky nose. Fullish body. Very rich on the palate. Very good grip. Long. Fine.

Clos de Vougeot,

Domaine Tortochot   Now to 2017   13.0

Full colour. Stewed nose. A touch of chlorine. Ungainly. Medium to medium-full body. Indifferent fruit. Only fair.

Clos de Vougeot,

Domaine de la Vougeraie   From 2016   17.5

Medium-full colour. Soft nose. Ripe and subtle. Medium to medium-full body. Generous and attractive. Classy and profound. Fine.

VOSNE-ROMANÉE GRANDS CRUS

La Grande Rue,

Domaine Lamarche   From 2018   20.0

Full colour. Rich, full, ripe, and oaky on the nose. Lots of depth and quality here. Splendidly opulent and seductive on the palate. Excellent grip. Full body. Great finesse at the end. A great wine.

La Romanée, Domaine

Vicomte de Liger-Belair   From 2017   19.0

Medium-full colour. Closed-in; oaky nose. Ripe and succulent. Medium-full body. Not as structured as some of these Vosne *grands crus*. Very fine fruit. Very good grip. Complex, elegant, multidimensional, and very lovely.

Romanée-Saint-Vivant,

Domaine de L'Arlot   From 2016   18.0

Medium-full colour. Gamey, nutty nose, showing evidence of vinification with the stems. Fullish body. Excellent grip. Lovely, intense, pure fruit. No undue tannins. Real finesse. Long and complex, but it perhaps could have done with a little more weight and concentration. Fine plus.

Richebourg, Domaine Grivot From 2018 19.5

Full colour. Splendidly concentrated and complex on the nose, but still very closed-in. Full body, finely tuned, fragrant, understated, and very harmonious. Vigorous, intense, and very classy indeed on the follow-through. This is excellent.

Richebourg,
Domaine Anne Gros From 2020 20.0

Fullish colour. Backward, very concentrated nose. Very lovely pure fruit. Quite structured, but very, very classy. On the palate, just about perfect. Fullish body. Very harmonious. Vigorous, profound, and multidimensional. Utterly delicious concentrated fruit. A great wine.

Richebourg,
Domaine Gros Frère et Soeur From 2018 19.0

Very full colour. Rich, fat, concentrated nose. Full body. Backward. Tannic. Very youthful. Excellent grip. This got better and better in the glass. Splendid fruit and a very lovely finish.

Richebourg,
Domaine Thibaut Liger-Belair From 2017 18.5

Full colour. Closed-in nose. But there is plenty of fruit and substance here. Slightly adolescent at present—like most of the rest, it improved significantly in the glass—but rich and concentrated and full and profound. Very good grip. Needs time. Very fine.

Romanée-Conti,
Domaine de la Romanée-Conti From 2018 20.0

Medium-full colour. Ethereal nose. A lighter wine than many of these Vosne *grands crus*. Less new oaky also. This is highly individual and very, very delicious. Rich, fragrant, and complex. Impeccably textured. A great wine.

BONNES-MARES AND MUSIGNY

Bonnes-Mares,
Domaine Francois Bertheau From 2016 18.0

Full colour. Rich, lush, oaky nose. Fullish body. Oaky on the palate. Fresh. Very good acidity. Lovely fruit. Long and lingering at the end. Great charm here. Fine plus.

Bonnes-Mares,
Domaine Groffier From 2016 17.5

Good colour. Ample, plump nose. Elegant fruit and a lot of class. Good attack, but then it tails off just a bit. It lacks the complexity of Roumier, for instance. Fine, nevertheless.

Bonnes-Mares, Domaine
Jacques Frédéric Mugnier From 2017 18.5

Good colour. Quite closed on the nose but a less substantial wine than Roumier's example. Fullish body. Lovely fruit and very good harmony. A little adolescent at present but very fine, I'm sure.

Bonnes-Mares,
Domaine Georges Roumier From 2020 19.5

Very good colour. Marvelous fragrant Chambolle fruit on the nose. Really delicious. Splendidly abundant on the palate. Full body. Very good grip. Lots of energy and intensity, especially at the end. Yet, for once, Musigny-ish rather than Bonnes-Mares-ish. Excellent.

Bonnes-Mares, Domaine
Comte Georges de Vogûé From 2018 19.0

Good colour. Firm, quite closed nose. Full body. Rich. Profound. Backward. Gently oaky. Splendidly balanced and with very lovely fruit. Very fine plus.

Musigny, Domaine
Jacques Frédéric Mugnier From 2017 19.0

Good colour. Quite oaky on the nose. Fullish body. Lovely fruit, if a little closed at the moment. Underneath, there is a wine of splendid harmony, complexity, and great elegance. Very fine plus.

Musigny, Domaine
Comte Georges de Vogüé From 2020 20.0

Full colour. Closed-in nose. Very lovely fragrant fruit, yet quite sizeable. Full-bodied. Backward. Very, very concentrated and very, very high-class. Marvelous fruit. Very, very long, complex, and pure. Potentially a great wine. But currently merely an infant.

Clos des Lambrays,
Domaine des Lambrays   From 2017   18.5

Fullish colour. A surprisingly big wine for Clos des Lambrays. Rich, profound fruit on the nose. Fullish body. Very elegant and with really lovely harmonious fruit and very good grip. Lovely finish. Very fine.

Clos de la Roche,
Domaine Joseph Drouhin   From 2016   18.0

Fullish colour. Rich, fat, but very Drouhin fragrance on the nose. High-class fruit. Medium-full body. Very ripe tannins. This is quite accessible. Concentrated, harmonious, and stylish. Not a blockbuster but fine plus.

Clos de la Roche,
Domaine Dujac   From 2016   18.5

Full colour. Rich, concentrated nose. Nice and fat. Compared with earlier Dujacs, this has more backbone and intensity. Excellent fruit and really profound. Very fine.

Clos de la Roche,
Domaine Louis Remy   From 2016   17.5

Medium-full colour. Elegant and intense on the nose. By no means a blockbuster, but stylish and harmonious. Medium to medium-full body. Refined and rich. Well-balanced. Long on the palate. Fine.

Clos-Saint-Denis,
Domaine Dujac   From 2016   18.0

Very good colour; rather more than the Dujacs we were used to. Ample, ripe nose. Fullish body. Rich and balanced. Very good tannins. Fresh, complex, long, and with lots of energy. Fine plus.

Clos de Tart,
Domaine Mommessin   From 2018   19.0

Full colour. Fine, rich, concentrated nose. Lots of depth and quality here. Full body. Very good tannins. Quite masculine in character compared with rest of this flight. But not a bit tough or four-square. A backward wine with very fine depth, concentrated fruit, and lots of grip. The best Clos de Tart for a generation. Very fine plus.

Charmes-Chambertin,
Domaine Bachelet   From 2017   18.0

Medium-full colour. Ripe, concentrated nose. Medium-full body. Some tannin. Still very young. Attractive, cool, minerally fruit. But somewhat reserved. Very good grip. Lots of depth, and a very lovely finish. Fine plus, perhaps better still.

Charmes-Chambertin,
Domaine Camus   From 2013   13.5

Good colour. Quite rich, plump nose. Medium body. Not a lot of depth and structure and less finesse than it showed at first on the palate. Fair at best.

Charmes-Chambertin,
Domaine Claude Dugat   From 2020   18.0

Fullish colour. Full on the nose too, with a touch of cooked fruit and a little more extraction than most. But still very delicious. Full body. Plenty of tannin and concentrated fruit, held together by very good grip. This is energetic, intense, pure, and very long on the palate. Very fine.

Charmes-Chambertin,
Domaine Humbert Frères   From 2015   17.0

Fullish colour. Fresh, plump, ripe, cassis-flavoured nose. Medium-full body. Good tannins. Good ripe attack. Slightly less good at the end, but long and positive nevertheless. Very good indeed.

Charmes-Chambertin,
Domaine Maume   From 2015   16.0

Medium to medium-full colour. Soft, round nose. Attractive fruit, if not a blockbuster. Medium to medium full body. Fresh. Very good but lacks the definition and class for great.

Charmes-Chambertin,
Domaine Serafin   From 2017   18.5

Fullish colour. Lots of depth and concentration on the nose. Full body. Splendid old-viney fruit. Very fine tannins. Lovely balance. Very, very long, classy, and complex. Very fine.

Charmes-Chambertin,
Domaine Armand Rousseau   From 2015   16.5

Medium colour. A little evolution. Clean and stylish, but a bit unforthcoming on the nose. Medium body. Not a lot of backbone, but fresh and balanced and not a bit short. Elegant finish. Very good plus.

Charmes-Chambertin,
Domaine Taupenot-Merme   From 2015   16.0

Medium to medium-full colour. Fresh, ripe nose. Plump and attractive. Easy to enjoy. Medium to medium-full body. Not a blockbuster. Clean and fruity. Very good.

Mazoyeres-Chambertin,
Domaine Taupenot-Merme   See note

Medium-full colour. This was a little reduced and so difficult to assess. Medium to medium-full body. Good grip. Decent tannins and no lack of fruit. Perhaps very good but to be seen again.

Charmes-Chambertin,
Mazoyeres,
Domaine de la Vougeraie   From 2017   18.0

Medium-full colour. Firm, rich, gently oaky nose. Good depth here. Medium-full body. Good tannins. Attractive fruit. Freshly blanced. Long. Fine plus.

CHAPELLE, LATRICIÈRES MAZIS, AND RUCHOTTES-CHAMBERTIN

Chapelle-Chambertin,
Domaine Rossignol-Trapet   From 2016   17.5

Medium to medium-full colour. Round, ripe, velvety nose. Medium-full body. Good style and concentration. Very good fruit and grip. Long, positive, and classy. I like the vigour. Fine.

Chapelle-Chambertin, Domaine
Jean et Jean-Louis Trapet   From 2015   14.0

Medium to medium-full colour. A little evolution. Decent fruit but not the greatest of finesse on the nose. Medium body. Lacks real richness and concentration and, above all, vigour. Only quite good.

Latricières-Chambertin,
Domaine Simon Bize   See note

Medium to medium-full colour. Sweet and spicy and a little reduced on the nose. Medium to medium-full body. Quite a meaty wine, with good tannins and very good grip. Finishes positively, but it is difficult to assess the quality of the fruit. To be seen again.

Latricières-Chambertin,
Domaine Drouhin-Laroze   From 2016   17.0

Medium-full colour. Rich, fat, succulent, old-viney nose. Medium-full body. Quite austere at present. Good concentration. Very good acidity. Some tannin. Long on the palate. There is plenty in reserve here. Very good indeed, perhaps even better.

Latricières-Chambertin,
Domaine Faiveley   From 2020   18.5

Full colour. Ample, rich, and concentrated on the nose. Good class, weight, and depth, together with, as it evolved in the glass, the spice of this *climat*. Full body. Quite a bit of tannin. Backward. But vigorous, profound, and with very good grip. Fine classy fruit. Long. Very fine.

Latricières-Chambertin,
Maison Camille Giroud   From 2015 · 17.5

Medium-full colour. Rich, fat, concentrated, and full of fruit on the nose. Very elegant. Lots of depth and quality. Medium-full body. Very lovely, rich, gently oaky fruit on the palate. Complex and classy. Will develop quite soon. Fine.

Latricières-Chambertin,
Domaine Louis Remy   From 2016   17.0

Medium-full colour. Quite a substantial wine on the nose. Rich and ample as well. Fullish body. Good tannins. Nicely concentrated, succulent character, and good balancing acidity. Quite classy too. Very good indeed.

Latricières-Chambertin,
Domaine Rossignol-Trapet   From 2015   15.0

Medium to medium-full colour. Soft nose. Plump but not a lot of vigour. Decent attack but then it tails off a bit. Fruity, though, and not short. But good at best.

Latricières-Chambertin, Domaine Jean et Jean-Louis Trapet   From 2015   14.0

Medium to medium-full colour. Aromatic if not very assertive nose. Decent fruit and quite fresh on the palate. Medium weight. Pleasant but not serious. Quite good.

Mazis-Chambertin, Domaine Camus   From 2016   16.0

Good colour. A better wine than their Charmes. Medium-full body. Quite rich, ripe, and fruity. Good tannins and good balance. This is very good.

Mazis-Chambertin, Domaine Joseph Faiveley   From 2018   18.5

Full colour. Firm, rich, full, vigorous nose. This is quite a big tannic wine. Rich, oaky, concentrated, ripe, and profound on the palate. Lots of depth and energy. Lovely fruit. Very long. Very fine.

Mazis-Chambertin, Domaine Maume   From 2017   18.0

Medium-full colour. Classy fruit on the nose. Good concentration too. Fullish body. Rich, vigorous, and balanced. Needs time. Plenty of potential here. Fine plus.

Mazis-Chambertin, Maison Nicolas Potel   From 2017   17.0

Medium-full colour. Cool, classy, minerally nose. Medium-full body. Austere at present, but good tannins and plenty of fruit. Very good acidity. Lots of finesse. This is going to need time. It tastes more like a Ruchottes than a Mazis, but it's very good indeed.

Ruchottes-Chambertin, Domaine Christophe Roumier   From 2017   17.0

Medium-full colour. Slightly austere but rich and concentrated on the nose. Fullish body. Ample, meaty, and vigorous on the palate. Finishes well. Plenty of potential. Very good indeed.

Ruchottes-Chambertin, Clos des Ruchottes, Domaine Armand Rousseau   From 2016   18.0

Fullish colour. Cool, fragrant, very classy nose, with the slight leanness I associate with this *climat*. Medium-full body. Ripe tannins. Very good grip. Very pure and classy fruit. More generous at the end than on the attack. Very, very lovely stylish finish. Fine plus.

CHAMBERTIN, CLOS DE BÈZE, AND CHAMBERTIN

Chambertin, Clos de Bèze, Domaine Bruno Clair   From 2017   19.0

Medium-full colour. Closed-in but classy nose. Lovely fruit here and a touch of oak. Fullish body. Intense and vigorous. Very good tannins. High-class fruit and very good grip. Long. Harmonious. Very fine plus.

Chambertin, Clos de Bèze, Domaine Joseph Drouhin   From 2016   18.0

Fullish colour. A slight touch of austerity on the nose, and an absence of the real weight and concentration that Clos de Bèze should offer. Medium-full body. Classy and balanced but with the volume of a Charmes rather than a Clos de Bèze. Not exactly as voluminous or as concentrated as it should be. Fine plus but not great.

Chambertin, Clos de Bèze, Domaine Drouhin-Laroze   From 2016   17.5

Fullish colour. Firm, full, rich, high-quality nose. Fullish. Just a bit of astringency about the tannins. Yet very good acidity. Long and fine, but not great.

Chambertin, Clos de Bèze, Domaine Joseph Faiveley   From 2019   18.0

Full colour. Rich, full, firm, tannic, closed-in nose. Similar on the palate. Quite a lot of tannin. Underlying oakiness too. Very lovely fruit. Needs time. High-quality.

Chambertin, Clos de Bèze, Domaine Groffier   See note

Medium-full colour. The wine is a little reduced, but one can see some substance and no lack of richness. Medium-full body. Very good acidity.

It got better and better in the glass. Certainly at least very good. But I'll wait until I see it again.

Chambertin, Clos de Bèze,
Domaine Armand Rousseau   From 2018 19.0
Medium-full colour. Somewhat unforthcoming at first on the nose. But high-quality sings out. Medium-full body. Rich, generous, and succulent on the palate. Long, complex, and classy. Very good intensity. Very fine plus.

Chambertin,
Maison Camille Giroud   From 2017 18.0
Medium to medium-full colour. Not a blockbuster but concentrated, complex, classy, and harmonious on the nose. This is a lovely wine, which got better and better in the glass. Lots of finesse at the end. Not totally brilliant but fine plus.

Chambertin,
Domaine Rossignol-Trapet   From 2018 19.0
Medium-full colour. Ample, generous, creamy-rich nose. Fullish body. Old-viney concentra-tion. Poised and multidimensional. Long and classy at the end. One of the very few Chambertins I have had in years which is up to Rousseau's standards.

Chambertin,
Domaine Armand Rousseau   From 2019 20.0
Medium-full colour. Closed-in but rich, concentrated nose. Good grip here. Medium-full body. Ripe, balanced, fresh, and very profound and elegant. Exceptionally fine, complex fruit. Good as his Clos de Bèze is, this is, as always, just that bit superior. A great wine.

Chambertin, Domaine
Jean et Jean-Louis Trapet   From 2016 16.5
Good colour. A bit hidden on the nose. Medium-full body. The attack is presently a little blunt, but ripe, ample, plummy, and well-balanced on the follow-through. Not the class of Rousseau's Chambertin. But then, what's new? Very good plus.

The Ten-Year-On Tastings

2002 BURGUNDY

The 2002 red Burgundies, although not at the top levels in the same league as the great 1999s (or indeed 2005), have proved to be very popular on the market place. The red wines have a good colour, a refreshing acidity, medium-full body,

→ Rating for the Vintage ←	
Red	18.0
White	18.5

lots of plump fruit, and ripe tannins. They are relaxed wines. There is a French phrase, applied to people, "bien dans sa peau" (literally: comfortable within one's skin—that is, at ease with oneself), which is an apt description of the 2002s. The vintage is fine at the generic level. The village and *premiers crus* are also delicious. It is only at top *grand cru* level that there is a clear difference *vis à vis* 1999. But subtract 1999 (and 2005 and 2009) from the equation

and we have a year which is as good as anything else produced in recent memory. The vintage is also geographically consistent. Though some will suggest the Côte de Beaune is better than the Côte de Nuits, I do not agree. There are some lovely wines in Nuits-Saint-Georges and Chambolle-Musigny. For the third year in succession, said Jacques Lardière of Jadot, Gevrey-Chambertin is the best commune.

→ Size of the Crop ← (In hectolitres)			
	RED	WHITE	TOTAL
Grands crus	13,114	3,726	16,840
Village and *premiers crus*	170,522	62,385	232,907
TOTAL	183,636	66,111	249,747

The white wines, too, are extremely good, perhaps even better than the reds. There is a refreshing acidity which brings out wonderfully elegant complex fruit. This is coupled with good weight and potential to age well. All in all, a highly successful vintage.

Weather Conditions

It was a severe winter, very cold—but dry—both before and after Christmas. I remember it being minus 8.5°C at 8.30 a.m. in Savigny-Lès-Beaune several mornings running. This was followed by a mild February and March, allowing an easy bud-break, but this was succeeded by a cool May. This retarded the flowering, but fine weather after June 13 meant that this turned out successfully, though the crop would not be excessive. The next ten weeks were dry, but not too hot. And thankfully there were no hailstorms.

August was warm and still dry, and this led to a situation in the early days of September, where the development of the fruit—the Chardonnays more than the Pinots—was somewhat blocked. Then there was rain. This did no harm except in Ladoix, where it was somewhat excessive, reducing the concentration of the Cortons and such Charlemagnes as come from the top of this side of the hill. This was soon followed by fine weather. From mid-September, a cool north wind set in, accompanied by clear skies and cold nights. These conditions were similar to 1996 except that the crop in 1996 was larger and the weather had not been so fine in August. Volumes were reduced, and concentration and potential alcohol levels accelerated by this drying wind. The harvest began on September 15. It was over by October 1. The fruit was healthy but not in some cases completely ripe. The best growers waited a few days, benefiting from the continuing good weather, and then eliminated the berries that were not fully concentrated on the sorting table. It was hardly necessary to chaptalise. After October 1 the weather deteriorated, affecting the quality of the Hautes Côtes.

At first, there being quite a high level of malic acid, and the malos slow to complete, the 2002s were a bit aggressive. It was only after the malos had finished, and carbon dioxide levels started to decline—or were reduced by those who rack at the end of the summer—that the 2002s began to show their texture. These are wines of roundness and succulence as well as of pure fruit. Initially, there was somewhat less *terroir* definition than in the 1999s at the same stage, and although, according to Christian Gouges this aspect would improve, I feel, as Marie-Andrée Mugneret (Domaine Dr. Georges Mugneret) said, that the expression of the 2002s will always be more about Pinot Noir than exactly were they come from. It boils down to the weather pattern. A great vintage—which by definition is one of wines which speak loudly of their origins—is the product of a fine August (*août fait le mout*) as well as a fine September. August 2002 was good, but not brilliant. And the first two weeks of September were inclement as well. Many growers, despite malos which in some cases still had not finished by the time of the 2003 harvest, decided to bottle early, "to preserve the fruit."

Ten years on, it is quite clear that 2002 is a brilliant vintage for white wines in the Côte d'Or. It seems that the cooler weather in the first half of September concentrated the fruit and, most importantly, preserved the acidity. So we have wines which even ten years later are youthful, ripe, pure, vigorous, and profound. The best are hardly ready. The very best are quite sublime and will still improve. This is the best white wine vintage for a generation, and has not been equalled, let alone surpassed, since.

The red wines are also delicious. There is some very lovely fruit, plenty of concentration, and lots of elegance. The tannins are there, but not obtruding, and these are fully ripe and sophisticated. The 2005s have greater strength, but these 2002s are not far behind. Altogether a highly satisfactory vintage which will last and last.

The 2002 is also very consistent. There are lovely wines in both colours throughout the Côte d'Or and throughout the Côte Chalonnaise. Only in the Hautes Côtes, though here mainly highly satisfactory wines can be found, is the pattern less even. Stick to the best growers and you can hardly go wrong. The vast majority of the following wines were sampled at my usual ten-year-on tasting in June 2012. I have added notes on others tasted at around the same time.

TASTING NOTES
White Wines

Santenay, Beauregard,
Domaine Roger Belland   Now to 2017 15.5
Well-matured, ripe, fullish, and balanced. Good plus, but nothing special about it.

Saint-Aubin, En Remilly,
Domaine Hubert Lamy   Drink soon 16.0
Magnum. Not much nose. But crisp and ripe and stylish on the palate. Medium-full body. Good follow-through. Very good but drink soon.

Saint-Aubin,
Clos de la Chatenière,
Domaine Hubert Lamy   Now to 2019 17.0
Magnum. More depth and class and vigour than the En Remilly. Lovely fruit. Finishes well. Very good indeed.

Meursault, Domaine
Thierry Matrot   Drink soon 15.0
Full-bodied. Quite rich. Ripe. Balanced. Fully developed. Not the greatest class but good.

Meursault, Blagny, Domaine
Francois et Antoine Jobard   Drink soon 14.0
Magnum. Somewhat four-square. A little old. But good fruit and balance.

Meursault, Caillerets, Domaine
Fernand et Laurent Pillot   Now to 2018 16.0
Not a lot on the nose, but not four-square either. Medium-full body. Good freshness. Ripe fruit. Well-made and good energy. Surprisingly good for a Meursault from essentially red wine soil.

Meursault, Charmes,
Domaine Roulot   Now to 2020 18.0
Magnum. Slightly tight on the nose at first. But elegant and expansive underneath. Good

depth. Very fine. But not quite as exciting as his Tessons.

Meursault, Charmes,
Domaine Thierry Matrot   Now to 2020 15.5
Magnum. Good mature nose. Fresh and ample. Good grip. Tails off a bit at the end but no undue age. Good plus.

Meursault, Desirée,
Domaine des Comtes Lafon   Drink soon 13.5
Fresh and ripe. Balanced but the fruit has not much class.

Meursault, Genevrières,
Domaine Francois et
Antoine Jobard   Now to 2020 16.5
A slight touch of built-in sulphur at first. Fullish body. Ripe. A bit four-square, like his Porizots. And similarly it lacks a bit of fruit and high tones. But the finish is better.

Meursault, Genevrières,
Domaine des
Comtes Lafon   Now to 2022 plus 18.5
This is very lovely. Delicious fresh, full, complex fruit. A full-bodied wine. Concentrated and profound. Lots of energy. Very fine.

Meursault, Genevrières,
Domaine Francois Mikulski   Now to 2020 17.0
Magnum. Quite a deep colour. But supple and ripe and stylish and balanced. Good depth here. Good style. Very good indeed.

Meursault, Luchets,
Domaine Roulot   Now to 2020 17.5
Magnum. Full, vigorous, stylish, and concentrated. A very impressive example. Nicely poised and still vigorous. Lovely classy fruit.

Meursault, Perrières,
Maison Henri Boillot   Now to 2020 18.0
Closed-in, youthful, racy, mineral nose. Still unforthcoming. Fullish body. Very stylish. No undue oak. Crisp and lean in the best sense. Very complex. Lots of dimension and class. Fine plus.

Meursault, Perrières, Domaine Jean-Francois Coche-Dury   Now 2020 plus   19.5

Anyone who wants to know what all the fuss is about Coche-Dury wines needs to drink this. Closed-in but concentrated nose. Fullish body. Lots of racy fruit. Lots of vigour and depth. Still very young. Quite powerful. Marvelous and multidimensional.

Meursault, Perrières, Domaine des Comtes Lafon   Now to 2020 plus   18.5

This is still very young. Lots of depth and energy. Very fine fruit and class. This is even better than his Genevrières. A very lovely, really profound wine. Lots of life ahead on it. Very fine.

Meursault, Perrières, Domaine Pierre Morey   Drink up   12.0

This is ripe but the follow-through is flat. Disappointing.

Meursault, Poruzots, Domaine Francois et Antoine Jobard   Now to 2019   16.0

Fullish, fresh, youthful nose. Just a touch four-square and a touch of sulphur dioxide. Backward. Ripe. Lacks a little personality and fruit. A touch inflexible.

Meursault, Tessons, Clos de Mon Plaisir, Domaine Roulot   Now to 2020 plus   18.0

Magnum. Very lovely and very classy. Excellent concentrated fruit. Medium-full body. Splendidly balanced. This is long and complex, fresh and youthful. Vigorous and very lovely.

Puligny-Montrachet, Domaine Jean-Marc Boillot   Now to 2020   17.5

Ripe fresh, stylish, and with very good fruit and class for a village wine. Plump, vigorous, and *à point*. Fine

Puligny-Montrachet, Clos des Caillerets, Domaine des Lambrays   Now to 2020   18.5

A full, opulent, quite profound wine. Gently oaky and very classy. Balanced. Lush. But very good grip and energy. Very fine.

Puligny-Montrachet, Les Caillerets, Domaine de Montille   Now to 2025   19.0

Magnum. Rich, concentrated, classic, youthful. Splendid depth. A very lovely wine with a long future. Real finesse and multidimensional. Brilliant!

Puligny-Montrachet, Champ Canet, Domaine Etienne Sauzet   Now to 2020   18.0

Fresh colour. Ample, ripe, luscious, plump, and just about ready. Fullish, juicy, balanced, and succulent. Delicious. Fine plus.

Puligny-Montrachet, Les Combettes, Domaine Jean-Marc Boillot   Now to 2020 plus   18.0

This is very fine. Lovely fruit. Ripe, full-bodied, vigorous, and concentrated. Lovely finish.

Puligny-Montrachet, Les Combettes, Domaine Etienne Sauzet   Now to 2020   17.0

At first a little funky, and I feared prematurely oxidised on the nose. But this seemed to resolve itself in the glass. Rich and ripe and quite full on the palate. And it got better and better in the glass. Will still improve. A second bottle, on a separate occasion, was discreet at first but concentrated and very elegant.

Puligny-Montrachet, Les Folaitières, Domaine Louis Jadot   Now to 2025   18.5

Note: This is from Jadot's own domaine. Very delicious. Fullish body. Rich, concentrated, excellent fruit. Ample, lush, and very well-balanced. Very fine grip. Complex and classy. Lots of life. Very fine.

Puligny-Montrachet, Les Folatières, Domaine des Lambrays   Now to 2020   18.0

Full concentrated nose. A little less rich and oaky than the Clos des Cailerets. But lots of dimension. Lots of vigour. Lots of depth. Lovely peachy fruit. Fine plus.

**Puligny-Montrachet,
Clos de la Garenne,
Domaine Duc de Magenta,
Maison Louis Jadot**   Now to 2020 plus   19.0

Lovely nose. Pure, concentrated, and multidimensional. Very finely balanced. Real depth. And very high-class. Very long, intense follow-through. Very fine plus.

On two occasions in the United States I had a chance to retaste this wine shortly after the opportunity above. The samples were sadly rather more evolved. The wines not nearly as exciting. Once again, one wonders what goes on between landing and final delivery to customers' cellars.

**Puligny-Montrachet, Les Perrières,
Domaine Louis Carillon**   Now to 2020   18.0

Classy nose. Ample, ripe balanced, juicy, and peachy. Medium-full body. Lovely style. Very well put together. Long. Fine plus.

**Puligny-Montrachet,
La Truffière, Domaine
Michel Colin-Déleger**   Now to 2018   17.0

Plump, soft, and abundantly fruity without the grip of his En Remilly. Medium-full body. Fresh. Good acidity. Very good fruit. Fine finish. *À point.*

**Puligny-Montrachet, La Truffière,
Domaine Bernard Morey**   Now to 2016   17.0

Crisp, stylish nose. Quite concentrated. Peachy and lemony. Classy and harmonious. Fullish, balanced. Good depth and grip. Fat, yet minerally. Just about ready. Very good indeed.

**Chassagne-Montrachet,
Domaine Marquis de Laguiche/
Maison Joseph Drouhin**   Now to 2020   17.5

Fullish body. Good rich fruit. Concentrated, classy, and vigorous. A lovely plump, succulent wine. Still youthful. Lots of depth. Fine.

**Chassagne-Montrachet,
Les Dents du Chien, Domaine
Du Château de Maltroye**   Now to 2020   18.5

Fullish, rich, very concentrated nose, with very good grip. Very lovely fruit. High-class vigour and splendid balance. Intense and classy. Still has plenty of life. Very fine.

**Chassagne-Montrachet,
Les Caillerets,
Domaine Blain-Gagnard**   Now to 2020 plus   18.0

Fresh colour. Vigorous nose. Rich and concentrated and still very youthful. Fullish body. Ample, ripe fruit. Very well-balanced. Lots of depth and very high-class. Lots of life ahead of it. Fine plus.

**Chassagne-Montrachet,
Les Caillerets, Domaine
Fontaine-Gagnard**   Now to 2019   17.5

Just a litle flat on the nose at first. Rather better on the palate. Elegant, balanced fruit. Medium-full body. Flowery and peachy. Very gently oaky. Long. Fine.

**Chassagne-Montrachet, Morgeot,
Clos de la Chapelle,
Domaine Duc de Magenta,
Maison Louis Jadot**   Now to 2018   17.5

Some development on the colour. Full on the nose. Really quite rich. Almost over-ripe. Fully ready. Lovely fruit. Succulent and accessible. Fine quality.

**Chassagne-Montrachet,
En Remilly, Domaine
Michel Colin-Déleger**   Now to 2020   17.5

Attractive juicy-peachy fruit on the nose. Ripe, stylish, very good grip. Medium-full body. Long and persistent. Lots of energy. Fine.

**Chassagne-Montrachet,
Les Ruchottes,
Domaine Ramonet**   Now to 2020   18.5

Youthful colour. Rich nose, at first quite oaky, even little sweet. But less so in both respects as it evolved on the glass. Full-bodied. Still firm. Rich and concentrated. Very good depth and grip. A very fine example. Elegant and sumptuous. Lots of life ahead of it.

**Chassagne-Montrachet, Les Vergers,
Domaine Jean-Marc Pillot**   Now to 2018   17.5

A little development on both the colour and the nose. But firm and fresh on the palate. Fullish body. Rich and profound. Very good, plump, peachy, elegant fruit. Long and vigorous. Fine.

Chassagne-Montrachet,
Les Vergers,
Domaine Ramonet　　　　Drink soon　14.0
A little developed and a little built-in sulphur on the nose. Fullish on the palate. Quite ripe, rich, and vigorous on the palate but not the greatest grip or distinction.

Chassagne-Montrachet,
En Virondot,
Domaine Marc Morey　　Now to 2020 plus　18.0
Some evolution on the colour. Ripe, plump, vigorous, crisp nose. Very good fruit. Fullish body. Ample, complex, and abundant. Still youthful. Balanced and rich, yet mineral. Really quite concentrated. Fine plus.

Morey-Saint-Denis, Les Monts
Luisants, Domaine Dujac　　Now to 2018　15.0
Ripe full of fruit. Stylish and balanced, if a little one-dimensional. Still has plenty of life.

Corton, Blanc, Domaine
Chandon de Briailles　　　Now to 2020　16.5
Stylish, individual, but without the minerality of Corton, Charlemagne. Slightly four-square at the end. Youthful. Very good plus.

Corton, Charlemagne,
Domaine Bonneau du Martray　　From 2015　19.5
A very lovely example. Rich, ample, balanced, poised, and relaxed. Marvelous plump fruit. Very classy and very complex. Lots of life ahead of it. Indeed, it will still improve.

Corton, Charlemagne, Domaine
Bouchard Père et Fils　　　Now to 2025　18.5
Ripe youthful. Very good fruit on the nose. Succulent and lively. Fullish body. Only barely ready. Classy and very pure. This is very fine.

Corton, Charlemagne,
Domaine Jean-Francois
Coche-Dury　　　Now to 2025 plus　20.0
Closed-in, very concentrated nose. This really is very special. Still amazingly young. Great power—in the best sense of the word—in per-

sistence and intensity. Marvelous depth and concentration. A splendidly pure aristocratic fruit. Quite brilliant!

Corton, Charlemagne,
Domaine Faiveley　　　Now to 2020　18.5
Nicely steely and not a bit too oaky (which I had feared) on the nose. Fullish body. Very stylish. Lots of dimension. Properly cool and mineral. Still very young. Very fine.

Corton, Charlemagne,
Domaine Patrick Javillier　　From 2015　18.5
Magnum. Firm, full-bodied, rich, and concentrated. Very youthful still. A lot of depth and a true Corton, Charlemagne character. Took a while to come out of the glass. Very fine.

Corton, Charlemagne,
Domaine Rapet　　　　　See note
One bottle a little tired; a second even worse, and a deep colour as well. A pity, as the 2008 served alongside it was delicious.

Hospices de Beaune,
Corton-Charlemagne,
Cuvée Francois de Salins,
Maison Louis Jadot　　　　See note
Seen in the United States. Quite evolved on both colour and nose (poor storage?). Ripe and succulent at first. But it lacked the minerality of Corton-Charlemagne. Oxidised rapidly in the glass.

Bâtard-Montrachet, Domaine
Bouchard Père et Fils　　Now to 2020 plus　18.5
Full, rich, lively, and concentrated on the nose. Very impressive fruit. Profound and well-balanced. Pure, firm, and classic. A lovely wine.

Bâtard-Montrachet,
Domaine Jean-Noël Gagnard　Now to 2025　19.0
Fine, full, and lush on the nose and on the palate. Nothing a bit four-square here. Full-bodied, ripe, classy, and profound. Very good grip. Long. Very fine plus.

Chevalier-Montrachet,
Maison Henri Boillot　　　Now to 2020　17.5
Full, rich, ample, exotic but lots of grip. Very fresh. Fat and opulent. Very, very ripe. Even

a touch sweet. Fine but not great. Still very youthful.

Chevalier-Montrachet, Domaine
Michel Colin-Deléger et Fils Now to 2017 17.5
Quite a developed colour. The nose similar. Full, rich, and concentrated. Good grip. But fully *à point* and without the sheer class of Chevalier-Montrachet. Fine finish though. And a second bottle was better. This is a producer whose wines since the 1995 vintage have been regularly disappointing as they have aged.

Chevalier-Montrachet,
Domaine Leflaive Now to 2017 17.5
Some evolution here. But there is ample fruit. Lots of fat and concentration. A touch of oak. Fine but by no means great, and without the vigour to last. For Chevalier, a bit of a dissapointment.

Chevalier-Montrachet,
Maison Frédéric Magnien Drink soon 14.0
This is a disappointment. Fresh in appearence, but now fully ready. Medium-full body. Rather artificial fruit, with an aftertaste of boiled sweets. Ripe and balanced but an absence of class.

Le Montrachet,
Domaine Marquis de Laguiche,
Maison Joseph Drouhin 2016 to 2030 20.0
This is quite brilliant. Marvelous concentration, depth, and finesse. Aristocratic on the nose. Fullish body. Splendid grip. Very lovely, long, complex finish. Great class. A great wine.

Red Wines

Givry, Clos Jus,
Domaine Francois Lumpp Now 2018 17.0
Good colour. Still youthful. Lovely soft, graceful, fragrant, juicy fruit. Medium to medium-full body. Balanced, stylish, ripe, and succulent. Delicious. Really fine for a Côte Chalonnaise. Just about ready.

Givry, Clos Salomon,
Domaine du Clos Salomon Now to 2020 15.0
Medium, mature colour. Medium to medium-full in weight. A touch of tannin. Clean, vigorous, and stylish. Good.

Mercurey, Champs Martin,
Domaine Lorenzon Now to 2020 plus 17.0
Good colour. Quite a firm nose. Some oak here. Some tannin too. Medium-full body. Rich and ripe. Plenty of energy. Lots of depth. Will still improve. Long. Very good indeed.

Mercurey, Les Montots,
Domaine A et P Villaine Now to 2018 15.5
Medium, mature colour. Soft, ripe, fragant nose. Lovely fruit. Balanced and elegant. A delightful example.

Chassagne-Montrachet,
Clos-Saint-Jean,
Domaine Ramonet Now to 2020 16.0
Good colour. Soft nose, full of fruit. Almost sweet. Medium to medium-full body. Elegant and balanced. No great pretension but fresh, stylish, and well-balanced. Delicious now.

Savigny-Lès-Beaune,
La Dominode,
Domaine Bruno Clair Now to 2022 plus 16.5
Good fullish colour. Good rich, backward, stylish nose. Quite fat. Quite firm. Plenty of depth. Long. Very good indeed.

Savigny-Lès-Beaune,
La Dominode,
Domaine Jean-Marc
et Hugues Pavelot Now to 2020 plus 15.5
Medium-full colour. Quite a different wine from their Guettes, but also fullish and ample and full of fruit. No lack of depth or character. But a different fragrance.

Savigny-Lès-Beaune,
Les Golardes, Domaine
Fougeray de Beauclair Drink soon 13.0
Medium to medium-full colour. Somewhat clumsy on the nose. Medium-full body. Earthy. Lacks fruit. A bit sour. No joy here.

Savigny-Lès-Beaune, Les Guettes,
Domaine Jean-Marc et
Hugues Pavelot Now to 2020 plus 15.5
Medium-full colour. Rich, meaty, quite firm. Fullish body. Plenty of wine here. Very stylish too.

**Savigny-Lès-Beaune,
Les Narbantons,
Domaine Maurice Ecard**   Now to 2022   15.5
Good colour. Sturdy nose. Ripe and medium-full bodied. Good grip. A meaty wine with good depth and vigour. Good plus.

**Savigny-Lès-Beaune, Les Peuillets,
Domaine Lucien Jacob**   Now to 2020   14.0
Medium-full colour. A bit rustic on the nose. But it is fresh and fruity. Quite good.

**Beaune, Les Cent Vignes,
Domaine Lucien Jacob**   Now to 2022 plus   16.0
Medium to medium-full colour. Still youthful. Quite a concentrated example. Full body. Some tannin. Rich and meaty. Plenty of depth. Very good. Will last well.

**Beaune, Clos des Couchereaux,
Domaine Louis Jadot**   Now to 2025   17.0
Medium to medium-full mature colour. Fragrant nose. Slightly higher volatile acidity than is normal these days. Medium-full body. Very ripe fruit. Almost sweet. But very good grip and vigour. An opulent, seductive wine. Very good indeed.

**Beaune, Clos des Ursules,
Domaine Louis Jadot**   Now to 2025   17.5
Medium-full, mature colour. Rich, opulent, ripe, profound nose. Fuller, firmer, and richer than the Couchereaux. Somewhat less evolved too. But more energy. Real depth and class. Lovely finish. Fine.

**Beaune, Les Cras,
Maison Champy**   Now to 2018   13.5
Rather coarse at the end after a reasonably substantial fruity attack.

**Beaune, Grèves,
Vigne de l'Enfant Jesue,
Domaine Bouchard Père et Fils**   From 2015   17.5
Medium-full colour. Ripe and round on the nose, with a touch of gingerbread. Medium to medium-full body. Good energy. Stylish harmonious fruit. Good ripe tannins. Long and complex. Fine.

**Beaune, Grèves,
Domaine Michel Lafarge**   2015 to 2025 plus   16.0
Medium colour. Still youthful. Still rather closed on the nose. Full body. Good ripe, meaty fruit. Good grip. Just needs time. Very good.

**Beaune, Pertuisots,
Domaine Devevey**   Drink soon   13.5
Medium colour. Fully evolved. Pleasant fruity attack, but a bit weak and lean at the end.

**Beaune, Teurons,
Domaine Rossignol-Trapet**   Now to 2022   16.0
Medium-full colour. Round, ripe, stylish. Quite concentrated. Good definition. Attractive fruit. Very good.

**Volnay, *Premier Cru*, Domaine
Regis Rosssignol-Changarnier** Now to 2018   14.0
Medium colour. Fully mature. Soft nose. Ripe and quite spicy. Medium body. Fruity. But no great distinction. Balanced but not very elegant.

**Volnay, Caillerets,
Domaine Lucien Boillot**   Now to 2025   17.5
Medium-full mature colour. Rich, ripe, stylish, quite profound nose. Fullish body. Rich, ample, and energetic on the palate. Good grip. Lovely finish. Just about ready. Fine.

**Volnay, Caillerets, Ancien
Cuvée Carnot, Domaine
Bouchard Père et Fils**   Now to 2025 plus   18.5
Medium-full colour. Lovely, fragrant, soft, classy nose. Very Volnay. Medium-full body. Splendid ripe fruit. Very good grip. Intense and vigorous and rich and succulent. The tannins are now soft. Very lovely.

**Volnay, Les Caillerets,
Domaine Michel Lafarge**   From 2016   17.5
Medium-full colour. Somewhat unforthcoming on the nose at first. Still a bit closed and austere. Plenty of depth and quality though. Medium-full body. Concentrated. Very good grip. Long satisfying finish. Just needs time.

Volnay, Caillerets,
Domaine de Montille   Now to 2025   16.0
Magnum. Good fullish mature colour. A good classy, aromatic nose with a touch of the stems. Medium-full body. Good grip. Very good.

Volnay, Champans, Domaine
des Comtes Lafon   2016 to 2025 plus   17.5
Fullish colour. Ripe, rich, fullish, ample nose. Lovely fruit here. Stylish and balanced. Lots of class and depth. Fine.

Volnay,
Clos du Château des Ducs,
Domaine Michel Lafarge   From 2016   18.0
Fullish colour. Closed-in but full and rich and ample on the nose. Fuller and richer than the Caillerets, with a bit more depth. Lovely fruit. Very good grip. Splendid finish. Fine plus.

Volnay, Clos des Chênes,
Domaine Michel Lafarge   2016 to 2025 plus   18.0
Fullish colour. Still youthful. Very tight on the nose at first. Splendidly concentrated, full-bodied, rich, and classy fruit on the palate. But still backward. Fine plus.

Volnay, Clos des Chênes,
Domaine du
Château de Meursault   Now to 2019   16.0
Good colour. The nose was still a bit closed at first. Medium-full body. Ripe, round, and well-balanced with nice plummy fruit. Underneath, the tannins are not greatly sophisticated but the wine is ample and satisfying. Very good.

Volnay, Clos des Ducs, Domaine
Marquis d'Angerville   From 2016   18.0
Medium-full colour. Still youthful. Broader flavoured than their Taillepieds. Richer and spicier. Medium-full body. Slightly more austere at the moment. Long, stylish. Fine plus.

Volnay, Les Santenots,
Domaine Thierry Matrot   Now to 2025   17.5
Magnum. Medium-full, mature colour. Just a touch clumsy on the nose. Lovely, ripe, meaty fruit on the palate. Rich and full-bodied. Quite firm. A lot of depth. Just about ready. Fine.

Volnay, Les Santenots,
Domaine Francois Mikulski   Now to 2022   17.0
Magnum. Medium-full, mature colour. Good plump, fragrant nose. Stylish. Medium-full body. Balanced. Long and complex. Succulent and classy. Fully ready. Very good indeed.

Volnay, Taillepieds,
Domaine Marquis d'Angerville   From 2016   18.5
Medium-full colour. Still youthful. Delicious fragrant nose. Lovely fruit and balance and subtlety. Medium to medium-full body. Ripe, intense, and very classy. Very long. Very fine.

Pommard, Les Chaponnières,
Maison Jaffelin   Now to 2020   14.5
Fullish, ample; rich and quite closed. Good attack but then it tails off. Quite good plus.

Pommard, Clos des Epeneaux,
Domaine des Epeneaux   2016 to 2030   18.5
Full colour. Rich, ample, and concentrated on both nose and palate. Splendid tannins. A very lovely, full, flamboyant wine. Lots of depth. Excellent.

Pommard, Les Fremiers,
Domaine Louis Boillot   Now to 2020   15.0
Medium to medium-full weight. Fruity and stylish. Balanced. Lacks a little flair but good.

Pommard, Les Grands Epenots,
Maison Vincent Girardin   Now to 2020   18.5
Fullish colour. Classy nose, balanced, and profound. Lovely fruit. Fullish body. Harmonious and potentially lovely and velvety. Very fine. Indeed, quite brilliant for what it is.

Pommard, Les Jarollières,
Domaine Jean-Marc Boillot   Now to 2018   14.0
Medium colour. Fully mature. Soft nose. Ripe and quite spicy. Medium body. Fruity. But no great distinction. Balanced but not very elegant.

Pommard, Les Pezerolles,
Domaine A. F. Gros and
Francois Parent   2016 to 2025 plus   17.5
Magnum. Full colour. Good pure, stylish nose. Nothing too clumsy here. Clean, fullish-bodied, positive, and elegant. Lovely fruit. Fine.

Pommard, Rugiens,
Domaine de Montille   Now to 2025   17.0
Medium colour. Fully ready. Still tight on the nose. No great punch. Better on the palate. Round, rich, not very stemmy. Good grip and good depth. Ripe long finish. Very good indeed.

Pommard, Rugiens,
Fernand et Laurent Pillot   Now to 2020   16.0
Medium colour. Now mature. Ripe fruit on the nose. Good style and balance. But not a blockbuster. Medium body. Still a little firm on the attack. More flexible and succulent on the follow-through. Good long, vigorous finish. Very good.

CÔTE DE NUITS

Marsannay, L'Ancestrale,
Domaine Sylvain Pataille   Now to 2020   16.0
Full body, rich, stylish, and concentrated. Good old-viney depth. This is impressive. Very lovely fruit at the end.

Marsannay, Les Favières, Domaine
Fougeray de Beauclair   Now to 2016   14.0
A little pinched on the nose. Not as attractive or as round and fruity as the wine below, but better fruit on the palate than the nose would suggest.

Marsannay,
Les Saint-Jacques, Domaine
Fougeray de Beauclair   Now to 2018   15.0
Magnum. Medium to medium-full body. This has pleasant fruit. Fresh and attractive.

Fixin, Clos Marion, Domaine
Fougeray de Beauclair   Now to 2016   13.5
Magnum. Clumsy on the attack and then there is a lack of fruit on the palate. Lean finish.

Nuits-Saint-Georges, Domaine
Georges Mugneret-Gibourg   Now to 2022   16.0
Magnum. Medium-full colour. Plump, fruity, balanced nose. Medium to medium-full body. Very good grip. Stylish. Lovely finish. Very good, especially for a village wine.

Nuits-Saint-Georges,
Les Boudots, Domaine
Gerard Mugneret   Now to 2025 plus   17.5
Medium-full colour. Ripe, gently oaky, quite mellow nose. Lovely seductive fruit. Medium-full body. Abundant and almost sweet. Rich. Very good grip. Fine, long aftertaste. Just about ready. Fine. On another occasion I found it not as balanced or as classy as his Chaignots and gave it 16.5.

Nuits-Saint-Georges,
Les Boudots,
Domaine Jean Tardy et Fils   Now to 2020   16.0
Vieilles Vignes. Medium-full colour. Ripe, plump, oaky nose. Mocha flavours. Medium-full body. Round and attractive. Yet a touch short. Very good at best.

Nuits-Saint-Georges,
Aux Chaignots,
Domaine Faiveley   Now to 2020   16.0
Medium-full colour. Good class on the nose. Plenty of volume and depth. Still young. Medium-full body. Good ample attack. Rich and balanced. But then it doesn't have quite the grip on the follow-through. Very good at best.

Nuits-Saint-Georges,
Les Chaignots,
Domaine Gerard Mugneret   2015 to 2030   17.5
Full, barely mature colour. Rich, even opulent, potentially velvety nose. Lovely fruit. Very good grip. Fullish body. Well-balanced. Profound and most attractive. Plenty of energy and lots of depth. Very ripe at the end. Fine. Will still improve.

Nuits-Saint-Georges,
Clos des Forets-Saint-Georges,
Domaine de l'Arlot   Now to 2016   13.5
Medium to medium-full colour. The usual sweet stemmy stuff. Some fruit but lacks grip.

Nuits-Saint-Georges,
Clos des Porrets-Saint-Georges,
Domaine Henri Gouges   2015 to 2030   17.5
Fullish, youthful colour. Ripe, plump nose. At first a little reduced but this soon blew off. Full-

ish on the palate. Still a litte tannin to resolve. Concentrated and vigorous. Lots of depth and very good grip. Needs time but fine.

Nuits-Saint-Georges, Les Hauts Pruliers, Domaine Bertrand Machard de Gramont   Now to 2022 16.0
Fullish body. Ample and fruity. Quite rich. Good balance. Nice fresh, positive follow-through. Very good.

Nuits-Saint-Georges, Les Perdrix, Domaine des Perdrix   From 2015 17.5
Fullish colour. Quite a backward nose. Rich and spicy. Full-bodied. Ripe. Firm but classy tannins. Lots of ample fruit. Quite a meaty wine but very classy for a Premeaux. Fine.

Nuits-Saint-Georges, Les Porets-Saint-Georges, Domaine Alain Michelot   2015 to 2025 16.0
Fullish colour, still immature. Sturdy nose. Good grip and plenty of fruit, but not the greatest sophistication. Fullish, meaty, and balanced. Finishes well.

Nuits-Saint-Georges, Les Pruliers, Domaine Robert Chevillon   2015 to 2030 17.5
Fullish colour. Quite a firm, sturdy nose. Yet rich underneath. Fullish, vigorous, very classy, meaty structure. Lots of grip and depth. Lots of energy. Fine long aftertaste. Now getting mellow.

Nuits-Saint-Georges, Les Pruliers, Domaine Henri Gouges   2015 to 2030 18.0
Fullish colour. Still youthful. The nose still has the rawness of a five- or six-year-old wine. Fullish body. Still some tannin. Lots of energy. Abundant fruit. Very good grip. Very classy. Lovely long finish. Fine plus.

Nuits-Saint-Georges, Les Saints-Georges, Domaine Faiveley   2015 to 2030 17.5
Medium-full colour. Barely mature. Rich, concentrated nose. But still a bit tight. Medium-full body. Some tannin to resolve. Good grip and plenty of depth and class. Civilised for a middle

Nuits-Saint-Georges. Very good fruit and a long finish. Fine.

Nuits-Saint-Georges, Les Saints-Georges, Domaine Henri Gouges   From 2017 18.5
Fullish colour. Full, very rich, concentrated, tannic, backward nose. Very impressive. Full body. Some tannin. Splendidly profound. Very fine grip. Needs time but lots and lots of dimension.

Nuits-Saint-Georges, Les Vaucrains, Domaine Robert Chevillon   2015 to 2030 17.5
Medium-full colour. Stylish nose. Fullish, plummy, balanced, and profound. Lovely fruit. Lots of vigour and class. Fine.

Nuits-Saint-Georges, Les Vignerondes, Domaine Georges Mugneret-Gibourg   Now to 2025 17.5
Magnum. A lovely example. Rich, round, fragrant, and Vosne-ish. Lots of style. Fullish body. Balanced, profound, and classy.

Vosne-Romanée, Domaine Emmanuel Rouget   2015 to 2025 16.5
Medium to medium-full colour. Still youthful. Good firm, rich, vigorous nose. Fullish body. Lots of energy and depth. Still some tannin. Good concentration. Lots of dimension and class. Fine for a village wine.

Vosne-Romanée, La Colombière, Domaine du Vicomte de Liger-Belair   Now to 2020 plus 16.5
Medium to medium-full colour. Crisp, clean positive, fruity nose. Lots of class and depth for a village wine. Medium to medium-full body. Very harmonious. Classy and delicious.

Vosne-Romanée, Aux Réas, Domaine A. F. Gros et Francois Parent   Now to 2025 16.5
Magnum. Medium-full colour. Ample nose. Ripe and rich and gently oaky. Medium-full body. Good energy. Balanced and complex. Very good indeed for a village wine.

Vosne-Romanée, Les Beaux Monts, Domaine Grivot From 2016 18.5

Medium-full colour. Splendidly classy fruit on the nose. Intense and fragrant. Fullish body. Ample. Abundant. Excellent harmony. Very, very stylish. Complex and long. Quite splendid.

Vosne-Romanée, Les Beaumonts, Domaine Emannuel Rouget 2017 to 2035 18.5

Full, immature colour. Splendid nose. Rich and concentrated. Expansive and abundant. Lovely, really profound fruit. Rich and lush on the palate, but full and firm. Very fine.

Vosne-Romanée, Les Brulées, Domaine René Engel Now to 2025 18.0

Medium to medium-full colour. Now mature. Lovely fresh, fragrant, almost flowery nose. Medium-full body. Delicious ripe fruit. Balanced. Intense and classy all the way through. Lots of vigour. Fine plus.

Vosne-Romanée, Les Brulées, Domaine Michel Gros 2015 to 2030 18.5

Magnum. Fullish colour. Splendid rich nose. Very lovely multidimensional fruit. High-class. Fullish body. Now getting soft. But intense and classy and very long on the palate. Very fine.

Vosne-Romanée, Les Brulées, Domaine Méo-Camuzet 2015 to 2030 18.0

Full colour. Still youthful. Lots of oak on the nose. But no lack of volume and richness as well. Less oaky as it evolved in the glass. Full body. Still a bit of tannin. Rich and succulent. Lots of vigour. Fine finish. Fine plus.

Vosne-Romanée, Au Cros Parantoux, Domaine Méo-Camuzet 2016 to 2035 19.0

Full colour. Still youthful. Rich, quite powerful, but closed-in nose. Fatter, fuller, richer, more profound, and more opulent than their Brulées. Most impressive. Excellent grip. Not a bit too much oak. Very fine plus.

Vosne-Romanée, Clos des Réas, Domaine Michel Gros 2015 to 2025 18.0

Magnum. Medium-full colour. Lovely fragrant nose. Rich, profound, and balanced. A splen-

didly integrated, stylish wine with a very lovely finish. This is fine plus.

Vosne-Romanée, Aux Malconsorts, Domaine Sylvain Cathiard 2016 to 2035 19.5

Magnum. Fullish colour. Still quite closed-in on the nose. Medium-full body. Marvelous depth of very classy fruit on the palate. Very lovely balance. Complex and intense and splendidly integrated. Great wine here.

Vosne-Romanée, Les Suchots, Domaine Robert Arnoux 2015 to 2035 19.0

Full colour. Still youthful. Rich nose. But still hidden. Very lovely, intensely concentrated, old-vine fruit. Full body. Excellent grip. Lots of wine here. Great depth. Great class. Very fine plus.

Vosne-Romanée, Les Suchots, Domaine Jacques Cacheux et Fils 2015 to 2030 17.0

Full colour. Quite a full, rich but slightly extracted nose. Some tannin. Fullish body. Good fruit. Highish acidity. May get more generous as it evolves. Finishes promisingly. But at present only very good indeed.

Vosne-Romanée, Les Suchots, Domaine Grivot From 2017 18.5

Slightly fuller colour than the Beaumonts. Lots of very concentrated fruit on the nose. Fatter and fuller and richer. Just a bit more tannin. Slightly more austere. But also very profound and multidimensional. It will need a bit longer. Very fine too.

Vosne-Romanée, Les Suchots, Domaine Alain Hudelot-Noëllat 2015 to 2030 18.0

Medium to medium-full colour. Still quite youthful. A bit tight on the nose at first. Medium-full body. Plenty of depth and vigour. Very lovely ripe, rich fruit. Still a little tannin to resolve. Lots of energy. Still needs time. Very fine.

Vosne-Romanée, Les Suchots, Maison Nicolas Potel Now to 2025 18.0

Medium-full colour. Some development. Fine, pure, classy nose. Lots of vigour. Finely balanced. Medium-full body. Quite round and mellow. Fully ready. Very lovely fruit. Long and complex. Fine plus.

Chambolle-Musigny, Les Amoureuses,
Domaine J. F. Mugnier   From 2016   19.0

Medium to medium-full colour. At first it was a little pinched on the nose and the whole thing didn't quite sing. So I left it until the next day. Then it was glorious. Medium-full body. Very lovely fragrant, almost sweet fruit, with excellent supporting acidity. Long and subtle and very harmonious.

Chambolle-Musigny, Les Amoureuses,
Domaine Georges Roumier   2015 to 2035   18.5

Fine colour. Still youthful. Quite a firm nose. Aromatic. Spicy. Still unresolved. Fullish body. Still some tannin. This still needs time. Underneath, there is very fine classy fruit, balance, and intensity. Very fine.

Chambolle-Musigny, Les Amoureuses, Domaine
Comte Georges de Vogüé   From 2016   19.0

Fullish colour. Rich, fullish, concentrated, velvety-oaky nose. A lot of vigour and substance. Full body. Lovely fruit, balance, and class.

Chambolle-Musigny, Les Cras,
Domaine Ghislaine Barthod   Now to 2025   18.5

Medium-full colour. Lots of depth on the nose. Full body. Rich, classy, concentrated, and fragrant. Lots of dimension. Very lovely.

Chambolle-Musigny, Les Fuées,
Domaine J. F. Mugnier   From 2014   17.5

Medium to medium-full colour. Soft, ripe, fragrant, stylish nose. Very typically classy, intense Chambolle. Medium to medium-full body. Attractive, complex, elegant, and delicious. Fine.

Chambolle-Musigny, Les Gruenchers,
Domaine Digioia-Royer   Now to 2020   14.5

A bit of sulphur here. Medium to medium-full body. Ripe and plump. But it lacks a bit of style and the usual Chambolle fragrance. Quite good plus.

Chambolle-Musigny, Les Varoilles,
Domaine Ghislaine Barthod   Now to 2022   17.5

Medium-full colour. Poised and full of fruit on the nose. Medium-full body. Just a bit more loose-knit than her Cras. Just about ready. Fine.

Morey-Saint-Denis,
Domaine Dujac   Now to 2020   16.0

Good colour. Just about mature. Soft, intense nose. Ripe and succulent. No undue Dujac or stemmy flavours. Mellow. Fully mature. Fresh, balanced, classy, and long on the palate. Very good indeed for a village wine.

Morey-Saint-Denis, Les Faconnières,
Domaine Lignier-Michelot   Now to 2021   17.0

Medium-full colour. Ripe, fresh, abundant nose. More forward than some. Medium body. Stylish and fragrant. Balanced and full of charm. But it lacks a bit of vigour at the end.

Gevrey-Chambertin,
Mes Favorites, Vieilles Vignes   Drink soon   13.0

Magnum. A bad bottle? The other magnum was the same. Medium to medium-full colour. A bit shitty on the nose. Rather better after oxidation, but nevertheless somewhat astringent. I can't shine to this.

Gevrey-Chambertin, Les Cazetiers,
Domaine Bouchard Père et Fils   From 2015   18.0

Medium-full colour. Rich, quite firm, elegant nose. No lack of depth and dimension. Full-bodied, vigorous, classy, and balanced. A lovely profound example with a very fine finish.

Gevrey-Chambertin, Les Cazetiers,
Domaine Bruno Clair   2016 to 2035   18.5

Medium-full colour. Good rich, plummy nose. Plenty of depth, concentration, and class. Medium-full body. Ripe and vigorous. Lots of depth. Long. Very fine.

Gevrey-Chambertin, Les Cazetiers,
Domaine Christian Serafin   2015 to 2035   18.5

Good colour. Rich, ripe nose. A touch of oak. Lots of depth and class. Fullish body. Concentrated. Fat. Rich and lovely. Very fine.

**Gevrey-Chambertin,
Les Cherbaudes,
Domaine Fourrier** Now to 2020 plus 17.0

Medium-full colour. Just a touch of reduction on the nose at first. Rich, ripe, ample, and full of fruit on the palate. Good structure. Very well-balanced. Very good grip. Classy, succulent, and just about ready. Very good indeed.

**Gevrey-Chambertin,
Clos du Fonteny,
Domaine Bruno Clair** 2016 to 2030 17.5

Rich nose, with a touch of ozone. Medium-full body. Classy, poised, fruity, and balanced. Long, satisfactory finish. Slightly aloof, but fine.

**Gevrey-Chambertin,
Clos-Saint-Jacques,
Domaine Louis Jadot** 2015 to 2030 19.0

Medium-full colour. Very lovely, harmonious, rich, gently oaky nose. Fullish body. Approaching maturity. Lovely, ripe, balanced fruit. Vigorous, profound, and very classy. Very fine plus.

**Gevrey-Chambertin,
Clos-Saint-Jacques,
Domaine Armand Rousseau** From 2015 18.5

Medium to medium-full colour. Ripe, rich, succulent, and gently oaky on the nose. High-class. Very intense and fragrant. Not a blockbuster—indeed, it lacked just a bit of energy for great—but elegant and poised.

**Gevrey-Chambertin, Les Corbeaux,
Domaine Denis Bachelet** 2016 to 2035 18.0

Medium-full colour. Splendid rich, concentrated nose. Very classy tannins. Lots and lots of depth. Really very fine fruit on the palate. Lots of energy. A beautiful example.

**Gevrey-Chambertin,
Estournelles-Saint-Jacques,
Domaine Humbert Frères** Now to 2025 18.5

Fullish colour. Still youthful. Fresh nose. Plump. Balanced. Classy. Fullish body. Lots of concentration. A lovely vigorous, harmonious, profound wine. Really very good fruit. Very fine.

**Gevrey-Chambertin,
Lavaux-Saint-Jacques,
Domaine Bernard Dugat-Py** See note

Full, youthful colour. Rich, concentrated, old-viney, oaky nose. Still young. Fullish body. Rich and concentrated, but the tannins are rather burly. This is not easy to drink. Good acidity. But essentially overdone. I don't think it will ever soften satisfactorily.

**Gevrey-Chambertin,
Lavaux Saint-Jacques,
Domaine Claude Dugat** From 2016 18.5

Very full colour. Full, rich, firm, and concentrated on the nose. Lots of depth here. Fullish body. Some tannin. A lot of vigour and substance and a lot of dimension. Lovely energetic finish. Very fine.

**Gevrey-Chambetrin,
Lavaux-Saint-Jacques,
Domaine Denis Mortet** 2015 to 2030 18.0

Full colour. Full, rich, but just a little reduced on the nose at first. Fullish body. Very rich. Quite oaky. Very good but not a brilliant grip. Yet very lovely rich fruit, and no undue extraction. Lots of energy. Very fine. Another bottle was not reduced. No worries about the grip.

**Gevrey-Chambertin, Les Perrières,
Maison Nicolas Potel** 2015 to 2030 18.0

Fullish colour. Rich, ample, ripe, succulent nose. Lots of depth and distinction. Very seductive. Fullish body. Very good grip. Ripe tannins. Long and complex. Fine plus.

**Gevrey-Chambertin, Le Poissenot,
Maison Humbert Frères** 2015 to 2025 17.0

Good colour. Ripe, rich, fresh, positive nose. An attractive example. Very good fruit. Medium-full body. Balanced. Quite concentrated. Lovely finish. This is very good indeed.

Grands Crus

Le Corton,
Domaine Bouchard Père et Fils From 2015 15.0

Medium to medium-full body. Not a lot on the nose. Ripe but a little flat. Lacks a bit of grip.

Medium-full body. A touch astringent. Lacking richness. A little thin at the end. Pretty at best.

Corton, Maréchaudes,
Domaine Chandon de Briailles   From 2015   17.5
Medium-full colour. Fully mature. Ripe, sweet nose. Classy and composed. Medium-full body. Balanced. Very good, rich fruit. Long and fine.

Corton, Pougets,
Domaine Louis Jadot   From 2016   16.5
Good colour. Quite a firm, rich nose. A meaty wine. Good tannins, but it lacks a bit of real flair. Very good plus.

Echézeaux,
Domaine Bouchard Père et Fils   From 2015   18.0
Medium-full, youthful colour. Rich, spicy nose. Lots of depth. Very fine fruit. Full body. Ripe and concentrated. Lots of dimension. Fine plus.

Echézeaux,
Domaine René Engel   Now to 2025   18.0
Medium colour. Soft, plump, but fresh and stylish nose. Medium-full body. Lovely fragrant, balanced, very elegant fruit. Round and yet very persistent. Long. Fine plus.

Echézeaux,
Maison Vincent Girardin   From 2016   18.5
Fullish colour. Fresh, vigorous, ripe nose. Medium-full body. Lovely classy, balanced, ripe fruit. Some new oak. Lots of depth. Medium-full body. High-quality. Very lovely finish. Fine plus.

Echézeaux,
Domaine Emmanuel Rouget   From 2017   18.5
Medium-full colour. Still young. Splendidly rich, full, lush, abundant nose. Still quite closed. Succulent but some tannin still to resolve. This is very fine. But it needs time.

Echézeaux,
Domaine Jean Tardy   Now to 2022   16.5
Magnum. Good colour. Rich nose. Round and ripe but just a bit loose-knit. Ripe and oaky. Medium-full body. Easy to drink. A little astringency at the end. Very good plus.

Grands-Echézeaux,
Domaine Joseph Drouhin   From 2015   18.5
Good colour. Expansive, succulent nose. Very lovely fruit. Ample and delicious. Medium-full body. Lots of concentration and lots of class. Very fine.

Grands-Echézeaux,
Domaine René Engel   From 2015   18.5
Medium-full colour. Just a little less maturity than his Echézeaux. More depth. More concentration. More quality and a bigger wine. Some tannin. Rather less evolved. But real vigour and intensity. Needs time. Very fine.

Grands-Echézeaux,
Domaine de la Romanée-Conti   From 2015   18.0
Fullish colour. Rich, concentrated nose. Quite spicy. Fullish on the palate. Lots of depth, class, and complexity. Classic DRC. Very long and complex. Fine plus.

Clos de Vougeot,
Domaine Guy Castagnier   From 2014   17.0
Medium-full colour. Ample, fresh nose. Medium-full body. Ripe, balanced, and stylish. Not the greatest depth, but long and quite persistent. Very good indeed.

Clos de Vougeot,
Domaine René Engel   Now to 2025   18.0
Medium-full colour. Fully mature. Round, mellow nose. Not the intensity and depth of the Grands-Echézeaux. A charming wine. Closer in quality to the Echézeaux than the Grands-Echézeaux. Fresh. Good vigour. Elegant finish. Fine plus.

Clos de Vougeot,
Domaine du Clos Frantin   From 2015   18.5
Good colour. Fragrant nose. Medium-full body. Ripe tannins. Classy and profound. Lovely complex fruit. Ripe, vigorous, and delicious. Just about ready. Very fine.

Clos de Vougeot,
Domaine Grivot   From 2016   18.5
Fullish, vigorous colour. Full, firm, profound, nose. Very lovely fruit. Lots of dimension. Excellent finish. Very fine.

Clos de Vougeot,
Domaine Anne Gros   From 2015   19.5
Medium-full colour. Splendidly high-class, concentrated nose. Fullish. Excellent vigour and very profound fruit. Marvelous multilayered finish. Brilliant.

Clos de Vougeot, Domaine
Alain Hudelot-Noëllat   From 2016   18.0
Medium-full colour. Quite a soft, round, plummy nose. Medium to medium-full body. Good grip. Just a little tannin. Not the greatest succulence at present, but long and harmonious and improved in the glass. Fine plus.

Richebourg, Domaine Grivot   From 2017   20.0
Medium-full colour. Splendid nose. Really vigorous and concentrated. Very lovely fruit. Full body. Crammed with fruit. Very fine grip. Vigorous and classy and multidimensional. Excellent.

Richebourg,
Domaine Anne Gros   From 2017   20.0
Full colour. Still quite austere on the nose. But quite brilliant. Enormous drive and intensity. Great class. Very pure. Full-bodied. Splendid concentration and dimension without being a bit over-extracted. Very lovely long finish. A great wine.

Richebourg,
Domaine Gros Frère et Soeur   From 2015   17.0
Magnum. Fullish colour. Plump nose. Ripe, soft, round, and rich. Good meaty fruit, if without the usual Richebourg distinction. Fullish body. Good grip. But very good indeed at best.

Richebourg,
Domaine Méo-Camuzet   From 2020   19.5
Good full colour. Rich, full, backward, very profound nose. Lots of wine here. Full body. Splendid black fruit flavours. Still some tannin to be resolved. Oaky but not excessively so. Great depth and great energy. Still very youthful. Excellent.

Romanée-Saint-Vivant,
Domaine Robert Arnoux   From 2018   19.5
Good colour. Still rather closed on the nose. Fullish body. A little reticent at first, but not a blockbuster. Very lovely concentrated fruit, splendidly profound and balanced. Very, very long and complex. Very, very distinguished. Excellent.

Romanée-Saint-Vivant,
Domaine Sylvain Cathiard   From 2017   19.5
At first the bottle did not show well. I left it on ullage. There appeared to be a little built-in sulphur. It was just as it should be the next day. Medium-full colour. Still youthful. Soft, ripe, intense, very subtle, fragrant nose. Medium-full body. Very lovely complex, classy flavours. Not a blockbuster. Composed and very long on the palate. Very fine indeed.

La Romanée, Domaine
du Vicomte de Liger-Belair   From 2016   20.0
Medium-full colour. Lovely nose. Splendidly laid-back concentrated fruit. Very elegant. Ripe and rich and harmonious and classy. Very lovely finish. Excellent.

La Romanée, Domaine du
Vicomte de Liger-Belair,
Bouchard Père et Fils   From 2016   20.0
Medium-full colour. Splendid fruit on the nose: rich, profound, and creamy, with a touch of oak. Fullish body. Very, very concentrated and multidimensional. Great intensity and lovely harmony. Brilliant.

Bonnes-Mares,
Maison Vincent Girardin   From 2017   18.0
Good colour. Intense, fragrant nose. Not a blockbuster, but balanced and classy. Medium-full body. Very lovely Chambolle fruit. Long, lingering finish. Quite accessible already. Fine plus.

Bonnes-Mares,
Domaine J. F. Mugnier   From 2015   18.5
Medium to medium-full body. Ample, ripe, harmonious nose. Good substance. Good grip and intensity. This is particularly good this year. Medium-full body. Long. Intense. Very fine.

Bonnes-Mares,
Domaine Georges Roumier   From 2017   19.5
Fullish colour. Very lovely nose. Concentrated, rich, and very profound and classy. Still back-

ward. Full body. Multidimensional. Lovely balance. Lots of depth and heaps of finesse. Excellent.

Bonnes-Mares, Domaine
Comte Georges de Vogüé   From 2017   18.0
Very full colour. Still immature. Quite closed on the nose. Oaky and minty. Full body, rich, concentrated, and meaty. But in a good sense. Lots of wine here. Even quite powerful. Fine plus, but not as good as Roumier.

Le Musigny,
Domaine J. F. Mugnier   From 2016   20.0
Medium-full colour. Now just about *à point* compared to the Vogüé. Marvelous fragrance on both the nose and the palate. This is just what Musigny should be. Fullish. Splendid intensity and class. Very, very lovely finish. Brilliant.

Le Musigny, Domaine
Comte Georges de Vogüé   From 2017   19.5
Very fine, backward colour. At first a bit sweaty. But this blew off. The second bottle was cleaner: just what it should be. Full body. Meaty. Oaky. Very concentrated. Lots of wine here. Excellent grip and very lovely fruit. Still youthful. Very fine indeed.

Clos de Tart,
Domaine Mommessin   From 2016   17.5
Full, vigorous, immature colour. Rich nose. Almost over-ripe touches. Cooler on the palate. Full body. Good grip. Lots of concentration. Fine but not as classy as the wines are today.

Clos des Lambrays,
Domaine des Lambrays   Now to 2030   18.5
Magnum. Good colour. Ripe, stylish, fragrant nose. Medium-full body. Very good concentration and very lovely, elegant, balanced fruit. This is not a blockbuster but intense and very fine.

Clos-Saint-Denis,
Domaine Dujac   Drink soon   14.0
Only medium body. Fragrant but a bit light-weight. Especially compared with their Clos de la Roche. Disappointing.

Clos de la Roche,
Domaine Dujac   Now to 2025   18.5
Medium-full colour. Rich, fullish, ample, and stylish on the nose. Well-balanced. Lovely fruit. Just about ready. Very fine.

Clos de la Roche,
Maison Vincent Girardin   From 2018   18.5
Medium-full colour. Fragrant, intense nose. Very lovely fruit. Very composed, subtle, and concentrated. Very lovely fruit. Fullish body. Vigorous. Ripe and impressive. Very fine.

Charmes-Chambertin,
Domaine Arlaud   From 2014   17.0
Good colour. Fat, rich, ripe nose and attack. Just a touch of astringency on the follow-through. But ample enough and long enough. Medium-full body. Very good indeed.

Charmes-Chambertin,
Domaine Denis Bachelet   From 2017   19.0
Medium-full colour. Still vigorous. Still very youthful on the nose. Full body. Rich, ripe, and profound; but still closed. This is all in potential. Marvelous depth on the finish.

Charmes-Chambertin,
Domaine Bernard Dugat-Py   From 2017   16.0
Full, immature colour. Concentrated, oaky nose. Just a little forced. On the palate, not too much over the top. At least drinkable. Full body. Oaky. Tannic. Lots of grip. The fruit is fine and concentrated. But I find it unrelaxed—and it always will be.

Charmes-Chambertin,
Domaine Humbert Frères   From 2017   18.5
Fine, full, youthful colour. Splendidly rich nose. Quite tannic still. Lots of depth and concentration. This is still very youthful. Plenty of wine here. Very fine.

Charmes-Chambertin,
Vieilles Vignes,
Domaine Olivier Jouan   From 2018   18.0
Medium-full colour. Rich, ripe, round nose. Yet no lack of tannic structure. Fullish body. Lovely fruit. Lots of vigour. The tannins are

now beginning to soften. Long on the palate. Plenty of depth. Fine plus.

Charmes-Chambertin, Vieilles Vignes,
Domaine Perrot-Minot   From 2016   15.5
Full, immature colour. Rich, extracted, oaky, vigorous nose. Full and ripe, but rather forced and ungainly on the palate. Very good grip and concentration. May soften eventually, but I doubt it.

Charmes-Chambertin,
Domaine Taupenot-Merme   From 2014   15.5
Good colour. Somewhat pinched on the nose. Better on the palate, but a bit lean and one-dimensional. Medium to medium-full body. Fresh. Decent finish. Good plus.

Griotte-Chambertin,
Domaine Claude Dugat   From 2018   19.5
Fullish colour. Just a hint of maturity. Very beautiful, composed, concentrated, full nose. Excellent depth of fruit. A lot of dimension. Fullish body. Splendid class and harmony. Intense and fragrant and very long on the palate. Excellent.

Griotte-Chambertin,
Domaine Ponsot   From 2020   18.5
Medium-full colour. Expansive fruity nose. Fresh and generous. Medium-full body. Some tannin. Very good grip. Closed-in, even adolescent. Lovely fruit though. Very pure. Lovely finish. Very fine.

Latricières-Chambertin,
Domaine Rossignol-Trapet   From 2016   18.5
Medium-full colour. Now evolved. Ripe, accessible, plump, stylish, balanced, and fruity on the nose. Good depth and very good balance. Classy and concentrated too. Very fine.

Mazis-Chambertin,
Domaine Bernard Dugat-Py   From 2017   18.5
Big colour. Big wine. Powerful, very extracted, tannic nose. Not as bad as his Charmes, however. I can tolerate this. Fullish body. Lots of grip. Not too tough on the aftertaste. Multidimensional finish. Even class. Very fine.

Mazis-Chambertin, Maison Louis Jadot
   2015 to 2035 plus   18.0
Fullish colour. Lovely rich, aromatic nose. Pure, quite sturdy Pinot. Will still improve. Ripe. Lots of energy. Full body. Balanced, vigorous, and concentrated. Fine follow-through. Fine plus.

Ruchottes-Chambertin, Domaine Georges Mugneret Gibourg
   From 2015   18.5
Magnum. Fullish colour. Full, quite firm, concentrated nose. Full body. Ripe, ample, fresh, and very stylish and harmonious. This is intense, fragrant, and has a lovely finish. Very fine.

Ruchottes-Chambertin, Clos des Ruchottes,
Domaine Armand Rousseau   From 2015   18.0
Medium-full colour. Just a whiff of reduction at first. Fullish body. Very good grip. Nicely austere. Very lovely, slightly cool fruit. Fragrant at the end. Fine plus.

Chambertin, Maison Camille Giroud
   Now to 2030   18.5
Magnum. Fullish colour. Rich, full, spicy, and meaty nose. Fullish body. Ripe and abundant. Lots of depth. Now just about *à point*. Very long. Very fine.

Chambertin, Domaine Rossignol-Trapet
   Now to 2030   18.5
Medium-full colour. Fullish, ample nose in a similar vein to their Latricières. Full body. Very good grip. Lots of style if not the depth and concentration of Rousseau. Yet very long and very fine.

Chambertin, Domaine Armand Rousseau
   From 2017   20.0
Magnum. Medium-full, backward colour. This is brilliant. Full body. Rich. Concentrated and very youthful. Excellent grip. Very lovely finish. Very, very elegant.

Chambertin, Domaine Jean et Jean-Louis Trapet
   From 2016   19.0
Very good colour. Still youthful. Rich, full nose. Still a bit closed. Meaty. This is very fine plus. There is very lovely concentrated fruit and lots of flair.

There are four types of vintages: those which are obviously better than most, right from the outset, and fulfil their early promise; those which are indifferent at the beginning and always will be; those, sadly, which appear to be

rather good but fail to live up to original indications (1997 red Burgundy, for example); and lastly, those which seem to lack what it takes, but which go on just getting better and better. A prime example of this latter category is the 1991 red Burgundy vintage. It was decried at the outset but in fact has turned out very well indeed. The best wines are still delicious now, holding up surprisingly well. Another, I feel, is 2001.

Faces were long in September 2001, at the time of the Burgundy harvest. The weather pattern had by no means been perfect. The fruit, while ripe, was not really concentrated. The

| Size of the Crop | | | |
| (In hectolitres) | | | |
	RED	WHITE	TOTAL
Grands crus	13,955	3,935	17,890
Village and			
premiers crus	174,216	60,185	234,401
TOTAL	188,171	64,120	252,291

health of the grapes was not up to 1999 standards. And the musts registered a very high degree of malic acidity. Not a good vintage, we were told. The parallels were 1997 and 1994, not 1996 and 1998; far from 1999. Somewhat surprisingly, while the whites are only fair, the 2001 red Burgundy harvest has shown itself to

be really very good, especially in the Côte de Nuits. There is more substance, definition, and character than in the 2000s, though the 2002s are more regular and even better. In the 2001s there is a most appealing fresh, pure fruit, well-balanced by a good acidity. The tannins are ripe; and the wines speak of their origins. They have evolved in the medium to long term, but the very best are still vigorous, ten years after the harvest.

Weather Conditions

Generally speaking, 2001 was a wet, cool, and cloudy year in Burgundy. February and March were both rainy but mild, April and May—all except the last few days of the latter month—rainy and cool. The flowering was late and drawn out, and though the weather was for the first time in the year reasonably warm, the humidity left by all this wet weather produced outbreaks of mildew, as well as causing *mille-randage*, reducing the size of the crop.

July was miserably cold and wet, only heating up in the last ten days of the month. This resulted in a hail storm on August 2 which severely reduced the crop in Volnay, Monthélie, and the vineyards on the Auxey-Meursault border. The effect in parts of the Côte Chalonnaise was even worse, especially in Bouzeron. The last half of August was again warm, but most of the first three weeks of September were once again grey and cool, though reasonably dry.

The Ban des Vendanges fixed the first date of the harvest as Monday, September 17, in the Côte de Beaune and Thursday, September 20, in the Côte de Nuits. This was before the fruit was fully ripe, especially in those vineyards not green-harvested, but no one forced you to start on that date. While some of the less thoughtful rushed to pick, the better growers waited. There was a little rain on the September 19, rather more on September 26 and 27, but mainly at night. But in between it was windy, drying up the fruit, and after September 28 it became much warmer and sunnier. While the weather conditions were not ideal, the vines' leaves remained green, right up until the middle of the harvest. Photosynthesis was continuing to take place, making up for a blockage in this progress towards maturity occasioned by the cool weather earlier. Moreover, the wind helped concentrate the fruit, even if it was not initially very sunny.

While some of the Pinot Noir vineyards in the Côte de Beaune were picked earlier, while waiting for the white wine grapes to mature fully, much of the Côte de Nuits was not cleared until after September 28, in the best of the vintage conditions. This was a year to favour the late-pickers. This is the main explanation why not only is it a better year in red than in white, but why the Côte de Nuits is more successful than the Côte de Beaune. The other is a crucial difference in precipitation between the northern and the southern sectors of the Côte d'Or during the harvest and in the weeks which ran up to it. However, once one did begin, it was essential to clear the vines quickly before the grapes turned. Some doubled the number of pickers in order to get all the fruit into the winery at its best. The 2001 red wine harvest is 3.5 percent less in volume than the 2000, 8.4 percent lower than the 1999. This is less of a difference than the white wine yields (the 2001 is 9.7 percent less than the 2000), but it certainly plays a part in ensuring that the fruit approached a decent level of concentration rather than being merely ripe.

Triage, of course, was vital. Unlike the 1999, which was marvelously healthy, but like the 2000, there was, in 2001, an ever-present danger of rot. Sorting tables are now becoming more and more efficient. They vibrate, shaking off excess water. They have wind tunnels, which dry fruit that is moist. They can be lit from underneath, assisting the elimination of fruit which may have changed colour but not be fully ripe. The fruit is then destemmed (except in some top domaines such as the Domaine de la Romanée-Conti) but hardly crushed at all, then poured onto a second sorting table. Here it can be examined again, berry by berry. This ensures that only the perfect fruit is vinified.

The next step, in many cases in 2001, as in 2000, was a *saignée*: the bleeding off of excess juice, not only to improve the solid to liquid ratio but also, as in years like 2000, to eliminate the oxidise enzymes. As with the 2000s, 2001 was not a year for over-extraction, over-oaking, or over-chaptalisation. Despite the good acidities, the wines were essentially quite fragile. By this I do not mean that they were weak, but that the balance—and therefore the inherent elegance—risked, with over-manipulation, being easily compromised. Equally, this was a vintage for early bottling, to preserve the freshness of the fruit.

Where are the best wines? The vintage is better in the Côte de Nuits than the Côte de Beaune, and better in the Côte de Beaune than in the Côte Chalonnaise. Hail damage halved the harvest in some *climats* in Volnay, almost wiped out Bouzeron, and had severe effects in Rully and parts of Mercurey. The vines which survived were nevertheless unsettled as a result. Even putting these villages aside, the Savignys are proportionally better than the Santenays. There are some fine Cortons. Nuits-Saint-Georges is a village which has produced lovely 2001s, and these are better, proportionately speaking, than those in Vosne-Romanée and Chambolle-Musigny, where one or two wines are just a little *tendre*. The vintage is at its best in Gevrey-Chambertin.

At the outset, the red wines did not show very comfortably. There was a lot of malic acid, and the malo-lactic fermentations were slow to complete. As so often these days, one had to wait until the following autumn before one could confidently predict the eventual quality of the wines. This applied to the whites as well as the reds. If for the former the previous vintage, the 2000, is to be preferred, it is certainly the case that the red wines are better in this vintage. There are more than a few very attractive bottles, and these, just about ready ten years on, can safely be held. What is interesting to see is how the style of the vintage has affected the usual characters of the *communes*. This is particularly apparent in Pommard, where the wines, without having lost their usual size, seem to have more generosity and more sophisticated tannins. It also explains the success of the Nuits-Saint-Georges.

TASTING NOTES

The following wines were sampled at my usual ten-year-on tasting for the growers in Bouilland in June 2011. Once again, my thanks to Becky Wasserman and Russell Hone for permitting us to use the premises, and to Russell for his lentil cassoulet.

White Wines

Saint-Aubin,
Clos de la Chatennière,
Domaine Hubert Lamy   Drink soon   16.0
Magnum. Just a little fade on the nose. Better on the palate. Fresh, ripe, fruit-salady fruit. Balanced and stylish. Medium to medium-full body. Very good.

Saint-Aubin, En Remilly,
Domaine Hubert Lamy   Now to 2015   16.5
Magnum. A little more colour, but a little more vigour than the Chatennière. Fuller, richer, and with more grip. Today better. I usually prefer the above. Good depth. Lovely concentrated fruit. Holding up well. Very good plus.

Meursault, Maison Morey Blanc   See note
Past its best.

Meursault, Clos de la Barre,
Domaine des Comtes Lafon   Drink soon   15.0
Ripe, round, rich, and quite fresh, if without any real personality. Good.

Meursault, Limouzin,
Domaine Francois Mikulski   Drink up   13.5
Some fruit but a little tired. A little past its best. Somewhat four-square now.

Meursault, Meix Chavaux,
Domaine Roulot   Now to 2016   16.0
Ripe, clean, crisp, and classy. Holding up well. Lovely fruit. Can still be kept. Very good.

Meursault, Tête de Murger,
Domaine Patrick Javillier   Drink soon   15.0
Magnum. Rich, full, vigorous nose. Good substance, class, and depth. Good fruit. On the palate the wine is somewhat four-square and the finish is a bit coarse. Good at best.

Meursault, Les Charmes,
Domaine des Comtes Lafon   Now to 2017   17.0
Youthful colour. Fresh, succulent, and balanced, with attractive fruit if no great concentration. But there is depth and vigour here. Very good indeed.

Meursault, Les Charmes,
Domaine Roulot   Now to 2018   17.5
Magnum. Lovely, gentle, fresh nose. Soft and plump and elegant. Sumptuous, very harmonious fruit. Holding up well. Fine.

Meursault, Les Genevrières,
Domaine Francois Jobard   Now to 2016   16.0
Slightly more four-square on the nose than his Poruzots but better on the palate. More minerally. Good grip. Fresh. Quite vigorous. Can still be kept. Very good.

Meursault, Les Genevrières,
Domaine des Comtes Lafon   Now to 2015   16.0
Well-matured but still fresh. Ample, ripe, fullish. Not as fresh as the last example which came my way (or the 2000) but ripe and stylish.

Meursault, Les Perrières,
Domaine Thierry Matrot   Now to 2017   16.0
Labelled as Pierre Matrot. Ample, plump, and rich. Fresh and meaty. Good fruit. No great elegance but succulent. Medium-full body. Can still be kept. Very good.

Meursault, Les Perrières,
Domaine Pierre Morey   See note
Rather too reduced on both nose and palate for comfort.

Meursault, Les Poruzots,
Domaine Francois Jobard   Drink soon   14.5
Quite a firm, youthful nose. But a little age on the palate now. Fullish. Good grip. But rather rigid at the end.

Puligny-Montrachet,
Le Champ-Canet,
Domaine Jean-Marc Boillot   Drink up   13.0
Somewhat concocted nose. A bit rigid. Better on the palate, except that it is a bit sweet. Lacks class.

Puligny-Montrachet,
Les Champs-Gain,
Domaine des Comtes Lafon   Drink soon   17.0
Fullish, stylish nose. Ample, balanced, ripe, and still quite vigorous. Tails off a bit at the end. But very good indeed.

Puligny-Montrachet,
Les Demoiselles,
Domaine Guy Amiot et Fils   Now to 2016   16.5
Quite a developed colour, but the wine is fresh and stylish on both nose and palate. Medium-full body. A touch of new oak. Plump and fruity and balanced. Good depth. Very good plus.

Puligny-Montrachet, Les Pucelles,
Domaine Leflaive   Now to 2017   17.0
Fresh nose. Nicely crisp attack. Plump, balanced, and vigorous. Holding up well. Medium-full body. Some concentration. Good grip. Not enough flair for "fine" but very good indeed.

Puligny-Montrachet, La Truffière,
Domaine Jean-Marc Boillot   Drink soon   14.0
Better than his Champs-Canet. More relaxed. Fresher. Better grip. Medium-full body. But the fruit lacks class, especially at the end.

Chassagne-Montrachet,
Les Caillerets, Domaine
Richard Fontaine-Gagnard   Now to 2017   17.0
Youthful colour. Fresh nose. Ripe and balanced and elegant. Medium-full body. Good acidity. Crisp and stylish. No lack of depth. Finishes well. Very good indeed.

Chassagne-Montrachet,
Morgeots,
Domaine Lamy-Pillot   Now to 2018   17.5
Surprisingly fresh and peachy for the vintage. Classy, ripe, and delicious. Clean and fruit-salady. Very good grip. Long and well-balanced. Fine.

Morey-Saint-Denis,
Les Monts-Luisants,
Domaine Dujac   Now to 2018   16.0
Fresh colour. Fresh nose. Full of interest, depth, and vigour. Youthful and stylish. Still plenty of life.

Corton-Charlemagne, Maison Champy   See note
Prematurely oxidised.

Corton-Charlemagne, Domaine
Bonneau du Martray   Now to 2015   17.0
Ripe, rich, fresh, fullish, concentrated nose. Medium-full weight. This starts off well but then it tails off.

Red Wines
CÔTE DE BEAUNE

Givry, Clos Salomon,
Domaine du Clos Salomon   Now to 2016   15.0
Medium colour. Mature. Gamey nose. Fully mature on the palate. Slight sweet-sour notes. Medium body. Good fruit. Ripe and no weakness. Positive finish. Very good for what it is.

Santenay, Les Gravières,
Vieilles Vignes,
Domaine Vincent Girardin   Now to 2017   15.0
Good colour. Still vigorous. Quite a rich, oaky nose. Just a bit over-extracted, but this has given it a volume missing in some of the wines from the more celebrated communes further north. Medium-full body. No lack of fruit. Good acidity. But a certain element of the rustic. Good.

Savigny-Lès-Beaune,
Les Guettes, Domaine
Jean-Marc et Hugues Pavelot   Now to 2020   16.5
Magnum. Very good colour. Lovely fruit on the nose. Fresh, plummy, energetic, and complex. Really quite classy too. Medium-full body. Long. Very good plus.

Savigny-Lès-Beaune,
Les Marconnets,
Domaine Simon Bize   Now to 2018   16.0
Good colour. Somewhat subdued on the nose at first. But stylish. Medium body. Balanced.

Good vigour. Quite rich. Positive at the end. Long. Very good.

Savigny-Lès-Beaune,
Les Peuillets,
Maison Champy Now to 2016 14.0
Good colour. Round, ripe nose. Slight touch of bonfires. Medium-full body. Quite rich. Not much refinement but still vigorous. Quite good.

Savigny-Lès-Beaune,
Les Vergelesses,
Domaine Lucien Jacob Drink soon 14.0
Medium colour. Quite an evolved nose. A touch of astringency on the palate. Medium body. Good grip. But not quite enough fruit and class.

Pernand-Vergelesses,
Ile des Vergelesses,
Domaine Rapet Now to 2017 16.5
Medium to medium-full colour. Ripe nose. No great strength but classy and balanced. Medium body. Good follow-through. Very good plus.

Aloxe-Corton, Domaine
Maillard Père et Fils Now to 2018 15.0
Medium colour. No lack of vigour. Ripe, fruity, mellow nose. Medium to medium-full body. Plenty of fruit. Nicely balanced and stylish. Very good for a village wine.

Beaune, Les Cent Vignes,
Domaine Lucien Jacob Now to 2018 15.0
Medium colour. Soft nose. Ripe. Positive. Stylish and plump. An ample, medium-bodied wine with good vigour. Shows well.

Beaune, Les Cent Vignes,
Domaine René Monnier Now to 2017 15.0
Decent, mature colour. Sweet, soft nose. Nicely fruity, but not much depth or distinction. Medium body. Fresh and balanced. Good length.

Beaune, Aux Cras,
Maison Champy Drink soon 13.5
Magnum. Decent colour. But getting a bit old on both the nose and the palate. Somewhat loose-knit. Quite fruity. But some astringency.

Lacks a bit of grip and class and probably always did.

Beaune, Les Grèves,
Domaine Michel Lafarge Now to 2017 16.0
Good colour. Quite rich, spicy nose. A touch of astringency on the palate. But good depth and vigour and grip. Nice aromatic, ripe fruit. Finishes well. Cleaner than the attack. Very good.

Beaune, Les Pertuisots,
Domaine Devevey Drink soon 14.5
Magnum. Medium colour. Quite an earthy, developed nose. Medium body. Ripe. Reasonably positive and stylish. But it doesn't really sing. Quite good plus.

Beaune, Les Teurons, Domaine
Bouchard Père et Fils Now to 2020 16.5
Good colour. Ample fruity nose, now just about ready, but with plenty of vigour. Fullish for the vintage. Ripe, even rich. Good grip. Fresh and satisfying. Long positive finish. Very good plus.

Volnay, Caillerets,
Ancien Cuvée Carnot, Domaine
Bouchard Père et Fils Now to 2016 14.0
Medium colour. Fully mature. Soft nose. Elegant and fruity. But a little lightweight and diffuse. Their Teurons has a lot more going for it. Decently balanced. Not short. But a pretty wine: no more.

Volnay, Clos des Chênes,
Domaine Michel Lafarge Drink soon 13.5
Medium colour. Quite brown. Nothing much on nose and palate. Not as good as their Grèves. Somewhat dilute. Disappointing.

Volnay, Santenots,
Domaine Sylvie Esmonin Now to 2019 16.5
Very good, barely mature colour. Rich, earthy nose. This has been vinified with the stems. This has given it a backbone and depth missing in many of the other Côte de Beaunes. Fullish body. Ripe. A touch rigid. But a very good meaty wine. Good grip. Plenty of dimension on the finish.

Volnay, Santenots du Milieu,
Domaine des Comtes Lafon   Drink soon   15.0
Magnum. Medium-full colour. Soft nose. Ripe and stylish, but less depth and substance than usual. Medium body. Decent fruit on the attack, but no great dimension or interest. Good at best.

Volnay, Santenots du Milieu,
Domaine Francois Mikulski   Now to 2019   16.0
Magnum. Medium colour. Quite developed. A slight hail-taint on the nose, but not enough on the palate to render the wine undrinkable. Indeed, otherwise the wine is quite rich, full, and meaty. Fat at the end and with good grip. Very good.

Pommard, *Premier Cru*,
Domaine Billard-Gonnet   Now to 2018   15.0
Fresh, medium weight, mature colour. Soft, ripe, balanced, stylish nose. Medium body. An attractive harmonious wine with good support and a positive finish. Surprisingly good fruit. Good.

Pommard, Les Chaponnières,
Vieilles Vignes,
Domaine Billard-Gonnet   Now to 2019   16.0
Medium-full, mature colour. Soft, round, attractively balanced, ripe, fruity nose. Medium to medium-full body. Mellow. Stylish. Long on the palate. Very good.

Pommard, Les Charmots,
Maison Olivier Leflaive Frères Now to 2018 14.0
Good, fresh, medium-full colour. Ripe and balanced on the nose. But something not entirely clean here. Yet it wasn't corked. Medium to medium-full body. Good balanced acidity. Quite ripe fruit. And a decently positive finish. But only quite good.

Pommard, Clos des Arvelets,
Domaine Rebourgeon-Mure
Medaille d'Or, Concours des
Grands Vins, Mâcon, 2003   Now to 2020   17.0
Medium-full, mature colour. Lovely vibrant, succulent fruit on the nose. Medium-full body.

Round, ripe, rich, balanced, and stylish. The tannins very sophisticated. Mellow, complex finish. Very good indeed.

Pommard, Clos des Epeneaux,
Domaine des Epeneaux   Now to 2020   17.0
Magnum. Medium-full colour. Lovely fruit on the nose. Plump and ripe. Quite concentrated. Even sweet. Fullish. Fresh. Lovely finish. Very good indeed. Somewhat less exciting out of bottle six months later: only 16.0.

Pommard, Grand
Clos des Epenots,
Domaine de Courcel   Now to 2018   16.0
Magnum. Fully developed colour. Good energy on the nose. Ripe, rich, positive, and succulent. Medium-full body. Not as fresh or as classy as the Epeneaux, but very good.

Pommard, Clos du Verger,
Domaine Billard-Gonnet   Drink soon   15.0
Medium colour. Developed nose. Ripe, spicy. Fully ready, if not approaching its end. Medium body. Succulent and attractive. Positive at the end.

Pommard, Epenots,
Maison Olivier Frères   Drink soon   14.5
Medium colour. Quite a fresh fruity nose, but little in the way of depth or concentration. Light to medium body. But a bit dilute and one-dimensional. Yet what there is, is quite elegant. A pretty wine but no more than that.

Pommard, Les Pezerolles,
Domaine A. F. Gros   Drink soon   14.5
Medium body. Fully developed. Lacks energy. Soft and fruity. More to it on the palate. Medium-full colour. Balanced and spicy. But not a lot of style.

Pommard, Rugiens,
Domaine Jean-Marc Boillot   Now to 2017   15.5
Medium-full colour. Plump, succulent nose. Quite rich and meaty. Medium-full body. A slight touch of reduction on the palate. But good character and a positive finish. Good plus.

**Pommard, Rugiens, Domaine
Bouchard Père et Fils** Now to 2017 15.5
Medium-full, mature colour. A fragrant nose, without much weight behind it, and with a little over-extraction. Medium body. Just a touch dry. But quite fresh and fruity. Positive follow-through. Good plus.

CÔTE DE NUITS

**Marsannay, Les Longerois,
Domaine Bruno Clair** Now to 2016 15.0
Medium colour. Clean, precise nose. Attractive fresh fruit. Ripe, plump, balanced, and stylsh. A delicious picnic wine. Serve a little chilled. Very good for what it is.

**Marsannay, Cuvée l'Ancestrale,
Domaine Sylvain Pataille** Now to 2019 15.0
Medium to medium-full colour. Ripe. Plenty of vigour. Medium-full body. A meaty wine, especially for a Marsannay, but not over-extracted. Very good for what it is.

**Nuits-Saint-Georges,
Les Cailles, Domaine
Bouchard Père et Fils** Now to 2020 16.5
Very good colour. Soft and mellow on the nose. No great concentration or richness, but balanced and elegant. Medium to medium-full body. Still very fresh. Fully ready. Very good plus.

**Nuits-Saint-Georges,
Clos des Forêts-Saint-Georges,
Domaine Arlot** Now to 2020 15.5
Medium colour. Fully developed. Soft, ripe, almost sweet, stemmy nose. Medium body. Ripe. Fresh. Balanced. Good plus, but for me it lacks a bit of depth and concentration. Others liked it better than I.

**Nuits-Saint-Georges,
Les Pruliers,
Domaine Lucien Boillot et Fils** Drink soon 14.0
Medium-full colour. Some development. Not much on the nose. This has lost some of its fruit. Plump and quite rich, but a bit coarse.

**Nuits-Saint-Georges,
Les Saint-Georges,
Domaine Henri Gouges** Now to 2025 18.0
Fullish colour. Splendidly concentrated nose. Great style and class. Rich, full-bodied, meaty, and profound. Only just ready. Will still improve. Lovely finish. Fine plus.

**Nuits-Saint-Georges,
Les Vaucrains, Domaine
Robert Chevillon** Now to 2020 plus 17.5
Medium-full colour. Fully mature. Rich, full-bodied, and vigorous. Doesn't quite have the flair of the Gouges but a fine wine here. Plenty of life ahead of it.

**Vosne-Romanée, Les Brulées,
Domaine Michel Gros** Now to 2025 18.0
Magnum. Medium-full colour. A bigger, meatier, and less advanced wine than their Clos des Réas. And at present a little more clumsy. Still needs a couple more years. Fullish. Good tannins. Very good grip. Lots of energy and a lovely rich finish. Fine plus.

**Vosne-Romanée,
Clos des Réas,
Domaine Michel Gros** Now to 2025 18.0
Magnum. Medium-full colour. Soft, ripe, stylish nose. Lovely fruit. Medium-full body. Fresh, rich, harmonious, and energetic. Great harmony and great class. Fine plus.

**Vosne-Romanée,
Les Malconsorts, Domaine
Sylvain Cathiard** Now to 2025 plus 19.0
Magnum. Very good colour. Very lovely pure, classy nose. Concentrated and vigorous. Fullish body. Now just about ready. Very fine fruit and a lovely harmonious character. Splendid.

**Vosne-Romanée,
Les Malconsorts,
Maison Camille Giroud** Now to 2025 17.5
Medium-full colour. Classy fresh fruit on the nose. Pure. Concentrated. Poised. Harmonious. Medium-full body. Very elegant. Fine quality.

Vosne-Romanée, Aux Reignots,
Domaine Robert Arnoux   Now to 2025   17.0
Good colour. Just about mature. Fragrant nose. Still a little unforthcoming. Medium to medium-full body. Balanced and understated. Ripe and classy. Lovely fruit. Very good grip. Complex and subtle. Very good intensity at the end. Very good indeed.

Vosne-Romanée,
Aux Reignots, Maison
Bouchard Père et Fils   Now to 2025   17.5
Good colour. Fullish nose, nicely substantial. Ripe and rich. On the palate, only just about mature. Fullish body. Just a little tannin. Lots of vigour and depth. Quite a meaty wine for a 2001. Good energetic finish. Fine.

Vosne-Romanée, Les Suchots,
Domaine Robert Arnoux   Now to 2025   18.0
Fullish colour. Still youthful. A fullish, concentrated, still a little backward wine on the nose. Lovely rich, profound fruit. Lots of depth and dimension. Fullish body. Still a bit of unresolved tannin. High-quality underneath. Very good intensity at the end. Fine plus.

Vosne-Romanée, Les Suchots,
Domaine Grivot   Now to 2025 plus   18.5
Magnum. Very good colour. Rich, concentrated nose. Still a bit to go. Very lovely cool, plummy fruit. Fullish body. Complex and very classy. Lovely long, vigorous finish. Delicious.

Vosne-Romanée, Les Suchots,
Maison Louis Jadot   Now to 2025   17.5
Good colour. Ripe, fragrant, round but intense nose. Lovely elegant fruit. Medium to medium-full body. Soft tannins. Good grip. Lots of style and no lack of depth. Long and positive. Fine.

Chambolle-Musigny,
Domaine J. F. Mugnier   Now to 2018   16.0
Light-medium colour. Soft, classy, mature nose. Gentle, plump, and fruity. Ripe. Sweet. Medium body. Balanced. No great weight but lots and lots of charm. Lovely long finish.

Chambolle-Musigny,
Les Amoureuses,
Domaine Joseph Drouhin   Now to 2019   16.5
Medium to medium-full colour. Delicate but very classy on the nose. Quite developed. Good fruit. On the palate, a little undernourished. It lacks real intensity.

Chambolle-Musigny, Les Charmes,
Domaine Ghislaine Barthod   Now to 2019   17.0
Magnum. Medium-full colour. Lovely plump, succulent nose. Very stylish and very well-balanced. Long and very charming. Very good indeed.

Chambolle-Musigny, Les Cras,
Domaine Georges Roumier   See note
Fullish colour. First bottle round and ripe but both clumsy and a bit oxidised. The second bottle was cleaner but not really very exciting either.

Chambolle-Musigny,
Les Fuées, Domaine
Ghislaine Barthod   Now to 2020 plus   18.0
Magnum. Fullish colour. Firm on the nose. Rich, full-bodied, and profound. Lovely fruit on the palate. Medium-full body. Lots of energy. Ripe, balanced, and very good grip and depth. Classy and intense. Fine plus.

Chambolle-Musigny, Les Fuées,
Domaine J. F. Mugnier   Now to 2020 plus   18.0
Medium-full, mature colour. Splendidly clean, fragrant, balanced, vivacious nose. Very lovely fruit. Fullish. Very good grip. Round yet energetic. Long and lingering finish. Very lovely.

Chambolle-Musigny,
Les Groseilles,
Domaine Digioia-Royer   Now to 2020 plus   17.5
Medium colour. Lovely, fresh, plump fruit on the nose. Very elegant. Lovely style. Medium to medium-full body. Fresh and succulent. Long and lovely.

Chambolle-Musigny, Les Sentiers,
Domaine Arlaud   Now to 2017   16.0
Medium to medium-full, fully mature colour. At first a little spicy and flat on the nose, though

with no lack of acidity. Just a lack of freshness and sparkle. As it developed, the wine became more interesting and more elegant. Medium-full weight. Plump and fruity. Reasonable grip. Finishes positively. Very good.

Morey-Saint-Denis, *Premier Cru*,
Domaine Dujac   Now to 2019   17.0

Quite Dujac-y, despite the changes going on at the time. Soft, sweet, fresh nose. Medium body. No great depth or complexity—yet alone power—but very good indeed.

Morey-Saint-Denis, Aux Charmes,
Domaine Lignier-Michelot   Now to 2020   17.5

Medium-full colour. Fully ready. Intense, very pure, abundantly fruity nose, if no great weight or concentration. But balanced and very stylish. Now round, but fresh and complex. Fine.

Morey-Saint-Denis, Les Ruchots,
Domaine Arlaud   Now to 2019   17.5

Good colour. Soft, fragrant, intense nose. Gently oaky. Very lovely ripe fruit. Medium-full body. Balanced and elegant. Mellow but vigorous. Long. Fine.

Gevrey-Chambertin,
Mes Favorites (Vieilles Vignes),
Domaine Alan Burguet   Now to 2020   16.0

Medium to medium-full colour. Plump, fresh nose. Good meaty fruit. Medium-full body. Quite succulent. Fresh. Good grip. Plenty of wine here. Good vigorous finish. Very good.

Gevrey-Chambertin,
Vieilles Vignes,
Domaine Christain Serafin   Now to 2020   16.5

Good full colour, still vigorous. Quite an oaky wine on the nose, but fresh, fruity, and well-balanced. Medium-full body. Plenty of energy and succulence. Good long, positive finish.

Gevrey-Chambertin, Les Cazetiers,
Domaine Christian Serafin   Now to 2025   17.5

Fullish colour. Aromatic nose. Ripe, plump, not too oaky, as Serafin's wines can be. Ripe. Full-bodied. Balanced and very succulent. Not quite as brilliant as usual, but a fine 2011.

Gevrey-Chambertin,
Les Cazetiers,
Domaine Armand Rousseau   Now to 2018   16.5

Medium colour. Very soft but fresh on the nose. Lots of very ripe, balanced fruit, yet not much backbone. Medium body. Most enjoyable, if no real consequence.

Gevrey-Chambertin,
Les Cherbaudes, Domaine
Lucien Boillot Père et Fils   Now to 2020   16.0

Good fresh colour. Ripe, rich nose. Quite stylish. Well-balanced. A meaty wine with more depth and quality than usual at this period. Good fruit and good energy.

Gevrey-Chambertin,
Clos du Fonteny,
Domaine Bruno Clair   Now to 2025   17.5

Magnum. Good colour. Very lovely nose. Pure and poised and cool and very elegant. Lovely fruit. Very harmonious and persistent. It lacks just a little strength in the middle, but the finish is long and positive.

Gevrey-Chambertin,
Clos-Saint-Jacques,
Domaine Bruno Clair   Now to 2025   18.5

Magnum. Medium-full colour. Aromatic nose. Some new oak here. Medium-full body. Slightly spicy. A much more ample and substantial wine than the Clos du Fonteny. Lots of depth. Lots of energy. Lots of quality. Needs another two years.

Gevrey-Chambertin,
Clos-Saint-Jacques,
Domaine Sylvie Esmonin   Now to 2025   17.0

Full colour, still very vigorous. Really quite oaky on the nose. For my taste this almost dominates, but on evolution in the glass it didn't seem to take over unduly. Fullish body. Firm. Rich. Good grip. Plenty of depth and ripe, quite stylish fruit. Again, it seemed to get more sophisticated on evolution. Long and vigorous. Very good indeed.

**Gevrey-Chambertin,
Clos-Saint-Jacques, Domaine
Armand Rousseau** Now to 2025 plus 19.0

Medium-full colour. Rich, concentrated, high-quality nose with a touch of new oak. Fullish body. Profound. Youthful. Excellent grip. Very impressive finish. Splendid quality as usual. Will still improve.

**Gevrey-Chambertin,
La Combe aux Moines,
Domaine Fourrier** Now to 2020 17.0

Medium-full colour. Just about mature. Charming, mellow, vibrant, fruity nose. Medium-full body. Round but fresh. Very good fruit. Elegant and long on the palate. Very good indeed.

**Gevrey-Chambertin,
Aux Combottes,
Domaine Arlaud** Now to 2018 16.5

Good colour, full, and barely mature. Fully mature on the nose and on the palate. Medium-full body. A touch of spice. Round, ripe tannins. Good acidity, but it lacks a little grip on the attack. The finish is better. Plenty of ripe fruit. Very good plus.

**Gevrey-Chambertin,
Les Corbeaux,
Domaine Denis Bachelet** Now to 2025 18.0

Full colour. Ample, rich, meaty nose. Lots of depth here. Fullish body. Lots of class. Very lovely fruit. Great harmony and intensity. Will still improve. Fine plus.

**Gevrey-Chambertin,
La Petite Chapelle, Domaine
Dupont-Tisserandot** Now to 2018 16.0

Good colour. Ripe, rich, and with a slight gingerbread spice on the nose. Medium to medium-full body. Lacks a little energy on the follow-through, but still reasonably vigorous.

**Gevrey-Chambertin, Le Poissenot,
Domaine Humbert Frères** Now to 2020 16.5

Medium to medium-full colour. Soft, succulent, plump nose. Juicy-fruity. Full of charm, if not too much substance and energy. Balanced and fruity and elegant.

GRANDS CRUS

**Corton, Bressandes, Domaine
Chandon de Briailles** Now to 2020 17.5

Magnum. Medium colour. Fresh nose. Ripe and plump and stylish. Good fruit. Medium to medium-full body. Plenty of complexity as well as originality. Long. Fine.

**Corton, Clos du Roi,
Domaine Thénard** Now to 2020 17.5

Good colour. Soft, fruity, elegant nose, but not a lot of weight behind it. Medium-full body. Balanced and succulent. More to it than seems on the nose. Good persistence. Long on the palate. Fine.

**Corton, Renardes,
Maison Camille Giroud** Now to 2020 17.0

Full colour, barely mature. Rich, fat, opulent, meaty nose. Good grip and plenty of energy. Full-bodied. Still a little tannin to absorb. Stylish, rich, ripe fruit. Perhaps it could have been a bit more elegant. But very good indeed.

**Grands-Echézeaux, Domaine
de la Romanée-Conti** Now to 2020 18.0

Good, fullish colour. Aromatic, spicy, slightly burned nose. But most enticing red fruit behind it. Full body. Now mellow but with plenty of vigour. Very good acidity. Cool and classy. Lots of depth. Medium-full body. No enormous grip, but it evolved well in the glass. Fine plus for the vintage.

**Grands-Echézeaux,
Domaine Thénard** Now to 2018 17.5

Good colour. Soft, ripe, oaky, attractive nose. Medium-full body. Good acidity. Good depth. The wine is succulent and balanced. Positive at the end. No hard edges. Stylish. Fine.

**Clos de Vougeot,
Domaine Dr. Georges
Mugneret-Gibourg** Now to 2018 16.0

Medium-full colour. Full, rich, fat, ample nose. Fresh on the palate. Lots of depth at first. But not the greatest of intensity on the follow-through. Indeed, it tails off. A pity. Decent finish. But it could have been a lot better.

Romanée-Saint-Vivant, Maison Camille Giroud
Now to 2018 17.0

Medium-full, mature colour. Round, ripe nose. Medium to medium-full body. Juicy and succulent. Balanced and quite vigorous. Good class. Long and positive. Most attractive, but very good indeed rather than great.

Romanée-Saint-Vivant, Domaine Alain Hudelot-Noëllat
Now to 2020 18.0

Medium-full, mature colour. Fragrant, stylish, round nose. Balanced and with good intensity. Even better on the palate. Very lovely fruit. Plenty of vigour. Medium to medium-full body. Even quite rich. Very good grip. Succulent and energetic. Long classy finish. Fine plus.

Richebourg, Domaine A. F. Gros
Now to 2019 17.5

Fullish colour. Ripe and seductive on the nose, but a bit too soft for a Richebourg. Medium-full body. Balanced and stylish. But the attack lacks a little intensity. The follow-through is better. But fine rather than great.

Richebourg, Domaine Alain Hudelot-Noëllat
Now to 2020 plus 19.0

Good, mature colour. Rich, profound, concentrated, very well-balanced nose. Very lovely fruit here. A fullish 2001. Very elegant. Lots of vigour. Lots of depth. This is really classy and very fine indeed. Very lovely finish.

La Tâche, Domaine de la Romanée-Conti
Now to 2020 18.5

Fullish colour. Delicate but intense on the nose. Lovely fruit but a lack of real power. Balanced. Very classy nevertheless. Very fine.

Bonnes-Mares, Fougeray de Beauclair
Now to 2020 plus 17.5

Good colour, still youthful. The nose is still closed-in. On the palate a full-bodied meaty wine, still with a bit of tannin to resolve, but rich and full of blackberry and plummy fruit. Very good grip. At the end it lacks a little refinement, but a fine wine nonetheless, which will be better still in 2015.

Bonnes-Mares, Domaine Georges Roumier
Now to 2025 19.0

Full colour. I much prefer this to the Vogüé. It is fresher, riper, cooler, and classier. Fullish body. Lots of energy. Lots of depth. Very fine plus.

Bonnes-Mares, Domaine Comte Georges de Vogüé
Now to 2020 18.0

Full colour. Rich, fullish, plump fruit. Plenty of substance and depth. A slight lack of real class but no lack of wine here. Fine plus.

Musigny, Domaine J. F. Mugnier
Now to 2020 19.5

Medium-full colour. Fragrant, very lovely fruit. Delicate but intense. By no means a blockbuster. But ripe, succulent, harmonious, and very, very long and classy. Lovely. The wine of the vintage?

Musigny, Domaine Comte Georges de Vogüé
Now to 2025 18.0

Full colour. Quite a full, indeed aggressively oaky nose. Quite structured, but the fruit underneath is a little rigid. Good grip. Still needs time. Fine plus. But not great.

Clos de Tart, Domaine Mommessin
Now to 2020 plus 17.5

Fullish colour. Full, rich, meaty nose. Some stems evident. A sturdy wine. Full body. Rather more sophisticated on the palate than on the nose. Lots of vigour and energy here. Only just ready. Long on the palate. Ample, rich, and spicy. Fine.

Clos des Lambrays, Domaine des Lambrays
Now to 2018 18.0

Medium-full colour. Now fully mature. Lovely ripe, fragrant nose. Very lovely, complex, delicate fruit. Medium-full body. Lots of depth and dimension. Vigorous but now velvety. Very long. Not as concentrated as the wines produced today but fine plus.

Clos-Saint-Denis, Domaine Arlaud
Now to 2020 18.5

Medium-full colour. Delicious, soft, but intense and classy, fragrant fruit on the nose. Medium-full body. The tannins are now nice and mellow. Very harmonious. Profound. Lovely long finish. Very fine.

Clos-Saint-Denis,
Domaine Dujac   Now to 2020   18.5

Medium to medium-full colour. Higher-toned on the nose than their Clos de la Roche. Medium-full body. Complete, balanced, fragrant, and composed. Ripe and almost sweet. Very long on the palate. Lovely.

Clos de la Roche,
Domaine Dujac   Now to 2020 plus   18.5

Medium-full colour. A little fuller-bodied than their Clos-Saint-Denis. Meatier. Slightly less sweet but more vigour and a better grip. Will last longer. Lovely.

Charmes-Chambertin,
Domaine Arlaud   Now to 2020   17.5

Good, vigorous colour. Round, charming, ripe, stylish, intense nose. Plenty of depth. No hard edges. No weakness. This is balanced and full of fruit. Very gently oaky. Good grip. Fine.

Charmes-Chambertin,
Domaine Denis Bachelet   Now to 2025   18.5

Fullish colour. Plenty of energy and substance on the nose, but at present a little ungainly. This still needs time. Better on the palate. Fullish, rich, fat, and succulent. Very good grip. Very fine.

Charmes-Chambertin,
Domaine Humbert Frères   Now to 2020   18.0

Fullish colour. Full and rich, ample, and succulent. Plenty of depth and class. This is very well made. Lots of energy. Medium-full body. Very good fruit. Lovely vigorous finish.

Charmes-Chambertin,
Domaine Armand Rousseau   Now to 2018   16.5

Medium to medium-full colour. Soft nose. Slightly lean, but balanced and classy. Medium body. Round and attractive and well-balanced, if not exactly fat or rich. But fresh and positive, long and elegant. Very good plus.

Chapelle-Chambertin,
Domaine Rossignol-Trapet   Now to 2019   16.0

Medium to medium-full colour. Soft and a little loose-knit on the nose. Medium body. Fruity and reasonably fresh. But a lack of personality.

Griotte-Chambertin,
Domaine Joseph Drouhin   Now to 2020   18.5

Medium-full colour. Some maturity. Very lovely nose. Fragrant, intense, and very elegant and persistent. Round and ripe and complex and energetic. Medium-full body. Only just about ready. Real *grand cru* class. Very fine.

Ruchottes-Chambertin,
Clos des Ruchottes,
Domaine Armand Rousseau   Now to 2020   17.5

Medium to medium-full colour. Fragrant nose, showing lovely ripe fruit. Medium to medium-full body. Round, soft, silky-smooth. Fresh, balanced, ripe fruit. Plenty of class, if no great weight or concentration. Long and positive. Fine.

Chambertin,
Clos de Bèze, Domaine
Bouchard Père et Fils   Now to 2025   19.0

Medium-full colour. Very fine nose. Lots of class and depth. Profound, concentrated, fresh, and impressive. Medium-full body. Very good tannins. Very good grip. Long, complex, and high-class. Excellent.

Chambertin, Clos de Bèze,
Domaine Pierre Damoy   Now to 2020   18.5

Full, vigorous colour. Distinguished, very youthful, crammed-with-fruit nose. Fullish body. Very good tannins. The oak is just right, as is the extraction. Very fresh. Lovely.

Chambertin, Clos de Bèze,
Domaine Armand Rousseau   Now to 2025   19.0

Magnum. Medium-full colour. Splendidly rich, ample nose. Succulent and profound. Fullish body. Lots of energy and particularly lovely fruit. Very fresh. Lovely balance. Very classy indeed. Will still improve.

Chambertin, Domaine

Rossignol-Trapet   Now to 2020 plus   18.5
Fullish colour. Rich, fresh, plump, fullish nose.
Plenty of depth. This is *à point*. Fresh, juicy, and
balanced. Lots of plummy fruit. Long and positive and classy.

Chambertin,

Domaine Armand Rousseau   Now to 2025   19.5
Full, youthful colour. Lovely rich, ample, classy
energetic nose. Fullish body. Round and fat and
succulent. Lots of vigour here. Splendid fruit.
Quite delicious. Even better than the Clos de
Bèze. Will still improve. Very fine indeed for a
2001.

Chambertin, Domaine

Jean et Jean-Louis Trapet   Now to 2019   17.0
Medium-full colour. Still youthful. One bottle
a bit evolved and ungainly. The second better
but nevertheless not quite as pure and classy
as one hoped for. Fullish. Youthful. Good grip.
Plump and energetic, but a bit chunky. Very
good indeed rather than great.

2000 BURGUNDY

It was perhaps inevitable that after the glorious gifts on offer in the 1999, the 2000 should
prove a disappointment, and further, that
it should have been unduly criticized at the
outset, especially from those who had widely

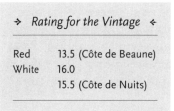

→ *Rating for the Vintage* ←

Red   13.5 (Côte de Beaune)
White   16.0
        15.5 (Côte de Nuits)

bought in the previous campaign and who were
disinclined to put more than a token toe in the
waters of the 2000. In fact, the vintage is not
at all bad. Only so-so in the Côte de Beaune as
far as the red wines are concerned, but very satisfactory in white and highly agreeable in the

→ *Size of the Crop* ← (In hectolitres)			
	RED	WHITE	TOTAL
Grand cru	14,199	3,989	18,188
Village and premier cru	180,748	59,353	240,101
TOTAL	194,947	63,342	258,289

Côte de Nuits. We all need wines which evolve
in the medium term, like the 2000s, not just
the restaurant business. Moreover, the size of
the crop, as can be seen in the table, was generous, leading to price stability, at least in euros.

Weather Conditions

The first few months of the year were warm
(February was wet; March was dry), leading
to an early bud-break. April was cool—but not
so cold that there was any frost damage—and
inclement; but after the middle of May, the
weather improved. The vines flowered rapidly
and uniformly in the first week of June, promising a large and early harvest. Then came July—
cold and miserable; one of the coolest in recent
years, and with no lack of rain. Nevertheless,
the evolution of the fruit remained ahead of previous vintages. August was warm, setting the
platform for a potential quality which, despite
the rain in September, would not be washed out
entirely. *Août fait le moût* (August makes the
must), as the French *vignerons* point out.

The harvest started in the Côte de Beaune
on Monday, September 11, and was immediately halted by a storm in the afternoon and evening of Tuesday. As much as 75 millimetres of
rain fell in some of the Côte de Beaune villages.
Volnay seems to have weathered the worst of
it. This immediately compromised what a few
days previously had looked very promising.
Less rain fell in the white wine villages, and in
the Côte de Nuits, which in general had had a
drier summer anyway, and was to remain drier

in the unsettled period which followed. The Côte de Nuits also benefited from the fact that the vintage normally follows a week or so after the Côte de Beaune. The effects of the great downpour could be allowed to drain away and the fruit to dry out. As a result, the incidence of rot was a great deal reduced, and some *cuvées* in the Côte de Nuits attained natural alcoholic levels of 13° or more.

It says a lot for the perfectionism which you see just about everywhere in today's Burgundy—sorting tables and so on—that there is little evidence of botrytis in the 2000s. Yes, some wines are a bit loose and soft-centred, others just plain dull and one-dimensional, and acidities in the Côte de Beaune are rather low. But from the motorway north—the dividing line being here rather than between Ladoix and Corgoloin—the wines are more than satisfactory: indeed fresh and succulent and even quite *terroir* specific. At ten years old, they are now fully ready. Open your bottles and enjoy them.

TASTING NOTES

The notes which follow come in the vast majority from my annual ten-year-on tasting, held in June 2010. I have added notes on other 2000s which came my way on separate occasions that year plus those tasted at a session organised by Tom Black of Nashville, Tennessee, in April 2011.

White Wines

Montagny, *Premier Cru* Selection, Domaine Stéphane Aladame   Drink soon   15.5
Fresh, plump, and stylish. Easy to drink. Holding up well. Very good fruit. Good plus.

Saint-Aubin, Clos de la Chatenière, Domaine Hubert Lamy   Now to 2015   17.0
Magnum. Very good grip. Attractive peachy fruit. Lots of depth and style. Could be a first-division Puligny. Plenty of life still. Very good indeed.

Beaune, Sur les Grèves, Domaine du Château de Chorey   Drink soon   15.0
Magnum. Ripe, nutty nose. A slight touch of reduction on the palate. Some evolution. But good.

Meursault, Clos de la Barre, Domaine des Comtes Lafon   Now to 2014   16.5
Quite a firm, energetic nose. Fullish body. Plenty of depth. Good grip and lots of style. Long. Very good plus.

Meursault, Blagny, Domaine Thierry Matrot   Drink soon   14.0
Losing energy on the nose. Better on the palate but it lacks a bit of style.

Meursault, Charmes, Domaine des Comtes Lafon   Now to 2018   17.5
Fresh, very stylish. Profound. Fullish body. A touch of oak. Very vigorous. Fine. But Lafon's Genevières and Perrières are superior this year.

Meursault, Charmes, Domaine Thierry Matrot   Drink up   14.0
Medium-full, fresh nose. Decent style. But not special.

Meursault, Charmes, Domaine Roulot   Now to 2015   16.5
Magnum. Fullish, firm, juicy, and ample. A wine for food. Good energy at the end. Very good plus.

Meursault, Genevrières, Domaine Francois et Antoine Jobard   Drink up   14.0
Magnum. Very fresh on the nose. Decent attack but then rather flat and one-dimensional at the end.

Meursault, Genevrières, Domaine des Comtes Lafon   Now to 2020   18.0
Fresh colour. Rich nose. Spicy in the usual citrus-peel way. Fresh and balanced and classy. Does not have the minerally energy of their Perrières but a lovely wine, and better than their Charmes.

Meursault, Genevrières,
Domaine Francois Mikulski   Drink soon   16.0
Magnum. Evolved colour. Yet fresh and juicy
on the nose. Very flowery. Good acidity. Individual. Very good.

Meursault, En Lurale,
Domaine Joseph Drouhin   Drink up   14.0
Soft, evolved. A little old on the palate. Never
had the greatest strength.

Meursault, Meix Chavaux,
Domaine Roulot   Drink soon   14.5
Clean, attractive nose. Very good fruit. Fresh at
first but a little less life on the follow-through.
Quite good plus.

Meursault, Perrières,
Domaine des Comtes Lafon   Now to 2020   18.5
Medium-full youthful colour. Fullish, rich,
concentrated, and profound on both nose and
palate. This is very impressive. Very lovely ripe
fruit. Lots of life ahead of it.

Meursault, Les Tessons,
Domaine Pierre Morey   Drink up   13.0
A touch reduced on the nose. A bit dead on the
palate.

Meursault, "Tête de Murger,"
Domaine Patrick Javillier   Drink soon   15.0
Magnum. Good nose if a little evolved. Ample.
Balanced. Lacks a little grip. But good.

Puligny-Montrachet,
Les Combettes,
Domaine Jean-Marc Boillot   Drink soon   15.0
Good nose. Some concentration. No lack of
vigour. Fullish. Firm. A little aggressive. But
good.

Puligny-Montrachet,
Les Demoiselles,
Domaine Guy Amiot   Drink soon   16.5
Fresh colour. Soft, plump, gentle nose. Plenty of
fruit, if no great depth or grip. A most agreeable
wine. Stylish and balanced. Very good plus.

Puligny-Montrachet,
Les Folatières,
Domaine Joseph Drouhin   Now to 2016   17.5
Ripe, fresh, gently oaky nose. Good vigour and
concentration and plenty of class and depth.
Fine.

Puligny-Montrachet,
Hameau de Blagny,
Domaine Martelet de Cherisey   Drink soon   15.0
Delicate, but not too delicate on the nose.
Attractive peachy fruit. Soft and ripe on the
attack. Then it tails off a bit. But good.

Puligny-Montrachet, Les Pucelles,
Domaine Paul Pernot   Drink soon   15.5
Well-matured nose. Lush, quite exotic. But
not exactly very elegant. Slightly blowsy. Fully
ready. Reasonably good grip on the palate, and
held up better in the glass than I had expected.
But good plus at best. It lacks both energy and
purity.

Puligny-Montrachet, Les Referts,
Domaine Jean-Marc Boillot   Drink up   13.5
A bit oxidised on the nose. Ripe though. Good
fruit.

Chassagne-Montrachet, Boudriotte,
Domaine Ramonet   Drink soon   16.0
Well-matured, but still fresh. Fruity and full
of interest. Not brilliant but a lovely bottle, still
holding up.

Chassagne-Montrachet,
Les Caillerets,
Domaine Fontaine-Gagnard   Drink soon   16.0
Quite a mature colour. On the nose this is
beginning to lose a bit of its fruit. But on the
palate, still ripe and balanced and juicy enough.
There is no lack of style here. Just a slight
absence of vigour. Very good.

Nuits-Saint-Georges, Clos de l'Arlot,
Domaine de l'Arlot   Drink soon   15.0
Fresh nose, but sweet and oaky, and with little
terroir expression. Lacks depth. Curiously confected. Yet good nevertheless.

Corton, Domaine

Chandon de Briailles   Drink soon 15.0

Quite fresh ripe fruit but a little one-dimensional. Lacks vigour at the end. And class. Good at best.

Corton-Charlemagne, Domaine

Bonneau du Martray   Now to 2020 18.5

A delicious wine. Full and very vigorous. Very lovely fruit. Complex and classy. A yardstick example. Very fine.

Note: Both the Wine Society and Berry, Bros and Rudd were forced to return parcels of this wine, where there were too many prematurely oxidised examples. They were, of course, fully compensated.

Corton-Charlemagne,

Maison Champy   Now to 2016 17.5

Magnum. Fullish, fresh, stylish, and nicely minerally. Very good energy. Plenty of quality fruit. Fine.

Corton-Charlemagne,

Domaine Antonin Guyon   Drink soon 15.5

Youthful colour. Somewhat neutral on both the nose and the palate. Fresh, clean, and quite stylish but a lack of *grand cru* depth. Good plus.

Corton-Charlemagne,

Domaine Patrick Javillier   Drink soon 17.0

Fresh colour. Good attack. No lack of vigour. Plenty of elegant fruit. Fullish body. It just slightly fades away at the end, especially after half an hour in the bottle.

Bâtard-Montrachet,

Domaine Joseph Drouhin   Now to 2020 18.5

Fresh colour. The nose is still closed. Not much evidence of new oak. Youthful. Fullish-bodied. Very good acidity. Very lovely fruit. Ripe and rich. Minerally and still very vigorous. Very fine.

Bâtard-Montrachet,

Domaine Jean-Noel Gagnard   Now to 2020 18.5

Magnum. This is delicious. Very lovely, concentrated, pure, vigorous fruit. Fullish. Classy. Long. Very fine.

Bâtard-Montrachet,

Domaine Leflaive   Now to 2016 18.0

Magnum. Not very forthcoming on the nose. Medium-full body. Ripe. Fresh and attractive. Very good fruit. Good energy. Fine plus.

Le Montrachet,

Domaine Marquis de Laguiche,

Maison Joseph Drouhin   Now to 2020 19.0

Youthful colour. Rich, fresh, succulent nose. Very classy and full of fruit. This is now *à point*. The wine is fullish-bodied, ripe, profound, and delicious.

Red Wines

Bourgogne Côte Chalonnaise,

La Digoine, Domaine

A. and P. de Villaine   Drink soon 14.0

Light to medium colour. Soft, fresh, cherry-type nose. Just a little suave. Medium body. Holding up well. Can still be kept.

Givry, Clos Salomon,

Domaine du Clos Salomon   Now to 2015 15.0

Magnum. Soft, stylish nose. *À point*. Balanced, supple, and fruity. Good.

CÔTE DE BEAUNE

Saint-Romain,

Domaine Emmanuel Giboulot   Drink up 13.0

Decent fruit at first. Light. Beginning to get dry and coarse.

Savigny-Lès-Beaune,

Domaine Lucien Jacob   Drink soon 15.5

Ripe, spicy, and attractive on both nose and palate. Good fruit. A very nice, mature wine. Very good for a village example.

Savigny-Lès-Beaune,

Les Bas Liards,

Maison Champy   Drink up 13.0

Magnum. Rather coarse on the nose. The fruit has dried up.

**Savigny-Lès-Beaune,
La Dominode,
Domaine Bruno Clair** Drink soon 15.0
Lovely nose. Rich and succulent. Very good
fruit. Not much underneath, but good.

**Savigny-Lès-Beaune,
Aux Gravains, Domaine
Jean-Marc et Hugues Pavelot** Drink up 13.5
Slightly disappointing. A lack of fat and vigour.
So not as fruity as I would have liked, as well as
slightly astringent.

**Savigny-Lès-Beaune,
Les Marconnets,
Domaine Simon Bize** Drink soon 14.0
Magnum. Somewhat lacking elegance. Medium
body. Decently fresh. But astringency lurks.

**Pernand-Vergelesses,
Ile des Vergelesses,
Domaine Chandon de Briailles** Drink soon 15.0
Magnum. Clean nose, not astringent. Quite
fresh, cherry-like fruit. Medium body. Decent
weight and follow-through. Good.

**Beaune, Cent Vignes,
Domaine Lucien Jacob** Now to 2015 16.0
Good colour. Quite full for a 2000 Côte de
Beaune. Ample and a lot more than one-dimen-
sional. Long and positive. Still plenty of vigour.

**Beaune, Champs-Pimont,
Maison Champy** Drink up 12.5
Rather too dry and astringent.

**Beaune, Aux Cras,
Maison Champy** Drink up 13.0
Magnum. A little thin on the nose. Not yet
astringent but fades away. Unexciting.

**Beaune, Aux Cras, Domaine
du Château de Chorey** Now to 2016 15.5
Magnum. Some fruit on the nose. A decent,
quite meaty wine. A lot better than most. Will
still last.

**Beaune, Grèves,
Domaine Michel Lafarge** Drink soon 14.0
A bit lightweight on the nose. Fruity but thin
and one-dimensional.

**Beaune, Lulune,
Domaine Emmanuel Giboulot** Drink soon 14.5
Attractive soft fruit on the nose. Light to
medium-bodied. Fresh. Not great but good for
a village wine.

**Volnay, Les Caillerets,
Domaine Michel Lafarge** Drink soon 14.5
Good colour. Fresh, elegant fruit on the nose.
A gentle wine. Medium body. Fragrant attack.
Then it tails off a bit to become rather one-
dimensional at the end. Lacks intensity.

**Volnay, Clos des Chênes,
Domaine Michel Lafarge** Drink soon 14.5
Very stylish fruit, but a touch astringent at the
end. A good effort for the vintage. Quite good
plus.

**Volnay, Fremiet, Domaine
du Marquis d'Angerville** Drink soon 14.0
Fresh, plump nose. Ripe and stylish. A little
suave but a decent finish. No astringency. Quite
good.

**Volnay, Santenots du Milieu,
Domaine des Comtes Lafon** Now to 2017 17.0
Magnum. The first bottle was fresh, if no great
weight. A bit slight and a bit over-oaked. Decent
fruit and no undue astringency. I marked it
good. Dominique Lafon was not satisfied with
it, so we opened another. This was a lot fresher
and more vigorous. Very good indeed.

**Pommard, Chaponnières,
Domaine Billard-Gonnet** Drink soon 15.0
Magnum. A little bit astringent after his
Clos du Verger, but a decent follow-through
nevertheless.

**Pommard, La Chatenière, Domaine
Catherine et Claude Maréchal** Drink up 13.5
Magnum. Spicy nose. Ripe on the palate but
some astringency now.

**Pommard, Clos des Epeneaux,
Domaine du Comte Armand** Now to 2018 17.0
Magnum. Ripe nose. Medium weight. Good
grip. Not the greatest of style but positive at the
end. Very good for a Côte de Beaune. A second

bottle was fresher and more vigorous. Rich, meaty, classy, and very good indeed.

Pommard, Clos du Verger,
Domaine Billard-Gonnet　　Now to 2016　16.0
Magnum. Good nose. Fresh and ample. Good fruit. Positive. Finishes well. Very good. Can be kept.

Pommard, Jarollières,
Domaine Jean-Marc Boillot　　Drink up　12.5
A bit too clumsy. Artificial fruit. Drink up.

Pommard, Pezerolles,
Domaine A. F. Gros　　Drink up　13.5
Quite a decent attack. But it lacks style on the follow-through. Slightly astringent.

CÔTE DE NUITS

Marsannay,
Les Saint-Jacques, Domaine
Fougeray de Beauclair　　Drink soon　13.5
Rather weak but quite fresh. Decent fruit. Not bad.

Nuits-Saint-Georges,
Aux Boudots, Domaine
Jean-Jacques Confuron　　Drink soon　14.5
Lacks a little energy on the nose. On the palate, medium-bodied. A little sweet. But it doesn't really impress and the follow-through is a little weak.

Nuits-Saint-Georges, Les Boudots,
Domaine Denis Mugneret　　Now to 2017　15.0
Medium colour. Soft fragrant nose. Stylish and fruity, but a bit on the slight side. Medium body. A touch of oak. Good but not great.

Nuits-Saint-Georges, Les Boudots,
Domaine Jean Tardy　　Drink soon　14.5
Medium body. Decent fruit and grip but some signs of astringency at the end. Quite good plus but a bit one-dimensional.

Nuits-Saint-Georges,
Les Chaignots, Domaine
Georges Mugneret-Gibourg　　Now to 2018　17.0
Plump, fresh, positive, and succulent. Only medium body but good style. Quite complex and elegant. Very good indeed.

Nuits-Saint-Georges,
Clos des Forêts Saint-Georges,
Domaine de l'Arlot　　Drink soon　16.0
Round, ripe, sweet, and fresh. Medium body. Balanced. Plenty of fruit. Very good.

Nuits-Saint-Georges, Les Pruliers,
Domaine Robert Chevillon　　Now to 2018　17.5
Medium weight. Ripe and fruity. Balanced, fresh, and stylish. Not the greatest of thrust but pure and classy. Lovely.

Nuits-Saint-Georges, Les Vaucrains,
Domaine Henri Gouges　　Now to 2020　17.5
Good structure. Rich and meaty. Very good ripe fruit. Medium-full body. Good tannins. Good grip. Lots of wine here. Long. Fine.

Vosne-Romanée, Aux Brulées,
Domaine Michel Gros　　Now to 2017　17.0
Fatter, richer, and sweeter than his Clos des Réas. Fullish body. Nicely fresh and meaty. Good style and depth. Long. Very good indeed.

Vosne-Romanée, Clos des Réas,
Domaine Michel Gros　　Drink soon　16.0
Lovely fragrant nose. Medium body. Ripe and balanced. Not the greatest of energy but fresh and classy. Very good.

Vosne-Romanée,
La Colombière, Domaine
du Vicomte de Liger-Belair　　Drink soon　16.5
Light but fresh and elegant on the nose. And on the palate too. But fragrant and positive and stylish on the follow-through. There is no shortage of interest and quality here. Very poised. A splendid effort for a first vintage. Very good plus.

Vosne-Romanée, Cros Parentoux,
Domaine Emmanuel Rouget　Now to 2020　18.0
Good, virile colour. Ripe, stylish, concentrated nose. I prefer this to the Henri Jayer Echézeaux. Good balance and depth. Fresh and high-class. Long and lovely.

Vosne-Romanée, Aux Malconsorts,
Domaine Sylvain Cathiard　　Now to 2018　18.0
Very lovely understated and persistent nose. High-class fruit. Medium to medium-full body.

Lovely balance. Lots of vigour. Very long and very lovely. Fine plus.

Vosne-Romanée,
Les Suchots,
Domaine Grivot Now to 2018 17.5
Fragrant, medium to medium-full bodied wine with just a touch of oak. Lovely classy, balanced fruit. Very good grip. Lots of energy. Fine.

Chambolle-Musigny,
Les Beaux-Bruns,
Domaine Ghislaine Barthod Now to 2017 16.0
Soft nose. Not the greatest grip of class but a good, mellow, medium-full bodied wine. Ripe, round, and quite sweet. Lots of charm if not much grip or depth. Very good.

Chambolle-Musigny, Les Cras,
Domaine Ghislaine Barthod Now to 2020 17.5
Much more serious than the Beaux-Bruns. Much better grip and class. Medium-full body. Ripe, very Chambolle fruit. Fresh on the follow-through. Lovely finish. Fine.

Chambolle-Musigny,
Les Gruenchers,
Domaine Digioia-Royer Now to 2016 16.0
A bit weedy on the nose. Medium body. Quite fresh, pleasant fruit. Better on the palate than on the nose. Good follow-through. Quite classy. Very good.

Chambolle-Musigny,
Les Gruenchers,
Domaine Dujac Now to 2016 17.0
Good colour. Soft, ripe, very Dujac nose. Good acidity. Almost sweet. Medium to medium-full body. Aromatic. Very fresh. Good energy. This is surprisingly positive at the end. An attractive wine.

Morey-Saint-Denis,
Domaine Dujac Now to 2016 16.0
Medium colour. Round, fresh, ripe, and vibrant on the nose. Lots of quality and depth for a village 2000. Lovely balance. Succulent and classy. Long. Very good.

Morey-Saint-Denis,
En La Rue de Vergy,
Domaine Bruno Clair Drink soon 16.0
Decent substance. Good fruit. Good style. Medium body. Fresh. Good acidity. Very good length. Attractive. Very good.

Morey-Saint-Denis, *Premier Cru,*
Cuvée Romain Lignier, Domaine
Lucie et Auguste Lignier Now to 2018 17.0
Ample, ripe nose. Medium-full body. Some oak. A meaty wine but with good grip and depth. Plenty of wine here. Long and satisfying. Very good indeed.

Gevrey-Chambertin, Mes
Favourites, Vieilles Vignes,
Domaine Alain Burguet Now to 2018 16.5
Good nose. Very clean and with very good grip. Medium to medium-full body. Rich, balanced, stylish, long, and impressive. Very good plus.

Gevrey-Chambertin, Cazetiers,
Domaine Christian Serafin Now to 2020 17.5
Magnum. Rich, ample, nicely substantial, and full of fruit on the nose. Fullish body. Good grip. Round and most attractive. Very harmonious. Classy too. Fine.

Gevrey-Chambertin, En Champs,
Domaine Denis Mortet Now to 2017 15.5
Slightly clumsy on the nose. But no lack of substance. Medium to medium-full body. Rich, slightly oaky, ripe, and meaty. Good plus.

Gevrey-Chambertin,
Clos-Saint-Jacques,
Domaine Bruno Clair Drink soon 14.0
Seems a bit weedy on the nose. Pleasant fruit but it tails away. Lacks substance and depth. Stylish but disappointing.

Gevrey-Chambertin,
Les Corbeaux,
Domaine Denis Bachelet Now to 2018 18.0
Fragrant nose. Not a lot at first. Elegant, discreet, composed, and with very good intensity. Excellent grip. Lovely fruit. Only medium to medium-full body, yet lots to it. Fine plus.

Gevrey-Chambertin, Crapillot,
Domaine Humbert Frères   Drink soon   15.0
Soft, round, stylish nose. Medium body. Ripe pleasant fruit on the attack, but then it tails off. Good.

Gevrey-Chambertin,
Lavaux-Saint-Jacques,
Domaine Denis Mortet   Now to 2020   17.0
Fat, meaty, quite structured nose. Some tannin. Fullish body. Nice and rich and substantial. Very good grip. Plenty of depth. Finishes very well. Very good indeed.

Gevrey-Chambertin, Poissenot,
Domaine Humbert Frères   Now to 2016   16.5
A little less on the nose than the Crapillot. But more grip on the palate. Lovely pure, juicy fruit. Good grip. This is very good plus.

GRANDS CRUS

Le Corton,
Vieilles Vignes, Réserve,
Domaine Marius Delarche   Now to 2016   14.0
Medium colour. Soft nose. Not a lot of fruit. And very little richness. Medium body. A little more charm on the palate. But it lacks concentration and depth.

Corton, Bressandes,
Domaine Comte Senard   Drink soon   14.0
A little more meaty than the Clos du Roi, but not the class. A slight touch of astringency. Decent freshness but only quite good.

Corton, Clos des Cortons-Faiveley,
Domaine Faiveley   Now to 2018   15.5
Fullish colour. Fragrant, stylish nose. Medium-full body. Somewhat rigid tannins. Decent grip and style nevertheless. But a bit astringent at the end.

Corton, Clos de Roi,
Domaine Comte Senard   Now to 2016   16.5
Pretty, but a touch weedy on the nose. Ripe, elegant, and balanced on the palate though. Not too weak. Very good grip. Finishes well. I like the fresh style here. Very good plus.

Corton, Rognets,
Domaine Bernard Ambroise   Now to 2018   17.0
Medium-full colour. Still youthful. Quite full and concentrated on the nose. A little burned, bitter oak. Better on the palate. Fullish, yet soft. Rich, balanced, ripe, and fresh. Good energy. Very good indeed.

Corton, Rognet,
Domaine Méo-Camuzet   Now to 2019   15.0
Full, immature colour. Quite extracted and some oak on both nose and palate. Fullish body. Meaty. But lacks class. An ungainly wine.

Corton, Rognet,
Domaine Dupont-Tisserandot Now to 2016   15.5
Nicely rich, meaty nose. A touch sweet, perhaps. But good depth and good substance. Decent class and good tannins and grip. Good plus.

Echézeaux,
Domaine Bocquenet   Now to 2019   16.0
Full, immature colour. Ripe, meaty nose. Good depth. Slightly rigid tannins, and so a bit clumsy, but a decent finish.

Echézeaux, Domaine Dujac   Now to 2019   17.0
Medium colour. Now mature. Some stems on the nose. Medium weight. Ripe. Elegant. Good follow-through. Good dimension for a 2000.

Echézeaux,
Domaine Henri Jayer   Now to 2018   17.5
Good colour. Lovely, classy, intense fruit. Ripe, fullish body. Concentrated. No great depth, but positive and fully ready. Impressive.

Echézeaux,
Maison Dominique Laurent   Now to 2018   16.5
Fullish colour, still youthful. Ripe, rich, nose. Somewhat clumsy but good vigour. Fullish body. The tannins are ripe and there is plenty of fruit. A meaty wine. Good grip. Got better as it evolved, but essentially it lacks grace.

Echézeaux,
Maison Frédéric Magnien   Now to 2018   15.5
Medium-full colour. Somewhat soupy nose. Ripe, even rich. Medium-full body. Slightly concocted, because of being slightly extracted.

Echézeaux,
Les Rouges du Bas,
Domaine Méo-Camuzet   Now to 2017   15.5
Fullish colour. Ripe, rich, and meaty on the nose. Good depth. Fullish body at first, but it lacks grip, and falls away quickly.

Echézeaux,
Domaine Dr. Georges
Mugneret-Gibourg   Drink soon   17.0
Good colour. Pure, fresh nose. No lack of fruit or depth. Succulent, elegant, and harmonious. Medium body. Lovely fruit, if no great vigour at the end. Very good indeed.

Echézeaux, Domaine
de la Romanée-Conti   Now to 2020   18.0
Quietly composed and classy. Lots of depth and very stylish fruit. Fullish body, rich, balanced, and very ripe. Excellent grip. This really is an example of how the 2000s should have been made. Lovely.

Grands-Echézeaux,
Domaine Gros
Frère et Soeur   Now to 2018   18.5
Good colour. Lovely fresh nose. Balanced and full of fruit. Good backbone for the vintage. Juicy and complex. Long and very elegant. Ready but no hurry to drink. Very fine.

Clos de Vougeot,
Domaine Réné Engel   Now to 2018   18.0
Good colour. Ripe, round, gently oaky, slightly spicy nose. Medium-full body. Soft on the palate. Most attractive, if not with a lot of grip and concentration, but stylish and not short.

Clos de Vougeot,
Domaine Faiveley   Now to 2020   17.0
Good colour. Firm, tannic nose. Quite marked by the new oak. Full body. Balanced. May still improve as is softens further.

Clos de Vougeot,
Domaine Anne Gros   Now to 2020 plus   18.5
Good colour. Very lovely nose and palate. Super fruit. Composed and harmonious. Lovely finish. Real class and depth.

Clos de Vougeot,
Domaine Louis Jadot   Now to 2020   17.5
Good colour. Firm, rich, concentrated, and vigorous on the nose. Fullish, ripe if not very rich on the palate. Lacks a little fat. But good depth.

Clos de Vougeot,
Domaine Leroy   Now to 2020   18.0
Good colour. Ripe and fruity and balanced on the nose. Intense, fullish, and harmonious on the palate. Long. Fine plus.

Clos de Vougeot,
Domaine Méo-Camuzet   Drink soon   12.0
Good colour. Firm nose. Rich but exctracted. Reduced. Sweet and rather concocted on the palate. I can't enjoy this.

Richebourg,
Domaine Anne Gros   Now to 2020   19.5
Medium-full colour. Good vigour for 2000. Lovely nose. Not even a hint of weakness. Good depth and volume and, above all, fruit and fragrance. Even quite concentrated. Still some tannin to resolve. Fullish, rich, and energetic. Lots of class. Only just ready. Still very fresh. Excellent.

Richebourg,
Domaine A. F. Gros   Now to 2020   17.5
Ripe, stylish, and ample on the nose. Very well-mannered. Rich, concentrated, and fullish-bodied on the palate. Rather more style than I had expected, as usually I rate this rather lower than the other Gros domaines. Though it is a touch hot at the end. Fine nevertheless.

Richebourg, Domaine
Gros Frère et Soeur   Now to 2020   19.0
Rich, quite substantial nose. Fresh and classy, intense and ripe, and concentrated on the palate. Fullish body. Lots of depth. Vigorous and very lovely.

Romanée-Saint-Vivant, Domaine
Jean-Jacques Confuron   Now to 2020   18.0
Classy fruit. Not a bit over-oaked. Much more together than their Boudots. Balanced, fresh, medium-full body. Just a touch sweet perhaps,

but with very good grip. Nicely intense at the end. Fine plus.

La Tâche, Domaine de la Romanée-Conti — Now to 2025   19.5
Full, very fresh colour. Marvelous depth and concentration on the nose. Rich, vigorous, crammed with fruit. Impressive grip. Really profound for a 2000.

Clos-Saint-Denis, Domaine Bertanga — Now to 2018   17.5
Good fresh colour. Attractive, ripe, succulent nose. Medium body. Good fruit. Quite classy. Positive at the end. Fine.

Clos-Saint-Denis, Domaine Michel Magnien et Fils — Now to 2016   14.0
Full colour. Too extracted on the nose. Slightly reduced. Meaty but coarse.

Clos des Lambrays, Domaine des Lambrays — Drink soon   17.5
Soft, ripe, intense, and very lovely on the nose. But fully *à point*, and without a lot of vigour and grip at the end.

Clos de la Roche, Domaine Arlaud — Now to 2017   17.0
Medium colour. Open, fresh nose. Quite classy, if quite light. Medium body. Balanced. Positive and very good indeed.

Clos de la Roche, Domaine Dujac — Now to 2018   18.0
Medium to medium-colour. Good depth, freshness, and concentration for a 2000. Fullish, aromatic, and youthful. Good grip. This is less Dujac than the Gruenchers. Long, complex, and stylish. Fine plus.

Clos de la Roche, Domaine Jean Raphet — Now to 2016   15.0
Medium colour. Ripe nose. A bit too sweet. Lacks energy and class. But a pleasant bottle.

Clos de la Roche, Domaine Armand Rousseau — Now to 2020   18.5
Medium to medium-full colour. Fully mature. Quite a rich nose. Plummy still a little austere.

Very good acidity. Very classy. More to it at the end than the Dujac. Lovely finish. Very fine.

Bonnes-Mares, Maison Champy — Drink soon   12.5
Fullish colour. Sweet, ungainly nose. Somewhat concocted. Lacks style.

Bonnes-Mares, Domaine Dujac — Now to 2020   18.5
Magnum. This is a fuller and more vigorous wine than the Clos de la Roche. Better grip. Medium-full body. Very lovely complex fruit. Very classy. Very fine.

Bonnes-Mares, Domaine Georges Roumier — Now to 2025   19.0
Full colour. Virile, concentrated, very fresh, high-class nose. Full body. Very harmonious. Full-bodied. Still a little austere, but a lovely wine.

Bonnes-Mares, Maison Frédéric Magnien — Now to 2020   18.0
Medium-full body. Round, ripe, quite extracted, but good grip. Lots of depth. Fine plus.

Bonnes-Mares, Domaine Comte Georges de Vogüé — Now to 2018   17.5
Fuller colour than their Musigny. Quite an ample, substantial, oaky nose. Decent fruit. But slightly weak on the follow-through. It lacks intensity. Only fine.

Musigny, Domaine J. F. Mugnier — Now to 2020   18.5
Medium-full colour. Lovely fragrant nose. Excellent fruit. Medium-full body. Balanced. Classy. Multidimensional and long on the palate.

Musigny, Vieilles Vignes, Domaine Georges de Vogüé — Now to 2025   19.0
Rich, fullish, very composed nose. Very lovely complex fruit. This year it is substantially better than the Bonnes-Mares. Fullish body. Very good tannins. Excellent quality and particularly fine ripe fruit. Long and very lovely. Very fine plus.

Charmes-Chambertin,
Domaine Denis Bachelet   Now to 2018   18.5
Ripe, rich, understated and very elegant on the nose. Fullish body. Lovely fruit. Ripe and ample on the palate. Not the greatest of energy but very classy and nicely intense. Lovely finish. Very fine.

Charmes-Chambertin,
Domaine Dujac   Now to 2017   17.0
Good colour. Classy nose. No weakness. Fully ready. Medium body. Ample, soft, and succulent. Slightly oaky. No great grip, power of vigour, but that is 2000. Balanced and classy and positive. Very good indeed.

Charmes-Chambertin,
Domaine Taupenot-Merme   Drink soon   15.0
Fullish, meaty nose if with no great finesse. Medium-full body. Decent fruit, but just a little astringent. Good but not great.

Griotte-Chambertin,
Domaine Joseph Drouhin   Now to 2018   18.0
Fine colour. Very pure, elegant fruit. Cool and very lovely. Medium to medium-full body. Only medium in intensity and thrust, but very lovely fruit. Very well-balanced. Very classy. Fine plus.

Latricières-Chambertin,
Domaine Faiveley   Now to 2020   18.0
Full colour. Ample, rich nose. No undue dried-out oak here. Rich, meaty, concentrated. Very good grip. Fine plus.

Latricières-Chambertin,
Domaine Rossignol-Trapet   Now to 2020   18.0
Fresh classy fruit on the nose. Good depth. No lack of energy. Fullish. Very good grip. Lovely fruit here. Vigorous and fine plus.

Mazis-Chambertin, Hospices de Beaune, Cuvée Madelaine
Collignon Henri Boillot   Now to 2020   19.0
Full colour. Very classy nose. Rich and concentrated. Excellent fruit. Succulent, energetic, and with lots of dimension. Very stylish. Very long. Very lovely.

Mazis-Chambertin,
Domaine Faiveley   Now to 2017   17.5
Fullish colour. Still fresh. Fresh on the nose too. Plump. Good tannins. Ripe and stylish and with good depth. Medium to medium-full. Well-balanced. Good energy. Fine.

Mazis-Chambertin,
Maison Dominique Laurent   Now to 2015   14.0
Medium to medium-full colour. Full, rich, meaty, almost Northern Rhône nose. Too much so. Good grip. But coarse.

Mazis-Chambertin,
Domaine Armand Rousseau   Now to 2020   18.5
Fullish colour. Ripe, rich, classy nose. Pure, vigorous, profound, and lovely on the palate. Ripe and succulent. Aromatic and lovely.

Mazoyères-Chambertin,
Domaine Taupenot-Merme   Drink soon   13.5
Broader-flavoured, more stemmy, and with less grip than their Charmes. Coarse on the palate. Full and fresh nevertheless. But not for me.

Ruchottes-Chambertin,
Domaine Dr. Georges
Mugneret-Gibourg   Now to 2020   19.0
Lovely nose. Very ripe. Very pure. Very sophisticated. Medium-full body. Lovely composed fruit. Great class and harmony. Impressive complex finish. Very fine plus.

Chambertin,
Clos de Bèze,
Domaine Faiveley   Now to 2017   16.0
Medium-full colour. Somewhat rigid on the nose. Full-bodied, youthful, ripe, and rich on the palate. But clumsy. Yet a long finish suggests it might get a bit more sophisticated as it evolves further.

Chambertin,
Clos de Bèze,
Maison Frédéric Magnien   Now to 2020   16.0
Full colour. Ripe, extracted, lumpy nose. Fullish. Good grip. But rather clumsy. Fresh and balanced though.

Chambertin, Clos de Bèze,

Domaine Jean Raphet et Fils   Now to 2019   17.0

Fullish colour. Fresh and positive on the nose and palate. Not quite enough concentration but pretty good class. Very good finish.

Chambertin,

Domaine Denis Mortet   Now to 2025   19.0

Good colour. Fragrant, classy nose. Medium-full body. Lovely depth and balance. Not a bit too much over-extraction. Very lovely. This was the vintage for which Mortet took his foot off the accelerator to produce less-extracted wines. What a tragedy he didn't live to see how well the wine would turn out.

Chambertin, Clos de Bèze, Domaine

Armand Rousseau   Now to 2020   See note

First bottle: Good nose but not the greatest of energy. On the palate this lacks a bit of thrust, grip, and dimension. The fruit is there, but not the weight or energy. Fine at best. Second bottle: This was very much better. It had all the vigour and strength I expected. Lovely finish. Very fine.

Chambertin,

Domaine Rossignol-Trapet   Now to 2020   18.5

A classier wine than Jean-Louis Trapet's example, and a bigger wine too. Medium-full body. Excellent grip. This is long, complex, stylish, and very lovely. Very fine.

Chambertin,

Domaine Armand Rousseau   Now to 2020   19.5

Magnum. Very fine fragrant nose. But not as big a wine as some this year. Significantly better than the Clos de Bèze (I wrote this before I had seen the second bottle of that wine). Medium-full body. Very good grip. Lovely fruit. Lots of flair and energy and dimension. Very fine indeed.

Chambertin, Domaine

Jean et Jean-Louis Trapet   Now to 2017   17.5

Good colour. Fresh nose. Good structure and depth. Very classic. Very good grip. Medium body. Gentle. Balanced. Classy. Fine. But it needs a bit of weight and dimension.

1999 BURGUNDY

The 1999 was a gift from the gods: a vintage both plentiful and successful; not only of high-quality but consistent geographically and hierarchically; delicious from the Mâconnais (not to mention the Beaujolais) to Marsannay; and fine, within its context, from generic up to

⇥ *Rating for the Vintage* ⇤	
Red	18.5
White	17.5

grand cru. The wines have volume as well as concentration, richness and balance, intensity and class. And the whites are almost as splendid as the reds.

They are now fourteen years old. The lesser wines are ready, by which I mean most of the red *premiers crus* of the Côte de Beaune downwards, the village wines of the Côte de Nuits,

⇥ *Size of the Crop* ⇤ (In hectolitres)			
	RED	WHITE	TOTAL
Grand cru	15,297	4,187	19,484
Village and			
premier cru	208,830	67,051	275,881
TOTAL	224,127	71,238	295,365

and nearly all the white wines. But the senior bottles still need a few years. Yet such is the sophistication and ripeness of the tannins, that even the very top wines can be enjoyed now, though obviously it is a pity to open them so soon. Such also is the harmony of all the wines that even many of only minor pretension (Aubert de Villaine's Bourgogne Côte Chalonnaise, La Digoine, or Patrick Javillier's Bourgogne Blanc, Cuvée Oligocène, for instance) will still last well.

I started pulling out odd bottles, particularly white (as much because of the problem of premature oxidation as the tenth birthday), from January 2009. When I began, I came across one white wine which was still very tight. I gave it two hours in the decanter. The improvement was startling. I have always believed in carafing wines (even Burgundy, which the locals frown on, and equally whites as well as reds). It had not occurred to me what a difference it would make to a ten-year-old *blanc*. But that is the vintage. I have since been decanting all my white 1999s two hours in advance.

Harmony is the key to longevity. When it is supported by good structure, the time span, the window of opportunity of optimum drinking, can be much more extended than we expect. All good reds of a good vintage, plus most of the whites of *premier cru* level and above, require ten years to show their paces. This is very true of the 1999s. As you will see, there are very few disappointing wines. To those who possess stocks of the vintage, I say, Yes, you can start drinking, but don't be in too much of a hurry to empty your bins. There are plenty of bottles which will still be in a vigorous prime in 2019.

TASTING NOTES

The following notes come in the main from my ten-year-on tasting, a party for the growers I hold in Burgundy in June every year. I have added notes on other important wines which came my way in the first few months of 2009.

White Wines

Montagny, *Premier Cru*,
Cuvée Selection,
Domaine Stéphane Aladame   Drink up   13.5
Good colour, but now a little tired. I tried two bottles.

Bourgogne, Cuvée Oligocène,
Domaine Patrick Javillier   Drink soon   15.0
Ripe, rich, and full-bodied. Lots of class, depth, and interest. Holding up well. No hurry to drink.

Saint-Aubin, En Remilly,
Domaine Hubert Lamy   Now to 2016   17.5
Magnum. Holding up very well. Rich, medium-full body. Fresh and concentrated. Lovely fruit here. Peachy and classy. Delicious. Still has plenty of life.

Beaune, Clos des Mouches, *blanc*,
Domaine Joseph Drouhin   Now to 2016   17.0
Fullish but youthful colour. Very fresh on the nose; ripe and concentrated with a flavour of candied peel. Fullish body. Rich but crisp. Lots of depth and plenty of life ahead of it. Very good indeed.

Beaune, Teurons, *blanc*,
Domaine Bouchard Père et Fils   See note
Old before its time. Oxidised.

Meursault,
Domaine Pierre Morey   Drink soon   14.0
Ripe and quite sizeable. Still fresh. But I don't get much style and distinction.

Meursault,
Domaine des Comtes Lafon   Now to 2018   16.0
This is very impressive. Lovely fruit. Fullish body. Fresh and vigorous. No sign of age. Positive and harmonious at the end. And classy too.

Meursault, Blagny, Domaine
Thierry et Pascale Matrot   Now to 2017   16.0
Slightly four-square on the nose. Full and ample, but a slight suggestion of reduction on the palate. Fresh though. Improved in the glass. Very good.

Meursault, Bouchères,
Domaine Roulot   Now to 2016   15.5
Magnum. Not as fresh or as interesting on the nose as the Tessons. Slightly four-square. Medium-full body. Good plus.

Meursault, Charmes,
Maison Louis Jadot   Now to 2019   17.5
Quite an advanced colour. Rich, fat, and just a little blowsy on the nose. Fullish body. Nutty. No blowsiness on the palate. Rich, ample, generous, long. Very good acidity. Fine.

Meursault, Charmes,

Domaine des Comtes Lafon   Now to 2020   18.5

A little tight at first, but I had decanted it, and after an hour it was showing magnificently. Medium-full body. Crisp and firm on the attack, with plenty of backbone and good acidity. Lovely, minerally-flowery fruit. Long and high-class. Now mature but still has plenty of life ahead of it.

Meursault, Genevrières, Domaine

Bouchard Père et Fils   Now to 2018   18.5

Rich, full, abundant nose. Classy and profound. Ample, vigorous, and full-bodied on the palate. Concentrated, profound and very fine.

Meursault, Genevrières,

Maison Louis Jadot   Now to 2020   18.5

Quite a developed colour. But very good acidity and intensity on the nose. Full and firm. Profound and gently oaky. Succulent and rich. Very fresh and classy. Very fine.

Meursault, Genevrières,

Domaine Francois Jobard   Now to 2018   17.5

Magnum. A full, meaty example, but a lot of vigour after ten years. Lots of depth and quality too.

Meursault, Genevrières,

Domaine des Comtes Lafon   Now to 2018   17.5

Ripe and rich on the nose, with hints of oak and candied peel on the follow-through. Full, meaty, rich, almost voluptuous. Good grip. High-quality. No hurry to drink.

Meursault, Goutte d'Or, Domaine

Bouchard Père et Fils   Drink soon   16.0

A little oxidised on the nose, though rather better on the palate. Ripe and fruity. Not too tired. Ample, peachy, and with decent acidity. Very good.

Meursault, Perrières, Domaine

Bouchard Père et Fils   Now to 2020   18.0

Beautifully made. Just about *à point*. Fullish, fresh, crisp, and minerally. Quite concentrated. Lots of depth and class. Just the faintest suggestion of oak. Balanced, long, and with plenty of life ahead of it. Fine plus.

Meursault, Perrières, Domaine

Jean-Francois Coche-Dury   Now to 2020   18.5

Just about mature on the nose, though not quite focused, which it became after an hour or so. Rich but minerally. Concentrated and just a little appley, but in the best sense. Improved and expanded in the glass. Profound, youthful, and eventually delicious. Certainly very fine plus.

Meursault, Perrières,

Domaine Darviot-Perrin   Now to 2017   17.5

Fully evolved but no sign of undue age. Medium-full body. Round. Ample. Ripe and rich. Underneath minerally and fragrant. Balanced and very good depth and length. Fine.

Meursault, Perrières,

Maison Louis Jadot   Now to 2016   17.5

Rich and fat for a Perrières. Fully developed. But good grip. Reserved on the nose. Medium-full body. Long and complete. Lovely fruit, but not as ample or as complete as the Genevrières.

Meursault, Perrières, Domaine

des Comtes Lafon   Now to 2020 plus   18.5

Expanded considerably in the glass like most top 1999s. Fullish body. Rich but steely. Ample but racy. Splendid fruit, depth, class, harmony, and energy. Very fine. Still a great deal of life ahead of it. Very fine.

Meursault, Perrières, Domaine

Thierry et Pascale Matrot   Now to 2018   17.5

Rounder than Roulot. But rich and ripe and satisfying. Full and ample. Needs food. Fine quality, especially at the end.

Meursault, Perrières,

Domaine Roulot   Now to 2020   19.0

This is quite brilliant. Composed. Youthful. Splendidly minerally. Very long and very classy. Fullish body. Very fine indeed.

Meursault, Poruzots,

Domaine Francois Jobard   Now to 2018   17.5

Magnum. Ripe, rich, full-bodied. Just a little rigid at first. Would have been better decanted in advance. Classy fruit underneath. Developed considerably in the glass. Fine quality.

Meursault, Tessons, Clos de Monplaisir, Domaine Roulot Now to 2016 18.5
Magnum. Just a hint of fatigue on the nose, but none on the palate. Fresh, round, ripe, gentle, and stylish. Medium-full body. Very long and most lovely. Absolutely *à point*.

Puligny-Montrachet, Domaine Jean-Marc Boillot Drink soon See note
Fully mature. Ripe and well-made. Quite fresh. Certainly fruity. One bottle had a bit more zip than the other.

Puligny-Montrachet, Les Caillerets, Domaine de Montille Now to 2020 18.5
Splendid nose. Ripe, rich, concentrated, fresh, and vigorous. Very classy, very profound, and very lovely. Very fine quality.

Puligny-Montrachet, Les Champs-Canet, Domaine Ramonet Now to 2020 18.0
Youthful colour. A touch of sulphur at first. Full, firm, rich, backward nose. Very good grip. A masculine wine. Very lovely concentrated fruit. Got better and better as it evolved in the glass. Will still improve. Fine plus.

Puligny-Montrachet, Les Champs-Canet, Domaine Etienne Sauzet Now to 2020 17.5
Youthful colour. Fresh, fullish, ripe, and succulent. Lovely fruit. A bit more advanced as well as more peachy than the Combettes. Concentrated and very well-balanced. Lots of depth, class, and vigour. Fine.

Puligny-Montrachet, Les Combettes, Domaine Louis Jadot Now to 2016 18.0
Ripe, abundant, quite rich, well-matured but good grip. Fullish fresh, stylish, and vigorous. Fine plus.

Puligny-Montrachet, Les Combettes, Domaine Etienne Sauzet Now to 2020 18.0
Youthful colour. As with a lot of 1999 whites at this time, a bit tight at first. Rich, ripe full nose, gently oaky, and as much apricoty as peachy.

Full body. A lot of depth and class and very good grip. This is still young. Long and complex and very elegant indeed. Just about ready. Fine plus.

Puligny-Montrachet, Les Demoiselles, Domaine Michel Colin-Déleger See note
Prematurely oxidised.

Puligny-Montrachet, Les Enseignères, Maison Vincent Girardin Drink soon 14.0
Mature colour. Medium-full bodied, quite fresh, quite stylsh, and quite Puligny-like. But not a wine of great depth and finesse. A decent village example, but nothing special.

Puligny-Montrachet, Les Folatières, Domaine Leflaive See note
One bottle prematurely oxidised. The other a bit too developed on the nose, but slightly better on the palate. Okay but essentially lacking freshness. A third bottle was as it should be. Full, rich, ripe, and distinguished. This you could keep until 2017.

Puligny-Montrachet, Clos de la Garenne, Domaine du Duc de Magenta/Louis Jadot Now to 2020 18.5
Fresh, concentrated, vigorous, and very lovely on the nose. Fullish, profound, and energetic. Lots of dimension. Very lovely fruit. Lots of life ahead of it. Very fine.

Puligny-Montrachet, Les Perrières, Maison Louis Jadot Now to 2015 17.0
Really quite well-matured now. Even just a bit flabby on the nose, though better on the palate. Ripe, nutty, good grip. Plenty of depth. Very good indeed.

Puligny-Montrachet, Les Referts, Domaine Jean-Marc Boillot See note
A bit old on the nose. And curiously sweet on the palate. A second bottle was a bit more vigorous. But just as sweet.

**Chassagne-Montrachet,
Domaine du
Château de Maltroye**   Now to 2016   15.5

This is really very good for a village wine. Medium-full body. Still very fresh, yet fully mature. Ripe and full of fruit, with an interesting background spice. Balanced and vigorous at the end. Will still last a few years.

**Chassagne-Montrachet,
Les Blanchots Dessus,
Domaine Darviot-Perrin**   Now to 2020   18.0

The colour is still fresh. Expanded considerably with some aeration in the glass. Rich, vigorous, concentrated nose. Touches of crab apple and a little of the exotic. But very good grip and depth as well as class. Fullish body. Just a faint touch of oak. The finish is long, positive, and profound. Lovely. Lots of life ahead of it. Fine plus.

**Chassagne-Montrachet,
Les Caillerets,
Domaine Blain-Gagnard**   Now to 2020   18.0

Fresh colour. Full, vigorous nose. Lots of wine here and still very youthful. A fullish wine of depth and concentration. Lovely fruit. Very good grip. Lots of dimension. Fine plus.

**Chassagne-Montrachet,
Les Caillerets,
Domaine Duperrier-Adam**   Now to 2017   16.0

Fat, evolved, somewhat four-square nose, with a bit of built-in sulphur. Better on the palate. Fullish, rich, good grip. Fully ready. Good oaky base. Improved in the glass. Very good, if not a wine of great nuance.

**Chassagne-Montrachet,
Le Cailleret,
Maison Vincent Girardin**   Now to 2016   17.0

Quite a well-developed colour, but no undue oxidation. Rich, fat, quite oaky, but fresh nose. Fullish body. Ample. Plenty of ripe fruit. Peachy and apricoty. Good grip. Not a wine of the greatest distinction. It's a little clumsy. But certainly very good indeed.

**Chassagne-Montrachet,
Les Fairendes,
Vieilles Vignes, Domaine
Vincent et Francois Jouard**   Now to 2016   17.0

Good fresh colour. Some development on both nose and palate. Fullish body. Rich and spicy, even opulent and voluptuous. Good grip. Not the greatest finesse, but very good indeed.

**Chassagne-Montrachet,
En Remilly, Domaine
Michel Colin-Deleger**   Now to 2017   17.0

A bit flat on both the nose and the palate at first, though no undue oxidation. After aeration in the glass, the acidity seemed to come out and the wine was then medium-full bodied, ripe, balanced, and full of fruit. Very good indeed but not quite the precision of fine. A subsequent bottle was fine. I should have decanted it. After a couple of hours rather tight, it opened up to show classy, concentrated fruit and lots of depth.

**Chassagne-Montrachet,
Les Grandes Ruchottes,
Domaine Bernard Moreau**   Now to 2018   17.5

Fresh, stylish nose. Lovely fruit. This is a wine of high-quality. Medium-full body. Balanced. Very good acidity. Ripe and stylish, complex and vigorous. Very pure. Very lovely. A fine example.

**Chassagne-Montrachet,
Les Grandes Ruchottes, Domaine
Fernand et Laurent Pillot**   Now to 2020   18.5

This is very delicious. Splendid freshness coupled with ripeness and concentration and class on the nose. Ample, succulent, and vigorous. Lovely fruit. Long and complex. Splendid quality.

**Nuits-Saint-Georges,
Clos de l'Arlot, *blanc*,
Domaine de l'Arlot**   Now to 2015   15.0

Magnum. Soft, fresh, quite oaky, and very pleasant, but rather one-dimensional after all these top Côte de Beaunes. Not peachy enough. Good but not great.

Corton-Charlemagne, Domaine
Bonneau du Martray   Now to 2028 20.0
Full-bodied, crisp, very youthful. Firm, with a
great deal of depth, and a long way (in 2009)
from being ready for drinking. Very aristocratic fruit. Profound and very lovely at the end.
Excellent.

Corton-Charlemagne, Domaine
Bouchard Père et Fils   Now to 2018   17.5
Youthful colour. Ripe, mature, and gently oaky
on the nose. Plenty of depth and finesse. Fullish body. Good minerality. Very good peachy
fruit. High-quality here and plenty of reserves
for the future. Fine. Just about ready.

Corton-Charlemagne,
Maison Champy   Now to 2020 plus 18.5
Magnum. Very fine on the nose. Concentrated,
crisp, and vigorous. Full-bodied. Youthful.
Properly minerally. Very fine grip. Very fine.

Corton-Charlemagne,
Domaine Patrick Javillier   Now to 2020 18.5
Magnum. Rich, round, minerally, and essen-
tially harmonious on the nose. Ample, full-
bodied, and rich. Splendid grip. Very classy.
This is very fine.

Corton-Charlemagne, Domaine
Christophe Roumier   Now to 2018   15.0
Quite developed on the colour. A little lean on
the nose. A touch of oak. Austere and doesn't
really sing. Merely good. But it may round off
to its advantage.

Corton-Charlemagne,
Maison Vincent Girardin   Now to 2020 16.0
Fully mature on the nose with just a touch of
reduction, which did not blow away. Fullish,
rich, very gently oaky, and well-balanced. But
at the end of the day, neither the complexity nor
real class of this *grand cru*. So only very good
within its context.

Corton-Charlemagne,
Maison Verget   Now to 2016 16.0
A Corton from the Aloxe side, to judge by the
honeyed, slightly blousy nose. Full body. Some
evolution. Ripe. Almost exotically fruity. Good

acidity, but not really classy. Fresh at the end
but essentially a bit overblown. Very good at
best.

Bienvenues-Bâtard-Montrachet,
Domaine Sauzet   Now to 2020   18.0
The colour shows some development. Still
vigorous on the nose though. Ample, stylish,
ripe, rich, and profound. Very good grip. Lovely
fruit. Medium-full body. Long on the palate.
Fine plus.

Bâtard-Montrachet,
Domaine Ramonet   Now to 2020 plus 19.0
Firm, concentrated, youthful nose. High-class.
Very fine grip and depth. Long and intense and
harmonious. A beautiful wine. Very fine plus.

Bâtard-Montrachet,
Domaine Leflaive   Now to 2016   17.0
Fresh colour. But really quite evolved on the
nose. It lacks a bit of zip. Better on the palate.
Fullish body. Ripe. Some of the four-square-
ness of Bâtard. Decent follow-through but not
special.

Le Montrachet,
Domaine Marc Colin   Now to 2025 18.5
Made by Pierre-Yves Colin. This got better and
better in the glass. Excellent grip. Still very
youthful. Very high-class fruit as well. Fullish,
concentrated, balanced, and complex. Perhaps
not quite the depth and power of a great Montrachet but very fine. Will still improve (in 2009).

Red Wines

Bourgogne, Côte Chalonnaise,
La Digoine, Domaine
A et P Villaine   Now to 2016 16.0
Magnum. Fresh colour. Fullish, ripe, quite
meaty. Some tannin. Quite a big wine, really.
Very good fruit. Only just ready. Very good
indeed for what it is.

Bourgogne, Hautes Côtes de Beaune,
Domaine Lucien Jacob   Drink soon 15.0
Medium colour. Fragrant, classy fruit. Juicy
and attractive. *À point*. Delicious.

Givry, Clos Salomon, Domaine
du Clos Salomon   Now to 2016   15.0
Magnum. Fresh nose. Earthy. Fullish. Good grip. Ripe tannins. Plenty of energy. Very good.

Marsannay, Longeroies,
Domaine Bruno Clair   Drink soon   14.0
Medium colour. A gentle, quite succulent wine. Fresh and juicy. *À point*. Good.

Marsannay, Longeroies,
Domaine Fougeray de Beauclair Drink soon   13.0
Medium colour. Lightish but quite fresh at the end. Slightly empty in the middle. Lacks sophistication. Quite good.

Marsannay,
Les Saint Jacques, Domaine
Fougeray de Beauclair   Drink soon   12.5
Medium-full body. Slightly ungainly. Lacking class. Lumpy at the end. Only fair.

Chassagne-Montrachet,
Clos de la Boudriotte,
Domaine Ramonet   Now to 2018   16.0
Medium-full colour. Classy, round, fragrant nose. Medium-full body. Balanced, fresh, and attractive. No hard edges. Long and positive. Very good indeed, especially for what it is.

Savigny-Lès-Beaune,
La Dominode, Domaine
Jean-Marc Pavelot   Now to 2020   15.5
Very good colour. Plenty of size and energy on the nose. Rich, fullish, vigorous, and ample on the palate. Good tannins. Only just ready. Plenty of wine here. Very good plus.

Savigny-Lès-Beaune,
Les Fourneaux, Domaine
Chandon de Briailles   Now to 2015   15.0
Good colour. Soft, fragrant, sophisticated nose. Medium weight. No great energy or intensity, but fresh and harmonious. A wine which is full of charm. Good plus.

Savigny-Lès-Beaune, Les Guettes,
Domaine Simon Bize   Now to 2017   16.0
Good colour. Very good fruit on the nose. Complex, harmonious, fresh, and positive. Intense but not a blockbuster. Lovely long finish. Very good indeed.

Savigny-Lès-Beaune, Les Peuillets,
Maison Champy   Drink soon   12.5
Magnum. Good colour. Quite a firm, if not rigid nose; even a bit hard and green. Medium to medium-full body. Slightly astringent. Lacks a bit of charm and succulence and may now dry out. Unexciting.

Savigny-Lès-Beaune,
Les Vergelesses,
Domaine Lucien Jacob   Now to 2015   14.0
Medium colour. Interesting spice and baked jam nose. Medium-full body. Ripe. No great class but a satisfying, meaty bottle.

Beaune, Les Champs-Pimont,
Maison Champy   Drink soon   13.5
Good colour. Soft, ripe, quite graceful nose. Decent fruity attack, but then it tails off a bit. The finish lacks finesse. Quite good at best.

Beaune, Grèves, Vigne de
l'Enfant Jesus, Domaine
Bouchard Père et Fils   Now to 2017   16.5
Medium-full colour. Still youthful. Soft, ripe, round nose. Attractive, charming, and with good depth. Cool, composed. Medium-full body. The tannins just about absorbed. Good richness at the end. Harmonious. Just about ready. Very good plus.

Beaune, Grèves,
Domaine Michel Lafarge   Now to 2020   16.0
Medium-full colour. Round, rich, quite sizeable nose. Plenty of fruit and depth. Fullish body. Some tannin. Quite a muscular wine, as always. But rich and vigorous. Only just ready. Very good.

Beaune, Teurons,
Domaine Louis Jadot   Now to 2020 plus   17.0
Vigorous colour, beginning to show some signs of maturity. Succulent, sumptuous nose. Very ripe. Medium-full body. Soft and velvety. The tannins now absorbed. Very good acidity. Classy. Really very good indeed. Just about ready.

**Blagny, La Pièce
Sous Le Bois, Domaine
Thierry et Pascale Matrot**   Now to 2017   16.0

Medium-full colour. Round nose. Soft and juicy. Medium to medium-full weight. Good fruit. Plenty of personality, harmony, and even class. Long finish. Very good.

**Volnay, Vieilles Vignes,
Maison Nicolas Potel**   Now to 2018   16.0

Good colour. Fresh, engaging, supple, very fruity nose. Charming and balanced. Medium-full body. Ripe and stylish. Really very good, especially for a village wine.

**Volnay, *Premier Cru*, Hospices de
Beaune, Cuvée Général Muteau,
Bottled by Thomas Frères**   Now to 2020   16.5

Fullish, barely mature colour. Rich, full nose. Quite substantial, but the oak is not overdone. Fullish body. Good grip. Some tannin still to evolve, but the tannins are ripe and reasonably sophisticated. This is quite a meaty wine for a Volnay, but it has plenty of depth and no shortage of finesse. Long and quite concentrated on the finish, though it is a little inflexible. Still needs a few years. Very good plus.

**Volnay, Cailleret, Ancien
Cuvée Carnot, Domaine
Bouchard Père et Fils**   Now to 2020   18.0

Good fullish mature colour. A classic Volnay: fragrant, stylish, ripe, and harmonious. Medium-full body. *À point*. Complex. Vigorous and fine plus.

**Volnay, Cailleret,
Domaine Nicolas Rossignol**   Drink soon   14.0

Fullish colour. Just a touch vegetal and herbal on the nose. Slightly rigid on the palate. Medium to medium-full body. Suspicions of astringency. Lacks real class. Quite good at best.

**Volnay, Champans, Domaine
du Marquis d'Angerville**   Now to 2020 plus   18.0

Medium-full colour. Lovely complex, complete nose. Lots of lovely ripe fruit. Absolutely *à point*. Splendidly harmonious. Lots of energy. Fine plus.

**Volnay, Chevret,
Domaine Nicolas Rossignol**   Now to 2016   15.5

Full colour. Stylish nose. Plenty of weight and very good fruit. Medium-full body. A little sweet on the palate. But balanced and fragrant. Positive at the end. Good plus.

**Volnay, Clos de la Bousse d'Or,
Domaine de la Pousse d'Or**   Now to 2020   17.0

Good colour. Quite a substantial nose. Ripe and full of fruit, if without the nuanced elegance of a fine wine. Medium-full body. Now just about *à point*. Plenty of wine here but a little four-square.

**Volnay, Clos du Château des Ducs,
Domaine Michel Lafarge**   Now to 2025   17.5

Good colour. Very lovely fragrant nose: typical high-class Volnay. Ripe, succulent, harmonious, and elegant. Fullish body. Rich and almost voluptuous. Fullish body. Vigorous. Long on the palate. Better still in two years. Fine.

**Volnay, Clos des Ducs,
Domaine Marquis d'Angerville**   Now 2020   18.5

Fullish, vigorous colour. Lovely fragrant, ripe, harmonious, complex, and classy nose. Soft. Very subtle and elegant. Medium-full body. Very fresh. A lovely wine. Very fine.

**Volnay, Clos des Chênes,
Domaine Michel Lafarge**   Now to 2025   18.0

Good colour. Surprisingly open and accessible. Not a bit too firm and tannic. Fullish body. Lots of lovely concentrated fruit. Balanced, long, and very lovely. Better still in two years. Fine plus.

**Volnay, Taillepieds, Domaine
Marquis d'Angerville**   Now to 2020 plus   18.0

Medium-full colour. Lovely round, ripe, fragrant nose. Very Volnay. On the palate, medium-full body. Just about ready. Lots of very lovely, complex fruit. Good energy. Very good harmony. It will continue to improve. Long and laid-back at the end. Fine plus.

**Volnay, Taillepieds,
Domaine de Montille**   Drink soon   15.5

Medium-full colour. Soft nose. Classy but not very vigorous. Decent fruit on the attack. But then it tails off a bit. Elegant though. But only good plus.

Pommard, Chaponnières,

Domaine Billard-Gonnet   Now to 2018   16.5
Medium to medium-full colour. Ample, rich, quite meaty nose. Good class. Good tannins. Rich, balanced, sophisticated, and long on the palate. Very good plus.

Pommard, Les Croix Noires,

Domaine Lucien Boillot et Fils   Drink soon   15.5
Good colour. Decent fruit but not very sophisticated on the nose. Better on the palate. Juicy, fresh, and balanced. Good depth. At least some finesse. Good plus.

Pommard, Clos des Epeneaux,

Domaine Comte Armand   Now to 2030   17.5
Full immature colour. Full, tannic, backward nose. Now beginning to soften up on the palate. Firm and full-bodied but rich and concentrated. Tannic but the tannins are very sophisticated. Very good grip. This is very classy for a Pommard. Splendidly profound and abundant. Fine.

Pommard, Grand Clos des Epenots,

Domaine de Courcel   Now to 2016   16.5
Good colour. Fine fruit but quite soft and round on the nose; especially after the above. Medium-full body. Rich, succulent, and intense. Fresh and enticing. Very good plus.

Pommard, Pezerolles,

Domaine Billard-Gonnet   Now to 2016   16.0
Medium to medium-full colour. Classy, ripe nose. Good vigour. Medium-full body. Ripe. Sturdier than his Chaponnières. Very good.

Pommard, Les Rugiens,

Domaine Jean-Marc Boillot   Now to 2020   17.5
Full colour. Fullish, rich, complex, meaty nose. Lovely on the palate. Quite firm still, but rich and concentrated, with lovely balance. Lots of vigorous fruit. Long. Fine.

Pommard, Les Rugiens,

Domaine de Montille   Now to 2016   16.0
Medium colour. This is a lot better than their Taillepieds. Quite rich and complex on the nose. Good fruit. No great energy but intense and classy. Very good.

Côte de Nuits Villages,
La Robignotte,

Domaine Gilles Jourdan   Now to 2016   15.5
À point. Fullish. Very good grip. Fresh, velvety, ripe, and succulent. Lovely finish. Fine for what it is.

Nuits-Saints-Georges, *Premier Cru*,

Domaine Michel Gros   Now to 2019   17.5
From Aux Murgers and Aux Vignerondes. Good colour. Fullish, intense nose. Some of the rusticity of Nuits-Saint-Georges nevertheless. Fullish body. Ample, succulent, and ripe. Most attractive. Classier on the palate than on the nose. Fine.

Nuits-Saint-Georges, Les Boudots,

Domaine J. J. Confuron   Now to 2025   18.0
Fullish colour. Rich, almost sweet nose. Fresh, elegant, and medium-full bodied. Very good tannins. Very good grip. Gently, but quite markedly oaky. Plenty of quality and depth. Lots of vigour. Fine plus.

Nuits-Saint-Georges,
Les Boudots, Domaine

Dominique Mugneret   Now to 2015   15.0
Developed colour. Soft nose, slightly reduced. Not very sophisticated underneath. Better as it aerated in the glass. Not very classy nonetheless on the palate. Difficult to judge, but it is certainly not brilliant.

Nuits-Saint-Georges, Les Boudots,

Domaine Gérard Mugneret   Now to 2025   17.0
Good colour. Mellow nose. Soft and just a bit anonymous at first on the nose. But on the palate, medium-full bodied. Very fresh and well-balanced, and no lack of energy. Ripe, round, and succulent. Lovely stylish finish. Very good indeed.

Nuits-Saint-Georges, Les Boudots,

Domaine Jean Tardy   Now to 2017   16.0
Good colour. Ample, soft, round nose. Seductive if not serious. Medium-full body. Balanced; quite fresh. Nice and ripe. Very good.

Nuits-Saint-Georges, Les Cailles,
Domaine Robert Chevillon   Now to 2020   18.0
Good colour. Ripe, round, ample, harmonious, and unexpectedly classy on the nose. Medium-full body. Fresh. Balanced. Very good fruit and very good grip. Long, complex, and sophisticated. Lovely finish. Fine plus.

Nuits-Saint-Georges, Aux Chaignots,
Domaine Faiveley   Now to 2025   17.0
Full colour. Fragrant if slightly tough nose. There is still a little unresolved tannin here. Fullish body. Ripe and well-balanced, indeed rich and of high-quality. A little rigid, but it still needs time. Plenty of depth and length. Very good indeed.

Nuits-Saint-Georges, Les Chaignots,
Domaine Georges Mugneret   Now to 2020   17.5
Jeroboam. Good colour. Lovely nose. Ample, concentrated, and rich. Delicious fruit. Still very vigorous. Fullish body. Rich. Very good grip. Balanced and very classy. Long and lovely. Fine quality.

Nuits-Saint-Georges,
Clos des Forêts Saint-Georges,
Domaine de l'Arlot   Now to 2019   16.5
Good colour. Ripe, fresh, plump nose, with a touch—but not in a perjorative sense—of apples. Medium-full body; ripe, quite rich, very fresh. Individual. Long and complex. Very good plus.

Nuits-Saint-Georges,
Les Hauts Poirets,
Domaine Jayer-Gilles   Now to 2020   16.5
Medium-full colour. Still youthful. Ripe. Oaky. Slightly aggressive but still rich on the nose. Medium-full body. Somewhat roasted. Ripe and quite profound. The oak does not dominate on the palate. Very good plus.

Nuits-Saint-Georges,
Clos-Saint-Marc, Maison
Bouchard Père et Fils   Now to 2020   17.5
Fullish colour. Just a touch of maturity. Ripe if slightly closed nose. Fullish body. Meaty. Con-centrated and full of fruit. Good grip. Good energy. Rich and very vigorous at the end. Complex. Fine.

Nuits-Saint-Georges,
Les Pruliers,
Domaine Robert Chevillon   Now to 2020   17.5
Good fullish colour. Rich, full, succulent nose with a lot of depth. Now *à point* but with plenty of vigour. Fullish body. Ample, balanced, ripe, and delicious. Lovely finish. Fine.

Nuits-Saint-Georges,
Les Saint-Georges,
Domaine Faiveley   Now to 2028   17.5
Full colour. Like their Chaignots, the nose is a little austere, but not as tough. The tannins seem richer. Fullish body. Good grip. A true Nuits-Saint-Georges, with the weight and muscle typical of this *climat*. But ample and rich and balanced. Long on the palate. Fine.

Nuits-Saint-Georges,
Les Saint-Georges,
Domaine Henri Gouges   See note
Very good colour. Firm, closed, immature nose. Rather hard and green still. Fullish body. Still unresolved tannins. Adolescent. Doesn't sing. It is difficult to see the class and harmony. We'll have to wait and see.

Nuits-Saint-Georges,
Les Vaucrains,
Domaine Robert Chevillon   Now to 2016   15.0
Good colour. I prefer their Cailles, but this is still very good or better. Full, ample, ripe nose. Just a little stringy on the palate. Suspicions of astringency here. Not quite enough grip. Yet the finish is positive.

Nuits-Saint-Georges,
Les Vignerondes, Domaine
Daniel Rion et Fils   Now to 2018   15.0
Medium-full colour. Just a little lumpy on the nose. Lacks fresh, juicy fruit. Better on the palate. But slightly rigid. Decent grip. Medium-full body. Good vigour. But good at best.

Vosne-Romanée,
Aux Réas, Domaine
A. F. Gros et Francois Parent   Now to 2016   15.0
Magnum. Medium to medium-full colour.
Decent volume and class. Ripe, good vigour.
Not the greatest harmony and sophistication
but good.

Vosne-Romanée, Les Beaux Monts,
Domaine J. J. Confuron   Now to 2025   18.0
Medium-full colour. Round, rich, profound
nose. Full of fruit. Lots of class and depth. Fullish body. Just a little tannin still to be absorbed.
Very lovely fruit. Very harmonious too. This is
fine plus.

Vosne-Romanée, Les Beaux Monts,
Domaine Jean Grivot   2014 to 2030   18.5
Fullish colour. Vigorous, intense nose. Very
profound and high-class. Very fresh. Still
youthful. Fullish body. Some tannin. Lots of
lovely fruit underneath. But still needs time.
Potentially very fine.

Vosne-Romanée,
Les Beaumonts, Domaine
Alain Hudelot-Noëllat   Now to 2025   18.0
Medium-full colour. Very stylish, fragrant,
fresh, and succulent on the nose. Medium-full
body. Good backbone but the tannins fully
mature. Ripe, gently oaky, complex, and most
seductive. Fine plus.

Vosne-Romanée,
Les Beaux-Monts, Domaine
Daniel Rion et Fils   Now to 2026   17.0
Medium-full colour. Barely mature. Ripe, firm,
stylish nose. Medium-full body. Good grip. The
tannins are now mellow. Stylish and balanced.
Long. Very good indeed.

Vosne-Romanée, Les Brulées,
Domaine Engel   Now to 2025   18.0
Medium-full colour. Mellow, soft, rich nose.
But no lack of vigour. Lovely succulent fruit.
Medium-full body. Ripe, fresh, very pure, and
just about ready. A classic. Long and lovely. Fine
plus.

Vosne-Romanée, Les Brulées,
Domaine Michel Gros   Now to 2020   18.5
Good colour. Very lovely nose. Ripe, rich, succulent, classy, and harmonious. Fullish body.
Ripe and rich on the palate, vigorous, and balanced. Profound Pinot fruit here. Very long and
very lovely. Very fine.

Vosne-Romanée, Les Brulées,
Domaine Méo-Camuzet   Now to 2012   18.0
Fullish colour. Full, quite oaky nose. Not quite
so oaky on the palate, but nevertheless just
about at the limit. Still some tannin. Rich,
spicy, and earthy on the palate. Full body. Lots
of fruit and concentration. Vigorous. Fine plus
(for those who like markedly oaky wine).

Vosne-Romanée, Les Chaumes,
Domaine Jean Tardy   Now to 2018   16.0
Medium-full colour. Soft, ripe, succulent nose.
Gently oaky. Not the greatest concentration or
vigour. In fact, it eases off at the end. But fresh
and agreeable. Very good.

Vosne-Romanée, Clos des Réas,
Domaine Michel Gros   Now to 2020   18.5
Medium-full colour. More vigorous than his
Nuits-Saint-Georges, *Premier Cru* on the nose.
Energetic. Concentrated. Full of fruit. Long and
lingeringly perfumed. Very classy. Medium-
full body. Splendidly balanced and very classy.
Very fine.

Vosne-Romanée, Les Gaudichots,
Maison Nicolas Potel   Now to 2030   19.0
Very lovely, rich, splendidly concentrated, old-
viney nose. Full body. Splendid balance. Still
some tannin. Real depth and *grand cru* quality.
Very fine plus.

Vosne-Romanée, Les Malconsorts,
Domaine Sylvain Cathiard   Now to 2030   19.5
Magnum. Good colour. Marvelous nose. Very,
very lovely, harmonious, and profound fruit.
Essence of Pinot here. Full, vigorous, and balanced. Very fine grip. Very fresh. Splendid
class. Great length. Only just ready. This is
quite brilliant. Very fine indeed.

Vosne-Romanée, Les Malconsorts,
Domaine Clos Frantin/
Maison Albert Bichot   Now to 2025   18.5
Magnum. Good colour. Firm, rich nose. Lots of depth and a touch of new oak. Only just ready. Full body. Concentrated, rich, and quite meaty. Lots of energy. Plenty of class. Very fine.

Vosne-Romanée,
Les Malconsorts, Domaine
Alain Hudelot-Noëllat   Now to 2016   14.0
Medium colour. Fully developed. The wine is a bit slight for a 1999 on the nose. The oak shows, and there is even a bit of astringency. Medium body. Fruity and quite stylish but no great vigour or depth. A bit of a disappointment. Only quite good. (Given the success of Hudelot's two other Vosnes, I am tempted to suggest this was a bad bottle.)

Vosne-Romanée, Les Reignots,
Domaine du Vicomte de Liger-Belair,
Bouchard Père et Fils   Now to 2025   17.0
Full colour. Slightly four-square, even a little clumsy on the nose. Medium-full body. Fresh. Just a little unresolved tannin. Good grip and full of fruit. But not the greatest of finesse. Finishes well though. Very good indeed.

Vosne-Romanée, Les Suchots,
Maison Alex Gambal   Now to 2016   14.0
Full colour. Still immature. Clean but rather one-dimensional, if not anonymous for a Suchots. Ready. Medium-full body. Lacks depth and richness. Boring.

Vosne-Romanée,
Les Suchots, Domaine
Alain Hudelot-Noëllat   Now to 2025   18.5
Fullish colour. Rich, succulent, fullish nose. Ripe and concentrated and well-balanced on the palate. Lovely, very ripe, rich fruit. Lots of depth and energy. Very long. Very fine.

Vosne-Romanée, Les Suchots,
Domaine Gérard Mugneret   Now to 2028   17.5
Good colour. Quite firm on the nose. Rich, aromatic. Still with a touch of astringency here. There is still some unresolved tannin. But a lot

of concentration underneath. Long and complex and lots of vigour. Fine.

Chambolle-Musigny, *Premier Cru*,
Domaine J. J. Confuron   Now to 2026   17.0
From Les Châtelots and Les Feusselottes. Medium-full, youthful colour. Ripe, stylish, mellow nose. Proper Chambolle fruit here. On the palate, medium to medium-full body, but still a little austere. Good acidity. Ripe tannins. Lovely fruit. A very elegant wine. Very good indeed.

Chambolle-Musigny,
Les Amoureuses, Domaine
Jacques-Frédéric Mugnier   Now to 2030   18.5
Fullish, barely mature colour. Delicious, plump, naturally sweet nose. Fullish body. Succulent, balanced, classy, and lots of depth. Lots of vigour. Fragrant, subtle, and red fruity. Very fine.

Chambolle-Musigny,
Les Amoureuses,
Domaine Roumier   Now to 2030   19.0
Very full colour. Still immature. Rich, concentrated, oaky nose. Still a bit austere. Full and firm on the palate, but underneath excellent grip and depth and a touch of spice. Not as seductive as Mugnier or Vogüé at present. The least open of the three. But very fine plus.

Chambolle-Musigny,
Les Amoureuses, Domaine
Comte Georges de Vogüé   Now to 2030   19.5
Full colour. Quite firm on the nose at first. Rich, mellow, profound, very concentrated, and very classy. Full body. Splendid balance and depth. More black-fruity than the Mugnier and purer than the Roumier; marvelous energy at the end. A great wine.

Chambolle-Musigny,
Les Beaux Bruns,
Domaine Ghislaine Barthod   Now to 2020   17.0
Good colour. Ample, rich, still quite youthful nose. Fullish body. Gently oaky. Fresh and balanced. Good attack. Could have had a bit more class at the end, but very good indeed.

Chambolle-Musigny,
Les Beaux Bruns,
Domaine Thierry Mortet   Now to 2016   15.5
Medium-full colour. Ripe oaky nose. Clean
and agreeable. Medium to medium-full body.
Decent attack and quite fresh and positive. But
a little one-dimensional. Good plus.

Chambolle-Musigny, Les Charmes,
Domaine Ghislaine Barthod   Now to 2020   17.5
Good colour. Lovely nose. More succulent than
her Beaux Bruns. Ripe and very seductive. Full-
ish body. Plenty of energy. Rich and succulent.
Balanced and classy. Long. Fine.

Chambolle-Musigny,
Les Charmes, Domaine
Alan Hudelot-Noëllat   Now to 2020   16.0
Medium-full colour. Some development. Ripe,
ample, raspberry fruit. Nicely intense, if not
that vigorous. Medium-full body. Now ready.
Balanced and quite stylish, but not the depth
and richness of some. Very good.

Chambolle-Musigny,
La Combe d'Orveau,
Domaine Bruno Clavelier   Now to 2010   17.0
Fullish colour. Still quite youthful. Just a little
rigid on both the nose and the palate. Fullish
body. Good grip, and ample stylish fruit. But just
a little clumsy. Very good plus. Only just ready.

Chambolle-Musigny, Les Cras,
Domaine Ghislaine Barthod   Now to 2030   18.0
Fullish colour, still youthful. Full but still compact and slightly hard on the nose. There is still
tannin to be absorbed. Fullish body. Rich, tannic, and concentrated, but still firm and a bit
unyielding. Very lovely Chambolle fruit. Very
good grip. Potentially fine plus. But it needs
time.

Chambolle-Musigny, Les Cras,
Domaine Roumier   Now to 2030   18.0
Full, firm colour. Full firm nose. Still a little
unresolved tannin. Fullish body. Rich but backward. Very good grip. Underneath abundant,
pure, and classy. This is going to be fine plus.
But it needs time.

Chambolle-Musigny,
Les Fuées, Domaine
Jacques-Frédéric Mugnier   Now to 2025   18.5
Good colour. Lovely fragrant, Chambolle nose.
Delicate but firm enough to lead you to the
proximity of Bonnes-Mares rather than Amoureuses. Very fine, classy fruit. Medium-full
body. Just a touch of residual tannin. Very well-
balanced and very profound. Lovely now but
will still improve. Very fine.

Morey-Saint-Denis, Domaine
Lucie et Auguste Lignier   Now to 2018   16.0
Ripe, fat, attractive nose. Good vigour. Rich
fruit. Clean, harmonious, profound, and complex. Very good indeed for a village wine. Bravo!

Morey-Saint-Denis, *Premier Cru,*
Cuvée des Alouettes,
Domaine Ponsot   Now to 2030   18.5
Full, youthful colour. Firm nose. Still very
young. Fullish body. Still some tannin. Quite a
mouthful. Very lovely, cool fruit. Complex and
classy. Long and very lovely. Very fine.

Morey-Saint-Denis, Clos Baulet,
Maison Frédéric Magnien   Now to 2020   16.0
Medium-full colour. Slightly rigid on the nose.
Lots of oak. Decent fruit and grip. But a little
too structured. Yet it finishes better than it
starts. And the fruit is fresh. Very good.

Morey-Saint-Denis,
Clos de la Bussière,
Domaine Georges Roumier   Now to 2018   15.5
Good colour. Rich, full, ample nose. More
sophisticated than hitherto. (Something I
noticed last year.) Yet a little constrained on the
palate. A bit tight. Decent grip. Good fruit. It
may evolve out of this, but it's only good plus
today.

Morey-Saint-Denis,
La Faconnière,
Domaine Jean-Paul Magnien   Now to 2019   16.0
Medium-full colour. Mature, fruity nose. Quite
sylish, but without the depth or concentration
of a fine wine. Medium to medium-full body.
Good fruit. Good grip. Very good.

Morey-Saint-Denis, La Riotte,
Cuvée Romain Lignier, Domaine
Lucie et Auguste Lignier   Now to 2020   17.0
Medium-full colour. Lovely nose. Harmonious, vigorous, succulent, and gently oaky. On the palate, not the greatest grip and concentration, but lovely fresh, stylish fruit nonetheless. Positive at the end. Very good indeed. Just about ready.

Gevrey-Chambertin, Vieilles Vignes,
Domaine Denis Bachelet   Now to 2020   17.0
Good colour. Very lovely, harmonious, fresh, intensely flavoured wine. Real finesse. Medium-full body. This is very lovely.

Gevrey-Chambertin, Mes Favorites,
Vieilles Vignes,
Domaine Alain Burguet   Now to 2018   16.0
Good colour. Just a little four-square. But full of fruit. Good structure. Plenty of energy at the end. Very good.

Gevrey-Chambertin,
Les Cazetiers,
Domaine Bruno Clair   Now to 2028   See note
Two samples on different occasions. The first as follows. The second a bit weak. Full, barely mature colour. Ripe, rich nose, but still a little austere. Fullish body on the palate. The tannins now just about absorbed. But the wine is still a little raw. Lovely fruit. Very long and complex. Ripe, pure, and balanced. Richer and richer as it developed in the glass. Very lovely.

Gevrey-Chambertin,
Les Cazetiers,
Domaine Christian Serafin   See note
Good colour. Spicy nose. With a touch of oak and bonfires. Still a bit closed. Slightly strange, cardboardy aspects on the palate and a touch of reduction. Difficult to judge.

Gevrey-Chambertin,
Les Cazetiers,
Domaine Michel Magnien   Now to 2020   18.0
Good colour. Very clean, fresh, pure nose. Not a hint of over-extraction, yet made by Frédéric Magnien (see elsewhere). Medium-full body.

Very good grip. Complex. Long. Very promising fruit. Lovely finish. Fine plus. Just about ready.

Gevrey-Chambertin, En Champs,
Domaine Denis Mortet   Now to 2017   14.0
Very good colour. Fullish, rather reduced nose. Quite oaky. A bit overdone. Big, extracted, and burly. Lacks grace. No lack of energy though.

Gevrey-Chambertin,
Clos Prieur,
Domaine Thierry Mortet   Now to 2016   15.5
Village *appellation contrôlée* (AC). Medium-full colour. Round, ripe, succulent, and full of juicy fruit. Not the greatest finesse but balanced, long, and positive. Very good for a village wine.

Gevrey-Chambertin,
Clos Prieur,
Domaine Rossignol-Trapet   Now to 2025   18.0
Premier cru. Good colour. Fresh, vigorous, classy nose. Only just ready. Fullish body, meaty, balanced, and classy. Plenty of depth and lots of style. Long and positive. Fine plus.

Gevrey-Chambertin,
Clos-Saint-Jacques,
Domaine Bruno Clair   See note
Medium-full colour. Classy and fragrant but a little delicate on the nose. Like the Cazetiers at the ten-year-on tasting, I would have expected more vigour and depth. To be reviewed.

Gevrey-Chambertin,
Clos-Saint-Jacques,
Domaine Louis Jadot   Now to 2030   19.5
Fine, barely mature colour. Very lovely nose. Very rich, full, intense, and concentrated. Medium-full body. The tannins just about absorbed. Splendid fruit. Excellent grip. Very, very classy. Very fine indeed.

Gevrey-Chambertin,
Clos-Saint-Jacques,
Domaine Armand Rousseau   Now to 2030   19.5
Full colour. Intense, youthful, pure, harmonious, and very elegant. No obvious oak. Just about *à point*. Fullish body, long and complex. Great finesse. This is very fine indeed.

**Gevrey-Chambertin,
Aux Combottes,
Domaine Dujac**   Now to 2030   18.0

Medium-full colour. Soft, fragrant, ripe, fresh nose. Medium-full body. Rich. Still youthful. Plenty of energy and lots of class. Fine plus.

**Gevrey-Chambertin,
Les Corbeaux,
Domaine Denis Bachelet**   Now to 2030   18.5

Medium-full colour. Marvelous fruit on the nose. This is full-bodied, rich, and very, very concentrated. It will still improve. Splendid class and real harmony. Very long finish. Very fine.

**Gevrey-Chambertin,
Les Corbeaux, Domaine
Lucien Boillot et Fils**   Drink soon   13.5

Medium-full colour. Slightly dead fruit on the nose. Somewhat astringent on the palate. Medium body. Rather coarse.

**Gevrey-Chambertin,
Estournelles-Saint-Jacques,
Domaine Humbert Frères**   Now to 2020   18.0

Good colour. Classy nose. Very fresh, but soft. Slightly more open than the majority of these Gevreys. Medium-full body. Now *à point*. Lovely complex, classy, fresh fruit. Lots of depth. Long finish. Fine plus.

**Gevrey-Chambertin,
Lavaux-Saint-Jacques,
Domaine Claude Dugat**   Now to 2030   18.0

Full immature colour. Backward but very rich and concentrated on the nose. Very lovely fruit. Fullish body. Still some tannin. But very fine fruit and lots of depth. Very lovely finish. Fine plus.

**Gevrey-Chambertin,
Lavaux-Saint-Jacques,
Domaine Denis Mortet**   Now to 2022   16.0

Full colour. Quite full and extracted on both the nose and the palate. But not too much so. Rich and meaty, yet fresh and succulent. Not the greatest of class but very good.

**Gevrey-Chambertin,
Petite Chapelle, Domaine
Dupont Tisserandot**   Now to 2025   17.0

Medium-full colour. Ripe, positive, fresh, vigorous nose. Fullish, meaty, fresh, and rich on the palate. Not the greatest of depth and personality but clean and well-made. Very good indeed.

**Corton, Bressandes,
Maison Champy**   Now to 2020   17.0

Medium-full colour. Just about ready. Meaty nose. Good fruit, if not the greatest of finesse. Medium-full body. Decent balance. Good energy and depth. Finishes well. Very good indeed.

**Corton, Bressandes, Domaine
Chandon de Briailles**   Now to 2025   18.5

Medium-full colour. Rich, aromatic nose. Obviously whole-cluster maceration. Lovely balance and classy depth. Fullish body. Ripe, complex, and very delicious. Just about ready. Lovely finish. Very fine.

**Corton, Clos des Cortons,
Domaine Faiveley**   Now to 2025   16.0

Full, barely mature colour. Full nose, but rich underneath. Quite oaky. Fullish body. Tannic. Slightly rigid. Very good fruit. But I don't think the armour will ever soften.

**Corton, Renardes,
Domaine Marius Delarche**   Now to 2016   17.0

Medium to medium-full colour. Fresh nose, not a blockbuster. Cool, composed, very good fruit. On the palate, quite full-bodied. Ripe and balanced and succulent. Very fresh and most attractive. Leaner at the end than most 1999s of this weight. And so it lacks a little richness. But very good indeed.

**Corton, Clos du Roi,
Maison Vincent Girardin**   Now to 2028   17.5

Full colour. Still immature. Quite a tough nose. Some tannin. Still raw. Fullish body. Meaty. Very good, cool fruit. The tannins on the palate are more sophisticated than the nose would indicate. Very good grip. Classy. Fine.

Corton, Pougets,

Domaine Louis Jadot Now to 2030 18.0

Good colour. The merest hint of maturity. Some tannin on the nose. Still firm. But rich, fragrant, and classy. Fullish body. Lots of depth. Ripe and potentially succulent. Good acidity. Very pure. Really good for a Corton. Fine plus.

Echézeaux, Domaine Dujac Now to 2018 16.5

Medium colour. Rather more Dujac on the nose than Echézeaux, in contrast to Dujac's other wines. Medium to medium-full body. Intense and fragrant. Fresh and balanced. But a slight lack of personality and *terroir* definition. Very good plus. Just about ready.

Echézeaux,

Domaine René Engel Now to 2025 17.5

Soft, ripe, rich, generous, nose. Medium to medium-full body. Fragrant. Still some tannin. Balanced and classy. Lots of depth. Lovely finish. Very pure. Fine.

Grands-Echézeaux,

Maison Champy Père et Fils From 2015 18.0

Good colour. Rich, concentrated, classy nose. Lots of depth and quality here. Full-bodied. Still some tannin. Will still improve. Good backbone and very good class and grip. Fine plus.

Grands-Echézeaux,

Domaine du Clos Frantin/

Maison Albert Bichot Now to 2030 18.0

Good colour. Rich, firm nose. Lots of class. A little oak. Not yet ready. Full body. Fresh. Very good grip. Round and profound. Still some tannin to resolve. Distinguished. Long. Fine plus.

Grands-Echézeaux,

Domaine René Engel 2014 to 2030 19.0

This is quite a big wine, in contrast to his Echézeaux. Full colour. Plenty of weight and still quite a bit of tannin to resolve. Very fine concentrated fruit. Very good grip. Vigorous and profound and very high-class. Very fine plus. Still quite a way from maturity.

Grands-Echézeaux, Domaine

de la Romanée-Conti Now to 2025 19.0

Medium-full colour. Now just about mature. Fullish, slightly four-square nose. This softened up quickly. Fragrant, relaxed, poised, and elegant. On the palate, fullish body. Very lovely fruit. The tannins now resolved. Lots of intensity and energy. Long and complex. Very fine plus.

Clos de Vougeot,

Domaine Robert Arnoux

(now Arnoux-Lachaux) Now to 2020 18.0

Good, fullish, vigorous colour. Aromatic, classy nose. Good grip. Fullish. Quite spicy. Mellow tannins. Rich, vigorous, and classy. Lovely complex, long finish. Delicious now. Fine plus.

Clos de Vougeot,

Domaine René Engel Now to 2030 18.5

Good colour. Like his Grands-Echézeaux, this is quite a big wine. Rich, full, meaty nose. Plenty of class and plenty of fruit. Still a little unresolved tannin to be absorbed. Good grip. Fullish body. Ripe and succulent. Long and satisfying. Very fine.

Clos de Vougeot, Maupertuis,

Domaine Anne Gros Now to 2030 19.5

Good colour. Very, very lovely rich, concentrated, poised, gently oaky nose. Quite a marvelous perfume here! Fullish body. Very fine ripe tannins. Excellent fruit and impeccable harmony. A great wine. Is this the best Clos de Vougeot since Jean Gros's 1985?

Clos de Vougeot, "Musigni,"

Domaine Gros Frère et Soeur Now to 2025 17.5

Good colour. Ripe, quite open, succulent nose. Very good fruit. Fullish body. Still a little tannin to resolve. Rich and spicy. Still a little hard on the palate. Not the very greatest class but fine.

Clos de Vougeot, Domaine

Alain Hudelot-Noëllat From 2014 18.5

Fullish colour. Lots of depth on the nose. Fullish body. The tannins are still vigorous but properly ripe. This will still improve. Very harmonious and very classy. Very fine.

Clos de Vougeot,
Domaine Jadot   Now to 2028   18.0

Full colour. Rich, quite substantial nose. Very good tannins. Lots of virility. On the palate, medium-full body. Ample and harmonious. Lots of depth. Plenty of wine here. Fine plus.

Clos de Vougeot,
Domaine Leroy   Now to 2030   18.5

Fullish colour. A little maturity now. Ripe, round nose. Not unduly tannic. Lovely, classy fruit. This is fullish-bodied, ample, rich, exotic, and aromatic. Just a smidgen of tannin still to resolve. Very good grip. Lots of depth. Ripe, cool, and very fine.

Romanée-Saint-Vivant, Domaine
Alain Hudelot-Noëllat   Now to 2020 plus   19.0

Full, rich colour. Just about mature. Classy, fragrant, intense but not heavyweight nose. Medium-full body. Very lovely fruit underpinned by subtle oakiness. Now soft and round, but with plenty of energy. Very good tannins. Very good grip. Complex, long, and high-class. Very Chambolle-ish. Very fine plus.

Romanée-Saint-Vivant, Domaine
de la Romanée-Conti   Now to 2030   19.0

Good colour. Very lovely nose. Now just about ready. Splendid fruit here. Medium-full body. Marvelously intense, harmonious, and classy. Very long. Very complex. Very fine plus.

Richebourg,
Domaine Anne Gros   Now to 2035   20.0

Full colour. Still youthful. Marvelous, poised, concentrated, aristocratic nose. Immense depth. Rich, fat, full-bodied, and very beautiful on the palate. Excellent grip and vigour. Multidimensional and very complex. Indisputably great.

Richebourg, Domaine
A.F. Gros et Francois Parent   Now to 2028   17.5

Fullish colour. Decently fruity, but without the class, depth, and concentration it should have. Medium-full body. Good grip. On the palate it is rather better than on the nose. Lovely fruit,

and certainly has distinction. Fine but not great.

Richebourg,
Domaine Gros Frère et Soeur   Now to 2030   18.5

Magnum. Good colour. Rich, full, ample, and really quite classy on the nose. Fullish body. Still needs time. Finely concentrated and very good grip. Rich and vigorous and lovely at the end. Very fine.

Richebourg, Domaine
Alain Hudelot-Noëllat   Now to 2025   19.5

Strangely, the colour is more advanced than his Romanée-Saint-Vivant. Yet this is a much bigger wine. Distinct signs of brown at the rim. But full, rich, and vigorous on the nose. Succulent, classy, and black-fruity. Aromatic, fat, and quite structured. Plenty of energy, especially at the end. This has a very lovely multidimensional finish. Very fine indeed. Another bottle was not quite so good: 18.5.

Musigny, Domaine
Jacques-Frédéric Mugnier   Now to 2035   20.0

Good colour. Lovely, round, ripe, complex nose. Very classy wine here. Fullish body. Intense, refined, and fragrant. Very lovely harmony. Very long. Excellent.

Musigny,
Vieilles Vignes, Domaine
Comte Georges de Vogüé   Now to 2040   20.0

Good colour. Firm, full, rich, and fresh on the nose. Still very youthful. Fullish body. Rich. Excellent tannins. Very harmonious and very concentrated. Very lovely finish. Brilliant.

Bonnes-Mares, Domaine
Fougeray de Beauclair   Now to 2020   16.0

Medium-full colour. Slightly four-square but no lack of class on the nose. Medium-full body. Decent fruit. Ample and fresh, but without the concentration and finesse it should have. Very good at best.

Bonnes-Mares,
Maison Frédéric Magnien   Now to 2020   15.0

Good colour. Slightly over-extracted and rather too oaky on the nose. A bit brutal. Fullish body.

Rich but tough and rigid. But underneath lovely balanced fruit. A pity.

Bonnes-Mares,
Domaine Georges Roumier   Now to 2038   19.0
Good colour. Full, firm nose. Rich but still closed-in. Lots of class. Fullish body. Very lovely fresh, concentrated, distinguished fruit. Still a bit of tannin to resolve. Long. Very, very lovely. Very fine plus.

Bonnes-Mares, Domaine
Comte Georges de Vogüé   Now to 2040   19.0
Good colour. Very closed-in, more so than their Musigny. Yet very lovely, concentrated rich fruit here. Quite a different flavour from the Roumier. Slightly less spicy. Still very youthful. Full body. Rich. Very long and lovely. Very fine plus.

Clos de Tart,
Domaine Mommessin   Now to 2030 plus   19.0
Good colour. Full and still immature. Very fine super-concentrated nose of great class and depth. Excellent grip. Still a little tannin to be absorbed. Intense, vigorous, and very lovely. Very fine plus.

Clos des Lambrays,
Domaine des Lambrays   Now to 2025   18.5
Good colour. Very lovely, silky-smooth, rich, ripe fruit on the nose. Balanced and very classy. Medium-full body. Fragrant and intense. Very harmonious. Lots of finesse. Very fine.

Clos-Saint-Denis, Maison
Champy Père et Fils   Now to 2020 plus   17.0
Good colour. Plump, ripe, stylish nose. Medium-full body. Good depth. Now *à point*. Balanced, vigorous, full of fruit, and very good indeed.

Clos-Saint-Denis,
Domaine Michel Magnien   Now to 2025   17.5
Good colour. Ample, rich, succulent nose. No undue extraction here. Classy, but not quite the dimension of Dujac's Clos de la Roche. But lovely fruit nevertheless. Medium-full body. Long at the end. Fine.

Clos de la Roche,
Domaine Pierre Amiot   Now to 2028   17.5
Good colour. Rich, fat, ample nose. Fullish body. A nice creamy aspect to the fruit. Fresh, harmonious, and classy. Fine.

Clos de la Roche,
Domaine Dujac   Now to 2028   18.5
Good colour. Rather more personality and originality than their Echézeaux. Very good, ripe, rich, fresh fruit on the nose and palate. Medium-full body. Long and stylish and complex. Very fine.

Clos de la Roche, Domaine
Lucie et Auguste Lignier   Now to 2030   18.5
Good colour. Full, rich, and a touch of new wood on the nose. Still very youthful. Full body. Still has tannin to resolve. Rich and meaty. Long. Vigorous. Potentially very fine.

Clos de la Roche, Vieilles Vignes,
Domaine Ponsot   2015 to 2030 plus   18.5
Fullish colour. Firm, rich, very vigorous, and very concentrated on the nose. Excellent grip. Still lots of life ahead of it. Very classy. Very profound. Very fine. Still needs time.

Clos de la Roche,
Domaine Armand Rousseau   Now to 2020   17.5
Medium colour. Soft, rich, ripe, and now fully mellow on the nose. Medium-full body. Very good grip. But essentially soft-centred. Long on the palate. Fine.

Chapelle-Chambertin,
Domaine Louis Jadot   Now to 2020   18.5
Full colour. Now some development. Complex, classy, full, rich nose. Lots of quality here. Full-bodied. Still some tannin. Splendid depth and vigour. Very good grip. Long, rich, and concentrated. Very lovely, plump cassis fruit. Very fine.

Chapelle-Chambertin, Domaine
Jean et Jean-Louis Trapet   Now to 2025   17.0
Full colour. Rich, full, ample, meaty nose. Still a little closed. Fullish body. A little tannin still to resolve. Meaty but not *that* classy. Yet good grip and plenty of depth. Very good indeed.

Charmes-Chambertin,

Domaine Denis Bachelet   Now to 2040   19.5

Good colour. Still a bit tight on the nose, but great class here. On the palate, full body. A little closed-in. There is all that there should be even if it doesn't quite sing today. Potentially excellent.

Charmes-Chambertin,

Domaine Camus   Drink soon   13.0

Fullish, well-matured colour. Evolved nose. Smells of *boeuf à la Bourguignonne* and stewed prunes. Medium-full body. Decent grip. Soft tannins and no undue evidence of new oak. Quite fresh. It's not rustic, but it lacks class and depth. Only fair.

Charmes-Chambertin,

Maison Joseph Drouhin   Now to 2025   18.0

Medium to medium-full colour. Now just about mature. Soft, elegant, Chambolle-ish nose. Very fragrant. Surprisingly intense. Admirable fruit. Medium-full body. Long, subtle, and laid-back. Lovely. Just about ready.

Charmes-Chambertin,

Domaine Dujac   Now to 2030   18.0

Good colour. Plenty of depth on the nose. A little more backbone than the Clos de la Roche. Fresh, plump, generous, and vigorous. Fine plus.

Charmes-Chambertin,

Domaine Humbert Frères   Now to 2025   18.5

Good colour. Plump, ripe, and concentrated on the nose, if no great volume or backbone. Balanced and stylish. Gently oaky. Medium-full body. Creamy rich, long, and complex. Very fine.

Charmes-Chambertin,

Domaine Armand Rousseau   Now to 2018   16.0

Medium colour. Fully developed. Soft, ripe, mellow nose. No great energy, depth, or even *grand cru* class. But a delicious easy-to-drink wine. Balanced and fully ready. Tails off a bit on the aftertaste.

Griotte-Chambertin,

Domaine Joseph Drouhin   Now to 2025   19.0

Good colour. Rich, fragrant, succulent nose. Good weight. Still a bit of tannin to resolve. At first slightly austere but mellowed in the glass. Medium-full body. Lovely fruit and balance. Long, classy, and delicious. Very fine plus.

Latricières-Chambertin,

Maison Vincent Girardin   Now to 2028   18.0

Fullish colour. Now just about mature. Ample, ripe, and fragrant on the nose. Fullish body. Concentrated. Very lovely, ripe, concentrated fruit. The tannins now just about absorbed. Rich and complex at the end. This is fine plus.

Latricières-Chambertin,

Domaine Louis Remy   Now to 2025   17.5

Good colour. Still very youthful. Ample nose. Full and rich with a touch of spice. Fullish body. Ripe tannins. Lots of juicy fruit and plenty of depth. Really quite high-class too. Good grip. Long. Slightly earthy. Lovely finish. Fine.

Mazis-Chambertin,

Maison Champy   Now to 2016   13.5

Medium colour. Pedestrian nose. Herbaceous in the sense of lawn-mower clippings. Astringent. Medium to medium-full body. Ripe but rather coarse.

Mazis-Chambertin, Domaine

Dupont-Tisserandot   Now to 2030   17.5

Good colour. Fresh, ample, vigorous nose. No lack of depth or quality. Fullish body. Balanced. Quite meaty. Fine quality.

Mazis-Chambertin, Hospices
de Beaune, Cuvée Madelaine

Collignon, Louis Jadot   Now to 2030   18.5

Full, barely mature colour. A bit closed-in on the nose at first. Full, rich, ample, and concentrated. Very fine classy, profound fruit. A full-bodied wine which still has great vigour. Excellent grip. Very rich and succulent on the palate. Lovely long, distinguished finish. Very fine.

Mazoyères-Chambertin,

Domaine Camus   Drink soon   14.0

Fullish, well-matured colour. A little fuller, fresher, and less pruny than their Charmes. Firmer and with a better grip and more vigour. But no better than quite good.

Ruchottes-Chambertin, Domaine

Christophe Roumier   Now to 2028   18.5

Full colour. Still very youthful. Cool, full-bodied, rich, and concentrated. Very fine, classy fruit here. Intense and pure. Balanced and profound. The tannins just about absorbed. Vigorous, long, and complex. Very lovely. Very fine.

Ruchottes-Chambertin,

Clos des Ruchottes,

Domaine Armand Rousseau   Now to 2025   18.0

Medium-full colour. Hints of maturity. Lovely high-toned, fragrant nose. Medium-full body. Harmonious. Subtle. By no means a blockbuster. Full of soft, plump, very well-balanced fruit. Long. Fine plus.

Chambertin, Clos de Bèze,

Domaine Joseph Faiveley   Now to 2038   18.5

Full colour. The nose is still closed-in, but not a bit rigid. Lots of wine here. Full body. Very good tannins. Very good grip. Rich, concentrated, backward wine. Very fine quality.

Chambertin, Clos de Bèze,

Maison Frédéric Magnien   Now to 2025   18.0

Good colour. Fresh, ripe, and balanced on the nose. Even classy. But not the depth of this *climat*. Very lovely fruit on the palate though. Not overdone. Medium-full body. Fresh, balanced, and stylish. Fine plus.

Chambertin, Clos de Bèze,

Domaine Armand Rousseau   Now to 2030   19.0

Good colour. Slightly more aromatic on the nose than their Chambertin. Higher-toned. Less backbone, tannin, and structure. Very lovely fruit. Fullish, rich. Balanced and very, very lovely. The Chambertin is better, as it always is. But this is more approachable today. Very fine indeed.

Chambertin,

Domaine Rossignol-Trapet   Now to 2040   19.5

Magnum. Full colour. Very lovely, rich, concentrated nose. Not yet fully mature but highly promising. Full body. Excellent fruit. This really is splendid. Real class and very fine grip. Very fine indeed.

Chambertin,

Domaine Armand Rousseau   Now to 2035   20.0

Fullish colour. Splendid rich, concentrated, profound nose. Very impressive! Fullish body. Lovely ripe tannins. Very harmonious, simply delicious fruit. A great wine.

Chambertin, Domaine

Jean et Jean-Louis Trapet   Now to 2035   18.5

Full colour. Fine, full closed-in nose. Rich and concentrated. Still needs time. Rich and meaty. Quite structured and powerful. Lovely fruit. Full body. Very fine.

1998 BURGUNDY

By no means was 1998 the easiest vintage the growers have been presented with recently, but as the right things happened at the right time, the eventual result has proved to be highly satisfactory, with a good if not over-abundant crop

↛ Rating for the Vintage ↚	
Red	16.5
White	14.5

of ripe, balanced fruit producing geographically consistent high quality in *rouge* and good quality in *blanc*. At the outset some feared that the tannins in the red wines were a little too aggressive. Happily this has turned out not to be too prevelant. At fifteen years on, the wines are now—in all but a handful of cases—fully ready for drinking, and the wines show well. The tasting of some one hundred wines in June 2008 was not too exhausting: indeed, rather less so than both the 1995 and 1996 equivalents. There is an appealing fresh fruit here, and both elegance and harmony. There is neither the volume and richness of the 1999s, nor the grip of the 1996s, nor the depth of the 1995s. But there is much to enjoy, and plenty of scope for cellaring the best bottles for at least another decade.

The year got off to a bad start. Easter Monday brought severe frost to the Côte d'Or. Just about all the communes with the exception of Savigny-Lès-Beaune and Chassagne-Montrachet were blighted, and, the frost being early, it was the best exposed slopes—that is, the *grands* and *premiers crus*—which were the most

⇢ Size of the Crop ⇠ (In hectolitres)			
	RED	WHITE	TOTAL
Grand cru	11,907	3,605	15,512
Village and			
premier cru	168,473	51,430	219,903
TOTAL	180,380	55,035	235,415

affected. Here the eventual harvest would be 10 percent less than in 1997. The village wine crop was 10 percent higher.

After this the summer was uneven: fine in May and the first half of June, so a successful flowering. Dismal for the next six weeks, leading to *coulure* and *millerandage,* which would mean that some first-growth wines would have to be grouped together rather than separately vinified. Then in August it was almost too hot, and very dry, leading to hydric stress in the young vines. Humid conditions returned at the beginning of September, threatening rot, but in fact the weather then cleared up, and the harvest took place under sunny skies. You have to be a philosopher to be a winemaker!

Overall, 1998 is a very good vintage for red wines. There are few great wines, but there are very few duds. The very best 1996s and 1995s are clearly superior, but these are less even vintages. And of course there are many very splendid 1999s, as we were to discover twelve months later. At my ten-year-on tasting, the whites showed rather better than I had expected, offering both more depth and better balance—and, incidentally, as far as our samples of the white wines were concerned (we had three bottles of each wine), no examples of

premature oxidation. I had rather written the 1998 whites off—drink up before they die on you—but given our by-no-means-comprehensive selection, I have changed my mind.

TASTING NOTES

The following wines were sampled at my annual tasting for the growers in June 2008. A few notes date from other occasions in 2008.

White Wines

Mâcon, La Roche Vineuse,
Vieilles Vignes,
Domaine Olivier Merlin   Drink soon   15.0
Magnum. Brisk, fruity, no undue age. Good depth. Good.

Montagny, *Premier Cru*,
Cuvée Sélection,
Domaine Stéphane Aladame   Drink soon   15.0
Ripe, even rich. Plenty of personality. Very good fruit. An attractive wine.

Pernand-Vergelesses,
Les Combottes, Domaine
du Château de Chorey   Drink soon   15.0
Magnum. Showing a little age on the nose. But quite crisp and stylish on the palate. And decent weight.

Saint-Aubin,
Clos du Chatenière,
Domaine Hubert Lamy   Drink soon   16.0
Magnum. Well-matured but not tired. Quite rich and fruity. Good depth. Very good.

Meursault,
Domaine Jean-Marc Boillot   Now to 2016   17.0
Lovely nose. Ripe and mature and really quite profound. Fullish. Very good fruit. Long and fine. No hurry to drink.

Meursault,
Maison Morey Blanc   Now to 2017   16.5
Reticent nose. Quite firm. Very good depth and style. Still vigorous. Very good indeed.

Meursault, "Tête de Murgey,"
Domaine Patrick Javillier Drink soon 15.0
Magnum. Spicy. Good depth. But it lacks a little
grip. Good though.

Meursault, Desirée,
Domaine des Comtes Lafon Now to 2015 15.0
Fresh. Lots of fruit. Quite exotic, but not too
tarty. Good plus. No hurry to drink.

Meursault, Les Tessons,
Clos de Mon Plaisir Now to 2018 17.5
Magnum. Very delicious. Lovely fruit. Good
substance. Balanced, long, and subtle. Still
virile.

Meursault, Les Poruzots,
Francois and Antoine Jobard Drink soon 13.5
Somewhat austere. Slightly hard. Not enough
fruit.

Meursault, Les Genevrières,
Francois and Antoine Jobard Now to 2017 16.0
Good fruit. Firm, full, and rich. Still lots of life
ahead of it. Very good.

Meursault, Les Perrières,
Domaine Guy Roulot Now to 2020 18.0
Magnum. Very lovely nose. Ripe and elegant.
Ample, fullish, profound, and very fine. Lots of
life ahead of it.

Meursault, Les Perrières,
Domaine des Comte Lafon Now to 2020 18.0
Fullish, rich, multidimensional. This is excellent. Minerally and yet very ample. Lovely. Will
still keep very well.

Chassagne-Montrachet,
Clos du Maltroye,
Domaine Jean-Noël Gagnard Drink soon 16.0
Fresh, ripe, good vigour. This is very good.
Long and balanced.

Chassagne-Montrachet,
Les Blanchots Dessus,
Domaine Jean-Noël Gagnard Drink up 15.5
Very good depth, but just a hint of age now.
Ripe and stylish.

Puligny-Montrachet,
Domaine Jean-Marc Boillot Drink soon 16.0
Ripe full of fruit. Vigorous and fresh. Lovely
finish. Very good indeed.

Puligny-Montrachet, Le Cailleret,
Domaine de Montille Now to 2018 18.5
Very lovely fruit. Lots of life and complexity.
Lovely minerally style. Very, very long. Excel-
lent. Lots of life ahead of it.

Nuits-Saint-Georges,
Clos de l'Arlot,
Domaine de l'Arlot Drink soon 15.0
Soft and elegant on the nose. Ripe and abun-
dant. Even a touch sweet from the new oak.
Ultimately lacks a little zip and flair.

Corton-Charlemagne, Domaine
Bonneau du Martray Now to 2020 18.5
Firm, fresh nose. Lots of depth. Fullish, vigor-
ous, clean, and very stylish. Long on the palate.
Very fine. Lots of potential still here.

Bienvenues-Bâtard-Montrachet,
Domaine Leflaive Drink soon 16.5
Some evolution here. Ripe and abundant. Gently oaky. Fine but I would have liked a bit more
minerality and freshness.

Red Wines

Givry, Clos Salomon,
Domaine du Clos Salomon Drink soon 15.0
Magnum. Lightish, but pretty, fresh nose.
Medium body. Ripe and fruity. Stylish. An
attractive bottle.

Savigny-Lès-Beaune,
Les Marconnets,
Domaine Simon Bize Now to 2015 15.5
Magnum. Slightly reduced on the nose. Better
on the palate. Good grip. Plenty of fruit and
backbone. Long; very good.

Savigny-Lès-Beaune, Les Gravins,
Domaine Jean-Marc Pavelot Now to 2015 16.0
Fine, stylish nose. Good depth and grip. Medium
to medium-full body. Very ripe. Ample, slightly

spicy fruit. Balanced, long, elegant. Very good plus.

Savigny-Lès-Beaune, La Dominode, Domaine Jean-Marc Pavelot
Now to 2018   16.5

Profound nose. Rich and succulent. Lots of character. Ample, cool fruit. Medium-full body. Vigorous. Very good indeed.

Pernand-Vergelesses, Ile de Vergelesses, Domaine Chandon de Briailles
Drink soon   16.0

Magnum. Soft, ripe, ample, stylish nose. Medium body. Good intensity. Vigorous and succulent. Long. Very good plus.

Beaune, Lulure, Domaine Emmanuel Giboulot
Drink soon   14.0

Soft, attractively fruity nose. Quite developed. Ripe. Medium body. Not the greatest depth but a pleasant bottle.

Beaune, Les Champs Pimont, Maison Champy
Drink up   13.0

Magnum. Somewhat pedestrian on the nose. Some developement. Somewhat suave. Astringency lurks underneath. Only fair.

Beaune, Les Cents Vignes, Domaine Lucien Jacob
Drink soon   15.5

Vigorous but somewhat artisanal nose. Better on the palate. Fresh and amply fruity. Medium to medium-full body. Positive follow-through. Good plus.

Beaune, Les Cras, Domaine du Château de Chorey
Drink soon   15.5

Magnum. Strangely lean on the nose. Medium body. Cool. Slight elements of astringency. Quite stylish underneath, and no lack of charm. Good plus.

Beaune, Les Bressandes, Maion Camille Giroud
Now to 2016   16.0

Ripe nose. Lots of fruit. Medium-full body. Ample, rich, and spicy. Long and vigorous on the palate. Very good.

Beaune, Les Grèves, Domaine Michel Lafarge
Now to 2018   17.0

Still quite closed on the nose. Fullish body. Lots of very lovely, succulent fruit. Lots of depth too. Rich and satisfying. A real triumph. Very good indeed.

Volnay, Les Carelles, Maison Camille Giroud
Drink soon   14.0

Good fruit on the nose if a little four-square. Medium body. A touch astringent. Only quite good.

Volnay, Les Champans, Domaine du Marquis d'Angerville
Drink soon   16.0

Soft nose. Some evolution. Elegant fruit. Ripe. Medium body. Long and stylish. But not for the long term. Very good.

Volnay, Clos des Chênes, Domaine Michel Lafarge
Now to 2020   18.0

Rich, ripe, vigorous nose. Still firm, but just about *à point*. Fullish body. Lots of depth and energy. A lovely stylish wine. Fine plus.

Volnay, Clos des Chênes, Domaine des Comtes Lafon
Now to 2016   17.0

Good, fresh colour. Just about mature. Gentle, plump, quite oaky, fruity nose. Medium to medium-full body. Ripe, indeed rich, and with lots of charm. No hard edges. Very good indeed.

Volnay, Les Fremiets, Domaine du Comte Armand
Now to 2016   17.5

Very Volnay on the nose. Fragrant, soft, and fruity. Medium to medium-full body. Intense and very elegant. Long and lovely.

Volnay, Les Santenots, Maison Champy
Drink up   13.0

A bit dried-out on the nose. The fruit is artificial too. Lacks style. Medium to medium-full body. Only fair.

Volnay, Les Santenots du Milieu, Domaine des Comtes Lafon
Now to 2020 plus   17.5

Very good colour. Firm vigorous nose. Rich and full. Still very youthful. Lots of energy, lots of fruit, and lots of depth. Fine. Will still improve.

Volnay, Taillepieds,
Domaine de Montille   Now to 2020 plus   17.5
Youthful colour. Soft fragrant nose. Stylish Volnay fruit here. Medium to medium-full body. Balanced and stylish. Very good energy. Still just a little raw. But very good grip and vigour. Very complex and elegant. Long. Fine.

Pommard, Clos des Epenots,
Domaine du Comte Armand   Now to 2020   18.0
Magnum. Very good colour. Splendid nose. Full, concentrated, rich, and vigorous. This is a profound, multidimensional wine. Both a true Pommard and very elegant. Fine plus. Just about ready.

Pommard, Les Jarollières,
Domaine Jean-Marc Boillot   Now to 2016   16.0
Odd flavours on the nose. More "natural" on the palate. Fullish, ripe, good depth and vigour. Very good.

Pommard, Les Rugiens,
Domaine Jean-Marc Boillot   Drink soon   13.5
Rich, slightly over-ripe nose. Medium to medium-full body. Somewhat overdone. Slightly astringent. Lacks style.

Pommard, Les Rugiens,
Domaine de Montille   Now to 2016   16.5
Lean but quite stylish nose. Good fruit on the palate. Ample, balanced, long, and intense. Very good plus.

Marsannay, Longeroies,
Domaine Bruno Clair   Drink soon   14.0
Soft, ripe fresh and *à point* without being aged. Not the greatest depth but stylish and attractive. Very good for what it is.

Marsannay,
Les Saint-Jacques, Domaine
Fougeray de Beauclair   Drink soon   13.0
Magnum. Pedestrian nose. Some fruit on the palate but no depth and no flair. Medium body. Only quite good.

Fixin, Clos Marion,
Monopole, Domaine
Fougeray de Beauclair   Drink up   12.0
Magnum. Soupy nose. Medium body. Unstylish and unexciting.

Nuits-Saint-Georges,
Clos de l'Arlot,
Domaine Clos de l'Arlot   Now to 2016   16.5
Soft, ripe, attractive nose. Medium body. Quite rich. Not a bit stemmy. Good balance and vigour. Attractive and fully *à point*. Very good plus.

Nuits-Saint-Georges, Les Boudots,
Domaine Jean Grivot   Now to 2020   17.5
Quite a firm nose still. Lovely ripe fruit on the palate. Fullish body. A little tannin still to mellow. Rich. Very good grip and class. Very Vosne-ish. Long. Fine.

Nuits-Saint-Georges, Les Boudots,
Domaine Leroy   Now to 2020   18.0
Ripe nose with a hint of austerity still. Fullish body. Firm but rich underneath. Ample, succulent, classy fruit. Generous at the end, balanced, and with plenty of dimension. Long. Fine plus. Just about ready.

Nuits-Saint-Georges, Les Boudots,
Domaine Gerard Mugneret   Now to 2017   16.5
Quite an evolved nose. Plump and fruity on the palate. Medium to medium-full body. Quite rich. Positive and vigorous on the palate. Very good plus.

Nuits-Saint-Georges, Les Boudots,
Domaine Jean Tardy   Now to 2015   16.0
Soft nose, quite evolved. More freshness on the palate. Medium to medium-full body. Good fruit. Ample and attractive. Very good.

Nuits-Saint-Georges,
Les Porêts-Saint-Georges,
Domaine Alain Michelot   Now to 2020 plus   17.5
Medium-full colour. Rich, vigorous, full nose. Still youthful, though now just about ready.

Fullish body for a 1998. Typical Nuits-Saint-Georges structure and grip. Lots of fruit. Lots of vigour. But perhaps could have had a little more charm. Fine.

Nuits-Saint-Georges, Les Pruliers, Domaine Henri Gouges   Now to 2020 plus   17.5
Vigorous nose. Clean, pure, firm, and fresh. Slightly austere still. Will still improve. Medium-full body. Lots of depth. Classy. Fine.

Nuits-Saint-Georges, Les Vaucrains, Domaine Robert Chevillon   Drink soon   15.0
Soft nose. Quite evolved. Ripe and mellow. Medium body. Decent fruit but not enough vigour. Good at best.

Vosne-Romanée, Les Beaumonts, Domaine Alain Hudelot-Noëllat   Now to 2018   17.5
Soft, aromatic nose. Medium to medium-full body. Ripe, mellow, balanced, and classy. Long and complex. Fine.

Vosne-Romanée, Les Brulées, Domaine Engel   Now to 2017   17.5
Soft; smoky nose. Medium body. Now fully mature. Aromatic. Lots of fruit. Harmonious, complex, and stylish. But fine rather than great. Yet most seductive.

Vosne-Romanée, Les Brulées, Domaine Grivot   From 2016   18.0
Full, vigorous colour. On the nose still quite firm, with some oak. Fullish body. Very good grip. Round, ripe tannins, but still immature. Lots of depth, quality, and energy. Fine plus.

Vosne-Romanée, Aux Brulées, Domaine Michel Gros   Now to 2020   18.0
Lovely nose, if not quite as intense and individual as the Clos des Réas. Medium-full body. Very good grip. Succulent and very classy. Long. *À point.* Fine plus.

Vosne-Romanée, Les Chaumes, Domaine Daniel Rion et Fils   Now to 2016   16.5
Good plump nose. Medium-full body. Ripe, succulent, stylish, and fresh. Long. Very good plus.

Vosne-Romanée, Les Malconsorts, Domaine Sylvain Cathiard   Now to 2020   18.5
Magnum. Still quite closed on the nose. But very high-class. Fullish, rich, and concentrated. Vigorous and profound. Very lovely finish. Very fine.

Vosne-Romanée, Clos des Réas, Domaine Michel Gros   Now to 2020   18.5
Delicious fruit and very gently oaky on the nose. Medium-full body. Vigorous and intense. Ripe and rich. Very elegant. Lovely Vosne fruit. *À point.* Very fine.

Vosne-Romanée, Aux Reignots, Domaine Robert Arnoux   Now to 2020   17.5
Good colour. Fresh, ripe, stylish nose. Good depth. Medium-full body. Ripe tannins. Balanced. Very good fruit. Vigorous finish. Fine.

Vosne-Romanée, Les Suchots, Domaine Robert Arnoux   Now to 2020 plus   18.5
Good colour. Rich, fat, concentrated nose. Very classy old-vine Pinot. Gently oaky. Very good backbone. Fullish body. Just a little tannin still to resolve. Fat, rich, concentrated, and succulent. Vigorous and full of finesse. Very fine grip and lots of dimension. Lovely. Really remarkably good for a *premier cru*. Will be yet better in two years.

Chambolle-Musigny, Les Amoureuses, Domaine Jacques-Frédéric Mugnier   Now to 2016   17.5
Very lovely, soft nose. Very classic. Smooth and mellow and medium to medium-full bodied on the palate. Not the concentration and intensity for great but certainly fine.

Chambolle-Musigny, Les Beaux-Bruns, Domaine Thierry Mortet   Now to 2015   15.5
Round, quite oaky, succulent nose. Medium body. Decent fresh fruit but not a great deal of dimension. Good plus.

Chambolle-Musigny, Les Charmes,
Domaine Ghislaine Barthod Now to 2018 18.0
Poised, elegant, fragrant nose. Medium to medium-full body. Very lovely balanced, Chambolle fruit on the palate. Lots of finesse and depth. Lovely and intense. Fine plus.

Chambolle-Musigny, Les Cras,
Domaine Ghislaine Barthod Now to 2020 18.0
Rich, fat, quite substantial. Lots of depth and class. Fullish body. Intense, stylish. Lots of vigour. Very lovely. Fine plus.

Chambolle-Musigny,
Les Fuées, Domaine
Jacques-Frédéric Mugnier Now to 2020 18.0
Firmer than his Amoureuses on the nose. Seems richer as well as fuller on the palate. Medium-full body. Very lovely intense fruit. Lots of depth. Fine plus. For once, better than the Amoureuses.

Chambolle-Musigny, Les Sentiers,
Maison Frédéric Magnien Now to 2018 17.0
Fragrant nose. Not too over-extracted. Good grip. Medium-full body. Rich and succulent. Balanced. Vigorous. Long and stylish on the palate. Very good indeed. Just about ready.

Morey-Saint-Denis,
Clos de la Bussière,
Domaine Georges Roumier Now to 2018 17.5
Vigorous colour. Rich, fat, cool, and stylish on the palate: more so than in the past. Fullish. Balanced. Lots of energy and a lovely finish. Fine.

Morey-Saint-Denis,
Les Chaffots, Domaine
Lucie and Auguste Lignier Now to 2016 16.5
Good vigorous colour. Quite a chunky wine. Slightly four-square. Medium-full body. Good fruit here and plenty of energy. But very good plus at best.

Morey-Saint-Denis, Clos Sorbé,
Domaine Fourrier Now to 2015 16.0
Quite a developed colour. Quite evolved on the nose too. A little too much so. Medium body.

Fruity and stylish and positive on the palate, though. But very good rather than fine.

Gevrey-Chambertin, Clos Prieur,
Domaine Thierry Mortet Drink soon 14.5
Good colour, but somewhat tired and faded on the nose. Medium-full body. A little astringent on the palate. Decent fruit. Quite good plus.

Gevrey-Chambertin, Mes Favorites,
Vieilles Vignes,
Domaine Alain Burguet Now to 2018 16.0
Firm nose. Plenty of wine here, if not a great deal of class. Better on the palate. Rich, fullish, balanced, and very good for what it is.

Gevrey-Chambertin, Les Cazetiers,
Domaine Bruno Clair Now to 2018 18.5
Very lovely, intense, classy fruit on the nose. Fresh and harmonious. Vigorous and fragrant. Medium to medium-full body. Long, subtle, and multidimensional at the end. Very fine.

Gevrey-Chambertin,
Les Cazetiers, Domaine
Dupont-Tisserandot Drink soon 14.0
Slightly diffuse on the nose. Soft and sweet on the attack. Somewhat tired and soupy on the finish. Medium body. Quite good at best.

Gevrey-Chambertin, Les Cazetiers,
Domaine Faiveley Now to 2020 17.5
Good colour. Fullish on the nose. No undue oak. Fullish body, rich, meaty, and still with some tannin. Lovely fruit underneath. Still (in 2008) needs two years. Fine.

Gevrey-Chambertin, Les Cazetiers,
Domaine Christian Sérafin Now to 2020 17.5
Good colour. Ripe, vigorous, and succulent on the nose. Full, rich, very gently oaky and profound on the palate. Lots of energy. Fine.

Gevrey-Chambertin,
Les Cherbaudes, Domaine
Lucien Boillot et Fils Now to 2016 15.5
Slightly pedestrian nose. Ripe and succulent on the palate but not very classy. Medium to medium-full body. Good plus at best.

**Gevrey-Chambertin,
Les Combottes, Domaine
Lucie and Auguste Lignier**   Now to 2015   16.5
Lightish colour. Not a lot of backbone here. Medium body. Round, ripe, sweet, and gently oaky on the palate. Very seductive. Good grip. Long. Very good plus.

**Gevrey-Chambertin,
Estournelles-Saint-Jacques,
Domaine Humbert Frères**   Now to 2016   17.0
Soft, stylish nose. Good fruit. Fragrant and succulent. Medium to medium-full body. Balanced and elegant. Long and positive. Very good indeed.

**Gevrey-Chambertin,
Clos du Fonteny,
Domaine Bruno Clair**   Now to 2018   18.0
Lovely, cool, stylish nose. Lots of depth and class. Medium-full body. Balanced, poised, intense, and multidimensional. Lovely. Fine plus.

**Gevrey-Chambertin,
Lavaux-Saint-Jacques,
Domaine Denis Mortet**   Now to 2016   16.0
Magnum. A little reduced on the nose at first. Medium-full body. Not as exciting as I had expected. Ripe and rich but a certain lack of flair. Very good at best.

**Gevrey-Chambertin,
Clos-Saint-Jacques,
Domaine Louis Jadot**   Now to 2025   19.0
Firm, rich, profound nose. Very lovely fruit and great style here. A full, meaty wine; still with some tannin to resolve. Lots of energy. Real *grand cru* class. Long. Very fine plus.

**Gevrey-Chambertin,
Clos-Saint-Jacques,
Domaine Armand Rousseau**   Now to 2020   18.5
Rich fruit, gently oaky, and very classy on the nose. Medium-full body. Just about ready. Ripe and complex and profound. Very long. Very lovely. Very fine.

Grands Crus

**Le Corton, Domaine
Bouchard Père et Fils**   Now to 2020   17.5
Medium-full colour. Still vigorous. Fullish, quite sturdy nose. Rich and meaty. Very good grip. On the palate, full body, still a little unresolved tannin. This will soften up and get more generous if kept another couple of years. Very good grip. Long. Very good indeed.

**Corton, Les Bressandes,
Maison Champy**   Drink soon   14.0
The colour is quite evolved. A bit more elegant on the nose than the other Champys. But not really the depth of a *grand cru*. Medium to medium-full body. Somewhat soupy-sweet. Quite good.

**Corton, Clos des
Cortons-Faiveley,
Domaine Faiveley**   Now to 2020   18.0
Full, firm, backward nose. Lots of depth here. Full-bodied. Some tannin. But not dry. Vigorous, elegant, profound. Still needs time. Fine plus.

**Corton, Les Perrières,
Maison Nicolas Potel**   Now to 2016   16.5
Fresh but slightly weak nose. Fruity and stylish and not too ephemeral on the palate. Medium body. Ripe and balanced. *À point*. Very good plus.

**Echézeaux,
Domaine Robert Arnoux**   Now to 2020 plus   17.5
Rich, ripe, and classy on the nose. Lots of depth. Medium-full body. Very good grip. Lots of character. Now just about ready. Nicely fat and concentrated, with a long, positive finish. Fine.

**Echézeaux,
Domaine Jean Grivot**   Now to 2020   18.0
Firm, full, ample, concentrated nose. Lots of depth and quality here. Fullish body. Still just a little tannin. Vigorous and classy. Very lovely fruit. Excellent harmony. Fine plus.

Echézeaux,
Domaine A. F. Gros   Now to 2016   16.5
Magnum. Plump, stylish nose. But without much nuance. Better on the palate. Ripe. Medium-full body. But very good plus at best.

Echézeaux,
Maison Nicolas Potel   Now to 2015   16.0
Somewhat nondescript on the nose. Medium body. But pretty rather than serious. Lacks depth and dimension, though balanced and stylish. Very good but not *grand cru* quality.

Grands-Echézeaux,
Domaine Engel   Now to 2020   18.0
Ripe, rich, classy, and intense on the nose. Fullish body. Excellent concentration, grip, and depth. Vigorous and fine plus.

Grands-Echézeaux,
Domaine Gros Frère et Soeur Now to 2018   17.0
Rich and meaty but not very elegant on the nose. Fullish, ripe, and quite succulent on the palate. Some tannin. Good energy. Very good indeed.

Clos de Vougeot,
Maison Champy   Drink up   11.0
Somewhat lumpy nose. Poor. Astringent and evolved on the palate. No.

Clos de Vougeot,
Domaine Engel   Now to 2016   17.0
Softer on the nose than his Grands-Echézeaux. Plump, attractive, stylish fruit. Medium-full body. Aromatic and seductive. Not quite the energy but very good indeed.

Clos de Vougeot,
Domaine Jean Grivot   Now to 2016   17.5
Magnum. Very fine composed nose. Laid-back. Lovely fruit. Not the greatest weight, but balanced and energetic, fragrant and classy. Fine but not great.

Clos de Vougeot,
Domaine Anne Gros   Now to 2020   18.0
Full, firm, still backward on the nose. Full body. Still a bit closed, but very lovely, rich, intense fruit. Lots of depth and vigour. Still (in 2008) needs two years. Fine plus.

Clos de Vougeot,
Domaine Michel Gros   Now to 2020   18.5
Some evolution on the nose. Very lovely fruit on the palate. Succulent and ripe and intese. Lots of depth. Generous and very lovely. Very fine.

Clos de Vougeot, Domaine
Alain Hudelot-Noëllat   Now to 2018   18.0
Good vigorous colour. Round, ripe, slightly spicy, soft, and mellow on the nose. Good class, depth, and grip. Medium-full body. Fresh, long, and seductive. Balanced and fine plus.

Clos de Vougeot, Domaine
Georges Mugneret-Gibourg   Now to 2018   18.0
Elegant nose. Ripe and fragrant and stylish. Good depth. Vigorous and generous. This has a lot of personality. Long. Complex and elegant. Fine plus.

Clos de Vougeot, Domaine
Daniel Rion et Fils   Now to 2015   15.0
Decent fruit on the nose but a lack of flair and depth. Medium to medium-full body. Succulent but slightly four-square. Good at best.

Romanée-Saint-Vivant,
Domaine Robert Arnoux   Now to 2025   18.5
Full, youthful colour. Complex, very classy, profound nose. Fullish body. Mouth-filling fruit. Just a little tannin still to absorb. A wine with harmony, depth, concentration, and lots of dimension. It still (in 2008) needs a couple of years. Very lovely, long lingering finish. Very fine.

Romanée-Saint-Vivant, Domaine
Sylvain Cathiard   Now to 2025 plus   19.0
Good colour. Very lovely nose. Elegant and subtle; fragrant and profound and splendidly well-balanced. Fullish body. Very ripe. Gently oaky. Rich and concentrated and multidimensional. Very, very long on the palate. Just about ready. Very fine indeed.

Romanée-Saint-Vivant, Domaine
Alain Hudelot-Noëllat   Now to 2020 plus   18.0
Medium-full colour; just about mature. Fat and succulent on the nose with a touch of oak.

Fullish body. Just about ready. Rich and concentrated. Long and harmonious. Fine plus.

Romanée-Saint-Vivant, Domaine
de la Romanée-Conti   Now to 2025   17.5
Very full colour. Still youthful. Surprisingly firm on the nose. Even a bit austere. Fullish body, still some unresolved tannin. It doesn't really sing today. Yet fine fruit and very good grip. Fine.

Romanée-Saint-Vivant,
Domaine Nicolas Potel   Now to 2016   16.0
A bit slight for a Romanée-Saint-Vivant on the nose. Pretty but no real depth. Medium body. Elegant and fruity and well-balanced. But it doesn't have the depth for a *grand cru* of this potential. Very good.

Richebourg,
Domaine Anne Gros   Now to 2025   20.0
Still very closed on the nose. But great richness and depth here. Full body. Will still improve. Hugely concentrated and very finely balanced. Real finesse. A great wine.

Richebourg, Domaine
Gros Frère et Soeur   Now to 2020   17.0
Slighty lumpy and reduced on the nose. But better on the palate. Fullish. Quite rich. Quite stylish. Just a little four-square. Still needs two years. Very good indeed at best.

Richebourg, Domaine
Alain Hudelot-Noëllat   Now to 2025   18.5
Good vigorous colour. Fine, rich, very classy, old-viney nose. Long and very lovely. Full body. Still a little unresolved tannin. Very good grip. Lots of energy. Elegant and profound. Oaky at the end. Just about ready. Very fine.

Richebourg, Domaine
Dominique Mugneret   Now to 2020   18.5
First bottle a little flat. The second bottle was rich and fat. Gently oaky. Ripe and classy. Not a blockbuster but fullish body and very seductive fruit. Balanced, long, and very fine.

La Romanée, Domaine du
Château de Vosne-Romanée/
Bouchard père et fils   Now to 2020 plus   19.5
Fullish colour. Splendid concentration. Very classy, minerally fruit. Lovely balance. Ample, ripe, really complex, and very stylish. Very lovely fruit. Still youthful. Very fine indeed.

Clos des Lambrays,
Domaine des Lambrays   Now to 2016   16.5
Good colour. Fragrant, soft nose. Elegant fruit here. Medium body. Balanced and stylish but needs more vigour and concentration. Very good plus.

Clos de la Roche,
Domaine Dujac   Now to 2017   18.0
Classy nose. Fully *à point*. Very lovely, fragrant, intense fruit here. Medium to medium-full body. Rich and vigorous. Very classy and harmonious. Long and very lovely. Fine plus.

Clos de la Roche, Domaine
Lucie and Auguste Lignier   Now to 2020   17.5
Fat, rich, quite oaky nose. Slightly four-square. Fullish on the palate. Rich. Meaty. Lacks a bit of flair and nuance but good depth and concentration. Just about ready. Fine.

Clos de la Roche, Vieilles Vignes,
Domaine Ponsot   Now to 2020   18.0
Medium-full colour. Fully developed. Fragrant and vigorous on the nose. Medium-full body. Very good grip. Rich and ripe. Not quite silky but subtle and complex. Now quite round. Individual and lovely. Fine plus.

Bonnes-Mares, Domaine
Fougeray de Beauclair   Now to 2020   16.5
Ripe, rich, full, and succulent on both the nose and the palate, if without much flair. Yet balanced and vigorous. Very good plus.

Bonnes-Mares,
Maison Frédéric Magnien   Now to 2020   16.0
Good colour. Somewhat over-extracted, oaky nose. But rich and full and fat on the palate. Plenty of wine here. Still (in 2008) needs two years. Very good.

Bonnes-Mares, Domaine
Jacques-Frédéric Mugnier   Now to 2016   17.5
Very lovely ripe fruit on the nose. Very Chambolle. Medium to medium-full body. Soft and fragrant and classy, but lacks a bit of vigour perhaps. Fine but not great.

Bonnes-Mares, Domaine
Comte Georges de Vogüé   See note
All the samples were decidedly odd, and quite different from previous experiences. Soupy nose. Lumpy and astringent on the palate. Some built-in sulphur. Not "off" but certainly not very good. And it will just get drier and drier.

Musigny, Domaine
Joseph Drouhin   Now to 2020   19.0
Very lovely nose. Full, rich, subtle, and fragrant. Similar on the palate. This is very delicious. Intense and full of fruit. Not a blockbuster but very complex and very lovely. Very fine plus.

Musigny, Domaine
Jacques-Frédéric Mugnier   Now to 2017   18.0
Soft and intense on the nose. Understated and very classy. Medium to medium-full body. Like the Bonnes-Mares this is fine—indeed fine plus—but it lacks the vigour and real flair for great.

Musigny Vieilles Vignes,
Comte Georges de Vogüé   Now to 2025   17.5
This is a lot better than their Bonnes-Mares, but nevertheless a bit rigid on the nose. Fullish, sweet, a little overdone after the Drouhin. Lacks the nuance and sheer fragrance of a Musigny. Fine but not great. Still (in 2008) needs time.

Charmes-Chambertin,
Domaine Denis Bachelet   Now to 2025   19.5
Very lovely nose. Rich, ripe, full, and concentrated. Above all, great style and depth. Fullish.

Marvelous succulent fruit. Really very lovely. Multidimensional. Excellent. Will still improve (in 2008).

Charmes-Chambertin,
Domaine Humbert Frères   Now to 2020   19.0
Soft and fragrant and classy on the nose. Fresh, balanced, and intense on the palate. Very lovely fruit. Long. Very fine plus. (Emmanuel Humbert's first vintage: he got it spot on.)

Charmes-Chambertin,
Domaine Taupenot-Merme   Now to 2018   16.5
Slightly lumpy but basically good depth on the nose. Similar palate. Good meaty fruit. Quite classy underneath. Very good plus.

Chapelle-Chambertin,
Domaine Trapet Père et Fils   Now to 2020   18.0
Fresh, rich, fullish nose. Good class here. Medium-full body. Still a little tannin. Rich and fat and succulent on the palate. Very good grip. Lots of depth and style. This will still improve (in 2008). Fine plus.

Chambertin, Clos de Bèze,
Domaine Armand Rousseau   Now to 2025   19.5
Good colour. Very lovely nose. Rich and succulent, profound and gently oaky. Fullish body. Lovely balance. Excellent grip and great class. Lots of energy. This is very fine indeed. Will still (in 2008) improve.

Chambertin, Domaine
Armand Rousseau   Now to 2025   20.0
Full, rich, backward nose. Still youthful. Full body. Very good grip. Still needs time (in 2008). Splendid intensity, vigorous concentration and class. Very, very long. It's all here. A great wine.

Other Tastings

1995 BURGUNDY

This shows a drop of some 10 percent compared with the average and is similar to 1991, but the deficit was more marked in village and *premier cru* than in *grand cru,* and among those in the Côte de Nuits who picked late. "Plump,

↦ *Rating for the Vintage* ↤	
Red	18.5
White	18.5

ripe, and succulent yet nevertheless with the ability to age well," was how I described the 1995 red Burgundies at the outset. Three years subsequently, as usual, the tasting group gathered together a representative selection to see how the wines were progressing in bottle. "Watch out," said many. They have tightened up. The backbone and tannins we all knew were there are now to the fore. You will find it hard work.

Well, it wasn't *too* hard, for the wines were generally very good, and we took our time over the tasting, sampling the wines in flights over a day and a half. It was a small crop, and the wines are concentrated and balanced and the

↦ *Size of the Crop* ↤ (In hectolitres)			
	RED	WHITE	TOTAL
Grands crus	11,720	3,286	15,006
Village and *premiers crus*	173,727	46,575	220,302
TOTAL	185,447	49,861	235,308

tannins are ripe. The tasting confirmed that 1995 followed 1993 and preceded 1996 as yet another highly successful red Burgundy vintage for keeping.

There was no real winter in 1994 and 1995. The early months of the vegetative cycle were dry and mild, indeed fine in March and April.

This produced a good *sortie* of buds in both the Chardonnay and Pinot Noir. The bad weather arrived in the middle of May. It snowed, the snow remaining on the upper slopes, on May 13. Two days later, there was frost on the flatter land below. The weather remained cool and unsettled right through until June 21 or so—indeed, throughout my visit to sample the 1994 whites in cask I was wearing a jacket or pullover, rather than the normal short-sleeved shirt. The result, naturally, was a long and drawn-out flowering with the inevitable losses due to both *coulure* and *millerandage*. The harvest in parts of Chassagne, Chambolle, Gevrey, and Marsannay was reduced even further by hail. There were also sporadic outbursts of mildew all the way up and down the Côte. Again, Gevrey-Chambertin was particularly badly affected. The bad flowering affected the red wine crop more than the white. It produced an uneven fruit-setting, leading to irregular maturity.

After June 21 the summer arrived, and thereafter it became, paradoxically, too dry and too hot: to the extent of placing a stress on the vine and blocking the progress towards maturity. The fine weather continued until September. The two weeks after September 4 were unsettled, the latter half of this fortnight distinctly rainy, but after September 18 the weather cleared. Bouchard Père et Fils began to collect their Pinots on September 21, their Chardonnays on September 23. Drouhin followed two days later. Most of the Côte de Beaune was picked in dry but cool weather during the following week. By September 30 the harvest was well under way in the Côte de Nuits, and it was at this time that weather broke again. There was a thunderstorm which quickly "turned" the fruit. It became essential to perform a *triage* to eliminate the rotten grapes, both in the vineyard and then later in the winery. Some decided to wait, hoping for a return to finer weather and a gain in sugar content—this did eventually come, but a little too late. Most, however, managed to escape at the cost, at the Domaine de la Romanée-Conti,

of having to reject 30 percent of their crop in their last picked vineyards, Echézeaux and Grands-Echézeaux.

At the outset the 1995s, were certainly a bit tannic and burly, but all of a sudden, as they began to approach their ninth birthday, they began to soften up. When I did my ten-year-on tasting, I had already begun to sample the 1995s, so I was not surprised to find the tasting less tiring than others were expecting. The vintage was delicious then and it remains so today. There is plenty of life still in the best. The other matter is the state of play of the 1996s. At the outset nearly all the palates I respect, in Burgundy and elsewhere, opted for the 1996s over the 1995s. The former are less graceful and less well-balanced, we said. The later vintage may not have the volume but it is more elegant. We have changed our minds since. Firstly, as I have described, the 1995s have turned out much more civilised than predicted. Secondly, the 1996s are beset by a rather dominating acidity. This was always tastable among the lesser wines, particularly the whites, but it is a failing that is present even at *premier cru rouge* level. When one comes to a 1996 which is properly rich, generous, and succulent, it comes as a relief.

Where are the best 1995 wines? Given that generalisations can be cramping, and do more harm than good, I would say that there are in 1995 some lovely wines in Volnay and in the whole of the southern Côte de Nuits up to Bonnes-Mares. The Gevreys are spotty, even at the top levels. Yet there are some lovely wines here. I was impressed at the outset by the quality and consistency of the Côte Chalonnaise and the lesser villages in the Côte d'Or such as Santenay, Chassagne-Montrachet, and Savigny-Lès-Beaune. But I have not had much experience at this level in recent years.

TASTING NOTES

The vast majority of the following wines were offered at a tasting of *grands crus* organised by Tom Black in Nashville in April 2012. It was a splendid event, as you will see. My very grateful thanks to him and his friends.

Beaune, Boucherottes,
Domaine Jadot Now to 2018 16.0

Good, vigorous colour. Ripe, succulent nose, but good backbone to support it. Just a touch of volatile acidity. Medium-full body. Good grip. Good energy and good style. Softened as it expanded in the glass. Very good.

Nuits-Saints-Georges,
Les Vaucrains,
Domaine Henri Gouges From 2018 17.0

Full, deep, immature colour. The nose is still very tight and tannic, as is the wine on the palate, giving one fears that it will never come round. But underneath there is a lot of concentrated fruit, good grip, and no lack of class. Rather tough at present.

Chambolle-Musigny,
La Combe d'Orveaux,
Domaine Henri Perrot-Minot Now to 2018 17.0

Full colour. Meaty, slightly clumsy nose, though not as much so as some of the domaine's wines at this period. Medium-full body. Balanced, juicy, and with good class and fruit at the end. Very good indeed.

Gevrey-Chambertin,
Les Cazetiers,
Domaine Dupont-Tisserandot Now to 2015 15.5

Good colour. Ripe, balanced nose. Medium-full body. Good grip. Lacks a bit of real class, but juicy and attractive and quite concentrated. Good plus.

Corton, Maison Louis Jadot Now to 2022 16.0

Medium-full colour. Some maturity. A ripe, succulent nose, but without the interest of their Pougets. Medium to medium-full body. It tails off. There is a lack of grip and *grand cru* depth. Decent fruit and balance on the attack but very good at best. Fully ready.

Corton, Clos des Cortons,
Domaine Faiveley Now to 2025 18.0

Full colour. Ripe, ample nose. Rich and succulent. Medium-full body. Lovely ripe fruit on the palate. Rich and generous and just about ready. Lots of elegance and dimension. Fine plus.

Corton, Hospices de Beaune,
Cuvée Charlotte Dumay,
Maison Dominique Laurent Now to 2030 17.5

Medium-full colour. Some maturity. A touch of reduction on the nose. Medium-full body. Vigorous. Very good grip. Ample fruit. Long on the palate. Ripe and stylish. Just about ready. Fine.

Corton, Pougets,
Domaine Louis Jadot Now to 2030 18.5

Medium-full colour. Some maturity. Very lovely nose. Pure, ample, succulent. Lots of depth and class. Medium-full body. Very good energy. Lovely balance. Lots of dimension. Very long. Very impressive. Very fine. Just about ready.

Corton, Rognets,
Domaine Méo-Camuzet Now to 2022 17.5

Fullish colour. Barely mature. Ripe, oaky nose. Rich but quite a lot of oak on the palate. Medium-full body. Fully ready. Ample and generous. Ripe and stylish and balanced. But fine rather than great. Pity about the oak.

Echézeaux,
Domaine Régis Forey Now to 2030 18.5

Medium to medium-full colour. Fully mature. Attractive, fresh nose. Supple, stylish ripe fruit. Medium-full body. Fully ready. Balanced, fresh, rich, and ripe. Long and elegant. Much more so than Forey usually is. Very fine.

Echézeaux,
Domaine Henri Jayer Now to 2030 19.0

Medium-full colour. Fully mature. A quite different wine from the Rouget. High-toned. Fresh. Now soft and succulent. Balanced and very lovely. Great class, depth, and harmony. Long, subtle, and excellent.

Echézeaux,
Domaine Emmanuel Rouget From 2015 18.0

Medium-full colour. Fully mature. Full, concentrated, backward nose. Fullish body. Still closed-in. Plenty of grip. Lots of wine here and still not yet ready for drinking. Lots of fruit. But does it lack a bit of elegance?

Grands-Echézeaux,

Domaine Réne Engel   From 2015   18.0

Fullish colour. Rich, ripe, and concentrated on the nose. Now round. Lots of depth and class. Lovely fruit. Vigorous and classy. Very intense. Will still improve. Fine plus.

Clos de Vougeot,

Domaine Bertanga   From 2015   15.5

Full colour. Barely mature. Ripe, rich, still youthful nose. Not perhaps the greatest of class. Fullish body. A little astringent. Still a little unresolved tannin. Good acidity but a lack of generosity. Good plus at best.

Clos de Vougeot,

Domaine Bouchard Père et fils   From 2015   18.0

Medium-full colour. Fully mature. Aromatic nose. Very good fruit. Fullish body. Nice and firm. Very good grip. Lots of depth. Will still improve. I like the vigour and the elegance here. Fine plus.

Clos de Vougeot,

Domaine Anne Gros   From 2015   19.0

Full colour. Splendid nose. Rich, concentrated, succulent, and profound. Full body. Lovely concentrated fruit on the palate. Very good grip. Lots of elegance. Still youthful. Very fine plus.

Clos de Vougeot, Domaine

Alfred Haegelyn-Jayer   Now to 2030   18.0

Fullish, mature colour. Rich nose. Just about softened now. Medium-full body. Ready. Very lovely succulent fruit. Very good acidity. Stylish, balanced. Fine plus.

Clos de Vougeot,

Domaine Louis Jadot   From 2017   18.5

Full, immature colour. Fine nose. Rich, concentrated, and backward. Full body. Still some tannin. Lovely vigorous balanced fruit. Lots of depth, dimension, and energy. Lovely finish. Very fine.

Clos de Vougeot,

Domaine Georges Roumier   From 2015   17.0

Fullish colour. Barely mature. Quite a soft nose. But good succulent fruit. Fullish body. Not exactly 100 percent clean on the palate. A slight touch of astringency. Good grip, but lacks generosity at the end. Very good indeed at best.

La Romanée,

Bouchard Père et Fils   From 2015   18.5

Fullish colour. Rich, concentrated, youthful, and backward on the nose. Fullish body. Still some tannin to resolve. Very fine grip and complexity of fruit. Quite a sturdy wine but lots of depth. Elegant too. Very fine.

Romanée-Saint-Vivant,

Domaine de l'Arlot   Now to 2020 plus   14.0

Medium to medium-full colour. Now mature. Typically Arlot stemmy nose. No *terroir* definition. Medium to medium-full body. Round, ripe, sweet. But anonymous. Not my style. A waste of an opportunity.

Romanée-Saint-Vivant,

Maison Louis Jadot   From 2015   19.0

Full, immature colour. Splendid concentration and depth on the nose. Full body. Still some tannin. High-quality on the palate. Lots of wine here. Abundant, vigorous, rich, ripe, fat fruit. Still needs time. Very fine plus.

Richebourg,

Domaine Jean Gros   From 2015   20.0

Medium-full colour. Rich, abundant, ripe, creamy nose. Very, very lovely. Fullish body. Excellent acidity. Marvelous fruit. A brilliant wine.

Richebourg,

Domaine Denis Mugneret   Now to 2025   18.5

Medium-full colour. This is evolved but delicious. Ripe, round, balanced, and very elegant on the nose. No lack of class and dimension. Lovely fruit. Medium to medium-full body. Perhaps not quite enough power and vigour at the end, but the wine is complex, classy, and lovely.

Musigny, Domaine

Joseph Drouhin   Now to 2030 plus   19.5

Medium-full colour. Just about mature. Soft, subtle, rich, abundant, delicate, and very, very classy on the nose. Medium-full body. The tannins just about resolved. Understated, intense, and very, very lovely. Very, very long, lingering finish. Very fine indeed.

Musigny, Domaine
Comte Georges de Vogüé　　From 2016　20.0
Fullish colour. Just about mature. Full, rich, concentrated, and youthful on the nose. Quite structured. Full body. A little oak. Very fine grip. Excellent fruit. Still needs time. Quite splendid.

Bonnes-Mares,
Domaine d'Auvenay　　Now to 2020　16.0
Medium-full colour. Still youthful. Just something a little weak on the nose. Medium-full body. Ripe on the attack. Ample but it finishes a little astringently. It lacks vigour. I'm underwhelmed.

Bonnes-Mares,
Domaine Dujac　　Now to 2030　18.5
Good, fullish colour. Ample, fresh, ripe, juicy nose. Profound and stylish. Medium-full body. The tannins now resolved. Delicious fresh, balanced fruit, and lots of class. This is not as obviously Dujac as some. Very fine.

Bonnes-Mares,
Domaine Groffier　　From 2015　18.0
Full colour. A slight touch of ginger biscuits on the nose. Medium-full body. Lots of ripe, stylish fruit, if just a shade four-square. Medium-full body. Very good acidity on the palate. Good energy and lots of depth. The tannins are almost resolved. Fine plus.

Bonnes-Mares,
Domaine Georges Roumier　　From 2018　19.5
Full, immature colour. This is a brilliant wine. Full, rich, and concentrated on the nose. Still fresh and youthful. Splendid fruit. Real depth, vigour, and dimension. Real class. Will still improve. Very fine indeed.

Clos de la Roche,
Maison Dominique Laurent　　Now to 2030　17.0
Full colour. Plump, ample, succulent nose. Plenty of juicy fruit here. Stylish too. Medium-full body. The tannins now resolved. Good grip. Balanced and round, yet plenty of vigour. Lots

of attraction at first, but it is a little flat at the end. Just about ready.

Clos de la Roche,
Domaine Hubert Lignier　　From 2015　18.5
Very full colour. Still very youthful. Rich, very concentrated, gently oaky. Lots of depth and class. Fullish body. Still some tannin to resolve. Very good grip. Plenty of wine here. Rich, concentrated, and profound. Very fine.

Chapelle-Chambertin,
Domaine Louis Jadot　　From 2018　19.0
Fullish, immature colour. Full, rich, concentrated, and backward on the nose. Fullish body. Still some tannin. Excellent fruit. Very profound. Lots of depth and energy. Very, very long and multidimensional. Very fine indeed.

Charmes-Chambertin,
Domaine Denis Bachelet　　From 2015　19.0
Fullish colour. Still youthful. Closed-in but very stylish and concentrated on the nose. Very lovely, multidimensional fruit. A beautiful example. Full body. Lots of depth. Lots of energy. Above all, great composure and class. Very fine plus.

Charmes-Chambertin,
Domaine Dugat-Py　　From 2015　18.0
Very full, immature colour. Rich, ripe, full concentrated nose. Not over-extracted (as is the 2002). Lots of energy. Full body. Lots of depth. Fine plus.

Charmes-Chambertin,
Domaine Geantet-Pansiot　　From 2015　17.5
Full, immature colour. Fresh, quite gentle, plump, stylish fruit on the nose. Fullish body. Still some unresolved tannin. Ripe and rich. Very good acidity. Lots of vigour. A little four-square but fine.

Charmes-Chambertin,
Maison Frédérick Magnien　　Now to 2025　17.0
Medium to medium-full colour. Fully mature. Soft, mellow nose. But not a lot of weight. Medium to medium-full body. Ripe and plump but a little one-dimensional. Balanced and positive but it lacks a bit of definition.

Charmes-Chambertin,
Domaine Serafin   From 2015 18.0
Medium-full colour. Still youthful. Ripe, gently oaky nose. Lots of fruit. Now getting soft. Medium-full body. Ripe, creamy-rich. Just a little oak. Good concentration. Most seductive.

Griotte-Chambertin, Domaine
Chezeaux, Réné Leclerc   Now to 2022 plus 16.0
Medium to medium-full colour. Soft, ripe, stylish, and balanced but fully evolved on the nose. Medium-full body. Decent balance but a touch of astringency and a lack of real class. Very good at best.

Griotte-Chambertin, Domaine
Frédéric Esmonin   Now to 2020 plus 17.0
Fullish colour. Youthful. Only a hint of brown. Ripe, slightly spicy, ample nose. Plenty of depth. But a slight lack of real finesse. Fullish body, meaty, youthful. Still a little tannin to resolve. The follow-through is more elegant than the attack. Good grip and balance. Plenty of energy. Will still improve. Very good indeed but not fine.

Griotte-Chambertin,
Domaine Ponsot   Now to 2030 plus 19.5
Fullish colour. Individual fruit on the nose. Lots of style and interest. Fullish body. Ripe, pure, marvelously poised, and harmonious. Not a blockbuster but lots of energy and dimension. And great class. Very fine indeed.

Mazis-Chambertin, Hospices
de Beaune, Cuvée Madelaine
Collignon, Frédérick Esmonin   From 2015 18.5
Full, rich, vigorous colour. Very lovely, classy, fruit on the nose. Now accessible, but the wine will still improve. Full body. The tannins are ripe, if still present, and the wine is oaky, but not excessively so. Potentially this is very fine.

Mazis-Chambertin,
Domaine Frédérick Esmonin   From 2015 15.0
Medium-full colour. A little maturity. Ripe, rich, but just a little four-square on the nose. Fullish body. The tannins not quite absorbed.

On the palate it is a bit lumpy. Good grip. But a lack of distiction. Good at best.

Mazis-Chambertin,
Domaine Maume   From 2015 18.0
Very full, immature colour. Rich, full, nicely high-toned nose. Lots of class here. Lots of depth. Fullish body. Ample fruit. Still some tannin. Very good grip. Long and succulent and delicious, especially at the end. Fine plus.

Mazis-Chambertin,
Domaine Joseph Roty   From 2018 20.0
Very full, immature colour. Rich, impressively concentrated, and profound on the nose. Very high-class too. Old-viney and multidimensional. Full body. Very fine fruit. Lots and lots of depth and energy. Will still improve. Very excellent.

Ruchottes-Chambertin,
Domaine Christophe Roumier   From 2016 19.0
Medium-full colour. Still youthful. Lovely fresh nose. Delicious fruit. Lovely balance. Very classy. Medium-full body. Splendid concentration of ripe, rich fruit. Excellent grip. Lots of dimension, distinction, and complexity. Still needs time. Very lovely.

Chambertin, Clos de Bèze,
Domaine Pierre Gelin   From 2015 18.5
Fullish colour. Only a suggestion of maturity. Ripe, quite high-toned nose. Fullish, fresh, supple, attractive, and very well-balanced. Plenty of class. This has a lovely long, energetic finish. Will still improve. Very fine.

Chambertin, Clos de Bèze,
Domaine Armand Rousseau   From 2015 19.5
Medium-full colour. Very vigorous. Splendid fruit on the nose. Really profound and classy. Medium-full body. Very concentrated, creamy-rich fruit. Very good grip. Very fine indeed. Will still improve.

Chambertin,
Domaine Joseph Drouhin Now to 2030 plus 19.0
Surprisingly deep colour for Drouhin. Pure, composed, ripe, classy nose. Very lovely. This

is delicious. Fullish, backward, fragrant nose with real finesse. Splendid balance. Discreet, laid-back, and very lovely. Very fine indeed. Only just ready.

Chambertin,
Domaine Denis Mortet   From 2015 18.0

Fullish, immature colour. Rich, but a little closed-in on the nose. Just a touch of oak. Medium-full body. Ripe, rich, balanced, and really quite classy. But fine plus rather than great. There is a nuance missing. Will still improve.

Chambertin,
Domaine Armand Rousseau   From 2015 20.0

Fullish colour, with now a touch of maturity. Quite brilliant on both nose and palate. The complete wine. Marvelous old-vine fruit. Beginning to get really velvety. Great concentration and excellent grip and dimension. Wine doesn't come better than this!

1990 BURGUNDY

The 1990s decade was bookended by two large and highly satisfactory vintages: 1990 and 1999. Both years were easy for the *vignerons*, the weather conditions being pretty well ideal.

→ Rating for the Vintage ←	
Red	18.5
White	16.5

All you had to do was not screw up nature's bounty. If 1999 can be criticised, it is that the harvest was just too large to give that final snap of real concentration that separates the splendid from the really great. If one was to cast aspersions on the 1990s, it is that the fruit is a little cooked—in the sense of the difference between a fresh plum and a cooked plum tart; and hence that the wines taste more of 1990 than they do of their origins. Nevertheless, there is no lack of differentiation between, say, the Chambolles

and the Gevreys. Furthermore, the red wines are consistently good both geographically and up and down the hierarchy.

An early and mild start to the growing season produced a prolific *sortie* of buds, but the weather then deteriorated in June and the flowering was long and drawn out, producing both *coulure* and *millerandage*. Thenceforth, it was both hot and very dry, causing some hydric stress among the younger plants and disallowing the tardy parts of the Burgundian *vignoble*

→ Size of the Crop ←			
(In hectolitres)			
	RED	WHITE	TOTAL
Grands crus	14,117	3,668	17,785
Village and premiers crus	188,573	51,926	240,499
TOTAL	202,690	55,594	258,284

the chance to catch up. Rain was essential, and happily at the end of August, 80 millimetres fell in one week. Just what the doctor ordered. Thereafter the vines rapidly finshed their cycle and the harvest was able to take place under sunny skies and in ideal conditions.

From the outset the 1990 vintage threatened to be too large. In retrospect, it was essential to cut down the potential quantity, and as early as possible—at the time of the fruit-setting after the flowering at the latest. Those who restricted their vines to below 40 hectolitres per hectare produced wines of concentration and longevity. Others were forced to perform a *saigner*, which is a useful technique, but one which by its very nature must be approximative guesswork. In fact, 1990 turned out to be a vintage where a small error in the yield did not have too deleterious affect on the wine's quality. The fact that the vast number of the *premiers crus* (let alone the *grands crus*) the team unearthed from their own cellars could still be held twenty years after the harvest is testimony to the success of the vintage. It was a splendid tasting.

TASTING NOTES

A group of us meet in Guilford, Connecticut, towards the end of March, every year, at a tasting hosted by Bob Feinn of Mount Carmel Wine and Spirits. This is what we tasted in 2010. On the same trip to the United States, I sampled other 1990s in Atlanta and Pittsburgh. Strangely, there were no duplicates.

White Wines

Auxey-Duresses, Les Boutonniers,
Domaine d'Auvenay   Drink soon   15.0
Rich, fat, full, vigorous, and with just a hint of oak on the nose. On the palate, the fruit has faded a bit, and the wine lacks a little charm. Better with food. Still good.

Meursault, Les Charmes,
Domaine des Comtes Lafon   Now to 2015   17.5
Quite a developed colour and nose, but on the palate the wine is fresh and juicy with a nice touch of underlying oak. Very much still alive. Full-bodied, complex, and classy. Fine. Can still be kept.

Meursault, Perrières,
Maison Louis Jadot   Now to 2015   17.0
Very good, youthful colour. Ripe, mineral, very gently oaky nose. Lots of depth and energy. Fullish body. Just a little age beginning to show on the palate. Rather better with food. Lacks a bit of charm and is getting a bit four-square, yet still very good indeed.

Puligny-Montrachet, Les Pucelles,
Domaine Leflaive   Drink soon   15.0
Quite a developed colour. Rather neutral on the nose. No great class or definition but balanced and reasonably fresh. Positive at the end, but a lack of vibrancy and class. Good rather than great.

Puligny-Montrachet, Les Referts,
Domaine Etienne Sauzet   Past its best
Old colour. Too maderised to be enjoyable any longer. Yet good fruit and depth. Other bottles may still be very good indeed.

Corton-Charlemagne,
Domaine Bonneau du Martray Now to 2015   18.5
This is very fine and still has plenty of vigour. Fullish, round, rich, and well-balanced. Very stylish. Lots of dimension. Lovely.

Corton-Charlemagne,
Domaine Louis Latour   Now to 2015   17.5
Broad nose. Not very Corton-Charlemagne. Fullish on the nose. Oaky and youthful. Quite concentrated on the palate. Profound and complex and nicely ripe at the end. Fine.

Bienvenues-Bâtard-Montrachet,
Domaine Ramonet   Now to 2020   18.5
Fresh, green-gold colour. Profound nose. Still youthful for a twenty-year-old wine. Lots of quality here. Very fine grip. Multidimensional. Full body. Very fine. Seems as if it will last for a good ten years yet.

Bâtard-Montrachet,
Domaine Pierre Morey   Now to 2015   18.5
Ripe, rich, concentrated, and vigorous. This is very lovely and still has bags of life. Very fine, long, lingering finish.

Chevalier-Montrachet,
Les Demoiselles,
Domaine Louis Latour   Past its best
Old, orange colour. Very oxidised. Undrinkable.

Musigny Blanc, Domaine
Comte Georges de Vogüé   Now to 2018   19.0
No undue maturity on the colour. Fresh nose. Rich and individual, with just a hint of oak. Ripe, complex, and classy. Very delicious and not a bit like a Meursault or a Puligny. No hurry to drink.

Red Wines
CÔTE DE BEAUNE

Santenay, Clos des Tavannes,
Domaine de la Pousse d'Or   Past its best
Quite an old colour. Old on the nose. This was a fullish wine with good ripe, sturdy fruit. Now well past its best.

**Chassagne-Montrachet,
Les Morgeots, Domaine
Duc de Magenta/Louis Jadot**   Drink soon   15.0
Good colour. Full, rich, healthy nose. A meaty wine with a lot of depth and vigour. Fresh on the palate. A sturdy wine for food. Good energy at the end. Good.

**Savigny-Lès-Beaune,
La Dominode,
Domaine Bruno Clair**   Now to 2020   15.5
Rich and meaty on the nose. Plenty of vigour. A full, fresh, wine which, if no great finesse, has ample fruit and plenty of depth. Still vestiges of tannin. Good plus.

**Beaune, Les Epenottes,
Domaine André Mussy**   Past its best
Fullish, well-matured colour. Somewhat rustic nose. Dried out on the palate. Was reasonably ripe, if never very elegant. Now past its best.

**Beaune, Grèves, Domaine
Thomas-Moillard**   Now to 2020   17.0
Big, rich nose. Full, concentrated, very typically 1990 on the nose. Lots of depth and lovely fruit. Fully ready, but with plenty of vigour. Impressive.

**Beaune, Clos des Mouches,
Domaine Joseph Drouhin**   Now to 2015   16.0
Full colour. No undue age; rich, balanced nose. Good grip, good fruit. Fullish body. Meaty. This is a wine which needs food, but it is very good. Still plenty of future.

**Volnay, Les Champans, Domaine
Hubert de Montille**   Now to 2015 plus   17.0
Full colour; still youthful. Ripe, very Volnay on the nose. Fullish body. Still lots of vigour. Good energy and very good grip. Impressive fruit. Lovely harmonious finish. The most vigorous of his Volnays. Very good indeed.

**Volnay, Clos des Chênes,
Domaine Michel Lafarge**   Now to 2020   18.5
Full colour. Still very vigorous. Rich, full, energetic nose. Splendidly succulent, fresh, and youthful. Very lovely fruit. Intense and classy

and multidimensional. Bags of life ahead of it still. Very fine.

**Volnay, Les Mitans, Domaine
Hubert de Montille**   Drink soon   16.0
Full colour, still very fresh. Good nose. Fragrant and a bit more delicate than the Champans. Medium body. Soft. Balanced. Still round and vigorous but getting towards the end. Very good.

**Volnay, Les Taillepieds,
Domaine Hubert de Montille**   Drink soon   15.5
Full colour; *à point*. A bit more evolved than the Champans on the nose. And on the palate too. Just a little astringency taking over. Yet ripe and balanced and classy. This was perhaps even better than the Champans originally, but it is beginning to lack fruit. Best with food.

**Pommard, Clos des Epeneaux,
Domaine du Comte Armand**   Now to 2020   17.5
Very full colour. Rich, sturdy nose. Good tannins. Full body. Ripe, plummy, vigorous, and profound. Long and meaty and still very virile on the palate. Bags of life. Fine.

**Pommard, Grand Clos des Epenots,
Domaine de Courcel**   Now to 2015   17.0
Full, mature colour. Good classy, fragrant nose. Medium-full body. Good grip. Well-balanced if without the weight and intensity of the Comte Armand. Still plenty of life. Very good indeed.

**Pommard, Clos des Epenots,
Maison Camille Giroud**   Drink soon   17.5
Full, mature colour. Rich nose. Succulent. Very good tannins. Typical Epenots. Not the power of the Clos des Epeneaux but with very elegant fruit. Very good grip. Just a suggestion now of impending astringency. But fine.

**Pommard,
Les Jarollières, Domaine
Jean-Marc Boillot**   Now to 2020 plus   16.0
Full, vigorous colour. A big, somewhat ungainly wine. But rich and fruity on the nose and better on the palate. Full body. Good tannins. Lots of meaty fruit. Good acidity. Finishes well. There is even some elegance at the end. Very good.

Pommard, Les Rugiens,
Domaine Hubert de Montille   Now to 2015   17.5
Full colour. *À point*. Ripe, rich, succulent nose.
Full body. Vigorous. Elegant for a Rugiens.
Splendidly rich. Good follow-through. Long.
Fine. No hurry to drink.

CÔTE DE NUITS

Nuits-Saint-Georges, Aux Meurgers,
Domaine Méo-Camuzet   Now to 2015   16.0
Full, youthful colour. Sizeable on the nose. A
little four-square, but neither too macerated nor
too oaky. Fullish body. A little too extracted on
the palate. Yet good grip and an intense follow-
through. Really quite concentrated. Very good
but by no means fine. A bit tiring to drink.

Nuits-Saint-Georges, Les Perrières,
Maison Camillle Giroud   Now to 2020   17.5
Good colour. Ripe, fresh, stylish nose. Plenty
of wine here and plenty of finesse. Nicely pure.
Fullish body. Very good grip and vigour. Good
tannins. Lots of energy. And life ahead of it.
Fine.

Nuits-Saint-Georges,
Les Saint-Georges,
Domaine Henri Gouges   Now to 2020 plus   18.5
Good, full, mature colour. Vigorous nose. Rich,
complete, classic, ripe Pinot fruit. Fullish body.
Very sophisticated tannins. Smooth and vel-
vety. Fine grip. A very lovely wine. Nuits-Saint-
Georges doesn't come better than this. Very
fine.

Vosne-Romanée, Les Brulées,
Domaine Méo-Camuzet   Now to 2016   16.5
Fullish mature colour. A slight reduction on
the nose. A bit four-square as well. Not as rigid
as the Meurgers and somewhat more together.
Fullish. A bit over-macerated nevertheless. And
this detracts from the style. Good grip though.
Very good plus.

Vosne-Romanée, Les Chaumes,
Domaine Jean Tardy   Now to 2015 plus   17.0
Medium colour. Fully mature. Ripe nose, soft
and gently oaky. Fresh and stylish. Medium-

full body. Still lots of energy. Just a little sweet.
But good grip and balance. Tardy's wines today
can be a bit bland. This isn't. It's a most enjoyable, charming wine.

Vosne-Romanée,
Les Malconsorts, Domaine
Hudelot-Noëllat   Now to 2018 plus   17.5
Fullish, mature colour. Smoky, mocha nose.
Attractive and vigorous. Fullish body. Good
balance. Lots of depth and style and energy.
Complex. Long on the finish. Fine.

Vosne-Romanée, Clos des Réas,
Domaine Jean Gros   Now to 2018 plus   18.0
Medium-full colour. No undue age. Very lovely
rich, definitive fruit. Real elegance and complexity. Medium-full body. Fresh. Very harmonious and stylish. Lovely.

Vosne-Romanée, Les Suchots,
Domaine Grivot   Now to 2018   17.0
Clean and clear on the nose. Poised and classy.
Medium to medium-full body. Good grip. Bal-
anced and full of fruit. Not the greatest of com-
plexity and flair but very good indeed.

Chambolle-Musigny,
Les Amoureuses,
Maison, Pierre Bourée   Now to 2016   18.0
Fully mature colour. Yet quite full. Ripe, aromatic nose. Quite developed now but no undue
age. Fresher on the palate. Lovely fruit. Fragrant. Very Chambolle. Fresh and long at the
end. Fine plus.

Chambolle-Musigny,
Les Amoureuses, Domaine
Joseph Drouhin   Now to 2016   See note
Good colour. Rather old and tired and oxidised
on the nose. Still judgeable on the palate. There
was once very lovely fragrant fruit here plus a
very good grip. This bottle is past its best.

Chambolle-Musigny,
Les Gruenchers,
Domaine Dujac   Now to 2016   17.0
Medium colour. Quite developed. Much more
Dujac than Chambolle. The stems, a little
sweetness, purity, and good acidity. Spicy, but

less substance and richness than, for example, their Clos-Saint-Denis. Very fresh and long on the palate. Very good indeed.

Morey-Saint-Denis,
En La Rue de Vergy,
Domaine Bruno Clair   Now to 2015   15.5
Medium-full colour. Fully mature. Quite an evolved nose. More character than the Henri Perrot-Minot. Good fruit. Good freshness. Clean and long. Good plus.

Morey-Saint-Denis,
En La Rue de Vergy,
Domaine Henri Perrot-Minot   Now to 2015   14.0
Medium-full colour. Fully mature. Plump nose. Good succulence. Medium body. Good freshness. But not a great deal of depth or interest. Quite good. No hurry to drink.

Morey-Saint-Denis,
Premier Cru, **Vieilles Vignes,**
Domaine Hubert Lignier   Now to 2015   16.0
Medium-full colour. Fully mature; not much on the nose at first. Round, ripe, fresh, plump fruit with a touch of wood. Good depth. Medium-full body. Positive follow-through. Very good.

Gevrey-Chambertin, Les Cazetiers,
Domaine Joseph Faiveley   Now to 2015   17.0
Very good colour. Inexpressive and somewhat rigid nose. The usual rather dry, woody hints of Faiveley wines at this time. Good substance and ripe, rich fruit nonetheless. Very good indeed.

Gevrey-Chambertin, Les Cazetiers,
Domaine Christian Serafin   Now to 2020   17.5
Magnum. Good colour. Full, plump nose with more than a touch of new wood. Fullish body. Lovely ripe fruit. Good energy and depth. Long and classy. Fine.

Gevrey-Chambertin,
La Combe Aux Moines,
Maison Michel Couvreur   Now to 2018   16.0
Good colour. Slightly reduced on the nose at first. Medium-full body. Good grip. Stylish and balanced. Good depth. But it could have been a little richer and more concentrated.

Gevrey-Chambertin,
Aux Combottes,
Domaine Dujac   Now to 2016   17.0
Good colour. Well-developed, typically Dujac nose. Sweet, very good acidity, slight hints of bubble gum. Plus the stems, of course. Medium to medium-full body. Balanced. Very ripe. Still very fresh. Most enjoyable but lacks a little *grand cru* dimension.

GRANDS CRUS

Corton, Clos des Cortons Faiveley,
Domaine Joseph Faiveley Now to 2015 plus   18.0
Full, mature colour. Rich, very oaky nose. Less oaky on the palate and the oak here less rigid. Vibrant, lush, balanced. Very good acidity. Fullish body. Still vigorous. Long and stylish. Fine plus.

Château Corton Grancey,
Domaine Louis Latour   Drink soon   16.5
Developed, medium to medium-full colour. Spicy, mocha nose, a little loose-knit now. Not much class. Better on the palate. Medium body. Not a lot of vigour, but soft and ripe and fresh and enjoyable.

Corton, Perrières,
Domaine Michel Juillot   Drink soon   16.0
Good fresh colour. Not a lot of generosity on the nose, which is a little bitter. Medium to medium-full body. Slightly dry. Decent fruit, class, and freshness but a lack of richness on the aftertaste.

Echézeaux, Domaine Dujac   Now to 2020   18.5
Good, fullish colour. Ripe, fragrant, fat, and rich on the nose. Lovely fruit. Medium-full body. Vigorous nevertheless. Sophisticated, intense, and beautifully balanced. Fine plus.

Echézeaux, Domaine
de la Romanée-Conti   Now to 2020   18.0
Good, vigorous colour. Splendid ripe, rich, concentrated fruit on the nose. Round and succulent. Lots of depth. Fullish body, rich, vigorous, and classy. Lots of depth and, above all, vigour. Still young. Lovely.

Grands-Echézeaux,
Domaine Joseph Drouhin   Now to 2020   19.0
Good colour. Very lovely, rich, ripe, almost sweet, classy nose. Splendidly balanced complex fruit. Ripe and fullish and intense and harmonious. Lots of finesse. Disarmingly delicious. Great purity.

Clos de Vougeot,
Domaine Robert Arnoux   Now to 2018 plus   18.5
Medium-full colour. Fragrant nose. Quietly stylish but slightly gamey. Medium-full body. Ripe, round, good grip and tannins. Mellow but vigorous. Really quite concentrated. Long, complex, and energetic. Lovely fruit. Very fine.

Clos de Vougeot,
Domaine Joseph Faiveley   Now to 2018   17.0
Good colour. Rich if a little rigid on the nose. Good ripe fruit but a slight lack of nuance. Fullish body. Balanced. Ripe and juicy. A touch of unresolved tannin. Yet very good fruit. Long. But the oak tends to dominate, especially at the end. Very good indeed but not fine.

Clos de Vougeot,
Maison Camille Giroud   Now to 2019   16.5
Full, vigorous colour. Rich, full but somewhat four-square nose. A bit inflexible. Full body. Some residual tannin which will, I fear, never completely integrate. Good grip. But not exactly succulent. Very good plus.

Clos de Vougeot,
"Maupertuis," Domaine
Anne et Francois Gros   Now to 2020 plus   19.0
Fullish colour. Very high-class fruit on the nose. Fullish body. Marvelous equilibrium. Concentrated, energetic, harmonious, and profound. Vigorous, complex, and multidimensional. Lovely finish. Very fine plus.

Clos de Vougeot, "Musigni,"
Domaine Gros Frère et Soeur   Now to 2018   17.5
Medium-full, mature colour. Not a lot on the nose. Medium to medium-full body. Ripe and balanced. Round and classy. Fragrant and charming. Long and positive. Fine.

Clos de Vougeot, Domaine
Alain Hudelot-Noëllat   Now to 2018   17.5
Medium-full mature colour. Nicely spicy on the nose. Interestingly gamey. Medium-full body. Balanced. Good grip. Vigorous. Fine.

Clos de Vougeot,
Château de la Tour,
Domaine Labet   Now to 2014   17.0
Fullish, fresh nose. Ripe nose. Good vigour. Good depth. Medium-full body. It has lost a little of its fruit, but was not as austere with food as it was on its own, and still very enjoyable. The finish is quite profound and quite classy.

Clos de Vougeot,
Domaine Daniel Rion et Fils   Now to 2018   17.0
Full colour. Still youthful. Ripe, slightly spicy nose. Attractive gamey character. Medium-full body. Balanced and most enjoyable, if no great depth and finesse. Long and vigorous. Very good indeed.

Romanée-Saint-Vivant,
Domaine J. J. Confuron   Now to 2018   17.5
Fullish colour. A touch of reduction at first but this blew off. Not, though, really top *grand cru* quality. It is a bit four-square. Rich, concentrated, and really quite intense and powerful nevertheless. But a touch rigid at the end. Fine at best.

Romanée-Saint-Vivant,
Maison Louis Jadot   Now to 2020 plus   20.0
Very fine, full, just about mature colour. Marvelous nose. This is very fine indeed. All the glory of great Burgundy. Fullish body. Multidimentional. Excellent harmony. Splendid fruit. Real energy and complexity on the follow-through. Brilliant!

Richebourg,
Domaine Jean Grivot   Now to 2020 plus   20.0
Fullish colour. Still quite closed-in on the nose. Marvelous concentration on the palate. Full body, creamy and rich. Great class and marvelous fruit. Very, very long and energetic. Everything in place. A truly great wine. (Another

bottle, sampled *chez* Grivot, did not sing as much. It was too introverted and slightly reduced.)

Richebourg,
Domaine A. F. Gros   Now to 2020 plus 19.0
Fullish colour. Just a touch of reduction at first, but very fine concentrated fruit underneath. Lovely harmony. Fullish body. Splendid fragrance as it developed. This is the same wine as that labelled Jean Gros.

Richebourg,
Domaine Jean Gros   Now to 2020 plus 20.0
Fullish colour. This is cleaner, richer, fuller, more complete, and more classy than that labelled A. F. Gros. Marvelous harmony, concentration, vigour, and class on the palate. Quite splendid fruit. Multidimensional. Indisputably great.

Richebourg, Domaine
Alain Hudelot-Noëllat   Now to 2018 18.0
Medium-full, mature colour. Interesting, slightly odd grilled-meat flavours on the nose. Medium-full body. Soft and ripe and rich and succulent. Very velvety. Lovely harmony. Yet it misses a bit of finesse. So it is not totally convincing.

Richebourg,
Domaine Leroy   Now to 2020 plus 19.5
Full, vigorous colour. Very lovely concentrated fruit. Cool and balanced. Lots of finesse. Fullish body, excellent grip, lovely fruit. A profound, classy wine, but more Leroy than Richebourg. What it lacks is real originality.

Richebourg, Domaine
Thibaut Liger-Belair   Now to 2018 18.5
This wine was made and bottled by Denis et Dominique Mugneret, before the lease came to an end in 2002 and Thibault got the vines back. Medium-full colour, still youthful. Ample, round nose. Quite substantial. Rich and balanced. Fullish body. A meaty wine with a good grip. Good concentration and intensity, if not the class of the very best.

La Romanée, Domaine du
Château de Vosne-Romanée/
Bouchard Père et Fils   Now to 2020 19.5
Fullish, mature colour. Rich nose. Some oak. Great class here, if without the concentration of fruit of the best Richebourgs. Very good grip. Just the slightest bit austere. But a lovely balanced, intense, and vigorous wine.

La Tâche, Domaine de
la Romanée-Conti   2015 to 2030 20.0
Splendid colour. A touch of reduction at first but this quickly blew away. Pure and definitive and very fine indeed on the nose. Marvelous fruit. Indisputably a great wine. A big wine of huge concentration, splendid tannins, and very good grip. Very fine, long finish. Very youthful still. Will still improve.

Bonnes-Mares,
Maison Pierre Bourée   Now to 2020 17.5
Full colour. Fresh and vigorous. Slightly dense and four-square on the nose. Ripe and rich and full but a bit solid. Fullish body. Better than the nose. Almost exotic. Even a little sweet. An earthy wine but balanced and energetic and fine.

Bonnes-Mares,
Domaine Joseph Drouhin   Now to 2016 19.0
Good colour. Rich, fat, full, succulent nose. Lots of juicy fruit here and a touch of oak. Fullish body, opulent, very ripe. Exotic and sensuous. Very lovely finish.

Bonnes-Mares,
Domaine Robert Groffier   Now to 2015 14.0
Good, full, vigorous colour. Quite spicy but a little coarse and cooked. A sturdy wine, not exactly elegant, and showing some bitterness and vegetal elements at the end. Full and rich, but rather ungainly.

Bonnes-Mares,
Domaine Roumier   Now to 2020 plus 19.5
Fine, full colour. Very lovely nose. Marvelous pure fruit. Full body. Not too big, but a bit tough at first, but soon developed into a mellow and multidimensional wine with splendid

complexity, class, and harmony. Very fine, long finish. Excellent.

Bonnes-Mares, Domaine

Comte Georges de Vogüé   Now to 2020   18.5
Very full colour. Rich, fresh, very full, and at first slightly four-square nose. Still very vigorous. Good tannin and very good grip. Lots of fruit and a touch of oak. At first I was less enthusiastic, but it got better and better in the glass as it mellowed. Very fine.

Musigny, Domaine Drouhin   Now to 2020   20.0
Medium-full, mature colour. Very delicious. Complex, classy, and fragrant on the nose. A delicate wine compared with some but very lovely, intense fruit on the palate. Excellent grip and balance. Very, very long. Quite gorgeous.

Musigny, Domaine

Comte Georges de Vogüé   2015 to 2030   19.5
A bottle from my own celler in France. Full, still very youthful colour. The nose is quite splendid but still very young. Marvelous depth and concentration. It seems as if it will still improve. Full body. A little tannin to resolve. Great class. Does not have the voluptuous charm of the Drouhin today, and I think it may always be a touch rigid, but quite splendid nevertheless.

Musigny, Domaine

Comte Georges de Vogüé   Now to 2014   16.0
A bottle from an American cellar. I am convinced something untoward happened to the shipment. Bottles in the United States have never sung. Full, rich colour. Still vigorous. Still a little dumb—or is it just tight?—on the nose. Fullish body. Some evidence of unresolved tannin. Vigorous, rich and meaty, but rather four-square. Did not hold up very well in the glass.

Clos-Saint-Denis,

Domaine Dujac   Now to 2017   18.0
Medium colour. Fully mature. Soft, fragrant, stylish, well-balanced nose. On the palate this is round and harmonious, but this bottle is beginning to show a little age. There is a slight lack of vigour, and the acidity is beginning to show at the end. Held up well in the glass, however.

Clos-Saint-Denis,

Domaine Georges Lignier   Now to 2014   17.5
Medium to medium-full colour. Fully mature. Ripe nose. Quite stylish. By no means a blockbuster, but still fresh. Medium to medium-full body. Good acidity. Fully *à point*. Good plump fruit. Good class. Fine.

Clos de la Roche,

Domaine Dujac   Now to 2018   18.5
Full, rich, vigorous colour. Lovely fragrant nose. Lots of quality and lots of energy. On the palate, ripe and medium-full bodied. Plenty of vigour. Long, velvety, intense, and very elegant. Very fine.

Clos de la Roche, Vieilles

Vignes, Domaine Ponsot   Now to 2020   19.0
Full, vigorous colour. Ample, round, ripe, succulent nose. Silky and harmonious. Intense, fresh, vigorous, and very lovely. Fullish body. Lots of energy at the end. Very profound. Very fine plus.

Clos de la Roche, Domaine

Armand Rousseau   Now to 2016   18.0
Good colour. Fresh, plump nose. Succulent, ripe, medium-full weight. Just a touch of oak. This is ample, round, and full of charm. Very good grip. Lots of intererst. Holding up well. Lovely.

Charmes-Chambertin,

Domaine Bernard Dugat-Py   See note
Very good colour. A rich, full wine, if a touch rigid. But badly corked.

Charmes-Chambertin,

Domaine Frédéreic Esmonin   Now to 2020   18.5
Full, rich, vigorous colour. Still very youthful. High-quality. Full and concentrated and vigorous on the palate. Lovely fruit and lots of energy. Long and complex and very classy. Very fine.

Charmes-Chambertin,

Maison Roland Remoissenet   Now to 2014   16.0
Fullish colour. Fresh, ample, plump nose. Good fruit and good grip. Medium to medium-full weight. Lacks the energy of the best of the rest. Fresh and fruity, but a bit one-dimensional.

Mazis-Chambertin,
Hospices de Beaune, Cuvée
Madelaine Collignon   Now to 2020 plus   18.5
Bottled by Maison Rodet. Fine, full, vigorous colour. Full, energetic, fresh, very black-fruit nose. Quite oaky, but the oak integrated. Very rich. Full body. Youthful. Concentrated and with very good grip. A big wine, but no aggressive tannins nor over-maceration. Voluptuous. Impressive. Splendid fruit.

Mazy-Chambertin,
Domaine Armand Rousseau   Now to 2018   19.0
Full, mature colour. Ripe, rich, ample, seductive nose. Good fat and concentration here. Restrained, understated, cool, and complete on the palate, especially after the Hospices Mazis above. Medium-full body. Very lovely fruit and excellent harmony. Very classy indeed. Long and quite lovely.

Ruchottes-Chambertin, Domaine
Dr. Georges Mugneret   Drink soon   18.0
Fullish, vigorous colour. Quite developed but in an exotic rather than in a deleterious extent. Medium-full body. Ripe. Very good grip. Quietly classy. Just a suggestion of astringency at the end. So drink quite soon. This does not have the intensity for great but it has lovely balance, and is long and complex.

Ruchottes-Chambertin,
Clos des Ruchottes,
Domaine Armand Rousseau   Now to 2015   18.5
Fullish colour. Like the Dr. Georges Mugneret example, this is more gamey than the Mazy. Nor does it have the volume and concentration. It is a little leaner than the Dr. Georges Mugneret, but it is fresher, longer, more intense, and more elegant at the end. Medium-full body. Lovely.

Griotte-Chambertin,
Domaine Ponsot   Now to 2018   19.5
Very full colour. Almost black to the rim. Very, very rich, ripe, and exotic on the nose. Silky but gloriously fruity. Fullish body. Very intense and concentrated without being a blockbuster. Very lovely, individual black-fruit flavours. Lots

of depth and energy and splendid balance. Excellent.

Chambertin, Clos de Bèze,
Domaine Joseph Faiveley   Now to 2016   17.0
Full youthful colour. Again, rather blunt, dry, and rigid on the nose. Fullish body. Slightly astringent. A lack of suppleness. Good fruit and good grip, but rather tiring to drink.

Chambertin, Clos de Bèze,
Domaine Louis Jadot   Now to 2020 plus   20.0
Fullish vigorous colour. Profound nose. Rich and fat and very concentrated. Still very youthful. Very lovely fruit; succulent and multidimensional. Great class. Full body. Splendid depth of character. This is truly excellent. Still has years of life ahead of it.

Chambertin, Clos de Bèze,
Domaine Armand Rousseau   Now to 2016   18.0
Full, mature colour. Full, mature nose. Rich and succulent but a slight touch of the farmyard. Fullish, aromatic, very good grip. Slight rigidity nevertheless on the follow-through. Lots of energy, if not the purity and elegance of the best bottles of this wine.

Chambertin, Domaine
Bouchard Père et Fils   Now to 2020 plus   19.0
Fullish colour. Very lovely nose. Fragrant, classy, fullish, intense, and balanced. Still very youthful. Very composed. Multidimensional. Very fine plus.

Chambertin,
Domaine Joseph Drouhin   Now to 2018   19.5
Full colour. Very, very lovely nose. Marvelous, poised, ripe fruit. Great finesse and purity. Lots of dimension. Really very profound. Excellent harmony. Long on the palate. Very, very fine.

Chambertin,
Domaine Armand Rousseau   See note
Very full colour. This has always been a 20/20 wine. But like the Clos de Bèze above, this bottle has not been well stored. It starts off well enough on the nose, but then is weak, loose, and even coarse on the palate. What a pity!

PART FOUR

Observations

Premature Oxidation of White Burgundy

SOME FIFTEEN YEARS AGO, it began to become apparent that some of what should have been the best *premiers crus* and others were not holding up as they should have been. Fine white Burgundy, after all, is the supreme dry white wine for aging. Anything halfway decent should be better at ten years rather than five. While one might be prepared to accept certain other chardonnays which were already aging at five years, if this occurred in a top Puligny or Meursault, it just wouldn't do. At first these bad bottles appeared merely to be some unfortunate one-offs. But as time went on, reports began to circulate of more and more oxidised bottles, and from just about every single estate, even the very prestigious—Lafon, Bonneau du Martray, Roulot, Ramonet. No one seemed to be spared. It was rather like a very contagious plague.

I've had my own experiences. In Atlanta, at a dinner of the local Confrérie de Tastevin some years ago, we had to open a full case of Puligny-Montrachet, Les Combettes, from Domaine Etienne Sauzet, to obtain four decent bottles. *Chez* Ramonet, with a group, and Noël generous enough to offer a vertical of his Ruchottes, the two of us were holding bottles of the 1998 (or was it the 1997?) up to the light to find a wine with a clear youthful colour. In my cellar I had a dozen bottles of 1999 Puligny-Montrachet, Les Demoiselles, Domaine Colin Déleger. I tried three. All excessively oxidised before their time. Then I discovered that six of what I thought was twelve were in fact Chassange-Montrachet, En Remilly. No problem. But what do I do with the three remaining bottles of Demoiselles? I can't sell them. Happily, thankfully, these are the only off bottles in my cellar.

But a story from Dominique Lafon: In April 2011 he found himself in a bistro in Burgundy. His meal was interrupted by a stentorian (American) pronouncement—"Prematurely oxidised"—from the other side of the room. He looked up and saw that the wine was his. He called the wine waiter over. The wine was his basic Meursault 2004. He tasted it. Not a bit brilliant. And now aged. But not "prem-ox." Just a bit old. He went over to the American table. "This is my wine," he said. "And the wine is getting old [and it was by no means a great vintage], but it is what I would expect it to be after seven years. Obviously you prefer your wines younger and fresher. Please accept a bottle [nod to the wine waiter] of my Clos de la Barre 2008 with my compliments." The moral here: not all so-called "prem-ox" bottles are prematurely oxidised.

Naturally, alongside the evidence of oxidised bottles came the theories. Why had this happened? Why had there been no previous warning? What, indeed, were growers doing today that they had not been doing pre-1995, the vintage when all the problems seemed to begin? The first culprit was the cork. We are all agreed that the standard of cork supply has dropped. The bark was being stripped to soon. The stripping was occurring too near the base of the trunk. No one, it was pointed out, had experienced a prematurely oxidised screw-top bottled white Burgundy. Moreover, those who wax the ends of their bottles, like Raveneau in Chablis, seem to have fewer bad bottles. While the incidence of bad bottles at Roulot and Lafon, in my experience and theirs (and I believe them), was confined to one or two isolated examples, elsewhere there was rather more (at Colin-Déleger and Leflaive and Sauzet) or very many fewer (at Leroy, Coche-Dury, and the Domaine de la Romanée-Conti).

Corks can vary, even within the same batch, if the winemaker is not vigilant enough. Growers have been horrified to find that in some instances the sulphur level applied at bottling had practically disappeared a month later, while in a companion bottle, it was all it should be. You can weigh corks to ascertain their density. The heavier the better. Philippe Prost of Bouchard is one who did this before Bouchard Père et Fils switched over to the DIAM closures in 2009. More and more people are changing to DIAM or Guala closures, and to screw cap for their more basic wines, and a good thing too—it also avoids the problem of corkiness.

A second series of explanations concerned the winemaking. Generally speaking, growers were using less sulphur, a protective and anti-oxidant. But they were employing *batonnage*,

itself oxidising. With the new, at the time, horizontal bladder presses, the juice produced was squeaky clean and perhaps more vulnerable. Some growers used to deliberately allow a little oxidation of the must right at the beginning. The theory was that it prevented oxidation later on. With global warming, vines were being harvested early in Sepember when the weather was better—longer days and warmer ones too than three weeks later—and the gallop towards maturity was speedier. So did the wines have enough acidity? Was there too much of a touch of botrytis? Indeed, why did just about everyone in Burgundy urge the malo-lactic fermentation? They don't in Bordeaux and Alsace and even in Champagne. Finally, the soaking liquid used for making the corks more supple prior to bottling had changed from a sort of paraffin, seen as carcinogenic, to silicone or peroxide, again oxidative.

Moreover, there was a related further complication. The incidence of prem-ox bottles was and continues to be distinctly higher in the United States than in France and Great Britain. How much did bad storage come into the equation? It cannot be excessively high temperatures during shipment over the Atlantic, for all is shipped in refrigerated containers these days, nor in the customers' private cellars, for surely these all have temperature control, if not at 12° Celsius (55° Fahrenheit) which is the ideal, then at 15°C (60°F). No, I am talking here about the temperatures in the van and the warehouse between port and private residence. There can be no other place where things can go wrong.

Some allege further mistakes in winemaking. Don Cornwell and John Gilman (see http://oxidised-burgs.wikispaces.com/corks) have addressed this in some depth. There are two distinct oxidation processes going on. One is the oxidation of flavonoid phenols. These come from the grape skins, seeds, and stems, and more vigorous pressings will result in higher levels of these compared with whole-cluster pressing and other less extractive techniques. The oxidisation of these phenols results in the colour change in white wines from light-greenish yellow to golden brown. The other, larger group of phenols are the nonflavonoid ones. They are found in the pulpy part of the grape. They will oxidise over time but will not produce detectable changes in colour, flavour, or aromas.

The second type of oxidation is the oxidation of ethanol. Ethanol is oxidised by the hydrogen peroxide present in the wine, producing acetaldehyde. The source of the hydrogen peroxide is from the oxidation of phenols. At a certain level of acetaldehyde, the taster can perceive "oxidised" aromas. The process can be protected by the use of sulphur dioxide, as can the SO_2 prevent oxidation of the flavonoid phenols. But sulphur's more important role is to react and effectively remove hydrogen peroxide. It is generally agreed that the flavonoid and nonflavonoid phenols play a greater part as the barrier to oxidation.

There are techniques such as hyperoxidation which can and are being used, both in Burgundy and California. This is sometimes called "browning of the must." The idea is to remove 99 percent of the phenols from the wine. Fine, I would suggest for a Mâcon Blanc, but is it really going to result in a Corton-Charlemagne that tastes as we have come to expect at ten years old? This is where the change in the sort of wine produced today comes in. They are lighter, they mature quicker, they contain less sulphur. They are therefore less protected. They will oxidise sooner. Wines are offered for tasting earlier, and so it is self-defeating to bottle them with the sort of sulphur content we used in the 1970s. They would not attract any sales. It would be idiotic to expect today's wine to be both delicious at a year and a half and to hold up for fifteen years thereafter. Something has to give. I regret that it seems to be the aging potential of the wine.

Since the worst of the vintages for prem-ox (1996, 1997, 1998), there has been a welcome reduction in the incidence of bad bottles, but it still does occur. And yet there has been little scientifically published in France. More research, translated into a more rigorous understanding of what oxidation actually is, and how this specifically applies to *premier* and *grand cru* Burgundy, and this being taught in the wine schools of Beaune and the oenological degree couses at Dijon, is essential.

Biodynamism

BIODYNAMISM FOLLOWS the precepts of the educationalist and social philosopher Rudolf Steiner (1861–1925). Applied to viticulture, it follows on from the biological approach, acknowledging that not only should one be as environmentally friendly as possible, eschewing the use of herbicides, pesticides, insecticides, chemical fertilisation, and the rest, and that the land should be ploughed in order to be given back its natural level of micro-fauna and micro-flora; but that there are further interests to be persued—most importantly, the influence of the moon, stars, and their astrological position *vis à vis* the earth, and that the vine will respond and flourish if given what are often homeopathic doses of certain naturally occurring plants and other elements.

There are four elements in any plant: the root, the leaf, the flower, and the fruit. Indeed, there are four types of plants: those reared for their root, like a carrot; for their leaves, like spinach; for their flowers, like the flower of a courgette; and for their fruit, like the vine. These respond to the four elements of Earth, Water, Air, and Fire, as follows:

Earth	Root	Taurus, Virgo, Capricorn
Water	Leaf	Cancer, Scorpio, Pisces
Air	Flower	Gemini, Libra, Aquarius
Fire	Fruit	Aries, Leo, Sagittarius

Every nine days the moon passes in front of one of these constellations; its force will be greater or lesser depending on the wax and wane of the moon itself and the position of the planets. What this all boils down to is that there are certain dates when the efficiency of a treatment can be much greater than others, certain dates which are appropriate and others which are not. A friend of mine in Burgundy, no mean gardener, once planted three rows of new potatoes at ten-day intervals. The first and the third, she later found out, happened to coincide with a biodynamically recommended day. These thrived. The second row, which didn't, was a disaster.

By and large, fruit and flower days are days which should be set aside for plant work: pruning, debudding, desuckering, cluster thinning, removal of surplus leaf growth, and of course for harvesting. Leaf and root days are the opposite. On these days you would plough or hoe, or remove old plants where a vineyard is to be replanted. The lunar mode also dictates. The best periods are the first and last quarters; the other two are less auspicious.

With the knowledge of this, a biodynamic lunar calendar can be created. I have found by experience that fruit days are the best for tasting wines, and root days the worst. I am not the only one: in Britain the supermarket groups and others now only offer their wines for tasting by the media on a fruit day. We know that the wines are harder, more closed-in, and less charming on a root day. The use of sulphur and copper sulphate, against oidium and mildew, is permitted. Against other depredations biodynamicists may employ all or any of the following. I list what their use counteracts:

Yarrow	Oidium
Camomile	Mildew
Lavander, Absinthe, Citronelle	Insects
Rhubarb	Insects
Lucerne	Hydric stress
Nettle, Horsetail	Reinforces the cell wall
Comfrey (rich in Boron)	For a more efficient flowering
Nettle, Valerian	A better recovery from hail damage
Silica	Aids light

Homemade compost, based on cow dung, is recommended. In some cases the treatment may be placed in a cow horn on one special date and dug up on another, before being diluted by ten million parts before being applied. However, this is not an immediate process. It takes seven years for a vineyard to become completely biodynamic. Most domaines go through a trial period, before transforming entirely, and quite a number, as I write, are still within this preparation period, even if they started experimenting as far back as 2002.

It would seem odd, on the face of it, that Burgundy, the most disperse and fragmented of all France's *vignobles,* should have such a large proportion of its territory now cultivated biodynamically—1,600 hectares, or 5.3 percent of the total surface, at the last count. After all, what your neighbours do, only a few rows of vines away, is bound to impinge on what you have done with your vines. How biodynamic is it possible to be in this situation? But then Burgundy, God bless, is nothing if not a vineyard area of individualists. The refreshing fact is that here the proprietor is the winemaker, the *chef de cave* and the *chef de culture,* as well as probably the bookkeeper in his or her spare time. Decisions can be taken, perfectionism persued, without reference to endless committees of finance wizards and shareholders.

Biodynamism works, though it is more expensive than the *lutte raisonnée* (the ordinary, sensible, reactive viticultural approach). The wines are better and more representative of their origins. As important, the vines are hardier, less susceptible to rot and crytogamic diseases. And the wines that they produce are more robust; they hold up better. Sometimes the extremes of biodynamism sound like black magic. But the point is, it works. We should not be in too much of a rush to stand and scoff. Within a decade, I predict that 10 percent of Burgundy will be biodynamic.

———————

Here's a story—a true story—which will infuriate the sceptics. It concerns Nicolas Joly of Savennières' Coulée de Serrant, one of the pioneers of biodynamics. Back in the 1980s, he had a problem with rabbits, an infestation in one of his vineyards. A friend told him what to do. Firstly, capture and kill a couple of them (and you can make a good rabbit stew). But preserve the skins. Burn these up until you are left with the ash. Dynamise the ash (stirring it up over a hour, firstly in one direction for a minute and then in the other). Then—and I don't know whether you have to do this at midnight under a full moon, but I don't see why not—sprinkle a coffee-spoon of the ash at all four corners of the vineyard and in the centre. You have to do this for three years in succession. And then, as *chez* Joly, you won't see any rabbits ever again.

So You Think Today's Burgundies Are Brilliant?

BURGUNDY HAS NOT had a bad vintage since 1984. It is as if *Le Bon Dieu* is smiling on the region and rewarding the growers for their dedication and individualism, their refusal to submit to uniformity and indulge in petty jealousies, and their reasonableness with prices. The standard of the wines, and the very large number of praiseworthy domaines and merchants is far higher than it has ever, ever been in the past. Yet things can only get better—much better. While everyone is well-equipped in their cellars—sorting tables, temperature control, attention to the minute details of *élevage*, and so on; and is as exigent about dispensing with herbicides and systematic sprays, and is, indeed, as biological if not as biodynamic as one could wish, the raw material, the vines themselves, leaves much to be desired.

Today's "old vines" are no longer, for the most part, those planted in the 1900s, the 1910s, and the 1920s—that is, the first generation of grafted vines planted after the original *vignes francaises* died out. They are more likely to be the infamous Pinots Droit planted in the 1960s or the first generation of clones, reared for quantity as much for disease resistance. Neither, of themselves, produce fine quality. Nor, for the most part, were the rootstocks they were grafted on to, for instance, the SO_4, the most desirable, we can say with hindsight. A vine on SO_4 tends to race to maturity as September evolves, rendering the window of perfect opportunity very narrow indeed. Moreover, there is still much of the Burgundy vineyard, over-fertilised on the 1960s and 1970s, which is still today, forty years on, over-burdened with potassium, resulting in wine with a deficiency of acidity.

So, if you find your 1999s delicious, and are licking your lips in anticipation of your 2005s and 2009s, just think how more brilliant the Burgundies are going to be in the 2040s, when today's carefully selected newly planted vines, chosen with the highest care and all the viticultural know-how we have today, are the "old-vine" backbone of the wine. Of course, some of us will no longer be around. And there is the threat of global warning. But it's a nice thought.

What Are Winemakers Doing about Global Warming?

THERE MAY STILL BE a few nutters out there who believe that the world is flat. There are certainly those who, astonishingly enough in view of the contrary scientific evidence, persist in believing in Intelligent Design, whom we used to call Creationists. There may indeed be some left who still consider it a good idea to sell arms to corrupt and oppressive regimes, on the basis that the mad dictators who rule them are, temporarily at least, against the same people that we are. As at least one American president has said: he may be a nasty bastard, but at least he's our nasty bastard!

But surely there can be no one left who does not accept global warming? Who or what is resposible for shrinking glaciers and rising sea levels is an argument which has no place in this book. But the effect of global warming on viticulture and viniculture, the potential threat to wine styles and wine and food matches is another matter, and that is what I am going to attempt to address in this chapter. It is ironic that, just as we are now beginning to produce good wine from almost any grape variety you could care to mention in almost every country

in the world—just as, to put it in a nutshell, humans have finally mastered the art or science of winemaking—nature should be skulking round the corner ready to bludgeon us with a blunt instrument called climate change. We are going to have to go back to square one and think through our ideas all over again.

Until relatively recently, life for all those involved in the wine business was very different. We didn't understand the science. We didn't have the treatments we needed to keep our vines and their fruit healthy. We hardly knew whether it would rain tomorrow or not. Only a limited few were interested in consuming better wine than the local jug stuff. And none of those at the production end made a profit.

Like any other agriculturalist, the viticulturalists' aim was to produce quantity: to encourage nature to do its thing. But there was very little to encourage perfectionism. Nothing, indeed, but *amour propre*. Thank you to the proprietors of Lafite and Romanée-Conti who realised that someone had placed something sacred in their hands.

Today at the top level, estate managers are spending a great deal of time and money *reducing* the crop, and then isolating the issue of the junior vines into a second wine. We are fighting against the energies of nature. It's a great paradox. We are in more command of the science, and we certainly have all the controls over temperature and so on that we would wish. Weather forecasting could be a lot more reliable, but for the next five days, it is reasonably accurate. Most importantly, all the world drinks wine, and with today's techniques there is nothing to stop us producing something enjoyable almost anywhere we like, and for all those in the pipeline to make a good living on the way.

Perhaps for the majority of the world's wines, global warming, provided it does not get too excessive, will not do any harm. In lands like Chile, for example, vineyards at the northern end of the country, if they become too warm and too dry, will just be abandoned in favour of new plantations further south. This principle will be applied all over the world. It will be expensive to relocate, of course: planting a vineyard from scratch is not cheap. Access to water will become even more important than it is today. And water, clearly, is going to become more and more expensive in the decades ahead. But I don't consider that the wines which will result will become greatly different in character than they are today. They'll just come from different places. Alaska or Tierra Del Fuego, any one?

Where the threat really lies is at the Great Wine end. What, after all, is it that distinguishes a great wine from the competently made bottle that sits next to it on the shelf? The answer, I suggest to you, is a question of depth and complexity, elegance and a sense of "somewhereness." In short, *terroir*. Just as, in *Animal Farm*, some animals are more equal than others, so some *terroirs* are superior to others. It's not all the vineyards in Burgundy or Bordeaux, to take two areas I know something about. But those vineyards on which lie the classed growths and their equivalents, or which are already designated *grand cru* and *premier cru*, these bits of land are special. You won't find a

convenient substitute a couple of hours away where it is a little cooler.

The winemaker has a dual task here. The first, obviously, is to make the very best wine he or she can. The second is to preserve, even enhance, the integrity and signature of the *terroir*. Why have all these *permiers* and *grands crus*—550 in the Côte d'Or alone—if they are not going to produce individual wines, each with its own special nuance? While modern methods are making life easier for the winemaker to more consistently come up with something fine, global warming is tending to impose a uniformity on the results.

Sixty years ago, the vintage in Bordeaux and the Côte d'Or began in the last week of September. Whether it actually started on the twenty-fifth or the twenty-eighth often merely depended on which day was a Monday. It was just more convenient to begin at the beginning of the week. If you take the average since 1945—irrespective of the fact that 1945 itself, followed by 1947 and 1949, were all hot vintages—you can see that every decade the vintage begins three or so days in advance of the previous one, so that the average is now a harvest date in the first week of September. In the last decade we have had three vintages which began in August: 2003, 2007, and 2011. The only previous August vintage in anybody's records is 1893.

The days at the start of September are both sunnier and warmer, plus more likely to be drier, than they are three or four weeks later. In fine weather, ripeness gallops towards fruition in any case, but today faster than ever. For the white wine grower this is a potential nightmare. In the production of white wine, the acidity is all important. Miss the optimum day and your wine is compromised. It is the explanation why 2008 and 2006 are better vintages, overall, in the Côte de Beaune than 2005 and 2009, despite the much better weather conditions in these latter vintages. Many white wine vineyards were cleared too late. Christian Moueix will tell you that he picks Petrus only in the afternoons. By this time the dew has evaporated and his fruit arrives in the winery with another half a degree of potential sugar. I can envisage Burgundian white wine makers considering doing the opposite!

What the best of the white winemakers can do, and the recent epidemic of prematurely oxidised bottles has encouraged this, is to produce less ephemeral wine. If you are, say, a grower in a Puligny *premier cru,* you are getting enough for your bottle not to be forced to squeeze every last drop out of every single grape. Press more gently and you'll get a better and more concentrated wine. Think of Champagne or think back, if you are as decrepit as I am, to 1973, 1979, and 1982. These were all three huge vintages. Pressing didn't have to be continued to the maximum. There was enough juice anyway. The result: three excellent white wine vintages. A further feature would be to avoid, or halve, the malo-lactic fermentation. Jadot does this. Why not others?

Red wines, in Burgundy at least, are so far benefiting from the earlier harvests, though for how long, given the notorious fragility of the Pinot Noir, I hesitate to guess. We can today expect better colours, healthier and more concentrated fruit, and in all but the very hottest vintages, a more enhanced relationship between the wine and its *terroir.* Moreover, the red Burgundy producer can play around and permutate between long or short cold soaking before fermentation, the use or rejection of the stems, the temperature—28°C, 30°, 32°, and upwards—and length of the fermentation and maceration, and the amount of new oak. With 2009 it became obvious that a large number of young men and women in the Côte d'Or were doing little experiments on the side. Were the techniques they had performed for the last decade or more really the best? Should they be more flexible?

Bordeaux is another matter. It tends to be hotter than Burgundy in August and September, and the varieties employed—principally Cabernet and Merlot—tend to be more tannic, and in the case of the latter, less acidic, than Pinot Noir. For thirty years I have participated in three- and ten-year-on tastings of the best.

The first growths and their equivalents are served at the end. In the 1980s most of us, a group of buyers of the leading UK wine merchants, would be disappointed if we had not guessed at least four out of the eight correctly. Today the only *château* I would feel confident of isolating would be Haut-Brion. I'm not the only Bordeaux lover who finds the wines increasingly similar.

If the acidity level is what is all-important in top white wine production, it is the level of alcohol in the reds which often separates the fine and elegant and *terroir* expressive from the merely rich and fruity. Here global warming poses another threat. We want the habitual hundred days or more between flowering and harvest. This is the length of time (which we didn't have in 2003) we require for the tannins to become ripe and sophisticated. A first of September harvest means a first of June midflowering, and that requires benign weather conditions in the spring. If April and May are cool, and June, July, and August uneven—which they are not all every year in the middle of France, but still in the majority of cases—we are sitting comfortably. Nothing will ripen properly before September 18 or so.

But if the spring is precocious, as it was in 2011, or if the summer is very hot, the fruit will ripen rather earlier. There is a limit to how long we can delay picking before the fruit begins to rot. The danger is that the tannins are still only marginally ripe but the wine weighs in at 14.5° or so. About the only solution, given overall temperature control in the winery, is to multiply the number of pickers by a factor of three or four, and once you have started picking, to continue twenty-four hours out of twenty-four until every grape has been collected. And, oh yes: You'll have to double the size of the winery and the number of fermentation tanks.

Too many wines, all the way around the world, are already made with acidity levels which are for my palate too low, and with alcohol levels (ditto) which are too high. Is this really what the customer wants, or is it more that these wines are picked out by the critics?

The bigger wines stand out alongside those with less muscle and guts. But this is in the absence of food and leisure time, which is the real point. These wines are certainly much less food friendly than the fresher, less tannic, less alcohol-hefty examples you are more likely to find in France and Italy than California. These we can match with food. These are made for drinking, not analysing. We may even enjoy them so much we'll order another bottle; while even the first representative of the opposite category goes unfinished.

Sadly, global warming is not helping the production of food-friendly wines. Yet I remain an optimist. An elitist optimist perhaps. For the time being, there are enough of these wines. What I say is give the customer not what they think they like, but what they should like. The task is ours. Once we have convinced them, they can encourage all those involved in the prodution and sales of food-friendly wines, however strange the provenance may seem at the outset. There may well be all sorts of so far undiscovered great *terroirs*; inconceivable today, but which may be eminently suitable for the wine industry in 2112.